OTTO KLEMPERER

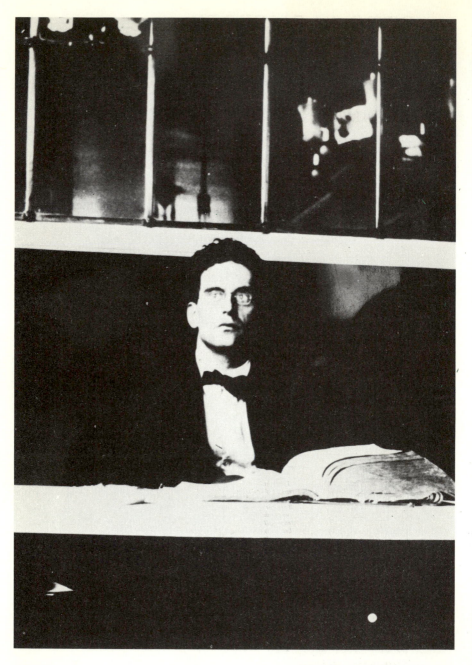

1   Klemperer in the orchestral pit in the Strasbourg theatre, c. 1915

OTTO KLEMPERER

his life and times

VOLUME 1   1885–1933

PETER HEYWORTH

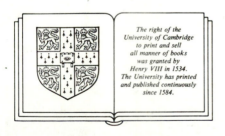

The right of the
University of Cambridge
to print and sell
all manner of books
was granted by
Henry VIII in 1534.
The University has printed
and published continuously
since 1584.

CAMBRIDGE UNIVERSITY PRESS

Cambridge
London   New York   New Rochelle
Melbourne   Sydney

Published by the Press Syndicate of the University of Cambridge
The Pitt Building, Trumpington Street, Cambridge CB2 1RP
32 East 57th Street, New York, NY 10022, USA
10 Stamford Road, Oakleigh, Melbourne 3166, Australia

First published 1983
Reprinted 1984

Printed in Great Britain by the University Press, Cambridge

Library of Congress catalogue card number: 83–1992

British Library Cataloguing in Publication Data

Heyworth, Peter
Otto Klemperer.
Vol. 1: 1885–1933
1. Klemperer, Otto—Biography
I. Title
789'.092'4   ML422.K67
ISBN 0 521 24293 2

Contents

Illustrations

List of illustrations

The publishers wish to acknowledge the following for permission to reproduce illustrations: Frau Lotte Klemperer nos. 1, 2, 3, 6, 9, 12, 13, 17, 20, 21, 28, 34, 36, 38; Gustl Breuer no. 7; no. 10 Copyright Dr Wolfgang and Ingeborg Henze, Campione d'Italia; Frau Martha Dix no. 14; Ullstein Bilderdienst nos. 16, 22–4, 29, 36; Allgemeiner Deutscher Nachrichtendienst no. 30; Frau Ursula Dülberg, nos. 11, 26, 31 and 33; Frau Lucia Moholy nos. 25 and 34.

Extracts from Arnold Schoenberg's diary and a letter from Schoenberg to Klemperer are used by permission of Belmont Music Publishers, Los Angeles, California 90049.

viii

Preface and acknowledgements

Otto Klemperer would have raised an ironic eyebrow at the length of this biography. A man of few words, he detested verbiage. Unlike most of his colleagues, he also regarded his occupation with a degree of ambivalence. As his comment on Pierre Boulez, 'He conducts splendidly; [but] my goodness, that shouldn't be so terribly important for him', implies, conducting was for him a lower (and more ephemeral) activity than composing.

Yet there seem to me to be valid reasons for writing at length about Klemperer's life and career. During the first fifty years of his life he had close ties with many of the main creative figures of his time. It was, of course, Mahler who launched him on his way. But composers as various as Busoni, Pfitzner, Schoenberg, Stravinsky, Hindemith and Weill also played a part in his career. Even in his eighties, long after he could have included their music in his repertory, he preserved an interest in composers of a younger generation, such as, notably, Boulez and Stockhausen.

From this association with some of the most vital creative forces of the first half of the twentieth century, came a deep involvement in the profound change in musical climate that swept Europe in the decade after the First World War. In his youth a musician of an intensity that could be described as 'expressionist', Klemperer was more profoundly affected than he later liked to admit by the neo-classicism that came to prevail in the twenties. In later years he attained an equilibrium between these two components in his musical character: 'Nirgends brennen wir genauer', as his friend, Ernst Bloch, put it in a phrase that became celebrated. But in 1927, when he was finally called to Berlin at the age of forty-two as director of the Kroll Opera, he was a controversial figure, attacked and praised as an arch-exponent of *die neue Sachlichkeit*.

Klemperer's entire career up to that point can be seen as a preparation for the unique experiment of running a major opera house that would be contemporary in the fullest meaning of the word: his four years at its head represent the keystone of his life and hence of this volume. The Kroll (or, to give it its proper title, the Staatsoper am Platz der Republik) was from its start as a quasi-independent theatre every bit as controversial as its director, and on political as well as musical grounds. The right-wing radicals who became increasingly vocal in the last years of the Weimar

Republic regarded it as a cesspool of *Kulturbolschewismus*. Conversely, to 'progressive' circles it seemed the very embodiment of a new world they hoped to call into existence. Since the war the Kroll has indeed come to acquire mythological status as a fountainhead of operatic modernism. In an attempt to discuss in a more detached spirit what remains one of the most remarkable chapters in the chequered history of twentieth-century opera, I have examined its origins and end, its achievements and failures, in some detail. That accounts in large part for the length of the biography.

When I embarked on the task, I had no conception of the work it would involve. In the course of a career ranging over sixty-five years, Klemperer was active in cities as far apart as Los Angeles and Moscow, Budapest and Buenos Aires, Berlin and London. Much vital material was destroyed in the course of the Second World War. In Cologne, for instance, where he was permanently engaged between 1917 and 1924, the daily programme of the opera house had disappeared and no extensive collection of press cuttings existed. His activities could therefore only be reconstructed by literally turning every page of local newspapers and periodicals. For this purpose the University Library kindly gave me direct access to its stacks, but its officials plainly regarded the Englishman who returned at intervals to thumb his way for days on end through countless journals as something of a freak. There were similar problems elsewhere. Furthermore, many of the people who had known Klemperer in the earlier stages of his career were either dead or had been scattered across the face of the earth by political events in Germany.

In the course of these labours I received much help and personal kindness. I have attempted to list below the many libraries, archives and other institutions that provided material and guidance, and the even more numerous individuals who granted interviews, answered enquiries, made letters available and otherwise gave advice and support. I am, however, painfully aware that there are gaps in these lists, notably in the case of individuals to whom I have spoken and institutions I have visited without prior or subsequent correspondence. I would beg anyone who finds their name not listed to accept my apologies for this oversight and to accept this expression of gratitude for the help they gave. I have thought it better to reserve the names of those I have already consulted in connection with Klemperer's career after 1933 for inclusion in the concluding volume of the biography.

I have, however, incurred debts which demand more detailed acknowledgement. I would like in the first place to express my gratitude to those who undertook research on my behalf. They include: †Arňost Mahler and Mr Jan Graf (Prague), Mr N. P. H. Steffen (Holland), Signora Milena Benedetti (Italy), Fräulein Renate Voit (Vienna), Señor Pablo Andrés Spiller (Buenos Aires), Mrs Svetlana Sigida and Mr Stuart Campbell (Moscow). I need hardly add that the views expressed on the basis of the material they provided are mine alone.

Others helped in a variety of ways. Dr C. G. Curjel kindly permitted me to examine the *Nachlass* of his father, Hans Curjel, and Mrs Rosemarie Cave gave valuable assistance in ordering the huge quantity of photo-copies and press cuttings relating to the Kroll that I borrowed from this source. Substantial gaps nonetheless remained in the latter and these I was able to fill through the help and patience of Frau Hildegard Boldt (Berliner Landesarchiv) and Frau Eva Trapp (Ullstein-Archiv). †Eigel Kruttge, who had unrivalled knowledge of Klemperer's years in Cologne and Berlin, gave unsparingly of his time and wisdom. Dr Jitka Ludvová and Dr Alena Němcová (Janáček Archives, Brno) similarly provided valued help. Mr Harold Rosenthal suffered persistent enquiries with unfailing patience. With a generosity that I deeply appreciate, Mr David Drew and Dr Stephan Stompor allowed me to read unfinished typescripts listed in the bibliography. I am also much indebted to individuals and an institution that provided hospitality during research expeditions, notably to Mrs Dorothy Huttenback (Los Angeles), Dr Gerd Köhrmann (Cologne) and the Akademie der Künste (West Berlin).

Mr Terence Kilmartin, Mr Francis King and Mr John Warrack all did me the great service of reading the typescript from beginning to end; I owe a great deal to their pertinent observations. I am also indebted to my publishers. Mr Michael Black found time to give detailed consideration to a basic problem in the book's structure. Mrs Rosemary Dooley has seen the typescript through to publication with meticulous efficiency and firmness of purpose; an author who finds the support of a sub-editor as perceptive, informed and clear-headed as Mrs Penny Souster is fortunate indeed. I would like to thank Mrs Joan Goldsbrough, who typed and retyped the volume through what must have seemed an unending series of revisions.

I have also received generous financial support, without which I could not have sustained the research involved, and would like to express my gratitude to the following: EMI Ltd (Sir Joseph Lockwood), The I. J. Lyons Charitable Trust, The Arts Council of Great Britain, Stifterverband für die Deutsche Wissenschaft. I would also like to express appreciation of the help given by the Earl of Drogheda, Lord Bullock, Mr Peter Nestler and Mr Shephard Stone in procuring these grants, also of the journeys to Los Angeles and Germany facilitated by Mr Ernest Fleischmann and Dr Brigitte Lohmeyer respectively.

Finally I owe an incommensurable debt to Frau Lotte Klemperer, who not only made available all relevant family papers, but supported my labours in ways too various to enumerate.

*   *   *

Acknowledgements

Aachen: Internationales Zeitungsmuseum. *Amsterdam:* Concertgebouw Orchestra (Dr E. J. G. Zwarts). *Arnhem:* Gemeente Archief.

Bayreuth: Festspielhaus (Dr Oswald Georg Bauer). *Berlin (GDR):* Akademie der Künste (Dr Manfred Grabs). Brechtarchiv (Frau Ramturn). Deutsche Staatsbibliothek (Dr Hedwig Gittag, Dr Jutta Teurich). Deutsche Staatsoper (Professor Dr Hans Pischner, Herr Werner Otto, †Erdmann H. Treitschke). Märkisches Museum (Herr Dreifuss). *Berlin (W):* Akademie der Künste (Dr Wünsche, Herr Manfred Schlosser, Dr Dirk Scheper). Alex Springer Verlag, Ullstein Archiv (†Hans Wallenberg). Archiv der Berliner Konzert- und Theaterreklame. Freie Universität, Musikwissenschaftliches Institut (Professor Dr Rudolf Stephan). Freie Volksbühne (Dr Günter Schulz). Geheimes Staatsarchiv (Herr Eckhard Henning MA). Philharmonisches Chor (Frau Marianne Buder MA). Philharmonisches Orchester (Frau Gisela Huwe). Staatliche Hochschule für Musik und darstellende Kunst (Frau Steffen). Staatliche Institut für Musikforschung. Staatsbibliothek (Herr May). *Bonn:* Katholischer Akademiker Verband (Dr Hans Heinrich Kürth). Stadt- und Universitätsbibliothek. *Boston:* Symphony Orchestra (Mr Daniel R. Gustin). *Brno:* Janáček Archives.

Cambridge (Mass.): Harvard University, Widener and Houghton Libraries (Miss Elizabeth Ann Falsey). *Chicago:* Lyric Opera (Mr Danny Newman). *Cologne:* Historisches Archiv der Stadt Köln (Dr Kleinertz). Kunsthistorisches Institut (Dr Cocks). Museum Ludwig (Dr Evelyn Weiss). Musikwissenschaftliches Institut (Dr Gerhard Heldt). *Stadt Anzeiger,* Archiv (Frau Weesen). Theaterwissenschaftliches Institut (Herr Helmut Grosse, Frau Flatz). Universitäts- und Stadtbibliothek (Frau Daisy Teutenberg).

Dortmund: Institut für Zeitungsforschung. *Dresden:* Staatstheater (Herr E. Schmidt). Philharmonie (Frau Renate Wittig). *Duisburg:* Stadtarchiv (Herr Buschmann). *Düren:* Stadtarchiv (Dr Domsta). *Düsseldorf:* Dumont-Lindemann Archiv (Herr Heinrich Riemenschneider). Stadtarchiv (Dr Weidenhaupt).

Erfurt: Stadtarchiv (Herr Fischer).

Frankfurt am Main: Paul Hindemith Institut (Dr Dieter Rexroth). Stadtarchiv (Dr Andernacht). Stadt- und Universitätsbibliothek (Dr Hartmut Schäfer). Stiftung Hoch's Konservatorium (GMD Klaus Volk).

Göttingen: Niedersächsische Staats- und Universitätsbibliothek. *Groningen:* Rijksuniversitait, Institute voor Musiekwetenschaf (Drs P. M. Op de Coul).

The Hague: Gemeente Archief. *Hamburg: Der Spiegel,* Archiv. Einwohner-Zentralamt (Herr Kolman). Gelehrtenschule des Johanneums (Herr

Acknowledgements

Bregulla). Hotel Vierjahreszeiten (Herr Gert Prantner). Musikbücherei (Frau Möller). Staatsarchiv (Herr Sielemann). Staatsoper (Dr Joachim Wenzel). Staats- und Universitätsbibliothek (Dr Stockmann). Theatersammlung der Universität (Dr Diedrichsen).

Jerusalem: Jewish National and University Library (Dr M. Nadav).

Karlsruhe: Badische Landesbibliothek (Herr Klaus Häfner). Badisches Generallandesarchiv (Dr Schwarzmeier). *Kassel:* Stadtarchiv (Dr Litterschied). *Koblenz:* Bundesarchiv (Frau Hanne Marschall, Herr Verlande).

Lausanne: Bibliothèque cantonale et universitaire (Monsieur Jean-Louis Matthey). *Leipzig:* Museum für Geschichte der Stadt Leipzig (Dr H. Wenzel, Dr K. Sohl). *Leningrad:* Saltykov-Schedrin State Public Library (Mrs F. Davidovna-Bartnovskaya, Mrs I. F. Grigorieva). State Theatre Museum (Mr G. Z. Mordison). *London:* British Institute of Recorded Sound (Mr Eric Hughes). British Library, Department of Manuscripts (Mrs A. Payne); Newspaper Library, Colindale. Central Music Library. *Financial Times* Library (Mr Keith Moore). German Historical Institute (Dr Lothar Kettenacher). Goethe Institute Library (Frau Inge Niemöller, Frau Mechthilde Offermanns). Great Britain–USSR Association (Mr J. C. Q. Roberts). London Library. Royal Academy of Music (Miss M. J. Harington). Royal Philharmonic Society (Mrs Shirley Barr). Wiener Library. *Los Angeles:* Arnold Schoenberg Institute (Professor Leonard Stein, †Clara Steuermann, Mr Jerry McBride). Public Library (Miss Katherine Grant, Mr Robert Riley). UCLA Music Library (Mr Stephen Fry, Miss Marsha Berman). *Ludwigshafen:* Stadtarchiv (Dr Brennig).

Mainz: B. Schott's Söhne (†Ludwig Strecker, Frau Dr Gertrud Marbach, Frau Dorothea Härtter, Mr Ken W. Bartlett). *Mannheim:* Musikalische Akademie (Herr Fritz Bunge). Stadtarchiv (Dr Schadt). Städtisches Reiss-Museum (Herr Wilhelm Herrmann). Universitätsbibliothek (Herr Alfred Götz). *Marbach am Necker:* Deutsches Literaturarchiv (Dr Joachim W. Storck). *Marburg:* Universitätsbibliothek. *Maria Laach:* Abtei Archiv (Professor Dr Emmanuel Severus). *Moscow:* Bol'shoy Theatre Archives (Mrs Marina Tshurova). The British Embassy (Mr Terry Sandell, Mr Michael Sullivan). *Munich:* Bayerische Staatsbibliothek (Dr Dachs). Institut für Zeitgeschichte (Frau Ingrid Baass).

New York: Library and Museum of the Performing Arts (Mr Frank Campbell, Miss Jean Bowen). New York University, Elmer Holmes Bobst Library (Mrs Ruth B. Hilton); Department of Music (Mr Jan La Rue). Performing Arts Research Center (Mr David Hall). Philharmonic Symphony Society (Mr Frank Milburn, Miss Mary de Camp). Public Library, Newspaper

Acknowledgements

Division. Solomon Guggenheim Museum (Mr Ward Jackson). State University at Binghampton, Max Reinhardt Archive (Miss Marianne J. Janauer).

Paris: Bibliothèque de l'Arsenal. Bibliothèque nationale (Monsieur François Lesure). *Philadelphia:* Balch Institute Library (Mr J. L. Sanders). Pennsylvania University, Charles Patterson Van Pelt Library (Mr Rudolf Hirsch). *Prague:* Ceske Filharmonie (Professor Jiří Pauer). Divadelni Ustav (Dr Eva Hermannova). Národní Muzeum v. Praze (Dr Milan Poštolka).

Strasbourg: Archives municipales (Monsieur J. Fuchs). Bibliothèque nationale (Madame Lang). Opéra du Rhin (Monsieur J. P. Wurtz). *Stuttgart:* Institut für Auslandsbeziehungen (Frau Elvira Pflüger). Staatsgalerie (Dr Karin Frank von Maur).

Tel-Aviv: University, Department of Musicology (Professor Herzl Shmueli).

Vienna: Gesellschaft der Musikfreunde. Österreichische Nationalbibliothek, Musiksammlung (†Franz Grasberger, Dr Günter Brosche, Frau Ingeborg Feichtinger); Theatersammlung. Österreichisches Staatsarchiv (Frau Hofrat Dr Anna Benna). Stadt- und Landesbibliothek, Musiksammlung (Dr Ernst Hilmar). Universal Edition (Herr Alfred Schlee, Frau Marion von Hartlieb). Wiener Philharmoniker (Herr Mario Beyer).

Washington: Library of Congress (Mr Wayne D. Shirley). Smithsonian Institute, Archives of American Art (Miss Nancy Zembala). *Wiesbaden:* Hessische Landesbibliothek. Hessisches Staatstheater. Wiesbadener Stadtarchiv. *Wiesbadner Tagblatt,* Library (Frau Rosenbaum). *Wupperthal:* Stadtarchiv. Stadtbibliothek (Dr Werner). *Würzburg:* Stadtarchiv (Dr Dunkhase).

Zurich: Zentralbibliothek (Dr Günter Birkner).

Frau Hilda Abendroth; Mrs Dorothea Alexander; Señor Claudio Arrau.

Professor Dr Rolf Badenhausen; Professor Joachim Beck; Professor Dr h. c. Hellmut Becker; Herr Franz W. Beidler; Dr Jürgen Bengsch; Madame Jacqueline Bensard; Mr Lionel Bentley; Miss Elisabeth Bergner; †Herbert Binswanger; †Simon Bischheim; †Charlotte Bloch; †Ernst Bloch; †H. J. Blum; †Karl Böhm; Dr Werner Bollert; †Luise Bontemps; Professor Dr Knut Borchardt; †Adrian Boult; Mr Philo Bregstein; Mr Gustl Breuer; Professor Dr Reinhold Brinkmann; Mr Andrew Brown; Mr Richard Buckle; Herr Wolfgang Burbach; Frau Hedwig Busch; †Lord Butler of Saffron Walden.

Herr Peter Cahn; Monsieur Roger de Candolle; Mr Alfred Clayton; Dr Michael de Cossart; Miss Jeanne Courtauld; Mr Robert Craft; Mr Edward Crankshaw; Dr Karoly Csipák; †Hans Curjel.

xiv

Acknowledgements

Signor Fedele D'Amico; Mr David Denny; †Paul Dessau; †Max Deutsch; Herr Ulrich Dibelius; Frau G. Dichgans; †Willi Domgraf-Fassbänder; Mr Frederick Dorian; Mr Nigel Douglas; †Peter Dülberg; Frau Ursula Dülberg.

Herr Georg-Albrecht Eckle; Miss Eva H. Einstein; Miss Irene Eisinger; Mr Herman Z. Elbin; Herr Martin Elste; Frau Julia Erdmann.

Mr H. Federer; Herr Hugo Fetting; Frau Hilde Firtel; †Grete Fischer; †Fritz Fischer; Mr M. H. Fisher; Frau Moje Forbach; Dr Alfred Frankenstein; Herr J. Hellmut Freund; †Max Friedemann; Frau Ilse Fromm-Michaels; Herr Gerhard Fürst; Frau Elisabeth Furtwängler.

Mr Patrick Gardiner; Herr Paul Gergely; Herr Michael Gielen; Dr Ruth Gladstein; Frau Rosemarie Gless; Dr Detlev Gojowy; Professor Michael Goldstein; Mr Michael H. Gray; Frau Josefina Grimme; †Helmut Grohe.

Herr Willy Hahn; Mr Chris Hailey; Herr Bruno Hauer; Mr Gerhard Haurwitz; Miss E. B. Heemskerk; Mrs Olga Heifetz; Frau Erika Heinisch; Miss Eva Heinitz; Professor Hans Heintze; Mr Hans W. Heinscheimer; †Clara Herstatt; Dr Rosemary Hilmar; Dr E. E. Hirschler; †Max Hofmüller; Mr Alex Hubert; Mlle Marguerite Hugel.

Professor Seymour W. Itzkoff; Mr Charles Jahant; Mr C. A. Johnson; Professor James Joll.

Herr Alfred Kaine; Dr Joachim Kaiser; Frau Inge Karsch; Frau Magda Kemp; Frau Dr Elisabeth Kessler-Wellesz; Madame Léon Kien; Dr Herfrid Kier; Frau Hedy Klein; Dr Derek Klemperer; Mr O. E. Klemperer; Mr Werner Klemperer; Herr H.-H. Klihm; †Olga Knack-Brandt; Monsieur Boris Kochno; Mr Irvine Kolodin; Dr Peter Konstam; Mr George Korngold; Frau Dr Annie Kraus; Mr Ernst Krenek; †Lotte Kruptat; Frau Margarete Kruttge; Mr Henryk Krzeczkowski; †Charles Kullman; Monsieur Roger Kunzinger.

Monsieur Henry-Louis de La Grange; Professor H. H. Landau; Mrs Eva Lande; Mrs Carlotta Landsberg; Monsieur Henri Lazare; Mr Vladimir Lébl; Mr Tom van Leeuwen; Frau Magda Legal-Krevenov; †Lotte Lehmann; Mrs Eva Lehnsen; †Lotte Lenya; †Richard Lert; Miss Julie Levy; Mrs Else Lewertoff; Dr E. G. Lowenthal.

Professor Dr Wilhelm Mader; Mrs Charlotta Mahler; †Igor Markevich; Dr Micha May; Professor Dr Hans Mayer; Sir Robert Mayer; †Peter de Mendelssohn; †Theodore E. Merrill; †Gerhard Meyer-Sichting; Mrs Mercedes Meyerhof; Mr Jan Meyerowitz; †Thomas Michaels OSB; †Paul Mies; Professor Donald Mitchell; Frau Lucia Moholy; Señor John Montés; Frau Eva Morel; †Elisabeth and †Susanna Müller-Hartmann; Mr William Muschenheim.

Acknowledgements

Frau Charlotte Naef; Frau Agnes Nierendorf; Herr Gerhard Niess; Frau Jarmila Novotna; Mrs Else Nürnberg; Mr W. Norwood.

Herr Werner Oehlmann; Mr Igor Oistrakh; †Cissie Oppenheim; Herr Walther G. Oschilevsky.

Professor E. E. Papst; Mrs Ruth Passer; Herr Willi Pempel; Mr Peter Piccaver; Herr Hans Piroth; Professor Dr Helmuth Plessner; Mr K. A. Pollak; Herr Jörg Polzin; Mr Gerd Puritz.

Professor Arthur-Maria Rabenalt; Professor Dr Hans Rectanus; Mr Henry Rée; Miss Anneliese K. Reich; Professor Wilhelm Reinking; Dr Helmut Reinold; Mrs Ruth Ries; Mr Jack Robinson; Mr John Rockwell; Madame Marie Romain Rolland; Mrs A. Rookwood; †Eduard Rosenbaum; Miss Gudula Rosenbaum; Mr Gennadi Rozhdestvensky; Frau Rudolf; Professor Josef Rufer.

Mrs Natalia Satz; Mrs Ruth Scherk; Dr Edgar von Schmidt-Pauli; Professor Dr Arnold Schmitz; Professor Hans-Peter Schmitz; Mr Karl Ulrich Schnabel; Dr Hans Schrank; †Maria Schreker; Señora Heidy Schreker-Bures; Professor Oskar Fritz Schuh; Dr Willi Schuh; Frau Gerda Schüler; Herr Klaus Schulz; Dr Hagen Schulze; Dr Boris Schwarz; Monsieur Georges Sebastian; Dr Wolfgang Seifert; Signor Sandro Sequi; Mr Roger Sessions; Professor Howard Shanet; Mr Desmond Shawe-Taylor; Mr Geoffrey Skelton; †Hilde Sluzewski; Mlle Jacqueline Starer; Frau Dr Gertrud von Steeg; Mr Francis Steegmuller; Mrs Olga Sternberg; Mr Ronald Stevenson; Frau Alice Strauss; †Hugo Strelitzer; Dr Wolfgang Stresemann; Herr Erich Streubel; Frau Hilda Strobel; Professor H. H. Stuckenschmidt; †Margot Stuckenschmidt.

Mr Leon Temerson; Dr Rainer Theobald; Herr Rolf Tiedemann; †Heinz Tietjen; Herr J.-P. Tonger; Monsieur André Tubeuf.

Mrs Louise Varèse; Herr Claus Vaternahm; Mrs Eliso Virsaladze; Monsieur Vladimir Vogel; Herr Bernd Vogelsang; †Bruno Vonderhoff.

Dr Franz Wallner-Basté; Professor Dr Horst Weber; Frau Friedrike von Wedelstädt; Professor Dr Herbert Weichmann; Mr Eric Walter White; Professor Hermann Wiesler; Frau Erna Wildermann; Herr Erich Wilke; Mr John Willett; Dr Karlheinz Wocker; †Ernst Wollheim; Professor Dr Heinrich Wollheim; Professor Richard Wollheim; Mr John E. Woolf; Mr and Mrs Stephen Wright.

Mr Gabriel Yudin; Frau Herrat Zeinecke; Mrs Louise Zemlinsky; Frau Claudia Zenck; Mr and Mrs Fritz Zweig.

*   *   *

Acknowledgements

Footnotes are separated from endnotes, so that the former are confined to matters of substance. References and sources are given in endnotes, which the general reader can therefore safely ignore, should he choose to do so.

Hinton St Mary
25 January 1983

1   *Childhood*

Otto Klemperer was about nine years old when he first saw the man who
was to be the central inspiration of his entire life as a musician.

> I remember as though it were yesterday, seeing Mahler on the street when I was
> quite small. I was on my way to school. Without anyone pointing him out to me,
> I knew it was him. At that time he had a habit of pulling strange faces, which made
> a tremendous impression on me. I ran along shyly after him for about ten minutes
> and stared at him as though he were a deep-sea monster.[1]

The schoolboy also noticed that his hero held his hat in his hand and walked
with a jerky gait, as though he had a club foot. After that initial encounter,
he frequently saw Mahler, who since 1891 had been First Conductor at
the Hamburg Stadttheater and had lived in the west of the city close to the
Grindelallee. Two years before his arrival the boy's parents had settled
nearby.

Otto Klemperer's father, Nathan, was a newcomer to Hamburg. Like all
his recorded ancestors he had been born in the Prague ghetto.* The family
name had originally been Klopper, which was derived from *Schulklopfer*,
the synagogue official whose task was to wake members of the Jewish
community for early service and its children for school. In 1787, however,
as part of the reforming Emperor Joseph II's attempts to integrate the Jews
into Christian society, the head of each family was obliged to assume a
family name and every member of it also to take a first name. Hence Otto's
great-great-grandfather, who had been born Gumpel the Klopper in 1758,
died in 1803 as Markus Klemperer.

Otto Klemperer never knew his paternal grandparents. His grandmother
died young, having given birth to nine children of whom four died in
infancy. His grandfather Abraham (1809–87) was an austere, ascetic
character – qualities that, after skipping a generation, were to stamp the
grandson. A portrait, now lost, showed a dark face with black eyes and
compressed lips. Abraham Klemperer is described as a teacher, versed in
the Talmud. However he gained his living, it cannot have amounted to
much, for his second son, Nathan, who was born in 1846 and was to be
Otto's father, started work as an errand boy at a Jewish trading house at
the age of only eleven, before he had even finished elementary school.

---

* Prague, the capital of the kingdom of Bohemia, had been longer established as a centre of
Jewry than the imperial capital of Vienna.

1

That premature end to his formal education can hardly have been in accordance with Nathan's own wishes. Even as a boy he revealed a passion for theatre and for music, and while still a penniless apprentice managed to attend performances of Schiller in the gallery. But his own artistic ambitions were to remain thwarted. His pious father refused to countenance a career as an actor, which was still not considered a respectable occupation. And, when he began to reveal an attractive baritone voice, his own unwillingness to become a cantor barred the only form of professional training open to him. Thus he never learnt to read music and was all his life to remain something of an artist *manqué*, although his accomplishment as a singer was to play a part in winning him his wife.

Nathan Klemperer's heart was not, and never was to be, in business. But in 1864, at the age of eighteen, he left Prague for Germany to earn a living as a commercial traveller in Silesia. At night in lonely hotel rooms he was able to make up for some of the shortcomings of his education by avid reading. After five years of this peripatetic existence he finally settled in 1869 in the provincial capital of Breslau,* where he and a younger brother, Hermann, opened a small shop that sold haberdashery and toys.† The frequency with which the business moved its premises suggests that it was never very firmly established. The brothers also manufactured dolls and at the exhibition of Silesian handicrafts and industry that was held in Breslau between May and October 1881 they received a diploma of honour for their products. It was at this exhibition that Nathan Klemperer met his future wife, Ida Nathan, who had come from Hamburg to visit a married sister. Fräulein Nathan was a talented pianist and on the evening after they had met she accompanied Nathan Klemperer in some Schubert songs. Although they were both in their early thirties, it seems to have been a love match. Three days later they were engaged, and on 28 December 1881 they were married in Hamburg.

*   *   *

They were in some ways a strange couple. Ida Nathan, who was born in 1849, came from a background very different from that of the orthodox and impecunious Klemperer. Her father, Nathan Solomon Nathan (1805–78), was a tobacco broker. Her mother, Marianne Rée (1810–87), was descended from a family of Sephardic Jews who in the eighteenth century had established themselves in Altona, a part of Hamburg that remained Danish until the Prussians took it after the war of 1864, and in

---

* Since 1945 Wrocław, a Polish city. Until the annexation of Silesia by Frederick II of Prussia in 1740, Breslau had been Austrian, as part of the Historic Provinces of the Bohemian crown. Hence its close links with Prague.

† In the *Adressen- und Geschäftshandbuch der Königlichen Haupt- und Residenzstadt Breslau* for 1885, it is described as selling 'Galanterie-, Kurz- und Spielwaren'.

2

2   Nathan and Ida Klemperer

the course of the second half of the eighteenth century had built up a considerable trading company centred on Denmark.* Marianne's grand-father, Isac Hartvig Rée (1751–1825), had run the Hamburg end of the business, which dealt largely in corn. The well-to-do Rées were to play an important role in young Otto's development.

---

* Klemperer himself supposed the Rées to be of French origin, having been expelled at the time of the St Bartholemew's Day massacre (1572). Although there is no evidence for this belief, it probably accounts for his special sympathy for France in general and Paris in particular.

3

To these differences of background were added differences of temperament. In spite of chronic failure in business, Nathan Klemperer remained all his life a kindly, aimiable character. A bit of a *flâneur*, he was never happier in later years than when he could relax in an Austrian spa café, play cards and watch the world go by. However hard up, he never failed to take an annual 'cure' in Carlsbad.

His wife, brought up under the grey Hanseatic skies of Hamburg, presented a very different face to the world. Gaunt in appearance, obsessively conscientious, unyielding in her moral standards and deeply immersed in literature as well as music, she might have been a formidable schoolmistress. The austerity and dislike of fine words that she was to bequeath to her only son is evident in the way she chose to end her letters to her children. Whereas the ever-affable Nathan signed himself 'your deeply loving Papa', his wife remained more formally 'your loving mother, Ida'. Yet the same letters reveal warmth, humour and even, at moments, a degree of high spirits. In spite of her stern sense of right and wrong, the household over which she presided was neither prim nor repressive. In a later and more liberated age Ida Klemperer's sharp intelligence and formidable strength of character might have found fulfilment in an academic career or even as a professional musician. But marriage to a man who left to her the main responsibility of raising a family in circumstances that were often straitened served to underline the severer side to her character. Ida's unbending rectitude did not always make things easy for her husband or for her children.

On their return to Breslau the newly married pair moved into a first-floor flat on the Kaiser Wilhelm-Strasse* in the middle of the city, and Ida Klemperer, who may well have provided additional capital, became a co-director of the modest family enterprise. In August 1883 their first child, Regina, was born.† On 14 May 1885 Ida gave birth to a boy, who was to remain her only male offspring. The event is recorded in a family prayer book, where his names are given as Otto Nosom.‡ A second daughter, Marianne, was born in February 1889.

Later that year a decision was taken to return to Hamburg. The little business, in which Ida Klemperer also worked,§ had never prospered, the two brothers had never got on well (Hermann was notoriously stingy) and no doubt Ida welcomed the prospect of exchanging the remote, alien city of Breslau for the solid certainties of her birthplace. In 1887, her widowed

---

* Today Ul. Powstańców Śląskich 3. In all probability it was in this house that Otto Klemperer was born.
† Henceforth referred to as Regi, the name by which she was invariably known.
‡ Properly Nossan, which is the Ashkenazic spelling of the Sephardic Nathan.
§ In the *Breslauer Adressen- und Geschäftsbuch* she is listed as 'Prokurist', i.e. she was legally empowered to sign for the business.

mother had died and left each of her three children a useful inheritance*
that was invested in property. That no doubt provided the basis for the
move. But in Hamburg the young family could also look for support from
her well-to-do relatives. Accordingly, in October 1889 father, mother and
the three children, together with a nurse, set out on their journey. Regi,
at that time six years old, recalled the scene over half a century later.

My little cousin, with whom we played every day, bade us a tearful farewell, and
just before the train was about to leave a friend burst on to the platform to give
my mother a wool cap which she had knitted for the baby. Then Breslau sank into
the distance. I remember a long, long journey. I see the nurse rocking my sister
to keep her quiet. And then we arrived in Hamburg. It was late evening. We were
packed into a cab...Suddenly my mother cried, 'Look, children, there is the Alster.'†

What, however, seized the attention of the four-year-old Otto were the
round, red pillars, covered with concert announcements. As he gazed at
them in wonder, he had no notion of the part they were to play in his own
life. From this moment Breslau was forgotten. Henceforth he felt himself
a Hamburger.

*   *   *

A flat was soon found in the Bogenstrasse, in a western district of the city
that was predominantly Jewish, and on 12 October the family registered
with the police as residents. The Klemperers continued to live in the
Bogenstrasse until 1900, so that it was there that Otto spent his early
childhood. Today the area is entirely built-up. At the end of the last
century, however, the street ran into meadows, and the cows that grazed
there provided the young children with milk.

The family fortunes did not prosper. Nathan's original intention had
been to open a steam laundry, but the capital was not forthcoming, perhaps
because Ida's relations were not impressed by his business abilities. For
almost a year he scratched a living as an insurance agent, until in
September 1890 he found a job as a book-keeper with a firm of
haberdashers. Although he still held it four years later, when the family
took German nationality, it proved to be only the first of a succession of
modest positions, few of which lasted for long. There were periods when
he provided a small income for his family and periods when he earned
nothing. Without an allowance of 2,000M a year from two Rée cousins,
the young family would have found it difficult to make ends meet. As Ida
ruefully admitted, her husband was no business man.

Indeed, with his handsome head, topped by a leonine mane, his Austrian
affability and easy-going ways, he could well have been taken for an actor

---

* Marianne Nathan's estate was valued by her executors at about 62,000M, at that time
quite a substantial sum.   † Lake in the centre of the city.

of the old school, and in industrious, mercantile Hamburg he must have seemed an alien figure. Ida kept him on a short leash: she was so deeply shocked by his only recorded infidelity with a housemaid that thereafter, whenever she took the children on holiday, her husband was never permitted to stay alone in the flat. In other ways he was a good family man. At home he liked to recite from Goethe and Schiller, and even before breakfast, accompanied by his wife, he would sing Lieder by Schubert,

3　Klemperer with his sisters, Regi and Marianne, 1892

Loewe, Schumann and Brahms – then still a 'modern' composer. Indeed, their son's earliest musical memory was of his parents performing *Dichterliebe*. Though often financially straitened, the Klemperer household was *gebildet*.*

It was also a religious household, although the manner in which that faith was expressed changed subtly with the move to Hamburg. In Breslau, where, as in most of the cities of Eastern Europe, the Jewish community was still largely intact, the Klemperers' family life was later described by their younger daughter, Marianne, as 'old-fashioned Jewish': the Sabbath, feast days and dietary laws were all observed. In Hamburg, however, Nathan found employment in a Christian firm, which involved working on the Sabbath. From this time much religious observance was allowed to lapse. Though Nathan remained a member of a synagogue and observed fasts to the end of his life, Ida, who had grown up in the less hermetic Jewish world of Hamburg, was deeply imbued with the ideal of assimilation. Yom Kippur was observed by the male members of the family, but dietary restrictions were gradually abandoned and Ida took her young children to a reformed synagogue, where the services were partly in German. On his thirteenth birthday, Otto was formally received into the Jewish faith at the ceremony of bar mitzvah, but among the books he received as presents on that occasion were the complete works of Shakespeare. There was great emphasis on prayer, but the prayers were German. Grace was said at table in German. Traditional Hebrew songs gave way to German music. There was no mention of Zionism. Nor did Ida send her children to exclusively Jewish schools. Unlike his father, who had been raised in a closed Jewish society in Prague, Otto Klemperer was brought up as a German citizen of Jewish faith, a half-way house that was to fail to withstand the storms of the twentieth century.

Inevitably, the combination of an ineffectual husband and a strong-minded, over-conscientious wife produced tensions, and in later years Ida nursed resentment about Nathan's shortcomings. Yet it was not a quarrelsome family; at any rate visitors were never allowed to perceive any underlying strains. But Ida's rectitude sometimes proved over-strenuous. When Regi told her mother that a girl in her class was cheating, she promptly went to the teacher and demanded chastisement. When Regi failed to admit at school that a dirty ruler was hers but, tormented by conscience, confessed the misdemeanour to her mother, she obliged her to own up to the teacher. Otto, on the other hand, was not above a little cheating, at any rate in mathematics, at which he did not excel. But he took good care not to tell his mother or his elder sister. Nonetheless Ida

---

* The German concept of *Bildung* can only weakly be rendered into English as 'intellectual and inner formation'. *Gebildet* is thus (inadequately) 'educated, cultivated'.

7

Klemperer succeeded in imbuing her son with a devotion to truth from which he rarely deviated. It was to prove a precious asset, for from it stemmed a quality that was to lie at the heart of his stature as a musician. But his mother's rigorous standards undoubtedly imposed strains on his young psyche, and some glimpse into his inner life as a small boy is provided by two stories that he related in old age.

*   *   *

Klemperer's only recollection of Breslau, and hence the earliest memory of his childhood, was of being desperately frightened by a big black dog that had sprung on to his shoulders. It recurs in another form in a later memory that dates from about his tenth year.

I was very clumsy. Sometimes I fell and dirtied my clothes, and when I got home I got into trouble...I didn't like being reproached. So I invented a lie. I told my parents that a big man with a black beard had followed me and pushed me on to the ground...My parents believed me and my mother even went to the police. I often told this lie. But I was quite clear that I was doing something very wrong.* I thought, 'It's a terrible thing that I am always lying....' Then in an illustrated magazine I saw a picture of a man making a confession on his deathbed and I thought that it would be the same with me. Finally, I couldn't bear it any more, and one evening...I ran down to the living room and told my parents everything.[2]

They laughed and sent him back to his bedroom, supposing the whole story to be no more than a figment of a tired child's imagination. But Otto was not prepared to brush his 'crime', as he regarded it, under the carpet; he insisted that he be punished by being left behind when his mother took his sisters on holiday that summer. Nonetheless his lies remained on his conscience for many years.

These events were still vivid in Klemperer's memory over seventy years later, when he readily agreed that the black dog and the black man were closely linked in his imagination. Indeed, he admitted to feeling 'blackness' as an external power that threatened him.† A fear of dogs persisted until he was a man and, although quite free of racial prejudice in the usual sense of the word, black people disturbed him or were regarded as bad omens to the end of his life. It is also perhaps significant that he related the later story of the bearded man as though it were true, and only in the course of the narration did he reveal it to be a fabrication. Anxiety and guilt were to remain strong elements in his character.‡

---

* The memory of this wrongful deed was entwined with another: he had originally dirtied his clothes while burying an unfavourable school report.

† 'The black dog' is a common synonym for depression, from which Klemperer was to suffer greatly.

‡ In later years, when any misfortune occurred, Klemperer would tend to regard it as a 'punishment'. Thus, when ill, he would attribute a rise in temperature to the fact that he had taken an additional sleeping tablet without confessing his 'sin'.

8

Yet Ida was not a severe mother, at any rate in the conventional sense of the word. Punishment was virtually unknown, and if she heard her children's 'confessions' each night before they went to sleep, that was not to chastise them, but rather to bring them to recognise their shortcomings. For her time, she was a modern-minded woman, who aimed to bring up her children, not by nursery discipline, but by example. As her elder daughter, who was to inherit her rigorous moral standards, put it, 'Her example influenced us and we grew up around her, each in his own way.' But as the ten-year-old Otto's reaction to his 'crime' suggests, a very lack of chastisement may well have made the need for self-punishment all the more imperative. Yet, formidable as she was by nature and was forced to become by the limitations of her husband, Ida was also a mother who, as Regina later wrote, had 'a genius for love'. She was the hub of a closely knit family and all her children were deeply devoted to her.

This attachment was inevitably particularly strong between the mother and her only son. Otto had inherited his father's striking appearance and his humour. He also came to share to the full his love of the theatre. But in every other way he was 'ganz die Mama'. He inherited her ability, intelligence and powers of concentration, and, to a more ominous extent than he could have been aware as a child, her disposition. From his mother he received his musicality, and it is significant that he was said to resemble her above all when he was making music.*

Ida Klemperer was far more than is usually implied by the term 'musical'. She composed songs and was a pianist of considerable attainments. Later in life, when she herself was in her sixties and her son was already starting to make a name for himself, a young violinist who lived nearby came regularly to play with her. He has left this account:

Dear Mother, you should have heard that old woman play a Beethoven sonata with me. She played with such overwhelming fire that at moments she really made me forget my own playing and listen to her interpretation. Her 24-year-old son is said to have inherited some of her talent and has already been engaged as first conductor at the theatre here.[3]

Music was an integral part of Ida Klemperer's life. She gave piano lessons, accompanied her husband, taught her children, and regularly devoted Saturday afternoons to music for four hands. Music also inevitably figured on special occasions. On her birthday she played chamber music with members of a local conservatory and it was on one of these occasions that her son first heard and was overcome by the sound of strings. She was

---

* With the sexes reversed Goethe's lines from *Zahme Xenien* well describe the sources of his inheritance.

> Vom Vater hab' ich die Statur,
> Des Lebens ernstes Führen,
> Vom Mütterchen die Frohnatur
> Und Lust zu fabulieren.

9

also an avid concert-goer, and her comments in letters reveal an ability to express her perceptiveness with unusual precision.

*   *   *

From quite early it was decided that Otto should also be a musician. At the age of about five his mother started to give him piano lessons and within a year or so he could play, as he later put it, 'quite nicely'. Before long he was able to share in the musical activities of the household, performing Haydn symphonies in reductions for four hands with his mother and even joining in occasional chamber music. His greatest pleasure, however, was to put a book of poems on the piano and improvise on the ideas that these conjured up in his mind.

It soon became clear that the boy was not only a promising pianist but also possessed an exceptionally sharp pair of ears. A particular pleasure was to listen to the military bands that played in the Zoological Gardens. When, at the age of about seven or eight, he was standing behind a clarinettist, he became aware that the musician was not playing the notes in front of him. The small boy plucked up courage to point this out. Astonished, the musician explained that on the B flat clarinet the music sounds a tone lower than notated. That Otto observed this fact is evidence that he possessed perfect pitch at an unusually early age.

As he grew older, he began to develop surprisingly clear views on how a piece of music should be performed and this eventually led to friction with his mother. She sensibly decided that her precocious son would do better under a professional teacher and he was accordingly sent to Hans Havekoss,* with whom he had a daily two-hour lesson and continued to study until he was sixteen. Under Havekoss, Klemperer quickly mastered much of the keyboard literature from Bach to Schumann.

At some point, accompanied by his teacher, he played the solo part of a Mozart concerto to his cousin, Tante Helene. Helene Rée, his mother's first cousin, was the family benefactress. Born in Hamburg in 1839, she had married another member of the Rée dynasty and, after being widowed early in life, had settled in Paris. A wealthy, childless woman, she lived and dressed with almost eccentric simplicity, so as to devote her resources to the poor and to poor artists in particular. On this visit to her impecunious cousins she was so impressed by the boy's playing that she undertook to pay for his musical education. Klemperer never forgot his old cousin's benevolence. Whenever in later years he was eating *en famille* with

---

* Hans Havekoss (1860–?), who had previously been organist and choirmaster at Grabow in Mecklenburg, only registered with the police as a Hamburg resident on 8 April 1897. Hence, unless he made regular visits to the city for that purpose, it is unlikely that Klemperer studied with him before the age of twelve.

her relatives in Paris, he never failed to raise his glass to her memory. Tante Helene was similarly remembered with gratitude at his eighty-fifth birthday party in London in 1970.

Though the family (and that, of course, in the first place meant Ida) had decided that Otto was to be a musician, he at first had other ideas. As a child his great desire was to be an actor. It was an ambition that never entirely left him and that he was to some extent later able to gratify through a deep involvement with the staging of opera. No doubt the father's passion for the theatre served to stimulate a similar love in his son. At home all manner of 'performances' were frequently improvised under Nathan's supervision, sometimes drawing in other young people from the neighbourhood, and young Otto frequently 'produced'. As the children grew older, there were visits to the theatre. The Klemperers subscribed to an annual Schiller cycle and each took it in turn to accompany the parents. Otto's earliest theatrical memory was of weeping so loudly in the apple scene of *Wilhelm Tell* that his mother had to remove him.

Opera only came later, which is why Klemperer never heard Mahler conduct in Hamburg*. At the age of thirteen he was taken to *Fidelio*, in which the first act canon quartet (a piece of music not calculated to strike young ears) made a particularly deep impression. *Il Trovatore* followed; that he found splendid. He also heard *Lohengrin*, *Der Freischütz* and *Don Giovanni*. But at this stage of his life Mozart still had little appeal. On Havekoss's urging, his mother took him every Good Friday to a performance of Bach's *St Matthew Passion* at the Michaelis Church. Later, he started to accompany her to Hamburg's Philharmonic concerts. At the age of about fifteen he heard *Tod und Verklärung*, when it was given its first performance in the city. The sound of Strauss's opulent orchestration and the dramatic sweep of the music enthralled him.

At the end of the summer in which the incident of 'the black man' had occurred and Otto had foresworn the usual holiday with his mother and sisters, his father as compensation took him on a tour of the Holstein lakes, north-east of Hamburg. Ida Klemperer extracted a promise from her husband that they would go on foot to save money. But Nathan's budgetary sense was less stringent. Father and son took a train to Eutin and set themselves up in a comfortable hotel in Malente, where the sweet trolley made so deep an impression on Otto that he recalled it in a letter written almost forty years later. In the evening Nathan sang and his young son accompanied him on the piano. Their standards must have been tolerably high, for the guests assumed them to be travelling artists, who had been engaged for their entertainment.

*   *   *

* Mahler moved to Vienna in 1897.

At the age of six Otto had been sent to the Hamburg Stiftungsschule, which, although originally a Jewish foundation, was also attended by Christians.* He did not enjoy school and was by his own account 'a fairly undisciplined pupil'.⁴ It was only when he moved in 1895 to the Realgymnasium (where Latin and foreign languages, but not Greek, were taught) of the Johanneum that he began to make progress with his school work, although mathematics remained an ordeal. It was the world of the theatre that above all exercised his imagination. At a reading in class the hypocrisy of Mark Antony's speech in *Julius Caesar* made so deep an impression that he often referred to it in later life.

Klemperer was not particularly happy at the Johanneum, if only because it was not long before he became aware of anti-Semitism. In later years he maintained that as a Jew he had been unable to become head of his class.† On outings to Bismarck's nearby estate of Friedrichsruhe on the anniversary of the battle of Sedan, he was not permitted to carry the flag or the class emblem. At a drawing lesson, when he had difficulty in drawing a straight line, he later recalled that the master had remarked, 'No wonder, in view of your race.' He also encountered an early example of the sort of political reactions he was to experience later in life, in America as well as in Germany. Like many Jews at that time, Nathan Klemperer was a staunch Liberal and his son had imbibed his radical leanings. When he dared to criticise German expenditure on a vast navy, which had become a burning political issue, he was howled down by his classmates as 'a socialist'.

But Otto was clearly cut out for music rather than learning and when he was fifteen a decision had to be reached whether he was to continue at school or to study piano at a conservatory. Advice was sought from a friend of the family, Max Mayer, a German who lived in Manchester, where he was later professor of piano at the Royal Manchester College of Music. He heard the boy play sonatas by Carl Philipp Emanuel Bach and Beethoven, tested his ear and looked at some youthful compositions that did not much impress him. He reported to Ida Klemperer that her son had it in him to be, 'not, perhaps, a Hans Richter',⁵ but a good musician. Then, turning to the boy himself, he gravely told him that success should never be the measure of a musician's life; the essential thing was inner satisfaction. Klemperer never forgot those words.

In Hamburg, Ida Klemperer and her son had been impressed by a recital

---

* Under the headmastership of Anton Rée (1815–91), a relative of Ida Klemperer, the school had in 1852 opened its door to all denominations. It was the first Hamburg school to do so.

† This assertion has been challenged by H. J. Blum, another former Jewish pupil of the Realgymnasium, who attended the school at approximately the same time as Klemperer. In a letter to the author he maintained that, though a Jew, he had frequently been head of his class.

given by the well-known Dutch pianist, James Kwast,* who had established a considerable reputation as professor of piano at the Hoch Conservatory in Frankfurt am Main, and it was decided that Otto should try to secure a place to study under him. That meant leaving school in 1901 at the age of only sixteen without having taken the *Abitur* examination. At the time Otto was glad to escape from the Realgymnasium and he spent a blissful summer between leaving school and going to Frankfurt, devouring books, mainly by contemporary writers, such as Suderman, Halbe, Hartleben and Schnitzler, names that, with the exception of Schnitzler, have long since fallen into oblivion.

In later years, however, Klemperer came to regret the shortcomings of his formal education. As a result, he developed an almost exaggerated respect for learning and, as though in compensation for what he felt himself to lack, took special pleasure in the company of intellectuals. In particular he was drawn to philosophers with a literary bent, and some celebrated thinkers, such as Georg Simmel, Max Scheler and, above all, Ernst Bloch, were to become friends. Among musicians, Klemperer himself later came to enjoy something of a reputation as an intellectual. In fact, he lacked the intellectual discipline and powers of sustained self-expression that might have come with a university education. Yet he was to remain all his life an avid reader, a sharp and caustic observer of affairs, and, true to his Jewish heritage, a man deeply involved in the world of ideas.

* James Kwast (1852–1927) was married first to a daughter of Ferdinand Hiller. Their daughter later eloped with Hans Pfitzner to Canterbury, where they were married.

2   *A student in Berlin*

At the end of August 1901 Ida Klemperer took her son to Frankfurt. He was already enormously tall, a feature that was emphasised by his thinness, long arms and clumsy movements. The Hoch Conservatory, housed in a handsome new building in the style of a Roman *palazzo*, was at the height of its reputation. There he sat an examination and was accepted by what at the time was one of the leading institutes of its kind in Germany and thus in the world. Kwast proved a splendid musician (he also composed) and an admirable teacher. There were also theory and composition classes under Ivan Knorr.* 'To Kwast and Knorr', Klemperer later stated, 'I owe the whole basis of my musical development.'[1] The regime was demanding. For eight hours daily he practised the piano, a further hour was devoted both to the violin and to theoretical exercises. His progress must have been rapid, for in December 1901 he was singled out to play Beethoven's Sonata in D major, Op. 10 No. 3 at a conservatory concert and in the new year he was the soloist in a performance of Schumann's Piano Concerto.

Life in Frankfurt delighted him. He had an attic room to himself in the apartment of a retired piano teacher, where practising presented no problem, and, above all, he was free. The city had a good opera house and orchestra and as a student he had access to cheap tickets. For the first time he heard *The Ring* and was swept off his feet by it. Here was a new world, and for a while he became an avid Wagnerian, though in the course of his piano studies that passion ebbed, as he became increasingly drawn to Brahms. There were other excitements. He was given Grieg's Piano Concerto to play and even that sounded modern to ears that had been exclusively reared on the classics. He heard D'Albert perform the 'Emperor' Concerto, and Paderewski was another pianist who left a lasting memory. But the deepest impression at Frankfurt was made by Julius Stockhausen. Although in his mid-seventies, the celebrated baritone, who was particularly renowned for his interpretation of Brahm's Lieder, still gave private classes. Among his pupils was Klemperer's violin teacher, August Leimer, who was probably instrumental in securing for Klemperer the privilege of acting as accompanist. When the great man held up his phrasing as a model to his

---

* Ivan Knorr (1853–1917) had been appointed in 1883 on Brahms's personal recommendation. He was the teacher of the entire English 'Frankfurt School', which consisted of Cyril
Scott, Roger Quilter, Balfour Gardiner and Percy Grainger.

class, the young pianist flushed with pleasure. It was also at the Hoch Conservatory that he met a fellow pupil, the pianist Lonny Epstein, who was to remain a close friend until her death in 1965. Indeed, had not a love affair with a pupil* obliged Kwast to give up his position, there is no reason to suppose that Klemperer would not have completed his studies in provincial Frankfurt. In that case his career might have turned out very differently. But when in 1902 Kwast moved to the Klindworth–Scharwenka Conservatory in Berlin, Klemperer and a number of other pupils opted to follow him. Nathan Klemperer came to Frankfurt and family permission was given for a move in the autumn.

After the impressive Frankfurt institution, the Klindworth–Scharwenka Conservatory, modestly housed in the Potsdamerstrasse, seemed something of a come-down. Nonetheless the tuition was good. Klemperer joined the theory class given by Philipp Scharwenka† and worked on orchestration and score-reading under Wilhelm Berger.‡ For a while he persisted with violin instruction and was even persuaded to join a conducting class. When his turn came to take the baton he experienced so little difficulty that the instructor told him that he had no need of lessons in stick technique. But, for the time being at any rate, his piano studies under Kwast continued to be his main concern, and evidence of the attention his playing was beginning to attract was not long in appearing in the musical press.

On 30 June 1904 the *Allgemeine Musikzeitung*, whose editor, Otto Lessmann,§ taught musical history at the Klindworth–Scharwenka establishment (doubtless a reason why its house events were so assiduously covered in that journal), announced that Klemperer 'whose name occurs frequently in the college's concerts' had been awarded its piano prize of 200M for a performance of Bach's *Chromatic Fantasy and Fugue*. On 17 March 1905 the same periodical commented favourably on his accompaniment of the Dutch cellist, Jacques van Lier, in a performance of Tchaikovsky's *Variations on a Rococo Theme*.‖ Fourteen days later yet another review of an event at the conservatory described him as 'konzertreif'. In fact he had already made his first recorded professional appearance two months

---

* Frida Kwast-Hodapp (1880–1949), whom he married in 1902. Subsequently a well-known pianist.
† Philipp Scharwenka (1847–1917) enjoyed a reputation as a prolific composer as well as a pedagogue.
‡ Wilhelm Berger (1861–1911), composer and conductor. In 1903 he gave up his position at the Klindworth–Scharwenka Conservatory on succeeding Fritz Steinbach as conductor of the celebrated Meiningen Orchestra, a position in which he was followed by Max Reger.
§ Otto Lessmann (1844–1918) edited the *Allgemeine Musikzeitung* from 1882 to 1907. He also composed.
‖ Jacques van Lier (1875–1951) was in charge of the conservatory's chamber music class. A distinguished instrumentalist and later a member of the well-known Netherlands Trio, in 1907 he gave several public concerts with Klemperer. See pp. 26–8.

15

earlier, when on 10 January 1905 he had accompanied Lessmann's daughter, Eva, in a group of songs at the Berlin Singakademie.

Thus at this stage of his career Klemperer still seemed destined to be a concert pianist. Although his fingers were considered too large and thick, he was already a formidable technician and a fellow-student, Ilse Fromm,* has paid tribute to the extraordinary sense of musical equilibrium that already marked his performance of the 'Hammerklavier' Sonata.[2] In 1905, while he was at the Klindworth–Scharwenka Conservatory, Kwast entered him for the Rubinstein prize in Paris. This was a major international competition, for which the bashful young Klemperer considered himself inadequately equipped.† Founded by Anton Rubinstein in 1890, it offered substantial prizes for composers as well as pianists and took place every fifth year and each time in a different city. In Paris in August 1905 the winner was the 21-year-old Wilhelm Backhaus.‡ Bartók, who offered what eventually became his Rhapsody for piano and orchestra, Op. 1, received a mention for composition but no award as a pianist. About Klemperer 'opinions were divided'.[3] That is not wholly surprising as two movements of one of Rubinstein's own piano concertos (which were obligatory for all candidates) were hardly calculated to show off his talents to best advantage. A month later, however, he entered for the Mendelssohn Prize in Berlin, at that time the foremost competition in Germany, and on this occasion was commended by a jury that included Joachim for his performance of the 'Hammerklavier' Sonata, a work that was certainly more to his taste.

But nervousness hindered progress. When performing in public, Klemperer's hands grew wet with tension and his playing was considered by Kwast and others to be less impressive than it was in private. Even so, by the time of his first year at the Stern Conservatory, to which he transferred in 1905, (see p. 20) he had come to be regarded as a classical pianist of exceptional promise, while the future of another pupil, Edwin Fischer,‡ was at that time thought to lie in conducting. Heinz Tiessen, the composer, who also entered the Stern Conservatory in autumn 1905, later recalled the young Klemperer as already 'spell-binding'.[4] At the public examinations at the end of the school year, his account of the Schubert–Liszt *Wanderer-Phantasie* was described as 'absolutely mature'[5] and the term ended with a special commendation.

*   *   *

* Ilse Fromm-Michaels (1888–   ); pianist and composer. In 1912 the soloist in Klemperer's very first orchestral concert. See pp. 63–5.
† It 'was really nonsense, as I wasn't advanced enough' (*Conversations*, p. 28).
‡ Wilhelm Backhaus (1884–1969) and Edwin Fischer (1886–1960), both celebrated pianists, who subsequently played under Klemperer. Information about Fischer provided by Edmund Schmid, another contemporary at the Stern Conservatory.

16

Berlin naturally offered a far wider range of musical activities than more historically important but smaller cities, such as Frankfurt and Hamburg. Richard Strauss, still only in his late thirties, had since 1898 been First Conductor at the august Court Opera on Unter den Linden, and in April 1907 Klemperer had an opportunity to savour his fresh and lively approach to Mozart in a performance of *Don Giovanni* that took place at the Kroll Theatre, with which Klemperer's own name was to be so momentously connected a generation later. He would also have been able to attend the concerts that Strauss gave with the Berlin Tonkünstler Orchestra, a body the composer had himself set up in 1901 for the performance of contemporary works. The conductor of the Philharmonic Orchestra was Arthur Nikisch, the star maestro of his day,* whom the young Klemperer found 'a better conductor than he was a musician'.[6] But he was enthralled by Nikisch's interpretations of the romantics and in particular by the beauty of sound and controlled passion he brought to Tchaikovsky's *Symphonie pathétique*. Though already in his seventies, Joseph Joachim was still active as director of the Musikhochschule and as a moving spirit in chamber music. As a student Klemperer was able to attend the rehearsals his quartet always held in the Hochschule on the mornings of its concerts. On these occasions Klemperer was impressed by the passionate playing of an old man who had had intimate connections with Brahms and was generally regarded as a pillar of classicism.

Yet the gawky, shy young provincial, who walked around with an abstracted look, as though he always had something on his mind, was not at first much drawn to the German capital. It was, indeed, in many ways an unattractive place at the turn of the century. In the thirty-odd years that had passed since Bismarck had proclaimed the Second German Empire at Versailles, Berlin had been transformed beyond recognition. During that period a sober, straight-laced small city, imbued with Prussian virtues of discipline and restraint and dominated by officials and soldiers, had become a strident metropolis. Huge industries had arisen in the east and north. In the west beyond the Tiergarten a prodigious property boom had conjured into existence vast new suburbs with the Kurfürstendamm as their main axis. Here lived the new middle classes that had flocked to the city in their hundreds of thousands to seek their fortune during the *Gründerjahre*.

Berlin was the *parvenu* among the capitals of Europe and it set out to do on a bigger and better scale everything that had been achieved elsewhere, and above all in Paris, which until the French defeat of 1870 had been regarded as the great city *par excellence*. A vast cathedral, an even

---

* See biographical glossary.

17

vaster parliament were built. A first class museum was put together by Wilhelm Bode with truly American energy. Great arteries were opened up. Roads were broader, pavements more spacious, rooms larger and voices louder than anywhere in Europe. In a term of praise much favoured at the time, Berlin was *kolossal*.

Culturally, however this 'teutonic Chicago' was still overshadowed by older centres, such as Dresden and Munich, not to mention Vienna, all of whose reigning dynasties had traditionally shown themselves far more enlightened patrons of the arts than the hitherto relatively impoverished Hohenzollerns, based as they had been for centuries on the arid sands of the Mark of Brandenburg. Nor did the brash spirit of the new Empire prove more favourable to the arts. Like all court theatres, the Linden Opera was run by the imperial household, and the influence of the reigning emperor, Wilhelm II, was baleful. Productions still conformed to Meyerbeerian standards of spectacle, and, although Strauss was a royal Kapellmeister, favour was not extended to his music. The Kaiser's preferred composer was Leoncavallo, from whom he personally commissioned *Der Roland von Berlin*, which had its first performance at the Linden Opera in 1904, while permission was only granted to stage *Salome* on condition that, as the curtain fell, the Star of Bethlehem was seen to rise over the heroine's body. Up to the end of the First World War Berlin had a well-merited reputation for philistinism.

Klemperer was not entirely without support in this new Babylon. His first cousin, Georg,* had established a considerable reputation as a physician and the young student was invited regularly to lunch on Sunday. The children of the household found this strange, tall relative who ignored them and stamped noisily when he played the piano an alarming figure. But a warm mutual regard grew up between the two cousins. Though Georg was almost twenty years the elder and made no pretence of interest in music, the relationship came to assume a growing importance in Otto's life. Georg was the epitome of the sage physician and, partly owing to the limitations of Otto's natural father, came increasingly to be looked to for counsel and support as well as medical advice at moments of difficulty, of which there were to be many in the coming years. With Georg's younger brother, Felix,

---

* Georg Klemperer (1865–1946) was the eldest of three sons of Wilhelm, Klemperer's father's eldest brother, all of whom were to become well known. Georg was a distinguished physician, who in 1906 became director of the Moabit Hospital in Berlin, a position he held until 1932 (see also biographical glossary). Felix (1866–1925) was a chest physician of repute. Victor (1881–1960) was an author, who among much else (notably studies in French literature) wrote "*LTI*", *Die unbewältigte Sprache*, a fascinating study of the perversion of the German language in the Third Reich. Schoenberg set one of his poems to music in his Two Ballads for voice and piano, Op. 12. The three brothers, children of a liberal rabbi, were the first Klemperers to establish prominent positions for themselves within Christian society.

18

also a physician of repute in Berlin, relations were less cordial. Felix Klemperer, who had married a rich woman and lived in some style, invited his young cousin to a meal and afterwards obliged him to entertain the assembled company. That, it seems, was the last occasion he was given a chance to do so; young Otto did not see himself as a *salon* musician. But with Victor, who as by far the youngest of the three brothers was a near contemporary, there was more common ground and the two cousins saw a good deal of each other during their student days in Berlin.

Klemperer was also a regular visitor at the house of relatives of a Hamburg schoolfriend, Ernst Levy. Though the younger children laughed at his old-fashioned, elastic-sided shoes and general unconcern about his dishevelled appearance, a romantic attachment sprang up with Ernst Levy's sister, Anna. In the summer of 1904 they went together to the seaside. Almost twenty-nine years later, in an ironic little entry in the guest book of Anna Lippmann, as she had long since become, he recalled his bashfulness as a nineteen-year-old suitor.

> Gott, war ich ein dummer Jüngling,
> Schüchternster der Schüchternen...
> Wär ich damals keck gewesen,
> Stünd' ich heute anders da...
> Aber stünde ich besser da?*

But, for an impecunious young man used to a close family life, Berlin, like all large cities, could be a lonely, impersonal place. Klemperer practised to the exclusion of all else. In later years he came to regret that he had not profited more from the city's intellectual life. But, as he ruefully observed, he had lacked a mentor. Even at that early stage of his life he was a rather solitary figure, often lost in his own thoughts, and he seems not to have formed any close friendships during his student years. Yet solitude can be the fruit, as well as the seed, of depression; and it is significant that, when in 1905 he was obliged to look for new lodgings where he could practise freely and could for a long time find nothing he was able to afford, he grew deeply depressed.

That is not an uncommon affliction among introspective young artists. But even at this early point in his life Klemperer may have been aware that in his case depression was not just a matter of being down in the dumps. Years later, he commented that it was at this moment that he first understood the misery his mother suffered. That is evidence that he had already come to understand that he had inherited, though in a far more acute form, Ida Klemperer's depressive temperament. In her son's case this

---

* God, I was a silly youth,/Shiest of the shy./Had I shown a bit more courage,/Where might I not be standing now.../But would I be the better for it?

19

took the form of manic-depressive cycles.* It was an affliction that was to plague him throughout his life, and on several occasions was to come close to destroying his career.

*   *   *

In the autumn of 1905, James Kwast moved again, this time to the Stern Conservatory, and Klemperer once more moved with him. Housed in extensive new premises directly adjacent to the old Philharmonie in the Bernburger Strasse, it had flourished since 1894 under Gustav Holländer's direction and enjoyed a higher reputation than the smaller Klindworth–Scharwenka school. At the Stern Conservatory Klemperer naturally continued his piano studies under Kwast, but he also joined Hans Pfitzner's classes for conducting and for composition. Pfitzner,† who was still in his mid-thirties, was already regarded as one of the outstanding German composers of the rising generation.‡ Indeed, as the composer of two operas, *Der arme Heinrich* (1895) and *Die Rose vom Liebesgarten* (1901), both of which had enjoyed more recognition than Strauss's earliest essays in this field (*Guntram* and *Feuersnot*), Pfitzner had claims to be considered the most important operatic composer to have emerged in Germany since the death of Wagner, at any rate until Strauss swept the board with *Salome* only a few weeks after Klemperer had joined Pfitzner's class.

Klemperer studied with Pfitzner for two years. His master (as he later referred to him) was not an enthusiastic teacher; anything that stood in the way of composing was regarded with resentment. His conducting classes took an odd form. One pupil would play the piano (when it was Klemperer's turn the irascible Pfitzner constantly complained that he played too loudly), another would conduct, while Pfitzner, who had some talent for this sort of thing (see p. 90), would himself sing all the roles. Whether Klemperer's technique much profited is doubtful. But, as he himself later admitted, he learnt a good deal about the Wagner operas to which these strange sessions were mainly devoted. Even more important, a warm relationship sprang up between master and pupil that for a number of years survived differences of temperament and conflicting musical sympathies.

---

* A manic-depressive temperament is often hereditary: fifteen per cent of children of a manic-depressive parent are themselves manic-depressive, as compared to less than half a per cent of the general population (Bleuler, *Lehrbuch der Psychiatrie*, 1960 edn, p. 424). It is known that Ida Klemperer suffered from depressions as well as periods of hyper-activity, such as characterise a manic phase. The illness only manifests itself in adult life, generally between the ages of twenty (as in the case of Klemperer) and fifty.
† See biographical glossary.
‡ There were those who regarded him as a less meretricious figure than his more celebrated and brilliant rival, Strauss. Among them was Thomas Mann. See *Betrachtungen eines Unpolitischen*, pp. 398–418.

Pfitzner's composition class soon fired Klemperer's hitherto dormant creative ambitions. He had already written contrapuntal exercises and elementary essays in vocal polyphony. Now a deep love of Brahms that had developed with growing insight into his piano works led him to compose instrumental music. A piano trio was performed at the Stern Conservatory and Kwast himself was sufficiently impressed to offer to take it into his repertory. But Klemperer declined on the grounds that the work was too dependent on Brahmsian harmony and melody to stand on its own feet. He reacted in a similar way when in 1907 Karl Muck,* to whom he had played a concert overture, offered to perform it in Boston. Once again, Klemperer got cold feet. It was a curious reaction for a young musician with ambitions to compose and on the point of what might have proved a small breakthrough. But, as later events were amply to confirm, Klemperer's attitude to his own compositions varied with his psychological condition.

Nonetheless, they served to bring him into contact with a musician of far wider perspectives than any he had hitherto encountered and one who was eventually to exercise a deep influence on his own musical attitudes. Ferruccio Busoni had been living in Berlin since 1894, torn between the demands of his career as a virtuoso and a desire to compose. A refugee from the limitations of Italian musical life, he had been drawn to the homeland of the great classical masters from Bach to Beethoven, but had reacted sharply against the Wagnerian aesthetic that still dominated German musical life. In this and in much else, he stood at an opposite extreme from his future adversary, Pfitzner, who remained entirely incarcerated within the German romantic tradition. In contrast, Busoni, who in the orchestral concerts he had started to promote in 1902 had been among the first to bring to Berlin new French works, notably by Debussy and Ravel,† was already seeking a way out of what he regarded as the impasse confronting post-Wagnerian music.

A musician of such intellectual curiosity, who served as an anti-body within the complacent ranks of the German musical establishment, inevitably came to exercise a growing fascination on the young, and by the early years of the century his flat in the Augsburgerstrasse had become a meeting place. Busoni generously made himself available to students free of charge on one afternoon a week and it was perhaps on one of these occasions that Klemperer performed his overture. By Klemperer's own account, Busoni was more impressed by his playing than by his composition.

* Karl Muck (1859–1940), celebrated Wagnerian conductor. 1906–8 and 1912–18 conductor of the Boston Symphony Orchestra.
† One of the many paradoxes about Busoni is that he never seems to have included examples of the brilliant new school of piano music initiated by these composers in his own recitals.

4   Mahler and Oscar Fried. Berlin 1906

For his future development it was to prove important that, while still a student, he had come within the orbit of two such outstanding yet sharply contrasted musicians as Busoni and Pfitzner.

But in 1905 an event had occurred that was to lead Klemperer's career in a different direction. While he was still at the Klindworth–Scharwenka Conservatory, Philipp Scharwenka had recommended him as accompanist to Oscar Fried,* a former pupil, who had recently been appointed conductor of Berlin's oldest choir, the Stern Gesangsverein.† Fried's first concert (20 March 1905) was a performance of Liszt's *St Elisabeth*. Earlier he had travelled to Vienna to seek the advice of Mahler, who was performing the same work. Mahler seems to have taken to him, as he agreed to attend the final rehearsals for a performance of his Symphony No. 2 that Fried was to conduct that autumn. The young student who had been engaged to accompany rehearsals thus found himself conducting the off-stage orchestra that figures in the work's last movement in the presence of the composer.

At this point of his life, Klemperer was by no means a devotee of Mahler's music. In the previous season he had heard Nikisch conduct the Fifth Symphony and had not been impressed. But an encounter with the composer himself was to change the entire course of his career. The first rehearsal that Mahler attended did not go well.‡ But on the following day, largely, as Klemperer later suggested, due to the advice the composer had given him, Fried established a firmer grip on the score. When, however, Klemperer diffidently enquired whether the off-stage band had been to his satisfaction, Mahler abruptly told him that it had been far too loud. Klemperer protested that the music was marked 'sehr schmetternd' ('blaring'). But from a distance, replied Mahler. As it was physically impossible to play from the remoteness that Mahler clearly had in mind, Klemperer told his musicians to play softly. The performance on 8 November 1905 was the work's first unqualified success in Berlin§ and the composer was greeted with tumultuous applause. In the green room afterwards he caught sight of the enormously lanky youth who had been in charge of the off-stage band. He went over, shook his hand and said, 'Very good'. The young man glowed with pride.[7]

*   *   *

* See biographical glossary.
† The choir had no relationship to the conservatory of the same name.
‡ Doubtless due to inexperience, Fried devoted so much attention to the other works in the programme, which included two orchestral songs by Liszt, sung by Destinn, that by the end of the allotted time he had only reached the second movement of the symphony. Told that he must stop, Fried, who was given to tempestuous rages, hurled a chair into the auditorium.
§ Mahler himself had first conducted it there in 1895.

23

Although Berlin's musical life was by no means uneventful in the early years of the century, the real excitement lay in the spoken theatre, where the young Max Reinhardt was making a name for himself. At the small Neues Theater am Schiffbauerdamm, where forty years later Brecht was to launch his no less epoch-making Berliner Ensemble, Reinhardt, who was still in his early thirties, had in a series of productions (such as Maeterlinck's *Pelléas et Mélisande*, Wilde's *Salome* and, above all, the first of his many celebrated stagings of *A Midsummer Night's Dream*) shaken to its very foundations the decorative naturalism that had dominated German theatre in the second half of the nineteenth century. Later he proved to be less of a revolutionary than he had at first seemed. But the stir created by his early productions was immense and, as a student with a particularly lively interest in the theatre, Klemperer saw most of them.

Early in 1906, he received a letter from Fried. Reinhardt was planning to stage Offenbach's *Orpheus in the Underworld* with a cast of actors as his final production at the Neues Theater, before moving to the larger Deutsches Theater. He wanted to hear the music, which he did not know. Would Klemperer therefore accompany Fried, who would sing. Reinhardt's associate, Felix Holländer, later recalled 'a pale, thin, immensely tall young man', who appeared and was afterwards engaged as chorusmaster and deputy to Fried, who was to conduct.[8] After the audition Reinhardt asked how long it would take to prepare the chorus. 'About two weeks' Klemperer brashly answered. 'Sie sind wohl noch sehr jung' ('You really are still very young') was the withering reply. It was only then that it dawned on the young musician that the chorus would have to sing by heart.[9]

Rehearsals were lengthy, but Klemperer at once felt at home in the world of the theatre, where he found himself working with figures as famous as Tilla Durieux, Georg Engels and the great Alexander Moissi, who was playing the role of Pluto – still, it seems, with a trace of a foreign accent. Klemperer later recalled his singing voice as 'wonderfully expressive'.[10] He had, however, to learn that, unlike singers, actors were not accustomed to looking to conductors for their cues. In the course of those first weeks with Reinhardt, he also gained more fundamental insights that were to shape his entire approach to opera in later years.

My first impression of musical theatre was of a performance musically and scenically prepared down to the smallest detail...The great practical value of a series of performances (of a single production) was already then absolutely clear to me. My path led me to repertory opera where – in the sharpest contrast to serial theatre (Serientheater) – forty to sixty 'standing' productions, inevitably performed with virtually no rehearsal, were given...Twenty years as an operatic conductor have taught me that this sort of repertory opera is an impossibility.[11]

24

At that early stage of his career, however, Klemperer had no notions of the thorny path through the thickets of repertory opera in the German provinces that lay ahead of him.

The production opened on 13 May 1906 amid great excitement, for Offenbach performed and sung by actors was an event without precedent in Berlin. But on the second night the choleric Fried had a *contretemps* with a leading actress and refused to conduct the following performance. Reinhardt thereupon asked Klemperer to take over and, though he was embarrassed at the prospect of upsetting Fried, he did in fact take charge of the third performance on 16 May and continued to conduct the production until the end of the season. The twenty-fifth performance was attended by a critic from *Der Tag*, who on 10 June observed that, although Herr Fried conducted 'with vigilance', he could achieve similar results without 'throwing his limbs around like a windmill'. Two days later, *Der Tag* carried an announcement:

Kapellmeister Klemperer wishes to state that it was he who conducted the twenty-fifth performance of *Orpheus in the Underworld*...and not Herr Fried, as incorrectly stated in the programme.

Klemperer continued for many years to be criticised for the vehemence and even noisiness of his gestures as a conductor. But for a 21-year-old student to conduct fifty-odd performances of Reinhardt's first Offenbach production was, as he himself later put it, 'a very amusing occupation'.

*   *   *

In January 1907 Mahler, already in what was to prove the final season of his historic decade as director of the Vienna Court Opera, returned to Berlin. On this occasion he himself was to conduct his Third Symphony, and Klemperer was entrusted with the off-stage drum. The work itself did not greatly impress him.* But for the first time he experienced Mahler in rehearsal, and the impact on him was overwhelming.† On this occasion Klemperer was even able to spend a little time in the great man's company. After the morning rehearsal on 13 January, the day before the concert, Mahler was to lunch with Strauss, who, like Busoni, lived in the Augsburgerstrasse. As he did not know his way, Klemperer offered to accompany him on a recently completed line of the city's underground railway. Klemperer

---

* Significantly, Klemperer never conducted it.
† An article by Paul Bekker (*Allgemeine Musikzeitung*, 9 June 1905) on Mahler as a conductor at this comparatively late stage of his career suggests a striking resemblance to Klemperer at his most unyielding period in the later twenties. E.g. 'The thoroughness and conscientiousness of his preparation borders on pedantry...He provokes thought, he astonishes, ...but his light does not warm...one obeys and follows him unwillingly – one cannot do otherwise.' Perhaps significantly Bekker started his life as an orchestral player, indeed he led the orchestra in Reinhardt's *Orpheus*. For Bekker, see also biographical glossary.

25

was disappointed that Mahler evinced no interest in this technical marvel. Instead, he abruptly turned to his young companion and asked him whether he composed. Klemperer was far too diffident to admit that he did. But Mahler laughed, 'No, no, I can see you do.'[12]

After these experiences of Mahler as a man and a musician, Klemperer had only one ambition – to work under his hero. Fried advised that the best approach to Mahler was through his compositions, and Klemperer at once set about making a piano reduction of the Second Symphony.* An opportunity of presenting it to the great man was soon to occur. In February 1907 Klemperer set out as van Lier's accompanist on a tour that was to take them to Vienna on no less than three occasions. The first of their concerts took place in the Saal Ehrbar on 11 February. Klemperer's part in it was small and no sooner had he completed it than he rushed to the Opera, where Mahler was that night conducting the second performance of a new production of *Die Walküre* with a cast that included Anna Bahr-Mildenburg (Brünnhilde)[†] and Friedrich Weidemann (Wotan).[‡] He arrived in time for the second act.

It was indescribable. Mahler, who was his own producer, ruled over everything. I had never seen the close of the second act presented so lucidly on the stage. The woodwind trills at the beginning of the third act were more piercing than I could have believed possible, and during the great C minor episode ('Nach dem Tann lenkt sie das taumelnde Ross') the orchestra almost vanished into thin air. At the end of the magic fire the conductor seemed to surpass himself.[§]

Only three days later, Klemperer had a further opportunity to hear Mahler, this time as a pianist. On 14 February the composer returned to Berlin to accompany the Dutch baritone, Johannes Messchaert,[‖] in a recital devoted entirely to his songs. In spite of the singer's fame, the concert was poorly attended, which indicates how small was Mahler's following in the German capital during the early years of the century. But the event made sufficient impact on Klemperer for him to single it out for comment in a letter he wrote to Alma Mahler a few months after her husband's death. 'I have never', he recalled, 'heard anything so simple and straightforward

---

* Lost during Klemperer's American years.
† Anna Bahr-Mildenburg (1872–1947) was of all singers perhaps the closest to Mahler, to whom she was at one point reputedly engaged. She made her début under him in Hamburg in 1895 (in *Die Walküre*) and in 1898 followed him to Vienna, where she continued to sing until 1921. One of the great dramatic sopranos of her time.
‡ Friedrich Weidemann (1871–1919) was a leading baritone from 1903 until his death.
§ *Minor Recollections*, p. 15. For the innovations, notably in the field of lighting, made by Mahler and Roller in this production, see Ludwig Hevesi, *Altkunst, Neukunst – Wien 1894–1908*.
‖ Johannes Messchaert (1857–1922), Dutch baritone, who was one of the outstanding Lieder and concert singers of his generation.

(schlicht).'[13] Paul Bekker concurred. In a review he described Mahler's playing as 'unyieldingly objective (rucksichtslos sachlich)'.[14]

Van Lier and Klemperer were back in Vienna for their second concert on 15 March,* when their programme included Beethoven's Variations in E flat for Cello and Piano and Grieg's Cello Sonata. At the opera Mahler was preparing a new staging of Gluck's *Iphigenia in Aulis* with Marie Gutheil-Schoder† and Mildenburg in the principal roles. It was to be the last of his collaborations with his designer, Alfred Roller,‡ and as usual he himself was in effect producer as well as conductor. To Klemperer's young ears and eyes the performance was 'so perfect as to defy description'.§ Here on a far larger scale he found that unity of music and theatre that he had first experienced in Reinhardt's Offenbach production. It was to serve as an inspiration to his entire career as an operatic conductor.

Mahler's production of *Iphigenia in Aulis* was a development of the style in which he and Roller had approached *Don Giovanni* in the previous season. On that occasion the stage had been dominated on either side by two massive, permanent towers, which had enabled the opera's frequent changes of scene to be made with a minimum of delay, an innovation that represented a decisive break with the naturalism still dominant in opera in early years of the century. As Roller later recalled, Mahler had welcomed 'a stage on which everything is only intimated'.[15] To that extent his epoch-making productions of *Don Giovanni* and *Iphigenia in Aulis* reveal parallels to the *Stilbühne* that was in the process of emerging in the spoken theatre under the impact of the ideas of Adolphe Appia and Gordon Craig (see p. 83).

Mahler believed that 'in every performance the work has to be reborn'. His overriding concern was to achieve unity between the music and its visual manifestation on stage, and in this respect he was a true successor of Wagner. But he went beyond Wagner in his belief that 'modern art must serve the stage...must extend to costumes, props, everything that can revitalise a work of art',[16] and to this extent he did much to lay the foundations of twentieth-century operatic production. Yet it would probably be a mistake to suppose that he had any theoretical preoccupations about staging. Indeed Roller subsequently asserted that the subject bored Mahler. As his favourite phrase, 'Steht alles in der Partitur' ('It's all in the score')[17] suggests, his concern was first and foremost with the music and it is

---

* On the previous evening he had accompanied Eva Lessmann in a recital in his native city, Breslau. This may have been part of another brief tour.
† See biographical glossary.
‡ Alfred Roller (1864–1935). Chief designer at the Vienna Court Opera from 1903.
§ *Minor Recollections*, p. 15. The performance took place on 18 March 1907. Mahler himself wrote, 'I believe it is the best thing Roller and I have done so far' (Blaukopf, *Mahler*, p. 213).

significant that, according to Roller, he only gave his consent to his collaborator's designs for *Don Giovanni* after long reflection had convinced him of their relevance to the work's musical shape. And if he nonetheless attached more importance to staging than did any of his contemporaries in the field of opera, that did not mean that he was willing to abdicate his own powers to any producer other than himself. Because it was Mahler, the practical man of the theatre, rather than theorists such as Appia and Craig, who was to provide the central inspiration of his approach to opera, differences were later to open up between Klemperer and some of the more radical producers and designers who surrounded him at the Kroll Opera in the late twenties.

On his third visit to Vienna with van Lier,* Klemperer, armed with his reduction of the Second Symphony, presented himself to Mahler in his office in the opera house, where he sat down and played the scherzo without music. Mahler was impressed and moved that anyone should know his music by heart. He asked why a musician who was so formidable a pianist should want to be a conductor. Klemperer insisted that that was now his ambition. Mahler was already aware that his own days in Vienna were numbered† and the Court Opera did not in any case engage untried and unpaid staff. As he was unwilling to provide a written recommendation, he first sent Klemperer to see Rainer Simons, the director of the Volksoper. When, however, the young man returned from that interview empty handed, Mahler took a visiting card and on it wrote:

GUSTAV MAHLER recommends Herr Klemperer as an outstanding musician, who despite his youth is already experienced and is predestined for the career of conductor. He vouches for the successful outcome of a probationary appointment and is willing personally to provide further information.

That card was eventually to 'unlock every door'.[18] Klemperer kept it, and later a copy of it, in his wallet until his own death sixty-seven years later.

Back in Berlin the following day, he had the card photographed and sent a copy to every major opera house in Germany. The few that replied offered only unpaid posts, which he could not afford to accept and would in any case have been willing to take only under Mahler himself. Now that his studies had come to an end and the need to earn a living had become

---

* At their concert of 16 April 1907 at the Saal Ehrbar the programme included Beethoven's Cello Sonata in A major, Op. 69. Klemperer also played solos from Beethoven's Bagatelles, Op. 119 and 126. It was perhaps on this occasion that the well-known Viennese critic, Richard Specht, commented that it had been one of those rare events in which an accompanist had made a marked impression (*Skizzen*, April 1929. Interview with Klemperer. It has not been possible to trace the original review.)

† The Emperor 'graciously released' him in autumn 1907.

28

pressing, he found temporary work as an assistant to Artur Bodanzky* at a small-scale season of popular opera at the Lortzing Theatre in Berlin.

That engagement finished on 31 May. At the end of June, on the off-chance that some opening would present itself, Klemperer decided to attend the annual festival of the Allgemeiner Deutscher Musikverein, a meeting ground for the entire profession which was that year being held in Dresden. There he heard Ernst Schuch†conduct Strauss's most recent opera, *Salome*, and the Rosé Quartet give an early performance of Schoenberg's String Quartet No. 1, Op. 7, an event that rent the audience into sharply opposing factions. But no prospect of a job emerged. At the very end of the festival, while lunching alone, Klemperer overheard a conversation at a nearby table, where two men were discussing a vacancy for a junior conductor at the German Theatre in Prague. 'I would like to have stood up and shouted, "Here he is," but I didn't dare.'[19] After the men had left, Klemperer asked who they were. The waiter told him that one was the well-known Prague critic Richard Batka, who was also at that time serving as musical adviser to the German Theatre during the illness of its director, Angelo Neumann. After consulting Pfitzner who was also in Dresden, Klemperer rushed to Batka's hotel, only to discover that he had already left for the station.

In the waiting room I found this Dr Batka and gave him Mahler's card. He said, 'Go to Marienbad right away. Angelo Neumann, the director of the Prague theatre, is there. Tell him I sent you.'

I travelled third class through the night from Dresden to Marienbad. In the morning I presented myself to Neumann, who was in bed – he was suffering badly from prostate trouble.‡ I had a big package of compositions under my arm, as I felt that somehow I had to introduce myself musically. These didn't interest him at all, but Mahler's recommendation did a great deal. In his rather theatrical way, he said, 'I now offer you the position I offered twenty§ years ago to Nikisch. You will come to Prague in the middle of August as chorusmaster and conductor. What do you want to conduct?' No one had said that to me before! I said '*Carmen*, and perhaps *Rigoletto* and *Der Freischütz*.' He said, 'Bravo,' and the conversation seemed to be at an end. I said, 'Mr Neumann, I must have that in writing.' 'You don't need that with me,' he replied. 'No, no...if you don't put it in writing, I won't come.' He then gave me a piece of paper...I was engaged for five years at a salary that certainly wasn't high.[20]

---

* See biographical glossary.
† As music director of the Dresden Court Opera, Ernst von Schuch (1846–1914) conducted the first performances of a series of Strauss operas, including *Salome*, *Elektra*, and *Der Rosenkavalier*.
‡ Neumann was in fact plagued by kidney stones.
§ In fact thirty years earlier.

3 Apprenticeship in Prague

Prague was a city of two cultures and relations between them were far from relaxed in the early years of the twentieth century. The predominantly Czech-speaking capital of the Austrian kingdom of Bohemia and Moravia contained a substantial German minority of some 40,000 inhabitants, which represented about a tenth of the city's total population.

German culture was no newcomer to Bohemia: Prague had been an integral part of the Holy Roman Empire since the Middle Ages. Its university (founded in 1348) was the oldest in the German-speaking world and the German Ständetheater, where *Don Giovanni* had had its first performance in 1787, had remained the city's sole opera house until 1861. But with the rise of Czech national consciousness and an influx of Czech peasantry, drawn by industrialisation into a city that had hitherto been substantially German, the German-speaking inhabitants had in the course of the second half of the nineteenth century become a minority, consisting largely of an Austrian aristocracy and officialdom and a middle class that was more than half Jewish.* The wealth and influence of that minority still outweighed its lack of numbers, but as the scales tipped increasingly against it, it had started to place new emphasis on a sense of national identity it had hitherto taken for granted.† The German opera house, to which Klemperer had been appointed, had come to play a crucial role in the maintenance of that sense of identity. As an article that subsequently appeared on Neumann's death explained,

The German Theatre in Prague is more than a theatre...it is a political factor..., the focal point of our society, it is our *Volkshaus* and *salon*, the brace that holds together the various components of German Prague and the place where each of us is made most keenly aware of the greatness of German culture.[1]

    *   *   *

When Angelo Neumann was appointed director of the German opera house in Prague in 1885, he was already a well-known figure. A Jew, born in

---

* The balance had begun to tip after 1848. As late as 1856 almost half the population of Prague was German speaking. Fifty years later (1905) Baedeker states that five-sixths were Czech. Until 1914 the Jews identified themselves predominantly with the German-speaking minority.
† The German theatre only started to attach the epithet 'deutsch' to its title in the 1860s, after the first Czech national theatre had been established.

30

Vienna in 1838, he had been an undistinguished baritone at the Court Opera of his native city from 1862 to 1876, when what was described as 'an infection of his vocal chords' led him to seek lusher pastures. In 1876 he became opera director at the Leipzig City Theatre, where he rapidly made his mark as an impresario of exceptional energy and engaged the young Arthur Nikisch as conductor. In the same year as Neumann arrived in Leipzig, Wagner had been left deeply in debt by the performances of *The Ring* that had opened his new Bayreuth Festspielhaus that summer. Neumann, who had met Wagner when he had sung the role of the Herald in a production of *Lohengrin* that the composer had himself staged in Vienna in 1875, saw his opportunity. He persuaded Wagner to rent out the entire scenery and costumes and in 1878 mounted in Leipzig the first complete *Ring* to be seen outside Bayreuth. Having thus demonstrated that the vast tetralogy could be staged outside the Festspielhaus that Wagner had built specially to house it, he proceeded to take the entire production to Berlin and London, where it was seen in 1882. He then toured it in Germany, Austria, the Low Countries and Italy, and finally in 1889 visited St Petersburg and Moscow. These tours made Neumann a celebrity. Wagnerians complained bitterly of the cuts he imposed and of other deficiencies in the performances,* but the royalties the earlier ventures earned enabled Wagner to compose *Parsifal* in the comfort his creative powers required.

In 1882 Neumann left Leipzig and, after three years in Bremen, moved to Prague. He arrived at a difficult moment for the German Theatre. In 1881 the Czechs had opened an imposing National Theatre as an expression of their growing sense of cultural identity. Thenceforth a substantial part of the Czech majority deserted the German Theatre. But the German minority was determined to reply in kind and a new theatre,† which was already in construction on Neumann's arrival, was opened in 1888. Henceforth the two institutions were rivals; comparatively few German works were performed at the National Theatre, no Czech works whatever at the New German Theatre.‡

The New German Theatre was the property of a committee. It was supported principally by the German-speaking community, although the provincial government also provided a subsidy, as it did for the Czech

---

* Neumann did not hesitate to order an encore when a 'number' was applauded. In Bologna Mime's 'Sorglose Schmiede' was sung three times, and in Rome an entire Erda scene was repeated. (Felix Adler, 'Neumann als Operndirektor', *Bohemia*, 21 December 1910)

† Today the Smetana Theatre.

‡ In justice it should be added that a specifically Czech repertory only started to emerge towards the end of the nineteenth century. But no Czech works were heard at the German theatre until Zemlinsky became musical director in 1911, when one of his first moves was to stage *The Kiss* by Smetana.

5   Angelo Neumann

National Theatre. Like many city, as opposed to court, operas of the period, it was leased to a director, who was free to pocket any profits as long as his artistic policy met the approval of the committee. Thus to all practical purposes the German Theatre was a privately run venture.

It says much for Neumann's abilities that with the backing of a population that was the equivalent of no more than a small town he was able to establish a company that was not only able to face the competition of the National Theatre, but was widely regarded as the equal of opera houses in Frankfurt, Leipzig and Breslau, all cities with a population of some 400,000 people, and was even able to undertake guest performances

32

in Berlin. To achieve this he had to persuade the German-speaking minority to support its theatre with subsidies that amounted to more than four times per head those paid by the inhabitants of most purely German cities at that time. He was thus more dependent on public taste.

In fact his own artistic leanings were well matched to those of his public and his time. In spite of his Wagnerian connections and of the fact that he made something of a speciality of Wagner's operas at the German Theatre, he had no conception whatever of Wagnerian *Gesamtkunstwerk*. He was essentially a representative of an earlier period. He had eaten with Berlioz, he had witnessed Meyerbeer, Gounod and Verdi in rehearsal, and his knowledge of old-style, pre-Wagnerian opera was wide.[2] His taste was basically Meyerbeerian: stars and spectacle were his recipe for a full house and ensemble took a low priority. Producers remained unknown in his theatre until 1906; until that date programmes contained a note that 'Der Direktor führt die gesamte Regie' (The director assumes responsibility for all matters of production).[3] Neumann ran an entirely personal regime, controlling every detail in his theatre. Under his leadership the German Theatre never developed an artistic identity. It remained a *Betrieb* – a business enterprise.

Yet Neumann had artistic discernment of a sort. In 1887 he established a series of Philharmonic concerts and in 1899 he inaugurated the spring festival that has since remained a feature of the city's musical life. He had a sharp nose for talent, and particularly for young conductors, if only because his association with Wagner's music had led him to appreciate their growing importance as orchestras increased in size. The young Klemperer was by no means his first catch. In Leipzig he had enlisted the 23-year-old Nikisch. In Prague one of his first steps had been to engage the 25-year-old Mahler, and in succeeding years he acquired young men of the calibre of Muck, Blech,* Schalk and Bodanzky, all of whom were later to make large reputations.

But by the time the young Klemperer arrived in August 1907, Neumann's regime, which had earlier proved so successful according to its lights, had begun to attract criticism. Partly this was the result of advancing age and declining health. The director's self-importance had waxed with the years. In his earlier days an approachable and open-minded man, he had grown increasingly despotic. To those who accepted his rule, he could be a benevolent patriarch, but any expression of dissent was increasingly liable to be taken as a personal affront, and Klemperer was to experience both sides of his character. In the summer of 1907, Neumann, who was nearing seventy, had been taken seriously ill and was absent for several

* See biographical glossary.

33

months.* Thus Klemperer arrived at the German Theatre at a moment when his regime had reached a critical point.

*   *   *

On 15 August 1907 the new young chorusmaster duly reported for duty, only to be met by blank gazes: Neumann had forgotten to inform the theatre of his engagement. Thereupon he proudly presented the letter Neumann had given him and congratulated himself on his forethought in having insisted on written confirmation.† The following morning he was plunged into choral rehearsals for *Madam Butterfly*. A few days later he was told that, in accordance with Neumann's undertaking, he was to conduct a performance of *Der Freischütz*. In spite of the fact that he was given little notice, he was not unprepared. After his engagement he had gone to the Ammersee in Upper Bavaria, where Pfitzner was on holiday. There he had rented a room and worked daily with his former teacher on the operas he had told Neumann he would like to conduct. But his apprehension is evident in a letter he wrote on 25 August to Ilse Fromm, with whom he had been on friendly terms since they had both been in Kwast's piano class at the Stern Conservatory. 'I...start conducting at the beginning of September,...whether I can I still don't know. Cross your fingers for me.'

For Klemperer his first opera was naturally a momentous occasion. The administration saw it in less dramatic terms and he was informed that one rehearsal would be sufficient. It was his first encounter with the realities of life in a repertory opera house. He was appalled and demanded two rehearsals, one of them with the orchestra alone, and threatened not to conduct if they were not granted. As a result of this show of determination he got his way. The performance on 4 September was a success,‡ and Klemperer felt that he had learnt a vital lesson: 'one shouldn't always say "Yes"'.[4] The press of 5 September 1907 was favourable. The *Prager Tagblatt* described the performance as 'fairly smooth', though wishing for tauter rhythms and livelier tempi. *Bohemia* praised the conductor's 'healthy musical impulses' and found the result 'thoroughly satisfactory musically'. More revealing was the anonymous critic of the *Prager Abendblatt*, who wrote: 'This young man, whose firm hand and secure beat is apparent in the freshness and exactitude of the choruses, also proved himself as a

---

* During Neumann's illness the theatre was run by his wife with Richard Batka (see p. 29) as artistic adviser.
† In later years, when insisting on written confirmation of an agreement, Klemperer liked to add, 'I once before had a bad experience with a director.'
‡ Alfred Boruttau, who was a soloist in the first performances of Schoenberg's *Gurrelieder* and Berg's *Altenberg Lieder* in Vienna in 1913, sang the role of Max.

34

conductor. Already in the overture the dark romantic breath of the adagio and a fiery allegro showed...that he has individuality.'

But this performance of *Der Freischütz* was to remain a relatively isolated event in Klemperer's first season. The German Theatre had three other conductors on its staff, all of them his senior, and they naturally took charge of the most substantial works in the repertory. The bell boy was left with what remained and in the conditions in the theatre from the 1907/8 season that consisted overwhelmingly of operetta.

While Neumann had been away ill that autumn, trouble with the personnel over pay had culminated in an orchestral strike. On his return, he detailed his young chorusmaster to conduct an obscure operetta, *Das Wäschermädel*, with a piano accompaniment and waved aside Klemperer's indignant protests with an airy assurance that in his time he had even presented *The Ring* in this way. But the ill wind blew some good. Owing to the strike, it had proved impossible to rehearse the first performance in Prague of Mahler's *Kindertotenlieder*, which Johannes Messchaert was to sing at a Philharmonic concert on 16 October. The great baritone was persuaded to appear with a piano accompaniment, which Klemperer so successfully provided that henceforth in Prague he was to be in considerable demand in this role.

The strike lasted only three days, as Neumann had no alternative but to meet the musicians' demands. But the crisis proved a turning point in his regime. Feeling himself humiliated and under financial pressure, from this moment the ageing director's sole concern was to provide for his family.* Henceforth he gave operetta, which in his heart he despised, an even larger place in the repertory and Klemperer inevitably bore the brunt of that policy.

Neumann also expected his chorusmaster to turn his hand to any odd job that happened to crop up. Early in November Klemperer was, for instance, obliged to accompany two twelve-year-old prodigies at a concert at the German Theatre.† On Boxing Day he had to accompany on the piano the miniature concert that was traditionally inserted on feast days into the second act of *Die Fledermaus*. Two of the theatre's stars, Margarete Siems‡

---

* Richard Batka, 'Angelo Neumann', *Der Merker*, 1911, No. 7. It says something for Neumann that he did not in fact make much money out of the German Theatre and died a comparatively poor man. (Rosenheim, *Die Geschichte der deutschen Bühnen in Prag*, p. 189).
† One of them was Erwin Schulhoff (1894–1942), later a composer and pianist of repute. His parents were the subject of a story that Klemperer liked to tell in later years. Shortly before the concert they called on Neumann to ask about a fee. 'Oh', replied Neumann, quick to spot a threat to his pocket, 'I don't take fees.'
‡ Margarete Siems (1879–1952), who sang the Marschallin in *Der Rosenkavalier* at its first performance in Dresden in January 1911, was at the German Theatre from 1902 to 1908, after which she frequently returned as a guest.

and the newly engaged Alfred Piccaver,* contributed respectively what was described as an American song and a vocal arrangement of Johann Strauss's *Frühlingsstimmen*, and the accompanist rounded off the show with two caprices for piano that he had composed himself. The *Prager Tagblatt* described the concert as an oasis in a desert, but the next morning Klemperer was summoned by Neumann. His playing had been satisfactory, but his shirt was a disgrace. Neumann must have had a soft spot for the young man, for he told him to have six shirts made at his (Neumann's) expense.

Unsatisfactory working conditions and a meagre repertory were not the only difficulties Klemperer encountered during his first season in Prague. One of his first duties was to prepare the brass fanfares for a revival of *Lohengrin* that was to take place on 27 September. As the theatre declined to engage the trumpeters for the additional rehearsal that he considered necessary he paid their fee himself and summoned them to rehearse at his quarters in the Divisstrasse.† This they did with such gusto that a posse of outraged burghers soon gathered in the street, with a result that Klemperer had to seek accommodation elsewhere. Eventually he settled in the Pštrossgasse (today Ulice Anny Letenské) on the Königliche Weinberge, as the section behind the National Museum and the German Theatre was then called, and he continued to live there during the three seasons he was to remain in Prague.

He had, of course, relatives in the city from which the Klemperers stemmed and in which his father had been born. But, though he visited his uncle Philipp, he had little contact with them. Even as a young man Klemperer did not make friends easily. In Prague he grew close to only two men. Ferdinand Onno was that rare creature, an actor who was both erudite and well versed in music.‡ Artur Bodanzky, under whom Klemperer had already worked in Berlin during the spring prior to their simultaneous engagement by Neumann, was First Conductor at the German Theatre. Although he was eight years older than Klemperer, the two musicians were linked by a common devotion to Mahler, for whom Bodanzky had briefly worked as repetiteur at the Vienna Court Opera. Until the Bodanzkys left for America in 1915, their home, first in Prague and later in Mannheim, provided Klemperer with a refuge to which he frequently resorted.

*   *   *

* Alfred Piccaver (1884–1958), English tenor, who, like Klemperer, made his début in Prague in 1907. From 1910 to 1937 he was the leading tenor at the Vienna Court Opera.
† In the largely industrial suburb of Smichóv (today Radlická), where newcomers to Prague traditionally sought cheap accommodation.
‡ In 1968, when Klemperer conducted for the last time in Vienna, Onno, also in his eighties, was housebound. In spite of severe disablement Klemperer climbed many flights of steps to visit his old friend in his fifth-floor flat.

36

Following the example of the Vienna Court Opera, the German Theatre did not at this period print the name of the conductor on its programmes, so that such reviews as appeared in the daily press provide the only clue to Klemperer's activities. But posters for the Philharmonic concert of 11 March 1908 announced that the programme would open with his Overture for Large Orchestra (presumably the work he had earlier played to Busoni and Muck). At the last moment the performance was cancelled owing to the composer's illness, though it is not clear why it should not have been given in his absence. Had he again had last minute doubts about a work he had earlier offered to Muck and subsequently withdrawn? (See p. 21.)

That question remains unanswered. But it is significant that, like everything he had composed up to this moment in his life, the score has not survived. Later in 1908 an event occurred that was to prove crucial to Klemperer's attitude to his own compositions. On 28 September he attended the Austrian première of *Pelléas et Mélisande* at the German Theatre and its 'enormous impact'[5] on him may well have led him to destroy everything he had hitherto written. Only after this first encounter with Debussy's whole-tone harmony did Klemperer begin to compose music for which, as he put it more than sixty years later, 'I would stand up today'.[6] The two songs that are all that remain of the compositions that date from his years in Prague were both written in the wake of this experience.*

Illness may nonetheless have played a part in the withdrawal of his overture, as the poster had claimed. That spring he developed an infection of the thyroid glands that necessitated an operation from which he only recovered slowly. The surgeon recommended that he should recuperate in a sunny climate, but, as he had no money, Klemperer returned to work. Neumann was, however, so shocked by the young man's appearance that he sent him for a month to a sanatorium outside Merano and footed the bill. Once again, he had shown his benevolence to his new chorusmaster and, though the coming seasons were to bring tensions, Klemperer never forgot the old man's kindness.

In May, restored to health, he was back in Prague for a concert that Mahler conducted on 23 May to open the exhibition that had been mounted in celebration of the sixtieth anniversary of the accession of the Emperor Franz Joseph to the throne. This was the first and last occasion on which Klemperer heard Mahler conduct a classical concert programme; it included Beethoven's Symphony No. 7 and the prelude to *Tristan und Isolde*, and he was overwhelmed by the experience.

* 'Aus dem Dunkel', composed in October 1908 for his mother's birthday and subsequently published in a Christmas number of *Bohemia*, and 'Wenn die Rosen ewig blühten'.

I could only get to a rehearsal, but my one reaction afterwards was that one should abandon the profession if one could not conduct as Mahler did. In the Beethoven he took the second part of the allegretto at a slightly livelier pace than the main portion. It sounded like a new work. I have never heard the climax of the *Tristan* prelude (which he naturally conducted without any increase of tempo) played with such emotional impact and the same applied to the march in *Die Meistersinger* ...Everything was absolutely natural...you felt that it could not be better and could not be otherwise.[7]

Klemperer spent part of his summer vacation with his younger sister, Marianne, on Sylt, the island resort off the German North Sea coast. He had not long returned to Prague when there was another and even more enthralling encounter with his hero. Mahler had been so delighted with the playing of the Czech Philharmonic Orchestra at his concert in May that he had agreed to return to Prague in August so as to give with it the first performance of his Symphony No. 7. Klemperer attended every rehearsal he could. A Viennese critic who had come to Prague for the occasion later recalled a lanky youth who had shadowed Mahler and even begun to ape his hero's mannerisms.[8] But the great man was not displeased by his disciple's attentions. On 22 August he wrote to his wife, Alma.* 'The last days very agreeable. The orchestra good and willing. I am constantly surrounded by a staff of young (and very nice) people, among them Bodanzky and Klemperer, who has made a magnificent reduction for two hands of the Second Symphony.'[9]

Klemperer has also left an account of the preparation for the première, which extended over several weeks, as Mahler had some two dozen rehearsals.

Each day after rehearsal he used to take the entire orchestral [material]† home with him for revision, polishing and retouching. We younger musicians, Bruno Walter, Bodanzky, von Keussler and myself, would gladly have helped, but he would not hear of it...We usually spent the evenings with him at his hotel. He was relaxed and extremely amusing, holding forth uninhibitedly about his successor in Vienna. Weingartner,‡ the man in question, had made such enormous cuts in *Die Walküre* that patrons of the fourth gallery had hissed and booed.

Mahler also spoke at length about Hugo Wolf, whom he did not like at all. Young puppy that I was, I had the impudence to contradict him and to assert that the Mörike *Gebet* was very fine. Mahler shot me an angry glance. All I could say was 'With all respect, that's only my opinion'.§

*   *   *

* See biographical glossary.
† Klemperer inadvertently used the word 'score'.
‡ See biographical glossary.
§ 'Das war nur so meine Meinung, Herr – Halten zu Gnaden'. Schiller, *Kabale und Liebe*, Act 2, Scene 6. The account is taken from *Minor Recollections*, pp. 18–19.

The new season mercifully brought an occasional release from operatic routine. There were opportunities to accompany singers of the calibre of Julia Culp, Margarete Siems, Vittorio Arimondi and Felix von Kraus.* Bodanzky was to conduct Beethoven's Ninth Symphony and Klemperer was entrusted with the preparation of the chorus. To one young member the impression was still alive almost sixty years later.

An immensely tall figure rose up...with the most beautiful head I had ever seen. Klemperer...had a high voice that squeaked when he was excited and he was always excited. But the old rehearsal piano sounded under his huge fingers and from the first moment we followed him, enthralled....[10]

But within the theatre Klemperer found himself condemned to conducting

* The last-named in Brahms's *Vier ernste Gesänge*, an interpretation for which he was particularly celebrated.

6 Klemperer with his sister, Marianne. Sylt, summer 1908

an unending succession of ill-prepared *Spielopern*. Thomas's *Mignon* was followed by Lortzing's *Der Waffenschmied*, Kienzl's *Der Evangelimann* by Nessler's *Der Trompeter von Säckingen*. It was doubtless better than the almost unvaried diet of operetta he had endured in his first season, and the critics began to praise his growing ability to hold these ramshackle evenings together. But they remained a far cry from the perspectives opened up during the intoxicating hours with Mahler. Klemperer felt increasingly despondent and frustrated.

On 3 December 1908 he wrote in despair to Pfitzner. That autumn his former teacher had taken up his duties as head of the Strasbourg Conservatory and director of the city's concerts. Klemperer asked whether a job could be found for him at the theatre. His letter was full of the anguish of a young idealist confronted for the first time in his life with the harsh realities of repertory opera:

I am writing to ask you a great favour. Would you ask Herr Direktor Wilhelmi whether he would take me from Prague even if I am in *breach of contract*.* I don't dare to write that myself to Herr Direktor Wilhelmi, as I don't want to present myself to him in a false light. It is only an action of despair on my part, as I am well on the way towards losing all pleasure in my vocation because of the inartistic conditions here which are ruining me in every respect.

No position in Strasbourg was available, and Pfitzner seems to have tried to comfort Klemperer, who on 29 January 1909 wrote to thank him for his 'extremely kind' advice. But in that letter it is apparent that the cause of his despair lay deeper than the deficiencies of Neumann's regime. 'Please don't be angry on account of my long silence...That it has taken so long to reply is due to an indisposition that has already been tormenting me for about three months. I am suffering from a nervous depression which plagues me and has certainly been brought about by the sad artistic conditions in the theatre.'

This was the first acute manifestation of the manic-depressive rack on which he was to be stretched until the very end of his life. It was a condition that was often to make him disconcertingly unpredictable to those (and they remained an overwhelming majority of his acquaintances) who were unaware of his affliction. In depression, Klemperer was withdrawn and impenetrable. He set a wall between himself and the outside world and the deeper his melancholy the more he shunned human companionship. In such periods, he suffered from intense anxiety, night-sweats and stomach pains. Tablets had little effect on his chronic sleeplessness. He became obsessively neat, puritanical in his attitudes, careful – even mean – with

---

* Wilhelmi was the Intendant of the Strasbourg theatre. Klemperer was bound to Neumann by the five-year contract he had signed. Wilhelmi rejected his offer to break it (see p. 43).

40

money, and so intensely self-critical that at moments he came even to doubt his own abilities.

In manic phases these characteristics swung to an opposite pole. He grew hectically active, talkative and gregarious. It is to periods such as these that most of the many anecdotes about him relate. When 'high', his attention was easily distracted, he tended to spend irresponsibly, his eroticism was heightened, and any attempt to restrain him was liable to give rise to frightening rages. In such phases he was also accident-prone, in so far as mania tended to deprive him of a healthy awareness of danger, just as in depression he saw it at every corner.

These changes did not, of course, occur abruptly. Acute phases only built up and dispersed gradually.* Shafts of sobriety and self-awareness would occur in the most intense manic periods. Conversely, in depression the clouds would sometimes lift momentarily. Thus the gradations in Klemperer's psychological condition were often hard to determine, even for those close to him. Nor did the acute phases of his malady constitute his entire life: between extremes, themselves of varying intensity, he enjoyed lengthy periods of relative equilibrium, although, as an introvert, even at such times he remained a withdrawn character who welcomed and indeed needed solitude. The cause of this 'illness of the emotions'† was in Klemperer's case primarily endogenous, in the sense that its phases were not reactions to outer circumstances, although these could bring about a heightening of whatever condition he might be in.‡

At times of equilibrium Klemperer occasionally composed. But it was only when 'high' that he produced a torrent of music which he later almost invariably rejected, so that comparatively little of his output has survived. Indeed his attitude to his compositions provided throughout his life a remarkably reliable indication of his psychological condition. Thus his refusal to allow Muck to perform his overture in Boston (see p. 21) suggests a degree of depression, just as its subsequent inclusion in a Philharmonic concert in Prague indicates a measure of euphoria. Now, as his letter to Pfitzner made plain, the weathervane of his emotions had once again swung decisively towards depression.

As he grew older, Klemperer learnt to bear his affliction with silent fortitude, so that only his immediate family and a handful of close friends were aware of it. But the depression that struck him in the winter of 1908/9 (and worse by far were to follow) seems to have caught him unawares.

---

* Klemperer's case was atypical in that these phases, whether manic or depressive, were more lengthy than is usual. More than one depression persisted for over a year.

† Phrase used by Herbert Binswanger, a noted Swiss psychiatrist who was well acquainted with Klemperer, in conversation with the author, 21 November 1972.

‡ It is today widely considered that the manic-depression syndrome results from chemical changes in the body. In any case, it is in no sense a neurosis.

For the first time he sought medical advice. He also wrote to his mother, who hastened to her distressed son and could only with difficulty be dissuaded from telling Neumann to his face how badly he ran his theatre.

Meanwhile, however, Klemperer had been allotted a task that may have brought psychological benefit as well as artistic satisfaction. On 12 February 1909 the theatre mounted Pfitzner's opera, *Die Rose vom Liebesgarten*, and he was naturally in charge of the choral preparations. Mahler had been impressed by the work, when he had performed it three years earlier at the Vienna Opera, and the high opinion of it Klemperer held as a young man is evident from the ardour with which after the Prague performance he urged its merits on Oscar Fried. Bodanzky conducted 'splendidly', Klemperer wrote to Pfitzner on 15 February 1909 immediately after the first night. But in the course of the following six weeks the work had only two more performances: 'Neumann', Klemperer wrote to the composer on 22 March, 'has *absolutely no* relationship to your art.'

Another event also served to reconcile him to Prague, at any rate for the time being. Without warning, Bodanzky had announced that he would be leaving at the end of the season for Mannheim. Neumann was able to offer Klemperer promotion, and it was not long before it bore fruit. Towards the end of the season he was put in charge of a revival of *Lohengrin*, by far the most demanding task that had as yet been confided to him. On the first night he conducted with immense passion; years later a member of the audience recalled his clenched fists raised high in ecstasy. Whether the performance was entirely successful is open to doubt. Both the *Prager Tagblatt* and the *Abendblatt* noted untidinesses and an occasional lack of unity between stage and orchestra. But Felix Adler,* the critic of *Bohemia*, with whom Klemperer had become friendly, was more positive in his review of 14 June 1909.

The evening provided Herr Kapellmeister Klemperer with his first opportunity to prove himself as a Wagner conductor. Anyone who has observed the activity of this extraordinarily able young musician with attention could not have doubted that he would succeed. An artist with absolutely his own intentions, he puts these into effect with burning enthusiasm, not, admittedly, without a certain excess of gesturing that a little self-control would easily remedy...It is a long time since one has heard a *Lohengrin* played with so much warmth and life.

The season ended on 20 June and he returned to Hamburg. There he found his mother distressed. In her husband's absence (he was as usual 'taking the cure' in Marienbad) she had discovered that the family bank account was empty. Ida Klemperer told her son that he must confront his

* Felix Adler (1876–1928) had succeeded Batka as music critic of *Bohemia* in 1907. His incisive pen was to play a crucial role both in the undermining of Neumann's reputation in his declining years and in the increasing attention that Klemperer was beginning to attract (see pp. 44–6).

father with his irresponsibility, a task for which he had little stomach; close though he was to his mother, he sometimes found her attitude to Nathan unduly harsh. After a stop in Berlin, where he played *Die Rose vom Liebesgarten* to Oscar Fried, he dutifully proceeded to the Bohemian spa, where he found his father taking a siesta, doubtless after the strains of the midday session of *Skat*. Nathan, who was already in his sixties, was unperturbed by his son's sudden appearance. He explained that the money had gone on the expenses of the marriage of his elder daughter, Regi, to Ismar Elbogen, a Jewish historian. During this journey Klemperer also made a detour to Bayreuth, where he was able to hear Karl Muck conduct *Lohengrin*. Under Cosima Wagner's regime productions had long been vigorously stereotyped and the staging, as he wrote to Pfitzner on 11 August from Prague, seemed to be 'without insight. One could write volumes over conditions there.'

In the meantime the prospect had arisen of a position in Strasbourg, for which he had yearned during the previous winter, doubtless owing to the intervention of Pfitzner, who had been appointed director of the theatre there with effect from September 1910. But now the depression had passed and he felt more confident of his future with Neumann. As a result, he was less eager to work directly under a character as notoriously irascible and dogmatic as his old teacher, many of whose views on repertory and production were far removed from his own. He was in any case still unclear how he could free himself from his contract with Neumann as he explained in his letter of 11 August to Pfitzner.

So far as my coming is concerned, at the moment it is impossible to say anything decisive...It is just as unclear to me as it was a year ago how I should free myself. On the contrary, now that Bodanzky has left, Neumann places still more confidence in me. He [Neumann] has the theatre until 1912 and my contract lasts until then. He probably won't be appointed director again and so in these last years he wants to save any money he can scrape together. He has me at a *dirt-cheap* price and for that reason he holds on to me. In December I offered to break my contract, but Wilhelmi turned it down. So that is not a possibility. I can't behave like Bodanzky, who left in a very abrupt way, because I'm indebted to Neumann for his splendid behaviour during my illness. If at all possible, give me advance notice of a decision, and please let me know the last day for acceptance.

Nothing more was to come of Strasbourg until 1914, when Klemperer's caution at the prospect of working under Pfitzner was to prove well justified.

As Second Conductor, a position to which he had been formally appointed in August 1909, Klemperer was naturally allotted a share of the more substantial works in the repertory at Prague. His first task was a new production of *William Tell*. The 24-year-old musician still had a tendency to take himself *au grand sérieux*. At a rehearsal of the overture, he conducted the opening andante with such portentousness that Neumann called out impatiently, '*Much* too slow!' The young conductor felt affronted and answered, 'I take it differently.' Years later, when he recalled the incident, he laughed at his earlier self-esteem and agreed that Neumann had been quite right.[11] The criticism seems to have borne fruit. At any rate, on the day after the première (10 September) *Bohemia* noted that the overture had been played 'with real bravura', while the *Prager Tagblatt* praised its 'rhythmic verve'.

Such activities were far removed from the succession of operettas and *Spieloper* that had so lowered his spirits in the previous seasons. But his continuing dissatisfaction with the rough and tumble of repertory theatre is evident in a letter his mother wrote to her elder daughter, Regi Elbogen, on 21 November 1909:

Otto is overburdened, so that he has no pleasure in his work. He ought to rest for three weeks, as he has even more to do over Christmas, but that monster Neumann only starts to look after his employees when they are on their backs...He exploits Otto in a wretched way. Well, at the moment Otto is bound by his contract, but that he won't stay for his full five years is as clear as daylight (steht mir bombenfest).

Ida Klemperer's prophecy was to be fulfilled more rapidly than she can have supposed. During the autumn of 1909 complaints in the press about the repertory and standards of the German Theatre had been growing sharper. In particular, Felix Adler, the critic of *Bohemia*, launched an increasingly savage assault on Neumann's regime, while singling out Klemperer for praise.*

On 5 December a guest conductor, who in accordance with the usual formula was billed as appearing *auf* (i.e. with a view to) *Engagement*, took over a performance of *Die Zauberflöte*. In the following morning's number of *Bohemia*, Adler asked with feigned innocence what had happened to necessitate a new engagement in a theatre that already boasted four conductors. He must have been well aware that relations between Neumann and Klemperer had finally reached breaking point. In his later years a hot-tempered man, Neumann had become increasingly enraged by the combination of Adler's attacks on himself and praise of his Second Conductor. He knew that Klemperer and Adler were friendly and, leaping to the conclusion that the articles had been inspired by his young Kapellmeister (and, at any rate indirectly, he may not have been entirely wrong), he presented Klemperer with an ultimatum: either he ceased to

---

* That the critic of the other principal newspaper, the *Prager Tagblatt*, was more moderate in tone may be attributed to the fact that its editor, Heinrich Teweles, had for thirteen years been Neumann's *Dramaturg* and eventually succeeded him as director.

see Adler, or he would be dismissed. Klemperer naturally refused to give any such undertaking and was accordingly fired with effect from the end of the season.

Significantly, he did not turn to Pfitzner, with whom only three months earlier he had been in correspondence about a position in Strasbourg, but to Mahler, who was that winter conducting in New York. Mahler's response was prompt and effective. To Hamburg he sent a two-word telegram, 'Klemperer zugreifen' ('Grab Klemperer').[12] To Ferdinand Gregori, then Intendant in Mannheim, he wrote,

I recommend Herr Klemperer with pleasure. He has all the characteristics that go to make a great conductor. He is admittedly still very young, but he has a future and I am convinced that you could not make a better choice.[13]

That was high praise from so exacting a musician and it is hardly surprising that both Hamburg and Mannheim offered positions. Klemperer opted for Hamburg. It was, after all, his home town, his parents and young sister were living there, and the prospect of working under Gustav Brecher,* another former repetiteur under Mahler in Vienna, proved a greater attraction than a position under Bodanzky in Mannheim. On 11 January 1910 Klemperer sent a telegram to his joyful parents announcing that a contract had been signed. He was delighted to receive a letter of welcome from Brecher shortly after his appointment had been announced.

Meanwhile the season continued to run its course. It was symptomatic of Neumann's taste in his declining years that Julius Stern's *Narciss Rameau*, the only contemporary opera that Klemperer was allotted during his stint in Prague (on 26 January 1910), should have been dismissed even by one of the more accommodating critics as 'a nullity'.† But during his last months in Prague he conducted for the first time in his career works as substantial as *Les Huguenots*, *Der fliegende Holländer* and *Carmen*. All were tasks very much to his taste and in the reviews they evoked there are clear indications that a sense of musical identity was beginning to emerge.

The season ended with a final humiliation for Neumann's theatre in its role as a guardian of German culture in a predominantly Slav city. In January 1909 Strauss's *Elektra* had had a triumphant first performance in Dresden. To those with ears it was the most important new German opera since the death of Wagner. But Neumann became involved in a wrangle with the publishers over performing fees and finally announced that he

---

* See biographical glossary.
† Ernst Rychnovsky, *Der Merker*, 25 February 1910. The work had its first performance in Breslau in 1907. Julius Stern (1858–1912), Viennese operetta composer, is not to be confused with the identically named conductor and pedagogue (1820–1883), who founded the Sternsche Conservatory in Berlin, at which Klemperer studied from 1905 to 1907.

would not stage it. The Czech National Theatre leapt into the breach and on 25 April 1910 mounted a production that greatly impressed Klemperer. Neumann was reduced to inviting the Dresden Opera to perform the work in German at the Spring Festival nine days later. It was an ignominious close to what was to prove his last complete season,* which ended on 31 May.

On that day Felix Adler wrote a farewell tribute to Klemperer in *Bohemia*.

Today Otto Klemperer ends his present engagement...To have been able to follow the growth of this rich talent from its earliest beginnings to complete maturity has been a particular pleasure...Klemperer came to Prague as a graduate of the Berlin Stern Conservatory and he leaves it as a conductor of character and individuality. He has not developed according to any model. He has had to find everything that he has become from within himself...As a result, his performances have acquired a character of their own...Instead of handed-down traditions, something new and good has emerged in the operas he has conducted...Such conductors are rare and awake opposition...Otto Klemperer can take pride in having in most cases overcome these difficulties and where he did not succeed in doing so he indicated with energy what he wanted. Thus performances of *Lohengrin* and *Der fliegende Holländer*, which he conducted with inspiration and idealism, as well as of Italian and French operas, provided an abundance of stimulus. Under his direction the ensemble and the orchestra have been stretched to the limits of their abilities. Had he been used as he deserved to be, the theatre would have gained richly. Now the Hamburg City Opera will benefit from his gifts.

It was a remarkable tribute to a musician who had only two weeks earlier celebrated his twenty-fourth birthday.

---

* During the following winter Neumann caught a chill during rehearsals for a new production of *Fidelio* and died on 18 December 1910.

46

4 Hamburg: 'Himmelhoch jauchzend, zum Tode betrübt'*

On his way home Klemperer broke his journey in Berlin. There he visited his cousin, Georg, who told him that, as he was about to begin a career in Germany, the time had come for him to leave the Jewish community, as Mahler had done thirteen years earlier when the prospect had arisen of a Viennese engagement.† For Georg, as for many Jews who in the years following emancipation had risen to prominent positions in Christian society, Jewish faith had become an irrelevance. For him it was a mere relic of the ghetto mentality that Jews of his standing had discarded. With that trust in progress characteristic of men of science in the nineteenth century, he believed that assimilation must follow emancipation and tolerance, as day follows night. He himself had long since become a Lutheran, had married a Christian and was in the process of bringing up his children in such ignorance of their Jewish heritage that his eldest son was not even aware that his grandfather, who was still alive, was a rabbi.

Klemperer was at that time no more attached to the Jewish faith than was his cousin, whom he admired and respected. But the implication that it could be sloughed off like a suit of old clothes made him uncomfortable. Predictably, his father, whose ties to the Jewish faith were still close, was outraged at the advice Georg had given. What Ida thought is not recorded: more 'liberal' than her husband, she may well have attached greater importance to her son's musical career than to his religious denomination. For some weeks Klemperer took no action. Then, on 16 July, he wrote to the official body that supervised such matters‡ for permission to leave the Jewish community. This was duly granted. Significantly, he took no steps to join the Lutheran or any other church. Perhaps a subconscious awareness of the as yet dormant religious nature of his own character prevented him from adopting a creed for reasons of convenience.

*   *   *

In the middle of June Klemperer travelled to Munich. Two events drew him

---

* Goethe, *Egmont* III, 2. Literally, 'exulting unto the heavens, sad unto death'. A phrase that Klemperer later used to describe his manic-depressive syndrome. (CBC Transcript 8, p. 8)

† Mahler had become a Catholic, a necessary qualification for the director of the Vienna Opera under the Habsburgs.

‡ Not, as Klemperer himself wrongly recalled, directly to the chairman of the Jewish community, but to the Hamburg Aufsichtsrat für Standesämter.

47

there. His visit coincided with a Richard Strauss week at the opera, where on 24 June he heard Edyth Walker* sing the title role in *Salome* under the composer's direction. Her performance, Klemperer wrote to his elder sister on 6 July, 'was better than the work itself'. The other was more compelling: towards the end of June rehearsals for the first performance of Mahler's vast Eighth Symphony were about to begin. As the composer entered the hall he was delighted to find Fried and Klemperer waiting for him.[1] As two years earlier in Prague, evenings were spent with Mahler in his hotel, where among other issues Mahler defended his practice of making retouchings in classical works such as Beethoven's 'Pastoral' Symphony.† Turning to Klemperer, he said, 'At first, of course, you will conduct the work as it is written. But later on you will see that some instrumental retouching has to be done.'[2]

Again Klemperer was amazed at the countless small instrumental alterations that the composer made during rehearsals. 'He always wanted more clarity, more sound, more dynamic contrast. At one point during rehearsals he turned to us and said, "If, after my death, something doesn't sound right, then change it. You have not only a right but a duty to do so."'[3] Klemperer was also struck by the intensity of sound Mahler was able to draw from his forces at the entries of 'Veni, creator spiritus' without any apparent outward effort.[4] The impact of the music on Klemperer was immense: 'To be frank, it was not until then that I understood Mahler's music well enough to realise what a great composer he was.'[5] So enthralled was he with what he heard that he wrote, as he told his sister, 'a really detailed article',‡ on it. Yet it was a work that he was destined never to conduct himself.

Early in July, Mahler left Munich for Toblach in South Tyrol, where he was to spend his last summer holiday. This is probably the occasion on which he invited Klemperer to visit him there. That Mahler thought highly of his young disciple's musical abilities is apparent from his repeated efforts to foster his career. That there was also a more personal link is clear from the fact that on more than one occasion he told Klemperer how much he was reminded by him of his younger brother, also called Otto, who had committed suicide but whom Mahler always described as more talented than himself.[6] Klemperer was later to regret that he did not accept the invitation to Toblach. Instead he travelled to Mannheim, where he stayed for a few days with the Bodanzkys. He was at this period again composing,

---

* See biographical glossary (Brecher).
† Klemperer must have noted all that Mahler said. Years later in Cologne he had a score of the work that contained all Mahler's retouchings, mainly in the brass. (Information provided by Professor Arnold Schmitz, see p. 152, 153–4n.)
‡ Letter of 6 July to Regi Elbogen. The article was never published and has not survived.

a sure sign that his spirits were high. Two of a cycle of four songs that he later orchestrated, 'Ständchen' and 'Empfindungen beim Wiedersehen einer viel geliebten Stadt', date from this summer, as does a Ballad to be scored for large orchestra that, like so many of his compositions, did not survive an ensuing depression. By the middle of July he was back in Hamburg, but after renting a room on the Rothenbaumchaussee Klemperer again went to stay with the Bodanzkys, who by this time were on holiday on the Starnberger See. From there it was a short journey to Munich, where he was able to attend more rehearsals of the new Mahler symphony. By this time an extraordinary assembly of musical figures was beginning to gather for the first performance. But Klemperer could not stay for the great event, as his own rehearsals in Hamburg were due to begin on 25 August.* He was never to see Mahler again.

*   *   *

As the opera house of Germany's second largest city and biggest port, the Hamburg Stadttheater was a more substantial undertaking than the German Theatre in Prague. But in other ways it bore disconcerting resemblances to the theatre Klemperer had just left, for it was one of the few remaining privately owned civic theatres in Germany, still leased to a director, who, like Neumann, was at liberty to retain any profits he made. In this, the Stadttheater reflected the mercantile traditions of Hamburg. The great court operas of Central Europe were the offspring of absolutism, of reigning princes who had made little distinction between private and public funds and had spent as much on theatres as they felt inclined. In contrast, Hanseatic Hamburg had for centuries been governed by its merchants, who were concerned to keep public expenditure to a minimum and regarded a subsidised theatre with suspicion.† In this the city followed Anglo-Saxon rather than Central European traditions, and it is not mere chance that in 1910 conditions at the Stadttheater bore a disturbing similarity to those at Covent Garden in London. But there was one substantial difference. Whereas at the Royal Opera House Sir Thomas Beecham was able to limit his activities to a relatively brief international season, the Stadttheater was obliged to provide repertory opera for ten months of the year. The strain of doing so was already beginning to tell.

Its director, Max Bachur, had originally joined the theatre as an accountant and he ran it primarily as a business. Whereas Neumann, for

---

* The following were among those who attended the first performance of Mahler's Symphony No. 8 on 12 September: Schoenberg, Berg, Webern, Siegfried Wagner, Casella, Thomas Mann, Max Reinhardt, Roller, Fried and Stokowski (see Schreiber, *Mahler*, pp. 121–2).
† The anti-absolutist tradition of Hamburg also affected repertory. In the eighteenth century, German *Singspiel* was preferred to Italian *opera seria*, which flourished in the court theatres.

all his failings in his later years, had earlier proved himself an imaginative impresario, Bachur, who was already in his mid-sixties when Klemperer joined the staff, seems to have had limited artistic insight. His main means of attracting a public were the engagement of famous guest artists (in 1906 he had inaugurated an annual visit by Caruso) and a succession of trivial novelties. The theatre's standards had fallen badly (like Prague, it had no musical director on its staff) and by 1910 Bachur himself had reached the conclusion that it could no longer be run as a purely private undertaking. He had accordingly drafted a memorandum to the Senate, requesting a public subsidy. When that request was rejected within a few months of Klemperer's arrival, Bachur resigned. Thus in Hamburg Klemperer again found himself part of a regime on its last legs.

*   *   *

On 3 September Klemperer made his début with *Lohengrin*. That he chose to do so in a work with which he was already familiar is characteristic of the caution he was always to show on crucial occasions. From the start he caught the attention of the house by refusing to raise his baton until there was complete silence; and, having caught it, he held it throughout an evening of triumph such as few young and unknown conductors have experienced. In the *Hamburger Nachrichten* (5 September) Ferdinand Pfohl wrote of 'a meteor fallen from heaven'. In the *Hamburger Fremdenblatt* of the same day Heinrich Chevalley described Klemperer as

a musician of the utmost sensibility, of thrilling temperament and natural dramatic instinct, who follows the music drama with an inner attention that guarantees a close integration between stage and orchestra...He knows how to give an act logical shape, he feels each accent in the drama as well as in the music, and as a musician he misses no detail in the score.

Pfohl was particularly enthusiastic about the prelude:

How shatteringly Klemperer built up to the great climax...the brass theme was really overwhelming and came with all the majesty and brilliance of an opening in the heavens. At this point, as though carried away by an irresistible impulse, the conductor leapt to his feet and hurled cues at the brass with bold, uninhibited gestures.

The critics were electrified. Both Chevalley and Pfohl had experienced Mahler's years in Hamburg; indeed Pfohl had known Mahler since they had been students together in Leipzig. Both men were immediately struck by the new conductor's resemblance to his great predecessor. In Klemperer's refusal to begin until there was complete silence Pfohl saw something of Mahler's 'prachtvolle Rücksichtslosigkeit' ('magnificent ruthlessness').

Chevalley took his concern with expression rather than form to be characteristically Mahlerian.*

There were, of course, reservations. Klemperer's taste for dynamic nuances was felt to be exaggerated. Pfohl pointed to deficiencies of technique that had almost caused a derailment. Chevalley observed that Klemperer conducted 'with a complete lack of concern about his appearance. And in fact his movements were not attractive; there were moments when one wished that this unmannerly conductor might enjoy the protection of a hidden orchestra.' More than one critic felt that there was something disconcertingly untamed about this wild young man. Pfohl went even further: here, he suggested, was an artist whose features suggested the presence of twilit powers. This was more than a Hoffmanesque conceit, for there was indeed something disturbingly expressionistic about the burning black eyes in a white face, the strange high-pitched voice, the gangling gait and enormous height. But the evening was a triumph and the applause, as Pfohl put it, was like 'a storm at sea'.

Klemperer was not allowed to rest on his laurels. A junior conductor had to be ready to conduct a different work on most nights of the week and *Faust* (Gounod) and *Carmen* followed *Lohengrin* on three successive evenings. In *Carmen*, in particular, his manner of conducting again drew comment.

Herr Klemperer again offered a little piece of theatre in itself...At moments he towered up as though his limbs were impelled by a spring, at moments he sank back into himself; at moments he used his baton as a lance with which he stabbed at the favoured musicians...That in choral scenes Herr Klemperer also invoked the use of his feet to drum the beat into the ladies and gentlemen on the stage can hardly be reckoned an attraction...in a few years he will smile at this noisy expenditure of energy.[7]

As in Prague, his tempi in *Carmen* were found to be slow, but there was praise for the delicacy, colour and expressiveness of the orchestral playing. Even if not on the level of his *Lohengrin*, it was clearly a far from routine performance. Testing though the three evenings had been, they had at a stroke established Klemperer in Hamburg. Their impact was well summarised by Robert Müller-Hartmann in the *Allgemeine Musikzeitung* of 7 October.

The Hamburg Stadttheater has...a young conductor, who through ability and character has from the beginning awoken an exceptional response. Musically armed to the teeth, he entered the lists with prodigious passion and triumphed over all resisters on the stage and in the audience...The score, thrilling as sound and rhythm, is in his head; the sense is always directed towards the whole...His gestures are often unwieldy and wildly ecstatic, but they leave nothing to be desired in clarity, and what one must excuse as youthfulness has the appeal of spontaneity and honesty.

* Chevalley was, presumably, referring to Mahler's earlier years in Hamburg. Later, in Vienna, his conducting became much more economical.

Klemperer had won fame in his home town and outwardly he for a while assumed the role of a rising star. A photograph taken at this time shows him in an uncharacteristically 'artistic' pose, such as he subsequently came to abhor, with the aquiline profile and powerful hands displayed to best advantage. For the only time in his life he had letter paper embossed with his name and an address, a practice he scorned in later years.

But such outer marks of confidence were no more than a mask. To his dismay, he began to realise that success would bind him more closely than ever to the treadmill of repertory opera. Even the eulogies he had received served only to heighten a sense of oppression. How, he asked his colleague, Fritz Stiedry,* in a letter written on 9 September, immediately in the wake of his triumphs, could he hope to fulfil the expectations he had aroused? Hamburg, he wrote, offered only two consolations. The orchestra was willing and well trained ('one notices...that Mahler was here'), and relations with his senior colleague, Gustav Brecher, were cordial. 'He is happy that I am here and *together* we want to see what can be achieved.'†

There were other encounters of a more personal nature. At the stage door Klemperer was so struck by the appearance of a girl who passed by that he asked who she was.‡ Her name, he learnt, was Elisabeth Schumann,§ a young soprano who had joined the theatre the previous season but had yet to make much impact. She sang the First Page in his opening *Lohengrin* and six days later was the Aennchen in a performance of *Der Freischütz* that he conducted on 9 September. But he was too over-burdened, and perhaps also too low in spirits, to give attention even to such an exceptionally attractive girl. The girls, however, had eyes for him. Among them was another young soprano, also destined to make a great career, who had only just arrived in Hamburg. At first sight Lotte Lehmann ‖ fell in love with 'this thin young man, tall as a lamp post, with mournful burning eyes and pale cheeks.'[8] But the object of her devotion had no time for a plain Jane whom he later recalled as a notably clumsy actress. In despair she took to sending him anonymous poems, which a mutual friend, Paul Dessau,¶ obligingly set to music that Klemperer declared to be better than the texts (of whose provenance he was, of course, well aware).

The following weeks brought two illustrious guests to Hamburg. In the last days of September Arthur Nikisch conducted a cycle of *The Ring*.

---

* See biographical glossary.
† Subsequently Klemperer was less wholly enchanted with Brecher. In the summer of 1911 he told Fried that 'Brecher was often very kind to me and showed much sympathy for my work. I also found his way of music-making interesting and individual. But something that is hard to define repels me' (undated letter).
‡ Recounted to the author by Lotte Lehmann.   § See biographical glossary.
‖ See biographical glossary.   ¶ See biographical glossary.

Klemperer was deeply impressed in spite of what he regarded as an extravagantly over-romantic approach; but for him Nikisch was not to be compared in musical understanding to composer–conductors such as Strauss and Mahler. In the middle of the month Enrico Caruso arrived on a visit that had become an annual event. Between 15 and 20 October he sang the principal roles in *Rigoletto*, *Martha* and *Carmen* and Klemperer was detailed to conduct all three performances. He was surprised by Caruso's willingness to rehearse like any other singer and even to allow himself to be told that he was dragging. Caruso must also have been impressed by the young conductor. After he had left, Klemperer learnt that, in view of the approval that the visitor had expressed, he would not be required to repay an advance that he had received on his salary.

But the privilege of providing an orchestral accompaniment for the greatest tenor of his time had an unhappy side-effect. Although he had obtained three clear days in order to travel to Munich for the first performance of Mahler's new symphony on 12 September, Klemperer had been too exhausted by the strains of his first week in his new position to do so. There was, however, a chance that in October Mahler would sail for New York either from Hamburg or Bremen, eighty miles away. On 30 September Klemperer wrote to ask Fried for the date and place of Mahler's embarkation, 'as I would so much like to speak to him beforehand'. Mahler in fact left from Bremen on 18 October, the very evening on which Klemperer had to conduct a performance of *Martha*, with Caruso. It is therefore unlikely that he was able to travel to Bremen. In which case, he missed a last opportunity to bid farewell to the man and musician he revered above all others. Seven months later Mahler was dead.

*   *   *

As a junior conductor on the staff of a large opera house, Klemperer found himself allotted a seemingly unending series of ill-prepared repertory performances. Only at the end of November was he entrusted with a new production of a double bill, consisting of Offenbach's *Fortunios Lied* and *Robins Ende*, a recent work by the 25-year-old Eduard Künnecke.* Klemperer conducted with what Pfohl described as 'the finest understanding of the intimate delights of classical Offenbach'.[9] But in spite of a cast that included both Elisabeth Schumann and Lotte Lehmann in small *Hosenrollen*, the Hamburg critics savaged *Robins Ende*, which Max Loewengard dismissed as 'a bad, protracted joke with pretentious and noisy music'.[10]

Frustrating though such duties were to an idealistic young musician, they cannot have been as unprofitable as he himself supposed at the time.

---

* Eduard Künnecke (1885–1953); prolific composer of operas and, above all, operettas. *Robins Ende*, which was his first stage work, had had its first performance in 1909 in Mannheim.

For all its limitations, repertory opera provided a hard but effective schooling, and Klemperer still had much to learn. In a revival of *Mignon* on 8 November a lapse of memory on stage caused confusion in the orchestra and Pfohl's comment is revealing. 'Herr Kapellmeister Klemperer appeared nonplussed by this unexpected turn of events...In a few years he will learn to confront incidents such as this...with the assurance and presence of mind he lacks today.'[11] He also had to learn, as he later came to delight in doing, to make the best of conditions that were less than perfect. As Heinrich Chevalley wrote after his initial *Lohengrin*, he would come to accept the fact that there was no point in 'demanding things that in our conditions *must* miscarry'.[12]

But it was precisely those conditions that revolted Klemperer's idealistic character. As in Prague two years earlier, he felt trapped in a system that made it impossible for him to achieve what he felt to lie within his powers and he was appalled by the countless artistic compromises it involved. Shortly after Caruso's visit he again began to grow depressed, and as the season proceeded his gloom deepened. With it came an increasing sense of inadequacy. He began to believe that he was not up to the job. And there may even have been an element of truth in this belief; in low spirits he was less likely to show the resilience and resourcefulness necessary to pilot a series of ill-prepared performances, more likely to fuss excessively over detail. A vicious circle had set in: unfavourable conditions fostered depression and depression made him less able to cope with the conditions.

His melancholy deepened to a point where he so seriously considered abandoning his vocation that he wrote to a friendly bookseller in Prague to enquire if he would accept him as an apprentice. Fortunately, the bookseller declined to take his enquiry seriously. Finally Klemperer's elder sister, Regi, who was on a visit from Berlin, persuaded him to consult a specialist in nervous complaints, who promptly ordered four weeks of total rest in hospital. During the month of January 1911 Klemperer did not conduct.

On his return to duty in early February the Stadttheater treated him with consideration. Previously he had conducted anything up to fifteen performances a month. In February and March that number was reduced to eleven, so that there were frequently two clear days between performances. But he was no better. The depression was as intense as ever and with it went the attendant symptoms of anxiety, night sweats, lack of appetite and inability to sleep that were always to afflict him during such periods. His family observed his condition with deepening concern; as Ida Klemperer must have perceived, the cause of her son's suffering lay deeper than mere difficulty in adjusting to the conditions of repertory opera. Nathan Klemperer left for Berlin to consult the family oracle, Georg.

Georg's response was prompt and generous: he would provide money to enable his cousin to take a year's leave; if, at the end of that period, he was not better, he should go ahead with his intention of abandoning his career as a conductor. On 31 March, Klemperer conducted a new production of Delibes's *Lakmé*. Two days later he made what was to be his last appearance at the Stadttheater for eighteen months.

*   *   *

At this point Klemperer himself went to Berlin to consult his cousin, as he was later to do in so many critical moments in his life. Georg recommended that he spend a few weeks at a clinic at Königstein, in the Taunus mountains north-west of Frankfurt, which was run by Dr Oskar Kohn-stamm, whom he knew well. It was a shrewd choice, for Königstein was to become a retreat and refuge, to which Klemperer frequently returned in periods of stress. The sanatorium, which was situated on a small hill some thirty minutes' walk from the town, had come into existence more or less by chance. Kohnstamm, who had begun his career as an *Internist* (specialist for internal disorders), had early discovered himself to possess a talent for treating mental distress, and in particular for reactivating depressed patients at a time when psychoanalysis was in its infancy and chemico-therapy did not exist. He had started by taking patients into his own house and by 1906 had achieved such success that he had been able to build his own sanatorium, to which a further wing was added in 1912.

The sanatorium nonetheless remained small in scale, for the essence of Kohnstamm's treatment lay in the personal attention he gave to each of his patients. Although he practised and published papers on hypnosis, his approach was essentially empirical and depended in large part on the direct influence he was able to exert. By 1911 he had already established something of a reputation for his skill in treating artists. But the sanatorium was not just a refuge for the rich and the famous. Those who could afford it were charged heavily, others paid little. Königstein was run on idealistic principles. 'Edel sei der Mensch, hülfreich und gut', a Goethe quotation that might have come out of *Die Zauberflöte*, was inscribed over its entrance.*

Kohnstamm at first told Klemperer that he should regard his illness as the psychological equivalent of growing pains. That was true to the extent that a manic-depressive temperament often first reveals itself in youth, as it had done in Klemperer's case. But the implication that he would 'grow out of it' was to prove sadly unfounded: though there were to be lengthy

---

* Poem from the collection, *Das Göttliche* (1782).

periods of relative calm, he continued until his death at the age of eighty-eight to alternate between 'highs' and 'lows' of varying intensity. Whether Kohnstamm himself came to the conclusion later reached by psychiatrists that his illness was primarily endogenous (that is, not caused by outward circumstances) is uncertain. But he set about reactivating his patient with considerable success.

In the case of depression Kohnstamm attached particular importance to a strict daily routine that was intended to make it difficult for patients to lapse into the inertia that often accompanies despair. In the morning there was compulsory gardening, even for those who had never lifted a hoe. After lunch a pause for sleep was followed by an afternoon walk, which sometimes took the form of an excursion. Bedtime was early; there was no smoking or drinking. Crucial to this routine were meals, which were taken communally at a long table, together with the staff. Kohnstamm himself each morning personally supervised the seating, and Klemperer, whose bad table manners had attracted unfavourable comment,* was often put next to Frau Kohnstamm in the vain expectation that this might bring about an improvement.

From this rigid daily order Klemperer acquired a discipline that was to stand him in good stead whenever depression threatened to immobilise him. But Kohnstamm was no martinet. He had in abundance the kindness and patience required in the handling of manic-depressives; and in the case of artists and intellectuals, he recognised the value of inner stimulation. Early on, he referred his patient to the sanatorium's library, where to his delight Klemperer first encountered Fontane's *Effi Briest*. Kohnstamm also attached importance to learning poetry by heart, and in particular he drew Klemperer's attention to lines from Goethe's *Faust*, Part Two, that described the depressive phase of his affliction.† In an attempt to restimulate Klemperer's interest in music, he invited him to hear the *St Matthew Passion* in Frankfurt. Klemperer at first refused. But Kohnstamm, who was no Freudian and did not hesitate to use direct influence when that seemed indicated, insisted, and Klemperer went. Within five weeks he had resumed his piano-playing and Kohnstamm set aside a room where he could practise

---

* Dr Peter Konstam, Kohnstamm's son, has recorded that 'Klemperer went through his meals like a tornado, leaving his place...in utter devastation'. (Communication to the author.)

† Act 5. Mitternacht.

Sorge: Wen ich einmal mir besitze,
      Dem ist alle Welt nichts nütze,
      Ewiges Düstre steigt herunter,
      Sonne geht nicht auf noch unter,
      Bei vollkommnen äussern Sinnen
      Wohnen Finsternisse drinnen,

Und er weiss von allen Schätzen
Sich nicht in Besitz zu setzen.
...
Soll er gehen? soll er kommen?
Der Entschluss ist ihm genommen.
(The power of decision is taken from him.)

undisturbed. A very warm relationship sprang up between doctor and patient.*

         *   *   *

On 18 May Mahler died at the age of only fifty. Klemperer read the news in the paper and the sudden loss of the man who more than any other had been his mentor and inspiration came as such a shock that for a while it seemed as though he were about to relapse into the depression from which he had been emerging. But by summer he was well enough to leave Königstein. A year's leave was still considered advisable and the question arose of where he was to spend it. He had written to Pfitzner from Königstein, explaining his troubles, and Pfitzner had been understanding. Now that Mahler was dead, the presence of his old teacher in Strasbourg, where he was completing his second year as director of the opera, doubtless played a large part in Klemperer's decision to base himself there. In Strasbourg he could attend rehearsals, had an opera library at his disposal, and, although relations were not particularly intimate, Pfitzner was a man with whom he could discuss musical issues. Strasbourg proved to have another advantage: in Robert Wollenberg, director of the University's psychiatric clinic, Klemperer found a sympathetic medical counsellor, who shared Georg Klemperer's opinion that a prolonged rest from the stresses of theatrical life was essential to his well-being. Wollenberg was also close to Pfitzner and deeply involved in the city's musical life. During the coming year and later during his period at the Strasbourg opera, Klemperer was to be a frequent guest in his hospitable home.

With a view to improving his French, Klemperer took lodgings with a French-speaking family in Schiltigheim, on the outskirts of Strasbourg. His room was furnished with no more than a bed, a piano, a table and chair, and he imposed on himself a regime almost as severe as that at Kohnstamm's sanatorium. In the morning he studied in depth ('that means going into the work – not just looking at it')[13] operas he did not know, above all *The Ring*, but also works by Mozart and Strauss, none of whose music he had yet had an opportunity to conduct. He worked methodically and slowly, first with a vocal reduction, and only when he had mastered that turned to an orchestral score. At meal times there was French conversation, in the afternoon walking or (in summer) swimming. Klemperer also hired a viola so as to try out bowings; and with the intention, which he never realised, of translating the libretto of *Don Giovanni*, he embarked on learning Italian. He also attended lectures on aesthetics at the university. The year of retreat that had been enforced on him was to play a crucial part in his

* Long after Kohnstamm's premature death in 1917, Klemperer remained on terms of friendship with his widow and children.

development. As he himself later put it with characteristic terseness, 'one learns a lot when one is alone'.[14] Depressions such as he suffered in 1911 forced Klemperer in on himself, but in spite of the deep unhappiness they brought, they contributed much to a growing depth of musical insight.

*   *   *

In the middle of July, when his spirits were already beginning to revive, he went on a short holiday in south Germany. There he chanced to read an enthusiastic account in the *Frankfurter Zeitung* of a production of Gluck's *Orphée* at the summer Théâtre du Jorat at Mézières, a village some fifteen miles north-east of Lausanne. Because acceptable performances of the work were rare in Germany, he decided on the spur of the moment to travel overnight, and on 16 July he arrived in time to attend a performance that did much to open his eyes to the possibility of musical theatre.

The Théâtre du Jorat* was a rustic, wooden amphitheatre that had been erected only three years earlier. *Orphée* was the first opera to be presented there and the main instigators of the undertaking were Gustave Doret† and Lucien Jusseaume.‡ Saint-Saëns, who attended the first night, has recorded in his memoirs[15] that it was on his advice that Doret returned, with certain modifications, to the original Italian version of the opera, in which the main role is sung by a woman. The performance was, however, sung in French. An orchestra of Swiss and German musicians was engaged, the soloists were brought from Paris, a largely amateur chorus was recruited locally.

Klemperer was so enchanted by what he heard and saw that he attended no fewer than three performances. For the first time since he had experienced Mahler's performances in Vienna four years earlier he had encountered an opera production in which music and drama marched hand in hand. So great was his enthusiasm that he even embarked on an activity that did not come easily to him and wrote a lengthy article that provides the earliest evidence of his deep concern with operatic staging.[16]

Doret's measured tempi and the clear voices of the French soloists account for his approval of the musical side of the performances. What pleased his eye is less clear and must to some extent be a matter of conjecture. He was attracted above all to the simplicity of the production. The chaste colours and unadorned prospects of Jusseaume's sets (described by one commentator as being in the style of Puvis de Chavannes, though

---

* *Le Roi David* and other stage works by Honegger later had their first performance there.

† Gustave Doret (1866–1943); Swiss conductor and composer. Pupil of Saint-Saëns and Massenet. In 1894 Doret had conducted the first performance of Debussy's *L'Après-midi d'un faune*. From 1907 to 1914 he was conductor at the Opéra-Comique.

‡ Lucien Jusseaume (1851–1925) had in 1902 been co-designer of the first production of Debussy's *Pelléas et Mélisande*.

paradoxically one scene recalled Böcklin to Klemperer's mind) were far removed from the elaborate historical detail which still prevailed in Central European opera houses. In the dances the customary clichés of classical ballet were jettisoned in favour of movements in the manner of the *Ausdruckstanz* that Isadora Duncan had developed from Jacques Dalcroze's eurhythmics. Their lack of artifice seemed to Klemperer to match the essence of Gluck's music.

In his article he recalled that Wagner, after he had seen a particularly satisfying production of this very opera in Dessau in November 1872, had held it up as an example of how a modest theatre could achieve results that lay beyond the reach of the great court operas, provided that a single person was in charge of every aspect of the performance.[17] Klemperer drew the same conclusion from the Théâtre du Jorat. 'It was', he wrote more than thirty years later in America, 'the most beautiful opera performance I have seen.'[18] A seed had been planted in his mind that was to bear fruit at a later stage of his career. Mézières had restored his belief in the possibility of operatic reform.

It also did a lot to restore his spirits. On 17 July, enchanted by the performance and the Lake of Geneva, Klemperer wrote from Ouchy to Mimi Pfitzner, who was at a clinic at Leysin, nearby.

For the first time I have seen a proper theatrical performance. I have seen what I have long dreamt of. You absolutely must go to it. I have written to Pfitzner and begged him to come...Here it is perfect. I didn't know that the world had such beautiful things to offer as this lake and the performance on Sunday.

*　　　　　　　　*　　　　　　　　*

As he started once more to take pleasure in the outside world, so his appetite for activity revived. In early August he wrote to ask Fried if he could find him any odd engagements in the intervening period. That his mind again turned to composition was a further straw in the wind. On returning to Schiltigheim he set about writing incidental music, which Max Reinhardt had commissioned from him for a production of the *Oresteia* that he was to stage in Munich at the very end of August. That was not the only reason to go south: the Bodanzkys had again invited him to stay on the Starnberger See, where he arrived on 12 August. The rest of the month was spent in nearby Feldafing, where he orchestrated the two songs he had composed the previous summer (see p. 49), together with two others that have not survived. In Feldafing he was visited by Ilse Fromm. Together they planned to give an orchestral concert in Hamburg in the course of the coming winter. It was to be the first in Klemperer's career.

Rehearsals started for the *Oresteia* in nearby Munich. Sets were by Alfred

59

Roller, the cast included Else Heims, Gertrud Eysold, Alexander Moissi and Fritz Kortner; and from the fact that Alexander von Zemlinsky,* who was about to take up a new position as musical director of the German Theatre in Prague, was billed to conduct the Munich Tonkünstler Orchestra, one may assume that Klemperer's incidental music was elaborate in conception. It was through Zemlinsky that Klemperer met Schoenberg, of whose music he was still 'completely ignorant'.[19] That is perhaps one reason why Klemperer found him 'proud and distant'[20] and distinctly unappreciative of his *Oresteia* music. Conceivably as a result of Schoenberg's opinion, and in spite of Zemlinsky's support, it was abandoned before the first night and never subsequently performed.† For a young musician eager to make his mark as a composer it must have been a crushing rebuff. That this setback did not cause any relapse into depression is less surprising than may at first appear: had Klemperer not already been in at least a mildly manic condition, the work would not have been composed in the first place. But his unwillingness in later years to give any account of what took place suggests that the incident nonetheless left a scar.

A more agreeable memory of Munich was provided by performances of *Figaro* and *Così fan tutte*, which Strauss conducted at the Residenztheater in the course of the summer festival.‡ Klemperer was particularly impressed by Strauss's conducting technique. 'He only made very small movements, but their effect was enormous. His control of the orchestra was absolute ...He accompanied the recitatives himself on a harpsichord and made delightful little embellishments'.[21] To Klemperer, Strauss seemed to have a new approach to Mozart.

*   *   *

Strauss was at the pinnacle of his fame when Klemperer went to visit him in Garmisch in August or September 1911. In *Elektra* (1909) he had shown that his idiom was still capable of extension and in doing so had revealed an unexpected kinship to the new movement of expressionism that was beginning to make itself felt in literature and painting. If in *Der Rosenkavalier*, which in the previous January had enjoyed a triumphant first performance in Dresden and was in the process of sweeping the opera houses of the world, he seemed, under the influence of Hofmannsthal's cultural nostalgia, to have retreated from this radical position, he had in doing so provided the German operatic repertory with its most successful new score since Wagner.

---

* See biographical glossary.   † It has not survived.

‡ Felix Mottl (1856–1911), director of the Munich Court Opera since 1903, had died that summer while conducting *Tristan*, and Strauss, who spent his summers in nearby Garmisch, had assumed responsibility for a number of performances at the festival. Mottl, who regularly conducted at Bayreuth, also championed Berlioz's music in Germany.

Inevitably the conversation turned to Mahler, who had died less than three months earlier. Strauss, who greatly admired Mahler, commented on his obsession with redemption. That, he said, was a concept that meant nothing to him. 'I don't know what I'm supposed to be redeemed from.'[22] Nothing could more graphically illustrate the psychological gulf that separated the two greatest composer-conductors of their time, one a questing metaphysician, the other a man of robust horse sense.

Clearly, so earth-bound a character could never fill the gap that Mahler had left in Klemperer's life. But, at that time at any rate, the young conductor regarded Strauss's 'towering personality...with awe'.[23] Strauss, for his part, seems to have been impressed by his young visitor, for a few weeks later they met again at the annual Tonkünstlerfest in Heidelberg, which that year was dedicated to the centenary of Liszt's birth. On 24 October Klemperer heard Strauss conduct *Tasso* and then accompany Busoni in a performance of the Piano Concerto No. 2 in A major. Busoni, Klemperer wrote in an undated letter to his parents, had played 'unbelievably (unerhört) well'.[24] The next morning, he continued,

I fetched [Strauss] from his hotel and we went walking in the lovely Neckar valley...He advised me to look as soon as possible for a job at a large court theatre (Munich or, better still, Berlin) and for the time being not to attach importance to a big position...(I am still far from *mature* enough for that). It would, however, be extremely advantageous for me as a conductor to work with a first-class orchestra, like, for instance, that in Berlin. I told him that in that case *he* could certainly do more for me than I could do for myself, as I could hardly make an application for employment in Berlin.* He said that, particularly for *me*, a few years of 'Prussian drill' would be beneficial; as a young man he had also been just as wild and idealistic in his demands as I am.

Then we ate together and after the meal I played him my orchestral songs in the hotel. He read the score and was absolutely charming. The first and last songs he liked very much, although the last he found very Mahlerian, but, as he said, laid out in a masterly way. The two middle songs were too *outré* for him. Anyway, at the end he said that he would recommend the songs for *performance* at the next Tonkünstlerfest...You can imagine how pleased I was at his interest, because in the final resort he is the most important German musician *for the moment*.†

If the last three words of that letter indicate that Klemperer already felt an immanent reserve towards a composer who was capable of storming imaginative heights but also of lapsing into the rankest bathos,‡ Strauss's

* Strauss was at that time *Generalmusikdirektor* (in this case a title, not a post) at the Berlin Court Opera.
† Strauss was as good as his word. On 17 December Max von Schillings (see biographical glossary) wrote to tell Strauss that 'Otto Klemperer will be put on a special list for the ADMV (Allgemeiner Deutsche Musikverein) right away. I have not forgotten your opinion of his things.' In spite of Strauss's advocacy, the songs were not accepted. (*Conversations*, p. 41)
‡ Thus, over sixty years later, he wryly wrinkled his nose when he re-read the somewhat effusive tone (effusive at any rate by *his* standards) of the letter of thanks he had written to Strauss after their encounter in Heidelberg.

advice suggests that he for his part considered that the ardent, idealistic young musician who had sought him out would benefit from a few years' routine in a first class opera house.

*   *   *

On 20 November Mahler's *Das Lied von der Erde* had its first performance in Munich under Bruno Walter and Klemperer travelled overnight from Strasbourg to hear it. To his surprise, the work made relatively little impact on him. That, as he explained in a cautiously worded letter[25] to Mahler's widow, Alma, he attributed to his own slowness at grasping new scores. But perhaps, he implied, the performance under Bruno Walter also had something to do with it. 'If only we could have heard the work once under Mahler.'*

Klemperer spent the afternoon before the concert with Alma Mahler and from the tone of his reply to a letter she had written to him within a day or two of that meeting it is clear that a very warm relationship had sprung into existence. During the following three weeks Klemperer wrote several times to Alma, but the arrival on 7 December of a money order for the substantial sum of 2,000 Austrian crowns came as a complete surprise. Three days later Klemperer explained to his parents what had occurred:

You know that I was recently with Frau Mahler in Munich and she was extremely kind to me...Then on Thursday there arrived a money order for 2,000 Kronen from Vienna with a letter enclosed in which she wrote more or less the following: I had laughingly told her in Munich about my debts...She had told all that to a woman friend...who is very rich and loves her (Frau M) very much. This friend had spontaneously sent her 2,000 Kronen for me. She only asked me *not* to use the money to pay my debts but go to a nice, mild climate and stay there for as long as the 'stupid' money lasted...

Nothing that I can tell you about the letter can give you the remotest idea of how marvellously kind it is. At first I was almost shocked and wanted to send the money back. But now I shall keep it with a happy heart, for by whom, or better, through whom, would I prefer to be helped *in this way* than Mahler's wife? It will make things much easier for me; among other things I shall be able to start the new engagement [i.e. in Hamburg] without an advance...*No one* must know anything about this. When I see you again, *perhaps* I'll show you the letters from Frau Mahler, which are so moving (schön). On Friday I had another one.

Klemperer and Alma Mahler continued to correspond during that winter. Alma's letters have not survived. From Klemperer's it is, however, evident

---

* Writing to his parents the day before he travelled to Munich, Klemperer described Walter as a 'conductor whom I admire enormously'. That admiration seems at odds with his reaction to the first performance of *Das Lied von der Erde*, a work which Klemperer himself later conducted in an anguished manner far removed from Walter's more nostalgic approach. See also biographical glossary (Walter).

that he had come to regard her as a confidante to whom he could open his heart as he did to few people outside his immediate family circle.

*   *   *

Early in November the concert that Klemperer and Ilse Fromm had planned to give in Hamburg was announced for 30 January 1912. As this was to be the first time he would conduct an orchestra in a concert hall, the programme became a matter of anxious deliberation. From the start Klemperer was clear that the second half of the programme should consist of Mahler's Symphony No. 4, which had not been heard in Hamburg, with Eva Lessmann (see p. 16) as the soloist in the last movement. But what works should the first half include? Like so many inexperienced young artists Klemperer and Ilse Fromm at first tried to cram too much on the plate: Ilse Fromm was to play both a Bach and a Beethoven concerto. It was Ida Klemperer who brought a sense of reality to their deliberations. Three major works, she insisted, was one too many. Klemperer saw the wisdom of his mother's advice and on 3 December he wrote to tell Ilse Fromm that one of the concertos must go. It was finally agreed that the first half should consist of Beethoven's *Weihe des Hauses* Overture and Bach's D minor Piano Concerto. Yet even this reduced programme caused him, as he wrote to Fried (20 December), 'not a little anxiety'.

It remains a mystery how Klemperer was able to afford to hire the large Hamburg Musikhalle for a programme that required additional strings and was by no means popular by the standards of the day; in the early years of the century Bach's instrumental music was relatively rarely performed,* while the Mahler symphony was a lengthy and still little-known modern work. The engagement of the leader of the Hamburg opera orchestra and the number of rehearsals that Klemperer insisted on must also have been added to the expenses.† Did the generous Tante Helene once again dip into her capacious purse? Or did some other friend enable Klemperer to mount this costly undertaking?‡

There was laughter when, on the night, Klemperer sat to conduct. He did so, as he subsequently explained to Alma Mahler, simply because, owing to his great height, he was embarrassed to stand.[26] But to a conventionally minded provincial public it seemed eccentric and the critics inevitably made

---

* In his biography of Busoni, Edward Dent claims that the all-Bach recital that Busoni gave in Berlin in December 1914 was the first such concert in modern times (*Busoni*, p. 221).
† According to the plans he had detailed in his letter of 3 November to Ilse Fromm, he was to be in Hamburg for rehearsals with his soloist on 23 January; orchestral rehearsals were to begin two days later and would in that case have extended over no less than five days.
‡ Ilse Fromm told the author that support may have come from Walter Kantorowicz, a Hamburg doctor. Kantorowicz later helped Klemperer financially at a difficult period in 1917 (see pp. 93 and 119).

much of it.* In the *Hamburger Nachrichten* of 1 February Ferdinand Pfohl wrote:

Herr Klemperer enriched the concert hall with a new feature. He appeared, a towering figure...[whose] exceptional height for a moment aroused horror. Then he sank into a chair and there he sat, sat and conducted...But his chair...transformed itself into a mystical steed, on which he performed a fantastic ride. It recalled the scene with the flying horse in *Don Quixote*, in which the horse does not move but carries its rider into the clouds. Klemperer really made the motions of riding: he curbed, subdued, whipped and spurred. O charm of the unusual!

There was general criticism of a conducting technique that Pfohl described as both 'violent' and 'awkward'. In the *Hamburger Fremdenblatt* of the same date Heinrich Chevalley rebuked Klemperer for a mixture of pedantry and gratuitous vehemence.

The help that Herr Klemperer gives with his baton, the way in which he indicates absolutely self-evident entries...is almost offensive to an orchestra of any standing, and the exaltation with which he used his baton in a Bach concerto makes one fear that when he eventually conducts *Tristan* those within reach will be in danger of their lives...This outward animation which in the main stems from a laudable desire for absolute clarity and definition is accompanied by many negative effects on the orchestral sound. In so far as Klemperer over-anxiously and over-eagerly watches over an individual thematic entry, this entry is unavoidably accentuated strongly, so that the ear...loses contact with the general development. Something hard, angular and academic crept into the performance of Beethoven's overture, *Die Weihe des Hauses*, which nonetheless had a wonderful plasticity and was shaped with classical monumentality.

But, Chevalley continued,

Whatever one may say against the surplus energy that bursts in an elemental manner out of Klemperer, whatever one may find to reproach in individual aspects of what he does, one must unreservedly salute his fiery spirit and unequalled musical conscientiousness. There is here unmistakably a great conductor (Dirigent grossen Stiles) in the making. It is equally unmistakable that Klemperer is able to impose his intentions on the orchestra. Our Philharmonic Orchestra has rarely produced a *piano* such as it did yesterday; and from his mentor and master, Gustav Mahler, Klemperer has learnt how with a sudden movement to seize the entire orchestra and make it flash. Whether admiration...will later grow into love for his innermost musical being, whether...warmth of heart will eventually shine out of him and his art...only the future can determine. As things stand, Klemperer remains...the only hope for our opera, and from the course of this evening...we can be certain that these expectations will not be disappointed.

The Musikhalle was, inevitably, far from full, but Klemperer gained much from his first orchestral concert. To a greater extent than was possible in the opera house, he had succeeded in impressing on his audience

---

* Klemperer never again sat to conduct until he was compelled to do so in his mid-sixties by a broken hip.

a sense of his musical individuality. He had shown that, for all the demands he had made, he had it in him to win an orchestra's unstinted support. But he himself was far from content. On 7 February he wrote to Alma Mahler:

I wasn't really satisfied with myself in the rehearsals. I felt that my gestures were not sufficiently relevant. To rehearse well is the hardest thing of all. We both know who knew how to do that.

In the middle of January, a couple of weeks before his orchestral concert, Klemperer had accompanied Eva Lessmann in recitals in Munich and Prague, and on 8 February they repeated the concert in Hamburg. Their programme, which consisted of songs by Mahler, Pfitzner, Fried and Klemperer himself, bore the stamp of his musical loyalties and indicated how little concerned he was to win easy success. There was unanimous praise among the critics for Klemperer's prowess as an accompanist, less agreement about his abilities as a composer.

The critics were not the only people to be puzzled by his songs. A month before the event, Nathan Klemperer had admitted to his elder daughter that

I am very sceptical about Otto's songs. I don't like the texts at all and where songs are concerned I can't separate the text from the music...How much I wish that I could regard the matter with complete objectivity. But how can I? Every nerve in me trembles when I think of how he exposes himself to the power of the critics.[27]

In fact they proved, if not favourable, at any rate less devastating than Nathan Klemperer had feared. Chevalley found too much atmosphere and too little structure.[28] Robert Müller-Hartmann was more critical, 'Between a desolate radicalism on the one hand and a folkiness in the manner of Mahler on the other, he forgets the main thing: to evoke his texts in music.'[29] Only Ferdinand Pfohl noted any individual quality in the music.

What these extremely strange songs have in common is above all a harmony that mocks all traditions...In pursuit of character and atmosphere it does not shrink from the most biting dissonances...and clashes, such as until now one has experienced only in *Elektra* and the music of the secessionist Schoenberg.

Then in a comment that put a finger on the dark side of Klemperer's temperament, Pfohl continued:

Their other characteristic is a deep sense of tragedy. They sound as though they come from the grave...There are lullabies full of sorrow and mortal weariness, deeply affecting in their sense of pain and pessimism. Most terrible is the setting of Heine's poem, 'Ich will mich im grünen Wald ergehen'. The whole piece is built on a...repeated note, which suggests a man knocking on the lid of his own coffin...One freezes when one hears this song.[30]

*   *   *

In fact Klemperer's mood had been growing steadily darker throughout the late autumn and early winter. In the letter of thanks written to Strauss after their encounter in Heidelberg, he had alluded to his lack of confidence in his songs when he was not himself accompanying them. He had expressed the same fear that they would not survive without, as it were, his personal protection in an undated letter written at about the same time to Ilse Fromm. On 11 November 1911, shortly after his return to Schiltigheim from Heidelberg, he had again written to her, 'It is only in seclusion that I become aware of everything I am *not* capable of.' In another letter (19 November) of the same period to his sister, Regi, he had told her of his difficulties in composing. On the same day he wrote to his parents

I am a plodding worker, always have been and will probably remain so until my happy end. I don't get on sufficiently quickly, perhaps not even effortlessly enough; although this is a wrong thought, because what falls into your lap without effort is not always the best. That one's longings should remain unfulfilled is certainly good, otherwise there would be no ideal to strive for. One must have patience and persistence.

The self-doubt, the difficulties in working and the inability to compose were all straws in the wind: the comparatively buoyant spirits that had tided him over the summer and early autumn were ebbing. A new depression was on the horizon.

By early February it had deepened. In his letter of 7 February to Alma Mahler, he admitted that 'I really have "Erquickung not"'.* In yet another letter written soon after his return from Hamburg to Schiltigheim to Ilse Fromm, with whom he was on cordial but by no means intimate terms, he uncharacteristically confessed, 'At the moment I am in very, very bad need of a little comfort.' The depth of the depression that had set in can be gauged from the fact that, so far as can be ascertained, Klemperer only twice left Schiltigheim during the rest of the winter and the spring of 1912, on both occasions to visit the Bodanzkys in nearby Mannheim. Significantly, because depression was liable to bring almost total cessation of contact with outer world, only two letters have survived from the entire period between February and July 1912. Both were written to Alma Mahler. In that of 20 April, addressed to 'My dear, dear friend', Klemperer came closer to describing the impact of his depressions than he had done before or was ever to do in the future.†

* 'I really "need comfort".' A quotation from *Das Lied von der Erde* ('Der Einsame in Herbst').
† It was a subject on which he was to become increasingly clamlike, though he made oblique reference to it in *Conversations*, pp. 40–1. In November 1972, only a few months before his death, Klemperer was asked by the author what he had inherited from his parents. 'I look like my father.' 'And from your mother?' 'She was also thin.' This was as far as he was prepared to go towards intimating that he had inherited his mother's temperament. Like himself, she also lost weight during depressions.

66

I haven't written for so long because I'm so very down. I have lost all courage and all hope...Nothing is wrong with me physically. I've often been in this condition before, but it seems to me that it has never been so bad as it is this time. It was certainly also bad last year, but my main worry then (that I felt myself so unprepared as an opera conductor) was removed by the free year that was made possible for me. I had hoped to better myself considerably. Well, I have indeed worked, but probably not enough and too slowly. Now this crazy anxiety about next winter oppresses me again.* I believe that I'll fail miserably and what that means to me and above all to my parents you can imagine. I recently went to visit Bodanzky in Mannheim. He strongly urged me to go there as here I am much too much on my own. Only I cannot decide what I ought to do. I would see more people there than I do here, [but] now I'm nervous, even frightened, of meeting people. When I was with you in Vienna (in January), I was already not so lively as I am when I'm well, but I didn't want to give way to this frame of mind. When I returned here after the [Hamburg] concert, it was really bad. I work, I mean I learn works that I don't know, with such frightful difficulty that I feel that there isn't enough time in the whole of existence for me ever to become an accomplished conductor. I don't know what is going to become of me. It's probably a lack of ability or of energy and confidence (which is a form of ability)...*Please* don't be angry about this dreadful letter. I am certainly not worthy to have such a friend as yourself. Of course there's no question of composing. Travelling or going away to recuperate would, I think, be pointless, as I only find *some* peace when I study to make good my lack of knowledge of so many works. Again, I beg you to forgive this letter. I *could* not write otherwise.

Hardly had he penned this self-revelatory letter than he began to regret it. From Mannheim, where he had gone in early May to attend the rehearsals for two Mahler concerts that Bodanzky was conducting on the first anniversary of the composer's death, he wrote anxiously to Alma, who had not replied (probably because she had been in Paris).

I hope that through mischance the letter has not landed in hands other than yours. It was in all conscience written solely and exclusively for your eyes. Perhaps it would have been better if it had been left unwritten. I *couldn't* have written other than I did, and I thought that to you I could write exactly as I felt without any reserve...I feel that I may have told you more about myself than you wanted to know. In that case, *please* forget it and don't be angry.[31]

That was the last of a series of notably unreserved letters that Klemperer wrote during the six months following his encounter with Alma Mahler in Munich in November 1911.† They must have met when they were both in Mannheim for Bodanzky's Mahler concerts on 10 and 11 May. But thereafter their correspondence ceased as abruptly as it had begun. At some point Alma, never bashful in her approaches to the opposite sex, made an advance. Klemperer was deeply shocked: for him, she remained first and

---

* A reference to resuming work at the Hamburg Stadttheater.
† It is worth noting that the originals are lost and that the letters survive only as typescripts, which, to judge from Alma's treatment of Mahler's letters in her book, *Gustav Mahler: Memories and Letters*, may not be complete.

foremost the widow of the revered Mahler. He seems to have repelled her with a prudery characteristic of him in depression, and their friendship accordingly cooled.*

After his visit to Mannheim, Klemperer returned to Königstein. Kohnstamm told him that, in spite of his fears, he would be well enough to return to Hamburg for the coming season and early in July he travelled north to prepare for what he later referred to as his 'year of destiny'.

* In later years they were on amicable though never again close terms. The gleeful pleasure that Klemperer took in Tom Lehrer's scurrilous song, 'Alma', suggests that his feelings for her were at best ambivalent.

5   *Shipwreck*

In autumn 1912 the Hamburg Stadttheater came under new management. Much was expected of Hans Loewenfeld, the new director, who, unlike his predecessor, was an artist as well as an administrator.* Still in his thirties, he had studied composition and musical theory, and in Leipzig, where he had been opera director since 1908, had attracted attention with a series of productions of Strauss's operas and with a staging of *Die Zauberflöte*, which was notable for its departure from the customary monumental approach and freedom from naturalistic excess. An intelligent fellow-practitioner later described it as having 'brought the production of opera a good step forward'.[1] Loewenfeld was no world-shaker. But he promised to be a man who would bring the old-fashioned Hamburg Stadttheater into an age in which the public was no longer satisfied with vocal virtuosity alone, but was coming to attach importance also to the way in which a work was performed and staged.[2] Such a director was likely to be more sympathetic than his predecessor to the ideals of a radically minded young conductor.

Other factors were less favourable. Brecher had left for Cologne and been succeeded by Felix Weingartner, who though a distinguished conductor was not a man of the theatre.† Both the orchestra and chorus left a good deal to be desired, and the theatre itself was antiquated (a motion to rebuild it had gone before the Senate in October 1911). But the gravest limitation remained the fact that the Stadttheater received no public subsidies, so that Loewenfeld was as dependent as his predecessor on the box office. As Heinrich Chevalley noted at the start of the new season, it was the system, not the man, that was at fault.[3]

Nonetheless Loewenfeld's plans were more enterprising than those that had greeted Klemperer when he had first arrived at the Stadttheater two years earlier. In 1910 the 'novelties' had been the rankest trivialities. For the season of 1912/13 Loewenfeld had announced Strauss's *Ariadne auf Naxos*, even before it had had its first performance in Stuttgart in October of that year, Humperdinck's *Königskinder*, which had only won recognition

---

* On 6 November 1911 Nathan Klemperer had written to his daughter, Regi, 'Great things are hoped for from the new director. At any rate one thing is certain, that an expert has come to the helm, who has already given proof of his ability.'
† For Mahler's comments on Weingartner, see p. 38.

69

since its revised version had had its first performance in New York in 1910, and *Der Schneemann*, a pantomime that had been composed at the age of eleven by the Viennese *Wunderkind*, Erich Wolfgang Korngold.* The general repertory was also more substantial than it had been, so that Klemperer was now largely spared trivial novelties and *Spielopern*. This also reflected a material change in his own position in the theatre. In 1910 he had been no more than a junior conductor. Now he was listed immediately after Weingartner in the musical hierarchy. Clearly, his achievements in the earlier season had not gone unremarked. The auspices for 1912/13, the season which was to witness the shipwreck of his career, were promising.

*   *   *

On his return to Hamburg in early July Klemperer rented a room in Gross Flottbeck, a leafy suburb with large, spacious villas on the estuary of the Elbe beyond Altona. Feeling a need to be on his own, he enjoyed living in surroundings that were still quite countrified and yet near enough to the city for him to return home at midday. There his depression lifted; writing on 23 August to his sister, Regi Elbogen, he expressed a sense of contentment quite absent from letters written earlier that year. His opening opera was *Fidelio*, a work he had not previously conducted, and he set about preparing it with his customary intensity. Singers were invited to Flottbeck to study their roles and among them was Elisabeth Schumann, who was to sing Marzelline. Although Klemperer had been struck by her appearance two years earlier, he had then been too depressed to pay attention to any woman and in the meantime Schumann had married Walther Puritz, a young Hamburg architect. Now, as his spirits rose, he became aware of her abundant charm and warmth, the crystalline beauty of her young voice and the unaffected freshness of her musical responses. In the course of incessant rehearsals, the shy, recessive Klemperer 'opened up to her as a human being'† and she, too, began to fall under his spell. As the weeks passed their relationship grew increasingly intense.

The new season opened on 30 August with *Aida*, staged by Loewenfeld and conducted by Weingartner, with a cast that included Lucille Marcel, Ottilie Metzger (see p. 103) and Heinrich Hensel, all singers of repute. After so splendid an inauguration of the new regime, the performance of *Fidelio*, which Klemperer conducted on the following day, inevitably came as

* See biographical glossary.
† The phrase occurs in Alfred Mathis's unpublished biography, 'Elisabeth Schumann: the chronicle of a singer's life'. This describes in some detail the earlier stages of her relationship with Klemperer, though it passes over its painful *dénouement* in silence. As the biography was written in close collaboration with Schumann herself, it can however be assumed to reflect her view of her association with Klemperer.

7   Elisabeth Schumann as Susanna in *Le nozze di Figaro*

something of an anti-climax. With the exception of Elisabeth Schumann's Marzelline, the cast was undistinguished. The strongest impression of the evening, wrote Heinrich Chevalley, came from the conducting.

The whole way in which he animated (beseelte) the work, enlivened tempi in relationship to the stage and accentuated orchestral expression as the dramatic situation demanded, again revealed Klemperer as one of the most talented disciples of the Mahlerian school and a conductor whose prime principle is to achieve an intimate fusion of drama and music.[4]

Pfohl concurred. 'The real significance and artistic merit of the evening stemmed from the excellent conducting of Kapellmeister Klemperer: it was truly artistic music-making, full of spirit, character and warmth; tender and powerful; worthy of Beethoven.'[5] There was a difference of opinion about what some critics regarded as his exaggerated concern with nuances and others a laudable attention to detail. But Pfohl singled out for praise the 'charming ease' of the opening duet for Marzelline and Jaquino (apparently cut in earlier performances at Hamburg). The hours of loving labour at Flottbeck had clearly borne fruit. *Tannhäuser*, three days later, was less successful. Chevalley found the performance over-driven and attributed orchestral lapses to 'express train tempi'.[6] He approved the opening of customary cuts, but other critics did not. Lotte Lehmann, who sang the role of the First Shepherd, was roundly rebuked for faulty intonation, although Pfohl found her voice spring-like.[7]

For the next two and a half weeks Klemperer was immersed (during that period he conducted only twice) in preparing his first *Ring des Nibelungen*. In the two previous seasons no less a conductor than Nikisch had been in charge of this annual event. It was thus an expression of confidence that it had been entrusted to him at the age of only twenty-six. As must be the case in any young conductor's first *Ring*, the result was uneven. Tempi, in particular, were considered erratic, here too fast, there (notably in the prelude of the first act of *Die Walküre*) too slow. The opening section of the prelude to *Das Rheingold* went so awry that Pfohl described it as 'barely recognisable'.[8] He also complained about exaggerated *pianissimi* and deficiences of balance. Astonishingly, Klemperer's decision to open all cuts brought down the wrath of several critics on his head. The singers were felt by Chevalley to have been less amenable to his will than the orchestra. But at the end of *Siegfried* Edyth Walker, one of the great Brünnhildes of her day, insisted on sharing applause with the young conductor.

Only in *Siegfried* did the cycle get into its stride. Thereafter the notices were warmer. 'The accompaniment', wrote Chevalley, 'became more flowing and flexible, and, above all, more discreet without any loss of...precision and emphasis.'[9] After *Götterdämmerung* there was widespread recognition that, whatever its shortcomings, this *Ring* had not been a routine occasion. Klemperer's achievement, wrote Chevalley, was to be rated highly. 'A conductor of his calibre enriches an entire theatre...Even if these characteristics are not without their disadvantages in daily *Betrieb*,...even if they create friction, that is far outweighed by their artistic merits.'[10]

*　　　　　*　　　　　*

From that comment it can be deduced that Klemperer was not always an easy colleague. Members of the theatre at that time recall a withdrawn, serious *Eigenbrötler* (odd fish), who rarely laughed. Yet, in spite of his shyness, in artistic matters he appeared supremely self-confident, even authoritarian. He was also prodigiously exacting. But because his demands were always made on account of the music and never as a means of asserting his ego, they caused little resentment. On occasion, indeed, he could be surprisingly conciliatory; given a good reason why he was wrong, he would concede a point ungrudgingly.*

Klemperer was, however, not the only exacting young radical Loewenfeld had to deal with. As an adviser in visual aspects of productions (Ausstattungswesen), he had engaged Ewald Dülberg,† a young artist who, after completing his legal studies, had joined the theatre that autumn. Klemperer and Dülberg met in Loewenfeld's office. After brief courtesies Mahler was mentioned and the two young men discovered an immediate bond, for the first performances of Mahler's Eighth Symphony and *Das Lied von der Erde* had been the strongest musical impressions of Dülberg's student years in Munich. Both men left a record of an encounter that was to prove crucial in their careers. 'I still see him before me, a typically tuberculous youth who was consumed by his work,' Klemperer wrote after Dülberg's death in 1933 at the age of only forty-five.[11] 'Klemperer', Dülberg recorded in 1932, at a period when they had quarrelled, 'burst into my life with the inevitability of a natural force; he belongs to the same chapter as illness, wars and unhappy marriages.'[12]

During the few months that Klemperer was to remain in Hamburg a firm friendship grew up between the two men. Although twelve years were to pass before they would be able to work together, Dülberg's influence on Klemperer's conception of the operatic stage was to be profound and far-reaching. More than any other single person, he determined the style

---

* Olga Knack-Brandt (1885–1978), on whose memories some of these observations are based, became the theatre's ballet mistress in 1912. She recalled a dispute about a tempo in the ballet music at a rehearsal for *Aida*, which Klemperer conducted on 5 November. Once Klemperer was convinced that it was too fast for the dancers, he backed down. There was amazement at the young tyrant's sudden docility. It was, however, in accordance with his character to face facts.　　　　† See biographical glossary.

73

of production that came to be associated with the Berlin Kroll Opera, when it was under Klemperer's direction from 1927 to 1931.*

This crucial meeting must have taken place quite early in the season, for on 19 October 1912 Klemperer and Dülberg together attended the performance of *Pierrot Lunaire*, which Schoenberg conducted in the small auditorium of the Hamburg Musikhalle. The work had been heard for the first time only three days earlier in Berlin. In Hamburg, which was the first stop of a tour that was to take the composer, his vocalist, Albertine Zehme, and an instrumental quintet around Germany, barely a hundred people turned up.† The critics rose to the occasion. Having confided that he had not only known Hartleben (the translator of the poems), but had even set some of his verse to music and therefore did not wish to speak ill of a rival (sic!), Ferdinand Pfohl went on to denounce the work as 'abominable, simply abominable...harmonically absolutely incomprehensible'.[13] On Klemperer, however, who had hitherto given no sign of any special interest in Schoenberg's music, it made 'an overwhelming impression. The sound effects...were indescribable...sometimes it sounded like an orchestra of a hundred men.'[14]

On this occasion Schoenberg proved more approachable than he had been at his first encounter with Klemperer the previous year in Munich, no doubt because Klemperer had in the meantime become more familiar with his music. A discussion took place about the Five Orchestral Pieces, Op. 16, which he had been studying. Klemperer told the composer that 'he did not feel capable of mastering their complexity'.[15] Schoenberg replied that for the moment it was sufficient for a conductor to count the bars; understanding would come with time. He was, of course, right, but Klemperer remained unconvinced, and he never ventured to perform the work. Nonetheless, after the impact of *Pierrot Lunaire*,‡ his interest in Schoenberg's music grew more marked.

*   *   *

* Dülberg was later to make even larger claims. On 28 Feb. 1932 he wrote to Hans Curjel that, whereas in Hamburg he already had a clear conception of what he wanted to achieve in the theatre, Klemperer, who was 'rambling' and 'insecure', had not. That is an overstatement. In 1912 Dülberg had yet to evolve the cubism that was characteristic of his designs in the twenties, while Klemperer's account of *Orphée* at Mézières in 1911 shows that he at least knew what he did *not* want on the operatic stage. But Klemperer was undoubtedly impressed by Dülberg's sets for Goethe's *Faust* and Offenbach's *Orpheus* in productions he saw at the Altona theatre, which was run by the Hamburg Stadttheater. He was also much taken by sketches for *Tristan*, which stood in Loewenfeld's office but were never used, and his uncharacteristically Bakst-like designs for Weber's *Oberon*.

† Heinrich Chevalley, *Die Musik*, November 1912. But there was sharp competition for audiences in Hamburg that night. In the Stadttheater Caruso was singing in *La Traviata*; in the large auditorium of the Musikhalle Elena Gerhardt, accompanied by Nikisch, was giving a Lieder recital.

‡ Klemperer conducted it in Cologne in 1922 (see p. 156).

Towards the end of November the Elsa in *Lohengrin*, which Klemperer had revived on 11 November, fell ill. The First Page on that occasion had been sung by Lotte Lehmann, who, although in her third season with Hamburg, was still confined to tiny roles. In despair about her future, she had indeed already offered her resignation to Loewenfeld, who had accepted it with alacrity. Klemperer was alone in regarding the young soprano, who was considered to lack dramatic talent and secure intonation, as an artist of promise, and he succeeded in persuading a sceptical Loewenfeld that she should deputise in the role of Elsa. It was by far the most important assignment Lehmann had received, but, having studied the role, she turned up for her first rehearsal with Klemperer, as she has related, full of confidence.

...if I thought I knew the part, I realised my mistake within the first five pages. Klemperer sat at the piano like an evil spirit, thumping on it with long hands like a tiger's claws, and dragging my terrified voice into the vortex of his fanatical will. Elsa's dreamy serenity became a rapturous ecstasy, her timorous pleading, a challenging demand. For the first time I felt my inhibiting shyness fall away and I sank into the flame of inner experience. I had always wanted to sing like this.[16]

Sixty years later, Lehmann's memories of singing under Klemperer were still vivid. He had, she said, had 'the same magic as Toscanini...He belonged to the category of conductors who made one tremble, yet one was blissful when he was content...But Toscanini made one do things because it hurt him if one didn't. Klemperer one obeyed with gritted teeth...He was always a terrible demon...one was hypnotised...one can't explain it.'[17]

It would be an exaggeration to claim that the Hamburg critics enthused about Lehmann's first appearance in a major role on 29 November. But Chevalley wrote, 'Her lovely, bright soprano fills the house, even if it does not yet fill the part...the seeds are unmistakable, and it is to be hoped that the bud will develop into lovely blossom.'[18] Blossom it did. Lehmann's resignation from the Stadttheater was quietly forgotten. Within less than two years of those taxing but profitable rehearsals with Klemperer she had left for the Vienna Court Opera and a career as one of the very greatest singers of her time.

*   *   *

Earlier in November Klemperer had started to prepare his first Mozart opera, *The Marriage of Figaro*, in which Elisabeth Schumann was to sing the role of Cherubino. Again, there were lengthy, private rehearsals at Flottbeck. But by this time Klemperer's mood had swung from the severe depression he had suffered in the spring to an intense euphoria, a condition that always led to a heightening of his sexuality. Enchanted by Schumann's

Cherubino, which she first sang under him on 21 November, he cast her in another *Hosenrolle*, Oktavian in *Der Rosenkavalier*. It was a bizarre decision. Hitherto she had sung the part of Sophie, a role with which she was to be closely identified throughout her stage career. As she must have been aware, Oktavian demanded a voice heavier than hers. But Klemperer insisted with manic exuberance and unwisely she gave way.

A major new role naturally necessitated further periods of study at Flottbeck. Up to this point, neither Klemperer nor Schumann had given voice to their feelings for each other. At one rehearsal, however, Klemperer exchanged roles with Schumann, so as to demonstrate how he wanted Octavian to move in a scene with the Marschallin in the opera's first act. In the role of Oktavian he sang to her,

> Wo sie dich da hat,
> Wo ich meine Finger in ihre Finger schlinge,
> Wo ich mit meinen Augen ihre Augen suche,...
> Gerade da ist Ihr so zumut?

As their 'fingers intertwined' and they 'gazed into each other's eyes', they realised they were in love. Schumann felt that Klemperer 'saw into the depths of her artistic soul'.[19] He for his part rapidly persuaded himself that he could not live without her, and in his elated condition found it easy to brush aside the inconvenient fact that she was married.

Usually reserved to the point of inhibition, Klemperer threw caution to the winds. He and Schumann were frequently seen together, after rehearsals they would eat at the Alsterpavilion and, on one occasion, Klemperer entered Ehmke's, Hamburg's famous fish restaurant, where he had indiscreetly taken a *chambre séparée* shouting, 'Is Frau Puritz here?'[20] Walther Puritz was naturally not happy about his wife's association. But the affair was conducted in so open a manner that, paradoxically, people found it hard to believe that it was not innocent.

The first (and, as it transpired, the last) performance of *Der Rosenkavalier* that Klemperer conducted in Hamburg took place on 28 November. Predictably, Schumann's Oktavian was not a success. Pfohl commented that she 'has to learn that no one can overstep the limitations of their personality...even if Edyth Walker had not been her predecessor, this Rosenkavalier would have been a pocket edition of the role'.[21] Chevalley was no less critical. 'The opera depends on the illusion that Oktavian is a boy. This illusion Frau Puritz-Schumann cannot sustain for a moment... (her) voice is much more girlish than that of Fräulein Lehmann, who, incidentally, sang Sophie charmingly...'[22]

On the following evening Schumann was in the theatre to hear Lehmann make her début as Elsa, after which she was to join her husband and friends for supper.* When she failed to appear, Puritz returned to his apartment, where he found a maid in tears. Her mistress had eloped. Schumann wrote to tell her husband that, to avoid unpleasantness, she and Klemperer had taken several days' leave from the Stadttheater. Puritz, however, informed the police of his wife's disappearance, which may account for a report from Hamburg in the evening edition of the Berlin *Lokal-Anzeiger* of 2 December that 'Herr Otto Klemperer and the opera singer, Frau Puritz-Schumann have disappeared since yesterday. Both are in breach of contract and have informed the management that they have gone abroad.' The management of the Stadttheater denied the report, but made it plain that the elopers were not free to accept other engagements.

Where they travelled is hard to establish.† They may first have gone to Frankfurt, where they at one point turned up at the house of the conductor, Egon Pollak,‡ whom they both knew well. If so, they cannot have stayed there long, for on 3 December Klemperer wrote to Universal Edition, Mahler's publishers in Vienna, asking them to send some Mahler songs to Schiltigheim. It also seems that the couple appeared unannounced during a party at the Bodanzkys in Mannheim, at a moment when the assembled guests were discussing their elopment. By 5 December, when Schumann sang in *Königskinder*, they were back in Hamburg. She did not, however, return to her husband.

At this point Puritz challenged Klemperer to a duel with pistols, which Klemperer, after twice asking for a postponement, finally declined on the ground that Puritz had also sued him for abduction.§ But though he mocked Puritz ('he should shoot at ducks'), he was alarmed enough to travel only in cabs with the blinds drawn. He had probably got wind that, having been foiled of a duel, Puritz, normally a gentle creature not given to violence, had been urged by his *Bundesbrüder*‖ to find some other way of avenging himself. On 14 December Klemperer withdrew from a performance of *Il Trovatore* at such short notice that the *Tageszettel* had already been printed. Thereafter he did not appear in public at the Stadttheater for almost two weeks.

When Klemperer entered the orchestral pit on Boxing Day to conduct *Lohengrin*, he appeared nervous. But he was greeted by lengthy applause and the first two acts went well. After the second interval Elisabeth

---

* This account and what follows is based on a typescript of the reminiscences of the incident of one of the friends in question, Luise Bontemps, who also gave an interview to the author.
† Less than four weeks later they were again to leave Hamburg together. At a distance of seventy years and more reminiscences inevitably confuse the two events.
‡ See biographical glossary.
§ Dülberg was to have been Klemperer's second.
‖ Fellow members of his former student corps.

Schumann, who was in a box, was alarmed to notice that her husband, supported by a few friends, had occupied some hitherto empty seats in the front row of the stalls immediately behind the conductor. Realising that something was afoot, she tried in vain to warn Klemperer. It was, however, not until the twelve-bar coda to the final chorus of the opera that Puritz rose and shouted, 'Klemperer, turn round!' ('Klemperer, umdrehen!'). As Klemperer did so, Puritz drew a riding crop out of his sleeve and with it struck him twice on the left side of his face. Neighbours immediately surrounded Puritz to prevent further violence. Meanwhile, Klemperer, who had fallen into the orchestra pit under the impact of the onslaught, clambered up 'like a huge black spider'* and tried to attack Puritz, who was about to be led from the theatre by his friends. One of them, a pastor, who declared himself an intimate of the family, tried to explain the reasons for the assault, whereupon Klemperer, much to the amusement of the audience, shouted, 'Herr Puritz has attacked me, because I love his wife. Good evening.'

Shortly after midnight a hurricane howled through the streets of Hamburg. Paving stones were dragged up, window panes blown in, and in many districts a cascade of slates and tiles were hurled on to the streets. Klemperer and Schumann sought shelter in a hotel where Fritz Stiedry happened to be staying and was able to persuade the management to give the fugitives a room. The following day both parties issued statements. Puritz maintained that Klemperer's refusal to accept a duel had left him with no alternative but 'to administer a thrashing...in the presence of the public and in the place that had made his behaviour possible'. Klemperer's lawyer ridiculed the suggestion that Klemperer had brought any pressure on Schumann through his position in the Stadttheater and went on to declare that 'Frau Puritz and Herr Klemperer assured Herr Puritz in the most solemn manner that...no damage to his marital rights had occurred.'†

*   *   *

For the second time in less than a month the young couple fled from Hamburg. But on this occasion the Neue Zeitung announced on 28 December that 'Herr Klemperer will discontinue his activities as conductor forthwith'. To prevent the eloping couple from obtaining posts in the same theatre, Puritz wrote threatening letters to a number of managements. As

---

* The phrase is Lotte Lehmann's. In 1972 she gave a graphic eye-witness account of the incident to the author. The Hamburger Neue Zeitung and the Hamburger Fremdenblatt (27 December) contain reports.

† Hamburger Nachrichten, 27 December 1912 (evening edition) and 28 December 1912 (morning edition). Elisabeth Schumann subsequently told Gustl Breuer, a close friend in later years, that up to this point the relationship had indeed been platonic.

no German opera house would in any case offer engagements to artists who had broken their contract as well as caused a public scandal, the fugitives had to seek employment further afield. Their first destination seems to have been Vienna, where the romantically minded Alma Mahler could be relied on to respond sympathetically to their predicament. She in her turn sent them to a wealthy friend with a castle outside Prague, and at one point to general embarrassment Klemperer appeared at the German Theatre in a fruitless attempt to find work for both himself and Elisabeth Schumann. Eventually, they sought refuge in Kohnstamm's sanatorium in Königstein. Kohnstamm would not permit them to live together in the sanatorium itself, but accommodation was found in a pension in the village and meals were taken in the clinic.

Meanwhile Klemperer's euphoria had begun to wane and as it did so he became aware of the full extent of his predicament. He and Schumann had lost their jobs. Because so few people outside his immediate family circle were aware of the nature of his malady, wild rumours had begun to proliferate about the cause of his extravagant behaviour, as they were to do at comparable periods throughout his life. Worse still, the passion that had been due to his manic condition began to cool with declining euphoria. For his sake, Schumann had left her husband and endangered her career; now he found he no longer loved her. One day, while they were walking in the countryside at Königstein their path through a wood came to a dead-end. Klemperer turned to Schumann and observed, 'This is our life'.* Kohnstamm had the painful duty of explaining to her that Klemperer's feelings for her had changed. Her emotions were more lasting. Although she returned to her husband in August 1913 and bore him a son,† Klemperer was to remain in her memory as 'a great love'.‡ As she lay dying in New York almost forty years later, Klemperer telephoned. After the conversation was over, Schumann sighed, 'It was the red thread in my life.'§

For the rest of his life Klemperer remained extremely unwilling to refer to the events of the winter of 1912/13 and avoided anything that might have served to resurrect memory of them. To some extent this reticence was habitual; any untoward incident that had occurred during a manic phase was later discarded as though it had no part in his 'real' life. And it is true that for many years the episode continued to dog his career. Yet in this case the memory of what had occurred remained peculiarly painful. Not without reason, he felt guilt about the manner in which he had failed

* Recounted to the author by Lotte Lehmann, who had it from Schumann herself.
† The marriage finally ended in 1917.
‡ The phrase is taken from Lotte Lehmann's letter of 22 October 1972 to Lotte Klemperer.
§ 'Es war der rote Faden in meinem Leben.' Recounted to the author by Gustl Breuer.

Schumann after she had left her husband for him. He had also brought shame on his family in his mother's native city. He was therefore embarrassed when, almost half a century later, in Vienna in 1960, Schumann's son, Gerd Puritz, presented himself after a concert so as to meet 'the man my mother loved so much'. In 1966, when he was eighty-one, he declined an invitation to conduct at the Hamburg Opera that he might otherwise have welcomed because he was convinced that its Intendant, Rolf Liebermann, had deliberately proposed *Lohengrin* (of all operas!) and that the press would use the occasion to unearth the events of fifty-four years earlier. In the previous year he had even refused to contribute a few lines of appreciation to sleeve notes that were to accompany a reissue of Schumann's matchless Lieder recordings.[23]

Klemperer remained for a month in Königstein in a state of deep depression. Fortunately, Leo Biermann, a wealthy patron of the arts from Bremen, provided financial support. Landladies were alarmed at Klemperer's wild, Hoffmannesque appearance, huge height and penetrating voice, but with some difficulty a room was found in Frankfurt, where he seems to have remained sunk in gloom until well into the summer. That no letters or traces of journeys survive from these months suggests that the depression that had again overwhelmed him proved deep and persistent.

He nonetheless had to seek a new position. He applied for a post at Karlsruhe, and no doubt at other theatres, but their directors were wary of a conductor who had made himself notorious. One of the colleagues to whom he turned was Wilhelm Furtwängler.* The two young musicians who were destined to become the leading German conductors of their generation had probably got to know each other when Klemperer attended the first performance of Furtwängler's *Te Deum* at Strasbourg on 6 November 1911 and reacted warmly to the work.[24] A cordial relationship had sprung into existence and Klemperer accordingly travelled with his mother from Hamburg to nearby Lübeck, where Furtwängler was musical director, in a fruitless attempt to enlist his aid. Ida Klemperer did not care for her son's new comrade. On leaving the theatre, she observed, 'That man is no friend of yours', or words to that effect.†

In April 1913, perhaps through the intervention of Egon Pollak, an opening occurred at the modest opera house in Barmen, a city in the industrial area of the Ruhr. Klemperer accordingly travelled to a spa in Bavaria, where Otto Ockert, the theatre's director, was undergoing a

---

* See biographical glossary.
† Neither mother warmed to the other's offspring. In January 1912, Furtwängler's mother attended a recital in Munich, at which Klemperer accompanied Eva Lessmann. 'If you were my son', she is reported to have told Klemperer after the concert, 'I shouldn't sleep at night.' Both incidents were subsequently related by Klemperer to his daughter.

Kneipp 'cure', which involved immersion in water. Armed with flowers for the Frau Direktor, Klemperer duly presented himself at the side of the baths. Ockert invited him to enter and at the end of an aqueous interview he was engaged as First Conductor. It was a sorry come down, but at least it was a job.

Still in low spirits, Klemperer went that summer to Munich. There he stayed in solitude in a small pension, reading avidly and attending some of the Mozart performances (which he found oversweet) that Bruno Walter was conducting at the summer festival. Among the works he heard, probably for the first time, was *Così fan tutte*. He also saw something of Furtwängler, whose family home was in Munich. The two young men went on walking expeditions together and on one occasion Furtwängler demonstrated his tempi for a Beethoven movement. Klemperer was impressed, 'I felt that here was a born musician.'[25]

*   *   *

Barmen's only notable feature was its *Schwebebahn*, the overhead railway that journeyed along the valley of the Wupper, suspended, as it still is, from an overhead rail. Its theatre's one period of distinction had come in the years between 1898 and 1905, when Hans Gregor* had run it in conjunction with that in nearby Elberfeld.† Yet in comparison to equivalent cities in France or Britain in the early years of the century, Barmen was far from an artistic desert. During the season that Klemperer remained, the local concert society mounted a performance of Berlioz's *La Damnation de Faust*, Bruch's *Odysseus* was heard and no less a personage than Richard Strauss descended to conduct a concert of his own music.

The first problem was accommodation. Klemperer needed two rooms: one for two grand pianos and the other to sleep in. Ockert was finally able to persuade a family to take in the tall, thin young conductor with alarmingly penetrating eyes.‡ Characteristically, Klemperer's first act on entering his rooms was to check that both pianos were properly tuned. The young conductor was not a domesticated animal. In some ways he never became one; provided he could work, creature comforts remained of little importance.

---

* Hans Gregor (1866–1945) in 1905 founded the Komische Oper, Berlin, where he established a style of performance that laid more emphasis on drama as a component of opera than was habitual at the time. Director of the Vienna Court Opera 1911–18.

† The two theatres were finally united in 1919. Ten years later the two cities merged into the conurbation of Wupperthal.

‡ This description was given many years later by the young daughter of the house. She also recalled that Klemperer seemed exclusively preoccupied with his work at the theatre. Her initial fear of him seems, however, to have evaporated. One evening as he paused on returning home to gaze at the moon, she slowly poured water on him from an upstairs window.

Though the resources of Barmen's theatre were limited, Klemperer's position of First Conductor gave him a liberty of action he had not previously enjoyed; for that reason he later looked back on his season in the valley of the Wupper with more pleasure than he had expected on his arrival. Much of his time was inevitably occupied with preparing routine revivals of the standard repertory, but even this had the compensation of enabling him to conduct a number of works for the first time in his career.

Even in a musical backwater, Klemperer was temperamentally incapable of taking things easily, or of allowing himself to coast on a calm sea of routine. He reserved to himself most of the taxing works in the repertory and his preparations were as strenuous as ever. In a notice of *Tannhäuser*, with which he commenced his activities on 14 September 1913, the *Allgemeine Musikzeitung* of 31 October acidly observed that if the voices sounded tired that was no doubt the result of the incessant rehearsals that had been inflicted on them. *Tiefland* and *Il Trovatore* were followed by a performance of *Tristan und Isolde* (the first that he had conducted), in which, as usual, he opened the cuts that had become customary. Never a musician who learnt new scores quickly, the task of conducting many demanding operas for the first time would hardly have been possible for him, had he not devoted the long period of seclusion earlier in the year to study. The results were evident in the chorus of praise that greeted the orchestral playing in virtually all the performances he conducted. 'It is astonishing', wrote the *Barmer Zeitung* (25 November 1913) after *La Juive*, 'how the orchestral playing gains in beauty and subtlety under his direction, yet everything at the same time makes an impression of naturalness and lack of artifice: one has a feeling that it must be so....'

*   *   *

The copyright of *Parsifal*, which had hitherto scarcely been seen outside Bayreuth,* was due to expire on 31 December 1913, and opera houses throughout the world had started to plan their own productions.† Even before he had taken up his duties in Barmen, Klemperer had determined that the size and technical limitations of the theatre would not prevent him from doing likewise and a local banker and patron of the arts‡ agreed to subsidise the production. Sets were commissioned from Hans Wildermann, a young designer of radical leanings, who had already begun to make a

---

* The Metropolitan Opera in New York had been able to ignore an international copyright agreement to which the USA was not a party. A few other opera houses had done likewise.
† The race to be first past the post was won by a short head by the Liceo in Barcelona, where the performance (in Italian) began at the Spanish hour of a minute past midnight on 31 December/1 January. In Prague the German Theatre beat the Czech National Theatre to it by an hour.
‡ Eduard Freiherr von der Heydt (1882–1964); member of a prominent Elberfeld family.

name for himself in Cologne.* In Barmen, Wildermann, who was described in the programme as 'szenischer Oberleiter', seems to have exercised control over all visual aspects of the production. Thus for the first time Klemperer found himself preparing a new production with a colleague who, like himself, was influenced by the new ideas that were stirring in the German theatre.

A revolution in the Central European approach to theatre in the first years of the new century had been brought about largely by the appearance in German of two books, neither of which was by a German author. Adolphe Appia's *La musique et la mise en scène* was published in Munich in 1899 and Gordon Craig's *The Art of the Theatre* six years later.† The reforms they called for were radical. The stage would once again be treated, as it had been before the invention of the proscenium arch, as an open space. Stylisation would replace naturalistic detail. Flat, painted scenery would give way to three-dimensional sets, which (and this was crucial) would facilitate the exploitation of new lighting resources. These epoch-making innovations found a far more fertile soil in Germany than elsewhere, partly because of the importance traditionally attached to theatre in Central Europe, but partly also on account of technical advances. The first revolving stage, which facilitated the shifting of the heavy architectural, as opposed to painted, scenery that a three-dimensional approach to production called for, had been installed in the Munich Residenztheater in 1896. Similarly, the invention of the high-wattage, incandescent bulb had opened the way to wide-reaching developments in the use of light and colour, and in this sphere, too, Germany led the world.‡

There is no reason to assume that Klemperer was at that time even aware of the existence of Appia,§ whose approach to theatrical design

---

* In 1907 Wildermann (1884–1954) had designed sets for Hebbel's *Herodes und Mariamne* that consisted exclusively of curtains and cubic blocks. Irmhild La Nier Kuhnt (*Philosophie und Bühnenbild: Leben und Werk des Szenikers Hans Wildermann*) claims these to have been among the first in Germany to dispense entirely with painted scenery. In 1912 Wildermann had contributed to a pot-pourri of designs for a new production of *The Ring* that survived to plague Klemperer ten years later (see p. 163). The practice of assembling sets for a single production from diverse sources was still widespread in the early years of the century. That Wildermann's operatic ventures were less innovatory in Cologne than his Barmen *Parsifal* may be attributed to the constraints put on him by an Intendant notorious for his conservatism, as well as to the survival of such working methods.

† Both were prophets unhonoured in their own countries. The concepts of Appia (1862–1928), who was Swiss and particularly concerned with the realisation of Wagner's theatrical vision, were only fulfilled a generation after his death by Wieland Wagner at Bayreuth in the fifties. Though a son of Ellen Terry, Gordon Craig (1872–1966) similarly exercised little influence on the English theatre of his lifetime.

‡ Although the Savoy Theatre in London seems to have been the first (1881) to have installed electric stage lighting.

§ There is no record, for instance, that he attended the epoch-making production of Gluck's *Orfeo* that Dalcroze and Appia had together mounted in Hellerau in 1912.

Wildermann in any case rejected as too abstract. But both men were undoubtedly influenced, if indirectly, by his ideas; indeed, in his use of stylisation and of colour, Wildermann probably owed more to Appia than he recognised. As in Wieland Wagner's first production of *Parsifal* at Bayreuth thirty-seven years later, the trunks of the trees were transformed into the pillars of the temple of the Grail. The vivid greens and blues of the forest gave way to mauves and reds as the Grail approached. The disintegration of Klingsor's castle at the end of the second act was realised by flooding the stage with a desolate grey-green light.*

It is hard to determine how these conceptions worked in the theatre. The *Rheinisch-Westphälische Zeitung* (5 January 1914) reported that the sets had made a less unified impression than the designs that had appeared in a special *Festschrift* published for the occasion, in part because of the technical shortcomings of the Barmen theatre. Whatever the results, the intentions, as revealed in the sketches, throw light on Klemperer's radical approach to stagecraft. As the *Barmer Zeitung* of 6 January observed, 'he was able for the first time to follow his own sensibility, free from any hangovers from the past'.

Preparations extended over many weeks, and, as always before important events, Klemperer grew increasingly wrought-up as the day approached. His condition made itself felt in rehearsals. On 30 December a letter from a member of the chorus appeared in the magazine of the Christen-Verband, complaining of his abusive behaviour. Among other incivilities, he had, it was claimed, forbidden a member of the chorus to leave the stage to satisfy 'an urgent need'. He had told Parsifal that, if the flower maidens got in the way, he should 'just give them a kick'. There was also outrage that he should have abused the chorus in the presence of the supplementary amateurs who had been enlisted for the occasion. Tension seems to have reached a climax in a matinée performance of *Lohengrin*. Klemperer, who, the correspondent asserted, in any case 'had nothing to do with the stage' (a comment that throws light on the working habits of other conductors), had attempted to discipline the ladies of the chorus, 'who had justifiably tried to defend themselves against his shouting'.†

The theatre itself was shut for two evenings before the first night on 4 January. As at Bayreuth, the performance was heralded by fanfares from the balcony of the theatre, no applause was permitted until its end and the orchestral pit was covered. Nathan Klemperer came from Hamburg for the occasion. After the performance, the applause that flooded the auditorium reached a climax as Wagner's bust was trundled on to the stage and there

---

* The designs are in the Theatermuseum of Cologne University.
† Women in particular were liable to receive the rough edge of Klemperer's blistering tongue.

adorned with a wreath. In the course of the season *Parsifal* was given no fewer than twenty-three performances to packed houses, a measure of the general public's eagerness to experience a work that had for forty years been the preserve of well-heeled visitors to Bayreuth. Klemperer conducted without a score.

*   *   *

Klemperer's bad relations with the chorus may have led indirectly to his other main achievement in Barmen. A new production of Cornelius's *Der Barbier von Bagdad* had to be abandoned because the chorus insisted that it had no time to learn the work's relatively simple choral numbers.[26] In its place Klemperer was able to win acceptance of an opera that made minimal demands of the chorus and that was particularly close to his heart. In the nineteenth century *Così fan tutte* had been widely dismissed as an aberration on the part of Mozart. Beethoven had frowned on what he had mistakenly taken to be its cynicism, others had described it as 'stupid' and 'disgusting', and Wagner had blamed the text for what he took to be the work's musical inferiority. Because of its supposedly weak libretto, the opera had generally been performed (when it was performed at all) in a variety of reformed 'versions'. In 1863 the librettists of Gounod's *Faust* had adapted the score to a French version of *Love's Labour's Lost*. As late as 1909, it had been wedded to a play by Calderón and performed at the Dresden Court Opera under the title of *Die Dame Kobold*.[27] Strauss and Mahler had been among the first to rescue the opera from such misuse, but Klemperer was before his time in his special devotion to it.*

His enthusiasm for the project induced him to write a brief introduction to the work for a local newspaper.[28] In it he not only defended the music, but even asserted the merits of the text. Far from being superficial, it was, he insisted, profound in its insight. That was an extremely unconventional point of view in 1914; indeed, more than half a century later, it is only in the process of being generally accepted. He also pointed to the pre-Beethovenian character of the canon-quartet, 'E nel tuo, nel mio bicchiero', in the second act, and to the foreshadowing of Mendelssohn's *Midsummer Night's Dream* music in the trio. 'Soave sia il vento'. To his ears, the distinguishing mark of *Così fan tutte* was not frivolity but a 'sublimated spirituality' ('Geistigkeit').

For his production Klemperer used a *Stilbühne*. This was an arrangement of curtaining that divided the stage into sections of varying depths and thus permitted the work's many short scenes to be played virtually without

---

* That devotion never cooled. A concert performance in London on 21 February 1971 proved to be the last opera he conducted.

interruption.* Stage properties were correspondingly restricted to a minimum. He used the translation that Hermann Levi had published in 1897 and accompanied the recitatives on a harpsichord, a rarity in the orchestral pits of the period. For the first time in his career, he himself produced.

The theatre was not full for the first performance on 14 March and the audience at first sat in glum silence. Only gradually did enthusiasm begin to mount from scene to scene until the curtain finally fell to loud applause, which further increased when Klemperer appeared on stage and was presented with a laurel wreath. The critics were full of praise for his contribution, as producer as well as conductor, to the first performance of *Così fan tutte* that had ever been given in Barmen. But a majority had reservations about the work itself. As usual, the music was held to redeem an unworthy text. The Barmen *Freie Presse* (16 March 1914) attacked its 'cold, empty, rationalistic *Weltanschauung*...in which deep feelings have no place'. The critic of the *Barmer Zeitung* was alone in proclaiming the work a masterpiece. But its inability to appeal to the ordinary opera-goer before the First World War is only too apparent from the fact that the production was given only two performances.

*   *   *

Later in the month there followed a cycle of *Der Ring des Nibelungen*. From the enthusiastic comments of the local critics it is possible to deduce that Klemperer had started to achieve a restraint and authority that had eluded him in his earlier performances of Wagner. Although Barmen had at first seemed a cruel setback, it had provided a range of experience such as he would never have been able to gain so quickly in a larger theatre. For the first time in his career he had been, as he himself later put it, 'really able to get to grips with the whole material of an operatic theatre'.[29] But by February 1914 it was already clear that he would not be remaining for a second year. The season in Barmen ended on 13 April. Three days later he was in Strasbourg.

---

* The *Stilbühne* was a very recent innovation. In *Twentieth Century Stage Decoration* Fuerst and Hume date it from 1912. That Klemperer should have used it in 1914 is a further indication of his radical approach to the staging of opera.

6   *With Pfitzner in Strasbourg*

In January 1914 Hans Pfitzner decided to take a year's leave from his position of opera director in Strasbourg in order to orchestrate his new opera, *Palestrina*. He had held out an offer of an engagement to Klemperer in 1909; now he again saw a chance to help his former pupil to escape from Barmen and at the same time to procure a competent deputy for himself. An emissary was accordingly despatched. But, far from grasping the prospect of a position of some authority in a city he knew and liked, Klemperer hesitated. Much though he admired Pfitzner as a musician, he did not regard him highly as a conductor. He was also aware that his old teacher's abrasive character had made him a controversial figure in Strasbourg. He foresaw correctly that any success he might have would be used by Pfitzner's opponents and that the result would be, as he later put it, 'envy, rivalry and malice'.[1] But the emissary mocked the notion that a little-known young conductor would provide competition for a figure as celebrated as Pfitzner, and Klemperer was in any case uncomfortably aware that few theatres were willing to engage him. It was a matter of choosing between Strasbourg and a further year in Barmen, and he chose Strasbourg.

The announcement of the appointment on 27 January produced exactly the sort of repercussions that made theatres wary of him. Two days later, the Strasbourg *Freie Presse* asked whether the Herr Klemperer who had been appointed was the same as had been compelled to resign his post in Hamburg on account of a scandal. On 3 February, the paper followed this tendentious enquiry with details of the difficulties that had occurred in Barmen between Klemperer and the opera chorus, commenting that 'this conductor is not suitable for Strasbourg'. Nonetheless an agreement was signed whereby Klemperer was engaged as First Conductor at a salary of 5,000 Marks a year.* He also secured considerable prerogatives. He was to have the right to choose what operas he would conduct within the repertory. He was to be consulted in matters of casting and would be on equal footing with the producers. He would conduct no operettas.

*   *   *

* There is, however, no trace in the minutes of the Theatre Commission's sitting of 26 January 1914 of the 'great opposition' to the appointment, to which Walter Abendroth refers to in his biography, *Hans Pfitzner*, (p. 199).

87

In 1871 Alsace had been annexed to the newly formed German Empire after almost two centuries of French sovereignty. During that period the professional and trading classes in the towns, and particularly in the province's capital, Strasbourg, had become largely Frenchified. The peasants, in contrast, had remained overwhelmingly German and continued to speak (as they still do today) their Allemannic *patois*. Thus the situation in Strasbourg was the exact reverse of that which Klemperer had experienced in Prague. Whereas in Bohemia a small German and Jewish middle class confronted a Czech peasantry and urban proletariat, in Alsace the German-speaking rural population far outnumbered the predominantly French middle class in the towns. Hence the opposition to German rule centred on the 'old Alsatian' bourgeois families who remained loyal to France.

Alsace became German at a period when German music had already come to dominate concert life and Wagner had begun to challenge the Latin hegemony that had prevailed in the opera house for over two-and-a-half centuries. Thus musical life, which found a ready-made base in the old German style instrumental and choral societies that had existed before the centuries of French rule, provided a means of fostering the German loyalties of the Alsatian population, and opera naturally played a crucial role in this attempt to integrate the province into the new *Reich*.* Throughout the period that Strasbourg remained German its theatre received a special additional grant from Berlin. The city was thus a more significant centre of opera than its size might suggest.†

*   *   *

In 1906, Rudolf Schwander became *Oberbürgermeister* of Strasbourg. Himself an Alsatian, he proved to be an energetic and far-sighted head of his city,‡ who carried through many large-scale projects, including the canalisation of the Rhine. One of his first concerns was to establish Strasbourg as an important musical centre and it was at his instigation (he himself travelled to Munich to complete the negotiations) that Pfitzner was in 1907 appointed director of the city's conservatory and concerts, on the understanding that, as soon as the position fell vacant, he would also become director of opera at the Stadttheater. ¶

* Berlin accordingly paid for the reconstruction of Strasbourg's charming French-built theatre, only – with characteristic Prussian heavy-handedness – to forfeit any good will this might have won by imposing a new director without reference to the municipality. This was one reason why the old Alsatian bourgeoisie tended to give the theatre the cold shoulder.
† The population of Strasbourg in 1914 was 173,000.
‡ Rudolf Schwander (1868–1950), who in 1918 became the last *Reichsstatthalter* of Alsace, was a man in the mould of another powerful, reforming *Oberbürgermeister*, whom Klemperer was to encounter later in his career, when he was at the Cologne Opera and the city's head man was Konrad Adenauer.
¶ In the following account of Pfitzner's career as director of the Strasbourg opera the author

In 1910 Pfitzner was duly appointed to that position with well-nigh dictatorial artistic powers; only in substantial matters involving finance was he obliged to procure the agreement of the Intendant. His contract specifically stated that he would take over both the conducting and the production of German operas, so far as he considered it to be desirable. Casting, repertory and rehearsals were entirely in his hands. As head of all the principal civic musical institutions in Strasbourg, Pfitzner was, as Schwander intended him to be, the arbiter of the city's musical life. In 1908

has drawn on files in the city's archives municipales in particular Pfitzner's personal file (12–69) and on the minutes of the meetings of the Theatre Commission. These files also contain information relating to Klemperer's initial engagement.

8   Hans Pfitzner

he and his family moved to Alsace, where they continued to live until the end of the First World War, when the province returned to France.

It was in many ways an imaginative and bold appointment. Although Pfitzner, who was only just over forty years old, had had no experience of conducting in an opera house, he had clearly defined views on staging and performance. He saw opera, not as an exercise in virtuosity or spectacle, but as an organic unity of music and drama. A work was a living entity and the task of conductor and producer alike was to recapture the creative vision that lay behind it. His central principle was 'faithfulness to the work of art'.* His policy in Strasbourg was to provide a limited number of exemplary productions and to that end he himself often produced as well as conducted. On these occasions he worked in close collaboration with his designer, Georg Daubler. He established an opera school at the conservatory and it is indicative of his disdain for mere expertise and eagerness to achieve a freshness of approach that on a number of occasions he chose to use his pupils in preference to established singers on the payroll of the Stadttheater.

Pfitzner was undoubtedly inspired by real feeling for the theatre. He frequently held play readings (mainly of German romantic authors) in his home; and on one notable occasion, when he was conducting *Die Meistersinger* and the Beckmesser became hoarse, he handed over his baton to a deputy, had himself shaved and sang the role in the third act 'with exemplary articulation and accuracy'.[2] Even Klemperer, with whom he was to clash at Strasbourg over matters of staging among other issues, in later years came to regard his productions with greater respect than he had had for them as a young man.†

It has become customary to regard Pfitzner as the very archetype of the entrenched reactionary he became in later years. But that is only one side of the coin. He had experienced Mahler at work at the Vienna Opera and in his more limited way he, too, brought intellectual energy and artistic ideals to the very necessary task of reforming operatic production in the early years of the century. At Strasbourg he had been invested by Schwander with powers that might have enabled him to make his mark on theatrical history. That he finally failed to do so was primarily due to an element of dogmatic rigidity in his own character. He was also basically out of sympathy with the times and thus cut off, as Klemperer was not, from the most vital forces of the period.

---

* *Vom musikalischen Drama*, p. 178; a collection of Pfitzner's earnest if hardly original essays on music and drama.
† Klemperer's own production of *Fidelio* at Covent Garden in 1961 could indeed be said to be closer to Pfitznerian principles than to the more advanced styles generally associated with his period at the Kroll.

As a consequence, his concern for *Werktreue* tended in practice to lapse into a slavish faithfulness to stage directions that was sometimes hard to distinguish from conventional naturalism. Pfitzner was also extraordinarily limited in his musical sympathies. As he himself put it, when writing of his student days, 'Real music seemed to me to begin only with Beethoven. With him "old music" came to an end. He opened the gates to what came after.'[3] That perspective was characteristic of the nineteenth-century taste to which Pfitzner all his life remained loyal. His interest in eighteenth-century music remained as minimal as his concern with his contemporaries (*Così fan tutte* he regarded, significantly, as a bad opera). Even within the field of nineteenth-century music large segments, notably of French and Italian opera, were dismissed out of hand, although Boieldieu, Auber and Meyerbeer won limited approval. *Otello* and *Falstaff* he declared to be works that Verdi should 'have on his conscience'[4] on account of what he regarded as the debasement of Shakespeare's plays. Unable to read any foreign language and militantly anti-Catholic, Pfitzner's cultural horizons were exclusively German.

These limitations are reflected in the works he chose to stage in Strasbourg. His own productions were rigidly confined to works by Weber, Marschner, Wagner and himself. As a conductor, he added an opera apiece by Gluck, Mozart, Beethoven, Lortzing, Cornelius and Bruch as well as all Wagner from *Der fliegende Holländer* onwards. The same bias was apparent in his concert programmes.* It was, to say the least of it, a narrow platform from which to win over a disaffected French minority.

*   *   *

By the start of Pfitzner's fourth season, in September 1913, difficulties had arisen on a less ideological level. Six months earlier, the Intendant, Wilhelmi, with whom he had got on well, had been taken ill and Anton Otto, an actor with little interest in or knowledge of opera, appointed in his place. Otto undoubtedly resented the special powers wielded by his opera director and at the first signs of discontent took pains to dissociate himself from Pfitzner. The complaints centred on Pfitzner's use of pupils from the opera school in his Stadttheater productions. Objection was also taken to what, even by German standards, was felt to be an ill-balanced repertory. On 19 September 1913 Pfitzner offered his resignation, which Schwander refused to accept.

It was not long before a new series of events brought the issue back to the boil. Early in December Pfitzner announced that the title role in his

---

* Although he did in 1910 conduct the first complete performance of Berlioz's *Romeo and Juliet* to be heard in Strasbourg.

91

forthcoming production of *Parsifal*, which was of course a matter of intense expectancy, would be sung, not by an experienced member of the company, but by Max Hofmüller,* a handsome young tenor of unusual intelligence and musicality who had studied at his opera school. Later in the month Otto publicly disclaimed all responsibility for an unsatisfactory new production of Flotow's *Martha* on the grounds that Pfitzner alone determined repertory and casting. Schwander again loyally came to Pfitzner's defence. But hardly had he done so than the *Strassburger Neueste Nachrichten* (22 December 1913) reprinted an article that had appeared two days earlier in *Die Zukunft*. In it Paul Marsop† demanded that Pfitzner be given a life tenancy as opera director and that a *Festspielhaus* on the model of Bayreuth be built in Strasbourg to house his stage works.

Such a combination of events gave Pfitzner's opponents the opening they sought and he was subjected to a series of bitter attacks in the local press.‡ On 6 January 1914 his supporters rallied. Newspapers on that date carried a letter to Schwander from a number of leading citizens, among them Robert Wollenberg (see p. 57), pointing to Pfitzner's achivements in Strasbourg. But on 26 January Schwander had to inform the Theatre Commission that its opera director had requested a year's leave. On the following day new powers were given to Otto and the *Neueste Nachrichten* reported that on his return from leave Pfitzner's prerogatives would be reduced. Clearly, Pfitzner's wings had been clipped and his request for a year's leave had been motivated by more than a desire to score *Palestrina*.

Klemperer, who had contacts in Strasbourg and was on cordial terms with Pfitzner, his wife and Wollenberg, must have been well aware of the events that had led to the offer of a job in Strasbourg; hence his initial unwillingness to accept a position that must otherwise have seemed to offer a providential deliverance. He saw only too clearly that any success he might have would be used as a means of discomfiting his former teacher, and that he would then be dragged into the internecine conflict that was already rending the city's musical life.

Meanwhile Pfitzner – never a man to pour oil on troubled waters – went over to the counter-attack. In an interview in the *Frankfurter Nachrichten* (1 April 1914) that was duly reprinted in Strasbourg, he complained of the difficulties he had encountered in pursuing a coherent artistic policy. He ended his outburst by declaring that, for his opponents, 'a *Schmiere* (a

* A good friend of Klemperer at Strasbourg and again in his later years. See biographical glossary.
† One of the two critics whom Klemperer had overheard discussing a vacant position at the German Theatre in Prague (see p. 29).
‡ Abendroth's assertion (*Hans Pfitzner*, p. 192) that these were led by the 'socialist' *Freie Presse* is unfounded. The *Bürgerzeitung* and the *Neueste Nachrichten* were equally involved and both were 'bourgeois' organs.

hack company) was preferable to a theatre with a policy', and then for good measure added, 'But that's what you get in the provinces, in the *Sumpf*'.* Now the fat was really in the fire. The press demanded that Pfitzner be brought to account for his insulting references to Strasbourg and its theatre, and the city council insisted that the burgomaster deal with the matter. On 22 April Schwander rose yet again to defend his opera director, this time before the city council. He denied that Pfitzner had used the words reported; and then, in an unhappy afterthought, added that Pfitzner had only wished to settle scores with two critics, whose professional competence he questioned. That observation brought Pfitzner a writ from one of the critics in question. Belatedly, on 29 April, Pfitzner was induced to deny that the word 'Sumpf' had ever crossed his lips, an assurance he repeated two weeks later when he was called to account before the city council.

*   *   *

Thus the rumpus was at its height when Klemperer arrived on 16 April to hold preliminary rehearsals for *Elektra*, which was to be his first new production in the coming season. His presence in Strasbourg also provided an opportunity to secure the engagement as chorusmaster and assistant conductor of Werner Rudolf, a young musician he had got to know at the Barmen theatre and who was to become one of his closest friends. Klemperer only remained in Strasbourg until the end of the month, but in that period Pfitzner played to him the first part of Act One of *Palestrina*, which was already complete in full score. He was, he wrote to Willy Levin† from Paris on 14 May, 'intensely moved' by the music.‡

Klemperer's visit to Paris was his first since he had travelled there in 1905 to compete in the Rubinstein competition and, as on that occasion, he again stayed with Tante Helene. The purpose of his visit had originally been to prepare a production of *Der Rosenkavalier*, which an Anglo-American syndicate planned to stage in Paris and which Strauss himself was to conduct. The composer had recommended him as a musician who might hold the rehearsals and as a bait had offered the opportunity to conduct a single performance. The prospect of appearing in such company in the French capital was not without its attractions. Klemperer needed the money and he was eager to revisit Paris, especially as in mid-May

* Literally 'swamp', implying 'cesspool'.
† Willy Levin (18?–1926) was a close friend both of Strauss and of Pfitzner, which says much for his diplomatic talent. The role of the Commerzienrat in *Intermezzo* is based on his character and *Elektra* is dedicated to him. His daughter was married to Walter Kantorowicz, a Hamburg physician whom Klemperer knew well. Hence the connection.
‡ He was later less enthusiastic. See *Conversations*, p. 48.

Diaghilev was to stage the new ballet, *Josefslegende*, he had commissioned from Strauss. Nonetheless, he had hesitated and on 25 March had written from Barmen to ask Levin whether it might not make an unfortunate impression in Strasbourg, were the deputy director of the city's opera house to undertake the duties of a repetiteur elsewhere. On this ground he declined the offer.* But the idea of a visit to Paris remained attractive and he arrived there on 13 May, the day before Strauss was himself to conduct the première of *Josefslegende*. The music was coolly received. Klemperer contrasted its unenthusiastic reception with 'the storms of applause' that greeted *Petrushka* a few days later, and attributed both reactions to the anti-German sentiment that was growing on the eve of the war. But he had to admit that Strauss's score was 'a miserable piece'.†

By the beginning of June Klemperer was in Venice on his first trip south of the Alps. La Serenissima made strangely little impact. Perhaps because it was already hot and he hated heat, he stayed on the Lido. He was unable to buy a coat ('all the people here seem to be exactly half my size'); the sea was beautiful, but so it was everywhere, and for anyone used to the North Sea the Lagoon lacked movement.‡ Early in July he returned to Strasbourg for more orchestral rehearsals for *Elektra*. But when war broke out he had resumed his vacation in Munich, where he stayed in a small pension, occasionally attending festival Mozart performances, reading Schopenhauer, walking and studying Debussy's *Pelléas et Mélisande* in preparation for a production he was to conduct during the ensuing season at Strasbourg.§

Carried away by the wave of patriotic fervour that swept across Europe in the early days of hostilities, he volunteered for the armed forces and was accepted. Only when he had done so did the full implications of his action dawn on him. After a sleepless night, he rushed back to the recruiting centre and extricated himself on the plea that he would have to consult his parents in Hamburg. But, like most German intellectuals, he continued until the last months of the war to believe in the rightness of his country's cause and in its approaching victory.

*   *   *

* The project in any case came to nothing owing to a quarrel between the directors.
† Heyworth (ed.), *Conversations*, p. 61. Klemperer was, however, mistaken in supposing that he heard *Petrushka*, which was his first encounter with the music of Stravinsky (whom he also met), on the same evening as the première of *Josefslegende*. The two works were only paired once, on 21 May.
‡ Letter of 2 June to Charlotte Abraham (later Naef). In later years Klemperer grew to love Italy, though he was never so closely attracted to it as he was to France.
§ Owing to the war, it never took place. Although he was much drawn to it, Klemperer never conducted the work.

Only thirty miles from the front, Strasbourg was one of Germany's most important fortresses in the West. On the outbreak of hostilities the Stadttheater was turned into a depot for comforts for the troops and some of its artists and virtually all its technicians were called up. On 11 August the theatre dismissed those who remained, though a small allowance was made to any members of the company who agreed, as did Klemperer, to hold themselves in readiness for an eventual reopening later in the season. That autumn the city, which contained innumerable military hospitals, was virtually bereft of musical activities apart from concerts for the wounded. But when it became clear that this section of the front was likely to remain inactive, the military authorities agreed to the reopening of the theatre for three nights a week. On 8 December, Klemperer, who was in Mannheim, was accordingly requested to return and reminded that he would need a special permission to enter the fortress city.

When the season belatedly opened on 10 January 1915 in the presence of the imperial *Statthalter*, the evening was prefaced by an oration, given by the city's leading critic, Gustav Altmann, on 'the solacing spirit of German art' in 'this great time'. That was followed by a patriotic 'Kriegsvorspiel', entitled *1914* and produced by the Intendant. After these preliminiaries Klemperer conducted a revival of *Fidelio*. With the exception of Altmann in the *Strassburger Post*[5] (of the city's newspapers the most favourably disposed to Pfitzner), who commented adversely on Klemperer's slow tempi and dynamic exaggerations, the critics vied with panegyrics every bit as fervent as those that had greeted his début in Hamburg. The *Freie Presse*[6] saluted 'a conductor such as Strasbourg had not heard in years'; the *Neue Zeitung*[7] observed that Pfitzner had never drawn playing of such dynamic range from the orchestra; the *Neueste Nachrichten*[8] lamented that Klemperer was to remain in Strasbourg only during Pfitzner's year of absence; in the *Neue Zeitschrift für Musik*,[9] Stanislaus Schlesinger, who only a few months earlier had issued a writ for libel against Pfitzner, wrote that Klemperer had drawn 'sounds such as we have hardly heard from our already excellent orchestra'.

It is clear from these comments that, exactly as Klemperer had foreseen, a number of the Strasbourg critics welcomed his success as a means of pursuing their feud with Pfitzner. In fact relations between the opera director and his deputy had already grown tense. During the rehearsals for *Fidelio*, Pfitzner, who continued to live in Strasbourg during his year's leave, had been angered to discover that Klemperer had restored a substantial cut in the last act.* Pfitzner instructed Klemperer to perform

* Pfitzner had been in the habit of deleting the opening number, so that the curtain rose on the chorus, 'Heil sei der Tag '. It was a cut that Mahler had also considered but rejected.

'his' version. Klemperer tartly replied that he preferred Beethoven's.[10] That was not the only ground for dissension. In the introductory bars both to the quartet, 'Mir ist so wunderbar', and to the prisoners' chorus, 'O welche Lust', Klemperer reduced the number of strings so as to achieve an ethereal effect. Such divergencies from the letter of the score offended against Pfitzner's principle of *Werktreue*.[11] Thus by the opening night the two men were already at loggerheads. That did not bode well for a harmonious collaboration on Pfitzner's return at the end of the season.

The critics' enthusiasm did not stem solely from a desire to pursue their feud with Pfitzner. In Stanislaus Schlesinger's description there emerge the first indications of a style for which Klemperer was in later years to become famous:

Unlike so many famous colleagues he did not open the E major overture in the almost traditional precipitous manner, but with a moderate allegro. The following adagio was very broad and expressive and only in the eighteenth bar did he allow the music to surge forwards, so as to achieve a sense of jubilance, which then rose to the heights in the concluding presto. In the eight-bar *ritornello* that introduces the canon-quartet, 'Mir ist so wunderbar', Klemperer began with such an ethereal, barely audible pianissimo of muted strings that one listened...with bated breath. The entry march of the guards, not usually one of the outstanding numbers of the opera, was pointed with such style that it acquired new significance. In Leonore's great aria he achieved complete unity between the wonderful vocal line and the orchestra; in the melodrama the inexorable, hollow triplets of the accompaniment had an uncanny effect...Under Klemperer's careful yet sharply articulated conducting, every entry in the chorus, 'Heil sei dem Tag',....was sharp and clear.

A high point of the evening came in the great C major overture [No.3]...It had not merely a masterly unity, but through the extraordinarily fine and subtle gauging of the climaxes provided proof of a musical sensibility, an independence of mind and a fieriness of spirit that recall Klemperer's model, Mahler.[12]

Sixty years later Klemperer's *Fidelio* was still a living memory in Strasbourg and the *Carmen* he conducted there for the first time on 14 February 1915 left a scarcely less deep impact. The issue of 'enemy music' had already been raised in the German press and in Strasbourg it had been settled by smugly contrasting the behaviour of the supposedly 'civilised' French, who had virtually banned music by dead as well as living German composers, with the greater generosity of spirit shown in these matters by the Germans. 'Ein echter, deutscher Mann mag keinen Franzosen leiden', wrote one critic, parodying Goethe, 'doch seine *Carmen* hat er gern'.* Klemperer's performance was highly praised for its measured tempi, fine instrumental detail and overwhelming climaxes. Marguerite Hugel, a young musician who was studying composition under Pfitzner, singled out

* 'Ein echter, deutscher Mann mag keinen Franzen leiden, doch ihre Weine trinkt er gern' (A real German may not be able to stand the French but he likes their wines). *Faust*, Part I, Brander in Auerbach's cellar.

for comment a prelude that was taken more broadly than usual, but 'with colossal rhythmic sense'.[13]

Wagner naturally dominated a repertory that bore the stamp of Pfitzner's taste. After a period as a student when he had leaned towards Brahms, Klemperer (partially, as he later admitted, as a result of Pfitzner's influence) at this period of his life came closer to Wagner than at any time before or after. Even so, he was never a Wagnerian in the full sense of the word. But in a disputed city such as Strasbourg and in the first year of the war it was inevitable that virtually half the performances that the First Conductor directed should be by the composer, who, more than any other, embodied the spirit of German nationalism. *Tannhäuser, Die Meistersinger* and *Tristan und Isolde* followed each other within a matter of weeks. The performances were received with ovations such as Strasbourg had rarely experienced. If they left a less lasting mark than those of *Fidelio* and *Carmen*, it was perhaps on account of some inner reservation, which Altmann may have sensed when he commented on 'a lack of rapture and elemental passion' in *Tristan*.[14]

*   *   *

It was Mozart rather than Wagner who was henceforth to stand at the centre of Klemperer's operatic preoccupations, and, after conducting a revival on 25 April of Pfitzner's earliest opera, *Der arme Heinrich*, his energies were concentrated on a new staging of *Figaros Hochzeit*,* whose première took place on 15 May. With redesigned sets for the last two acts, this was as close to a new production as the Strasbourg Opera was to get in the first year of the war. He himself took charge of the stage as well as of the musical side of the performance and nothing he did during his three seasons in Strasbourg was to arouse such opposition.

Some of this reaction was rankly chauvinistic. In particular, Klemperer's restoration of the recitatives came in for criticism.† The *Freie Presse* (18 May 1915) claimed that these were no more than a modish Italianate malady of Mozart's time; *Figaro* should by rights have been a *Singspiel*. The *Neueste Nachrichten*[15] complained about 'this parlando sing-song, which gets on the nerves because it is against nature'. Altmann found the plot *passé*: it was a pity that Mozart had squandered his genius on 'this more or less frivolous foreign vaudeville'.[16] On the other hand, no exception was taken to aspects of the production that might have been thought open to question, such as Klemperer's use of a grand piano to accompany the recitative, or of his inclusion of two pages of recitative to which Mahler had set Beaumarchais's judgement scene.

---

* In German-speaking territory Mozart's Italian operas continued to be sung in the vernacular until some years after the Second World War.
† At that time they were often spoken.

With more reason the critics assailed the casting. In his eagerness to rescue the opera from rococo daintiness Klemperer allotted the main roles to far heavier voices than was customary. Thus Susanna was taken by a soprano who had sung Aida, and the Cherubino by an Elsa. Klemperer never repeated these ill-judged castings, which did much to turn opinion against the entire undertaking. Yet they were part and parcel of his approach to the work. For him, Mozart was a matter of 'Helligheit auf dunklem Grunde' ('Lightness on a dark background').[17] What he sought was a maximum of dramatic intensity compatible with the music's classical equilibrium. Strength had to be matched to grace.* This dark realism was far removed from the sweetness and light that had been regarded as the prime characteristics of le divin Mozart in the previous century. Thus Klemperer's Figaro came as a shock to Strasbourg, just as fifty-five years later it was to disconcert a London audience.† Outraged by its 'Mahlerian' style and in particular by the Mahler insert, Pfitzner and his friends left before the end of the performance.[18] In London the representative of The Times did likewise.

Of the Strasbourg critics only Fritz Brust conveyed any sense of Klemperer's stylistic intentions.

The performance was musically and scenically inspired by Otto Klemperer. I am as sure that it was not totally successful as that it was of real significance ...Klemperer drew out the score's richness in small musico-dramatic episodes. How many conductors never sense these small hidden storms. One might not have supposed that the strings could go wild in Figaro, as they did when Marcellina bursts with rage. In these minor features of the work's musico-dramatic life, as well as in the strong and powerful accents he brought to contrasts and climaxes, one was made aware of the great value of Klemperer's individuality, although in Mozart that can be a mixed blessing. In each number one felt conscious of his thoughtful and enlivening approach; elsewhere, however, there was a lack of simplicity and naturalness...But a conductor was at work who is versed in the art of musical expressiveness and does not dispense with it in Mozart.[19]

Klemperer was much cast down by the failure of what for him had been the most important undertaking of the season, and he was correspondingly cheered to receive from an unknown hand a letter addressed 'To the conductor of a Mozart performance'. Its author was Siegbert Elkuss, a post-graduate student who with startling perspicacity put his finger on features that later came to be recognised as characteristic of Klemperer's approach to Mozart. His ear was struck by the 'acoustic surprises' in the

* Comment made to the author in November 1972 à propos the Strasbourg Figaro.
† On the last occasion that Klemperer conducted the work, in a concert performance at the Festival Hall on 3 February 1970, critics and others were upset, not merely by the predominantly slow tempi that had become characteristic of his last years, but by what they took to be a lack of high spirits.

orchestra and in particular by the unusual prominence that Klemperer gave to the woodwind.* He sensed in the performance 'the underground rumblings of the Revolution...which give the rhythms of that society such enduring fascination'. Finally, it seemed to him that Klemperer had restored the German components in Mozart's supranational style.† Expressive detail and inner tensions had taken precedence over mere comeliness and grace.

Elkuss proved to be a man with whom Klemperer could discuss music in its widest terms and they became friends.‡ To him he could pour out his ideas on staging *Don Giovanni* (the finale to the first act would end with the three women gazing in ecstasy at the hero as he made his escape). They talked about the varying approaches of Gluck, Mozart and Wagner to the problem of creating a German opera, and the characters in *Figaro*. In their view, Susanna was not just a pretty lady's maid, but 'a serious woman struggling with every feminine wile to preserve her marriage'; it was therefore ridiculous to cast the role with a soubrette. Similarly, Cherubino was not a sweet child, but a vigorous boy in the throes of puberty, whose voice could do with a bit of harshness.[20]

*   *   *

As early as 30 January 1915, when Klemperer had only conducted two performances of *Fidelio*, a member of the Theatre Commission who had earlier led the opposition to Pfitzner raised the question of re-engagement. As, however, Pfitzner was due to resume his duties as director on 15 May, there was no longer a position for a deputy. Thus negotiations, which opened on 1 April, hung fire, supposedly awaiting Pfitzner's return from leave. Klemperer's determination to have a say in production may also have caused delay, for his personal file contains the following undated note in his own hand:

He [i.e. Klemperer] is to have the *determining influence on the production of works he conducts, and occasionally the right to produce himself.*

There was also already a party within the Theatre Commission that was in favour of abolishing Pfitzner's position and offering Klemperer a three-year contract.§ But a decision was precipitated by the news that on

---

* In 1915 this must have sounded startlingly new.
† The author made the same comment half a century later about the London *Figaro* (*The Observer*, 8 February 1970).
‡ The friendship was destined to be short-lived, as Elkuss died the following year on active service. But the reproduction of the Athene of Myron that Elkuss gave him hung in Klemperer's living room until his death.
§ The issue was discussed in a session of 15 May 1915, five days after Pfitzner had returned from leave.

14 May Klemperer proposed to travel to Darmstadt to negotiate a position there. Schwander acted quickly. On 8 May the Theatre Commision offered Klemperer a year's contract at a substantially higher salary. He would have the right of casting and of collaborating in the productions of operas he was himself conducting...'naturally in agreement with the Intendant and opera director'. Although that was less than he had demanded, it was enough to be going on with and on 27 May a contract was sent to him for signature in Hamburg, where he had returned at the end of the season for his first lengthy stay in his home town since the scandal of December 1912.

* * *

Still on vacation there in July, he bumped into Ilse Fromm on the Jungfernstieg. With her was a young piano pupil, Elli Sternberg, who promptly fell in love with him. He was, she wrote to a friend, 'so tall that you have to look into the sky' to see his face.* Short of cash, Klemperer jokingly asked her if she would like an additional teacher. Fräulein Sternberg was only too delighted. But she was to learn that the romantic young musician with a mop of black hair, dark eyes and sensuous lips had a disconcerting side to his character. All three went on to visit an elderly lady, where Ilse Fromm and Klemperer started to perform the Good Friday Music from *Parsifal* on a harmonium and piano. To Elli Sternberg's astonishment, Klemperer

suddenly became wild and furious and stamped and shouted. I was sitting behind and was terrified, really terrified. I thought that he was actually capable of killing Ilse. (Now I know there's absolutely nothing to be frightened of.) Then he suddenly got up and left.

A few days later Klemperer took his new pupil to lunch at his parents' flat, where she was again amazed by his behaviour, though on this occasion it was less menacing.

He's like an incredibly naughty child. He says frightful things, curses everyone, shouts, bangs on the table, teases the maid, makes fun of his mother in an unbelievable way and then takes her in his arms and makes himself small, so that she doesn't seem so tiny beside him...Today I was with him for four hours and I'm as exhausted as though I had been walking uninterruptedly for six days.[21]

Klemperer had entered another manic phase, the most acute he had experienced since 1912. As always in these phases he threw over all restraint and inhibitions, including the self-critical faculty that usually prevented him from composing. In the summer of 1915 Klemperer turned

---

* Undated letter to Else Nürnberg. Elli Sternberg died in December 1916 at the age of only twenty-five after an operation for appendicitis.

out more music than at any other period of his life. In Hamburg between 3 and 14 June he completed a large-scale cantata, *Die vier Elemente*, for soprano and orchestra. He had hardly finished it before he embarked on incidental music to Goethe's *Faust*, Part I. As he was hard up (a chronic condition in manic phases, when he spent money heedlessly) and needed a holiday, in July he rented a room at Königstein and there within nine days sketched an entire opera, *Wehen*.*

Hardly were the works on paper than he set about getting them performed. Reinhardt, to whom he played the *Faust* music, held out a possibility of using it in a production he was planning for the following season. In Munich Gustav Brecher pointed to immaturities in *Wehen* but was otherwise encouraging. Strauss, whom he also approached, eluded a visit with a last-minute telegram. From Königstein it was only a short journey to Mainz, whither Klemperer travelled in the hope of interesting the famous publishing house of Schott in his compositions. To Ludwig Strecker,† he resembled 'a wild, beautiful Arab', whose behaviour was so bizarre that as a citizen of repute he was embarrassed to accompany him on the streets as they went to lunch. The following day Klemperer returned. He had, he told Strecker, enjoyed their lunch so much that he had felt the need for a brothel, had enquired for one at a nearby grocers, and been taken into custody by the police.[22] In spite of these eccentricities, Schotts agreed to publish four songs (which eventually became six) for a fee of 100M.

Doubtless encouraged by this success, Klemperer set about composing a second opera, *Eros*, whose action was set in the sanatorium itself, and groups of Kohnstamm's patients gathered around his upright piano in the evening to hear the latest instalments. Back in Hamburg, he continued composing at extraordinary speed. Elli Sternberg reported that

he writes whole scenes, one after another, without stopping, as though someone were dictating to him. First the music (only the themes, not developed) and then the words. The working out comes later.‡

In this way an entire act was completed in eight days and even cautionary words from Strecker, to whom he had sent the text, that it bore 'a casual stamp'[23] did not stem the flow. By the time that Klemperer returned to Strasbourg on 10 September, *Eros* was virtually complete, although it was only to take its final form in the winter of 1928/9, when Klemperer completed the orchestration and retitled it *Das Ziel* (see pp. 289–90, 297–8).

*   *   *

* 'Birth-pains'(!). Only the vocal score has survived.
† Ludwig Strecker (1883–1978); director of Schotts.
‡ Letter to Else Nürnberg, 3 September 1915. Klemperer himself later (24 November 1972) commented that words and music had often come to him simultaneously.

Klemperer had grown attached to Strasbourg, in particular to the great Minster that soared over the old town and to the *Staden*, the banks of the river to which the women still came to do their washing in the evening. During his years there new intellectual vistas opened up, as though in a belated adolescence.* Partly as a result of his prematurely interrupted education, his concerns had hitherto been almost exclusively musical. At the Wollenbergs, who entertained handsomely, he now for the first time came into the orbit of a philosopher of significance. Georg Simmel, who occupied the chair at Strasbourg, was a man of great brilliance and wit, whose range of interests extended to literature and art.† As such, he was well suited to stimulate and guide Klemperer's untutored mind. Music, which Simmel cared for deeply, was also a bond. Skating was another. Klemperer attended his lectures and was a frequent visitor to his house, where Simmel introduced him to the ethical teachings of Spinoza. Yet, like so many other young men in the early years of the century, Klemperer was also intoxicated by the heady brew of Nietzsche. As he himself ruefully admitted, he was at this period of his life like a first-year philosophy student, eagerly tasting all that was put before him, without much sense of discernment or direction.

It was as part of this ferment that a new dimension entered his life: he became increasingly drawn to Catholicism. At first, the attraction was primarily aesthetic. He was impressed by the pageantry and music in Catholic liturgy. At nights he would wander around the Minster, as though drawn by a magnet. But the ethical preoccupations his mother had imbued in him also played a part and it was not long before he started to visit a Jesuit theologian with a view to conversion. In spite of Klemperer's own deep inner sense of guilt and retribution, the Catholic doctrine of sin proved a stumbling block. Naively, he asked whether Goethe was a sinner in the eyes of the Church. Told that he indeed was so regarded, Klemperer's ardour for Catholicism momentarily cooled. But henceforth issues of faith were in one form or another never far from his mind.

This new-found religious awareness also opened up fresh musical perspectives. Up to this period of his life Klemperer had been little

---

* It is perhaps significant that it was only in this period that his handwriting belatedly settled into its final form.

† Georg Simmel (1858–1918). Neo-Kantian philosopher, who attempted to subsume the interpretation of a wide range of historical and cultural phenomena under fundamental categories of thought. Hence the breadth of his interests, notably in the field of sociology. As a magnetic and witty lecturer, he attracted a wide following and was described by another friend of Klemperer's, Ernst Robert Curtius (see p. 102), as 'the last word in intellectual subtlety'. His career was nonetheless impeded by his Jewish origins (see Gay, *Freud, Jews and other Germans*, pp. 120–4), so that, in spite of the support of Max Weber among others, he was fifty-six when he was finally appointed in 1914 to a full professorship in Strasbourg.

concerned with Bach, whose music was still rarely performed in concerts. Strasbourg, however, was a city with a thriving Bach tradition based on the Wilhelmskirche, where, since he had been appointed organist and choirmaster in 1882, Ernst Münch had regularly performed the passions and the cantatas.* The style favoured by Münch and Schweitzer was too *altväterlich* for Klemperer's taste, but the impact of the music was nonetheless profound. Late at night, Klemperer would bang on Hofmüller's door or simply kick it open, throw himself into a sofa and demand compote. Then the lights would be put out – it had to be dark – and he would go to the piano and play Beethoven sonatas and symphonies, or his own paraphrase on themes from *Don Giovanni*. But above all he would play Bach.[24] It was only in Strasbourg that the field of eighteenth-century music ceased to be, as Elkuss put it, 'not a mere childhood memory, but part of the experience of living'.†

*   *   *

Klemperer's religious preoccupations were also apparent in the songs he had poured out during the summer of 1915 and which Schotts published that autumn. In particular, *Gebet* is a prayer for divine guidance in supporting 'ein traurig Leiden'.‡ No fewer than nine of his songs (all but one new) were included by Ottilie Metzger-Lattermann§ in a recital she gave in Hamburg's Conventgarten hall on 26 October 1915 with their composer as accompanist. That a singer of international repute was willing to devote the entire second half of her concert to the music of a young and untried composer is evidence of her regard for Klemperer. He for his part considered it an honour to accompany an artist of her calibre. That did not, however, prevent him from seeking to impose his musical intentions, even in songs not written by himself. The Hamburg critics found his playing self-willed and Pfohl was particularly scathing.

[Klemperer] imposed his tyrannical will, indicating bar lines and entries by stamping his foot or an imperious nod of his head, relentlessly insisting on an idiosyncratic sense of rhythm, without for a moment allowing the voice a right to its own development or self-enjoyment...One can only say that he gave a piano recital with vocal accompaniment. To put it mildly, he confused the concert hall with the rehearsal room.[25]

---

* Albert Schweitzer, who for a number of years was the organist in these performances, was a product of this tradition.
† The German is more elaborate! 'Das Erlebnis einer gegenwärtigen, täglich fortschreitenden Erkenntnis'.
‡ 'An unhappy affliction'. A reference to his manic-depressive temperament.
§ Ottilie Metzger-Lattermann (1878–1943?). Celebrated contralto whose career began in Hamburg (1903–15), where before her second marriage she sang under the name of Metzger-Froitzheim. From 1901–12 she sang at Bayreuth, where her Erda was esteemed, and as guest in Vienna, Berlin, London and St Petersburg. Died in Auschwitz.

Pfohl did, however, find that Klemperer's own songs had individuality. Even if they lacked measure, coherence and melodic invention, they arose, he considered, out of a personal need for expression. Other reviews were less favourable. Robert Müller-Hartmann[26] regarded them as expressions of a divided nature and noted the influence of Mahler in the spiritual situations they mirrored. Chevalley dismissed the harmony as mannered.[27] The Hamburg critics plainly found it hard to decide whether the surprising elements in the music were to be attributed to originality or lack of expertise.*

Klemperer, however, was delighted with the reception the songs had received from a large audience in Hamburg (several had to be encored), and, still spinning like a top, he left immediately for Berlin, where on 28 October he heard the first performance of Strauss's *Alpensymphonie* conducted by the composer. Eager to get his summer's harvest of new works performed, he bearded Max Reinhardt in the interval. Reinhardt told him that his plans to produce *Faust* during the coming season at the Volksbühne had come to nothing, so that, at any rate for the moment, he could not use Klemperer's incidental music.† Nonetheless, in the course of a busy day (for he left Berlin that night) Klemperer succeeded in playing parts of it to Strauss, who, as Klemperer proudly told Schotts, had been 'immensely interested'.[28]

The recitals in Hamburg and Frankfurt were not Klemperer's only extra-mural activity that autumn. His Strasbourg *Figaro* had attracted attention across the Rhine in Mannheim, where he was not unknown in musical circles owing to his many visits to Bodanzky,‡ and the city's Philharmonic Society invited him to give a concert with the Frankfurt Museum Orchestra on 1 December. Hofmüller and Elkuss accompanied him and to mark the occasion Klemperer was persuaded to remove the beard he had recently grown. The Frankfurt orchestra had a reputation for putting down opinionated young conductors and when in the Scherzo of the 'Eroica' Symphony Klemperer wanted a notoriously exposed horn

---

* There were similar reactions when Metzger-Lattermann and Klemperer presented an identical programme in Frankfurt on 9 November, and again when musical journals reviewed the six songs that were published by Schott more or less simultaneously.
† He never did. The sole performance took place at a concert in Strasbourg on 19 April 1917 (see pp. 118–19).
‡ He also subsequently visited Mannheim on several occasions to hear Furtwängler conduct after he had succeeded Bodanzky in 1915. Klemperer later said (interview with Joachim Beck in the *Hamburger Fremdenblatt* of 19 January 1953) that at that time he regarded Furtwängler as 'the first conductor in Germany, that is to say, the most delicate (zart)'. Furtwängler told Beck that Klemperer had come to Mannheim on account of a love affair, but that he had taken the opportunity to borrow money and clothes – on the small side, presumably (recounted to the author by Beck). From Elkuss's letters to his fiancée it seems that in 1915 Klemperer admired Strauss and Brecher above all other conductors.

9   Klemperer. Strasbourg, 1915

105

passage played by the horns alone, without supporting woodwind as had become customary, there was a confrontation with the first horn. It is one of the few recorded occasions on which Klemperer backed down in the face of rebellion.

The concert, only his second with an orchestra, was less than a total success. There was admiration for the style and luminosity he brought to the overture to *Die Zauberflöte* and the 'power and pace' of Strauss's *Don Juan*.[29] His piano accompaniment of Claire Dux* in a group of Strauss songs and in 'Dove sono' from *Figaro* was also highly praised. But his first attempt at the 'Eroica', a work with which he was later to become more closely identified than any other, was found less than wholly convincing. The loyal Elkuss wrote to his fiancée on the day following the concert that the fugato in the Funeral March had engendered such tension that, though not given to tears, he had longed to sob. He then went on to put his finger on a crucial ingredient of Klemperer's nature as an interpreter. 'Perhaps only someone unromantic enough to consider the dynamic significance of the smallest semi-quaver and in whose world ecstasy nonetheless plays a central role [can do full justice to Beethoven].' The critics were less enthusiastic. Although the middle movements were generally regarded as successful, the *Neue Badische Landeszeitung* (2 December) criticised a tendency to get lost in detail in the opening and closing movements, while the illustrious *Frankfurter Zeitung* (3 December) acknowledged Klemperer's gifts but noted that his temperament was apt to get the better of him. The *Badische General-Anzeiger* (2 December) praised the attack and precision of the playing but found the tempi arbitrary. In short, Klemperer seems to have revealed little of the classical equilibrium that was to distinguish his Beethoven in later years. After the concert he himself observed ruefully, 'I always knew that one shouldn't conduct the 'Eroica' before the age of forty'.[30]

*   *   *

In the second winter of the war musical life in Strasbourg was still circumscribed by the city's exposed strategic position. Access was only possible with a military permit, visiting artists were few and far between and the principal concert hall remained a military hospital. Conscription had reduced the size of the orchestra so that the repertory at the Stadttheater was largely confined to works that required no more than a Beethoven-sized band.[31] On that account, the new production of *Elektra* that Klemperer had been preparing before the war was yet again postponed.

His ambition to produce and conduct *Don Giovanni* came to nothing, and,

* Claire Dux (1885–1967), celebrated soprano, member of the Berlin Court Opera and a frequent guest at Covent Garden in the years immediately before the First World War.

apart from a series of chamber concerts in aid of war relief (Klemperer planned the programmes and acted as accompanist), he was exclusively occupied in the months before Christmas with routine revivals. It was not until the New Year that he was given a new production of Goldmark's *Die Königen von Saba* to prepare. But an occasion on which most of the theatre's spare scenery seems to have been trundled on to the stage, so that sphinxes and pyramids appeared in Solomon's Jerusalem, can hardly have aroused his enthusiasm.

No one had a sharper understanding of his frustrations than his mother, who watched anxiously over her son's career. On the day of the première she wrote to Elli Sternberg.

I am sitting here not exactly with drawn sword but with crossed fingers. Today in Strasbourg at 6 pm they perform *Die Königin von Saba* by Goldmark for the first time...How much I should like to attend. But perhaps it's as well that I can't, because I shouldn't be at all happy there, if I were to see how, quite apart from the psychological stress, he so wears himself out physically that he has to change his underclothes. It's such a terribly hard vocation, and often so thankless. The public only has ears for the singers and rarely, very rarely, grasps that the entire building stands on the foundations of the orchestra, and that the whole thing is only given inner coherence and dedication through the conductor.

Unlike most mothers of budding conductors, Ida Klemperer was singularly free of any romantic illusions.

But [she continued] Otto will probably have to remain in the theatre. Concert music is finer, but there's more life in the theatre...What he would like best would be a position in a theatre...in which he could also conduct concerts.[32]

There were more specific reasons for frustration and unhappiness. Pfitzner had returned to the theatre at the start of the 1915/16 season and Klemperer's prophecy that they would become rivals was to be all too rapidly fulfilled. Since he had gone on leave in May 1914, Pfitzner's position had weakened in one important respect. The local elections in that month had resulted in a majority on the Theatre Commission for the socialists and liberals, both of whom tended to be critical of the opera director. Now his contract was due for renewal. On 31 January 1916 the Theatre Commission decided that the system whereby authority was divided between the Intendant and the opera director must end and accordingly determined not to extend Pfitzner's engagement. Before it could make the decision public, however, the enraged composer played into the hands of his enemies by resigning all his offices.*

Pfitzner's friends inevitably implied that Klemperer had led, or at least

---

* Pfitzner was finally persuaded by Schwander (and, it may be, by Wollenberg, who also made strenuous efforts to keep him in Strasbourg) to remain as director of the city's concerts and conservatory, posts that he continued to hold until the end of German rule in November 1918.

107

been made the tool of, a conspiracy. Klemperer was certainly no admirer of Pfitzner's conducting and he was not above giving imitations of its more comical features.* As usual, he found it hard to resist mocking remarks that raised a ready laugh but were liable to find their way back to the ears of their targets, and his scurrilous pun on the title of Pfitzner's loftily romantic opera, *Die Rose vom Liebesgarten*,† went the rounds of Strasbourg to predictable effect. Tension had risen early in the season when Pfitzner had allotted *Fidelio* to another conductor. Enraged, Klemperer unwisely (as he himself later admitted) refused to conduct performances of *Hans Heiling* that Pfitzner was producing on the grounds that 'we had quite different conceptions of the scenic realisation of an opera'.[33]

Behind this clash there lay deeper differences. As Klemperer himself later put it, 'I had a very strange relationship to Pfitzner. Very near, in that I was his pupil. Very distant, which was brought about by his and my development.'[34] Though separated in age by only sixteen years, they were in effect men of different centuries. In the decade that had passed since he had first gone to study with Pfitzner, Klemperer had become much more aware of and sympathetic to new developments, in the field of both music and theatre. In contrast, Pfitzner, though still only in his mid-forties, had come to identify himself with the aesthetic of a fast-vanishing age.

It was just that quality which attracted Thomas Mann, who since the outbreak of war had become involved in a fierce polemic in support of the conservative values that (as he claimed) Germany was defending against the progressive spirit of the Entente. In Pfitzner Mann saw an artist, who, like himself at that stage of his development, 'anticipated the march of the new with intellectual melancholy' and in *Palestrina* a work that as 'the last stone in the edifice of romantic opera' was 'in love with death'.‡ Since the early nineteenth century, romanticism in Germany had been identified with national revival. It was therefore no chance that the 'verspätet-deutsch' (the epithet is Mann's) Pfitzner saw the world through nationalist spectacles. Under the impact of the war, that nationalism grew more strident.§

Klemperer was by no means without respect for Pfitzner.‖ Nor was it

---

* Max Hofmüller recalled that, while conducting, Pfitzner had a habit of picking his nose, as though in a trance. His baton was liable to disappear behind his neck and is said on one occasion to have stuck in the back of his collar.

† *Die Hose vom Liebeskater*. Literally, 'The trousers of the morning after'.

‡ *Betrachtungen eines Unpolitischen*, pp. 398–9, 423–4. The last comment might also be applied to Mann's own *magnum opus*, *Der Zauberberg*. See also Mann's letters to Pfitzner (19 May 1917) and Bruno Walter (24 June 1917) in *Briefe, 1889–1936*, pp. 135–8.

§ During the war Pfitzner refused to drink French wine, so that his hosts were obliged to remove the labels. (Information provided by Mlle Marguerite Hugel.)

‖ On the grounds that it would be disrespectful of his former master, he adamantly refused to allow a comment that one of the reasons for their differences lay in the fact that they were both enamoured of the same woman to be included in the *Conversations*.

108

in his essentially forthright character to participate in a conspiracy, as is evident from his refusal to sign a new contract until he had had an opportunity to talk to Schwander about the problems of his personal and professional relations with Pfitzner.[35] Nonetheless biographies of Pfitzner published during the Third Reich were not slow to present their differences as arising out of a clash between an honourable German composer and a scheming Jewish conductor. Josef Müller-Blattau asserted that 'the intrigue of the Jew Klemperer...brought it about that Pfitzner's contract at the opera was not extended'.* Walter Abendroth, in an account that he later claimed to have been based on information he had received from Pfitzner and his wife, was more cautious.

> Klemperer quickly noted which way the wind was blowing and, instead of supporting his teacher and patron, allowed himself to be used by the anti-Pfitzner party...He put it about that Pfitzner was a great composer but a poor conductor ...[Pfitzner] had proof of the treacherous role that Klemperer had played. When Frau Mimi [Pfitzner's wife] reproached him [Klemperer] for ingratitude, he replied...'Without a position I am nothing but a poor Jew of no importance.'[36]

This last accusation particularly angered Klemperer. Whether he learnt of it when the book appeared in 1935 is unclear, but by then he had in any case left Germany and was in no position to challenge Abendroth's version of events. But twelve years later, when he visited Pfitzner in Munich in the summer of 1947, he demanded that the offending passage be deleted from any new edition.[37] Pfitzner, however, pointed out that he was not the author of the book. By 1966, half a century after the events described, Abendroth himself seems to have become unsure of his ground.† On 11 April of that year he wrote to Klemperer, confessing that he might have been misinformed in good faith by Pfitzner, who had (he suggested) probably only repeated to him what he had been told at the time by friends and supporters, and promising to alter the offending reference in any new edition. He suggested that in the meantime Klemperer should put on paper his own version of the events that had led to Pfitzner's departure from the Strasbourg Opera.‡

---

* *Hans Pfitzner*, p. 66. There are, however, no references whatever to Klemperer in a further study of Pfitzner that Müller-Blattau published in 1969. *Tempora mutantur...*

† In his autobiography, *Ich warne Neugierige* (1966), Abendroth admitted that, owing to the time at which he was writing (1934), he had 'felt obliged to employ very ticklish catch words (heikelste Stichworte), which gave more emphasis to Pfitzner the German patriot than had the original text, and to emphasise certain excerpts from Pfitzner's own writings that brought him the undeserved reputation of an anti-Semite' (p. 184). It is hard to place complete confidence in a biographer who unabashedly confessed that he had loaded the evidence to make his book more palatable to the cultural arbiters of the Third Reich.

‡ Klemperer did not react to Abendroth's suggestion, nor has any reply to Abendroth survived. No new edition of what in many respects remains a valuable biography had appeared before Abendroth's death in 1973.

Relations between Pfitzner and Klemperer went from bad to worse. Pfitzner seems to have had Klemperer hauled before some sort of tribunal at the Conservatory, where he accused him of bribing critics.[38] He also made much of the fact that, while he himself had (unsuccessfully) volunteered for military service, the younger Klemperer was not in the army. His animosity waxed to a point where he even returned a book, given to him by a pupil[39] on his birthday, when he discovered that it was Klemperer who had suggested that he might like it. Klemperer was also fiercely attacked by one of Pfitzner's adherents in the Theatre Commission,[40] who argued that he had not only failed to fulfil the promise of his first season in Strasbourg but was not of good moral repute. A critic had written of a woman artist who had sung Lieder with him in a state of 'amorous ecstasy'. Was the Hamburg scandal about to be repeated in Strasbourg? Such a man was unsuited to hold a position of responsibility in a 'moral institution' like the theatre, etc. etc.

*   *   *

On 27 February 1916 Klemperer conducted *Un Ballo in maschera* for the only time in his career. Prior to the Verdi revival that swept Germany in the late twenties, the work was little performed in Central Europe, but there was general agreement among the critics that he had revealed a remarkably sure grasp of its rhythmic tensions and expressive fire, and had succeeded in bringing even its less inspired numbers to life. 'In Verdi', wrote Fritz Brust, 'Klemperer managed to make a chorus that incurs the odium of musical literati – I mean the mocking of Amelia...sound like an idea of genius.'[41] The Strasbourg press commented with equal enthusiasm on the freshness and stylishness of his approach to Auber's *Fra Diavolo*, when he conducted a new production on 2 April, and there was again unanimous praise for the musical penetration he brought to a revival of Gounod's *Faust* four weeks later.

But in spite of these successes in French and Italian works with which he had not hitherto been associated, the season brought Klemperer little satisfaction and his spirits cannot have been raised by the unfavourable reception his own songs received when on 7 April he and Metzger-Lattermann repeated in Strasbourg the recital they had earlier given in Hamburg and Frankfurt. The strains of the quarrel with Pfitzner had taken their toll and early in 1916 he started to move into one of the deepest depressions that was ever to afflict him.

By the middle of May Klemperer was back in Königstein, where a fellow-patient was Ernst Ludwig Kirchner.* Kohnstamm urged him not

---

* Ernst Ludwig Kirchner (1880–1938), celebrated expressionist painter, known also as a graphic artist, who had had a nervous breakdown after a period of military service, was one of Kohnstamm's patients from October 1915 to July 1916. By the summer of 1916

to take his differences with the notoriously quarrelsome Pfitzner so much to heart. But the depression proved unyielding. At meals he sat at Kohnstamm's table, silent, sunk in himself to a point where he seemed oblivious of the outside world.[42] Earlier that year he had in despair consulted the celebrated psychiatrist, Emil Kräpelin,* in Munich with a view to undergoing psychoanalysis. Kräpelin had strongly advised against it. But in the summer Klemperer again raised the question and with Kohnstamm's approval he travelled once more to Munich to see another specialist, who repeated what Kräpelin had told him: his problems were not due to neurosis and as such were not susceptible to analysis. In any case his unintrospective character made him an unsuitable subject for this form of treatment.† His cousin Georg endorsed the advice and Klemperer never again considered psychoanalysis.

Kohnstamm procured a grand piano in the hope that this would reactivate his patient's musical interests. At first Klemperer could not even be persuaded to touch it. But gradually Königstein had its usual therapeutic effect and in due course he was even prepared to give recitals for fellow patients. By the middle of July he was able to leave for Göttingen, where his younger sister was studying at the university and he remained for several weeks.

Before he had left Königstein Simmel had sent Klemperer a manuscript by a former pupil, Ernst Bloch. Its title was *Vom Geist der Utopie* and Simmel urged him to read it. Klemperer wrote that he was in no condition to digest a philosophical treatise. Simmel replied that in that case he should just read the chapters that dealt with music. Klemperer did so and was enthralled. Little though he was in agreement with some of its detail, he recognised it as 'the work of a man of genius'.[43] The book was duly published and made the reputation of a philosopher who became one of the leading Marxist thinkers of his generation.‡

he had produced no fewer than seven portraits of Klemperer, five drawings, one etching and a woodcut. Part of his therapy took the form of frescoing a courtyard on the theme of the pleasures of the sea (Frau Kohnstamm having forbidden an earlier plan that he should similarly decorate the dining room). In 1933 these frescos were painted over (as examples of decadent art) and damaged beyond restoration.

* Emil Kräpelin (1856–1926), famous for his contribution to the classification of mental disorders. He was the first to make a clinical distinction between schizophrenia and manic-depressive illness. His approach to psychiatry was mainly somatic.

† Lotte Klemperer has provided the following illuminating comment: 'He was basically an *introvert*, by which I mean that he had a great need of solitude, did not like and avoided so-called society, parties and all that, was generally reserved, even taciturn, not prone to talk about himself or his inner feelings...Even when manic this impenetrable reserve never quite left him. (But) he was not at all *introspective*, in the sense that he was not preoccupied with himself – no trace of narcissism. I don't recall him ever having looked in a mirror...I cannot imagine that he ever even thought of keeping a diary.'

‡ Ernst Bloch (see biographical glossary) later became one of Klemperer's closest friends and one of the very few men with whom he was *per Du*. They did not in fact meet personally

10 'Otto Klemperer at the piano'. Pencil drawing by Ernst Ludwig Kirchner, 1916

With his usual appetite for learning and eagerness to make good the deficiencies of his own education, at Göttingen Klemperer attended a number of lectures and seminars in philosophy and literature by, among other, Edmund Husserl.* On 28 July he travelled to Berlin for the celebration of Nathan Klemperer's seventieth birthday at the home of Regi Elbogen, and after a further ten days at Göttingen returned to Hamburg. By this time he had at least regained some of his ability to laugh. Nonetheless, disconcerted at the persistency with which ups had followed downs, he there consulted yet another doctor, Moses Goldschmidt, an *Internist* to whom he subsequently returned at other moments of psychological difficulty. Goldschmidt confirmed the importance that Kohnstamm attached to a regular schedule in periods of depression. He also recommended that Klemperer take an after-lunch siesta, which henceforth became an unfailing part of his routine. By the end of August he was well enough to return to Strasbourg for what was to be his last and most satisfying season there.

*   *   *

With Pfitzner's resignation Klemperer had become senior member of the musical staff. For the first time since his year in Barmen he was now in a position to exercise a determining influence on the repertory, and in Paul Legband, the director of the Freiburg theatre who happened to be serving in Strasbourg as a soldier, he at last found a collaborator with whom he saw eye-to-eye on matters of staging. The Strasbourg streets were still in darkness at night, when artillery could be heard rumbling beyond the Vosges. But by the third winter of hostilities the city had settled down to wartime conditions. In the absence of other diversions, musical life flourished and the fact that the Stadttheater's orchestra could when necessary be reinforced by garrison musicians meant that the repertory was no longer as restricted as it had been during the first two years of the war. The outlook for the season was good.

Klemperer's plans included *Così fan tutte*, Auber's *La Muette de Portici* and, for the third season running, *Elektra*. None of these events materialised. The first major production of the season was Verdi's *Otello* on 15 October 1916. It was a work that Klemperer much loved (although, paradoxically, he shared Pfitzner's view of the 'rape' it supposedly inflicted on Shakespeare) but was rarely to conduct. On 18 November there followed a double bill of *Violanta* and *Der Ring des Polykrates*, one-acters that the

until the twenties, when they were introduced by Furtwängler, with whom Klemperer was still on cordial terms, at the Romanisches Café on the Kurfürstendamm, a favourite meeting place of Berlin's intellectuals and artists during the years of the Weimar Republic.
* Edmund Husserl (1859–1938), founder of phenomenology and as such a determining influence on the existentialism of Heidegger and Sartre.

phenomenally precocious Erich Wolfgang Korngold had composed at the age of eighteen.* As elsewhere, they were hailed in Strasbourg as the product of a *Wunderkind* whom many critics compared to Mozart. Inevitably, Wagner again loomed large in the season and, after revivals of *Die Meistersinger* and *Der fliegende Holländer*, a new production of *Die Walküre* followed on 3 December. A calm and fruitful period was only briefly disturbed by instructions to report for a medical examination, but as psychiatric adviser to the army Wollenberg was well placed to intervene† and on 13 November Klemperer was declared unfit for military service. In the previous month the Theatre Commission had decided to offer him a three-year contract, so that for the first time since he had left Hamburg, his future seemed secure.

*   *   *

On 26 November, however, Gustav Brecher, who since his departure from Hamburg in 1911 had been First Conductor in Cologne, had abruptly indicated that he would be leaving for Frankfurt at the end of the season. Cologne was thus obliged to find a replacement at short notice and (maybe on Brecher's recommendation) Klemperer was invited to conduct a performance of *Die Meistersinger* with a view to an engagement. As so often at crucial moments in his career, he preferred to make his bow with *Fidelio*,‡ which was substituted at his request. The Cologne theatre committee did not, however, concede his demand that a decision on the appointment be reached within twenty-four hours of his appearance.[44]

When he arrived in Cologne early in January 1917, Klemperer was delighted to find that the city boasted a first-class orchestra. It, however, was less than enchanted by Klemperer's exacting rehearsals. In its other guise as the Gürzenich Orchestra,§ it had played to the satisfaction of some of the leading conductors of the day and resented the young visitor's corrections as well as what it took to be the 'modernistic' retouchings he imposed on the score.[45] The cast, which included some of Cologne's best voices, also found the piano rehearsal that Klemperer called superfluous and only a young soprano, Johanna Geissler,‖ who had joined the company

---

* A measure of the success enjoyed by Korngold at this stage of his career can be gauged from the fact that Bruno Walter had conducted the double bill's *première* in Munich on 28 March 1916 and that Vienna had followed suit only two weeks later with a cast that included Selma Kurz, Maria Jeritza and Alfred Piccaver.

† Wollenberg provided Klemperer with a letter stating that he suffered from cyclothymia (the clinical description of his manic-depressive illness). Neither of the two examining doctors had heard of it.

‡ As he was to do in Wiesbaden (1924), Berlin (1927) and London (1961) and had done in Strasbourg (1915).   § Under this name it gave the city's concerts.

‖ She had been engaged, not merely for her musicality and lively stage personality, but also, it may be, because she had declared her age as 23 (she was in fact 28) and had thus been accepted as an artist young enough to remedy her technical shortcomings. She never did.

only four months earlier and was to sing the role of Marzelline, deigned to appear. Klemperer was therefore obliged to begin with her opening number, 'O wär ich schon mit Dir vereint und könnte Mann Dich nennen'.* Within two and a half years she was to be able to do so.

The critics were given special seats on 6 January 1917, from which they could observe the conductor's control of the orchestra. What they saw left them in no doubt. Otto Neitzel,† the influential representative of the *Kölnische Zeitung*, the leading newspaper in the Rhineland, singled out for praise the precision and lack of affectation of Klemperer's conducting: 'every detail seemed to stem from the depths of a creative imagination'.[46] The more conservative Anton Stehle complained of the influence of the 'modern, nervous' school of Mahler and its exaggerated passion for detail. He also disapproved of Klemperer's retouchings (which, among other things, included the insertion of a jubilant horn part in 'O namenlose Freude'!). But, like Neitzel, he recognised that Klemperer was not only an exceptional musician but a man with unusual responsiveness to the stage. 'One felt', Stehle wrote, 'that the entire performance was given a unified impact by a unifying will.'[47] Three days later the Cologne theatre committee decided to offer Klemperer the job and his appointment was announced on 11 January.

That left a vacancy at Strasbourg to be filled at short notice. At the end of the month Klemperer travelled to Zurich, where on the 28th he heard Strauss conduct his new version of *Ariadne auf Naxos*‡ with a cast that included Jeritza and Gutheil-Schoder in the roles of Ariadne and the Composer. Klemperer's immediate purpose was to attend a performance of a work that he himself was in the process of preparing for Strasbourg. But his attention was attracted to the evident talent of the nineteen-year-old musician who was playing the important piano part in the orchestra. The pianist, whose name was Georg Szell,§ was already regarded as a possible candidate for the vacancy in Strasbourg. When Strauss telegraphed his endorsement of Klemperer's recommendation, Szell was invited to conduct two guest performances, as a result of which he was engaged as Klemperer's successor, having declared himself to be three years older than he was.‖

*   *   *

* 'O were I already united with you and could call you husband.'
† Otto Neitzel (1852–1920), who had been critic of the *Kölnische Zeitung* since 1887, also had some reputation as a composer, a pedagogue and a pianist. He had sat on the jury of the Rubinstein competition for which Klemperer had entered as a pianist (see p. 16).
‡ The new version had only had its première in Vienna on 4 October 1916.
§ See biographical glossary.
‖ Klemperer had probably heard Szell at an even earlier stage of his precocious career, when in Prague on 20 January 1910, Szell (then thirteen years old) had been the soloist in a performance of Chopin's F minor Piano Concerto. At the same concert Klemperer had accompanied Bronislav Huberman in some pieces for violin.

115

The second half of the season proved less tranquil. It so happened that both the new productions Klemperer was to conduct contained substantial roles, which the company's leading soubrette, Alma Saccur, regarded as her own. Klemperer particularly disliked Saccur and tension that had been rising during the preparations for *Die Entführung aus dem Serail*, in which she sang Blonde on 20 January, reached a climax at the dress rehearsal of *Ariadne auf Naxos* on 9 February, when Saccur announced that she was 'unwell' and would not be available to sing the role of Zerbinetta at the première two days later. Klemperer thereupon declared that her deputy would not only take over on the first night but would also sing in all the subsequent performances. A public quarrel ensued and Klemperer addressed the singer in such abrasive terms that he was obliged to make an apology to her in front of the assembled company on the morning of the première.

Such a scene was a sure sign that he was again moving into a manic phase, for only in this condition was he prone to rages or lack of control. No doubt overwork played a part: in his apology Klemperer claimed that since his new appointment he had been under stress imposed by the need to prepare for his first season in Cologne at a time when he still had responsibilities in Strasbourg. But the fact that, on the very day of his quarrel with Saccur, he wrote to Schotts, announcing that he had composed a number of new songs, which Lotte Lehmann would, he hoped, include in Lieder recitals she was to give in Hamburg and Vienna, was another indication of his condition. He was in fact already under Wollenberg's care and it was doubtless on his advice that on 18 February he was sent on a month's leave.

After a fortnight in Königstein he made two visits to Würzburg, where his younger sister was now studying. Marianne Klemperer, who was already in her late twenties, was a large young woman* whose high-spirited, ebullient character more than compensated for any lack of physical charm. Although she had many intimate women friends, her brother was the ruling passion of her life, and he in his turn was closer to her than to his straight-laced elder sister, Regi, who since her marriage had been drawn into the world of Jewish orthodoxy. In contrast, Marianne was emancipated in her ideas and conversation. She was less shocked by, and better able to cope with, the wilder side of Klemperer's character that became apparent in manic phases. As a university student, she was also better equipped to share his burgeoning intellectual interests, and the fact that she was the centre of a group of lively and intelligent young women was no doubt a further attraction. She was also an excellent pianist.

---

* By some freak of nature Klemperer and his two sisters towered over their parents and indeed their children.

But Marianne was not the main reason for Klemperer's second visit to Würzburg. On 13 March Johanna Geissler, the Marzelline he had encountered in his Cologne *Fidelio*, was to sing three guest performances as Cherubino in *Figaro*. She innocently supposed that Klemperer's presence in Würzburg was a matter of chance. That he made the three-hour journey from Strasbourg is evidence that his interest was already aroused. In manic periods his approaches to women he found attractive could be drastic in their directness. Significantly, on this occasion Klemperer made no advances.

The critics' comments on a revival of *Tannhäuser* that he conducted on 12 April suggest that the manic phase persisted. Complaints of his stamping in the pit were nothing new. On this occasion, however, he conducted with his feet on the desk before him, so that the singers were confronted by the soles of his inordinately large shoes. He also shouted and beat time so noisily that the *Freie Presse*[48] dryly asked whether he supposed himself to be without an audience. Three days later came the new production of *Don Giovanni*, on which he had so long meditated. In it he used curtained sets, similar to those he had chosen for *Così fan tutte* in Barmen. The critics found these practical rather than evocative. Another innovation, at any rate for Strasbourg, was the restoration of the final sextet, which had customarily been deleted in the nineteenth century, so that the opera should not end on a humorous note, and had only recently been reinstated at the Munich Mozart Festival. The evening was less than wholly successful. 'Klemperer...powerful as ever, but the performance is not very noteworthy', observed the alert young Marguerite Hugel in her diary. But Simmel, whose musical sympathies centred on Beethoven, was much struck by the unsuspected demonism that Klemperer revealed in the score.

To Strasbourg there indeed seemed something demonic about young Klemperer himself. His years in the city to which he had first come in 1911 form a period of *Sturm und Drang* in his life. Depression and euphoria had followed each other with greater rapidity and intensity than they were to do for many years, and his intellectual life was in ferment. In manic periods his huge stature, sudden rages and unpredictable behaviour made him an alarming figure. Yet he was hardly less disconcerting in depressions, when he presented a withdrawn and remote face to the world. 'Klemperer is a man who says little or nothing', wrote Marguerite Hugel when she first encountered him at the Wollenbergs. 'He doesn't laugh. The phrases, compliments and congratulations of a so-called musical public run off him, like water off a duck's back.' In a different mood, his behaviour could be mephistophelian.* Marguerite Hugel heard him offer profuse congratula-

---

* In the theatre his nickname was 'Lucifer'. (Information provided by Max Hofmüller.)

tion to a singer he had accompanied at a musical evening at the Wollenbergs. No sooner had she left, than Klemperer burst into wild, mocking laughter. It was, Mlle Hugel noted in her diary, the only occasion she had heard him laugh. Hilarious or silent, he was an alarming figure. Yet there was also something fascinating, and particularly to women, in 'this sinister giant',[49] who fixed a penetrating yet impenetrable gaze on whoever he was talking to. Rumours of his conquests and love affairs rippled round the town.

*   *   *

On 29 April Klemperer conducted *Die Rose vom Liebesgarten* for the only time in his career. But as Pfitzner was already in Munich for the rehearsals of *Palestrina* the revival seems to have led to no reconciliation between the two men. On 15 May Klemperer made his last appearance at the Strasbourg theatre with a revival of Gluck's *Orpheus*. Marguerite Hugel noted that the music's simplicity suited his fiery style less well than more passionate works. *Der Elsässer*[50] commented snidely on the endless applause of the conductor's many women admirers at the end of the evening.

But Klemperer had in effect already taken leave of Strasbourg a month earlier in a farewell concert he had himself mounted in the hall of the Sängerhaus on 19 April. The programme was a bizarre miscellany. It opened with the overture to Pfitzner's *Christelflein*, perhaps a peace offering to his old teacher. Two items that followed are less easy to explain by any but cynical motives. Otto Neitzel, who as critic of the *Kölnische Zeitung* was well placed to smooth Klemperer's path in his new appointment, appeared as soloist, first in Liszt's *Totentanz* for piano and orchestra and then in his own *Capriccio* for the same forces. Marguerite Hugel described the latter in her diary as 'a nullity'.

The second half of the concert consisted entirely of Klemperer's own compositions. These included two of the orchestral songs that had won Strauss's approval in 1911 and a 'Liebeslied' from his unfinished opera, *Eros*.* There followed items from the incidental music to Goethe's *Faust* that Klemperer had written for Reinhardt in 1915 but that had remained unperformed (Szell accompanied some of these pieces at the piano). The concert ended with a patriotic work, *Geistliches Kampflied*, for chorus, organ and orchestra, which Klemperer had written in memory of Kohnstamm's elder son, who had been killed in the previous year at the Battle of Verdun.†
There was much applause, but the critics were markedly more reserved. As though not wishing to sour a farewell occasion, they evaded the issue

---

* Lotte Lehmann also sang this with some success at a recital she gave in Hamburg on 14 May 1917 – Klemperer's thirty-second birthday.
† The score has not survived.

of the music's worth and contented themselves with pointing to the influence of Offenbach and Mahler. Ludwig Strecker of Schotts attended the concert and after it declined to publish the *Faust* music. In a letter written two days later from Mainz he stalled on the matter of the *Kampflied* and agreed to print the as yet incomplete opera, *Eros*, only in the improbable event of a theatre accepting it for performance. As a sop, he consented to publish two of a group of songs Klemperer had recently composed. In the privacy of her journal, the trenchant Marguerite Hugel noted, 'As a creative artist Klemperer is hardly worthy of consideration'. He did not, however, return to composition until special circumstances in the spring of 1919 were once again to liberate his creative energies.

*   *   *

As so often after a manic phase, Klemperer found himself in financial straits at the end of the season. An abortive plan for a concert in Hamburg had cost him 800M and his salary in Cologne was not due to be paid until he took up his post there at the end of the summer. His situation was further aggravated by the losses he had incurred on his farewell concert, when he had mistakenly expected the theatre orchestra and chorus to perform without a fee. On 9 May Schwander was able to persuade the Theatre Commission that he should receive a gratuity of 1,000M.

But his financial anxieties were not at an end. On the outbreak of war, his father, who was already in his late sixties, had formally retired.* Wartime inflation further depleted the family savings and in 1916 Ida Klemperer's remaining share in the property that had been left to her by her mother thirty years earlier was finally paid out in cash.† The ever-generous Tante Helene died in Montreux during the war and this may have still further reduced the family's income. Perhaps as a result of straitened circumstances, in the summer of 1917 Ida Klemperer fell into a depression that was severe enough to necessitate several weeks in hospital. During his Strasbourg years Klemperer had already begun to support his parents, but this illness placed a further burden on him at a moment when he was already hard-up. In his embarrassment he turned to well-to-do Hamburg friends,‡ who tided him over the crisis and enabled him to enjoy a brief summer holiday in the Bavarian mountains before he travelled north to prepare himself for new tasks in Cologne.

---

* From 1915 he described himself in the *Hamburger Adressenbuch* as 'Rentier'. By 1918, when the family capital and with it the 'rent' had largely evaporated, he had varied the description to the more nebulous 'Privatmann'.
† The sum amounted to 13,195.45M.
‡ Joseph Asch and Walter Kantorowicz.

7 Cologne: conversion and marriage

D'rum, O Jüngling, merk dir diese Lehre:
Komm nie in Kunst nach Köln gereist.
(Hans Pfitzner)*

Cologne liked to regard itself as the metropolis of the Rhineland. An ancient city and the seat of a Prince-Archbishop, who until the dissolution of the Holy Roman Empire in 1806 was *ex officio* an Imperial elector and remained unofficial primate among German prelates, it had become part of Prussia after the Napoleonic Wars. In the course of the nineteenth century an ecclesiastical capital had been transformed into a thriving industrial town, whose population had doubled between 1885 and 1900 and reached half a million by 1910. After Strasbourg, Klemperer found the city noisy and sombre; only its wealth of romanesque churches† gave him pleasure as he trudged round in search of accommodation that would provide the 'little light, air, cleanliness and quiet I must have'.[1]

In the process of growth the city had burst its old mediaeval boundaries. But whereas in Strasbourg a similar expansion under French rule in the eighteenth century had lent the new quarters a spacious, even elegant, air, Prussian taste and industrialisation had stamped a colder image on the face of Cologne. The walls that had stood for over seven centuries had been torn down in the 1880s to make way for a broad Ringstrasse, on which a new opera house was erected. When this heavy, ornamental building was opened in 1902 it was the largest theatre in Germany.‡ But because it lacked side and revolving stages that were only introduced in the early years of the century, it was already regarded as obsolescent when Klemperer arrived fifteen years later. Under Otto Lohse,§ a distinguished Wagnerian conductor, who had worked with Mahler in Hamburg and was musical director from 1904 to 1911, the Cologne Opera had enjoyed a

* 'Therefore, young man, note this lesson: come not to Cologne in search of art.' Concluding lines of a satirical poem written by Pfitzner on the morning of a recital of his songs for which not a single ticket had been sold. *Kölner Tageblatt*, 6 November 1907.
† During his years in Cologne he was to be particularly drawn to the numinous basilica of St Maria im Kapitol.
‡ Bombs destroyed it during the Second World War. The present (much smaller) theatre is on a completely different site.
§ Otto Lohse (1858–1925); director of German seasons at Covent Garden in 1894 and from 1901 to 1904.

120

fruitful period. In 1911 the city (unlike Hamburg) had introduced municipal subsidies. In the same year it had appointed Fritz Rémond as Intendant.

The Rhinelanders' approach to the theatre has been described as 'primarily sensuous',[2] and the Cologne public was notorious for its lack of interest in new works.[3] Opera was popular precisely because it so rarely provoked thought and Rémond was the man to give this public what it wanted. Originally an actor, who had later made a successful career as a tenor,* he was an experienced and practical man of the theatre, who understood voices, and as a result vocal standards in Cologne were high. He also made a speciality of spectacular productions that were much admired by the local critics. Even by the standards of the day, he was a rather old-fashioned, Wilhelmine figure, and, appropriately enough, had been given the title of *Hofrat* by the ruler of the tiny principality of Schaumburg-Lippe. With the dawn of a new world in 1918, the Herr Hofrat's approach to the theatre appeared increasingly anachronistic. Such a man was unlikely to prove a sympathetic superior to the ardent, modern-minded young Kapellmeister who had arrived from Strasbourg.

*   *   *

Klemperer was aghast at his initial experience of working with Rémond on the new production of *Figaro* that opened the season on 1 September. For the first time he realised how unjust he had been to have reacted so fiercely against Pfitzner's stagings.[4] Though basically traditional, they at least arose out of an understanding of the music, whereas Rémond was primarily concerned to decorate the action with business. But that was what the Cologne critics were used to, as their warm approval of this *Figaro* confirms. Unlike their counterparts in Strasbourg, they had, however, been taught by Klemperer's predecessor, Gustav Brecher, to accept the restoration of Mozart's recitatives, which Klemperer on this occasion accompanied on the piano.† Some newspapers found his interpretation too overladen with nuances. But there was general praise for the performance's unforced sense of movement and pace. And on this occasion Klemperer abandoned the idiosyncratic notions of casting that had aroused opposition in Strasbourg. The Countess was sung by a lyric-dramatic soprano, Wanda Achsel,‡ and the Susanna by Johanna Geissler, who had sung Marzelline in the trial

---

* Fritz Rémond (1864–1931) had from 1906 to 1910 been a member of the Cologne Opera and had also sung the roles of Lohengrin and Parsifal in Bayreuth.

† Probably *faute de mieux*. Two years later he used a harpsichord in a new production of *Così fan tutte*.

‡ Wanda Achsel (1891–1977) later established a substantial reputation at the Vienna State Opera.

121

Fidelio that Klemperer had conducted in Cologne the previous January. The production laid the foundations of the reputation Klemperer was to win in Cologne as a conductor who excelled above all in Mozart.

The season brought the usual quota of new productions. On 30 September Johanna Geissler sang the title role in *Carmen* and the fact that Klemperer was willing to tolerate a light soprano in a part that manifestly calls for a darker voice suggests that the interest she had aroused in him earlier in the year had not subsided.* That was followed on 11 October by the first production in Cologne of Strauss's new version of *Ariadne auf Naxos*, and on 27 January 1918 Klemperer was able to turn again to *Don Giovanni*, a work that much exercised his imagination at this stage of his life.

There was unanimous praise for the musical side of the performance and Neitzel[5] compared Klemperer's treatment of the recitative to the playful style that Strauss had initiated earlier in the century. His decision to perform the work as it had been heard at its first performance in Prague and to omit all the arias that Mozart had subsequently written for Vienna, was less well received, and to a man the critics savaged the curtained sets that he had introduced. Neitzel devoted a special article to an attack on the use of stylised settings in Mozart's operas.[6] Such innovations, he insisted, might work in the spoken theatre, but opera demanded colour and a clear indication of time and place. Stehle deplored 'the dull, pallid light' that played over all the scenes, 'whether by day or night, serious or comic'.[7] Klemperer's first attempt to introduce a measure of scenic innovation in the Cologne opera house had clearly misfired, in part, no doubt, because he was not his own producer, but was obliged to work with an old-fashioned *Spielleiter*.

Nor was he his own master in the choice of repertory and of new works. He was unable to persuade Rémond to stage the revised version that Pfitzner had recently made of his early fairy opera, *Christelflein*, but found himself involved in a series of flimsy novelties, such as Intendants with no understanding of contemporary music are all too liable to alight on. After a double bill of Weingartner's *Cain und Abel* and Klenau's homespun ballet, *Klein Ida's Blumen* in October 1917, spring brought Bittner's *Das höllisch Gold*, which was coupled with *Eight Dance Scenes*, a balletic pot-pourri devised and produced by the Herr Hofrat himself. After this undistinguished fare, there followed on 12 May 1918 *Die vernarrte Prinzessin* by Oscar von Chelsius. As lieutenant-general and adjutant to William II Chelsius

---

* He was to prove less indulgent after they had married. His opposition to his wife's desire to sing one of her favourite roles was to be a cause of marital friction. After her marriage Johanna Geissler began to concentrate on lighter, coloratura roles better suited to her vocal resources.

enjoyed such imperial favour that, even in the last months of the war, he was able to secure the release from military service of members of the Cologne opera.* Klemperer found the work so musically unworthy that he at one point walked out of rehearsals and finally conducted only under protest. But Rémond's spectacular production assured success with the critics. As it was contrary to etiquette for so august a personage to appear on a stage, the General acknowledged applause from Rémond's box.[8]

In time Klemperer was to be able to bring about some improvement in the choice of new works. But to the end of his seven years in Cologne the

---

* Claim made by Klemperer to the author.

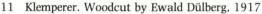

11   Klemperer. Woodcut by Ewald Dülberg, 1917

style of a vast majority of the productions was to remain a thorn in his flesh and the way in which one revival after another was thrown on the stage with little or no rehearsal continued to shock him.* To a greater extent than at any time since his first season at Hamburg he found himself a prisoner of the repertory system as it was (and to some extent still is) practised in the German provinces. The orchestra, which had given him such pleasure at his trial *Fidelio* in January 1917, had been depleted by conscription for the armed forces, while the public, he told Strauss after only a month in Cologne, he found 'sehr schlimm'.† 'I have a lot to put up with here,'⁹ he wrote to Dülberg towards the end of his first season.

The singers, for their part, found it hard to know what to make of their new conductor. If no one disputed his outstanding gifts, his methods were not always calculated to win affection. At the first ensemble rehearsal for *Die Meistersinger*, only a few weeks after his arrival in Cologne, he obliged the Masters to sing facing a wall, so as to become free of his beat.‡ Felix Dahn, who joined the company as producer in September 1918, found Klemperer 'rude to the point of boorishness, obstinate, fanatical – but a genius'.¹⁰ Even artists who admired him were alarmed by his appearance. To Julius Gless, the company's principal bass, his profile recalled that of the bust of E. T. A. Hoffmann in the restaurant of the Bamberg theatre. In the light of the conductor's desk singers saw a brow that 'calls to mind a dark bird of prey'.¹¹

Even before the end of his first season in Cologne, Klemperer may have had hopes of finding a position elsewhere. On 23 May 1918 Woldemar Runge, the Intendant of the Breslau theatres, wrote to Hans Gregor (see p. 81n), then in his last months as director of the Vienna Opera, to recommend Klemperer for a vacancy that was due to occur in autumn 1919.§ Gregor, it seems, was not favourably disposed, but Karl Lion, the secretary of the Vienna Opera, was instructed to send a confidential letter of enquiry to Sofie Wolf, a leading soprano in Cologne. Her reply was not calculated to further Klemperer's ambitions.

In *my* view Herr Kl. is not absolutely in the top rank...[He] is an excellent musician and a splendid theatre conductor who brings *nothing new*...I have, for instance, recently sung Isolde and Kundry under him and was rather unhappy...Whether

---

* In his first three months in Cologne he conducted no fewer than forty performances of thirteen different works.
† Letter of 30 September 1917, written in answer to a complaint from Strauss about the unsatisfactory standard of performance (not conducted by Klemperer in this season) of *Der Rosenkavalier* in Cologne.
‡ Information provided by Hugo Strelitzer (1896–1981), later Klemperer's chorusmaster in Los Angeles.
§ It has not been possible to establish why Runge should have interceded on Klemperer's behalf.

he or someone else is sitting there makes little difference; at the most he overdoes slow tempi in the most boring way...For the rest he refers to all the books he has read about the work he is conducting! I know my judgement is severe, but I think that all my colleagues are of the same opinion. His behaviour is certainly that of an educated man, also he lives in seclusion, so that in this respect there is nothing to be said against him [clearly a reference to Lion's enquiry about Klemperer's alleged eccentricities of behaviour]. All in all, he scarcely warrants your consideration as First Conductor...In the orchestra there is also no enthusiasm for him, as there was, for instance, for Lohse and often also for Brecher, whom I rate incomparably higher than Kl.*

For the moment that letter put an end to any possibility of an engagement in Vienna. Yet the issue was to arise again within a few months. In August 1918 Leopold von Andrian, a lifelong friend of Hugo von Hofmannsthal, briefly became Intendant of the Vienna court theatres. Never averse from a little Viennese intrigue, Hofmannsthal had mooted the possibility of Strauss as director in succession to Gregor.† For such an appointment to succeed, he stressed that Strauss would need 'a second conductor, who must nonetheless be absolutely first rate'. It was in this connection that on 24 September 1918 Hofmannsthal drew von Andrian's attention to Klemperer.

In the question of the conductor, I have been much occupied with gathering information from all sides...You must have...a younger but also extremely competent conductor to train the orchestra and the singers. For a proper regeneration this is absolutely necessary in addition to Strauss.
  I hear the best about Klemperer – Cologne...a passionate theatre conductor, with that an agreeable, adroit man, who brings the most out of singers and orchestra, and a tireless worker who in a short period has raised the Cologne Opera very high. Would, it seems, like to come to Vienna, even in a secondary post, as, though not vain, he is self confident and sure of winning a *de facto* front rank position. A leading virtuoso recently told me that he is the only conductor under whom he would play in an orchestra.[12]

Within six weeks the Habsburg Monarchy had collapsed and with it both von Andrian's appointment and any hopes that Klemperer had that the Vienna Court Opera might provide a means of escape from Cologne.

　　　　　*　　　　　　　　　　*　　　　　　　　　　*

On 30 June the season ended. In its course Klemperer had conducted no fewer than ninety-eight performances. In the last winter of the war food had become short in the big cities, and in March he had been ill with

---

* Sofie Wolf to Karl Lion, 1 June 1918. Sofie Wolf may have subsequently come round to Klemperer's abrasive personality and harsh methods of rehearsal. At any rate, on 8 October 1919 she gave the first performance of some of his new songs, which he himself accompanied.
† This came to pass. Together with Franz Schalk, Strauss was co-director of the Vienna Opera from 1919 to 1924.

bronchitis, which may explain why he chose to accept an offer from Carl Adler, a wealthy industrialist he had come to know in Strasbourg, of a month's holiday in Switzerland rather than financial help towards establishing himself in a flat in Cologne. Although now thirty-three, Klemperer was still an undomesticated animal, who felt no need of what he contemptuously dismissed as *Lebensgepäck*. On 11 July he arrived at the Waldhaus Hotel* in Sils Maria. In such unaccustomed comfort, his spirits, which had been low during the previous season, seem to have revived to a point where he was willing to play his own compositions to a fellow guest.

On his return from the Engadine five weeks later, he broke the journey in Zurich, where Busoni had taken refuge during the war.† A year earlier Klemperer had been in touch with him about the possibility of performing his two new short operas, *Turandot* and *Arlecchino* in Cologne.‡ Now that the project was coming to fruition, there were practical matters to be discussed.

That was probably not the only subject of conversation. Two years earlier, Busoni's *Entwurf einer neuen Aesthetik der Tonkunst*, which had attracted little attention when it had first been published in remote Trieste in 1907, had been reissued in a popular edition in Germany. In the intervening decade, which had seen much startling musical innovation, this essay on the future course of music had become more topical, and in the debate that had ensued Pfitzner had assailed what he took to be Busoni's modernism in a pamphlet entitled *Futuristengefahr*. The clash heralded a divide which was to rend German musical life after the war and Klemperer himself was to become inextricably involved in it. For Pfitzner, who henceforth increasingly became the mouthpiece for the most conservative elements in musical life, anything that threatened the hegemony of German romanticism was to be resisted on national as well as aesthetic grounds. Busoni, a more subtle and enquiring mind, had wider perspectives. Although he had yet to coin the phrase, 'Junge Klassizität',§ he had already outlined the contours of a new classicism. In his *Entwurf* he had attacked the literary influences that had since Wagner come to play so prominent a role in the development of music and advocated a return to 'absolute' music, whose course would be determined solely by musical laws.‖

---

* Much favoured by German intellectuals and musicians. Klemperer was often to stay there in the future.
† It was on this occasion that Klemperer was astonished to discover that Busoni did not know *Così fan tutte*. He sent him a score, which Busoni 'gulped down'. (*Minor Recollections*, p. 61)
‡ Klemperer had been prevented by commitments during his final week in Strasbourg from attending the premières, which had taken place in Zurich on 11 May 1917.
§ His essay of this title dates from 1920.
‖ Although Busoni scholars such as Ronald Stevenson are not in agreement, to this extent, at any rate, Busoni was a harbinger of the neo-classicism that subsequently came to

Klemperer did not later rate Busoni very highly as a composer. In his view, he had 'indicated the direction music must take, but as a creative artist could only give an indication of its course'.[13] But in this ominous dispute with Pfitzner he was, as he had earlier told Busoni in a letter written on 11 June 1917, wholeheartedly on his side.

That Busoni's ideas were already an influence on Klemperer's own musical attitudes is suggested by a perceptible change in his approach to Wagner. In a large and conservatively oriented theatre such as Cologne, his works inevitably figured prominently in the repertory. Klemperer was expected to conduct them, as he had done, happily enough, in Strasbourg, and he had some first class Wagnerian voices at his disposal.* Yet the critics frequently commented on an uncharacteristic lack of commitment in his performances. As early as 1917 Klemperer had made the revealing comment, 'Wenn Wagner mir gefällt, gefalle ich mir nicht'.† Three years earlier, he had preserved an embarrassed silence when Dülberg, an outright anti-Wagnerian, had demanded whether he would number Wagner among the very greatest composers, alongside Bach, Mozart, Beethoven and Schubert.[14] The heroic aspects of *The Ring* made little appeal. As he became increasingly drawn to Catholicism, he grew suspicious of Wagner's attempt in *Parsifal* to make religious ritual serve dramatic ends. Of the mature music dramas he was drawn most closely to the erotic world of *Tristan und Isolde*.

His approach to *The Ring*, which he first conducted in Cologne in June 1918, was felt even by admirers to be 'too sharply analytical to be entirely authoritative',[15] and a traditionally minded Wagnerian such as Anton Stehle complained on more than one occasion of what he regarded as Klemperer's 'Verzärtelung' (literally, 'coddling') of orchestral sound. Even in passages of great intensity he had a habit of highlighting detail to a point that threatened to undermine the balance and solidity of the music, a practice which, Stehle claimed, derived from Mahler.‡ Klemperer's abhor-

dominate much of the musical scene between the two wars. 'Words', said Stravinsky, wagging a finger in the present writer's face, 'are very dangerous. They have a life of their own.' That is a warning with which Busoni would have concurred. An historic meeting between the two composers occurred at the Weimar Bauhaus on 19 August 1923, when they sat side by side during a concert that ended with *L'Histoire du soldat*. Stravinsky told his friend, Ernest Ansermet, that Busoni had wept during the performance (letter of August 1923). But in his biography (*Busoni*, p. 283), Dent quotes Busoni's equivocal comment, 'There's something that achieves its aim! But let us take care not to imitate it.'

* Notably Sofie Wolf, Modeste Menzinsky, Julius Gless and from September 1918 Friedrich Schorr (1888–1953), the leading Wagnerian baritone of his generation.

† 'When Wagner pleases me, I don't please myself', an observation noted in her diary by Klemperer's sister, Marianne, after she had heard him conduct his trial *Fidelio* in Cologne on 6 January 1917.

‡ *Kölnische Volkszeitung*, 26 September 1918. Mahler's biographer, Henry-Louis de La Grange, has confirmed that Mahler was also criticised on this account. Yet, paradoxically, when

rence of rhetoric and love of clarity led him to react increasingly sharply against the upholstered orchestral textures which had come to be accepted as authoritative in the years after Wagner's death. On 6 June 1918, before a performance of *Götterdämmerung*, he put up a signed notice, requesting the orchestra to play all accompanying passages only 'half as loud as they are written, forte as mezzoforte, piano as pianissimo'. It is also relevant to observe that, apart from a single cycle in Buenos Aires in 1931, Klemperer was never to conduct *The Ring* after he left Cologne at the age of only thirty-nine. Towards the end of his life, he laconically observed that 'one shouldn't take Wagner's tragic pretensions all that seriously'.[16] In 1918 such a sentiment had subversive implications, at any rate for traditionally minded music lovers.

*   *   *

During the war Klemperer, like most German intellectuals, had firmly believed in the victory of the Central European powers.* It was not until his visit to Zurich in August 1918 that Busoni sowed doubts in his mind. But if defeat came to him as a shock, as it did to a vast majority of his compatriots, he nonetheless wholeheartedly welcomed the abdication of the Emperor and the foundation of a republic that eventually took the name of Weimar, the Thuringian city where its constitution was drawn up in 1919. 'I again see the future hopefully', he wrote on 28 November to Busoni, and at about the same time a musician visiting Cologne was startled to receive a lecture in democracy: a charwoman, he was told, was as important as a conductor.† From his youth Klemperer had had no time for bourgeois conventions or social distinctions. After the end of the war he became distinctly more radical in his sympathies.

But German society as a whole did not welcome the new era that seemed to have dawned. While many intellectuals were drawn to the new dances, new clothes, new music (jazz‡) and the new morals that had started to percolate from abroad, the middle classes tended to regard these alien innovations as an affront to German sensibilities. Tensions were further exacerbated by the fact that this cultural sea change was not accompanied by any equivalent transformation of the country's political arrangements. The apparatus of monarchy had disappeared and a republic had been established. But at a more fundamental level the fabric of German society,

---

‡ Klemperer performed and recorded the first act of *Die Walküre* in 1969, the sound was on a monumental scale that dwarfed even that of Reginald Goodall, who prepared the performance for him.

* *Conversations*, p. 52. See also the patriotic nature of his own *Geistliches Kampflied* (p. 118).

† A view Klemperer was to modify when, at about this time, the Cologne orchestra tried to determine the duration of rehearsals. (Transcript of CBC interviews.) The musician was Hugo Strelitzer (see p. 124).

together with the power structure that underlay it, survived more or less unchanged. The young republic inscribed the slogans of cultural innovation on its banners, but public taste remained essentially Wilhelmine. Hence the scene was set for a clash between an essentially conservative society and a radical culture, in which Klemperer's own career was to become inextricably entangled.

In the weeks immediately after the end of hostilities, left-wing groups were nonetheless able to seize the initiative. On 25 November a council of artists (Künstlerrat) was established in the Cologne theatre in imitation of the councils of soldiers and workers that had been set up earlier in Berlin and elsewhere and were soon to make a bid to take over the government of the country. The Cologne theatre council, however, contented itself with passing motions against the unrestricted powers enjoyed by the Intendant without attempting to replace him. It demanded 'human rights' for artists and in particular the abolition of the petty fines that were still often imposed for minor misdemeanours. It requested (but did not obtain) representation on the Theatre Commission and it established a tribunal to arbitrate in event of disputes between artists and the management. But it explicitly disavowed any intention of seeking a voice in artistic matters and thus failed to bring about any fundamental change in the way the theatre was run. The course of the 'revolution' in the Cologne theatre mirrors in miniature that which failed to seize power on a national level.

A widespread belief nonetheless persisted on the Left that art should cease to be the exclusive possession of the propertied classes but should serve as a means of spiritual regeneration for society as a whole. There was a concurrent expectation that a new society would produce new art and that a 'progressive' stance in politics called for support of new forms of cultural expression. Artistic and intellectual life should be 'the direct incarnation' of the new state.*

It was not long before such ideas found practical expression. On 28 December 1918 a society, which called itself 'Die Gesellschaft der Künste' ('The Society of the Arts') as a means of stressing its social commitments as well as its artistic aims, was established in Cologne. The arts, it announced in its manifesto, must become an expression of the people's will. They must be freed of any sort of regimentation,† and artists should determine how cultural subsidies were to be spent. The Society was to

---

* Paul Bekker, 'Die Kunst geht nach Brot' (1918), in *Kritische Zeitbilder*, pp. 212–17. Bekker, who was music critic of the *Frankfurter Zeitung*, was an influential spokesman for these ideas in the years immediately after 1918 and was singled out for attack by Pfitzner on that account (see p. 151).
† In 1918 it was doubtless pardonable to be unaware that no political system imposes cultural regimentation so severe as one that claims to represent 'the people's will'.

function as the Rhineland branch of the Arbeitsrat für Kunst that had been set up in Berlin, Karl Nierendorf* was appointed artistic director and a series of exhibitions, lectures and concerts was announced. At its first meeting on 15 February 1919 its founders emphasised that it had no political links. Nonetheless, it was not long before the Society incurred public wrath. On 4 March there was a disturbance in the theatre.† The Society was wrongly blamed for it in the press and Nierendorf was obliged to write a letter of disavowal to the *Oberbürgermeister*, Konrad Adenauer.‡

On 23 February the Society launched its first musical occasion, at which Bach was performed on the organ, interspersed with readings from the Bible, Hölderlin and Goethe. Perhaps aware that such an inauguration was more appropriate to a prayer meeting than a cultural group with radical leanings, the Society announced four days later that Klemperer had assumed responsibility for its musical activities and would himself take part in the first of three matinées.§ On 2 March in the Rococo-Saal of the Hotel Disch (Cologne boasted no other hall suitable for chamber music) Friedrich Schorr, accompanied at the piano by Klemperer, sang the *Kindertotenlieder* and other songs by Mahler. Neitzel chose to observe that, as a Semite who could not hide his feelings, Mahler bore a certain resemblance to Meyerbeer and Goldmark.[17] The remainder of the press received both the music and the performances with enthusiasm but commented that the *Kindertotenlieder* could only make their full impact with the original orchestral accompaniment. That Klemperer had had recourse to a piano was, however, due to the fact that the Society's application to Adenauer for permission to use the city orchestra had been turned down by the Theatre Commission on the grounds that the players were already overburdened. That refusal was to bring Klemperer's relations with Cologne near to breaking point before the end of the 1918/19 season.

*   *   *

The season had already seen a marked improvement in the choice of new works; in place of the ephemeral novelties that had plagued Klemperer's first year in Cologne, at his instigation recent operas by Janáček and Busoni were added to the repertory. *Jenůfa* was in preparation during the autumnal

---

* Karl Nierendorf (1889–1947), an early associate of Max Ernst and August Macke, established well-known galleries, first in Cologne and later in Berlin and New York. He was largely instrumental in the discovery of Otto Dix and became one of Klemperer's few close friends.   † In which Max Ernst took part.

‡ Konrad Adenauer (1876–1967), *Oberbürgermeister* of Cologne, 1917–33. As first Chancellor of the Federal German Republic (1949–1963) he, more than any single man, shaped the face of West Germany as it emerged after the Second World War.

§ Only two of these materialised. At the second concert Lonny Epstein (see p. 15) took part in a programme of violin sonatas by Pfitzner, Debussy, Busoni and Scriabin, an indication of Klemperer's broad musical sympathies.

weeks of 1918 when the war was finally drawing to a close.* The work could hardly have been put on at a less favourable moment. As Habsburg power disintegrated, the Czechs were in the process of throwing off Austrian rule, and in a rehearsal the Cologne chorus refused to take part in an opera by a composer 'whose fellow-countrymen were ruining German land and raping German women'.[18] The protest was echoed in the *Rheinische Musik- und Theaterzeitung* (23 November 1918), whose national-istically minded editor, Gerhard Tischer, asked whether it was right that Cologne should devote itself to Czech culture at a time when 'our Austrian brothers have to suffer so much under the effrontery of uncultured Slavs'.

The unfamiliar style of the music proved a further stumbling block to German ears. Casting around for 'influences', the critics surfaced with composers as remote as Mascagni (*Cavalleria Rusticana* was another village melodrama in *verismo* style), Debussy (whose vocal idiom also arose out of the spoken word) and even Schoenberg. In the *Kölner Tageblatt* (18 November) Karl Wolff maintained that what he took to be the crudity of the music was evidence that the Bohemians† were a people of *Musikanten* rather than true artists. Yet, in spite of such crass misunderstandings, the score's power and originality carried the day. The house was not full and there was only tepid applause after the first two acts, but in the last act the work fired the audience and by the end of the evening its success was assured. Klemperer himself wrote enthusiastically about the opera to Busoni.[19] Thereafter he was to be a leading advocate of Janáček's music at a time when it was still little appreciated outside Czechoslovakia.

On 6 December British troops entered Cologne, which became the centre of an occupied area that stretched from the Belgian border to the far side of the Rhine. On 8 December, three days before an early curfew obliged the theatre to shut for a week, Klemperer conducted a restudied revival of *Der Rosenkavalier* that he had promised Strauss a year earlier. When the theatre reopened on 18 December with performances that began at 5 pm or earlier, seats were reserved for the troops which the military authorities paid for at the usual subscribers' rates. The local press expressed surprise that they were invariably full.‡ For their part, the occupying forces were amazed at the breadth of the repertory and the passion that Klemperer

---

* After years of neglect, a revised version of the opera, which was first performed in this form in Prague on 26 May 1916, had belatedly brought the 62-year-old Janáček his first taste of success. The performance that Klemperer conducted in Cologne on 16 November 1918 was the first to be heard in Germany.
† Janáček was of course not Bohemian but Moravian.
‡ Perhaps Strauss, who felt his operas to have been neglected in Cologne and on 28 December 1918 ironically urged Klemperer to add *Salome* and *Elektra* to the repertory on the grounds that 'the troops would surely provide a more interested public...than the dear "Göllner" [local dialect for "Kölner"]', was nearer the mark than he may have realised.

brought to Mozart, though that did not prevent them from seizing orchestral interludes 'as an opportunity for conversation'.[20]

Military restrictions extended to all fields of communication. There was strict censorship of private correspondence as well as of newspapers, cars could only be used by special authority, all telephones were disconnected and – crowning example of colonial attitudes – the Rhineland was obliged to adopt Greenwich Mean Time.[21] On 6 January 1919 it became necessary to have special permission to enter or leave occupied territory. For a while Cologne and the Rhineland were virtually cut off from the rest of Germany.

These restraints were by no means the only difficulties confronting the Cologne Opera. The country was exhausted after four years of war in which it had suffered a loss of life proportionately greater than that it had inflicted on its enemies. There was a severe shortage of fuel and food,* an influenza epidemic raged in the early months of 1919, and the spectre of inflation was already raising its head.† Illness and travel restrictions made advance planning so difficult that on 4 March Rémond asked the Theatre Commission for permission to dispense with the monthly *Spielplan*. The chorus, underpaid and depleted by influenza, was in a rebellious frame of mind. Orchestral players, who were already suffering from rising prices, found that the early hours of the performances (*Götterdämmerung* started at 2 pm!) made it difficult to do the teaching on which they depended for an adequate standard of living.

In such circumstances a new production of Busoni's double bill on 26 January 1919 represented a considerable achievement. Always cautious in his approach to new works,‡ Klemperer had earlier travelled to Frankfurt to attend the dress rehearsal of the first German performance. But, though there was unanimous praise for Rémond's production and Klemperer's conducting, neither opera made much impression on the Cologne critics, who found *Turandot* too protracted and *Arlecchino* too contrived. Busoni's music, they maintained, appealed to the head rather than to the heart, and history has endorsed that verdict.

The choice of such new works clearly reflected Klemperer's taste; while staging remained the prerogative of Rémond, as senior member of the music staff he had gained a say in purely musical matters. On occasions he put that freedom to strange use. In a new production of *Die Entführung aus dem Serail* (29 September 1918) that further strengthened his reputation as a Mozartian, he dispensed with the bogus recitatives that were still in

* The Allies did not raise the blockade of Germany until June 1919.
† The black, or free, market price of theatre seats rose threefold within the first six months of the season.
‡ One reason why, for a conductor who was at any rate until the Second World War much involved in new music, he conducted relatively few first performances.

132

general use, but, alarmed at the prospect of raising the curtain on spoken dialogue, proceeded to compose pianoforte introductions to the second and third acts. That was not his only eccentricity. When on 15 March 1919 he conducted a new production of *The Barber of Seville*, a work he much loved, eyebrows were raised at the 'Berliozities' he had added to Rossini's storm music.[22] There were other anachronisms: in her singing lesson Rosina launched into Zerbinetta's aria from *Ariadne auf Naxos*. That at least Klemperer seems to have recognised as an error of taste, for at the second performance he substituted an aria from Verdi's *Ernani*. This also failed to satisfy him, for on 26 May Rosina sang an aria, 'Die überflüssige Vorsicht', composed by himself. In a letter to Bekker (5 November 1921) he later claimed to have stuck closely to Rossini's style. That, however, was not the impression of the Cologne critics, who frowned on the orchestral writing as reminiscent of Strauss's *Ariadne auf Naxos* and the dissonances as capricious. Klemperer the upholder of stylistic fidelity was a product of a later phase of his development.

*   *   *

By the spring of 1919 almost twelve years had passed since Klemperer had embarked on his career as a conductor, and in that period he had given no more than three orchestral concerts, two of which had been put on at his own expense or with the support of friends. Although very much a man of the theatre, he was acutely aware of the great orchestral repertory that was in effect barred to him and the frustrating conditions of his work in the opera house made him even more determined to seek artistic satisfaction in the concert hall.

In Cologne, however, orchestral concerts were the prerogative of the Konzert-Gesellschaft and its conductor, Hermann Abendroth.* Its Tuesday evening ceremonies with the city orchestra in the Gürzenich Hall (from which the opera house orchestra took its name when it abandoned the theatre for the concert platform) were the focal point of the city's musical life. Most seats were taken by subscribers, so that the public was overwhelmingly old and well-to-do, and its programmes appropriately conservative. The concerts had had an illustrious history since they had been established in 1850 by Ferdinand Hiller, whose successors had been Franz Wüllner and Fritz Steinbach, the leading Brahms conductor of his time. But by 1918 the Gürzenich concerts had become virtually a *geschlossene Gesellschaft* (closed society), which failed entirely to provide for the new and socially less exclusive public that had emerged during the war. A

---

* Hermann Abendroth (1883–1956) remained in Cologne until 1934, when he became conductor of the Leipzig Gewandhaus Orchestra, a position he retained until 1945.

133

demand arose for another series of concerts, and it was inevitable that its advocates should look to Klemperer to provide them.

A request by the Gesellschaft der Künste to use the city orchestra for popular concerts had already been turned down by the Theatre Commission on the ground that the orchestra was overburdened. But the issue arose again on 16 April when Georg Beyer,* the chairman of the progressively minded Vereinigung geistiger Arbeiter Kölns (Union of Intellectual Workers, Cologne), invited Klemperer to conduct three concerts in conjunction with evening classes run by the association. Klemperer accepted and planned to open the series with a performance of Mahler's Second Symphony on 18 May. Although these concerts were aimed at a public entirely different from that which attended the Gürzenich concerts, the Theatre Commission again rejected a request for use of the orchestra. It had grounds for doing so; but at a time when political feelings ran high its decision was widely regarded on the Left as due to political prejudice.†

Klemperer was informed of the Theatre Commission's refusal on 25 April and, regarding it as a rejection of his own claim to conduct concerts, he at once requested Rémond for freedom to look for another position. The following day under the title 'Klemperer leaves Cologne' the Rheinische Zeitung announced that he was already in negotiations with Aachen, Mannheim and Vienna. The news caused an outcry in the remainder of the press, which, irrespective of political leanings, agreed that his departure should at all costs be prevented. The heat was on the Theatre Commission. On 30 April Klemperer, the bit between his teeth, presented his demands to Rémond, which he put in writing two days later.[23] The first four and most essential were:

1. A seat on the city council's Theatre Commission and Music Commission.
2. The right to conduct at least three concerts every season with three to four rehearsals each and programmes to be determined by himself.
3. The right to choose the operas he would conduct and to conduct not more than three performances a week.
4. The right to take charge of the sets and production of at least two new productions each year. Here he added an illuminating rider: 'Opera is in my view a unified organism in which the orchestra and the stage must be in precise accord. As, however, it is in the first place a *musical* art, in so far as everything should flow from the music, I consider that the conductor is artistically justified in also taking charge of what happens on the stage.'

Although Klemperer was not granted a seat on the Theatre Commission and had to be satisfied with an assurance that every attention would be

* Georg Beyer (1884–1943) was until 1933 *feuilleton* editor of the socialist *Rheinische Zeitung* and Cologne city councillor with special responsibility for cultural affairs.
† The Catholic Zentrum party at that point had a majority on the Theatre Commission.

given to his wishes in the matter of the operas he conducted, his other demands were conceded on 21 May.*

That was, however, not the only conflict in which Klemperer was involved in the spring of 1919. On 23 April the assembled employees of the theatre announced that the theatre would be shut on 1 May.† This was regarded on the Right as a provocative move and the middle-class press, ever ready to scent revolution, denounced it as 'a *Putsch* in our cultural institutions'.[24] That it was politically motivated can hardly be doubted. But the *Rheinische Zeitung* of 29 April maintained that its purpose was also to express a lack of confidence in Rémond, no doubt an additional reason why Klemperer gave support to what in effect was a one-day strike. In the polemics that ensued, a correspondent alleged in the *Kölner Tageblatt* (3 May) that Klemperer himself had been the prime mover of the revolt. Paul Hiller, paradoxically music critic of the socialist *Rheinische Zeitung*, went further. In an article headed 'Agitation in the Cologne Theatres', he claimed in the *Allgemeine Musikzeitung* of 30 May that Klemperer, 'who to put it mildly is a left-wing socialist' had stirred up feeling against Rémond with a view to succeeding him. To an assembly of the employees he had declared, 'In the future the last shall be first and that will be you.' A month later Hiller was obliged to withdraw his allegations. Nonetheless, the events of 1 May, together with Klemperer's links with leftish associations like the Gesellschaft der Künste, led to a widespread belief that the First Conductor at the opera house was a militant socialist. Increasingly, there was a polarity between the conservative, middle-class concert-goers around Abendroth, and the Jewish, intellectual and radical circles that supported Klemperer.

*　　　　　　　*　　　　　　　*

In fact Klemperer's true commitment lay in quite another direction. Although he found Cologne in general unsympathetic, in one respect the city made a profound impact on him. For the first time in his life he found himself living in a bastion of intellectual Catholicism. The Rhineland was the centre of the liturgical movement, which opposed a merely personal

---

* In this connection it is relevant to mention that at the end of the season Klemperer wrote over Rémond's head directly to Adenauer to ask for assurance (which was rapidly forthcoming) that his position as head of the musical staff ('oberster musikalischer Leiter') was unaffected by the appointment, also as First Conductor, of Hans Hermann Wetzler (Historisches Archiv der Stadt Köln, Bestand 46/13/11, Nos. 136–8). Hence Professor Dietrich Kämper's assertion on p. 200 of the catalogue of the 1975 Cologne exhibition, 'Vom Dadamax bis zum Grüngürtel', that the two conductors were on equal level is incorrect.
† Although May Day had been a public holiday in France since 1889, the issue had remained a matter of dispute in Germany. Prior to 1914 employers had frequently resorted to lock-outs as a sanction against workers who took the day off. May 1 was not declared a public holiday in Germany until 1933 – by the National Socialist government.

piety, and in its emphasis on ritual advocated among much else a return to plainsong. Nearby Bonn was the seat of the Katholischer Akademiker Verband,* which under Prälat Franz-Xaver Münch† sought to establish links between intellectual and artistic circles and the Church. Münch became a friend and spiritual adviser and it was through him that Klemperer came into contact with the great Benedictine abbey of Maria Laach, some fifty miles south of Cologne.

The growing attraction that Catholicism had begun to exercise on Klemperer became apparent during Christmas 1918. To Marianne, the holidays with her brother in Cologne seemed like 'a weeklong conversion to Christianity'.[25] She had, she wrote to her friend, Leni Asch-Rosenbaum, listened with real Christian devotion to the carols Otto had played, and also to Bach arias, whose calm spirit she described (doubtless echoing his sentiments) as 'the purest essence of the German-Christian spirit'.

Immediately after Christmas another potent influence began to make itself felt. In January 1919 Max Scheler, the most celebrated Catholic philosopher of his time, was appointed professor at the newly established university of Cologne and by the following month both Klemperer and his sister had fallen under the spell of the intellectual brilliance of his lectures on the materialist view of history. Marianne found that there was 'something watchful (lauerndes) and sceptical about him that is hard for me to reconcile with his fervent Catholicism'.[26]‡ But Klemperer was fascinated by a man for whom philosophy was less an abstruse discipline than a means of reflecting on the great issues of life and death.§ Indeed, it was perhaps the very discursiveness of Scheler's thinking that appealed to his own untutored mind.‖ Scheler was no proselytiser and he played no direct part in Klemperer's conversion. But the closeness of these two restless, searching spirits is indicated by the facts that Scheler acted as witness to Klemperer's marriage in June 1919 and that the *Missa Sacra*, which Klemperer composed immediately after his conversion, is dedicated to him.

Early in 1919 Klemperer started to receive instruction from a Jesuit priest

* Its influence was widespread: both Heinrich Brüning (German Chancellor, 1930–2) and Robert Schumann (French Premier and Foreign Minister, 1948–52, who established the European coal and steel union and in doing so laid the foundations of the EEC) were members.

† Prälat Franz-Xaver Münch (1883–1940) was Secretary-General from 1916 until the association was banned during the Third Reich.

‡ Her observation was not unfounded. An unstable character, Scheler's turbulent personal and private life was to undergo many phases before his death in 1929 at the age of only fifty-four. At this period he was married to Furtwängler's sister, Maerit.

§ Scheler has been unkindly described as 'a *feuilleton* professor who conjured metaphysical meanings out of everyday events' (Wolf Zucker, *Die Weltbühne*, 15 February 1927).

‖ Scheler's comment on Klemperer's education (or lack of it) – 'So little capital, such a high return' – suggests that he nonetheless had regard for his intellectual capacity.

and on 17 March he was received into the Church. In one of those self-questioning moods to which he was prone, he later implied that he had taken the step in part as a means of distancing himself from his socialist associates in Cologne as well as from his Jewish background.* But all who knew him at this period of his life agree that, in contrast to Mahler who converted in furtherance of his career, Klemperer was inspired by faith and intellectual conviction. Henceforth a belief in the existence of God and the efficacy of prayer conditioned his entire outlook.

Throughout his career, he would unobtrusively withdraw before a concert to some point of refuge like a window and, as though momentarily absorbed, offer a silent prayer. Similarly, on leaving a city where he had perhaps fulfilled a taxing engagement, he would before leaving silently pause to give thanks for mercies received. He would on occasions likewise pray briefly before setting out on a journey, although a porter or a chauffeur who had entered the room to collect his bags might suppose him to be lost in abstraction. To the end of his life he remained a *homo religiosus*.

Yet a residual ambivalence remained. In every aspect of his life, Klemperer evaded dogmatism. Whether it was a matter of religious belief, political affiliations or musical issues, truth was too many-sided to admit of final conclusions. Thus his Catholicism did not hinder him from occasionally visiting a synagogue, long before he finally reverted to Judaism almost half a century after his conversion. Similarly, in his assiduous reading of the Bible, it was at all times the Old Testament to which he more frequently turned. Over the years his attendance at Mass grew increasingly sporadic. Outward religious observance was in any case largely confined to (was indeed a symptom of) a manic phase. When not 'high', Klemperer remained clamlike on all issues of belief. For him, these were, as he put it, strictly 'Privatsache'.[27]

Shortly before his baptism, he was assailed by a sudden crisis of faith. In his distress, he turned to Münch, who told him to remember that henceforth he would be in the hands of a loving Father. The words brought comfort, for they recalled a Hebrew text often cited by his mother, 'Adonai li velan vio'.† At the time of his conversion Klemperer accepted most of the doctrine of the Catholic Church. But the concept of free will gave him difficulty: to a man at the mercy of violent swings of temperament that were entirely beyond his control, it could have little meaning. Yet it was

---

* In a mocking reference to Klemperer's conversion, Amadeus, a would-be humorous columnist, maliciously observed in the *Kölner Tageblatt* of 30 March 1919 that 'our great Otto' had shown that Communism and Catholicism could go together. But Klemperer's support of the opera house strike five weeks after his conversion hardly suggests a desire to avoid a radical reputation. There was in any case no intrinsic conflict between his progressive leanings and the anti-capitalist overtones of Scheler's Catholicism at this time.

† Psalm 118/6. 'The Lord is on my side; I will not fear.'

perhaps an awareness that he was *not* free that led him to seek comfort and support in a beneficent deity through the dark and turbulent periods he knew himself condemned to face as long as he lived.

If that was his motive for conversion, his mother did not think much of it. 'Have yourself baptised, Otto', he later recalled her saying. 'It won't make any difference.' His devout father, who only seems to have learnt of his son's conversion over three months after it had taken place, simply asked, 'Who will say Kaddish for me when I am dead?'* Beyond that, the issue was never discussed in the family. It was not, however, to be the only bitter pill that Klemperer's ageing parents had to swallow in the spring and early summer of 1919.

* * *

On 12 April Klemperer went for a week's retreat to Maria Laach, where he remained throughout Holy Week.† His immediate purpose was no doubt to experience for the first time and to the full the culmination of the Christian year. The break also provided an opportunity to complete a setting of the Mass on which he had embarked after his baptism.‡ There can be little doubt that Klemperer was at any rate mildly manic during his stay in Maria Laach. To the priest charged with his care, he talked incessantly about theological issues, while simultaneously working on his Mass. There was an impression in the Abbey that he had not been prepared for conversion with sufficient thoroughness.§

While in Maria Laach Klemperer was visited by Johanna Geissler.‖ This was the first indication of the strength of his feelings for the soprano who had appeared in many of the operas he had conducted since his arrival in Cologne. At what point they decided to marry remains uncertain. Nor is it clear what precipitated the decision. The rise in Klemperer's spirits that seems to have set in in the course of the winter (on 7 February he had told Strauss in a letter that he was again composing)¶ would doubtless

* Both remarks were later reported by Klemperer to his daughter. Ida Klemperer's belief that conversion would not help her manic-depressive son proved wrong, at any rate in the short term. Kaddish is the prayer traditionally said by a Jewish son at his father's burial.
† He was accompanied by Ernst Robert Curtius (1886–1956), a distinguished scholar in the field of French literature.
‡ The theme of the Benedictus had come to him two or three years earlier during a service in the Strasbourg Minster.
§ The priest in question, Professor Dr Father Michels, who provided this information, implied that Prälat Münch was liable to be easy-going in such matters.
‖ When she left, he gave her portions of the newly composed Mass to take to Cologne for copying. Only on arrival there did she realise that in the course of the journey she had left them in a public lavatory, where they safely lay until she reclaimed them.
¶ Two songs, which were written at this period but have not survived, were sung by Cologne's leading heroic tenor, Modeste Menzinsky, at a recital on 20 February, in which he was accompanied by Klemperer. They were not well received in the press.

have led to a sharpening of his sexual responses and powers of decision. Perhaps the prospect of conversion turned his mind to the sacrament of marriage; he was, after all, now in his mid-thirties. Whatever the cause, Johanna Geissler seems to have been taken aback by the speed of events. Earlier that winter, a relationship with Friedrich Schorr had developed which had been sufficiently close for Schorr to assume that she would marry him. In his distress, he turned to Klemperer, unaware that it was he who had displaced him.

Johanna Geissler, who was thirty-one, had grown up in conditions of squalor and poverty. On her birth, her mother, whose name was Meyer, had advertised for foster-parents. An impoverished and elderly couple called Geissler (or Geisler, as it was sometimes spelt) agreed for a small monthly payment to adopt the infant, who was left by arrangement in a stable in the countryside outside Hanover. Johanna Geissler never knew her father and could only recall seeing her mother on two occasions, when a woman appeared without identifying herself. Her foster-father was a drunkard who was only occasionally in employment, her foster-mother harsh and brutal. Johanna rarely spoke about her childhood.

She left home and school at an early age, but a pretty, natural voice secured her a job in the chorus of the Hanover opera at the age of only fourteen. From there she graduated to tiny roles, started taking singing lessons, and after spells in Dessau and Wiesbaden was engaged in 1912 as soubrette in Mainz. There her success was such that four years later she was able to move to the far more renowned Cologne opera, where she rapidly made a reputation as an exceptionally lively performer. Technically her voice suffered from poor training and an incautious willingness to undertake a range of parts that extended from the Queen of the Night and Zerbinetta to Carmen and Butterfly. But she was a singer with strong musical responses.* Good-hearted, generous to a fault, resourceful and modest, she was the epitome of the 'good trooper', whose outward ebullience masked a deep inner shyness and sense of insecurity. Having herself known poverty, she was generous to a fault.† She had a weakness: though not an alcoholic, she was prone to drink more than was good for her and the habit grew more pronounced with the years.

Marianne, who only learnt of the wedding two weeks before it took place, described her future sister-in-law as being 'of medium height, with short hair..., a very lively face with an expressive nose and lips, but not particularly slender. You cannot imagine how vital she is – she must have

---

* A surviving record testifies to this.
† Her tips were notoriously lavish. In Leningrad in the twenties, Klemperer, who was alone but on a previous visit had been accompanied by Johanna, was accosted by a beggar. Having received little or nothing, the beggar asked, 'Et où est Madame?'

12   Johanna Geissler. Cologne, 1918

nerves of steel, she has *a lot* of humour and is very jolly. You would laugh
if you saw the two of them together...All in all, of all the women I have
known she seems to me to be the most suitable for Otto.'[28]

Marianne's intuition was better founded than she can have known. As
a result of the scandal that had rocked Hamburg in 1912 and of other less
spectacular incidents, Klemperer had acquired a formidable reputation as
a rake who was widely supposed to have chalked up an impressive list of
'conquests'. Such tales invariably originated in manic periods, when he
delighted in making remarks and advances of almost childish directness,

140

often with no intention but to shock. In fact Klemperer was anything but the Don Juan he liked to pose as when 'high'. Indeed, his sexual experiences up to this point of his life had been limited.

Marianne's lively circle of bluestockings had provided feminine companionship spiced with intellectual stimulus, and doubtless the ecstatic admiration with which they regarded their friend's handsome and shockingly unconventional brother was not unwelcome to him. Yet such friendships never acquired amorous overtones: high-minded young ladies did not at that time enter into relationships that were unlikely to end at the altar and Klemperer never seems to have shown sexual interest in girls whose background was perhaps too similar to his own to provide the stimulus of contrast to the world he had grown up in.

As for most young men of the middle classes in the early years of the century, prostitutes offered the accepted means of sexual release. In Hamburg Klemperer had of course visited the red light district, where his first encounter had filled him with such repugnance that months elapsed before he could bring himself to return. In fact the impression he liked to give in manic phases of an overburgeoning sexuality was the reverse of the truth. His energies were in general too absorbed by his work and musical preoccupations for him to have much time or even energy for a rampaging erotic life, while in depression he shied away from any form of human contact, sexual or otherwise. Thus, contrary to the general impression that he managed to create, the 33-year-old Klemperer, who early in 1919 seriously began to court Johanna Geissler, was no roué, but a chaste, even perhaps rather inhibited, suitor.

That indeed may in part account for the attraction she held for him. Like Elisabeth Schumann, Johanna was a woman whose sexual morals reflected the standards current in the theatre rather than in middle-class society. She was not a 'loose' woman, but her frank and open attitude to sex stood in sharp contrast to the more prim standards of the respectable and intellectual young ladies in Marianne's circle. As in the case of Elisabeth Schumann, that openness may have served to free him from the inhibitions that had hitherto made it hard for him to make serious (as opposed to show-off) advances to a woman of his own background. Significantly, Johanna took it for granted that they would sleep together before they were married. Equally significantly (and much to Johanna's surprise) Klemperer made no attempt to do so.

It was not until a couple of weeks before the marriage that Johanna Geissler told Klemperer that her thirteen-year-old 'sister', Carla, was in fact her daughter. At Carla's boarding school he met a plump, rather phlegmatic child, who had not settled happily in Cologne after her mother's move three years earlier from Mainz. Like most children, she remained shy of the huge and intimidating presence of her 'brother-in-law' and no doubt found it embarrassing to call a man more than twenty years her senior 'Otto'. That discomforture may account for the ingenuity with which she contrived over the years to address him neither as 'Du' (as would have been natural within a family circle) nor as 'Sie' (which would have implied a refusal to use 'Du').

If Carla felt uneasy about her position, Klemperer showed no such reservations; only a German law that forbad a man under fifty years of age to adopt a child prevented him from doing so legally. On his marriage he nonetheless assumed full responsibility for the education and upkeep of his 'sister-in-law', who until she married in the early thirties lived under his roof as a member of the family. In 1936 Carla and her first husband followed them to Los Angeles. It was shortly after their arrival there that, to the acute embarrassment of Johanna (whose Bohemianism paradoxically went hand in hand with a concern to observe conventions) and to the huge entertainment of his children, Klemperer made an improper remark that revealed Carla's true relationship to their mother.*

Carla was not the only appendage that Johanna Geissler brought to the marriage. Louise Schwab was the daughter of an innkeeper in Mainz, who had written fan letters to her during her period at the city theatre and had then started to do a variety of small services. The two women, who were the same age, became such close friends that Fräulein Schwab eventually moved into Johanna's flat as housekeeper to the busy young singer and her daughter. In that capacity she moved with them to Cologne. A paragon *Hausfrau* (which the untidy Johanna was not) and formidably efficient in everything she undertook, it was inevitable that after the marriage she should remain with Johanna. Klemperer did not at first welcome the arrangement: he was never attached to Fräulein Schwab, as he continued to refer to her. But a rare combination of talents soon rendered her indispensable. Fräulein Schwab cooked, sewed and immersed herself in every detail of the household. A competent book-keeper, she soon controlled the family finances, for which neither Klemperer nor his wife had much aptitude, as well as attending to correspondence. Indeed two weeks *before* the marriage she was already writing to Schotts about Klemperer's compositions in the inimitable tone of a minor German official.† With the arrival of children she acted as nurse, took them on holidays and, during

---

* Carla Metzner married twice and died in Los Angeles in 1963 at the age of fifty-seven.
† It is symptomatic of the role that this formidable woman came to play in the Klemperer household that on 4 February 1928 Willy Strecker (see p. 225) wrote to inform Hindemith that he had learnt from Fräulein Schwab, 'the inseparable friend and factotum of the Klemperer family', that Klemperer would be adding *Cardillac* to the repertory of the Kroll Opera later that season. The information proved accurate.

the absence of their parents on tours, assumed complete control of the household. Later she learnt book-binding, so as to be able to bind Klemperer's scores. With unhesitating loyalty, she left Germany when Klemperer and his family were obliged to emigrate in 1933 and continued to live with them until 1938.*

The civil marriage took place on 14 June. On the same day, Johanna Geissler, who had been brought up a Lutheran, was received into the Roman Church and for the first and last time in her life made a general confession. Two days later in the early morning the religious ceremony was performed in the small Jesuit chapel that then stood in the Albertusstrasse by the priest who had prepared Klemperer for baptism. Only a few close friends attended. Klemperer was observed to pray fervently throughout. Whether Johanna did likewise is unrecorded. Marianne, who characteristically described the occasion as 'dreamlike',[29] found it painful on her return home to pretend to her ailing father that the marriage had been a civil ceremony, but, as he was not even aware of his son's baptism, he could not be told that the marriage had taken place in church. It seems that Ida was also not present.

Afterwards Klemperer went straight to the Gürzenich Hall, where at 10 am he conducted a rehearsal of his *Missa Sacra* (as he called it until it was pointed out to him that all masses are sacred) that was described as private but seems to have been attended by a sizeable audience which included several critics. Johanna was the soprano soloist. Marianne sang contralto in the choir. As Klemperer had explained in a letter of 11 June to Paul Bekker, his intention was that the mass should have its first performance at a South German or Austrian church where a tradition of using orchestral music for liturgical purposes still survived.† Rudolf Kastner effusively declared that the work revealed Klemperer as one of the outstanding German composers of the day.[30] Anton Stehle was more cautious, but stressed the expressionistic elements in the music, notably in the anguished Miserere.[31] After the performance, which was enthusiastically received,‡ the bridal pair left for three days' honeymoon in Bonn. Early in July they set out for a six-week holiday in the Engadine. Johanna, who had had no experience of the closeness of Jewish family ties, was surprised that Marianne had arranged to stay for much of the time in a nearby hotel. On 25 July Johanna wrote to her father-in-law to tell him that she was pregnant.

---

* When she went to look after Georg Klemperer who had arrived in America in his seventies. Subsequently, she obtained a licence to deal in property in Los Angeles, which she did to such good effect that she died (in 1967) a wealthy, fur-caped American matron.
† That wish was never fulfilled.
‡ Schotts was sufficiently impressed to offer 2,000M for it and the coloratura aria, 'Die überflüssige Vorsicht' (see p. 133).

143

8   Cologne: galley years

As conditions in the great German cities had grown harder in the latter stages of the war,* Klemperer's parents had left Hamburg in May 1918 and moved to Würzburg, where their younger daughter was studying and fuel and food were less difficult to come by. In the winter of 1918/19 they moved to Cologne. Thus their son's marriage to Johanna Geissler cannot have taken them entirely by surprise. But that did not make it easier to accept. That he should have married a gentile was bad enough: mixed marriages were still frowned upon, even by liberally minded Jews. That his choice should have fallen on a woman of very modest (indeed, from a conventional viewpoint, dubious) origins, with little education and an illegitimate child, made it doubly difficult to swallow. The Klemperers were neither bigots nor snobs. But they were intensely respectable and Ida in particular attached great importance to *Bildung*.† Johanna was far removed from the sort of daughter-in-law they would have envisaged. The old people must have trembled for the happiness and welfare of their beloved only son.

For Johanna, these elderly Jewish folk must have seemed equally alien, and the intensity and closeness of their family ties oppressive to a woman who had grown up largely without them. Yet the letter she wrote to her father-in-law from Sils Maria on 25 July 1919 to announce her pregnancy betrayed a touching desire to win acceptance. In it she twice referred to her husband as 'dein Otto', as though to underline her acceptance of his family bonds. Her tactful mention of 'the one and only God to whom we all pray' may however have been made at the instigation of her husband. Johanna did indeed succeed in winning the heart of her kindly, father-in-law. But with the austere and rigorous Ida relations were never to be easy.

Whatever Klemperer's parents may have thought about Johanna's shortcomings, she brought new stability into their son's life. In contrast to the turbulent years that lay behind him, marriage and conversion ushered in a long period of relative tranquillity. In the summer of 1921, when he was on holiday, Klemperer told Johanna that a friend who had not seen him since the manic period in 1915 had found him so quiet as to be almost unrecognisable. 'You see, *mein Guter*, that I owe to you.'[1]

* The civilian death rate rose by 37 per cent in the winter of 1917/18.　　† See p. 7n.

So free indeed was Klemperer of the violent psychological oscillations which had marked his life in Hamburg and Strasbourg, that when trouble eventually recurred early in 1928, Johanna was at first unable to understand its cause. Similarly, some time was to pass before he became properly aware of his wife's propensity to seek comfort in the bottle.

These were not the only sources of tension. Johanna was far from being a meek and patient wife. She was almost pathologically jealous of her handsome husband and this weakness was exacerbated by his inability to resist a pretty face when in a condition of euphoria. When not manic, Klemperer was extremely careful with money and his wife's reckless generosity was a perennial cause of friction. Yet in spite of these underlying tensions and of the fearful strains it had to bear during severe manic periods in later years, the marriage stood the test of time. As Marianne sensed, Johanna's proletarian robustness and resilience made her a good match for a man whose psychological equilibrium was always precarious.* Klemperer particularly savoured the comic mixture of the Bohemian and the conventional in her character. He recognised her to be a woman with a keen sense of theatre and came to rely much on her advice. There was also something exposed and defenceless in her character that called out the knight errant in him: at the time of his marriage he told more than one friend that he had 'saved' her. It was in fact she who, more than any single person, was to 'save' him from the self-destructive elements in his character.

*   *   *

On 22 March 1920 Johanna gave birth to a son, having characteristically continued to sing until the eighth month of her pregnancy. Klemperer was present throughout the delivery, which was not easy. The boy was christened Werner after Werner Rudolf, who had died a few weeks earlier at the age of only thirty (see p. 93). With family and parents to support, Klemperer now had little alternative but to reconcile himself to Cologne. He had grown no fonder of the city and conditions in the opera house continued to irk him. But in the upheaval of the post-war years a better position was not easy to come by and in Cologne he had gained at least a measure of musical independence. Even more important, for the first time in his career he had secured the right to give an annual series of orchestral concerts.

* In a letter to Helene Asch-Rosenbaum of 31 May 1919, Marianne even wrote that the marriage was to be welcomed from a 'racial-hygienic standpoint'. It was a strange comment from a woman who later became a convinced Zionist and spent the last thirty years of her life in Israel, but it illustrates the degree to which racial thinking was current in Germany even before the rise of National Socialism.

His opening opera house concert on 4 October 1919 was devoted to Mahler's Symphony No. 2, the work which had first brought him to the composer's attention and continued to hold a special significance to him for the remainder of his life. The house was sold out; only the seats reserved for the occupying forces remained empty. The work itself, which had not been heard in Cologne since 1911, had a mixed reception. There were also minor criticisms of Klemperer's conducting: some critics found his contrasts of tempi and dynamics excessive. But for the first time in his career he clearly made an authoritative impression in a concert hall, and Marianne observed that his conducting had gained in a way that reflected his own development.[2] Indeed Neitzel, who had heard the work under Mahler himself, claimed that Klemperer had achieved an even greater clarity of detail.[3] Although acoustics presented a problem, the event established Cologne's opera house concerts as a challenge to the sedate programmes that Hermann Abendroth offered his well-upholstered audiences at the Gürzenich.

Thereafter Klemperer performed at least one major work by Mahler each season at Cologne.* The sixtieth anniversary of the composer's birth in 1920 and the tenth anniversary of his death in 1921 led to a renewal of interest in his vast symphonies and it was in the early twenties that Klemperer began to make a name for himself as an authoritative Mahlerian. But his advocacy of his hero's music was by no means indiscriminate. 'I'm not a silly, enthusiastic boy; I don't like everything he wrote', he later observed.[4] Some scores he never tackled. Among these are the Symphonies No. 3 (see p. 25), which he did not care for, and No. 5, whose impressive funeral march did not in his view compensate for an overlong scherzo and finale and an adagietto that came too close to salon music for comfort. Symphonies Nos. 6 and 8, which he admired but never conducted, fell into a different category. No opportunity to conduct the Eighth presented itself until he was too old to undertake so demanding a task. The Sixth was announced for a Cologne concert in 1922/3, only to be cancelled at the last moment, probably because he felt that he had not fully grasped it. It was a score towards which he remained ambivalent. In old age, he on one occasion dismissed the finale as 'a total failure',[5] on another he declared that he did not understand a movement that seemed to him 'a cosmos in itself'.[6] Nonetheless in 1969 he again toyed with the idea of performing the work, as he had done fifty-seven years earlier, only for a second time to abandon it. Owing to his dislike of its rhetorical finale, he never again gave No. 1 after the single performance he conducted in

---

* *Lieder eines fahrenden Gesellen* and Symphony No. 1 (1 June 1920), *Das Lied von der Erde* (30 April 1921), Symphonies Nos. 7 (18 May 1922) and 9 (17 May 1923), *Kindertotenlieder* (29 November 1923).

146

Cologne, and forty-six years were to pass before in 1968 he again conducted (and recorded) No. 7. For Klemperer, the Ninth, which, like Nos. 2 and 4 and *Das Lied von der Erde*, he continued to conduct throughout his career, represented the pinnacle of Mahler's achievement, and the performances he gave were widely regarded as standing among his highest achievements.

Though he also performed music by Schoenberg, Strauss and Pfitzner in his opera house concerts and on two occasions tried to persuade Busoni to appear as soloist in his mammoth Piano Concerto,* Klemperer was no less eager to make a reputation as a conductor of the classics. On 17 January 1920 he prefaced Schoenberg's *Pelleas und Melisande* with Mozart's Symphony No. 40 in G minor, the first concert work by Mozart he had conducted, and it was greeted by the critics with a paean of praise. Walther Jacobs, the new critic of the *Kölnische Zeitung*, observed that Klemperer's use of a reduced string section had served to emphasise the dark and bitter aspects of the score. It was Mozart 'played *con espressione*, yet with a translucency and a rhythmic and dynamic finesse of a true classical style'.[7]

But the triumph of the first season of the opera house concerts was a performance on 1 June 1920 of Beethoven's 'Emperor' Concerto, in which the soloist was Artur Schnabel.† No musician of his generation was to be closer to Klemperer. The two men had first met when Schnabel had given a recital in Strasbourg during the war. Even earlier, Klemperer's perceptive mother had singled him out as a young pianist particularly worth hearing.[8] The Cologne concert initiated a collaboration that was to last until Schnabel's death. Several critics commented on an uncanny affinity that had seemed to exist between the two musicians, and Marianne, who would have been privy to her brother's reactions, confirmed that there had indeed been complete unanimity between them.[9] Both were representatives of a generation which had started to react against what they took to be the interpretative liberties that had become habitual among conductors and pianists alike in the late romantic era. Both stood for a certain *rappel à l'ordre*, for a restoration of a more intellectual approach to music. Relations between them remained friendly rather than intimate, and occasionally there were difficulties. Both composed and neither esteemed the other's music highly; Schnabel, who attached more importance to his compositions than did Klemperer, was vexed when his friend failed to champion them. Yet in a real sense they remained comrades-at-arms, standing for similar values in the jungle of concert life.

*   *   *

* In 1920 Busoni's fee was too high for Cologne. In 1923, after he had agreed to play, declining health prevented his appearance.   † See biographical glossary.

The Cologne opera was not in a happy condition in the autumn of 1919. It had ended the previous season with a deficit twice as large as had been foreseen and the personnel was so exhausted by the strains of the winter that two new productions had had to be cancelled. The new season opened with a strike of the chorus and the *corps de ballet*, whose wages had not kept pace with the inflation. As a result the theatre was shut for a week in September. The city's only orchestra also felt itself to be overworked and underpaid and discussion of the need for an additional orchestra rumbled on throughout the winter until it was finally vetoed by Adenauer on grounds of economy.

Klemperer's assiduously rehearsed opera house concerts inevitably contributed to the orchestra's burdens and the resentment they caused among the players may well have sparked off an unpleasant incident that occurred only two days after the opening concert. On 6 October, during the first act of *Die Walküre*, the wind suddenly went off the rails at 'Ein Wölfing kündet Dir das', where horns and bassoons rise to a sustained fortissimo chord in which wrong notes would be particularly audible. The opera house subseqently denied that what it euphemistically described as a practical joke had been due to hostility to Klemperer, while the orchestral players' chairman vehemently asserted that relations between them and their conductor were good.[10] But, as the *Rheinische Musik- und Theaterzeitung* (11 October 1919) observed, only a person with access to the orchestral material and detailed knowledge of the score could have inserted wrong notes at a passage where they could not fail to be noticed. Klemperer himself later maintained that his own score had been stuck together at a similar point.* A malevolent little poem that was published a few days after the incident and a performance of Schoenberg's String Quartet No. 2, for which Klemperer, as musical adviser of the Gesellschaft der Künste, had been responsible, is further evidence that there was bad blood in the air.

> O Otto, take my advice, play Schoenberg.
> Then everything will be in order
> For all his notes are so wrong
> That no one could make them wronger.[11]

Less than two weeks after the incident Klemperer achieved one of his greatest triumphs in Cologne with a new production of *Così fan tutte* that he staged as well as conducted. In contrast to the hostile reception that his stylised treatment of *Don Giovanni* had met in his first season, on this occasion a similar approach was received with widespread approval. Again,

* Thereafter he made it a rule to go through all scores – page by page – before a performance. In later years his daughter performed this task for him, if possible in his presence.

148

the scenery consisted mainly of curtains,* and the work's burlesque quality was emphasised by a circular cut-out that separated the front and rear stages, so that the audience had an impression of looking at much of the action through a large key-hole.† The critics made their usual derogatory comments on the text, but the music evoked enthusiasm and the performance was much praised for the warmth, irony and Goethean *Heiterkeit* that underlay its high spirits.

Klemperer threw himself into every detail: at one moment he disappeared from the podium to conduct the off-stage band, reappearing 'like Dr Miracle' in time to play the opening chord of the following recitative, which on this occasion he accompanied on a harpsichord. The cast, in which Johanna Klemperer scored particular success as Despina, was on a notably high level, and the quality of the orchestral playing lent the evening an air of enchantment. Dramatically and musically, the performance was held fully to justify Klemperer's insistence that he himself should occasionally produce as well as conduct. Yet paradoxically it was the last occasion in Cologne on which he was to exercise his recently acquired right to do so. Was he so disheartened by conditions within the opera house, and in particular by its lack of suitable designers, that he preferred not to immerse himself in the visual side of productions?

Apart from a new production of Cherubini's rarely heard *Les Deux Journées*,‡ which Klemperer conducted on 21 March 1920, the main events of the season consisted of the first performances in Cologne of recent major works by Germany's two leading composers. *Die Frau ohne Schatten* was mounted on 10 December 1919, exactly two months after its première in Vienna and Strauss's opulent score gave the Herr Hofrat scope to exercise his flair for elaborate scenic effects. But though the critics thought well of the performance (some claiming that it was superior to those in Vienna and Dresden, both theatres with a flourishing Strauss tradition), Klemperer later described it as 'musically and visually very mediocre'.[12] He did not in any case care for the work, which he never again conducted.

The second new work, Pfitzner's *Palestrina*, was more to his taste. Immediately after the première of *Così fan tutte* he travelled to Berlin to discuss a Cologne production with the composer. They had not met since the time of their conflict in Strasbourg, three years earlier, but Pfitzner was

---

* There is evidence that the delay of a production that had originally been scheduled for the previous season may have been due to Klemperer's rejection of the sets that Rémond had ordered.
† Stehle (*Kölnische Volkszeitung*, 18 October 1919) contrasted the simplicity of these arrangements with the elaborate scenery used at the Munich Residenztheater in 1897, when Strauss conducted an historic production that in effect restored the work to the repertory.
‡ Performed in Cologne under its usual German title of *Der Wasserträger*.

appeased by Klemperer's eagerness to mount his *magnum opus* and agreed
to produce it himself if Cologne would guarantee him twenty-five clear days
of rehearsals. Thorough as ever, Klemperer started his musical preparations
on 15 January 1920, no less than four months before the première. On
9 April he himself collected Pfitzner from Cologne's railway station. As
British military regulations prohibited German citizens from staying for
more than seven days in an hotel, private accommodation had to be found,
a prospect that did not at first appeal to Pfitzner, who had not been able
to afford to bring his wife, and felt lonely and unhappy in a strange city.
But he found that 'the theatre makes a better impression than in Berlin*
[and] the roles are well cast'.[13] A week later he wrote with unaccustomed
buoyancy to tell his wife that the performance promised to be good. And
so it proved, although no reviews appeared in the daily press: as a reprisal
for the withdrawal of their free passes to the dress rehearsal the singers
had banned the critics from attending, and they in their turn declined to
review the performance on the basis of the première alone.† The Cologne
public never warmed to a work that it doubtless found excessively long and
lacking in erotic appeal. But for once Pfitzner was fully satisfied. Three days
after the première he wrote to Rémond praising every aspect of a
performance that 'has won Cologne a place among the leading German
theatres. To mention only one name: the consummate achievement of Otto
Klemperer.' Klemperer himself was less than wholly enthusiastic about a
work whose text‡ appealed to him more than its music. But the composer's
staging he later described as 'very impressive'.[14]

Pfitzner's visit to Cologne did not, however, pass off without incident.
To entertain his distinguished visitor, Klemperer gave a party to which he
also invited Max Scheler. After dinner Scheler had the unhappy idea of
reading aloud and in French a poem by Claudel. Pfitzner got up and left:
he was, he explained, not prepared to listen to a French poem at such a
moment in German history.§

Klemperer should have known better: among Pfitzner's many phobias
was anything that smacked of popery. But his reaction was more than an
isolated instance of petulance. In *Die neue Aesthetik der musikalischen
Impotenz*, which had been published only a few months earlier, Pfitzner had
allowed himself to be carried from purely musical issues on to political

---

* Where *Palestrina* had been produced earlier in the season.
† At the work's revival in the following season Stehle, however, wrote (*Kölnische Volkszeitung*,
  17 September 1920) that, notably in the elaborate council scene, Klemperer's feeling for
  line and rhythm had enabled him to bring a stronger sense of unity to the score than Walter
  had achieved at the first performance in Munich three years earlier.
‡ Heyworth (ed.), *Conversations*, p. 48. 'There are passages one can compare to Goethe.'
§ *Conversations*, p. 48. *L'Annonce faite à Marie* had been removed from the repertory of the
  city theatre on account of its author's 'anti-German' writings during the war.

ground. What had begun as an assault on Paul Bekker's sociological approach to Beethoven and more particularly on the slogan, popular in progressive circles, that a new age demanded new music,* ended in a wild onslaught on the influence of international Jewry on German musical life. For Pfitzner, as for many of his compatriots, the decline of German romantic music was a symptom of national decadence and those who precipitated it were agents of decay, if not traitors. Thus, paradoxically, he ended by adopting a sociological interpretation of music, different in viewpoint but in other respects comparable to that which he had attacked in Bekker's writings.† The intertwining of political and cultural issues, which was to play so fatal a role in the rise of National Socialism, had already begun and Pfitzner was one of its heralds.‡ His evolution during and after the First World War from a respectable musical conservative to a shrill and xenophobic nationalist was to mirror only too closely a transformation that occurred throughout much of the German middle class, which naturally included an overwhelming majority of German musicians.

A gulf that was no longer merely personal had opened up between Klemperer and his old teacher. He again made unsuccessful attempts to stage *Christelflein* in Cologne, and in the summer of 1921 planned to conduct Pfitzner's new cantata, symptomatically entitled *Von deutscher Seele*. The performance never materialised. Thereafter all contact ceased until the summer of 1947, when, both at the nadir of their fortunes, they met in the ruins of Munich.

*　　　　　　　*　　　　　　　*

* To which Bekker, paradoxically, failed to respond with much insight or enthusiasm when a style that could be said to be characteristic of the Weimar period finally emerged in the mid-twenties.
† In one form or another the attitude was widespread. In a speech he gave on 18 June 1919 at a dinner in celebration of Pfitzner's fiftieth birthday, Thomas Mann approvingly singled out the 'backward turning' quality in his music as 'in reality a turning inward into the depths of the national soul...' 'Tischrede auf Pfitzner', (*Gesammelte Werke*, Vol. 10, pp. 417–22). By the mid-twenties, after Mann had publicly declared his loyalty to the Weimar Republic, relations between the two men had cooled (see Mann's letter to Pfitzner of 23 June 1925, *Briefe 1889–1936*, pp. 241–2), although even then Mann declared his sense of spiritual affinity with Pfitzner. 'It is open to us to become enemies', he wrote, 'but we will not be able to prevent future times from often coupling our names.' Relations were finally severed in 1933, when Pfitzner was one of those (Strauss was another) who signed a 'protest of the Wagner City of Munich' against the critical yet deeply appreciative address on Wagner, 'Vom Grossen und Leiden des Meisters', which Mann had delivered at the University on 10 February, only a few days after the Nazis had come to power. Contrary to what these attitudes might suggest, Pfitzner was too idiosyncratic and rebellious to become a Nazi and as a result enjoyed surprisingly little favour during the Third Reich.
‡ It is thus not surprising that, with honourable exceptions such as *Die Musik* and the newly founded *Melos*, the tone of the German musical press in the Weimar Republic could be described as 'Pfitznerian'.

The season of 1920/1 proved the most dispiriting of Klemperer's years in Cologne. The difficulties confronting the theatre increased as inflation accelerated. Early in August, writing to Busoni from the Friesian island of Norderney, where he was on holiday, Klemperer complained that 'in the last few months it has been impossible for me to do anything in Cologne that doesn't guarantee to bring in money for the theatre'. Worse was to come. The rise in prices bit hard into the incomes of those who, like Klemperer and his wife, were on fixed salaries.* Singers increasingly sought foreign engagements, paid in hard currency, and a continuous flow of short-term replacements led to decline in standards. Many members of the regular public could no longer afford to attend and their place was increasingly taken by foreigners and others who had done well out of the collapse of the German currency but did not make discriminating audiences.†

Such conditions inevitably brought artistic restrictions in their wake, and, instead of the customary new production, the season opened on 1 September with a revival of the production of *Don Giovanni* that had failed to find favour in January 1918 (see p. 122). Nonetheless Klemperer went to work on the musical preparation with his usual fervour. Aware of his own lack of learning, he had earlier in 1919 appointed a young musicologist, Arnold Schmitz, as his assistant. Every detail of the opera was called into question. The rival merits of the Prague and Vienna versions were debated at length (in contrast to the cuts he had made in 1918, Klemperer on this occasion omitted only 'Per queste due manine'). There was also discussion about the use of appoggiaturas. Unlike most of his contemporaries, Klemperer was not wholly unaware of their expressive function. But at a time when there was no general agreement about their use, his approach seems to have been casual. He may also have been influenced by Mahler's aversion from any form of decoration.‡ The essential influence on the performance was, however, literary, for it was Kierkegaard's 'Diary of a Seducer' in *Either-Or* that shaped Klemperer's view of the opera's hero as an embodiment of demoniac sensuality. It was an interpretation that excluded both the tragic approach favoured in the nineteenth century and the comic emphasis placed on the work more recently. As Schmitz has recalled, 'Even in the catalogue aria, laughter vanished.'[15]

The musical side of the revival was received with the enthusiasm that

---

* In 1920 Klemperer earned 18,000M and his wife 13,000M. In contrast the leading tenor received a salary of 39,000M.

† The British occupying forces had a long tail of camp followers who profited from the decline of the mark (see F. Tuohy, *Occupied 1918–1930*, pp. 132–40).

‡ For Mahler, as for the architect Adolf Loos, 'Lack of ornament is a sign of spiritual strength' (see Blaukopf, *Mahler*, p. 174).

Klemperer's Mozart habitually aroused in Cologne. But he himself was not content. To Dülberg he wrote a few days later, 'Here in Cologne it is dirty (in every sense) and noisy. *Don Giovanni*, *Der Rosenkavalier* and *The Bartered Bride* have taken place – as performances for me unsatisfying evenings.' Nor was the next new production calculated to arouse his enthusiasm. On 4 December Cologne, simultaneously with Hamburg, gave the first performance of Korngold's *Die tote Stadt*, a work that marked the apogee of Korngold's meteoric career. The local critics were not exacting where new music was concerned. But, although Klemperer put a restraining hand on some of the most *kitschig* effects in the score, Korngold's amalgam of Puccini, Strauss and Viennese operetta for once called down their wrath. 'This...romantic hash is nauseating', the young Arnold Schmitz thundered in the *Westdeutsche Wochenschrift* (7 January 1921), while Heinrich Lemacher prophetically stated that the score was on the level of cinema music.*[16] The opera, whose principal role was describing as calling for the qualities of a Carmen and a Salome, extended Johanna Klemperer's resources to their uttermost but provided her with one of the greatest successes of her career. That, however, did not prevent her husband from refusing to acknowledge applause at the end of what he doubtless found a distasteful occasion.

*   *   *

Yet light dawned even in the gloom of post-war Cologne. Up to this point of his career Klemperer, who was already thirty-five, had only once conducted outside Germany and Bohemia.† But news of his achievements was beginning to spread, for the season of 1920/1 brought invitations to appear in Austria and Spain.

With characteristic prudence, Klemperer arranged to conduct in Cologne on 11 December 1920 a Beethoven programme almost identical to that with which he was to make his bow seven days later in Vienna. His account of the Symphony No. 2 was warmly received by the Cologne critics, but his retouchings in the Fifth provoked much discussion. On this occasion Klemperer doubled woodwind and horns and used no fewer than nine double basses. In the finale, especially, additions were made to the flute part as well as to the brass.‡ In a review of the concert Arnold Schmitz posed

---

* As another Viennese composer, Ernst Toch (1887–1964), later put it in a comment much savoured by Klemperer, 'Korngold has always composed for Warner Brothers, only he was at first unaware of the fact.' In spite of Klemperer's low opinion of Korngold's music, the two men were on cordial terms, when in the thirties they both found themselves in Los Angeles.

† On 14 December 1917 the Cologne Opera and the Amsterdam Concertgebouw Orchestra had combined to give a single performance of *Der fliegende Holländer* in The Hague.

‡ Klemperer's attitude to retouchings varied considerably in the course of his career. If in his earlier days he tended to follow Mahler's practices, in the late twenties and early thirties,

the question of whether such alterations were legitimate. But he himself provided an answer by adding, 'I freely admit that confronted by the gigantic stature of the first movement of the Fifth, doubts did not survive the opening bars'.[17] For Marianne 'the Fifth was so shattering that it took me days to get over it. It was not the usual smooth, classical Beethoven, but embraced the revolutionary as well as the man of feeling. It was heaven and hell, death and resurrection.'[18]

The Viennese critics were scarcely less impressed. In a city where Mahler was still a living memory, several of them commented on Klemperer's uncanny resemblance to him, in profile and gestures as well as in an ability to get to the heart of the music's thought and feeling. In the *Neue Freie Presse* (12 January 1921) Josef Reitler wrote,

He has the dynamic, energy-laden movements of the young Mahler... In the Second the lion already showed his claws...in a dark, headstrong account of the finale. In the Fifth dynamics were pushed to extremes and beyond; the last movement made one hold one's breath. Every ounce of power was extracted from each *sforzando*. Every drum beat heralded a calamity.

Heinrich Kralik found the performances fiery but violent and the style of conducting over-theatrical.[19] Victor Junck, on the other hand, maintained that the interpretation stemmed from a musician who had worked on, thought through and experienced the scores to a point where what he gave was no longer his version but Beethoven's own.[20] Only four days after the concert the *Kölnische Zeitung* announced that Klemperer had been engaged to conduct a series of concerts during the following season in Vienna.*

By that time, however, he was already in Paris, on the first leg of his journey to Barcelona, where he had been engaged to conduct three operas at the Teatro Liceo. Klemperer had originally proposed that, as the entire repertory was sung in Italian, he should conduct *Don Giovanni*. The proposal was turned down flat. Mozart, he was told, 'bored the Spanish public'.[21] What Barcelona wanted from a German conductor was Wagner and more Wagner. Accordingly, *Tristan und Isolde*, *Tannhäuser* and, perhaps as a concession, *Fidelio* were agreed on, all to be sung in Italian. As usual the French capital delighted Klemperer, even if he did not feel as close to it as he did to Vienna. 'The women are splendidly dressed. You'd be amazed', he wrote to his wife, and then, belatedly realising the impact of

when he came under the influence of stricter musicological attitudes and a more severe climate of opinion, he grew to attach far more importance to *Werktreue* (see pp. 300 and 371). Later again, after the Second World War and perhaps in response to the less vigorous atmosphere of London, he tended to a more empirical approach, which he himself summed up with the Goethean tag, 'Sehe jeder, wie er's treibe' ('Let each decide for himself what he does') (*Conversations*, p. 35).
* Nothing came of these engagements, perhaps because of inflation, which became acute in Austria earlier than it did in Germany.

154

such a remark on the jealous Johanna, added, 'But they don't interest me and I thank you, my good child, that my eyes are fixed in a different and better direction.'[22]

On arrival in Barcelona he wrote at once to his mother. The orchestra was excellent and had applauded him after the first rehearsal. On 30 December *Tristan* was scheduled to begin at 8.15 pm with a cast that included Marcel Journet as Kurwenal and Richard Schubert as the hero. Klemperer was amazed that the audience only began to assemble over an hour later, so that the performance did not end until the early hours of the morning. The public smoked and talked loudly, even in the boxes giving directly on to the stage,[23] but did not hesitate to hiss any isolated note that displeased it. Nonetheless the performance went exceedingly well, at any rate so far as Klemperer's contribution was concerned. 'Walther', the critic of the leading Barcelona paper, *La Vanguardia*, wrote (31 December 1920) that

He succeeded in imparting to the orchestra expression, colour, detail, grandeur and passion...In our opinion he was outstanding in the first act, at the end of which a tremendous ovation, such as is rarely heard in the Liceo, brought him repeatedly on to the stage...Some spectators may have found his performance overfull of effects, but a work as passionate as this needs them.

It was an auspicious début. But Klemperer's mind was already fixed on *Fidelio*, which was to receive its first performance in Spain. On the day after *Tristan* he wrote to Johanna, briefly mentioned that the evening had gone well and then went on to urge his wife, who was about to leave Cologne to sing Marzelline, to work on her virtually non-existent Italian – and on her top notes.* The first night on 11 January 1921 brought another triumph. *La Vanguardia* (12 January) described Klemperer as 'the heart and soul of the performance' and the Leonore Overture No. 3, which was played at the end of the second act† brought another tumultuous reception. But the fact that he had consented to conduct the work with recitatives in place of the spoken dialogue was a concession that he long recalled with discomforture.

Tannhäuser on 22 January 1921 proved less satisfying. A mainly Spanish cast was uneven and Klemperer found the scenery 'scandalous'.[24] A projected performance of Bruckner's Symphony No. 7 (a work he had not previously conducted) had to be abandoned owing to lack of rehearsal time, and in its place Klemperer was obliged to serve up a series of Wagner excerpts ('Miserable, isn't it?').[25] But there were compensations.

---

* His apprehension on Johanna's account was well founded: *La Vanguardia* singled her top notes out for criticism in an otherwise favourable notice. So did *La Publicidad*.
† The Liceu public valued its intervals and the final scene of liberation was performed as a separate act.

The sun had shone and he had been so enchanted by a visit to Montserrat that he had slept at the monastery, so as to be able to attend morning Mass as well as Vespers. If the artistic satisfaction of the visit had been meagre, he left Barcelona with hard currency in his pocket and a contract to return for six weeks in the course of the following season.

*   *   *

Of far more consequence for Klemperer's subsequent career were his first appearances in Berlin. In 1920, Otto Schneider, the editor of the Viennese periodical *Musikblätter des Anbruchs*,* who had established a series of concerts of recent music bearing the journal's name, invited him to conduct two programmes in the German capital. The first of these was to consist of Schoenberg's earliest orchestral works, *Verklärte Nacht* and the symphonic poem *Pelleas und Melisande*, which Klemperer had already performed in Cologne on 17 January 1920, when it had been tepidly received. That his choice should have fallen on two scores composed in a late romantic idiom around the turn of the century, rather than any of the series of great works in which Schoenberg had subsequently breached the frontiers of tonality, was not mere chance. To Klemperer's ears those scores sounded problematic, as they were indeed to remain for the rest of his life.†

During the winter of 1920/1 Schoenberg happened to be living less than a hundred and fifty miles from Cologne. As food and heat had grown increasingly hard to come by in Vienna, Dutch friends and admirers had invited him to spend the hard months at the small seaside resort of Zandvoort, where he gave private lessons as well as a course in Amsterdam. On 21 October 1920 Klemperer travelled to Amsterdam to attend a Concertgebouw concert of Schoenberg's music, consisting of *Verklärte Nacht* and the Five Orchestral Pieces, Op. 16. It may have been on that

---

* From 1929 simply *Anbruch*. Established in 1919 as a platform for the propagation of contemporary music by the publishing house of Universal Edition, which through the talents of its managing director, Emil Hertzka (1869–1932), had on its books most of the outstanding composers of the first half of the twentieth century. *Anbruch* fulfilled this role with *panache*, at any rate until 1933.

† The only occasion on which Klemperer ventured into this field was when he conducted *Pierrot Lunaire* in Cologne on 12 May 1922. In spite of the fact that the soloist was none other than Marie Gutheil-Schoder, one of the great Elektras of her time, the critics assailed the score as 'pathological', 'distorted' and 'without constructive powers', while Gerhard Tischer, the chauvinist editor of the *Rheinische Musik- und Theaterzeitung* (20 May 1922) denounced the performance of such a work 'at a time when the very existence of our nation and its culture are in question'. Klemperer himself remained ambivalent in his attitude to Schoenberg's masterpiece. Recalling the performance almost twenty-three years later, he described Gutheil-Schoder as 'wonderful' and the music as 'genial' ('of genius'). But he did not at all care for Giraud's poems. (Letter to Helene Hirschler, 4 February 1945.)

occasion that he arranged to return to Zandvoort to study the scores he had programmed for Berlin with the composer. For that purpose Klemperer visited Schoenberg in Zandvoort later in the winter.*

Thus equipped, Klemperer advanced on Berlin for his all-important début. For the Schoenberg concert, which took place in the Philharmonie on 16 April 1921, he had no fewer than five rehearsals. Adolf Weissmann, Berlin's most widely read critic, attended one of them and praised the ability of 'the most gifted of the younger conductors' to exact what he wanted from the Berlin Philharmonic Orchestra. 'No note, no pause is unimportant to him. [But] he is possessed, so that precision becomes poetry.' Yet the concert, which opened with *Verklärte Nacht*, did not begin without a contest of wills between the conductor and his audience, curiously similar to that which had preceded his first appearance at the Hamburg Stadttheater eleven years earlier. Weissmann wrote:

He wants to begin. No hurry. The well-to-do Berlin public does not regard a mixture of coughing, whispering and shuffling as constituting a disturbance. Not Otto Klemperer. He waits. Five minutes. Affectation? A real concert-goer shouts, 'Get on with it!' No hurry. And the D major pianissimo that opens the music like a breath justifies him. That is how it is. The spirit of Mahler lives on.[26]

The much respected Walther Schrenk considered that, although Klemperer was undoubtedly a fine musician of exceptional intelligence, he had not achieved complete clarity in the elaborate polyphonic web of *Pelleas und Melisande*.[27] But the verdict was overwhelmingly favourable. Two of the senior members of Berlin's formidable corps of critics vied with each other in their enthusiasm.† In the *Vossiche Zeitung* (20 April 1921) Max Marschalk wrote that

The way in which he mastered the Philharmonic Orchestra and secured extremely lively and plastic performances of both works corresponded with the reputation that had preceded him. From the first bars his conducting gave an impression of complete control...He has nothing of the rostrum virtuoso, yet he is too wise to be unaware that the fullness and power of a personality has to prove itself, even when a conductor dispenses with irrelevant gestures.

Oscar Bie, the shrewd and highly esteemed critic of the *Berliner Börsen-Courier* (21 April), noted that with years Klemperer's conducting had become quieter and more controlled. The orchestra, he wrote, had played with incomparable precision and clarity.

When Klemperer returned to Berlin scarcely a month later on 18 May it was to conduct a performance of Mahler's Symphony No. 2 in

---

* It has not proved possible to establish dates. In letters to the author, Max Deutsch, at that time Schoenberg's assistant, confirmed that the visit took place and that Klemperer studied *Pelleas und Melisande*, the Five Orchestral Pieces and *Erwartung* with their composer.
† During the Weimar Republic music criticism in Berlin reached a notably high level.

commemoration of the tenth anniversary of the composer's death.* No music was closer to his heart than this score, which had first brought him together with his mentor, and for Oscar Bie, among others, it was as though

Once again one had the impression of seeing and hearing Mahler. Klemperer's firm and serious approach, based on long and tireless rehearsing, gave the work a monumental greatness and incomparable musical clarity...And with that, no emotionalising, no trivialisation, no softness, no rhetoric, only power and necessity. Despite the summery heat and a packed hall there was full-voiced enthusiasm for this ardent, attractively individual and compelling conductor.[28]

In contrast to the Schoenberg concert, to which reactions had ranged from the guarded to the ecstatic, Klemperer's second appearance in Berlin was greeted by unanimous praise. In *Signale* (25 May 1921) Walther Hirschberg put his finger on what was to become a lifelong characteristic of Klemperer's finest performances.

Sobriety (Sachlichkeit) and ecstasy are the poles of his conducting. He has the ability to sink himself in a work so as to convey its innermost core, to place formidable competence and composure at the service of emotion, so that intellect and emotion become one...Never in a performance of a Mahler symphony have I had such reassuring certainty that it was entirely as its composer intended it to be.

As after his appearances in Vienna and Barcelona, Berlin also led to new offers. Schneider at once invited him to conduct Schoenberg's *Gurrelieder*† in Berlin and Bruckner and Franz Schreker evenings in Amsterdam, where a series of *Anbruch* concerts had also been established. There were abortive negotiations with Mary Garden, who was about to take over the artistic direction of the Chicago Opera.‡ Of more significance for Klemperer's future was the reputation he had established in Berlin. When, eight months later, Arthur Nikisch, the conductor of the Berlin Philharmonic Orchestra, died, three possible successors were discussed in the capital's press: Furtwängler, Walter and Klemperer. Weissmann wrote[29] that Klemperer was one of the strongest candidates, as a conductor who was both in the highest sense *suggestiv* and would meet the musical demands of the times. Schrenk[30] considered that Klemperer had the strongest claims of all. Furtwängler was appointed to the position, which, apart from a brief post-war interlude, he held until his death in 1954. But Klemperer had,

---

* In future years whenever possible he conducted a work by Mahler on or around this date.
† The project did not materialise. Klemperer never conducted the masterpiece of Schoenberg's earliest period, although on more than one occasion he planned to do so.
‡ Mary Garden (1874–1967), Scottish soprano who in 1900 became famous overnight, when in the middle of the first performance of Charpentier's *Louise* she took over the title role. Two years later she sang the role of Mélisande in the first production of Debussy's opera. A disastrous director of the Chicago Opera in 1922/3.

quite suddenly, come to be regarded as one of the country's outstanding young conductors.

*   *   *

On holiday that summer at Kampen on the North Friesian island of Sylt, Klemperer must have felt that a turning point had arrived in his fortunes. Had the day of liberation from Cologne at last arrived? At that very moment the position of music director fell vacant in the renowned Dresden opera house. Yet, paradoxically, he did not leap at the prospect. 'The moment may be ripe', he wrote to his wife (6 July 1921), 'but unfortunately not the solution.' A similar position in a more prestigious theatre held little appeal for him. What he hated in Cologne was less the grey city itself than the conditions of work at a repertory opera, and these would also have confronted him in Dresden. There were other reasons for staying put: the economic outlook in Germany was increasingly bleak. Klemperer (when not in a manic condition) was a cautious man and on this occasion his prudence proved justified. One by one, the prospects that had opened up so invitingly after his Berlin triumph faded. The *Anbruch* concerts collapsed, negotiations with Chicago came to nothing and the Dresden position went to Fritz Busch.* Within Germany Klemperer did not give a single concert in a major musical centre outside Cologne (his guest appearances were limited to Wiesbaden, Essen and Hanover) during the coming two seasons. Three years were to pass before he was again to conduct in Berlin.

From the fact that in the summer of 1921 he was already looking for a larger apartment, it is clear that he saw no prospect of deliverance from Cologne. More accommodation had in any case become a pressing necessity. After his marriage, Klemperer had moved into the small flat in the Mozartstrasse, a featureless late nineteenth-century street but conveniently close to the opera house, which Johanna had taken on her arrival in Cologne in 1916. With the birth of a child this accommodation had become increasingly cramped, but Klemperer, who was also maintaining his parents and younger sister in a separate establishment, could not afford to move into more spacious quarters. Marianne's engagement to be married† brought the problem to a head, for their parents, both well into their seventies, had become too old to live alone. In 1922 a move was made into a larger flat in the Mozartstrasse, where the family remained until Klemperer left Cologne in the summer of 1924.

There Johanna and Ida Klemperer lived for the first time under one roof,

---

* See biographical glossary. It has not proved possible to establish whether Klemperer in fact applied for the post.
† In 1922 she married Helmuth Joseph, a surgeon who had by chance attended Ida Klemperer when in 1921 she had been involved in an accident with a bicyclist.

an arrangement that brought predictable tensions in its wake. Ida was a strong-minded woman, used to running her own household. The Bohemian Johanna was far from a model housekeeper. There were abundant grounds for discord* between the two women and on more than one occasion Klemperer begged his wife to be patient.

If you find it difficult to get on with my mother, think of the basic differences in your characters and, as the young one, be the cleverer and more conciliatory. Be sure that anything you do for my parents, you do for *me*. And think of their age.[31]

* * *

The principal event of the first half of the 1921/2 season was the local première of *Der Schatzgräber*,† the first of three operas by Franz Schreker that Klemperer was to conduct in Cologne. In the years immediately after the war Schreker seemed set to challenge Strauss as Germany's foremost opera composer.‡ There were indeed those who rated him higher than Strauss. Among them was Paul Bekker who had hailed him as 'certainly the strongest musico-dramatic talent we have seen since Wagner'. Bekker's advocacy of Schreker's operas was based on his belief that they 'return to music written for the stage the rights that have been usurped by drama. They win back territory lost in the nineteenth century and return to opera its true vocation.'[32] According to this view they thus formed a variant of the general reaction against Wagnerian music drama and the subsequent preponderance of literary influence in opera, as exemplified in Strauss's collaborations with Hofmannsthal.§

In later years Klemperer was mildly embarrassed to be confronted with evidence of the warmth of this earlier advocacy of Schreker's operas and his more than cordial relations with the man. ‖ They had met before the war at Alma Mahler's in Vienna, where the encounter does not seem to

---

* Storms arose in the most improbable contexts. During the food shortage in 1922/3, Fräulein Schwab withdrew Ida's breakfast egg. Ida held it against Johanna, who remained blithely unaware of what had occurred.

† The first performance had taken place in Frankfurt in January 1920.

‡ See biographical glossary.

§ Bekker was by no means alone in his admiration of Schreker. In 1920 *Musikblätter des Anbruch* produced a Schreker number. By 1921, when Schreker was still no more than forty-three, two biographies and a study of his music had already been published.

‖ The references to Schreker in *Conversations* are all disparaging and in 1958 Klemperer declined to become an honorary member of the Schreker society. But the letters he wrote to Schreker in the twenties present a different picture. When, over forty years later, he reread these, he wrote to Schreker's widow (rather distantly, one might think, in view of his earlier reputed admiration for a notable beauty), expressing the hope that she had no plans for publication, as the opinions expressed therein were 'quite without importance' (letter of 1 December 1966). From the viewpoint of a biographer, however, they are of considerable importance, if only for the light they throw on the esteem that Schreker's music enjoyed immediately after the First World War.

160

have been over-friendly.* But during Schreker's presence in Cologne at the time of the final rehearsals for *Der Schatzgräber* and its première on 30 September 1921 mutual admiration led to something close to friendship. In a letter written to Bekker two days later Schreker was sharply critical of Rémond's production, which he found 'virulently tasteless'. But the musical side of the performance he described in lyrical terms.

Under Klemperer everything was of the greatest subtlety, precise, full of temperament, with complete freedom in the shaping and interpretation. In a word, complete bliss, joy – and amazement...The postlude I shall probably never again hear so beautiful and moving. It was...fulfilment. And in addition a great success. Even the press was decent.†

Klemperer was hardly less enthusiastic about the work itself. Two unusually warm letters that he wrote to the composer within a few days of Schreker's departure from Cologne went well beyond conventional politeness – never a commodity he dealt in – and in them the 'Sehr verehrter Herr Professor' became 'Lieber Freund'.[33] Indeed, the friends were now *per Du*, an intimacy that Klemperer accorded to few men in the course of his life.

When they met again in Essen in May 1922, plans were made for an extensive collaboration. In the coming season Cologne would mount a new production of Schreker's first opera, *Der ferne Klang*. The following year it would give the first performance of the as yet uncompleted *Irrelohe*, and in repayment for this honour would follow it with a week of Schreker operas.[34] The fact that Klemperer, usually so wary in the choice of new works, should on this occasion have accepted an unfinished opera suggests that his commitment to Schreker's music was more far-reaching than he subsequently liked to admit.

Schreker was not the only composer whom Klemperer performed that season in Cologne and whose music was subsequently to fall into unwarranted neglect from which it has only recently started to emerge. In 1921 he read with pleasure *Der Zwerg*, a one-act opera by Alexander von Zemlinsky, whom he had encountered in unhappy circumstances in Munich ten years earlier (see p. 60). The work impressed him, but Zemlinsky was at first unwilling to grant the right of first performance to an opera house that he plainly considered provincial. Only his respect for

* Alma Mahler, *Mein Leben*, pp. 62–3. After Schreker had played an excerpt from his early opera, *Das Spielwerk und die Prinzessin*, Klemperer unkindly told him that he could not distinguish any themes.
† The work indeed made a deep impression on the local critics. The *Rheinische Musik- und Theaterzeitung* (15 October 1921) saluted it as of 'incomparably greater significance than *Die Frau ohne Schatten*.' The level-headed Heinrich Lemacher asserted that, after Strauss and Pfitzner, Schreker was 'incontestably in the front rank of German opera composers' (*Rheinische Volkswacht*, 1 October 1921).

Klemperer's abilities and the assurance they provided of a first-rate musical performance overcame his hesitations.* The Theatre Commission made a special grant to enable Zemlinsky to attend rehearsals and a cordial relationship came into existence that was to bear fruit five years later when Zemlinsky agreed to serve as conductor under Klemperer at the Berlin Kroll Opera. At its first performance on 28 May 1922, the work was admired for its fine craftsmanship and delicate instrumentation†.

In contrast, *Petrushka*, which was its companion piece in the double-bill and had not previously been heard in Cologne, divided the critics. A few recognised it as a work of real, if alien, originality. Others dismissed it as 'a silly pantomime', 'wry and dehumanised', 'mere noise' and, strangest of all, 'the work of a Dadaist' (a familiar term of abuse in Max Ernst's home town). In Cologne, music was still widely equated with German music. A German musician who *was*, however, interested was none other than Richard Strauss. On 30 May he wrote to Klemperer from Karlsbad, congratulated him on the success of *Der Zwerg*, and asked where he could obtain the music of *Petrushka* and the permission to perform it, which, he claimed, he had been unsuccessfully seeking for two years.‡

Klemperer's performance of *Petrushka* marked the beginning of an association with the music of the twentieth-century composer to whom he was to feel closest.[35] Yet some of Stravinsky's scores he regarded as beyond him. When Arthur Bliss and Adrian Boult visited Cologne in March 1923 they were astonished to hear him admit in front of young members of his staff that he could not beat the irregular metres in *The Rite of Spring*, a work which he indeed never conducted.[36]

*   *   *

In November 1921 Klemperer returned to Barcelona to conduct three cycles of *The Ring*. On this occasion, however, the going was less smooth.

In the theatre everything is in a frightful muddle...No tubas, no horns, an impossible Fasolt, etc., etc. How Mestres§ conceives that *Das Rheingold* can be done without a producer, I cannot imagine. *Wie Gott will, halt ich still*‖ ... Barcelona is

---

* 'Klemperer ist *jemand*' ('Klemperer is *someone*') he wrote to Universal Edition on 10 May 1921 to inform his publishers that he had given the right of first performance to Cologne.
† At a revival in 1981 at the Hamburg State Opera (after more than half a century of total neglect) under the title of *Der Geburtstag der Prinzessin*, it also revealed itself as a work of macabre dramatic flavour and considerable theatrical impact.
‡ This surprising information would have gratified Auden, on the walls of whose Lower Austrian home portraits of his two house deities, Strauss and Stravinsky, confronted one another with apparent mutual distaste. In fact, Strauss never conducted *Petrushka* in spite of his concern in the early twenties to extend the meagre balletic repertory of the Vienna State Opera. See also p. 246n.
§ Joan Mestres y Calvet (1887–1955). Impresario of the Gran Teatro del Liceo 1915–47.
‖ As God wills....

162

beautiful, the sun does me good...and the cynicism is better than our (all too often) false seriousness.[37]

The general unfamiliarity of all concerned with the cycle, which was being sung in German for the first time in Spain,* made the rehearsals strenuous, and the brass, in particular, continued to be inadequate. To judge from notices in *La Vanguardia*, the orchestral playing improved as the cycle advanced, but 'Walther' was distinctly more temperate in his praise than he had been in the preceding season. At the end of Klemperer's visit there was discussion with Mestres about a Mozart season during the following winter. But the director of the Liceo would or could not meet his demands for rehearsals and the project foundered. Klemperer's thoughts had constantly been with his wife, who was making her début at the Berlin State Opera,† and he was glad when his visit ended. On this occasion the hard currency he had earned did not compensate for the artistic frustrations he had suffered.

Back in Cologne Klemperer was immediately confronted with another *Ring*. Since his *Così fan tutte* of October 1919 he had made no further attempt to bring about any reform of staging in Cologne. New sets, when they could be afforded, were ordered from the theatre workshops (*Malersaal*‡), which Rudolf Hraby had headed since 1902. Hraby's main function was to keep old sets in repair and to execute new productions as well as he could. In fact these were often assembled out of stock from an *Opernfundus*, a collection of sets that would meet most needs. Thus the Cologne *Ring* was a hotch-potch of designs provided over the years by Hraby and Hans Wildermann among others. The resulting lack of any stylistic unity irked Klemperer and on this occasion he was able to insist that at any rate some scenes be newly designed by Wildermann, with whom he had worked happily on the Barmen *Parsifal* of 1914. Significantly, Wildermann's name did not appear on the programmes and such comment as his mildly stylised set (or sets) aroused ranged from the tepid to the condemnatory.§ That seems to have been Klemperer's final attempt to achieve any visual renewal in Cologne.

*   *   *

* *Das Rheingold* was divided into two acts!
† In *Die Vögel*, a recent opera by Walter Braunfels, in which she had enjoyed great success when Klemperer had himself conducted it earlier that winter in Cologne (11 November 1921). In Berlin she was deputising for the celebrated Maria von Ivogün.
‡ The very title illustrates the extent to which stage design was still regarded as a function of painting.
§ It has not proved possible to ascertain precisely for which acts Wildermann designed new sets. In the catalogue to the exhibition (1975), 'Von Dadamax bis zum Grüngürtel', the design reproduced on p. 194 is said to be for *Die Walküre*. Reviews of the revival in January/February 1922 speak only of new sets for *Siegfried* and *Götterdämmerung*.

163

Up to the summer of 1922 inflation had brought great suffering to Germany but had been regarded as an aftermath of war. Now, however, a steady decline of the purchasing power of the mark started to snowball in a way that had no precedent in history. The collapse of the currency was triggered by the assassination on 22 July of Walther Rathenau, the German Foreign Minister, by right-wing extremists in Berlin. The period between that date and 26 November 1923, when a new currency was introduced, has been aptly described as 'the terrible year when money went mad'.[38] The very foundations of an ordered society (nowhere so highly rated as in Germany) seemed to tremble. By 31 August the exchange rate of the mark to the dollar had sunk from 350 to 2,000. Three months later it had reached 9,000.

This monetary debacle affected every aspect of life in Cologne. There had already been complaints that those with access to strong currencies were buying up luxuries, such as opera tickets. But by the summer of 1922 a sizeable part of the population could no longer afford the essentials of life. In contrast, the countryside, which had produce to sell, was prospering. More sinister in its political implications was the fact that all those living on fixed incomes, which included a sizeable part of the middle class, found themselves well-nigh dispossessed within a period of a few months. The public mood grew uglier and on 14 November food rioting broke out in Cologne.

The opera, which had a subsidy of five million marks, found itself confronted at the beginning of the 1922/3 season with a deficit of ten times that amount. The price of seats was raised threefold, a modest increase that caused bitter complaints about foreigners, who were estimated to form at least half the audiences.* Leading singers, such as Schorr and Achsel, left for other theatres. Others were often absent on guest appearances. Complaints about the level of performances grew increasingly sharp as the season advanced and at one moment towards the end of the winter the prospect of closure threatened. In April 1923 in an attempt to earn hard currency, the entire company travelled across the Dutch frontier to give a performance in Arnhem of *Figaro*, which Klemperer conducted.

That was not the only source of tension in Cologne's musical life. Difficulties between Klemperer and Hermann Abendroth, the conductor of the Gürzenich concerts, had existed since Klemperer had established a rival series in the opera house. These stemmed less from personal animosity (Klemperer was not an envious colleague) than from divergent musical sympathies and, above all, conflicting claims on the city's single orchestra. The fact that in the 1922/3 season Abendroth invited Klemperer to

---

* *Kölner Tageblatt*, 1 September 1922. On 14 October the occupying authorities belatedly consented to the introduction of special seat prices for foreigners.

conduct his Missa in C at a Gürzenich concert and himself conducted the remainder of the programme suggests that they were not on bad terms personally. But the underlying tensions came to a head in the autumn of 1922, when the two conductors held joint auditions for a new leader of the cello section and could not agree on an appointment. As neither would give way, in early December they were summoned before the *Oberbürgermeister*, Konrad Adenauer. Abendroth, who was the senior, threatened resignation if he did not have his way. Adenauer turned to Klemperer, 'Now we don't want Herr Abendroth to resign, do we?'[39] Klemperer could only murmur, 'Of course not.' Thereupon Adenauer endorsed Abendroth's choice and the audience seemed to be at an end, when he asked Klemperer to remain. 'I only wanted to tell you', he said, 'that the city has decided to grant you the title and function of *General-musikdirektor*.' There were few things that Klemperer hated more than to be addressed by subordinates as 'Herr General', as was then customary in Germany, but this civic accolade* represented official recognition of the position he had come to occupy in Cologne.

*   *   *

It says much for the deep roots of opera in German life and for the resilience of Rémond's leadership that at such a difficult period the Cologne theatre succeeded in mounting several new productions that could be regarded as enterprising even in easier times. On 1 November Weber's *Euryanthe* was staged in celebration of the work's centenary. Klemperer, who used Mahler's shortened version, conducted with dramatic fire, but even his committed advocacy could not gain much public support for this misshapen and dramatically flawed masterpiece.†

On 8 December there followed the first performance of Janáček's *Kát'a Kabanová* to be given outside his native Czechoslovakia.‡ Since he had conducted *Jenůfa* four years earlier, Klemperer had been eager to do another Janáček opera. The only work available was *The Adventures of Mr Brouček*, of which there was then, however, no German translation.§ *Kát'a*

---

* It was publicly announced on 8 December 1922.
† Although Klemperer described the work in a letter to Busoni (15 September) as a '*Ritterstück mit Musik*' (a 'tale of chivalry with music') and never conducted it after he had left Cologne, it was an opera he remained particularly fond of. In 1970, at the age of eighty-five, he made a determined but unsuccessful attempt to record it.
‡ The first performance had taken place in Brno on 23 October 1921.
§ In 1920 and 1921 Klemperer made three fruitless enquiries of the publishers, but Max Brod, Janáček's champion and the translator of *Jenůfa*, refused to translate *Mr Brouček* on the grounds that its second part glorified war. On 16 March 1921 Janáček wrote to tell the conductor, Otakar Ostrčil, that a translation had been commissioned from another source, as Klemperer intended to perform the work the following season. This translation never materialised and the work was not given in Germany until 1959.

Kabanová was also dogged by misfortune. In the course of the rehearsals Felix Dahn was taken ill, so that Klemperer assumed responsibility for the production. Then he himself fell sick, with a result that much of the musical preparation was undertaken by Hans Wilhelm Steinberg,* a young, locally born conductor, who had originally joined the back desk of the second violins of the city orchestra direct from Cologne Musikhochschule but in 1919 had been dismissed by Klemperer for disobeying his bowing instructions. Some months later, however, he had again attracted attention while accompanying at auditions, after which Klemperer took him on as an unpaid assistant. In June 1922 he at short notice conducted a performance of *La Juive*, in which Rose Pauly made her début in Cologne. After that performance Klemperer commented 'I admired the conviction with which you conducted the wrong tempi' and engaged him as conductor for the following season.†

Kat'a Kabanova was for the most part received with a hostility similar to that which had greeted *Jenůfa* four years earlier, and the Cologne critics yet again demonstrated their inability to assess foreign works by standards other than those they applied to German music. Walther Jacobs dismissed 'Janatschek' (as he insisted on writing the composer's name) as a musician with a primitive technique. He was, Jacobs maintained, unable to develop his ideas, so that the score remained a patchwork, the plot was *stockrussisch*, the characters were 'rooted in an alien tradition', the vocal writing was mere 'Sprechgesang'.[40] Anton Stehle asked whether it was appropriate to perform a Czech opera at a time 'when an association of Czech property owners has been set up in Germany'.[41] Only Heinrich Lemacher found praise for the music's intensity and individual construction,[42] but even he (like the rest of Cologne's critics) made no mention of the fact that the first scene of the second act had been omitted.‡ Rose Pauly scored a great success in the title role and Klemperer's conducting was highly praised. But, because the production had been delayed by illness, he was obliged to leave for Rome immediately after the opening night. Ostensibly on account of the death of a member of the cast and Klemperer's six-week absence, the first performance of the production proved to be its last. But it is hard to

---

* Later William Steinberg. See biographical glossary.
† Although relations subsequently cooled, Steinberg regarded Klemperer as having played a crucial role in his early development. 'What don't I owe to Klemperer, to his schooling, his example, to the comradely guidance of the still young master, to the fiery debates and analyses that continued throughout the nights, to the close collaboration of the days... You want to know my artistic creed...? Can I speak of a line from Weber to Mahler, and at a respectful distance from that of a Klemperer, as the practical realisation of music drama, of the dramatic idea...through a trinity of sound, sight and movement?' (*Prager Presse*, 26 June 1927).
‡ Janáček commented on this in a letter (19 February 1923) to Universal Edition and punctuated his observation with an exclamation mark.

avoid an impression that there was little enthusiasm for the work in the Cologne Opera House.

*   *   *

A new production of *Siegfried* was to open the Roman opera season on Boxing Day. In the autumn Klemperer had told Busoni[43] that he was apprehensive at the prospect of performing Wagner with Italian singers and an inexperienced orchestra. Busoni, sensing a German aspersion on Italian musical abilities, reacted sharply:

I am sorry to note that you expect so little. When an Italian orchestra puts its mind to it, it is second to none and quicker than most in grasping a point, a characteristic that in its turn explains why it lacks the patience for systematic rehearsing. Everything there is done on the spur of the moment. Personally, I regret that it should be *Siegfried*, which can only serve to deflect my country from (recognising) its true identity...[44]

As Busoni foresaw, matters went better than Klemperer had anticipated. After a dozen rehearsals the orchestra acquitted itself well, even if a number of tuba passages had to be simplified. Klemperer found his Siegfried, Amedeo Bassi, 'an excellent artist'* and Luigi Nardi (Mime) 'a small, highly gifted man with a fine voice'.[45] Only the Brünnhilde proved inadequate and Klemperer was obliged to put his objections to her on paper so that her contract could be revoked. He also much admired the energies of Emma Carelli, who since 1912 had been director of the Teatro Costanzi (where the Rome opera was housed). He had, he wrote to Johanna, witnessed her dressing down a prompter. 'It was amazing. *I* cannot make such a scene.'[46] That was a tribute from one master to another. The fact that the producer did nothing but await the conductor's instructions also met with his approval. He was, however, less than delighted to discover that it was customary for a new conductor to pay a call on the principal critics. Klemperer hired a car for the purpose, but was relieved to find only two of the gentlemen at home.

The opening night of the season was a great occasion.

You must realise [he wrote to Johanna on 28 December] that the traditional opening of the theatre on Boxing Day throws the entire city into a state of excitement. It's a topic of conversation days beforehand and on the evening itself there is enormous expectation...

[The performance] began at 8.30 pm. As soon as it was dark the conductor entered. Then the house lights became brilliant again and (as the Crown Prince was present at the head of the royal family) I conducted the Marcia Reale...The entire march was applauded. After that the fascist anthem was played...More applause. Then

---

* Amedeo Bassi (1874–1949). Sang Parsifal, Loge and Siegfried under Toscanini at the Scala.

it was dark again, whereupon there was a great hubbub – '*Luce, luce*'. A group of students in the gallery, who had scores, wanted the lights to remain up. Two minutes noise. I lift my baton. Deathly silence and *Siegfried* begins...In spite of this and that the performance in the main went well.[47]

For the Catholic convert, his first visit to the Holy City was a major event and for that reason (as well as economy) Klemperer at first lodged at a Franciscan monastery. It proved unexpectedly chilly (there was, he noted with surprise, no central heating) and it was not long before he took refuge in an hotel, although he did not feel able to afford a room with bath. In every other respect Rome enchanted him. He was particularly struck by the brilliant clarity of the interiors of the churches, in contrast to the half-light he was used to in Germany. He also shrewdly noted that, 'Everything that is said about "Italian passion" is untrue. The people are lively, but inwardly clear and rational.' He attended a rehearsal of a concert conducted by his old patron, Oscar Fried, whose self-preoccupation and musical limitations he had begun to find irksome.[48] There he met Alfredo Casella,* with whom he was to develop cordial ties. On New Year's Day he heard Mussolini speak from his traditional rostrum, the balcony on the Palazzo Venezia, and was much impressed by his programme of work and discipline. 'It's a face one doesn't forget', Klemperer wrote to Johanna two days later. He also indiscreetly told her that he had taken a carriage to the Pincio to enjoy the midday sun, whereupon she at once wrote to ask who had accompanied him.

Although there had been some questioning in the Roman press of the need to engage a German conductor for Wagner, who was himself still 'an ideological issue' in Italy,[49] and moments of tension in the rehearsals,† the visit was clearly a success, for Emma Carelli urged Klemperer's merits on her husband, Walter Mochi, who ran the opera season at the Teatro Colón in Buenos Aires. Klemperer turned down his offer: he now felt sure enough of himself to refuse to play second string to Strauss, who had already been engaged for the German season. In any case his mind was elsewhere: while in Rome the Deutsches Opernhaus in Berlin had offered him the post of director and he decided to return home by way of the German capital.

But he was in no hurry to do so. On 26 January 1923 Toscanini‡ was

---

* Alfredo Casella (1883–1947), a leading exponent of neo-classicism in Italy.
† The bass tuba, a *carabiniere*, sent a contra-bassoon as substitute. Klemperer is reported to have shouted, 'Lei non essere tuba! Io volere *mia* tuba. Con il *Sigfrido* di Wagner niente scherzare' (Frajese, *Dal Costanzi al Teatro dell'Opera*, Vol. 1, pp. 143–4, and *Musica* of 31 December 1922).
‡ Arturo Toscanini (see biographical glossary) had become omnipotent artistic director of the Scala in 1921, a position he retained until 1929. Thus Klemperer first heard him at the apogee of his operatic career. Nonetheless, Toscanini was still comparatively little

to conduct a new production of *Die Meistersinger* and a small detour enabled Klemperer to attend. In spite of a letter of introduction from Emma Carelli he failed to meet the great man, but the conductor made a deeper impression on him than any he had heard since Mahler. Six years later, on the occasion of Toscanini's visit to Berlin at the head of La Scala, Milan, Klemperer wrote of that *Meistersinger*, 'I have not heard a comparably complete performance of the work in any other theatre in the world'.[50] In an interview in the *Corriere della Sera* on the following day he declared that he had found Toscanini's style 'simple, natural and honest' – for Klemperer the highest praise. He had, he continued, rarely experienced such total unity between stage and orchestra. In Germany, where the season lasted ten months and the repertory was vast, such care could not, alas, be devoted to an individual production.

To Max Hofmüller, who met him at Munich station on the next leg of his journey, he admitted that he had found many of Toscanini's tempi too rigid and too fast, so that the finale of the second act had been barely singable. Notwithstanding this reservation, Klemperer recognised in Toscanini a man able to impose his will on the entire apparatus of opera so as to achieve an integrated musico-dramatic whole, such as remained his own as yet unfulfilled ambition. In that respect, at any rate, Toscanini was for him a model second only to Mahler. He was also not without influence on the more implacable musical style that Klemperer was to adopt as the decade advanced.[51]

known in Germany. In 1921, Nikisch, who had just heard him conduct *Tristan* in Milan, told members of the Leipzig Gewandhaus Orchestra that his was a name to remember. (Alfred Wallenstein, 'The Toscanini Musicians Knew', quoted by B. H. Haggin, 'Vienna's Great Conductors', *Encounter*, July 1977.)

9 Berlin beckons

By 1923 Klemperer, now almost thirty-eight years old, had established himself as one of the outstanding conductors in the German provinces and had made his mark in the concert hall as well as in the opera house. Yet for a man of his age and capacity advancement had been slow to arrive, and for this there were inner as well as outer reasons. Chaotic economic conditions had cast a blight over the country's musical life: thus the success he had enjoyed in Berlin in the spring of 1921 had led to no further engagements. But his own personal attitudes also played a part. The times were unsettled, he had heavy family responsibilities and in Cologne he at least had a position he could be sure of. Furthermore, he was determined not to leap from the frying pan into the fire. Any move would have to offer an escape from the repertory conditions that prevailed throughout Central Europe and had tormented him since the very start of his career. In his view,

Far, far too many operas were performed, they were almost all badly rehearsed, or not at all, and the general level was miserable. Not *all* the performances, of course; on a few evenings in the year, when there were new productions, they were well prepared and something was achieved. But the following evening there would be another opera – almost always badly performed.[1]

Yet Klemperer was also aware that, if he was to make his mark in the world at large, Berlin must be his target. That no doubt is why he decided to investigate the offer from the Deutsches Opernhaus,* unpromising though it in many ways appeared. Singularly lacking in charm but large and technically up to date, the theatre had been financed by public subscription, built on land provided by the Charlottenburg city council and opened in November 1912 with a view to bringing opera to the prosperous suburbs that had sprung up to the west of Berlin during the boom years after 1871. As it received no public subsidy, its director, Georg Hartmann, not unnaturally took it for granted that his first task was to satisfy his shareholders. The Charlottenburg Opera, as it was often called, was essentially a theatre for the middle class. Vocal standards were respectable, but the repertory was overwhelmingly conventional and such new works

* The appendix on p. 435 provides an outline of the evolution of the various Berlin opera houses during the Weimar Republic together with the varying names under which they went.

170

as found a place in it were generally trivial. There is no evidence that the least importance was attached to matters of production, which generally remained in Hartmann's own hands. His musical taste, or lack of it, may be gauged from a *Figaro* in which the recitatives were accompanied by harps and cello.[2]

In the post-war years the Deutsches Opernhaus had suffered from financial difficulties as well as artistic limitations. With the growing impoverishment of its overwhelmingly middle-class public, it had found the going increasingly hard. In a desperate attempt to raise funds abroad, Hartmann had in the autumn of 1922 embarked on an ill-fated American tour. In his absence he had in December been dismissed by his board, on which the shadowy figure of Ralph Littmann had become the dominating influence.* It was doubtless on Littmann's initiative that negotiations were opened with Klemperer, who arrived in Berlin on 28 January 1923 in a justifiably sceptical frame of mind.

Where were singers to come from at a time when even the greatest Central European theatres were having difficulty in maintaining an ensemble? Would a privately owned theatre have the will, let alone the means, to pursue the sort of artistic policy he had in mind? And how, for that matter, was he himself to reconcile his duties as director (for that was the position that was held out) with a pressing need to earn foreign currency by appearing abroad? Such were a few of the doubts that had run through his mind during the weeks in Rome.[3]

No record has survived of what transpired. Klemperer seems to have toyed with the idea of restricting his commitment to a limited number of new productions in each season, and it was doubtless with this in view that he proposed to open with a series of performances of *Così fan tutte*.[4] He also seems to have demanded that the entire auditorium be reconstructed.[5] Neither proposal was calculated to appeal to an opera house confronting bankruptcy and by 31 January Klemperer was back in Cologne. What was to prove only the first of a series of overtures from Berlin had come to nothing.

*   *   *

While Klemperer had been in Rome, his mother, in her seventy-fourth year, had been unwell, and he returned from a seven-week absence to find her in decline. Pneumonia set in, but death did not come easily. Ida Klemperer had never resigned herself to living under her daughter-in-law's roof and the resentments she had long stored up against her devoted but ineffectual

---

* Littmann had been Pierpont Morgan's representative in China and hence probably had access to foreign capital, the key to wealth and power in Germany during the years of inflation.

13   Klemperer, October 1923

14   Klemperer. Lithograph by Otto Dix

husband were now vented on his defenceless head. Perhaps unaware that she was dying, she refused to see him. Nathan was shattered, and Klemperer, deeply though he loved his mother, was unable to understand her harshness. Towards the end, he was able to bring her some comfort by telling her that he had found an apartment where she and her husband could once more live together on their own. It was not true, but she asked eagerly for details. When Ida Klemperer died on 13 February 1923, her son was at her side. His Catholic faith notwithstanding, he never failed to abide by the ancient Jewish custom of burning a small oil lamp or a candle on the anniversary of her death, as he was later to do on the anniversaries of the deaths of his father and his wife.

Ida Klemperer had followed every detail of her son's career with passionate concern. Unaware that women's voices were not used in Roman churches, she had written to him during his absence in Italy to ask whether it would not be possible to arrange for a performance of his Mass in C in Rome. The matter may have been uppermost in her mind, because, before leaving for Italy, he had already started rehearsals in Cologne for a performance that had been planned for a Gürzenich concert in early December, but had had to be postponed on account of his illness.

The first fully public performance of the Mass in C finally took place on 13 March 1923, almost four years after it had been completed in the monastery of Maria Laach. It aroused no more enthusiasm than it had done at the 'private' rehearsal that Klemperer had conducted immediately after his marriage. In the press there was, in particular, much adverse comment on the music's basic lack of stylistic unity. Harsh modern dissonances lay alongside the blandest diatonicism; austerely liturgical passages were matched to others whose anguish seemed personal; influences ranged from Gregorian chant to a Mahlerian use of folksong. Only the setting of the Benedictus drew general praise. The public reaction was no more than respectful.

When Klemperer conducted a further performance in Barmen on 21 April 1923, it was again the Benedictus that made the most favourable impression in a score that was otherwise regarded as too theatrical to appeal to German taste. A third performance, which Klemperer himself did not conduct, followed in Mainz on 2 April 1924, when for the first and only time the work was preceded by a setting of Psalm 42 that he had also composed in the summer of 1919 with the intention that it should serve as 'a sort of introduction to the Mass'.[6] On that occasion the critic of the *Mainzer Anzeiger* (4 April 1924) drew a perceptive distinction between 'older church music, which arose out of a deep, unshakable faith' and Klemperer's setting of the Mass, which was 'the work of an artist whose divided soul seeks refuge in the mystical gloom of a romanesque or gothic cathedral'.*

*   *   *

In spite of the speedy collapse of his negotiations with the Deutsches Opernhaus, there were other and more influential circles in Berlin who

---

* Thereafter the work remained unperformed, although from time to time, depending on his psychological condition, Klemperer's interest revived in a score that had been so intimately connected with his conversion and marriage. Thus on 9 May 1942 the Sanctus was performed with organ accompaniment at St Patrick's Cathedral in New York. In the early 1950s the staff at Schotts in London, where few people were aware of the existence of Klemperer's compositions, were startled when, unannounced, he entered the premises and imperiously demanded to inspect their stock of scores.

were determined to bring Klemperer to a central position in the capital's musical life. Scarcely more than four months later he returned for a new round of discussions, on this occasion with the Prussian Ministry of Culture and the State Opera House which had been built for Frederick the Great by Knobelsdorff on Unter den Linden.

Until 1918 the theatre had remained the personal property of the Hohenzollerns and as a student Klemperer had had first-hand experience of the lamentable influence that the last Emperor, William II, had exercised on its artistic policies. The Berlin Court Opera had had a particularly fine orchestra, first-rate conductors and an impressive array of singers. But under the monarchy its repertory had remained conventional and its productions 'prunksüchtig' (ostentatious).[7]

On 10 November 1918 the personnel proclaimed a workers' council, whose first act was to dismiss the royal Intendant. Four days later, the Prussian Ministry of Culture* assumed responsibility for the former court theatres. It was, however, ill-equipped to exercise control over its new acquisitions, as none of its officials had expert knowledge of theatre or opera. To make good the deficiency, technical advisers, or *Referenten*, were taken on the strength of the ministry. Ludwig Seelig, a mild-mannered lawyer, who had been an official of a union of theatrical employees,† was appointed *Referent* for theatrical matters. A far more forceful, imaginative and controversial figure, Leo Kestenberg, became his musical counterpart with joint responsibility for opera.

Kestenberg had been born of modest Jewish parentage in Slovakia in 1882. At the age of nine he had sensed what, in characteristically cloudy language, he later described as 'the oneness of socialism and music'[8] and this ideal was to be the lodestar of his life. He was trained as a pianist and, after a period of study with, among others, Vianna da Motta,‡ was admitted in 1900 to the master classes that Busoni held in Weimar. Kestenberg's devotion to Busoni, whom he briefly served as secretary, was unswerving. But though he soon started to establish a reputation as a pianist of promise, his main energies were increasingly absorbed by a variety of reformist causes, among them a commission for 'exemplary workers' furniture'. In 1905 he became a founder member of the central educational and cultural committee of the German Social Democratic Party (SPD). From this it was

---

* The Ministerium für Wissenschaft, Kunst und Volksbildung, to give it its full title, was generally referred to, as it will be here, as the Kultusministerium. In the Weimar Republic, all cultural and educational responsibilities were vested in the *Länder*, or provinces, of the *Reich*. Hence the Berlin State theatres were controlled by the Prussian, and not the central German, government.
† Genossenschaft Deutscher Bühnen-Angehörigen.
‡ José Vianna da Motta (1868–1948), Portuguese pianist and composer, who was one of Liszt's last pupils.

175

a natural step to the Berlin Volksbühne (see pp. 184ff), whose concerts he inaugurated in 1915 and continued to run until the Nazis came to power.* In these and other activities Kestenberg propagated a fusion of art and socialism that owed more to Ruskin and Morris than it did to Marx.

* Kestenberg emigrated to Czechoslovakia in 1933 and thence to Palestine in 1939. He died in Israel in 1961.

15   Leo Kestenberg

'I started from a conviction that there were creative powers in every human being that could be awoken and cultivated. It was through socialism and among the workers that I believed that this goal could be reached.'[9]

When the SPD split in 1915 on the issue of the war, Kestenberg's pacifism inclined him towards the smaller and more radical group of independent socialists (USPD) and it was as a nominee of the first USPD Kultusminister, Adolf Hoffmann,* that he was appointed *Referent* on 1 December 1918. In the ministry he found himself surrounded by old-style Prussian officials, who were deeply suspicious of him as a foreigner, a Jew and a left-wing appointee. Had not Carl Heinrich Becker† been appointed to the position of senior official in the ministry in April 1919, Kestenberg, able and energetic though he was, would certainly not have proved such an effective agent of musical and operatic reform. After initial mistrust, Becker gave his *Referent* unstinted support, and Kestenberg later gratefully described him as 'the only man who understood me at that time'.[10]

Kestenberg was a complex character and reactions to him ranged from devotion to suspicion. On the one hand, he was warm-hearted, generous and idealistic to the point of naivety. On the other, he was an operator with a finger in every pie and tactically adroit at securing his ends. He was also prone to promise more than he could fulfil. His most durable achievement was in a field of which he had direct knowledge: even the Third Reich left untouched the far-reaching reform of German musical education that he introduced in 1927 against widespread opposition. His enlightened views and sound musical judgement are also evident in a series of appointments that he inspired and that did much to give Berlin a musical primacy it had never before enjoyed with Germany, let alone Europe. It was he who instigated the appointment first of Busoni and after his death of Schoenberg as director of a master class in composition at the Prussian Academy of the Arts. It was his influence that brought Schreker and later Hindemith to the Hochschule für Musik. Kestenberg had also decided by 1923 that Klemperer was the broom he needed to cleanse the Augean stables of Berlin operatic life. Unfortunately, opera was a field of which he had no direct experience and in which he proved prone to underestimate the obstacles in his path.

Kestenberg inevitably incurred hostility. His innovations and reforms upset vested interests, and traditionally minded musicians saw him, not

* As the two socialist parties could not agree, two Kultusministers were appointed in November 1918, one by the USPD, the other (Konrad Haenisch) by the SPD.
† C. H. Becker (1876–1933), a liberally minded orientalist, who first as Secretary of State and subsequently as Minister was the dominant figure within the Kultusministerium until his resignation in 1930 (see p. 338) and hence in the cultural life of the Weimar Republic. Though nominally a member of the small Democratic Party (see p. 338n), Becker ran (or attempted to run) his ministry on non-political lines.

without reason, as the *éminence grise* of the young republic's musical life. His personal appearance undoubtedly played a part in the dislike he inspired. Kokoschka's striking portrait of 1926 shows a short, portly figure with large, fleshy features and a rather devious, myopic gaze. In the nationalist circles that were so strongly represented in the musical press he was regarded as the very embodiment of the growing Jewish influence in German music. When in 1932 Franz von Papen as Chancellor illegally dissolved the entire Prussian government,* one of his actions was to dismiss Kestenberg.

*   *   *

On 30 September 1919 the personnel of the State Opera startled the Kultusministerium by electing Max von Schillings as Intendant. A traditional composer of modest attainments, Schillings had from 1908 to 1918 served the King of Württemberg (who had knighted him) as music director in Stuttgart, whither Klemperer had travelled in 1915 to attend the first performance of *Mona Lisa*, his best-known opera. Schillings was neither an outstanding conductor nor an effective administrator. Conservative in his musical tastes, distinctly anti-Semitic in his opinions,† and reputedly under the thumb of the dramatic soprano, Barbara Kemp, whom he married in 1923, he was not a man to fulfil the still ill-defined operatic policies of the Kultusministerium. But in the autumn of 1919, when the constituent assembly of the new republic had only just completed its work in Weimar, the ministry had no alternative but to bow before this bizarre product of syndicalism in the opera house.

In fact Schillings did something to improve the lamentable standards of production at the Linden Opera. If his choice of new repertory was not notably adventurous (the five seasons between 1919 and 1924 did not include a single première), he at least introduced works by Busoni, Pfitzner and Schreker. But not even a Toscanini could have held together an ensemble at a time when inflation had led to the recurrent absence of many leading singers. Complaints about declining standards inevitably grew sharper and on 24 November 1922 Schillings wrote to his friend Richard Strauss (with whom he was *per Du*)‡ to express his resentment of the

---

* From 1918 to 1932 Prussia, which comprised no less than two-thirds of Germany, was (apart from a brief period in 1921) ruled by a coalition in which the Socialists were dominant. It was under this provincial government, and not under that of the Reich, that the cultural life of the Weimar Republic flowered and Kestenberg was able to exercise the influence he did.

† He liked to refer to Weimar Germany as 'Semitanien' (Raupp, *Max von Schillings*, p. 219).

‡ As conductor before the war at the Munich and Berlin opera houses, Strauss had been an early and assiduous champion of Schillings's music.

'Alberichs' in the ministry, who were fanning this criticism. 'There is', he complained, 'no league for protection against anti-Aryanism in the arts.'[11]

Matters were suddenly brought to a head by two resignations. On 18 April 1923 Furtwängler withdrew as conductor of the Staatskapelle concerts, which were given by the orchestra of the State Opera. Five weeks later, on 23 May, Leo Blech, who had since 1906 been a pillar of the house, resigned to take the post that Klemperer had earlier that year been offered at the Deutsches Opernhaus. It thus became necessary to find a replacement who would occupy both positions. Schillings, who was weary of his administrative burden, saw an opportunity to resume conducting on a wider scale. The ministry had other intentions and within three days of Blech's resignation Klemperer's name was mentioned as a successor in the well-informed *Berliner Börsen-Courier*. There can be little doubt that it was Kestenberg who had put forward his name; at any rate it was he who, acting on Becker's behalf, invited Klemperer to come to Berlin for negotiations.[12]

On his arrival in early June, Klemperer first saw Becker and Kestenberg, who told him that he was not only to have a leading position in the Linden Opera, but would also be conductor of the Staatskapelle concerts, second only in prestige to those of the Berlin Philharmonic Orchestra.[13] But detailed negotiations would be with Schillings, who as Intendant was directly responsible for all appointments within his own house. On 6 June the two men met. Simultaneously, the news of Klemperer's appointment was announced in (and fervently welcomed by) so many newspapers sympathetic to the ministry and hostile to Schillings that it is hard to resist an impression of an inspired leak, designed to force the Intendant's hand. If that was the plan, it misfired, for Klemperer, confident of the ministry's support, proceeded to overplay his cards.

On 11 June Schillings presented the ministry with a written account of the negotiations.[14] Klemperer had demanded a ten-year, irrevocable contract with the title of *Generalmusikdirektor*, which was to be accorded to no other member of the staff. He was to choose the works he would himself conduct and to have a voice in all matters concerning repertory, casting, and the engagement and dismissal of personnel. He was to produce two works each season and would choose the designer for these. He would be able to refuse to conduct performances for which there were fewer rehearsals than he deemed necessary, or performances in which guest artists took part. He was to be solely responsible for the Staatskapelle concerts and for the engagement and dismissal of orchestral musicians. Some subscribers to the concerts would be obliged to resign, so as to ensure a less conservative audience. Finally, he was to have the right to three months' leave during the season, in addition to the customary two months' summer vacation.

179

Not even Strauss had enjoyed such powers during his years as First Conductor. As Leopold Schmidt, the critic of the *Berliner Tageblatt*, commented (16 June 1923), Schillings would in effect only be able to enter his own theatre with the permission of his musical director. In his memorandum, Schillings sardonically observed that Klemperer appeared to regard himself as 'a saviour called to the bedside of a gravely sick patient'. He had even in the discussions openly admitted that he saw the role of *Generalmusikdirektor* as equivalent to that of a prime minister in a constitutional monarchy. In other words, all power would lie in his hands and not in those of the Intendant. 'Such a constellation', Schillings stiffly observed, 'would be incompatible with an artistic personality of my achievements.' On 14 June the *Kölnische Zeitung* reported that Klemperer had turned down an invitation to succeed Blech and would remain in Cologne.

Kestenberg may not at once have abandoned hope of resolving the differences between Schillings and Klemperer, for early in July he was in Cologne. But by this time Klemperer was resigned to the situation. Inwardly, he felt himself not yet ripe for the great responsibilities that had beckoned. He also suspected that he was being used by the Kultusministerium as an instrument in its desire to be rid of Schillings.* After fruitless approaches to Zemlinsky and Walter, Schillings finally turned to Erich Kleiber,† who, in spite of his youth and a trial *Fidelio* that aroused singularly little enthusiasm, nonetheless received the appointment. A year later, the ministry to general surprise announced the reappointment of Schillings as Intendant for a further five years. The renewal of his contract was, however, to prove no more than a truce. Kestenberg's first attempt to bring Klemperer to Berlin had misfired. But it was not to be his last.

*   *   *

Tired and depressed, Klemperer in the second half of July joined his wife, who was pregnant,‡ on the island of Sylt. In the course of a turbulent and unrewarding season the political and economic condition of Germany had gone from bad to worse. On 11 January 1923 the Franco–Belgian occupation of the Ruhr had put an end to any lingering confidence in the mark.§ On 31 January the Cologne authorities had given way to anti-French feeling and banned from the repertory any operas, such as

---

* 'I said to Becker, "You would like to be rid of Schillings. You want to break your marriage to him and I should be the marriage-breaker. I don't like that"' (*Conversations*, p. 54).
† See biographical glossary.
‡ Their second child, Lotte, was born on 1 November 1923.
§ When Regi Elbogen gave her father a dollar for his seventy-seventh birthday on 28 July it was worth a million marks.

La Traviata and *La Bohème*, that were set in Paris.* Klemperer had also found himself a butt of outraged nationalism: on his return from Rome, the *Rheinische Musik-und Theaterzeitung* (10 February 1923) had complained that he had absented himself to gain money and fame 'in a country whose engineers are busily engaged in ruining the German economy'. That was not the only criticism of his seven-week absence. On 6 April Johannes Meerfeld, the city official responsible for cultural matters, had written a sharply worded letter to Rémond about the low level of performances at the opera and the lack of any firm musical direction.[15] Nor had matters greatly improved after Klemperer's return. One projected new production after another had been dropped for lack of funds. It was not until 2 May that the first Cologne staging of Schreker's *Der ferne Klang* brought a breath of fresh air into a repertory otherwise given over to routine works.

By the time the Klemperers returned to Cologne from their summer holiday at the end of August 1923, there was concern about the winter food supplies, and French-instigated separatist movements were gaining ground in the Rhineland. By October bread was rationed, milk prices were soaring and potatoes no longer available. As prices rose, so did unemployment, and the atmosphere inevitably became more violent. Cars, lorries and shops were sacked and the police were stoned when they attempted to make arrests. Throughout the country there were disturbances which culminated on 8 November in an unsuccessful *Putsch* in Munich, led by General Ludendorff and Adolf Hitler, an agitator still unknown outside the lunatic fringe of Bavarian political life. In fact the corner had already been turned on 13 August with the appointment as Chancellor and Foreign Minister of Gustav Stresemann, who was committed to a policy of fulfilment of war reparations. On this basis, Hjalmar Schacht, subsequently president of the Reichsbank, was able to issue a new currency in November. But in autumn 1923 the country seemed on the brink of political and economic disintegration.

In the teeth of countless difficulties in daily life, Klemperer was nonetheless able to open the season with a new production of *Die Entführung aus dem Serail*, which was generally considered to rank amongst his outstanding musical achievements in Cologne. This was followed on 24 November by *Boris Godunov*, an opera that had been performed at only three German theatres since Diaghilev had first brought the work to Western Europe in 1908.[16] In his approach Klemperer was influenced by his new musical assistant, Eigel Kruttge,† who persuaded him to end the opera, as Mussorgsky had done, not with Boris's death, but with the

---

* Paradoxically, an archetypal French work, such as *Carmen*, continued to be given, presumably on the grounds that the setting was Andalusian.
† See biographical glossary.

revolutionary scene. Kruttge was also critical of Rimsky-Korsakov's revision of the score, but the original version was at that time not available.* Klemperer was, however, able to spare the work one of Rémond's Meyerbeerian stagings. The vivid, expressionist colours and bare stylised outlines of Heinrich Pützhofer-Ester's sets were among the most adventurous that had at that time been seen in the visually backward Cologne opera house.

Of more significance for his future than any of these operatic activities, however, was a performance of Bruckner's huge Eighth Symphony, which he conducted for the first time at an opera house concert five days after the première of *Boris Godunov*. Up to this point of his career Klemperer had performed little by a composer with whom he was to be so closely identified.† Several features of the performance, which he conducted without a score, were immediately recognised as new. In the first place he gave the work uncut; or, more precisely, unlike virtually all conductors at that time, he made no further cuts in the already abbreviated and doctored version that was the only form in which the work was then available.‡ William Steinberg later recalled[17] that Klemperer made extensive retouchings in the score, which may account for the almost Mahlerian luminosity he achieved,[18] in contrast to the rich Wagnerian carpet of sound that the bowdlerised version mistakenly aimed to produce. In contrast to the pathos-laden performances that were still general, Klemperer's approach was primarily architectural, so that even the problematic finale sustained its length. When, on 9 December, Klemperer repeated the performance with the orchestra of the German Theatre in Prague, his old champion, Felix Adler, observed that in his interpretation complaints about the formal coherence of Bruckner's music vanished into thin air.[19]

It is probable that these performances were in some degree rehearsals for a concert at which Klemperer was to make his début with the illustrious Leipzig Gewandhaus Orchestra on 24 January 1924, when he was to replace its permanent conductor, Wilhelm Furtwängler.§ On 30 December, however, an invitation arrived out of the blue to return to Barcelona at extremely short notice. An opportunity to earn foreign currency at a

---

* It only reached Germany in 1931, when Nikolay Mal'ko conducted a performance at the Berlin Radio.

† Hitherto the only Bruckner he had conducted were a few performances of the Symphony No. 7 in 1921, on the twenty-fifth anniversary of Bruckner's death.

‡ Scarcely more than two years later Klemperer changed his mind. In New York on 4 February 1926 he made a cut of several pages in the finale, as he again did in London on 17 November 1970, on that occasion on the bizarre grounds that 'the composer was so full of musical invention that he went too far' (Festival Hall programme). The Bruckner *Urtexte* only started to be issued in the 1930s.

§ Klemperer conducted Bruckner's Symphony No. 8 in Leipzig during the following season, on 1 January 1925.

moment when the mark still had no value outside Germany was not to be missed. Klemperer rushed to Frankfurt to collect visas, paused briefly in Paris to borrow journey money from Koussevitzky* and to send his apologies to Furtwängler, and within half an hour of his arrival in Barcelona on 5 January 1924 had plunged into rehearsals for *Parsifal*. The cast was strong and Helene Wildbrunn's singing as Kundry gave him particular pleasure.† But the orchestra was as ill-disciplined as ever, rehearsals were insufficient and the staging by Franz Ludwig Hörth, resident producer at the Berlin State Opera, struck him as weak. 'Ha! ha! *Alter*',‡ he wrote to Johanna on the day of his arrival in a reference to his abortive negotiations with Schillings during the previous summer, 'How right I was to demand independence.' *Der Rosenkavalier* followed on 19 January, but while it was still in rehearsal Klemperer received a telegram from his agent to tell him of yet another overture from Berlin.

       *   *   *

On this occasion the approach came from a source less august than the Berlin State Opera. The Grosse Volksoper had been launched immediately after the war, though during the earliest years of its existence it had consisted of little more than a grandiose title and an ambitious programme. Its founder, Otto Wilhelm Lange (1884–1975) had started life as a bank clerk, but after his marriage to Aline Sanden,§ he had for a couple of years worked at the Leipzig Schauspielhaus and during the war had run a theatre in German-occupied territory. In spite of his limited experience, Lange had a nose for opportunity and knew how to seize it. At the end of the war he had assessed the cultural climate of the hour with remarkable astuteness and on 16 August 1919 had boldly proclaimed the foundation of a 'Grosse Volksoper', which would provide good performances at cheap prices in a theatre (and this was essential to his plans) that would seat four thousand people.‖ Lange naturally had no such theatre. Indeed, he was never to have

---

* Serge Koussevitzky (1874–1951) was still a refugee conductor of an eponymous orchestra in Paris. Later in 1924, he was appointed conductor of the Boston Orchestra, a position he held until 1949.

† Helene Wildbrunn (1882–1971) was one of the outstanding dramatic sopranos of her time.

‡ Approximately, 'old dear'. From the outset of their marriage Klemperer and his wife addressed each other thus, in conversation as well as in letters, both using the masculine form of the adjective.

§ Aline Sanden (1876–1955) enjoyed her greatest period of success as a dramatic soprano at the Leipzig Opera from 1909 to 1921. In 1914 she sang Salome under Klemperer in Barmen.

‖ Such conceptions were in the air. Even Bruno Walter, who as a friend of Pfitzner and Thomas Mann could not be said to move in circles friendly to the newborn republic, briefly toyed with the idea of a huge Volksoper in Munich in November 1918. (Thomas Mann, *Tagebücher, 1918–1921*, 24 November 1918)

one, and this was to remain the Achilles' heel of his undertaking until its demise five years later. But that did not prevent him from announcing the appointment of architects to design a building with 'classless'[20] seating arrangements and from issuing shares to intending subscribers.

The Kultusministerium at first smiled on his plans. Its new men believed that an age had dawned in which the theatre (of which opera was of course an integral part) would at last be liberated from princely and commercial influences and would thus be able to fulfil its true function as an agent of spiritual and social rebirth, as had been envisaged by Lessing, Schiller and Wagner. Socialists like Kestenberg were convinced that a progressive state should seek to express itself in progressive cultural policies, which would not merely extend the availability of opera but would determine the course of creativity itself.[21] As he put it in characteristically heady language, 'Only when the people control opera will the coming generation of composers also belong to the people.'[22] The most immediate need was thus for an opera house that would embody the ideals of the new republic, as the court theatres had mirrored the age of absolutism.

Unfortunately the Kultusministerium found itself without the physical means of fulfilling that ambition. The only opera house at its disposal in Berlin was the venerable theatre on Unter den Linden, which like most eighteenth-century theatres had only a very limited number of cheap seats, many of them with poor sightlines. It was thus structurally ill-suited to serve the purpose of what in the jargon of the day was termed *soziale Kunstpflege* (literally, the cultivation of the social functions of art), and after a lost war and with a revolutionary upheaval on its hands the Prussian government was in no position to build a new opera house.

Kestenberg's agile mind saw a solution. Since 1908, he had sat on the artistic committee of the Berlin Volksbühne, an organisation close to the German Social Democratic Party (SPD) that had been set up in 1890 to make good theatre available to the masses at a price they could afford. But, whereas in the field of the spoken theatre the Volksbühne had succeeded in building a handsome theatre of its own,* its operatic activities, which were largely Kestenberg's responsibility, had hitherto been limited. The immediate post-war period saw a large increase in its membership and the times seemed propitious to its ideals. Thus it was not long before it, too, started to look around for an opera house of its own.

From 1918 Kestenberg had a foot in both camps, and it was he who brought the Prussian government and the Volksbühne together. In the Tiergarten, immediately beyond the Brandenburg Gate and adjacent to the

---

* It still stands on the Rosa-Luxemburg-Platz in East Berlin, where it fulfils its original purpose.

Reichstag, stood the Theater am Königsplatz, generally known as the Kroll Theatre, which the new republic had inherited as part of the confiscated properties of the crown. Originally built by one Joseph Kroll as an entertainment centre with an auditorium and banqueting halls, it had in the course of the nineteenth century come to be used as supplementary accommodation for the court theatres. Lacking the resources to rebuild the Kroll, the new republic, with Kestenberg as broker, did a deal with the Volksbühne. The Volksbühne would undertake the reconstruction and would in return be granted a twenty-five-year lease, during which period the state theatres would provide its members with performances. A contract to this effect was signed in April 1920. Both parties had reason to be satisfied. The state would be enabled to bring theatre and opera to the masses, the Volksbühne would have its own opera house.

As it was clearly going to take a year or two to reconstruct the Kroll Theatre, the Kultusministerium nonetheless cast around for more immediate means of providing opera at modest prices and Lange's Grosse Volksoper seemed to offer a useful instrument to this end. Though still a somewhat shadowy undertaking, it appeared to share the cultural and social ideals of the ministry and the Volksbühne. Accordingly, both Schillings and Georg Singer, the chairman of the Berlin Volksbühne, were encouraged to join its board, the State Opera lent sets and costumes for a number of improvised performances in the suburbs of Berlin, and in autumn 1920 Lange was able to instal his embryonic administration in a wing of the Kroll, alongside that of the Volksbühne.

In a petition he later (April 1923) presented to the Prussian Landtag, Lange claimed that the Grosse Volksoper had come into existence 'with the idea of being a sister to the Volksbühne'. If so, she proved to be a sister with predatory ambitions. In the Kroll, Lange saw the theatre he needed and access to foreign funds seemed to offer a means of acquiring it. The source of those funds remained something of a mystery, though in the Berlin press of the period there are allusions to shadowy financiers, who, it was claimed, stood behind Lange, as indeed they stood behind the Charlottenburg opera house. Inflation naturally strengthened the position of the Grosse Volksoper, for as the purchasing power of its foreign funds rose the value of the Volksbühne's savings in German currency fell.

The Volksbühne's difficulties were compounded by the long arm of Prussian bureaucracy: more than a year passed before, late in 1921, the various necessary permissions had been obtained so that reconstruction could begin, and by then the Volksbühne was beginning to feel the draught. Consequently, in November 1921 it found itself obliged to accept a sisterly loan from Lange, who plainly regarded the debt as a means of strengthening his foothold in the Kroll. A particularly hard winter caused

185

further delay and in June 1922 the Volksbühne borrowed another $10,000 from the Grosse Volksoper. Even that did not enable it to complete the job and in November it had to admit to the Kultusministerium that it was no longer in a position to fulfil its side of the agreement of April 1920.

To Lange, it seemed as though his hour had come. He had as yet no more than a two-year lease on the Theater des Westens,* in which his young company was, however, already playing with considerable success. Now a full-scale opera house seemed about to drop into his lap like a ripe plum. Accordingly, he offered the Volksbühne yet another $10,000 towards completing the Kroll, if it would agree to the Grosse Volksoper playing in it. The scheme had much to recommend it: the Volksbühne would have opera performances on seven nights of the week instead of the four that the State Opera had undertaken to provide and the Grosse Volksoper would have its theatre. But it did not appeal to the Kultusministerium. Its officials did not like the smell of Lange's backers, in whom they saw a recrudescence of commercial influences in the theatre. They also had doubts, which were to prove well-founded, about the long-term financial viability of the undertaking. If, on the other hand, contrary to the ministry's expectation,

* See appendix.

16   Exterior of the Kroll Theatre, *c.* 1935

the Grosse Volksoper were able to establish itself as a permanent institution, it might prove a dangerous rival to the ailing State Opera. Furthermore, the ministry already had plans to carry out a thorough reconstruction of the antiquated technical equipment of the Linden opera house and would accordingly need the Kroll Theatre to provide it with alternative accommodation.

The Volksbühne was eventually won over to the Kultusministerium's viewpoint, partly on account of its own suspicions of the 'capitalistic' Grosse Volksoper and partly by the ministry's assurance that it would match Lange's offer to provide seven opera performances a week. On 30 April 1923 the Prussian state and the Berlin Volksbühne signed a revised agreement. The state would complete the Kroll Theatre, which would remain its property. In return the State Opera would make half the seats available to the Volksbühne at a price that was to be geared to the wages of a 25-year-old manual worker (presumably based on the ministry's idealised notion of the sort of audiences that would be drawn to the Kroll). The repercussions of that agreement were to resonate throughout the operatic history of the Weimar Republic and to play a crucial part in Klemperer's own career.

No one was satisfied. The Volksbühne had lost its coveted opera house. On the other hand, the non-socialist parties in the Landtag believed that it had received preferential treatment from its friends (i.e. Kestenberg) in the Kultusministerium, and this suspicion was echoed in leading liberal papers, such as the *Berliner Tageblatt* and the *Vossische Zeitung*. Schillings, who had already proved a less than competent administrator, found himself saddled with the formidable task of running two opera houses in tandem. But it was, of course, Lange who had lost most, and he did not take defeat lying down. He campaigned vigorously, arguing, not without justice, that he had the resources to complete and run the Kroll without additional state subsidies and that he had already won his artistic spurs in the Theater des Westens. Even the left-wing *Sozialistische Monatsheft* gave him support. 'When one considers the work of the Berlin State Opera during the last winter', it wrote in May 1923, 'the Grosse Volksoper comes out better. Here is life. The performances are unequal...But there is a will to create.'

That the Grosse Volksoper was able to present so formidable a challenge to the combined resources of the ministry, the State Opera and the Volksbühne that its supporters were able to force a debate in the Landtag on 15 June 1923 reflected the undermining effect of inflation on established German institutions. But it also testified to the impact of Lange's first complete season at the Theater des Westens, which only eleven days earlier had culminated in a propitiously successful production of *Julius*

Caesar at a time when Handel's operas were still virtually unperformed.* Lange's nose for talent and his flair for enterprising projects were still more apparent in his second season. Having expanded his orchestral pit so that it could accommodate eighty-four players, he proceeded to engage two up-and-coming conductors: Eugen Szenkar† was appointed musical director and Fritz Zweig‡ First Conductor. Productions, which were in the hands of Hans Strohbach, were well in advance of their time in the use of stylised sets. Lange had also acquired the right to give the first German performance of Dukas's *Ariane et Barbe-bleu* and Ravel's *L'Heure espagnole*, and by early 1924 had announced the engagement as guests of singers of the calibre of Gutheil-Schoder, Slezak and Battistini. In a remarkably short period of time and with limited resources, he had begun to make a distinctive impact on operatic life in the German capital.

*   *   *

Thus when Lange's offer of a three-year engagement as director (and not merely *musical* director) of the Grosse Volksoper reached Klemperer in Barcelona early in January 1924, he was attracted by the proposition in spite of the organisation's lack of official status. For the first time in his career he would be in a position to control every aspect of artistic policy; and no doubt the prospect of being at the head of a lively young company that would be well placed to make rings round the cumbersome, demoralised State Opera, which had rejected his conditions, was a further inducement.

He was also well aware that, sooner or later, he would have to establish himself in the capital. Like countless actors, artists, writers and musicians from the German provinces and beyond, he felt drawn to the harsh, shabby city. In many ways it was not an attractive place. As Carl Zuckmayer later recalled, 'The people were irritable and bad-tempered, the streets were dirty and full of crippled beggars...while passers-by in elegant shoes or bootees walked hurriedly by...But Berlin had about it a taste of the future.' Above all, it had since 1918 increasingly come to assume Vienna's position as the musical metropolis of central Europe. 'Once you had Berlin, you had the world.'[23]

Klemperer was, however, well aware of the doubts that had been cast on the Grosse Volksoper's financial viability; he also knew of its short tenure of the Theater des Westens. Accordingly, he evaded a precipitate

---

* The Handel revival, which was to play a prominent part in the operatic life of the Weimar Republic, both in its influence on the approach of composers to operatic forms and in the field of stage design, dates from the production of *Rodelinda* in Göttingen in 1920.

† Eugen Szenkar (1891–1977). Hungarian conductor who was subsequently musical director in Cologne (1924–33) and Düsseldorf (1952–60).

‡ See biographical glossary.

188

decision. Meanwhile he asked his wife, who was about to leave for Berlin to sing the roles of Adèle (*Die Fledermaus*) and Gilda (*Rigoletto*) with the Grosse Volksoper, to inform him about the company's artistic attainments.* Back in Cologne, he turned again for advice to Willy Levin, who lived in Berlin and had business as well as musical connections (see pp. 93–4).

> Whether and to what extent artistic possibilities exist for me is something I still cannot assess. The most important thing for me to know is whether, *purely materially*, I can have confidence in this institution, and by that I mean whether it is financially sound...Would you, *Herr Commerzienrat*, be good enough to make enquiries as to whether the Grosse Volksoper is an undertaking to which I can confide my own fortune and that of my family for a number of years.

The course of events between 31 January when that letter was written, and 20 February, when the Cologne Theatre Commission met to consider Klemperer's application to be released from his contract, is unclear. Klemperer probably travelled to Berlin in early February for negotiations that proved inconclusive (at any rate he did not conduct in Cologne until 8 February). Subsequently Lange sent Zweig to Cologne as an emissary. His overtures must have had some success, for Klemperer returned with him to Berlin, where on 21 February he attended and was much impressed by the Grosse Volksoper's new production of *Boris Godunov*. His appointment as director was announced the following day. The news was greeted with enthusiasm in the capital's principal newspapers, although Weissmann found it ironic that Klemperer should be going to the Grosse Volksoper, while Kleiber, a conductor of lesser calibre, ruled at the State Opera.[24] There was also some puzzlement that Klemperer should have accepted a position with such a shaky organisation, and on 14 March the *Vossische Zeitung* carried a report (subseqently denied by the Kultusministerium) that his contract contained a secret clause, whereby he would be transferred to the State Opera once Kleiber's contract had expired.†

Klemperer lost no time in planning his opening season. The day after his appointment he approached the publishers of Ernst Krenek, a 23-year-old Austrian composer who was already making a name for himself.‡ His purpose was to request permission to give the première of

---

* Klemperer, who was aware of his wife's deficient technique and had earlier persuaded her to abandon heavier roles and to study with Oskar Daniel, a well-known Berlin singing teacher, did not think that Johanna was adequately prepared for the part of Gilda. When he failed to persuade her not to accept it, he sent her detailed instructions. 'On the first entry sing with concentration but without too much emotional agitation (so that you don't breathe too quickly); the duet with Rigoletto...*light* as drops of water, but with tone..."Caro nome" like *sighs*, *portamento* (!) and learn it *exactly* musically...Above all, *Alter*, don't work yourself up so much' (letter of 20 January 1924).

† It was frequently alleged that Kestenberg, whose hand was seen in every appointment, lay behind the Grosse Volksoper's approach to Klemperer. In view of Lange's bad relations with the Kultusministerium this is improbable.   ‡ See biographical glossary.

Krenek's first stage work, the 'scenic cantata', *Zwingburg*; this he planned to perform in a double bill with *Petrushka*. Back in Cologne, he wrote to ask Busoni if he might stage his early opera, *Die Brautwahl*.* Three days later it was announced that he would also conduct the first German performances of Bartók's *The Miraculous Mandarin* and *The Wooden Prince*. On 7 March Marianne wrote to tell Helene Rosenbaum that her brother was looking forward to the artistic independence his new position would bring. He was clearly determined to put it to good use.

But it was not long before clouds appeared on the horizon. On 19 March Issay Dobrowen† conducted a performance of *Boris Godunov* and Klemperer was incensed that he had not been consulted. More serious trouble arose when Lange took it on himself to instruct Zweig to make cuts in *Siegfried*. Zweig appealed to Klemperer, who insisted that the work be performed in full on 20 March. Two days later the *Vossische Zeitung* carried a report that, contrary to Lange's claim that he had acquired a twenty-year lease on the Theater des Westens, the Grosse Volksoper would find itself without a roof at the end of the season. That was not the only disturbing news. On 13 March Leo Blech had resigned as musical director of the Deutsches Opernhaus and rumours now began to circulate of a merger between Berlin's two privately run opera companies. Like the Deutsches Opernhaus, the Grosse Volksoper's viability had depended on inflation; with access to foreign funds Lange had thrived on the weakness of the mark. Hence its stabilisation in the course of the winter of 1923/4 had undermined the financial foundations of his company. Klemperer began to feel the ground uncertain beneath his feet.

*   *   *

At this point, however, he had to turn his attention to a major commitment in Cologne that had already suffered delay. When the score of Schreker's *Irrelohe* had arrived in October of the previous year, Klemperer had written (11 October 1923) to tell the composer of his enthusiasm for it, and Steinberg had started the musical preparations before Christmas. As this was the first opera that Schreker had completed since his meteoric rise to fame at the end of the war, expectations ran high and a great gathering of critics, conductors and theatre directors descended on Cologne for the première on 27 March 1924. Apart from an absence of foreign guests (for Schreker's reputation had not yet penetrated beyond Central Europe), the occasion had something of the glitter of a Strauss première in Dresden. A

* Letter of 25 February 1924. Klemperer had had premature ambitions of conducting the work (which was not yet complete) in Prague in 1909.
† Issay Dobrowen (1891–1953), a Russian-born conductor, who was an outstanding interpreter of Russian music and subsequently functioned as First Conductor of the Grosse Volksoper until its demise. Lange was not slow to spot talent.

190

particularly formidable contingent arrived from Berlin, eager also to hear the conductor who was shortly expected to take up a prominent position in the capital. They were not disappointed. 'Klemperer', wrote Paul Bekker after the première, 'is perhaps the best theatre conductor in Germany today, technically utterly secure, as an interpreter irreproachably painstaking, admirable above all in the way he puts his own personality behind the work.'[25] Heinrich Chevalley considered that 'orchestral playing of such fineness, beauty of sound and expressive power is today probably only equalled in [the opera houses of] Dresden and Vienna'.[26] 'In Klemperer', wrote Adolf Weissmann, 'there is a unity of instinct and understanding and a breath of greatness.'[27]

If the evening was a triumph for Klemperer, it proved a disaster for Schreker. *Irrelohe* marked the zenith of his career. Paul Bekker, who had done more than any man to create Schreker's reputation, stubbornly maintained that it was a work of maturity that happened to be out of touch with the new anti-romantic mood that had started to emerge.[28] Karl Holl indicated the limitations of the work and expressed a widely held view when he snidely described Schreker as 'the most remarkable musician in the German theatre of today – no less, but no more'.[29] It was, however, Weissmann's incisive pen that wrought the greatest havoc. The work, he declared, was pretentious *Kitsch*, musically impoverished and theatrically ineffective, a pseudo-modern concoction that was of significance only in so far as it threw light on a chapter of musical history. '*Irrelohe*', he concluded in a phrase of devastating finality, 'has no future.'[30] The five-year wonder was over.

By the time the première was behind him Klemperer also seems to have lost sympathy with a score he had praised so lavishly only a few months earlier. At any rate on 1 April, Nathan Klemperer, who had foresworn theatres and concerts (for him a considerable sacrifice) during a year's mourning for his wife that had only recently expired, reported on the event in a letter to his elder daughter, Regi, in Berlin. 'The worth of the opera', he wrote, 'stands in no relationship to the number of rehearsals (c. fifty) that were necessary and the to-do about the production...Otto bore the main burden. Weissmann was right when he said to him, "I congratulate you. You have triumphed over Schreker."' To the composer's annoyance, Rémond reneged on the plan to stage a cycle of his operas in Cologne; and, although by the end of the season he had given no fewer than ten performances of *Irrelohe*, Klemperer never subsequently conducted as much as a bar of his friend's music. In later years he unkindly dismissed Schreker as a composer of 'typical inflation music',[31] a comment that underlined the fact that his years of fame had uncannily corresponded with the years of inflation in Central Europe. As though some unseen hand had

191

pulled a switch, German musical life – and with it Klemperer's own career – was about to enter a new era. The failure of *Irrelohe* was prophetic of what was to come.

*   *   *

On 10 April Klemperer returned to Berlin to conduct his first concert in the capital for almost three years. His two previous programmes had been devoted exclusively to works by Mahler and Schoenberg. Now, as though to emphasise that he did not wish to be regarded primarily as an interpreter of contemporary music, he chose an exclusively classical programme of symphonies by Haydn (No. 95 in C minor), Mozart (the 'Jupiter') and Beethoven (No. 7 in A major). Aware of how much hung on the concert, he planned it with the meticulousness of a commander preparing for battle. As early as November 1923 he conducted the Haydn and Beethoven symphonies in Bonn.* On 1 April 1924 he gave the entire programme in Wiesbaden and four days later repeated it in Cologne.

This long and careful preparation was amply rewarded. Almost half a century later, Wolfgang Stresemann recalled the impact made by the concert that Klemperer conducted on 10 April in the Philharmonie.†

A packed hall was crackling with expectation as the outsize Klemperer appeared on the platform, recalling Mahler with his penetrating eyes...[He] proved himself a mature conductor who knew exactly what he wanted and whose almost excessively powerful character provided him with the means of obtaining it. His impressive control of the orchestra simultaneously communicated itself to the audience, which, as in the case of Mahler, fell entirely under his spell...Comment was almost wholly enthusiastic in spite of the fact that the interpretations were anything but traditional.

In contrast to the Philharmonic's usually soft, saturated tone, the orchestral sound was a little rough, although entirely transparent and balanced...Rarely in the Berlin of the twenties did a relatively young and little-known conductor make such an impact with a classical programme and in spite of the fact that his approach stood in almost diametrical contrast to those of Furtwängler and Walter. Klemperer was less concerned with expression and feeling. At the core of his interpretations stood form, structure and a relentless determination, which he imposed on himself as well as on the orchestra, to provide an objective realisation of the score...Outward emotion seemed alien to him; he rejected the least alteration of tempo that was not marked in the score...

Thus his interpretations, controversial though they were in many details, as in, for example, the very slow tempo at which he took the second movement of the Seventh, represented a sensational break in the ranks of those recreative artists whose late romantic approach...then dominated the scene. Indeed in the concert

---

* When Lonny Epstein (see p. 15) was the soloist in Mozart's Piano Concerto in A major, K.488.
† Wolfgang Stresemann (1904–), son of the German statesman Gustav. Conductor, composer and Intendant of the Berlin Philharmonic Orchestra (1959–78).

of 10 April 1924 seemed a sort of battle cry...against the generally accepted style of interpretation and simultaneously an attempt to replace it with a new approach. That in the prevailing conditions this was at first carried to excess cannot be denied....[32]

The press greeted the concert with immense enthusiasm. Leopold Schmidt, the doyen of the city's critics, observed that during his seven years in Cologne Klemperer had ripened into a well-defined personality. 'The way in which he controlled the orchestra with a masterly if not notably individual stick technique stamps him as a born leader. The Philharmonic Orchestra was fired to an exceptionally high level of playing and followed the guest even where he departed from what is customary.'[33] On occasions, Schmidt observed, Klemperer had a tendency to over-emphasise detail. The *Börsen-Courier* (15 April 1924) felt that rhythmic contrasts were sometimes carried to theatrical lengths. But Hugo Leichentritt hailed Klemperer as an authoritative interpreter of the classics. Musicianship, temperament, craftsmanship and intellect combined to make him 'one of those rare conductors...who are able to illuminate the spiritual experience that lies behind the notes'.[34] Virtually overnight, Klemperer had established himself in Berlin. The only question was the form that his association with the city was to take. Part of the answer was provided when, within a few days of this triumph, the all-powerful Berlin agents, Wolff und Sachs, announced that he would return during the following winter to conduct no fewer than six concerts with the Berlin Philharmonic Orchestra.

Meanwhile the newspapers were increasingly full of disturbing reports on the situation of the Grosse Volksoper and doubts were cast on whether Klemperer would be taking up his appointment. He himself already had reason to question Lange's artistic integrity. By the time of his Berlin concert he had also become aware of the full extent of his financial difficulties. On 14 April the *Vossische Zeitung* reported that Klemperer had altered his contract with the Grosse Volksoper to 'a loose connection', but would conduct a new production of *Die Zauberflöte* in the earlier part of the coming season.

Even that prospect was not to materialise. On 16 July 1924 the owner of the Theater des Westens brought bankruptcy proceedings against the Grosse Volksoper for non-payment of rent. Lange now had his back to the wall, but within two days he had succeeded in raising a loan from the Berlin City Council. This enabled him to stagger on into the following season, for which he had announced ambitious plans that included productions of *Bluebeard's Castle* and Hindemith's three early one-act operas. As late as 27 August it was stated that Klemperer would be appearing as a guest conductor.[35]

But by autumn the stabilisation of the mark that had been achieved in the course of the summer had finally cut the ground from under Lange's feet. In a last desperate attempt to acquire a theatre, he bought Littmann's sizeable share-holding in the Deutsches Opernhaus. To block this move, a shareholder in the Deutsches Opernhaus thereupon bought shares in the Grosse Volksoper. The validity of both sales was contested. On 8 November a general meeting of shareholders of the Grosse Volksoper called for Lange's resignation. A week later, in a final gesture of defiance, he appointed himself *Generalintendant*, only to be compelled on 5 December to resign. At a meeting called three days later, the shareholders learnt that Lange's principal backer, 'the Russian industrialist, Rubin' had earlier bankrupted himself in a vain attempt to save the Grosse Volksoper, whereupon Lange had threatened him with deportation as an undesirable alien.[36] But now the game was up; in spite of further assistance from the Berlin City Council, the Grosse Volksoper shut on 25 January 1925 with a performance of *Don Giovanni* conducted by Leo Blech.*

*　　　　　　　*　　　　　　　*

By the time that Klemperer returned to Cologne it was clear that, even if 'a loose connection' were preserved with the Grosse Volksoper, it would not provide him with a living. It was also clear that, at any rate for the time being, it could not offer the artistic independence that was his ultimate ambition. In that case, he must have asked himself, what purpose would be served by leaving Cologne for a similar position elsewhere? In February, when he had asked to be released from his contract, the Theatre Commission had done its utmost to persuade him to remain. Now that his reputation had received such a boost in the capital, might not Cologne offer a new engagement with some of the artistic powers he had sought in Berlin?

Pocketing his pride, he wrote on 23 April directly to Konrad Adenauer.[37] As a result of the unusual success of his concert in Berlin, he had received various proposals. Could not an attempt be made to reach a new agreement with Cologne before he made a decision on these offers? Adenauer referred the matter to the city's principal cultural official, Meerfeld, who in a memorandum dated 28 April advised against a new engagement.[38] Klemperer, he pointed out, had dissolved an existing contract, only

---

* No more was heard of Lange until November 1931, when his sharp nose for prevailing winds enabled him to reappear (brandishing his self-bestowed title of *Generalintendant*!) as director of a Deutsches Nationaltheater in Berlin that had Nazi support. Although Alfred Hugenberg and Joseph Goebbels attended the opening night, the enterprise lasted less than two months. In March 1933, after Nazi storm-troopers had occupied the Berlin Städtische Oper (as the Deutsches Opernhaus had since become) and evicted its Intendant, Carl Ebert, Lange attempted to instal himself as Ebert's successor. The Nazis, however, preferred Schillings, who was appointed on 26 March, four months before his death on 23 July 1933.

subsequently to discover that the conditions he had been promised in Berlin were not as he had been led to suppose, and these were by no means the first negotiations he had had in the capital. Now he wanted to remain in Cologne. In conversation with Meerfeld he had nonetheless let it be known that, not only would the initiative have to come from the city, but he would insist on an appointment as opera director, whereby he would assume responsibility for all aspects of opera, not, as hitherto, merely its musical side, as well as on longer periods of leave. The Theatre Commission, reported Meerfeld, was convinced that he would nonetheless take the first opportunity to leave for Berlin or Vienna. The opera house could not stand such uncertainty and was in any case suffering from tension between Klemperer and Rémond. Eugen Szenkar had accordingly been invited to conduct two guest performances with a view to engagement.*

The Theatre Commission was so eager to cut its ties with Klemperer that it did not even wait for Szenkar to make the second of these appearances before appointing him musical director on 9 May. This unseemly haste brought protests in the press and elsewhere and it is possible that Prälat Münch made an attempt through the ecclesiastical channels that always had Adenauer's ear to get the appointment reversed.[39] Klemperer himself was wounded by the city's lack of eagerness to retain his services (though in view of the number of attempts he had made to leave it, it can hardly have surprised him) and on 17 May went to complain of this to Adenauer himself. As on other occasions the great man received him with the cordiality he had always shown to a *Generalmusikdirektor* who had brought prestige to the city at a difficult period of its long history and with whom he had walked in the public processions on Corpus Christi that are a feature of its religious life. Nonetheless, he was not prepared to overrule his Theatre Commission. But he did not allow the leave-taking to be soured by mutual recriminations. Rejecting a long-winded, reproachful draft provided by Meerfeld, Adenauer on 19 May wrote Klemperer a cordial but decisive letter.

I deeply regret...your departure from Cologne. As you yourself told me personally when you asked to be released from your contract, it was your firm resolve to go to Berlin...An attempt to retain you seemed...hopeless...When, contrary to all expectations, your agreements with Berlin proved unrealisable, negotiations for a successor were fairly far advanced...To my great regret I see no possibility of retaining [you]...at the Cologne Opera. I would however like to take the opportunity to tell you that the accusations that have been made against you...have no basis in fact, and that the entire Commission is united in its extremely high esteem for your artistic abilities.

---

* Paradoxically, Szenkar had resigned as musical director of the Grosse Volksoper when Klemperer had been appointed director over his head.

On your departure from Cologne...I would like to thank you from my heart for all that you have given us during your seven years of activity here. You can be sure that your impact, your artistic character and your extraordinary achievements...will not be forgotten.[40]

On 11 June, in celebration of Strauss's sixtieth birthday, Klemperer conducted a new production of *Salome* with Rose Pauly in the title role. Three days later and with Schnabel as soloist he conducted the last of his opera-house concerts, which had become an established feature of the city's musical life. At its close there were repeated ovations and the stage was covered in flowers. Finally the safety curtain was lowered and Klemperer slipped out of the theatre, for the last time, by a side door. A crowd that had gathered hoped that he would speak to it. But he refused to do so, perhaps because, as the *KölnischeVolkszeitung* (16 June 1924) suggested, he was bitter that so little effort had been made to retain him in Cologne.

*   *   *

Among the approaches that Klemperer had received was one from Carl Hagemann, the Intendant of the Wiesbaden theatres. After the concert he had given there on 1 April, Hagemann had described him in an internal report as 'a conductor of genius'. Aware that Klemperer's engagement with the Grosse Volksoper was in question, he determined to bring him to Wiesbaden. A telegram on 5 April having elicited only an evasive reply, Hagemann pursued his quarry to Berlin. Discussions took place, but at that time Klemperer still hoped to resuscitate his Cologne engagement. Wiesbaden was in any case a smaller theatre and hence a step down in the German operatic hierarchy. On 29 April, by which date it must have seemed doubtful whether Cologne would re-engage him, Klemperer agreed to open negotiations, but warned Hagemann that 'a new constellation' had come into existence.[41]

That constellation consisted of offers from Vienna and Karlsruhe. Earlier in April there had been reports in Berlin newspapers that Richard Strauss, who was nearing the end of his five-year period as director of the Vienna State Opera, intended to engage Klemperer as an assistant conductor.* On

---

* *BZ am Mittag* (5 April) and *Vossische Zeitung* (11 April). But the most concrete evidence of negotiations with Vienna in April 1924 consists of a note in the files of the Karlsruhe Opera, which was also eager to engage Klemperer, to the effect that Vienna would have decided one way or another by early May.

Rumours of a Viennese engagement recurred early in 1925 (*Neue Freie Presse*, 20 January). That they were not groundless is indicated by a surprising outburst on the part of Strauss, who on 3 November 1924 had resigned as director of the State Opera. In a letter of 5 December to the Viennese critic, Ludwig Karpath, he wrote, 'If it is really wished not to break all bridges...they should desist from hostile actions: as such, I consider a

26 April Klemperer wrote to the Karlsruhe Intendant to suggest that the concert he was to give there on 6 May would provide an opportunity to discuss his offer of an engagement. Why Klemperer should have given Karlsruhe, another medium-sized theatre, preference over Wiesbaden, is unclear. It was in any case unknown territory and he accordingly cast around for someone familiar with operatic conditions there. He was given the name of Hans Curjel, a young art historian on the staff of the local Kunsthalle, who had also studied musicology and had ambitions to conduct.* Curjel advised against accepting a position in Karlsruhe and nothing came of the negotiations. But Klemperer was so impressed by his young adviser's intelligence and the breadth of his artistic horizons that he promised him a job at whatever theatre he went to.†That promise was to be fulfilled three years later, when at Klemperer's insistence he was appointed *Dramaturg* of the Berlin Kroll Opera, in whose fortunes he was destined to play a crucial role.

With Cologne, Karlsruhe and, presumably, Vienna out of the running, Wiesbaden was left in sole possession of the field. Klemperer arrived there for negotiations on 12 May and ten days later his appointment was announced. The musical world was surprised that a conductor who seemed on the brink of a brilliant career should have opted for a relatively small theatre. But Hagemann had proved willing to make substantial concessions to land a big fish. As a spa, Wiesbaden could afford to tolerate lower standards off-season, provided that the opera was at its best during the months when the town was full of visitors. This made it possible for him to offer a contract that bound Klemperer for no more than six months a year, thus enabling him to accept guest engagements on a scale that had been impossible in Cologne. He was to have an entirely free hand artistically. The orchestra was to be strengthened and he was to give six concerts a season with it. His salary (25,000M) was handsome.

Wiesbaden offered another advantage. In spite of its relatively modest size, the theatre enjoyed a special position among German opera houses. Originally the personal property of the Hohenzollern dynasty, it had, like all the Prussian court theatres, in 1918 passed under the direct control of

possible engagement of Herr Klemperer, a notoriously bad conductor of my operas and famously lazy (in Cologne they are glad to be rid of him).' (International Richard Strauss Society, *Blätter* No. 6, pp. 17–18.) The comment is surprising because before and after this date relations between Strauss and Klemperer appear to have been cordial, and laziness was certainly not one of Klemperer's shortcomings. No traces of either negotiation has come to light in the files of the Austrian federal theatres or of the Vienna State Opera.

* Curjel (see biographical glossary) had already conducted an early chamber work, *Frauentanz*, by Kurt Weill, at that time still a little-known composer.

† In a conversation with the author on 11 July 1973, Curjel stated that Klemperer subsequently offered him a post at Wiesbaden, which he could not accept as it was unpaid.

the Kultusministerium. When the question of Klemperer's engagement arose, there can be little doubt that the ministry looked favourably on it.* Though it had failed in the previous year to bring him to Berlin, it still had him in mind as a conductor who, once circumstances were more propitious, might reform the ailing Berlin State Opera. In Wiesbaden he would be directly under the ministry's eye. Conversely, Klemperer was doubtless aware that as a theatre controlled from Berlin, Wiesbaden made an ideal springboard for the capital.

*   *   *

Two days after the new engagement was announced, Nathan Klemperer died at the age of almost seventy-eight. Since he had suffered a mild stroke in 1919, he had been failing in body though not in mind, and the death of his wife fifteen months earlier had left a gap that the devotion of his children could not fill. Marianne and her husband lived close by, his two small grandchildren, and especially the infant Lotte, who had been born the previous November, were a source of unfailing pleasure. But Klemperer and his wife were busy at the theatre, so that he hardly saw them other than at mealtimes and often felt lonely. By the winter of 1923/4 a weak heart made it difficult to climb stairs or leave the house. Although the end came suddenly, his only son was with him when he died. Nathan Klemperer was buried in Cologne's Jewish cemetery alongside his wife.

Freud observed that the death of the father is the most crucial event in the life of a male child. Kind, gentle Nathan had never been a very effective *paterfamilias*, yet his death corresponded in time to a decisive turn in his son's career. Klemperer's galley years were over. Within twelve months not only Berlin but Moscow and New York would beckon.

* There is, however, again no evidence that the engagement was instigated by Kestenberg, as has often been asserted.

Klemperer and Carl Hagemann, his new Intendant, were by no means strangers. They had first met about 1909 in Bodanzky's home in Mannheim, where Hagemann was ending the first of his two periods as Intendant and the 24-year-old Klemperer had, as Hagemann later recalled, drawn attention to himself through his 'genialische Manierlosigheit'.* They had also encountered each other in Hamburg, where Hagemann was appointed director of the Deutsches Schauspielhaus in the same year as Klemperer arrived at the Stadttheater. There may well have been further contact during Hagemann's second period in Mannheim (1915–20), when Klemperer was a relatively frequent visitor to the city from nearby Strasbourg, and again when, after he had been appointed to Wiesbaden in 1920, Hagemann had invited him to conduct occasional concerts.

Hagemann greatly admired Klemperer's musical powers. But there was a more specific reason for his eagerness to bring him to Wiesbaden as musical director. A prolific writer, mainly on theatre and travel, Hagemann was a man of wider intellectual and cultural horizons than the conventional theatre director. He had started his career as a journalist and *feuilleton* editor, in which capacity he had in 1903 attended the production of *Tristan und Isolde* that was the first fruit of the collaboration between Mahler and Roller in Vienna. Its new emphasis on space, lighting and three-dimensional objects in place of the then customary painted coulisses had come as a revelation. Henceforth Hagemann regarded Mahler, not merely as a supremely great conductor, but as the man who had achieved on the operatic stage that unity of music and drama which Wagner had sought but failed to bring about at Bayreuth.[1] He himself had indeed played a part in the movement of scenic reform that swept the German theatre in the early years of the century. In 1907 he had staged *Hamlet* in Mannheim with a single set that with variations in lighting remained in position throughout the evening. What he termed an *Ideal-Bühne* thus formed a link in the chain of innovations that had led from the permanent features that Roller had devised for Mahler's *Don Giovanni* in Vienna in 1905 to the near-abstract *Stilbühne* that Klemperer had used in his Barmen *Così fan tutte* in 1914.[2] While Intendant in Mannheim he had, together with his First

* Freely translated, 'The mannerlessness of genius' (Hagemann, *Bühne und Welt*, p. 100).

Conductor Wilhelm Furtwängler, and his principal designer, Ludwig Siewert,* in 1917 in Baden-Baden staged a production of *The Ring* with projections that represented one of the earliest challenges to the naturalism still prevailing at Bayreuth.

It was as a man with a progressive reputation that Hagemann had been appointed Intendant in Wiesbaden by the Prussian Kultusministerium. The theatre enjoyed an exceptional status among German opera houses. After Prussia had annexed Hesse-Nassau in 1867, it had been placed under the direct control of the *Generalintendant* of the Berlin court theatres, who had continued to run it until the revolution of 1918. The Hohenzollerns had a special affection for the spa town at the foot of the Taunus mountains. William II built an opulent neo-baroque theatre and this became the focal point of an annual May festival, which he and the court regularly attended. Imperial patronage gave the theatre a prestige out of proportion to its size. Hohenzollern taste also permeated productions that became a by-word for lavish vulgarity.† After the Kultusministerium acquired the theatre at the end of the war, it gave Hagemann a brief to transform it into an institution more in tune with the spirit of the new age.

Like Klemperer, Hagemann was passionately opposed to the repertory system, which he regarded as incompatible with a high level of performance. His experience of Mahler in Vienna had led him to believe operatic salvation could only be achieved when one man, be he conductor or stage director, took overall responsibility for every aspect of a performance.[3] In Klemperer he believed he had found that man and for that reason he was prepared to concede him wide-ranging powers, in the field of staging as well as in musical matters. Klemperer was undoubtedly drawn to Wiesbaden by his awareness that in Hagemann he had at last found an Intendant who was not merely willing but eager to give him the prerogatives he had hitherto sought in vain.

*   *   *

Klemperer's plans for Wiesbaden centred on one man: Ewald Dülberg. Since they had first met in Hamburg in the autumn of 1912 (when Hagemann as director of the Schauspielhaus had commissioned sets for Goethe's *Faust* from Dülberg that were among his earliest work in the theatre) the two men had only been able to meet on isolated occasions. But over the years their friendship had deepened and around 1917 Dülberg

---

* Ludwig Siewert (1887–1966) was a leading expressionist designer. In 1950 Klemperer worked with him on a production of *Die Zauberflöte* at La Scala, Milan, but did not enjoy the experience.

† His Imperial Majesty even took a hand in designing sets for *Oberon* (Niessen, *Deutsche Oper der Gegenwart*, p. 46).

had produced a series of strikingly penetrating woodcut portraits of Klemperer. Both had waited impatiently for conditions in which they could put their ideas on the staging of opera into practice. Despairing of finding fulfilment in the theatre (for a brief and unhappy period, he had worked at the Berlin Volksbühne's Theater am Bülowplatz), Dülberg had in 1921 taken a post at the Staatliche Kunstakademie in Kassel, where, in addition to teaching painting, woodcutting and printing, he had developed sidelines in textile design, stained glass and mosaics.

As a stage designer, Dülberg stood 'between two periods'.* On the one hand, he was deeply opposed to conventional naturalism. 'My entire theatrical activity', he wrote, 'is based on a longing for space...not as an end in itself but as a framework for the movement of characters.'[4] That preoccupation with space suggests the influence of Appia, as indeed do the massive block formations that dominate many of Dülberg's sets. He also firmly believed that every age had a duty to reinterpret the masterpieces of the past. Yet this radicalism was tempered by a suspicion of new trends. Although he was closer to the Bauhaus than he liked to believe (and was frequently attacked by conservative music critics on that account), he remained fiercely critical of it. Although he practised drastic stylisation in his own designs, he remained opposed to it as a principle, arguing, with Schoenberg, that every score laid down a style. Dülberg was an abrasive, solitary character, who always remained his own man. As a result, he came to be attacked by radicals as well as reactionaries.

Dülberg's strong if rather puritanical musical sympathies were dominated by a detestation of emotional extravagance. He was deeply suspicious of Wagner (and influenced Klemperer in this respect) and contemptuous of Schreker.† He knew Busoni, and sympathy for Busoni's 'young classicism' paved the way for a later admiration of Stravinsky and Hindemith, whose flat in Berlin he decorated in the late twenties. His musical understanding led him to acknowledge the primacy of music in opera. In his view, the task of a designer was to provide a visual accompaniment to the score by means of form, colour and space.[5] No man did more to shape Klemperer's approach to the staging of opera.

Klemperer's first act after signing his contract was to summon Dülberg from Kassel and, so impatient was he to start work, that he was vexed to learn that his collaborator could only travel the following day.[6] For three

---

* Comment of the art critic, Heinrich Simon, which Dülberg quoted, presumably with approval, in his 'Versuch einer Selbstdarstellung', *Der Merkur*, 1951, No. 3, p. 257. It might equally well be applied to Klemperer.

† Three days after the première of *Irrelohe*, for which he had disdainfully declined to design sets, Dülberg wrote on 30 March 1924 to Kruttge, 'The *Irrelohe* muck (I have looked at a piano reduction with horror) has now certainly revealed its stench.'

201

days and three nights Dülberg laboured on designs for *Fidelio*, which was to open the new season. These aroused Klemperer and Hagemann to such enthusiasm that they then and there offered him an engagement to design any operas that Klemperer might conduct at Wiesbaden and to supervise the opera house's entire scenic activities. In Klemperer's mind he was to play a role similar to that which Roller had played under Mahler in Vienna.

As ill-luck would have it (and he was a man who drew ill-luck as a steeple attracts lightning), Dülberg was discovered early in August 1924 to be suffering from tuberculosis of the lungs and was obliged to leave for Arosa with only his sets for *Fidelio* completed. Klemperer, who was holidaying in Sils Maria, was aghast.* A projected production of Stravinsky's *L'Histoire du soldat* was postponed until later in the year. But Dülberg did not recover rapidly; he participated only in one further production (of *Don Giovanni*) during the three years that Klemperer remained in Wiesbaden and plans for him to work on a permanent basis in the theatre had to be abandoned.

The bold forms and harsh colours of Dülberg's sets for *Fidelio* set Wiesbaden by the ears when the new production was first seen on 3 September. Decoration in the usual sense of the word had disappeared. In its place stood vast rectangular blocks that formed varying patterns in each scene and in the finale rolled aside to reveal a huge open space. In the opening scene Rocco's quarters were entirely bare. Fierce red walls towered above the courtyard of the jail with entrances that were holes rather than doors. The prisoners formed an undifferentiated mass with shorn hair and whitened faces and in the finale the chorus was again deployed in static blocks, this time against a brilliant, blue background. Countless designers and producers have since staged the work in comparable ways, but in 1924 Dülberg's approach was revolutionary. Its stark monumentalism (together with the banishing of the cosy sentiment usually associated with the *Singspiel* elements in the opera) shocked the local critics, and even Klemperer later conceded that the production had been 'perhaps too drastic'.[7] But the *Frankfurter Zeitung* (13 September 1924) praised the production's 'revolutionary ethos' and welcomed the emphasis it gave to the epic elements in the drama. Although some critics complained that Klemperer had occasionally exaggerated dynamic shadings and other nuances, there was virtually unanimous praise for the musico-dramatic unity and urgency of the performance. It was, one critic wrote, an event that could only be compared to Mahler's deeds in Vienna.

---

* German currency being again acceptable abroad, the Engadine resort was teeming with German musicians. Among them was Bruno Walter, who, as Klemperer wrote to his wife on 4 August, was agreeable but 'somewhat alien'. Other visitors to Sils Maria were Elisabeth Schumann and her second husband, Karl Alwin. Klemperer went out of his way to inform Johanna that he had had little contact with her.

The essential in Klemperer's achievement...lies in the impact it makes above all on the stage...One has an impression of hearing the opera for the first time: the steadily growing tension of the first act, the dramatic charge of the prison scene, the immense impact of the *dénouement* and the almost hysterical fervour of the liberation. The ensembles become natural points of resolution in this great tension and development. Not for a moment does one have a feeling of music-making as an end in itself...All historical accretions, all implausibilities of plot and text are swept away. Myth emerges from an anecdotal story, archetypes out of operatic characters. Most splendid of all, Beethoven is reborn out of the experience of our own time, fashioned out of our feeling for space and sound. Maybe details of the staging are open to discussion...Maybe the personality cult of the present-day is overdone, particularly where performing artists are concerned...But in the case of Klemperer, the true servant of Beethoven's work, it is justified.[8]

In Wiesbaden Klemperer for the first time succeeded in freeing himself from the toils of repertory; almost without exception every opera performance he conducted was of a new production or of a revival he had himself prepared. Owing to commitments in Berlin and the Soviet Union as well as to Dülberg's illness, it was not until 10 December that he was able to stage Stravinsky's *L'Histoire du soldat*, which he coupled with a concert performance of the *Pulcinella* suite. With its foreshadowing of Brechtian theatre and its bony instrumentation, *The Soldier's Tale* came as a shock to eyes and ears reared on naturalistic productions and Wagnerian orchestration.* In his report on the evening, Hagemann, who produced, noted with evident relief that it had been heard without interruption and even been applauded by a minority, although the local critics shrugged it off as 'a box of tricks' and 'a symptom of cultural decline'. New productions followed of *Lohengrin* (11 January 1925), *Figaro* (22 February), which Hagemann also produced, and at the very end of the season an *Elektra* which Otto Dorn described as 'a fire storm'.[9] The season brought Klemperer himself a degree of satisfaction and fulfilment that he had never previously found in his work. In later years he was to look back on his time in Wiesbaden as the happiest of his life.

*   *   *

While Johanna had been busy establishing their new home in a villa in the Nerotal, a hilly, wooded area on the northern outskirts of the town in the summer of 1924, Klemperer had been preparing by far the most extensive series of concerts he had as yet undertaken. In addition to six concerts in Wiesbaden and a further half-dozen in Berlin, he had received an invitation from Furtwängler to deputise for him at the Leipzig Gewand-

---

* Only two months after Klemperer had conducted the work in Wiesbaden, a performance at the Hamburg Opera had to be abandoned owing to the violence of the reaction it provoked (*Wiesbadener Tageblatt*, 25 February 1925). See also pp. 276–7 for reactions in Berlin in 1928.

haus Orchestra's New Year's Day concert, and his Berlin agents, Wolff und Sachs, had enquired whether he would also undertake a tour in the Soviet Union. He had also contracted to make a series of acoustical recordings with the Berlin Staatskapelle for Polydor.*

Klemperer's concerts with the Berlin Philharmonic Orchestra represented a formidable challenge. They called for an extension of a repertory that was still extremely limited and he was not a quick learner of unfamiliar scores. Even the prospect of conducting Brahms's Fourth Symphony for the first time caused apprehension. He also found himself in a peculiarly exposed position. In spite of the fact that he had become the darling of the more radical critics, who hailed him with ever-increasing frequency as the man who would 'cleanse' the capital's chaotic operatic life, to Berlin audiences he was still little more than a name. The stabilisation of the currency had moreover brought about a sudden resuscitation of concert life, as famous musicians once again flocked to the German capital. Looking at the posters for the coming season, Adolf Weissmann commented that one might imagine oneself back in pre-war days.[10] On the other hand, as a result of drastic deflation, money was short. In such competitive conditions the series of concerts that now lay before Klemperer could make or break his reputation. Characteristically, he played for safety.

For his first concert on 17 October he chose Bruckner's Symphony No. 8, a work in which he had already triumphed in Cologne, Prague and Wiesbaden, and in Berlin his interpretation was again greeted by a well-nigh unanimous paean of praise. A senior critic wrote that not even Richter or Nikisch had given such an imposing account of the work.[11] Max Marschalk found it characteristically North German in its avoidance of sentimentality and exaggeration,[12] but Schrenk praised the brisk pace of the adagio, which had not endangered the music's solemnity, the demonic humour of the scherzo and the rare sense of unity in the finale.[13] A recording of the adagio, which was made at around this time,† confirms Marschalk's description: the music is unfolded with a magisterial spaciousness that is completely free of mannerism or affectation.

None of Klemperer's other concerts in Berlin in the winter of 1924/5 achieved such overwhelming success. His accompaniment of Edwin Fischer in a performance of Beethoven's 'Emperor' Concerto on 21 November was widely held to be exaggerated in its heroic attitudes.‡ Although the first

* See discography, nos. 1–4.
† The date is unverifiable, as the Polydor/Deutsche Grammophon archives were destroyed in the war.
‡ Karl Ulrich Schnabel (b. 1909) pianist son of Artur, who was hearing Klemperer for the first time at the age of fifteen, has recalled his accompaniment of the finale as so overwhelming that 'one entirely forgot that a pianist was playing' (interview with the author). Perhaps that was what the critics were complaining of.

performance in Germany of Krenek's recent realisation of two movements of Mahler's unfinished Symphony No. 10 (28 December) received enthusiastic notices as an interpretation, there was general agreement among the critics that these posthumous fragments should not have been performed. Klemperer himself was sceptical of their validity and subsequently came to believe that they had been published in direct contravention of Mahler's expressed wishes.*

Other attempts that he made to introduce contemporary works met with equally little success. Stravinsky's *Pulcinella* suite (26 January), a work that was henceforth to figure prominently in his programmes, was condemned by the older critics as bringing an air of levity inappropriate to the hallowed traditions of a German concert hall. Another essay in the new classicism, Krenek's attempt to resuscitate the spirit of Bach's Brandenburg Concertos in his recent Concerto Grosso No. 2 (8 February), occasioned a public uproar and found equally little approval in the press.†

The following winter of 1925/6 Klemperer returned to Berlin on three occasions, on each of which he conducted a huge work with which he was to become closely identified. On 27 September he again performed Bruckner's Symphony No. 8, this time at a Volksbühne concert in its theatre on the Bülowplatz. When, five days later, he conducted Mahler's Symphony No. 9 at the Philharmonie the hall was far from full.‡ Yet the critics were again virtually unanimous on the overwhelming impact of a performance that combined intensity and precision, architectural grandeur and grasp of detail. 'What Otto Klemperer achieved this evening', wrote Schrenk, a writer not given to high-flown phrases, 'can hardly be conveyed. Intellectually (geistig), musically and technically, he has completely measured up to his task... Those with ears to hear experienced the fascinating beauty and splendour of this "Ninth" with breathless astonishment.'[14]

But if Bruckner and Mahler was territory he had made very much his own, Beethoven's Ninth was another matter, for when he finally did conduct it for the first time in Berlin on 22 November, he faced a public

---

* After the only occasion on which he relented (London, 24 April 1961, as part of an all-Mahler concert, in which it was difficult to find an orchestral piece of appropriate length), he declared that he would never again conduct it, a decision to which he adhered. In later years Klemperer was even more passionately opposed to Deryck Cooke's reconstruction of the entire work from sketches, so much so that he refused to listen to a recording or even to receive Cooke. (*Conversations*, p. 35)

† It is indicative of Klemperer's diffidence when confronted with new works that a week before the concert he should have written to the twenty-four-year-old Krenek, offering to pay his hotel bill if he would come to Berlin for rehearsals, adding, 'Above all else, I want to know if I conduct your concerto correctly'. (Letter of 2 February 1925.)

‡ He had already conducted it in Wiesbaden (1922) and Cologne (1923).

and a press whose memories went back to Bülow, Mahler and Nikisch. Yet Leopold Schmidt, the doyen of the city's critics, had few reservations.

Even the first movement leaves no doubt that we are in the presence of an entirely individual interpreter, uninfluenced by his predecessors. And, make no mistake, there is no arbitrary fussiness, no conductor's presumptuousness in this sense of individuality, only a complete faithfulness to the score...Nothing is overlooked... nothing is added...I found the tempi gloriously right...the first movement is lively and compact, never dragged or emotionally padded out. The scherzo is taken at a speed that can be risked with the Philharmonic's excellent woodwind, and the trio is spared the error, still not completely eradicated, that the metronomic markings refer to semi-breves...These quicker tempi are particularly beneficial to the third movement...Klemperer fashions the melodic line with remarkable plasticity, even in passages where it is in the woodwind and usually obscured by string figuration...The tempestuous opening of the finale...corresponds to this overall approach. In the choral sections the theatre conductor became apparent, not to the disadvantage of their impact. One can conceive of the music more solemnly performed, but not more expressively....[15]

A few critics found the performance overdriven and its climaxes excessively violent. But they remained a minority. Rudolf Kastner, who wrote that the organ points in the first movement 'thundered with a Dantesque sense of terror',[16] was among those who were plainly overwhelmed, and so again was Schrenk.

I had never supposed that a work which one has heard a hundred times could have the impact of a revelation...The secret of the pulverising effect of [Klemperer's] Ninth lies simply in the fact that he fulfils Beethoven's will as laid down in the score with a fanatical objectivity. I can think of no performance that has...dispensed with any sort of personal 'interpretation' in order to realise the spirit of the music so purely.[17]

Neither Schrenk nor any of his colleagues took exception to the fact that Klemperer had not only used retouchings in the scherzo that had become traditional since they had been introduced by Wagner,* but introduced a number of his own.

In the course of these concerts in 1924 and 1925 there were fierce encounters with the Berlin Philharmonic Orchestra, which resisted Klemperer's meticulous rehearsing of works with which it considered itself familiar. And by no means everything he conducted found approval. His Schubert and Schumann were widely felt to lack romantic sweetness, his Mozart to be unduly Beethovenian in spite of its grace and ease. But he had established himself as a musician of arresting individuality. His largeness of conception and concern for detail, the sense of naturalness that tempered his fervour, the intensity of sound he drew from an

* In Dresden in 1846.

206

orchestra, the austerity and grandeur of his interpretations, seemed to express the new post-romantic age that was beginning to emerge.[18]

*   *   *

In the winter of 1918/19, while Germany was in the toils of defeat, occupation, civic strife and economic crisis, a new group of composers had emerged in Paris, who took, or at any rate accepted, the sobriquet of *Les Six*. Their model was Erik Satie, their spokesman Jean Cocteau, who in a provocative essay entitled 'Le Coq et l'arlequin' (1918) had heralded a new simplicity in music. Cocteau was as opposed to Debussy as he was to Wagner; the 'dense fog' of Bayreuth had merely been transformed into the 'sunlit mist' of impressionism. Both composers were dismissed as exponents of an elaborate and over-refined art. To what he considered the corrupt world of theatre and opera, Cocteau opposed the music-hall, the circus and negro jazz. 'The role of art', he maintained, 'consists...in finding an antidote against useless beauty which encourages the superfluous.'[19] He longed for an orchestra 'without the caress of strings', for a composer who would write for a mechanical organ.* Although *Les Six* included composers as diverse as Honegger, Milhaud and Poulenc, the sounding board of Paris and Cocteau's flair as a propagandist imposed a short-lived unity. In the years immediately after the war, the group were linked by a common interest in popular music and a revulsion against the 'high' view of art that had predominated throughout the late romantic era and reached its apogee at Bayreuth.

Nowhere was that view so deeply ingrained as in Central Europe, which is one reason why the new aesthetic took some years to cross the Rhine. That it failed to do so until about 1924 can be also attributed to the isolation, at once political, psychological and economic (a fee paid in marks being virtually valueless to foreign artists), that Germany suffered in the years immediately after the war. The first work in which Hindemith broke decisively from a late romantic idiom, the *Kammermusik No. 1*, was in fact composed as early as December 1921. But for the moment it remained little more than a straw in the wind; it was not until after the end of inflation and the subsequent success of Stresemann's policy of fulfilment in the Locarno Treaty of October 1925, which restored Germany to the community of Western European nations, that the impact of *Les Six* and of Stravinsky's new classicistic style began to make much headway in Central Europe.

German traditions imposed a distinctively national flavour on the new

* Cocteau seems in 1918 to have been blithely unaware of the fact that his friend, Stravinsky, had in fact already realised much of his programme. This accounts for the break in their relationship that occurred after the publication of *Le Coq et l'arlequin.*

French flippancy. Even composers as deeply immersed in chromatic harmony as Wagner and Brahms, not to mention Reger and Schoenberg, had never lost touch with the contrapuntal roots of German music. Thus it was natural that in Germany the reaction against chromatic harmony, lavish orchestration and 'high' art should express itself in a revival of eighteenth-century polyphony. Hindemith, in particular, matched the irreverent spirit of new French music, its rhythmic vigour, clearly defined tonality and direct tunes, with a return to neo-Bachian contrapuntal virtuosity, seemingly under an impression that Bach was 'inexpressive'. By 1925 this specifically German brand of neo-classicism was well enough established for Schoenberg to mock it in his *Three Satires* for mixed chorus. But his own music of the period* is evidence of how deeply even he had been infected by it. The world that Busoni had foreseen in his writings but failed to bring into existence in his music was coming to pass and, taking the title of an exhibition of post-expressionist painting mounted by Gustav Hartlaub in Mannheim in 1925, it embraced the tag of *die neue Sachlichkeit*. The agonies and exultations of expressionism had been succeeded by a new age of sobriety.

To a greater extent than perhaps any other major interpretative musician of his generation, Klemperer had a foot in both camps. The wild-eyed young man pictured in the orchestral pit at Strasbourg (see frontispiece) might be a figure in an expressionist film. Klemperer's very disposition, with its violent swings from exultant mania to bottomless melancholy, had an expressionist quality, and so did the flailing arms, stamping feet and fanatical fervour of his conducting as a young man. Even his deep attachment to Mahler and the attraction exercised by early Schoenberg carried expressionist implications.

By the mid-twenties Klemperer's musical attitudes, like those of so many of his more go-ahead contemporaries, had undergone a deep change. Already in Cologne his sympathy for Wagner had waned as Mozart had increasingly become the keystone of his operatic repertory, and, as the decade advanced, a commitment to Bach became steadily more apparent (see pp. 302–5). As early as 1922, he had expressed interest in a new work by Walter Braunfels, 'especially as it offers a welcome prospect of closed numbers, arias, etc.'.[20] In this evolution the influence on him of Busoni was paramount, as Klemperer himself acknowledged, when he described it as second only to that of Mahler.[21] Thus Busoni's death on 27 July 1924 came as a personal blow. 'How great the loss is', he wrote to Johanna immediately after learning of it, 'we have still to realise.'†

* For instance the *Serenade*, Op. 24. This had its first performance at the Donaueschingen Festival of 1924, which Klemperer attended.
† Letter of 29 July 1924. In spite of his veneration for Busoni, Klemperer nonetheless drew

17 From left to right: Schoenberg, Klemperer, Hermann Scherchen, Webern and Erwin Stein at the Donaueschingen Festival, July 1924

His style of conducting also underwent a corresponding evolution, as his youthful vehemence came increasingly to be tempered by a revulsion against anything that smacked of exaggeration or emotional indulgence. In part this was a reflection of growing maturity. But it also stemmed from a remarkable ability to span the apparently irreconcilable worlds of

a clear distinction between the man and his music. Although he attended the posthumous première of *Doktor Faust* in Dresden on 21 May 1925, he made no attempt to perform the opera himself. Not a bar of Busoni's music was performed at the Kroll during the four years that Klemperer was responsible for its artistic policy.

expressionism and *die neue Sachlichkeit*, an ability that was to provide the very basis of his individuality and stature as a conductor. It was this unique combination of romantic intensity and classical equilibrium that led him rather than Walter and Furtwängler, who already seemed representatives of an earlier generation, to be regarded as the conductor closest to the new world of feeling which had emerged since 1918. That did not prevent him from conducting romantic composers such as Brahms, Bruckner and Mahler as frequently as they did. But the interpretations were widely felt to be basically different in spirit.

This evolution also affected his attitude to new music. Composers such as Pfitzner, Schreker and even, in the late twenties, Strauss were discarded in favour of representatives of the up-and-coming neo-classical school, such as Krenek, Hindemith and, above all, Stravinsky. Confronted with the obligatory interview on his arrival in New York on 15 January 1926 (see p. 225). Klemperer expressed his belief that 'there will be a reversion to the old classical schools, to the kind of music that was written before the days of Mozart'.[22] That was, however, the closest he was to come to any explicit commitment. From first to last, Klemperer was a man who shied away from labels. He was to be every bit as resistant to attempts (and many were to be made in the coming years) to pin on him the slogans of the *neue Sachlichkeit* as to Trotsky's description of him as an expressionist (see p. 223). Just because his musicality spanned and drew nourishment from two worlds, he remained unwilling to commit himself wholeheartedly to either of them. This fundamental ambivalence could appear merely evasive, and it was to lead him to be attacked (like his friend Dülberg) on two fronts. To upholders of the old romantic world of feeling, his interpretations seemed alarmingly new in their analytical and intellectual rigour. To the new classicists he occasionally appeared faint-hearted in his advocacy of modernism.

The only clear commitment to emerge in the early twenties was to the music of Stravinsky, the contemporary composer to whom he was in the coming years to feel closest. And even in this case Klemperer character-istically refused to allow himself to be manoeuvred into a sectarian position. Asked in the Soviet Union about the discrepancy between Stravinsky's 'artistic brilliance' and the 'deeper emotionalism' of Schoen-berg, his reply was forthright:

I categorically reject the idea of an opposition between Schoenberg and Stravinsky. Both are geniuses, although representatives of different races. The difference between them lies more in the fact that they belong to different generations than in any explicit tendency of the one or the other.[23]

In 1925, the year in which Schoenberg and Stravinsky both attended the

ISCM Festival in Venice but failed to meet, that was a highly unusual point of view. To the musical world at large they had come to be seen as leaders of irreconcilable schools, as they were indeed to remain until Schoenberg's death in 1951.

That Klemperer's refusal to regard the two composers as mutually exclusive was more than an off-the-cuff observation is evident from his programme when on 17 November 1925 Stravinsky came to Wiesbaden as the soloist in his recent Piano Concerto.* In addition to the suite from *Pulcinella* and a Haydn symphony, he opened the concert with the two Bach chorale-preludes that Schoenberg had arranged for large orchestra in 1922. Nothing could have been further removed in style from the neo-classical view of Bach that Stravinsky offered in his new work than their cushioned sound and defiantly nineteenth-century spirit. Yet, to Klemperer's surprise, Stravinsky commented on them appreciatively. The first rehearsal of the concerto did not, however, start smoothly, for Klemperer, who had had only limited experience of the composer's recent works, took the concerto in a manner that Stravinsky found unduly romantic. Klemperer later recalled that after a few bars Stravinsky cried 'No! no! think of Savonarola.'[24] Thereafter matters must have gone to the composer's satisfaction. Two years later, when Klemperer invited him to perform the work in Berlin, Stravinsky telegraphed (9 September 1927), 'With you I am always happy to play my concerto.' But the Wiesbaden critics predictably did not warm to a work that marked a complete break with the romantic conception of a concerto. To Otto Dorn, who described the composer as a 'quiet, fair-haired young gentleman, smooth and elegant, but with an unworldly, almost apprehensive look', this deeply Bachian music seemed 'alien to German ways of feeling'.[25] So indeed it was.

Five days before this concert Klemperer and Dülberg had staged a new production of *Don Giovanni* that was to be one of their closest and most successful collaborations. Although Hagemann's name appeared on the programme as producer, it was Klemperer, who, with Hagemann's full consent, took effective charge of the stage as well as of the music.[26] Dülberg set out to provide space for action rather than stage decorations. To achieve dramatic unity, he followed Roller's example in Vienna twenty years earlier, flanking the stage with two permanent, towerlike structures whose doors, windows and balconies could be drawn into the action. The stage itself was divided into three sections, each of which could be curtained off and was used in its entirety only in the long finales of each act. Dülberg's

---

* Its first performance had taken place in May 1924. In view of Stravinsky's later reputation as a man who drove a hard bargain, it is worth noting that, in response to a special plea from Klemperer (letter of 5 September 1925), he agreed to come to Wiesbaden at a reduced fee.

designs avoided any suggestions of local colour beyond a stylised baroque.* In their production Hagemann and Klemperer set out to restore the comic elements to their rightful place, a feature that found little favour with the local critics. Johanna Klemperer, whose appearances on stage were much less frequent in Wiesbaden than they had been in Cologne, where she had been a full member of the company, sang Donna Elvira. Klemperer's conducting evoked enthusiasm far beyond the confines of the town. Indeed, few events did more to establish his reputation as an agent of operatic renewal, and among those who came to see it was Leo Kestenberg.

*   *   *

The immense success of the concert Klemperer had conducted in Berlin on 10 April 1924 attracted attention in countries beyond the comparatively limited area of western Europe within which he had already made a reputation. On 25 August Klemperer wrote to Schnabel, asking for an introduction to 'a person of authority' in Moscow, as his agents had held out the possibility of a Russian tour and he was anxious lest it misfire. Even before he had visited the Soviet Union, Klemperer was predisposed in its favour. Like many intellectuals of his generation he looked to the young Communist state as an experiment offering hope for a future free of prejudice, poverty and war, much as the young Wordsworth and Shelley had regarded revolutionary France more than a century earlier.[27] By 1924 developments in at any rate Soviet cultural life seemed to offer grounds for that optimism.

In 1917 Anatoly Lunacharsky had been appointed People's Commissar for Education.† In that position he headed a ministry that had taken over musical responsibilities recently discharged in the field of opera by the court and in concert life by a restricted circle of societies, patrons and publishers. The times were turbulent, as a result of widespread emigration the calibre

---

* The effect in black and white photographs at the Theatermuseum of Cologne University is stiff and lifeless. But eye witnesses, such as Curjel, Kruttge and Frau Eva Morel, who was attached to the theatre, concur that, when lit and peopled by characters costumed in materials that had been specially woven by Dülberg's pupils at the Kassel Kunstakademie, the effect was lively and unified, more so indeed than the production that Klemperer and Dülberg mounted at the Kroll Opera two seasons later. As in Dülberg's *Fidelio* of the previous year, a feature of both sets and costumes was the fierceness of the colours employed. (Hans Curjel, 'Zu Ewald Dülbergs Don Giovanni-Bühne', source unknown.)

† Anatoly Vasil'yevich Lunacharsky (1875–1933), poet, playwright, philosopher and lover of music, described himself as 'an intellectual among Bolsheviks, a Bolshevik among intellectuals'. Lenin, who was of course responsible for his appointment, is said to have referred to him in more equivocal terms: 'He has a sort of French brilliance. His light-mindedness is also French; it comes from his aesthetic inclinations' (quoted in Fitzpatrick, *The Commissariat of Enlightenment*, p. 2). In spite of the fact that he was never admitted to the inner counsels of the Party, he survived as Commissar until 1929. His twelve years in power saw a remarkable flowering of cultural life, in theatre and cinema as well as music. His dismissal marked the beginning of its end.

of the Commissariat's staff was not high, and a deep rift soon occurred in the interpretation put on the revolution's task in the field of culture. On the one hand, widespread if somewhat disorganised attempts were made in the immediate post-revolutionary phase to bring music to 'the masses'. On the other, Arthur Lourié,* who from 1918 to 1921 served as musical adviser to Lunacharsky, fostered modernism in the belief that a revolutionary state's prime duty was to support revolutionary music.[28] Rival organisations, the Russian Association of Proletarian Musicians (RAPM) and the Association for Contemporary Music (ACM), to which most active composers belonged, came into existence in support of these conflicting policies.

Until the end of the twenties, however, the Party preferred to stand above the fray, perhaps because its own internal power struggle, which had arisen after the death of Lenin in 1924, was as yet unresolved. On 18 June 1925 in a resolution that related primarily to literature but also applied to music, the Central Committee determined that 'the Party...cannot support any faction'. Therefore within the context of Communist ideology, 'it must advocate free competition between various groups'.[29] Trotsky's views were more sharply defined. Two years earlier, he had rejected the notion of 'proletarian culture' on the grounds that the proletariat would merge into a classless society before it had had time to produce a culture of its own. 'The cultural reconstruction,' he wrote, 'which will begin when the need of a dictatorship [of the proletariat]...has disappeared, will *not* have a class character. This seems to lead to the conclusion that there is no proletarian culture, that there never will be any, and in fact there is no need to regret this.' The Party, he wrote, must be vigilant to 'destroy any tendency in art...which threatens the Revolution', but within that context 'art must make its own way...and by its own means'.[30] He therefore advocated 'complete freedom of self-determination in the field of art'.[31] Lunacharsky similarly held that the less the state interfered in creative work the better and accordingly refused to support any one faction against another.

The relaxation that had set in after the introduction of Lenin's New Economic Policy in 1921 also brought about a resumption of contacts with the outside world and in particular with the young Weimar Republic. In April 1922 the two states, which for differing reasons felt themselves to be outcasts from the community of nations, signed a treaty of friendship in Rapallo. On 1 June 1923 a Soviet–German cultural association was set up with a committee that included, among others, Max von Schillings and Thomas Mann. As a direct result, German musicians began to visit

---

* Arthur Lourié (1892–1966) subsequently settled in Paris, where he became Stravinsky's 'closest musical friend from 1924 until the mid-thirties' (Robert Craft note in Stravinsky, *Selected Correspondence*, Vol. 1, p. 216). See also pp. 311–12 and 389.

the Soviet Union in ever-increasing numbers. Among them was a particularly large quota of conductors who helped to fill a gap left by post-revolutionary emigration. Klemperer was among the earliest and on his first visit in November 1924 he enjoyed success so overwhelming that he was to return to conduct in Moscow and Leningrad every season until 1929. His appearances in Russia thus correspond exactly with the brief flowering of its musical life that occurred after the country had begun to recover from political upheaval and civil war and before Stalin had secured a firm grip on its cultural life.

Nonetheless Klemperer's opening concert in Moscow with the orchestra of the Bol'shoy Theatre on 2 November attracted little attention. The Great Hall of the Conservatory was only half full and such critics as attended were not unduly impressed. In *Pravda* (6 November) Evgeny Braudo described his slow tempi in Beethoven's Symphony No. 7 as characteristic of German expressionism and made no comment on his accompaniment of Brahms's Violin Concerto. A week later, *Izvestiya* (14 November) followed suit. 'Otto Klemperer's conducting', wrote Khrisanf Khersonsky, 'bears the stamp...of the neurasthenic mood of contemporary Germany with its taste for expressionism.'

From Moscow, Klemperer travelled to Leningrad. With an alert and enlightened public, an illustrious concert orchestra and a purpose-built concert hall, the old capital was still *de facto* the centre of Russian musical life. His first encounter with its Philharmonic Orchestra did not, however, go smoothly. To a young student who was present at rehearsals, he seemed possessed by 'a kind of diabolic madness' that soon won him the sobriquet of 'the black devil'.* Throughout rehearsals he maintained 'a hellish degree of tension' that was also evident in the shrillness of his voice. Individual phrases were repeated until he had obtained exactly what he wanted. In the view of another young musician, Alexander Gauk, who as a conductor was later to be associated professionally with Klemperer, the submission he demanded of his players not only made for bad blood but deprived the playing of ease and joy.[32] A scene occurred in the final rehearsal, when additional players had failed to appear exactly at the determined hour. Klemperer threw down his baton, leapt into the stalls, where, for want of a better means of ventilating his fury, he hurled the fur-coat he had acquired for the journey to the ground. Two minutes later, when the instrumentalists had appeared, he climbed back on the platform, 'as black as a cloud'. Yet his dedication to the music was so complete that resentment soon evaporated.

Owing to the difficulties that had arisen in rehearsal Klemperer cancelled one of the two concerts he was scheduled to give in Leningrad, and

* G. Ya. Yudin (1905–   ), conductor, on whose illuminating memoirs, *Za gran'yu proshlïkh dney*, and obituary of Klemperer (*Muzïkal'naya zhizn'*, 21 November 1973) this account of his first visit to Leningrad is largely based.

214

conducted a solitary programme, consisting of Mozart's Symphony No. 40 in G minor and Brahms's Symphony No. 4 in E minor. Neither was calculated to arouse enthusiasm. In a country whose musical tradition had only come into existence in the course of the nineteenth century there was comparatively little taste for Mozart,* while the dominant influence of Liszt in the development of Russian orchestral music had caused Brahms to be regarded as a dry academic, whose symphonies were rarely played. Hence only a small audience turned out to hear an unknown German conductor make his bow on 5 November. The Philharmonic had rarely been so empty.

Yudin felt that, although there were no Beethovenian overtones in Klemperer's account of the G minor symphony, Mozart was constricting to his volcanic temperament. But the Brahms he subsequently described as 'an earthquake';[33] in a lifetime's concert-going he had never undergone such a shattering experience. At the end of his career Klemperer himself similarly recalled that neither before nor later had he witnessed scenes such as occurred at the end of the concert. 'It wasn't just that everyone stood. They surged around the platform [continued applauding] for about a quarter of an hour.'[34]

The critics were equally overwhelmed. In *Krasnaya gazeta* (8 November) N. Strel'nikov hailed Klemperer as one of the great conductors of the age, a musician who combined in equal parts constructive logic with dynamic power, a sense of detail with an amazing overall impact, all of which was achieved with gestures so unmannered as to be monotonous. *Rabochiy i teatr* (1 December) went further: in its view Klemperer surpassed Nikisch, Mahler and all the other leading Central European conductors who had been heard in Leningrad. The correspondent of *Die Musik* (March 1925) reported that the concert had 'given rise to ovations such as we have hardly ever experienced here'. 'Once bitten by such a performance', wrote the anonymous critic of the Party newspaper, *Leningradskaya pravda* (12 November)...'it is hard to return to workaday concert-life.' On a more factual level Gauk singled out for praise in the Brahms symphony the accuracy of the phrasing, the unusually pronounced dynamic contrasts, the relative absence of ritenutos, the differentiation of melodic lines, the expressiveness of inner parts.[35] After the concert Klemperer had supper with friends of Schnabel. Among those at table was Boris Asaf'yev, the Soviet Union's most influential critic and musicologist.† A card, which he

---

* Such at any rate was Klemperer's view.
† Asaf'yev (1884–1949), who wrote criticism under the name of Igor Glebov and also composed, was a crucial figure in the musical life of the Soviet Union in the twenties and a powerful advocate of modernism. In addition to influential studies of Russian nineteenth-century music, he also wrote the first (1929) monograph on Stravinsky to appear in the Soviet Union. For an account of his often difficult relations with the Party, see Olkhovsky, *Music under the Soviets*, pp. 81–2.

signed, was sent to Schnabel. On it a member of the supper party wrote, 'We have had a great day.'

With this triumph under his belt Klemperer returned to Moscow, where on 12 November he was due to conduct a performance of *Carmen* at the Bol'shoy Theatre. The new national opera house was not in a happy condition: Lunacharsky himself admitted at about this time that 'the repertory...has become so impoverished that I for one have completely stopped going'.* *Carmen* was not a new production and Klemperer was aghast to discover that in the first act the stage was littered with figures whose sole purpose was to lend 'local colour'. His insistence that they be eliminated did not endear him to extras who were only paid when they appeared. But the theatre was shut for a number of evenings and the performance further postponed for forty-eight hours so that he could prepare the performance dramatically as well as musically. Later he recalled that 'the orchestra was splendid, the singers excellent, the public indescribable'.†

By the time that Klemperer conducted his second concert in Moscow on 16 November word had spread and police had to be summoned to control the crowds who struggled to secure admittance.[36] In place of the first Russian performance of Mahler's Ninth Symphony originally announced (the two-day postponement of *Carmen* having eaten into available rehearsal time), Klemperer conducted a less demanding programme consisting of Bach's Brandenburg Concerto No. 1, Schoenberg's *Verklärte Nacht* and Brahms's Symphony No. 4. Although the sight of a conductor himself sitting in the middle of the orchestra with his back to the audience to play the continuo at a harpsichord in the Bach concerto occasioned surprise, the concert aroused immense enthusiasm. Both the main official papers had in the meanwhile also changed their tune. In *Pravda* (20 November) Braudo described the evening as 'a great occasion' and saluted Schoenberg as 'the leader of the Western European left front in music'. The following day in *Izvestiya* Leonid Sabaneyev hailed Klemperer as one of the outstanding conductors of the day. He also observed that while Germany nourished its talent, the Soviet Union was going through 'a critical patch as far as conducting is concerned'. Like Braudo, Sabaneyev praised *Verklärte Nacht*, but felt that a more recent work by Schoenberg would have been even more welcome. Modernism was still acceptable, even in the new regime's new capital city.

---

* A. V. Lunacharsky, *O teatr i dramaturgii*, Vol. 1, pp. 255–6, where Klemperer is cited as the 'great' new conductor, now working in Moscow.

† Klemperer regarded his Latvian Carmen, Amand Liberto-Rebané (1893–?), as one of the finest interpreters of the role he had heard. On 1 January 1925 *Izvestiya* published a letter that he had written to members of the Bol'shoy Opera, in which he stated that 'in my opinion only one orchestra can rival Moscow's and that is the Vienna Philharmonic'.

The repercussions of this success soon became apparent. Two days after *Carmen, Leningradskaya pravda* (16 November) announced that Klemperer would take charge of revivals of *Don Giovanni* and *Salome* in Leningrad early in the coming year. Subsequently it was stated that he would conduct *Die Walküre* and *Siegfried* at the Bol'shoy. Finally on 10 January 1925 *Pravda* broke the news that negotiations, which, it claimed, were going well, were in progress with a view to his appointment as principal conductor at both the Moscow and Leningrad opera houses. A subsequent report in the *Neue Freie Presse* (Vienna, 20 January) claimed that he was to be granted powers such as no foreign conductor had ever enjoyed in a Russian opera house and that negotiations would probably be concluded on his return to the Soviet Union at the end of the following month.*

Klemperer himself took to Russia as enthusiastically as Russian musical audiences had taken to him. He loved the passionate intensity of a public that 'listened with its heart'.[37] He sensed the excitement of a country in the throes of a far-reaching social experiment. And he was, in particular, enthralled by its theatrical life. Always an avid theatre-goer, both in Moscow and in Leningrad he seized opportunities to attend productions by Stanislavsky, whose naturalism struck him as 'now almost classical'.† He was impressed by Nemirovich-Danchenko's production of *Carmencita*, a version of *Carmen*, which he saw at the time he was himself rehearsing Bizet's opera at the Bol'shoy. He attended productions by Meyerhold and Tairov and performances at the Hebrew Theatre. He also made numerous visits to the Central Children's Theatre, with whose 22-year-old director, Natalia Satz, he became friendly. Her innovatory productions so impressed him that he later invited her to produce and assist him in productions in Berlin and Buenos Aires.‡ Soviet men of theatre reciprocated his interest. Nemirovich-Danchenko sent a laurel wreath at the end of his visit to Moscow in December 1925. Tairov later attended performances at the Kroll Opera (as did Lunacharsky), and, together with Meyerhold, was

---

* It has not been possible to ascertain why these negotiations came to nothing. They were still a live issue in March 1925, when *Pravda* (17 March) announced that Klemperer had arrived in Moscow to hold discussions with the directors of the Bol'shoy Opera. One possibility is that Johanna, who on this occasion accompanied her husband and did not wholly share his wide-eyed enthusiasm for the Soviet Union at the time, may have persuaded him not to accept a position that would probably have involved settling there.

† Letter to Carl Hagemann, Moscow, 30 March 1925. In a tribute, dated 25 April 1927 now in the Moscow TsGALI archives, Klemperer cited a production by Stanislavsky of Rimsky-Korsakov's *The Tsar's Bride* as demonstrating the validity of 'Seelentheater' ('theatre of the soul') at a time when the purely theatrical threatened to assume excessive prominence. The implication is that he found it impressive if a shade old-fashioned.

‡ See also pp. 370–1, 381. Klemperer later published a laudatory article on a performance he attended in the Central Children's Theatre in *Nowy zritel* (21 April 1929).

217

present at at least one of Kemperer's concerts in Moscow, after which the three men met at supper (see p. 314). Soviet avant-garde theatre undoubtedly opened new perspectives that influenced Klemperer's own approach to the stage when he became director of the Kroll Opera in 1927.

On his return to Berlin on 19 November, his elder sister, Regi, found him alarmingly exhausted. But the life of a new society had gripped his imagination to a point where he was even prepared to consider emigration. 'It turned out differently, and it is better that it did so' was his subsequent laconic comment.[38]

*   *   *

In contrast to his first visit to Leningrad only four months earlier, when he had appeared before a half-empty hall, on his return on 17 March 1925 crowds beseiged the Philharmonic building, vainly struggling to gain admittance.[39] The programme included the first performance in Russia of Stravinsky's *Pulcinella*, which was met with an enthusiasm that Klemperer himself described as 'unparallelled'. 'You can hardly conceive of the noise of the applause', he wrote the following day to Carl Hagemann. Both in Leningrad and in Moscow, where he again conducted the work on 29 March, it received a unanimously warm critical welcome. Asaf'yev described it as the impersonification of the *commedia dell'arte*; Braudo, who found the Moscow performance less than fully confident, was equally approving.[40] There was as yet no suggestion that the neo-classical idiom of the most recent music by the greatest of living Russian composers was incompatible with Soviet aesthetics.

During the following three weeks Klemperer, who on this occasion was accompanied by his wife, conducted concerts in both Moscow and Leningrad, commuting between the two cities. In the old capital he chanced his arm on 8 April with an all-Russian programme that, in addition to a repeat performance of *Pulcinella*, consisted of Mussorgsky's *A Night on a Bare Mountain* and Borodin's Symphony No. 2. *Rabochiy i teatr* criticised his account of the symphony as 'too European', but Yudin later recalled both performances as 'irreproachable' in their naturalness, sense of measure and choice of tempi.[41] On this visit, however, Beethoven provided the keystone of his programmes. Yudin later referred to the 'titanic merriment' of the Eighth Symphony.[42] Asaf'yev described the 'colossal intensity' of the Fifth as 'stupendous'; of the Ninth, which Klemperer conducted in Moscow on 6 April and in Leningrad in his final concert eight days later, he wrote that 'at moments the tensions of the performance were so great that it seemed as though Beethoven's music could hardly bear the pressures put on it'.[43] The Leningrad correspondent of *Die Musik* (September

18   Klemperer. Leningrad, 1925

1925) wrote that the performance had crowned Klemperer's visit, even if the tempi had been too fast for both chorus and soloists.

Klemperer had originally intended to arrive in Moscow in the first week of March to conduct *Die Walküre*, for which rehearsals had, as *Pravda* (25 February) announced, already started. Illness delayed his departure from Germany and the project was dropped. Shortage of rehearsal time similarly curtailed his operatic activities in Leningrad, where he was at first expected to take charge of revivals of *Siegfried* as well as of *Don Giovanni* and *Salome*. Rehearsals for *Salome* did indeed begin.[44] On 22 March, however, *Rabochiy i teatr* announced that Klemperer would only conduct *Carmen*, which he did on 24 March and 10 April, again with Rebané in the title role.

The performances aroused as much enthusiasm as that which he had earlier conducted in Moscow. In a week of rehearsals he again simplified the production and even succeeded in having the level of the orchestral pit raised by three feet so as to secure a more open quality of sound. In a detailed account of the performance, Yudin later recalled the surprisingly massive weight and measured tempo of the prelude, the brilliance of the entry of the factory girls, the Schubert-like delicacy of the strings in the card scene and Klemperer's insistence on precise articulation of the triplets in the Habanera. Gauk was impressed in particular by the manner in which

19   Klemperer in the Leningrad Opera House

Klemperer raised the drama to the level of tragedy.[45] *Rabochiy i teatr* singled out for praise the manner in which he had combined fieriness with precision and nervous vitality with compelling logic. *Zhizn' iskusstva* (7 April) hailed the performance as the outstanding event to have taken place in the former imperial opera in years.

By the end of his second visit to the Soviet Union Klemperer had become something of a public hero. 'To give you an idea of the enthusiasm of these people', he wrote to Hagemann on 30 March, 'we attended a performance of Tchaikovsky's beautiful *Pique Dame* at the Mariinsky.* After the second act the assistant director suddenly appeared in the stalls, made a speech about me and asked the public to give me three cheers, which they did with great warmth.' On the evening of his final concert in Leningrad on 14 April many of the city's leading musicians signed a letter, which was published the following day in *Krasnaya gazeta*. The signatories, who were headed by Glazunov, the director of the Leningrad Conservatory, and included Andrey Rimsky-Korsakov and Maximilian Steinberg (son and son-in-law of the composer), Asaf'yev, Rebané, Gauk, as well as the young pianist, Mariya Yudina,† thanked him for the 'splendid impetus' he had brought to the city's musical life and assured him of the deep sympathy his artistic character had awoken.

The letter produced an irritated reaction. In *Zhizn' iskusstva* (28 April), the organ of Lunacharsky's Commissariat, Nikolay Malkov,‡ who wrote under the pen name of 'Islamey', praised Klemperer unstintingly as a conductor who, in contrast to Nikisch, was 'of the era of struggles and social upheavals which have shaken mankind since the 1914 war'. Yet instead of appearing before audiences of workers, he had attracted gatherings reminiscent of 'civilised Europe'. This hero-worshipping had found expression in the 'collective curtsey' of the letter in *Krasnaya gazeta*. 'Thus', observed 'Islamey' acidly, 'do Leningrad musicians write in the eighth year of the revolution.' Asaf'yev took a more generous view. 'The enthusiasm that Klemperer has evoked...might be considered naive in Europe. But...an ability to derive intense enjoyment from art...is a token of a youthful *joie de vivre* that has not yet been obscured by European satiety or mere American curiosity.'[46]

Such *joie de vivre* is movingly evident in a tribute, written in faulty German and addressed to him by a group of young people in Moscow.

---

* The pre-revolutionary title of the Academic Theatre, which did not acquire its present name, the Kirov Theatre, until 1935.
† An unflinching champion of Schoenberg and Webern in the darkest years of Stalinism and thereafter. Klemperer was much impressed by her playing of Bach. (Anna D. Artobolevska, 'Vospominaniya uchenika', in Aksyuk (ed.), *Mariya Veniaminova Yudina*, pp. 130–40.)
‡ Not to be confused with the conductor, Nikolay Mal'ko.

You know us, you often hear our excited voices and applause. We applaud until we lose all physical sensation...After the concert we fly down from our gallery to the stalls. We surround you, we laugh with joy and our eyes say more than our hands. Don't imagine that we are star-struck young people who give way to hysteria through a surfeit of joy. In our time such naive young people don't exist. Our souls already have furrows...

Now to the main matter. Our [i.e. the Bol'shoy] orchestra is poor and feeble. It is made up of simple workers, wretched individuals on whom life has one and for all imposed a mundane existence...They don't play in tune...They are subordinates without enthusiasm. They are subdued by the power of your genius, but it is a victory you win with mercenaries. They don't understand you. You need love and devotion, not fear.

Have you considered the possibility of forming an orchestra of your own...of working with young people whose tempo and rhythm of life are like yours? We think of an orchestra of young people who would be ready to follow you far and wide...Brimming with life...such a collective would bestride the world as conquerors...And the main thing is that you would not be alone. We feel your loneliness when we see how you struggle to convey your splendid conceptions to our musicians...[But] they are half dead. Your sun blinds and burns them. Your voice is too powerful for them, your thoughts too dangerous. They are used to twilight. And it is surely not only in Russia that you lack the orchestra you need.

How is one to find talented musicians who are prepared to give themselves to a cause? This is not a chimera...Permit us to hope that the day will come when in our deafening applause one will hear the words, 'Long live the young fighters for the future of mankind and their leader, Otto Klemperer.' One gentle, foolish request. Please let us have an answer – only two words – so that we know that you have received our letter.

The letter reached Klemperer as he was leaving Moscow. Its authors were too timid to present it themselves, fearing that they would not be admitted. That Klemperer was touched by their youthful idealism is evident from the fact that it is one of the few documents he kept to the end of his life.

*   *   *

Before the end of the year Klemperer was back for his third visit within little more than twelve months. Once again, he was received with fervent enthusiasm and a packed house at his opening Beethoven concert in Leningrad on 1 December 1925. Never a man to boast about his own achievements, in a letter written the following day to his wife he described the evening as 'a prodigious success. While the 'Pastoral' received applause that was still on a European scale, after the Seventh it seemed as though the ovations would never end. Only when I appeared in my fur-coat did the audience take this gentle hint and let me go. I have no public better disposed to me than the people in Leningrad.' In Moscow it was the same story. 'Here in Russia', he wrote on 12 December to Walter Damrosch (see p. 225n), 'I have had an absolutely fabulous success. The

222

people here have an enthusiasm such as one rarely finds in Germany.' In an article written after this visit, Braudo confirmed that 'Klemperer's popularity in Russia is quite extraordinary – [it is] a kind of phenomenon – and has never been surpassed by [that of] any foreign conductor, including even Nikisch... There is something downright inflammatory about his manner of treating not only new music but the most venerable of the classics as well.'[47] Asaf'yev, who on 1 December had found the Leningrad Philharmonic so over-booked that he had been unable to reach his seat in time to hear the first movement of the 'Pastoral' Symphony, expressed a similar reaction. 'It is as though...he focusses the will of the masses... in the movements of his arms.'[48]

Success on such a scale inevitably attracted attention on the highest level of Soviet power. On 12 December Klemperer wrote from Moscow to tell his wife that Trotsky would be attending his performance of the Ninth Symphony the following evening. After the concert the great man came to the conductor's room,* and, perhaps echoing a phrase that Braudo had used only two days earlier in *Pravda*, told Klemperer that his conducting reflected the influence of German expressionism. Klemperer demurred; he did not care for type-casting. Trotsky then commented on the disturbance caused by a chorister, who had only taken his place in the course of the performance. Klemperer ventured to imply that Russian orchestras and choruses lacked discipline. 'You will never get discipline in Russia', replied the man who had successfully defended the infant Soviet state against overwhelming odds, 'I haven't succeeded either.'[49] Henceforth the figure of Trotsky much exercised Klemperer's imagination.†

Yet as the visit wore on a growing sense of disenchantment became evident in his letters to his wife. In part this was due to sheer fatigue: for almost four weeks he was obliged to travel frequently between two cities almost four hundred miles apart. He was also for the first time in his career confronted with an uninterrupted series of concerts. In particular, he was irked to find himself committed to conduct no fewer than four performances of the Ninth Symphony in as many weeks. 'I'm a little weary of conducting concerts', he wrote to his wife on 17 December in the closing stage of his visit. 'This journey has taught me how necessary the theatre is to me...I'm so exhausted that I can hardly write.'

This was not the only source of discontent. Moscow no longer appealed to him as a city, although he had to admit that conditions of living had improved.[50] There were disagreements with Rosfil, the state concert-

---

* Although Trotsky had ceased to be Commissar for War in January, he was still a member of the Politburo.
† Trotsky's autobiography (1930) made a particularly deep impression (Meyer-Sichting, *Partitur eines Lebens*, p. 48).

promoting agency, about programmes. He was exasperated to discover that on the same day as he was giving an afternoon concert with the Bol'shoy Theatre Orchestra, it was also scheduled to play in *Die Walküre* that very evening, and that rehearsals for both events had similarly been arranged to take place on the previous days. 'When I see how here in Moscow non-artistic factors, such as organisation and money, again and again compel compromise...I begin to wonder *where* one can make music. America? I suspect that the *Betrieb* (business) there is even worse than it is here.'[51] Back in Moscow a week later he found the chorus at his first rehearsal for the Ninth Symphony 'very bad'. A variety of factors, among which may have been depression, contributed to a mood of frustration and gloom.

Nor did all his concerts meet with virtually unvarying enthusiasm as they had on earlier visits. Braudo found him temperamentally unsuited to Haydn's Military Symphony and Schubert's Symphony No. 9 in C major, which formed a programme he conducted in Moscow on 6 December.[52] Two days later in Leningrad, where he substituted the 'Unfinished' Symphony for the Haydn, Asaf'yev, as Klemperer reported the following day to his wife, had not been convinced by his approach to Schubert, while a German visitor reported that his account of the C major symphony had lacked 'restraint (Vornehmheit) and clarity'.[53] A performance of Schumann's Symphony No. 3, which he conducted in Leningrad on 16 December, was similarly described as lacking in romantic lyricism by *Zhizn' iskusstva* (19 December), whose critic also found Klemperer's account of *Till Eulenspiegel* marred by an 'exaggerated dynamism'. In the same article 'incredibly fast tempi' in his performance of the Ninth Symphony on 19 December were described as 'at times neurotic and disorganised'. At any rate during the latter part of his visit, Klemperer was clearly not in his best form.

Before leaving Leningrad on 21 December he nonetheless signed a contract to return in April 1927 to conduct and produce *Fidelio* in commemoration of the centenary of Beethoven's death; Dülberg was to design sets. He also agreed to conduct a complete cycle of the symphonies, together with the *Missa Solemnis*.[54] But there can be little doubt that, on this occasion at any rate, Klemperer left the Soviet Union with a degree of relief. To that was added his joy at the prospect of spending Christmas at home with his family before, scarcely more than a week later, he set out, this time westwards, on a journey to another unknown land.

*   *   *

In the spring of 1925 Klemperer had received an invitation to conduct the New York Symphony Orchestra for a ten-week period during the following season. The link had been effected by Willy Strecker,* co-proprietor of the publishing house of Schott in Mainz, who lived across the Rhine in Wiesbaden. There he had been well placed to form an opinion of Klemperer's abilities and had recommended him to Walter Damrosch in such glowing terms that an offer of an engagement had followed.† On 30 March 1925 Strecker telegrammed Klemperer's acceptance. The contract that was signed a week later bears a note in Klemperer's hand stipulating that he was to have ten rehearsals for each fortnight of concerts he gave.

Klemperer did not arrive in New York at a propitious moment. The evening before he landed on 15 January 1926, Toscanini had given his first concert with the Philharmonic Orchestra, and henceforth the city was to be at his feet, as Moscow and Leningrad had been at Klemperer's a few weeks earlier.‡ Furthermore, in February Toscanini was followed by Furtwängler, who had made his *début* in New York during the previous winter. Matched against conductors who were widely regarded as the greatest of their time and a superior orchestra, Klemperer was to find the going tougher in New York than he had in the Soviet Union. Moreover, he did not care for the city itself. He spoke English only with difficulty and he did not warm to the wealthy patrons who surrounded – indeed financed – the orchestra. There were interviews and social events, for neither of which he had much aptitude. In New York conductors were already the subject of a personality cult that had not yet spread to Europe and it was not long before Klemperer's physical appearance attracted attention. For *The New Yorker* he was

the seven foot dynamo from Wiesbaden, the terror of the second trombonists, the caveman who yanks 'em by the collar and shakes sweet music from their quivering instruments, the wild bull of the symphony . . . and all the rest of it. We're not setting down our opinions; we're quoting *verbatim* some of the quaint phrases with which the Symphony Society's guest has been surrounded, and we hope we're not shooing you away from his concerts, for he's worth hearing and seeing.

Klemperer stoops down to his orchestra as though he were about to touch the floor with the palms of his hands, straightens up viciously, hurls his baton to the roof, crushes invisible nuts in his other hand, contracts and shudders . . . He wants certain things and he's going to have them if he breaks every bone in somebody's

---

* See biographical glossary.
† Walter Damrosch (1862–1950), German-born conductor who played a substantial role in New York musical life over many years. Among other posts, he held that of director and principal conductor of the Symphony Society from 1903 until its merger with the rival Philharmonic Society in 1928.
‡ Klemperer took the occasion to attend a number of Toscanini's concerts both in this and in the following season. He subsequently wrote that in New York he had heard him conduct a repertory extending from Haydn to Stravinsky and had 'always had the same happy impression of an uncontrived (absichtslose) rightness' (*Das Tagebuch*, 25 May 1929). For Klemperer that was the highest praise.

225

20 Otto and Johanna Klemperer on arrival in New York, 15 January 1926

body – perhaps his own. It's melodramatic, it's theatrical, it's exciting; and he gets what he wants.[55]

Although Klemperer had included a number of contemporary works in the draft programmes he had earlier sent to Damrosch from Moscow (11 December 1925), he once again elected to play safe and to open his season in Carnegie Hall with a classical programme, such as had in April 1924 done so much to establish his reputation in Berlin. The impact in New York was hardly less great. Olin Downes, the city's leading critic, wrote with particular enthusiasm.

With the proviso that no one orchestral concert is a test of a conductor it may be said that the *début* of Otto Klemperer...was an auspicious occasion. There was every evidence before the conductor had gone far with his program that the Symphony Society had introduced...a significant figure among the younger musicians of the day. Mr Klemperer...proved that he was not only letter-perfect in the scores he conducted from memory, but that...he had important things to say.

Mr Klemperer...now crouched, now rose to his full height or bent double like an immense bird over the orchestra...But there was never any question of the conductor's sincerity...Whether or not his gestures appealed to the gallery...the basic and important fact is that they drew immediate and precise response from the orchestra, that the men were infected with the conviction and the enthusiasm of their leader, and that his spirit was felt in turn by the audience.

The symphonies were played as if for the first, instead of the hundredth time – as if, indeed...their fate as well as that of the interpreter was at issue...nothing escaped the conductor and nothing was allowed to sink into commonplace. The result...was a concert which, instead of provoking the apathy of a thrice told tale aroused immediate and exceptional enthusiasm.

Haydn and Mozart were played in careful accordance with the letter of the score, but with what life, vivacity, eloquence...There could be differences of opinion concerning the allegretto of the [Beethoven's] Seventh Symphony...but it is hard to remember many readings of the symphony so great in spirit and fresh in feeling, so abounding in eloquence of detail...[56]

In a review that gives a striking picture of Klemperer's conducting at this stage of his career, Lawrence Gilman drew a revealing comparison between an outer demonstrativeness and an inner sobriety.

Conducting without a score he has no stand to impede him and he does indeed swoop and swirl and write his temperament in fiery scrolls upon the trembling air. He hovers over his orchestra like some fabulous, gigantic bird-man, menacing and inescapable. He growls audibly at his men, and once at yesterday's performance he almost roared...But these are external things. In Mr Klemperer's projection of the music we found nothing of the melodramatic, nothing of the sensational. On the contrary he seemed almost indecently reluctant to face the audience and acknowledge its greeting...His whole demeanor was that of a musician deeply...

227

intent...on the matter in hand and more than a little bored by the necessity of recognising the presence of an audience.

There was no doubt...of his exceptional ability, and of his success with his audience, which was little short of uproarious.[57]

With such reviews in the city's two principal papers – and they were widely echoed elsewhere – it must have seemed as though Klemperer's American reputation was made. Yet his success did not take fire as it had done in Russia. The critics were distinctly less enthusiastic on his second appearance at a matinée concert at Carnegie Hall on 28 January, which in contrast to the concert that Toscanini conducted there in the evening, was not well attended. Gilman in particular found his vehemence excessive and criticised a 'heavy-handedness' in Beethoven's 'Pastoral' Symphony.[58]

The first unfamiliar score that Klemperer ventured was no better received. His performance of Bruckner's Symphony No. 8 (4 February 1926), which had not been heard in New York for seven years, did not appeal to either the critics or the public. A blizzard played havoc with the attendance figures and many members of the audience walked out after the first and second movements.[59] With one exception, none of the critics found much pleasure in a further encounter with a composer whom most of them regarded as intolerably long-winded and repetitious. Only Pitts Sanborn wrote that Klemperer had conducted 'like a born believer' and even went on to complain of a six-page cut he had made in the finale.[60]

Although his account of Brahms's Fourth Symphony was enthusiastically received a fortnight later, Klemperer was cast down at his failure to achieve the impact he had made elsewhere and sought Damrosch's advice. Damrosch told him that he had made the same mistake as Walter and Furtwängler: New York preferred a mixed, international repertory, and, as though to underline that opinion, Downes in a review of one of Klemperer's concerts complained of the preponderance of German music in the city's orchestral programmes.[61] Klemperer clearly took the point, for at a few days' notice he cancelled a performance of Mahler's Symphony No. 9, which he had conducted with success little short of sensational earlier in the season in both Wiesbaden and Berlin, and substituted an uncharacteristically miscellaneous programme. His remaining programmes all included non-German works, some of them scores of meagre significance that he never again conducted, such as Saint-Saëns's *Rondo Capriccioso* for violin and orchestra and the overture to Respighi's opera, *Belfagor*.

Yet the Symphony Society was well satisfied. On 11 February its president, Harry Harkness Flagler, reported that among their guest conductors Klemperer had already made a particularly strong impression. And towards the end of his ten-week stint audiences began to respond more

228

warmly. Reviewing one of his last concerts, Lawrence Gilman commented on the applause that greeted all his entrances and exits. 'Mr. Klemperer has apparently made himself greatly liked...There is good reason for [his] popularity. He is transparently sincere; he has will, integrity and emotion; and he has a certain largeness of view that satisfactorily matches his largeness of physical aspect.'[62]

What then was lacking? The reviews of his last concert suggest that his style did not meet an American taste for highly sheened surfaces and technical virtuosity. His reading of *Petrushka* was found powerful but lacking in subtlety, his account of Beethoven's Fifth Symphony, though 'on a scale of sonorous tonal grandeur, as yet not surpassed',[63] was widely held to lack polish. New York was not to be so easily subdued as Berlin or Moscow. But the concert nonetheless ended with an ovation so great that several papers commented on it. In his report on the visit Flagler stated that admiration for Klemperer's musicianship had grown with each week of his stay and that he would return for a further two months in January 1927.

*   *   *

Back in Wiesbaden, and still in poor shape after an attack of influenza that had marred his last days in America and obliged him to cancel what would have been his first orchestral concert in Hamburg since the scandal of 1912, his energies were in the main absorbed by opera. On 9 June he conducted a new production of *Der Freischütz* to mark the centenary of Weber's death. Although it was a resounding success and Klemperer was particularly attached to the work, he was never again to do so. On 1 July, in the final week of the season, a double bill consisting of Ravel's *L'Heure espagnole* and Busoni's *Arlecchino* divided critical opinion and evoked more interest than enthusiasm among the public. The only new ground that he had been able to break in his concerts that summer was Debussy's *Ibéria* (a work that had not previously been heard in Wiesbaden), which he included in his programme of 22 June. Klemperer did not, however, intend to lay himself open again to a charge in New York that his concert repertory was too limited and too exclusively German. He customarily devoted much of his vacation to the study of unfamiliar works and the season had scarcely ended when he began to bombard Universal Edition (and no doubt other publishers) with requests for scores that he might perform in New York. The fruits of his labours were at once apparent in the programmes he conducted that autumn in Wiesbaden, where he could give unfamiliar works a trial run in relative seclusion.

It was there on 30 September 1926 that he gave the first German

229

performance of Sibelius's recently composed Symphony No. 7.* His second innovation was even more surprising for a musician who had come to be regarded as an exponent of *die neue Sachlichkeit*: on 10 October Klemperer for the first time in his career conducted a Tchaikovsky symphony. Only a year earlier he had warned Damrosch that on no account could he be induced to include such music in his programmes. Whether his visits to Russia, where a more robust and less sentimental view is taken of Tchaikovsky than prevails in the West, had brought about a change of heart is uncertain, but his performance of the *Symphonie pathétique* caused such a furore in Wiesbaden on 10 October that a staid spa audience broke into cheers after the march that precedes the final adagio.

The next major addition to his repertory was more in accordance with his reputation as a modernist, but surprising for other reasons. Klemperer had met Alban Berg as early as 1908, when both men had attended the first performance of Mahler's Seventh Symphony.† Yet when the score of *Wozzeck* had been sent to him in Cologne, probably early in 1923, he had rejected it without close inspection.‡ The immense success that the opera subsequently enjoyed when Kleiber conducted its first performance in Berlin in December 1925 may have inclined Klemperer to include the *Three Fragments* which Berg had earlier made into a concert work, in a programme he gave in Wiesbaden on 3 November 1926 with Johanna as soloist. He was sufficiently impressed to speak highly of the music in an interview he gave a month later in Prague,[64] (where in a concert with the Czech Philharmonic Orchestra on 2 December he had further extended his French repertory by conducting for the first time a Debussy Nocturne ('Fêtes') and Ravel's *Alborada del Gracioso*§). He also declared that he would conduct the *Wozzeck* pieces that winter in New York. He did not, however, do so, either then or later. Nor did he ever conduct the opera. Klemperer was to remain as ambivalent towards Berg's music as he was to that of Berg's teacher, Schoenberg. Significantly, not a single work by Berg was

* Sibelius did not enjoy in Central Europe the esteem in which he was held in Anglo-Saxon countries between the wars. Klemperer, who in a letter to Damrosch (10 July 1926) had earlier described the new symphony as 'durchaus interessant' ('really interesting'), was one of the relatively few German conductors of his generation to perform him.
† Both their signatures appear on a card that the Mahlers sent Schoenberg on 20 September, the day after the event.
‡ As Berg had as yet no publisher, he himself sent scores directly to a number of conductors, shortly after he had completed the work in December 1922. (Information provided by Helene Berg, the composer's widow.) Klemperer's name occurs in a list of conductors to whom scores were sent. Half a century later, on 15 October 1972, he watched a television performance of the opera. When asked (meaningfully) by the author how he had found it, Klemperer took refuge in a delphic utterance, 'The music is as good as the text, no better', conceivably an oblique reference to the fact that Johanna is said to have drawn his attention to the merits of the libretto in Cologne.
§ He recorded both works, probably later in December 1926.

performed at the Kroll. Not until 1934, by which time he was living in Vienna, was Klemperer to show any further interest in his music.

With the last of the substantial novelties he had in mind for New York, he returned to more familiar ground. Though there had hitherto been no personal contact between them, on 13 July Klemperer wrote to Janáček, addressing the envelope simply to 'Herrn Leos Janáček, Komponist. Brünn'. He diffidently enquired whether the composer knew of him and asked to be entrusted with the American première of his new 'Military

21   Klemperer with his children, Werner and Lotte. Wiesbaden, 1926

Symphony', as the *Sinfonietta* was originally entitled. Janáček's cordial reply ('as though I do not know of you') came by return of post and with it his consent that Klemperer should give the work its first New York performance.[65]

By way of preparation Klemperer conducted its first German performance in Wiesbaden on 9 December. It was not, however, as warmly received as he had hoped. 'The music and the sound are too new', he observed shortly after the event.[66] Fritz Zweig, who had come from Berlin to hear the work, wrote on 14 December to assure the composer of the excellence of the performance and of Klemperer's enthusiasm for this and other works.* In contrast to his wavering attitude to the music of Schoenberg and Berg, Klemperer's commitment to Stravinsky and Janáček was steadfast and wholehearted.

*   *   *

Thus by the time that Klemperer arrived in New York on 29 December he was better placed to provide varied programmes than he had been on his first visit to America. Yet, inevitably, it was not in non-German works that he found most favour. His accounts of *Alborada del Gracioso* and 'Fêtes' were both considered heavy-handed. *Musical America* (3 March 1927) compared the effect of his performance of 'Les Parfums de la nuit' from Debussy's *Ibéria* to 'a searchlight...turned on a moonlit landscape'. The impact of Sibelius's Symphony No. 7 was diminished by the fact that Stokowski had given the work its first American performance during the previous season. The critics were not much taken with the charms of Stravinsky's Suite No. 2 or Casella's *Scarlattiana*. Even Janáček's *Sinfonietta* aroused no more than polite interest.

On this second visit to New York Klemperer also undertook a certain number of extra-curricular engagements, notably a concert of new music which he conducted for the International Composers' Guild† on 30 January 1927. Contact with Varèse no doubt accounts for a private performance of *Octandre* that he conducted at the composer's request,‡ for it was to be the only occasion on which he ventured on to musical territory that even in avant-garde circles was for many years to be regarded as lying on the borders of the incomprehensible. On 26 January Klemperer also accom-

---

* Klemperer's plans to give *The Cunning Little Vixen* in Wiesbaden and *The Makropoulos Affair* at the Kroll both came to nothing.

† The Guild had been founded by Varèse in 1922. It survived until 1927. The programme included the first American performances of Ravel's *Chansons madécasses*, Krenek's *Symphonische Musik* (1922) and a concert suite from Hindemith's ballet score, *Der Dämon*. Downes again wrote that Klemperer conducted 'as if the reputations of the composers and himself hung in the balance' (*New York Times*, 31 January 1927).

‡ At the home of Mrs Edgar Rossin.

panied his wife in a recital of songs by Brahms, Mahler, Strauss, Schoenberg and himself. The critics praised the expressiveness and musicality of her singing but found her upper register precarious.

Paradoxically, it was a Bruckner symphony (No. 7) that won the most enthusiastic plaudits. An overwhelming majority of the critics again rejected the music, but they acknowledged the eloquence and authority that Klemperer brought to it, and the audience applauded his advocacy 'as, it is safe to say, no conductor of a Bruckner symphony has ever been applauded in New York'.[67] Even if Klemperer's attempt to meet an alleged demand for non-German music had not been as successful as he must have hoped, his impact on public and orchestra alike had once again been considerable, in spite of the fact that during his period in New York the rival Philharmonic Orchestra had again been conducted by Toscanini and Furtwängler.

The board was also impressed. On 15 December 1926 Damrosch had announced his retirement at the end of the season after an association of forty-two years with the Symphony Society, and in its issues of 19 and 26 January the Berlin periodical, *Signale für die musikalischen Welt*, carried reports from New York that Klemperer had been invited to succeed him as musical director. But there is no evidence that negotiations took place. Indeed, the Kroll appointment (see p. 241) ruled out any such commitment, and on 5 May Flagler reported to his board that 'Mr. Klemperer's new duties in Berlin will prevent his again accepting an engagement with us'. On 11 March Klemperer sailed down the Hudson on his return voyage to Europe. Seven years were to pass before he was to conduct again in New York, and by then he would be a refugee from a National Socialist Germany.

11   *The call comes*

The reconstructed Kroll Opera finally opened its doors as a branch of the State Opera on 1 January 1924. The work had been entrusted to Oskar Kaufmann, who had made his reputation before the war as architect of the Berlin Volksbühne's Theater am Bülowplatz. The auditorium and stage had been enlarged, lighting controls had for the first time been integrated into the design of the theatre, the orchestral pit had been divided into three individually sinkable sections and the stage could similarly be sunk or moved sideways. Technically, the new Kroll was regarded as up to date, though Dülberg and his apprentice, Teo Otto, both subsequently complained of shortcomings.[1] Aesthetically, however, the restoration was less satisfactory. Brown painted woodwork and a red plush curtain gave a certain warmth, but otherwise the effect was anaemic and indecisive. Weissmann unkindly remarked that an attempt to match Volksbühne simplicity to the style of a boulevard theatre had resulted in a compromise that had nothing to do with the people and nothing to do with art.[2] The acoustics were generally judged to be indifferent.

From the start the theatre was dogged by misfortune and misjudgement. The opening performance of *Die Meistersinger* under Kleiber found little favour with the critics and the strain on the Staatsoper of providing seven performances a week (as the Kultusministerium had promised the Volksbühne in its determination to outbid the Grosse Volksoper (see p. 187)) in two theatres soon began to tell. Both the orchestra and the chorus had to be augmented and a larger number of soloists than Schillings had foreseen proved necessary. With the end of inflation, receipts also fell short of estimates.* Within a few weeks Weissmann was putting some pertinent questions. How was the chronically ailing Linden Opera to provide the resources the Kroll required? Where were the players to provide a good orchestra in each house, or the singers capable of rising above a level of mediocrity? 'The level of the performance', he insisted, 'is shamefully low.'[3]

It was not long before the question of Schillings's competence recurred in a more acute form. On 3 April 1925 C. H. Becker was reappointed Kultusminister, and he determined to grasp the nettle of the State Opera.†

---

* By 30 per cent (undated memorandum in the C. H. Becker-Archiv, Geheimes Staatsarchiv, Preussischer Kulturbesitz, Berlin (Dahlem).
† He had previously held the position between February and November 1921. Between 1919 and 1925 he had been Secretary of State (see p. 77).

Scarcely more than a week later it was announced that its deficit had risen to 2,750,000M and that Kestenberg had been installed as controller to make economies.[4] On 2 May Schillings was summoned by Becker and presented with a proposal whereby Heinz Tietjen, who had made a reputation as Intendant in Breslau, would become joint Intendant of the State Opera and assume sole responsibility for the ailing Kroll.

Heinz Tietjen was to play an important role both in Klemperer's career and in German operatic life. Born in 1881 in Tangier of a German father and a British mother, he was originally intended for the law. A chance meeting with Nikisch led to a period of study with him and at the age of twenty-one Tietjen embarked on a career as a conductor, for which he had revealed some ability. But his real talent lay elsewhere. At his first post in Trier he quickly revealed such administrative gifts that within fifteen years he had risen from chorusmaster to Intendant. It was as Intendant that after the war he first came to the attention of the Prussian Kultusministerium, which was concerned to bolster the theatres in the occupied Rhineland as an expression of the region's German culture. In 1922 Tietjen was despatched by the ministry to the even more exposed frontier province of Silesia, part of which was claimed by the new Polish state. As Intendant in Breslau, he acted as adviser to the ministry on all theatrical matters in the area.

Outwardly colourless, unobtrusive and reserved, Tietjen had an extraordinary capacity 'to emerge the smiling, modest victor from the most tricky situations'.[5] Bruno Walter, who worked with him during four rewarding seasons at the Berlin Städtische Oper (1925–9) described him as 'a man of medium height, with drooping eyelids, a constant sideways look of his bespectacled eyes, a narrow-lipped and tightly compressed mouth, and a nervously twitching face. Never a spirited or spontaneous – to say nothing of an interesting – word came from his lips.'[6] Walter did not like Tietjen, but he paid tribute to his formidable administrative powers, his efficiency as a conductor and his competence as a producer.

Tietjen's remarkable administrative and diplomatic gifts made him a natural choice for the difficult task of running the two houses of the Berlin State Opera in tandem with a character as prickly as Schillings. Schillings, however, rejected Becker's proposal. In 1923 he had barred the way to Klemperer's appointment as musical director. Now he refused to countenance Tietjen, and in doing so he once again proved an obstacle to the reform of the State Opera, which the ministry was determined to bring about.* Henceforth his days were numbered.

* A further attempt by the Kultusministerium to bring Klemperer to Berlin in the summer of 1925 was probably connected with its attempts to raise standards at both houses of the State Opera. What transpired is not clear, but it seems that at some point he travelled to Zurich to discuss the issue with Curjel. On 15 June Klemperer wrote to his wife, 'I don't

Meanwhile an event had occurred that was to transform the operatic scene in Berlin and force Becker to precipitate action. On 25 December 1924 the Deutsches Opernhaus in Charlottenburg had finally been declared bankrupt and the *Magistrat* (city council) of Gross-Berlin had come into possession of the theatre. Gustav Böss, since 1921 the city's

want to hear any more about Berlin. It would have been an all too complicated way of bringing me there...I think that it would be impossible for me to speak to Schillings without an invitation to do so.'

22   Auditorium of the Kroll Theatre at its reopening in January 1924

236

energetic *Oberbürgermeister*, had long nursed an ambition to set up a directly subsidised civic opera house. Now that a theatre had fallen into his hands, he did not delay in putting his plan into action. On 13 February 1925 it was announced that the Deutsches Opernhaus would reopen in the autumn as the Städtische (City) Oper under the control of a supervisory board, on which the *Magistrat* would have a majority. On 7 May, only five days after Schillings had refused to work with him at the State Opera, Tietjen was appointed Intendant of the Städtische Oper and his first action was to invite Bruno Walter to become musical director.* From the start Tietjen and Walter aimed at the highest standards and within a few weeks of the theatre's reopening on 18 September 1925 had succeeded so well that, to the acute discomfort of the Kultusministerium, the performances at Charlottenburg began to outshine those at the Linden Opera.

On 21 November Becker summoned Schillings to a meeting to discuss the budget estimates for the State Opera.† Schillings refused to appear and on 25 November the *Börsen-Courier* carried a report that he had also declined to resign. His authority directly challenged, Becker had no alternative but to dismiss his Intendant, which he did on the following day. Up to this point Schillings had enjoyed precious little support in the press. But, to Becker's consternation, virtually every Berlin newspaper, irrespective of political persuasion, now took up the cry of bureaucratic interference in artistic issues. The entire opera personnel also sided with Schillings (although Kleiber cannily issued a statement deploring only the *manner* of his dismissal).[7] Leopold Jessner, the Intendant of the state spoken theatres offered his resignation in sympathy, the Prussian Academy of the Arts and its president, Max Liebermann, declared their support, as did a meeting of twenty other Intendants. The right-wing Deutschnational Volkspartei (DNVP) seized the opportunity to table a motion of no confidence in the Kultusministerium.

* Tietjen later maintained that he had only accepted the position at the Städtische Oper after Becker had assured him that a means would later be found of bringing him to the State Opera. (Heinz Tietjen, 'Fünfzig Jahre Behörden-Intendant', typescript in the Tietjen-Archiv, Akademie der Künste, West Berlin). This duly came to pass in September 1926 (see p. 240). Tietjen subsequently showed a remarkable talent for advancement – and for survival. In 1930 he became *Generalintendant* of all the Prussian state theatres. He remained in this position after 1933 and continued until 1945 to work as smoothly with Göring as he had done with Becker. During the Third Reich he also administered the Bayreuth Festival, where he produced and conducted. At the end of the war he nonetheless emerged as a member of the resistance and in 1948 for the second time in his career became Intendant of the Städtische Oper in West Berlin. On retiring from that position in 1954 at the age of seventy-three, he was appointed Intendant in Hamburg for a further five years.

† Until 1925 the former court theatres had continued to be financed from the revenues of the Hohenzollern estate. Thus they did not appear in the Kultusministerium budgetary estimates until 1926, when for the first time they became a political issue. (Rockwell, 'The Prussian Ministry of Culture and the Berlin State Opera, 1918–1931' (diss.), pp. 78–9)

23   Heinz Tietjen

Becker had miscalculated badly. In his first confrontation with the opponents of his attempt to set up a socially oriented opera house in Berlin he found himself deprived of his natural allies both in and out of parliament. On 28 November he called a press conference but entirely failed to convince it that Schillings was not a victim of bureaucratic intrigue. While liberal opinion was preoccupied with the issue of artistic liberty, the Right was free to concentrate its guns on the Kultusministerium's policy and in particular on what it saw as the nefarious influence of Seelig and Kestenberg. They had, it was argued, set up the Kroll Opera against

238

the advice of Schillings to meet the wishes of their cronies in the Volksbühne and on conditions that were bound to result in a deficit.

The extreme nationalist press did not hesitate to introduce an anti-Semitic flavour into its attacks. Schillings, declared *Der Jungdeutsche* on 28 November, was 'the last man with German blood in the Prussian state cultural institutions'. At the opera he had been surrounded by a band of Jewish conductors. Behind them stood 'the dark figures' in the Kultus-ministerium, products of the November revolution, who were undermining the remaining bastions of German culture. 'A Jewish camarilla' lay behind the dismissal of Schillings.[8] The musical press was not slow to chime in. Paul Schwers, the editor of the *Allgemeine Musikzeitung*, wrote (4 December 1925) that 'the un-German Socialist, Kestenberg, is a threat to German culture' and called for the removal of 'that fatal remnant of an evil revolution'. Even Schillings's lawyer did not hesitate to fan the flames by asserting that the roots of the trouble lay in the *Weltanschauung* of Becker's advisers.[9]

So in a sense they did, for 'der Fall Schillings', as it had come to be known, was the first assault to be mounted on the young republic's musical policies. When the issue was debated in the Landtag on 14 December* Becker stoutly defended his *Referenten* and stressed that his policy aimed only to make good operatic performances available to a wider public at a price it could afford. But in this attempt to depoliticise the issue, he revealed his failure to grasp that the opponents of the Kroll were not primarily concerned with artistic issues: for them these were no more than a stick with which to beat Prussia's republican coalition. The right-wing parties supported a motion calling for Schillings's reinstatement, and four small extreme groups, one of them the National Socialist Workers' Party (commonly referred to as Nazis) urged that provision for the salaries of Kestenberg and Seelig should be deleted from the budget estimates.

At this stage, however, party loyalties reasserted themselves and both motions were defeated by the Socialist, Democrat and Zentrum coalition which was the mainstay of Braun's government. On 3 January 1926 a face-saving compromise was reached, whereby Schillings resigned and his dismissal was rescinded.† With his departure the way was at last open for

---

* By a curious coincidence the first performance of *Wozzeck*, the first première of major significance to have occurred at the Berlin State Opera for decades, took place that evening.

† After a period of decline, Schillings's career started to blossom once more in 1932, when he succeeded the painter, Max Liebermann, in the influential position of president of the Prussian Academy of the Arts. His appointment was in itself an indication of the way the wind was blowing and, when the National Socialists came to power in January 1933, Schillings proved a ready instrument in securing the resignation of those members, Thomas Mann among others, who had incurred the disfavour of the new regime. These services were duly rewarded by his appointment on 26 March 1933 as Carl Ebert's successor as

the Kultusministerium to bring administrative order and artistic purpose into the two houses of the Berlin State Opera. But 'der Fall Schillings' had revealed how deep and venomous was the opposition both in and out of the Landtag to the young republic's policy of bringing into existence at the Kroll an opera house that would reflect its own image.

For the time being, Becker had, however, lost the services of Klemperer and Tietjen, the two men he had chosen to achieve that end. The problem of bringing Tietjen back into the fold was adroitly solved. On 5 January 1926, only two days after Schillings had finally conceded defeat, the Kultusministerium announced that an *Interessengemeinschaft* would be set up to harmonise the functions of the State Opera and the Städtische Oper. Ostensibly, its purpose was to resolve differences about repertory and the dates of new productions, as well as to provide mutual assistance. Its longer-term purpose was to enable Tietjen to become Intendant of both institutions. His appointment as Intendant of the State Opera was duly announced on 16 September.

Meanwhile, it continued to coast under a committee (consisting of Blech, Kleiber, the producer, Franz-Ludwig Hörth and Georg Winter, an administrative official) that had temporarily assumed control on Schillings's departure. Standards remained unsatisfactory, particularly at the Kroll, and on 22 April 1926 an article in the *Berliner Tageblatt*, based on an interview with Hörth and thus representative of opinion within the State Opera, argued that the Linden and Kroll theatres could not be run in tandem with a single company. In July Hörth followed this up with a memorandum in which he gave reasons for the failure of the Kroll as a *Filialbetrieb** and urged that it should be established as a separate house with its own musical staff and company.† It was on the basis of Hörth's memorandum that the Kultusministerium finally determined to establish the Kroll as an artistically autonomous opera house, and Kestenberg was despatched to offer Klemperer the post of director.‡

Klemperer was spending his summer vacation in Sils Baselgia in the

Intendant of the Städtische Oper. On 23 May 1933 Schillings also wrote to inform Schoenberg that he had been relieved of his position as director of the Academy's master class for composition. His death two months later prevented him from enjoying the fruits of his 'come-back'.
* Literally, a branch of an undertaking.
† The author was unable to trace this memorandum in such files of the Kultusministerium and the State Opera as survive in the East German Zentrales Staatsarchiv in Merseburg. But its existence is mentioned on more than one occasion in the proceedings of the investigatory committee set up by the Landtag in 1931 (see pp. 362, 365–8), when it was proposed to shut the Kroll Opera (Preussischer Landtag, 1928/31, Nr. 7431, *Bericht des Unter-suchungsausschuss (Krolloper)* – henceforth referred to as *Untersuchungsausschuss* – column 319). Tietjen's support of the Hörth memorandum is mentioned in his evidence in column 324 of this report.
‡ Kestenberg subsequently claimed that this was the first occasion on which he had discussed

Engadine, where as usual a number of musicians were on holiday.* News of what was afoot must have reached him, for on 21 August he wrote to Curjel:

> You know that I am a burnt child and am firmly determined not to concern myself with unlaid eggs. I have been played with all too often for me to give any sign from my side before an official approach is made.
>
> You certainly know, better than almost anyone, what I have in mind. Will it be possible to realise it? *Aspettiamo.* How justified my reserve has been is also shown by the fact that no affirmative word has reached you from a responsible mouth. If Kestenberg wants to speak to me, he will certainly let me know and I shall be glad to see him. For the rest, just one request: *silentium* about all rumours.

The following day Klemperer left for Italy, planning to return to Wiesbaden on 31 August. On 28 August he was joined in Locarno by Kestenberg, who formally offered him the directorship of an independent Kroll, while they were swimming in the lake.†

*   *   *

Klemperer's engagement was made public on 22 September 1926, six days after Tietjen's appointment as Intendant of the Staatsoper had been announced. His contract,[10] which was to run for ten years, specified that he was to be director of the Kroll as well as its music director 'in vollem Umfang' ('in the full meaning of the word'), that the theatre was to be run independently and that he was to be consulted before Tietjen took artistic decisions relating to it. His salary was to be 55,000M. Klemperer also stipulated that he should give an annual series of concerts with the Staatskapelle (as the State Opera Orchestra was called when it emerged from the orchestral pit). At his behest Dülberg was put in charge of stage design. Curjel became *Dramaturg.*[11] Klemperer seemed finally to have achieved his ambition: he was to be sole master in his own house and free to put his ideas into practice.

The Kultusministerium had, however, omitted to secure the consent of two parties whose support was essential to the success of the undertaking. In spite of his close connections with the Volksbühne, Kestenberg seems

the issue of the Kroll with Klemperer (*Untersuchungsausschuss,* column 318). Klemperer himself maintained that Kestenberg had held out the prospect of an independent Kroll when he visited Wiesbaden earlier in 1926 to hear *Don Giovanni.* (Submission to Labour Tribunal, 24 March 1931)

* Edith Stargardt-Wolff's *Wegweiser grosser Musiker* contains an account of his playing Schumann's symphonies in a four-handed version with Joseph Rosenstock (his eventual successor in Wiesbaden) and then switching into 'Valencia', a hit tune of the moment.

† Kestenberg, *Bewegte Zeiten,* p. 67. The purpose of this curious choice of background was to preserve security. Kestenberg later discovered from his wife, who was sitting on the shore with Johanna Klemperer, that every word had been clearly audible over the water!

241

to have made no attempt to prepare it for Klemperer's appointment, let alone for his policies. In view of its humdrum cultural tastes that was to prove a serious omission. Even more grave was the failure of the Kultusministerium to secure the agreement of the Ministry of Finance to the establishment of an independent Kroll on the grounds that it was merely a matter of internal reorganisation.

It was not long before that bird came home to roost. On 29 November Tietjen and Klemperer met officials to consider in more detail the requirements of an independent Kroll. When the additional cost was estimated at 878,000M, the representative of the Ministry of Finance bluntly declared that he could not sanction expenditure on such a scale.[12] Tietjen adroitly averted a head-on collision. But for a while the entire project was in such peril that, before Klemperer left for New York a month later, it was agreed that Kestenberg would telegraph if the difficulties had not been overcome. Kestenberg later told Klemperer the situation had grown so threatening that at one point the telegram had lain on his desk, ready for despatch.[13] Disaster was eventually averted. But henceforth the Ministry of Finance, resentful at the Kultusministerium's failure to consult it, was to be counted among the most formidable of the Kroll's enemies. On 13 July 1927 Klemperer wrote to his wife from Berlin,

There have been some hot days here (in both meanings of the word). In spite of all my efforts the ceiling will *not* be altered. Fire regulations don't allow it to be covered with material and it can't be painted within six weeks. I don't believe it but have no means of enforcing my will. In the process there was a really very disagreeable discussion with an (all-powerful) *Ministerialdirektor* of the Ministry of Finance, who adopted a 'Prussian tone' that I – at least – am not used to.

Thus, even before an independent Kroll had opened its doors, the ineptitude of Becker's ministry had ensured that neither the Volksbühne nor the financial authorities felt committed to the project. That was to prove a crucial factor when the Kroll came under fire in the Landtag for its artistic policies.

Nor did its independence prove to be as unrestricted as had been suggested by the wording of Klemperer's contract. At the meeting in Berlin on 29 November 1926, the policy was defined as 'to establish the Kroll with its own ensemble on *as independent a basis as possible*' (author's italics)[12]. The most important limitation was financial. The Kroll was to be financed out of the general budget for the State Opera and hence Klemperer's much-prized artistic autonomy was from the start circumscribed by the fact that funds were not under his control, but Tietjen's. The Kroll was also obliged to share its orchestra and chorus with the Linden Opera, and this was to prove a potent source of friction during its opening season. Nonetheless Tietjen was committed to its artistic independence and

242

Klemperer was left full freedom to build his own ensemble. Among his most crucial appointments were those of Alexander von Zemlinsky and Fritz Zweig as conductors.

Curjel considered Zemlinsky 'not quite in the first class' as a conductor,[14] but among his admirers were Stravinsky, who later described a *Figaro* he had heard under him in Prague in the twenties as 'one of the most satisfying experiences of my life',[15] and Strauss, who was enchanted by a performance of *Salome* that he subsequently heard him conduct at the Kroll.[16] That Zemlinsky, who was music director at the German Theatre in Prague, was prepared to accept a subordinate position reflects his admiration for Klemperer. Zweig was to specialise in the lighter works (later he conducted the entire repertory), to which he brought a deft hand. This well-balanced and harmonious team of conductors remained unchanged throughout the four years during which Klemperer remained at the helm of the Kroll.

*   *   *

Among the new works that Klemperer brought to New York in 1926/7 was Hindemith's Concert Music for Wind Orchestra, Op. 41. At its first American performance on 10 February it was greeted by hissing and the criticisms were hostile. 'There are enough jagged figures and ugly passages for grunting wind instrumentation to stock the larders of a dozen... modern musical blacksmiths', wrote the critic of *The Sun* (11 February 1927). Feeling the work to have been misunderstood, at its second hearing three days later Klemperer urged his audience to listen to it 'in good humour and not too seriously'.[17] There is no evidence that his words had much effect, but that he took the unusual course of speaking up for the music was indicative of a commitment that was to become increasingly far-reaching in the coming years.

Given the thirty-year-old Hindemith's prominence as the undisputed leader of the rising generation of German composers and the proximity of Wiesbaden to both Hindemith's powerful publishers in Mainz and his home in Frankfurt, it is surprising that there is no evidence of any contact before April 1926, when Klemperer had made a belated and unsuccessful attempt to procure the first performance of his opera, *Cardillac*.[18] During the summer of that year he had been in contact with the composer about a new work, which turned out to be the *Konzertmusik* he conducted in New York. But it was not until he attended the première of *Cardillac* in Dresden on 7 November 1926 that Klemperer became a whole-hearted advocate of Hindemith's music.[19]

In *Cardillac* the post-war generation of German composers decisively elbowed its way to the forefront of the operatic scene and the production

243

that Klemperer conducted in Wiesbaden only seventeen days after the first performance in Dresden played a crucial part in that breakthrough. Hindemith's score marked the first major and consequential application of Busoni's belief that there was no such thing as specifically dramatic music (were not Mozart's operas at any rate in part symphonic and, for that matter, Bach's non-operatic Passions dramatic?). Music in opera, Busoni had argued, should cease to cling to the coat-tails of a text; inherent musical values should resume their primacy in closed numbers.[20] An equally important influence on the score of *Cardillac* was the rediscovery of the world of *opera seria*, notably at the annual productions of the Handel Festival in Göttingen. To Hindemith, its closed forms seemed to offer an escape from the dominating role played by the text in post-Wagnerian music drama and in *Cardillac* he set about reinstating them with a rigour, if not a crassness, that would have startled Busoni, let alone Handel*.

The local critics did not warm to a work that stood the Wagnerian relationship between text and music on its head. But visitors from Berlin and elsewhere concurred in finding the performance far more dramatically compelling than that in Dresden. The *Berliner Tageblatt* (26 November 1926), in particular, perceived a parallel between Hindemith's 'absolute', non-illustrative score and the rigorous thematicism that marked Klemperer's performances of classical scores in the concert hall. 'The performance', the writer continued, 'attained a complete blend of empathy and discipline.' The first night ended in scenes of enthusiasm such as have rarely greeted a radical new opera in the twentieth century. Henceforth Klemperer was to be one of Hindemith's most powerful champions. He also came to like him as a man, even if the relationship never progressed beyond cordiality.†　By the end of the following summer it was agreed that Hindemith would himself be the soloist in the first performance of a new viola concerto during the coming season at the Kroll. Thereafter no living composer figured more prominently in its programmes or came to be regarded as more representative of its spirit.

*　　　　　*　　　　　*

Hindemith was not the only young German composer to whom Klemperer looked for new works to perform at the Kroll. As three years earlier, when

---

* It was left to a former pupil of Busoni, the more flexibly minded Kurt Weill, to warn that the restoration of 'absolute' music values in the theatre (with which he in principle sympathised) carried with it a danger of transforming opera into oratorio ('Bekenntnis zur Oper', Heinsheimer and Stefan (eds.), *Universal-Edition Jahrbuch 1926*, pp. 226–8). It is a danger that *Cardillac* does not entirely escape, one reason why Hindemith in 1952 subjected the score to a drastic revision that Klemperer regarded as mistaken (*Conversations*, p. 63).
† In 1931 Hindemith for a while gave Klemperer's son, Werner, violin lessons.

it had seemed as though he was to become director of the Grosse Volksoper, he again turned first to the brilliant, versatile figure of Ernst Krenek. As early as September 1926 he expressed interest in three one-act operas that were still incomplete; at about the same time he even seems to have offered him a job at the Kroll, which he turned down because it was poorly paid.[21] But on 10 February 1927 Krenek hit the jackpot with the first performance of *Jonny spielt auf*, an ingenious and eclectic score, decked out with every current fad from jazz to neo-classical counterpoint. Its success was so prodigious that theatres from Moscow to New York clamoured to perform it.* Thereafter, Krenek and his publishers proved evasive. As a consolation prize, Hans Heinsheimer, head of Universal Edition's opera department, on 24 March 1927 offered Klemperer the first performance of Kurt Weill's *Photographie und Liebe*.† Weill was, of course, by no means unknown; Busch had performed his first opera, *Der Protagonist*, in Dresden in March 1926 and Kleiber had just given *Royal Palace* at the Berlin State Opera.‡ But Klemperer did not bite the bait. On the contrary, he continued to hammer on the door of Universal Edition for the first performance of Krenek's one acters while hesitating throughout the spring and summer of 1927 about *Der Protagonist*, which Weill's publishers had also offered. But on 17 July an event took place which overnight radically transformed his attitude to the two 27-year-old composers.

In 1927, the Donaueschingen Festival, which had served as a focal point in the spread of neo-classicism and *neue Sachlichkeit*, moved to more spacious quarters in Baden-Baden. As the town boasted a theatre, the festival seized the opportunity of commissioning four chamber operas, designed to explore what could be achieved with modest forces and the simplest of sets. Johanna Klemperer was engaged to sing in three of them.§ But it was the last work in this quadruple bill, Weill's *Mahagonny* Songspiel on texts by Brecht, that enthralled Klemperer, who had hastened from Berlin to be present. At a reception later that evening Weill's wife, Lotte Lenya, 'suddenly...felt a slap on the back, accompanied by a booming laugh. "Is there no telephone?" It was Otto Klemperer. With that, the whole room was singing the Benares Song, and I knew that the battle was won.'‖

---

* Together with Bodanzky, Tietjen and Kodály, Klemperer attended a performance in Leipzig on 1 May 1927. He nonetheless made no attempt to perform it at the Kroll.
† Subsequently re-entitled *Der Zar lässt sich photographieren*.
‡ Klemperer and Curjel went to see it, but walked out on account of a performance that Curjel described as *penetrant* (i.e. penetratingly awful) ('Erinnerungen um Kurt Weill', *Melos*, 1970, pp. 81–5).
§ Milhaud's *L'Enlèvement d'Europe*, Toch's *Die Prinzessin auf der Erbst* and Hindemith's *Hin und zurück*.
‖ Sleevenote to the Philips recording of *Der Aufstieg und Fall der Stadt Mahagonny*. 'Is there no telephone?' is a line from the Benares Song.

245

There and then discussions started about a full-length opera for the Kroll. Weill at first proposed *Na-und?*, which he had completed earlier that year, but the project was dropped after Curjel reported unfavourably on it.* It was only then that the question arose of performing a full-scale, operatic version of the *Mahagonny* Songspiel and on 4 August Weill reported to his publishers that he was setting to work with Brecht on what was to become *Der Aufstieg und Fall der Stadt Mahagonny.*†

But a Brecht–Weill opera was as yet an unborn child. What Klemperer needed was a major new stage work for his first season at the Kroll, and for this his hopes were pinned on Stravinsky. At the end of May 1927 he and Dülberg travelled to Paris to attend the first performance of *Oedipus Rex*, which was to be given in concert form after Stravinsky's failure to raise funds for a stage production.[22] On 29 May they attended a party given by the Princesse de Polignac,‡ at which Stravinsky and Prokofiev accompanied on two pianos an otherwise full-scale performance of the work. Klemperer was deeply impressed, more so, indeed, than he was the following evening by the première itself, which suffered from the composer's inexpert conducting.§ Neither a Latin text nor an overtly static dramatic action seemed obstacles to a staged performance, such as Stravinsky had originally envisaged, and that summer Klemperer and Dülberg worked together on the details of a production.‖

*   *   *

Wiesbaden had not seen much of Klemperer in the latter half of the season. In addition to his visits to New York, Moscow and Leningrad, the Kroll had demanded time-consuming visits to Berlin. Inevitably there were grumbles

---

* *Na-und?* was Weill's first full-length opera. On his hurried emigration in 1933, he left the score, which was never performed, in Germany. It has since disappeared (David Drew, 'Kurt Weill: life, times and works', unpublished study, typescript, p. 180).

† Curjel, who first met Weill at Baden-Baden, later claimed on more than one occasion that it was he who had instigated the 'big' *Mahagonny* (e.g. *Melos*, 1970, pp. 81–5). Yet as early as 4 April 1927 Weill had informed Universal Edition that 'the material of a large-scale tragic opera is already worked out'. If David Drew is correct in maintaining that this was in fact the 'big' *Mahagonny*, Curjel's claim must be rejected. It nonetheless remains probable that the prospect of a première at the Kroll gave Weill and Brecht a motive to press on with what had up to that point been no more than a project. It is significant that, after several months of inactivity, they should have set to work 'almost daily' (Drew, 'The History of Mahagonny', *Musical Times*, January 1963) soon after their encounter with Klemperer and Curjel at Donaueschingen.

‡ Winnaretta de Polignac (1865–1943), a celebrated patroness of the arts. The daughter of Isaac Singer, the manufacturer of the sewing machine, who left her a vast fortune.

§ Klemperer sat next to Cocteau, the author of the text, who whispered, 'He can't do it. This is impossible' (*Conversations*, p. 60). In later years, however, Klemperer considered Stravinsky a highly effective conductor of his own music.

‖ On the train from Paris Klemperer chanced to encounter Strauss, whom he told of the work and of his intention to perform it at the Kroll. Strauss turned up his nose in disgust. '*In Latein!*'

246

in the press about his long absences. But the season ended in a blaze of glory that stilled all criticism. On 25 March he conducted a Beethoven concert in commemoration of the centenary of the composer's death, which was attended by Chicherin, the Foreign Minister of the Soviet Union.* A triumphant *Meistersinger* followed on 15 May, and on 30 June at his last concert Klemperer conducted two works that he had not previously performed: Beethoven's *Grosse Fuge* and Bruckner's Symphony No. 5. Finally, on 3 July, he bade farewell to Wiesbaden with a performance of *Don Giovanni*. The ovations at the end of the evening seemed unending.

The house...rose applauding, but no one left their place...There was clapping, banging, stamping and shouting without end...Then Klemperer and after him Hagemann appeared and on each occasion the hurricane broke out anew. At length the curtain was raised and there they all stood in a sea of flowers and laurel wreaths...How often the curtain went up, I don't know – who could count amid such scenes! The lights were put out – it didn't help, the storm continued to rage. Then the lights went on and...the game began all over again, until, slowly but relentlessly, the iron curtain descended like a guillotine. But even that did not...cut off the stage from the auditorium. The iron curtain has a small doorway and through it they came again and again...Finally the door was shut and the lights put out. *Schluss*. No, it was still not the end. Hundreds of last-ditch resisters stormed to the artists' entrance, where they waited for half an hour to take farewell, now really for the last time.[23]

Twenty years later, Hagemann looked back at his association with the three great conductors he had worked with in Mannheim and Wiesbaden.

Whether Bodanzky or Furtwängler or Klemperer was the greatest...is something I would not presume to decide...But one thing I know and that with unshakable certainty: Klemperer is the greatest of them all as a theatre conductor; scenically and musically, he is simply a master. In this field he had no rival, never has had one. Even Gustav Mahler, however much one may esteem his artistic personality, was only his forerunner as an operatic conductor. Mahler showed the path and the goal...it was Klemperer who first brought fulfilment. He is a disciple who has become what the teacher again and again strove for and here and there achieved: the conductor-producer, the guiding stage-artist of the opera...

Otto Klemperer has been the only living musician I have known who in the theatre conducted...exclusively for the stage...At the piano and with models of the set before him he would try in open discussion with the producer and his assistants, the designer, the technicians, the lighting experts, the wardrobe personnel, to make clear his intentions down to the smallest detail. In the rehearsals

---

* Georgy Chicherin (1872–1936), Foreign Minister of the Soviet Union (1918–30). This was not the only occasion on which he heard Klemperer conduct in Wiesbaden, for in 1930 he completed a study of Mozart, in which he took Klemperer to task for what he considered an 'anachronistic' production of *Don Giovanni*. The book was not published in the Soviet Union until 1970 (German edition 1975). After the Beethoven concert, Klemperer, who was not addicted to social gestures, gave a supper party at his home for Chicherin (and enjoined the guests, who included the soloist, Joseph Szigeti, and Kestenberg, to address him as *Excellenz*).

he worked in closest partnership with the producer...and later conducted the performance as a unified work of art – not just the music, but the musico-dramatic *Gestaltung* as such...Otto Klemperer...was destined to be a leader of modern music theatre.[24]

That bold claim was to be tested to the full in the coming four years in Berlin.

12 *Klemperer's Kroll opens*

Early in the morning of 1 September 1927, Hans Curjel, *Dramaturg* of the reconstituted Staatsoper am Platz der Republik,* burst into Tietjen's office in the Oberwallstrasse and shouted excitedly, 'Der Betrieb läuft' ('The show's on the road').[1] The claim was premature. Since May 1926 the Kroll had been occupied by the Linden Opera, whose theatre had been shut for a reconstruction that was proving far more protracted than had been envisaged. It had originally been intended that it would have returned to its own quarters by the spring of 1927. Owing to a series of accidents and delays, it was not to do so until April 1928. Thus Klemperer faced the dual task of forming newly engaged artists into an ensemble and of mounting a series of entirely new productions while sharing his theatre with another full-scale and long established company. As Curjel later recalled, the joint rehearsal schedule was 'a minefield'.[2] Rehearsals at first took place in an ill-suited administrative building behind Unter den Linden. It was not until 10 October that an improvised stage became available in a disused exhibition shed in the grounds of Schloss Bellevue, some two miles to the west. Even the Kroll's small administrative offices were for a while housed in the *Generalintendanz*.

At half past ten the assembled company was greeted by Klemperer, who then launched into the preparations for *Oedipus Rex*. At midday four of the five men who were to run the Kroll during the four years of its existence as an artistically independent opera house assembled for lunch at Habel's wine restaurant on Unter den Linden. The only absentee was Alexander von Zemlinsky. Already in his late fifties, he was by far the most seasoned member of the Kroll's leadership. After sixteen successful years as musical director of the German Theatre in Prague, he had practical knowledge unrivalled by that of his colleagues, including Klemperer. Age and experience gave him special authority and made him 'the musical conscience' of the Kroll.[3] Klemperer never failed to show him respect, frequently consulted him when problems arose, and later paid tribute to 'an extraordinarily sympathetic and considerate colleague'.[4]

* In 1923 the Königsplatz, on which the Kroll stood, had been renamed Platz der Republik. As political tensions began to gather around the Kroll, it came to be referred to, by its friends as well as its enemies, as the 'Republikoper'. Indeed, at one point Klemperer wanted the Kroll to be officially known as the Republic Opera (Klemperer, 'Meine Tätigkeit an der Krolloper', in *Über Musik und Theater*, pp. 113–14).

249

24 Alexander von
Zemlinsky, 1930

Zemlinsky undoubtedly reciprocated these feelings in full measure.[5] Nonetheless he may have come to feel himself overshadowed as a conductor by the huge stature of Klemperer and grieved at his failure to cut more ice in Berlin. At any rate a sense of resignation is apparent in a letter he wrote to his old friend and former pupil, Alma Mahler, when the Kroll's days were numbered and he himself was oppressed by a sense of gathering years. 'I lack', he admitted to her, 'that certain something that one must have...in order to get to the very top. In such a throng it is not enough to have elbows, one must know how to use them.'[6] But Zemlinsky's sense of failure may have stemmed as much from psychological factors as from his subordinate position at the Kroll, for after it had closed he refused a post as musical director in Wiesbaden, where he would once more have been his own master.*

The remaining four formed a curiously diverse group. The most traditionally minded was Fritz Zweig, who remained largely aloof from the intellectual currents and conflicts that eddied around the theatre. Essentially a *Musikant*, Zweig's literal view of stagecraft led him to regard innovatory productions with suspicion, if not with downright distaste. Apart from his

---

* Zemlinsky's well-nigh indecipherable letters in the Library of Congress, which the author has not read, may reveal more about his situation at the Kroll.

250

staunch advocacy of his compatriot Janáček (both men came from Moravia), he also showed much less commitment than Klemperer and Zemlinsky to the music of his time. At the Kroll Zweig was to prove an accomplished and versatile conductor rather than a strong influence on his company's artistic policies. He did, however, serve an important non-musical function: he enjoyed good relations with Tietjen, under whom he had already worked at the Städtische Oper. When tension rose, as it not infrequently did between Klemperer and his *Generalintendant*, it was Zweig who often served as intermediary.

In contrast, the youngest member of the lunch table, Hans Curjel, who was to become the company's intellectual and ideological mainspring, shared Kestenberg's belief that 'art and society are now sweeping to a new synthesis'.[7] In his view, new modes of artistic expression would emerge out of the social and economic changes that as a man with strong socialist sympathies he believed to be both necessary and inevitable. Art would follow life and the role of the Kroll was to serve as midwife in this process.* His sympathies with the rising generation of German composers,

---

* The belief that there is a deep interrelationship between changes in the fields of arts and politics was not, of course, invented by Marx. Plato held that 'when the modes of music change, the fundamental laws of the state change with them' (*The Republic*, Book 4, 424C). Curjel's 'Neue Kriterien – neue Massstäbe' (*Melos*, March 1932) provides an account of his views at a later date in his career. It also illustrates his propensity to employ 'sociological' concepts as though they were scientific terms.

25   Hans Curjel, *c.* 1930

251

26 Ewald Dülberg,
c. 1928

and in particular his closeness to Weill, undoubtedly served to bolster Klemperer's leaning towards *die neue Sachlichkeit*. Through his links with and understanding of contemporary painters, he came increasingly to determine the visual image of the Kroll.

In this field, however, Curjel's influence was at first limited by the presence of Ewald Dülberg. Of the group Dülberg was personally by far the closest to Klemperer, on whose approach to the stage he had had a decisive influence. Klemperer had originally intended that, in addition to taking charge of the entire visual side of the theatre's activities, he should also design its principal productions, as he was indeed to do in the opening season of 1927/8.* But as he looked across the lunch table, Klemperer observed that his friend was a sick man; by the following summer the pulmonary tuberculosis from which he already suffered had spread to his bowels. Dülberg's perfectionism and inflexible character made him a slow

---

* Less important productions were handed over to Dülberg's young assistant, Teo Otto (see p. 285).

worker, ill-suited to the rush and improvisation that are an inescapable part of the theatre, and illness made him a difficult collaborator. As his influence waned, Curjel's star came into the ascendant.

But in the opening season Klemperer and Dülberg were the dominant artistic influences. They shared to the full Curjel's belief in the need for scenic renewal. But in spite of Klemperer's general leaning to the Left, which became more marked in the hard, radical air of Berlin and after his triumphant visits to the Soviet Union, neither of them sympathised with his avant-garde commitment. As Ernst Bloch later put it, 'Avant-garde...does not suffice to define Klemperer, on the contrary...he himself regarded such a description with a certain revulsion. More revulsion than was perhaps justified.'[8]

Klemperer's own attitude to the staging of opera was characteristically straightforward. His basic intention was 'to make good theatre. Not avant-garde theatre, but good theatre',[9] and as a means to that end he looked to thorough preparation as much as to stylistic innovation. He was eager to purge the operatic stage of grandiloquence and spectacle. But those aims were subordinate in his mind to purely musical considerations: he had been drawn to the Kroll above all by the possibility it offered of basing a repertory on a limited number of productions, all of which could be rehearsed with exceptional care and thereafter maintained in good repair.*

* Wilhelm Reinking (*Spiel und Form*, pp. 113–14) is in error when he alleges that the system did not work because members of subscribing organisations, notably the Berlin Volksbühne,

27   Fritz Zweig, *c.* 1930

He also attached paramount importance to ensemble: only thus could the standards reached on a first night be maintained throughout the season.

Klemperer himself was in some ways an improbable leader of such a heterogeneous group. To one later collaborator he embodied a baffling combination of qualities:

This thin man with burning, coal-black eyes and the head of a sparrow-hawk wedded the goodness of Nathan the Wise to the intolerance of a grand inquisitor ...He could be as cynical and sarcastic as any misanthrope and as naïve and childlike as any unworldly idealist. He had wit and yet was quite without humour. He combined sharp powers of understanding with the stubborn ignorance of someone who was unteachable. He had the driving power of a maniac, yet was...a plaything...in the hands of Tietjen. The divided nature of his character revealed abysses just where one least expected them. Basically, he was – as he himself insisted – conservative and anything but a revolutionary. And yet he and his interpretations had a revolutionary impact.[10]

But however baffling his character, Klemperer radiated an effortless sense of authority that commanded the loyalties of his collaborators. As Curjel later put it,

Otto Klemperer was revered by us all, although there was no kow-towing. His severe and unaffected (unverwaschenes) music-making, his freedom from any sort of self-aggrandisement or other vanity, his eschewal of musical and personal gush were greatly esteemed. The authenticity of his music-making, the self-control with which he conducted, instead of, like others, behaving as though he were officiating at High Mass, were a great example to us.[11]

Democracy rarely thrives in the opera house, and no man could be more ruthlessly autocratic than Klemperer when he felt artistic issues to be at stake. Yet, unlike most tyrants, he hated sycophants and (even in old age) his eyes would light up with interest when confronted by a surprising idea or even flat disagreement. Decisions at the Kroll (wrong as well as right) were taken in open discussion. With a couple of notable exceptions, operas were chosen and cast by personal agreement. All accounts are unanimous on one point: there was a truly remarkable absence of back-biting and intrigue.

*　　　　　　　　*　　　　　　　　*

In spite of the importance that Klemperer attached to ensemble, he at first intended to engage a few outstanding artists, such as Frieda Leider, whom he wished to cast as Leonore and Donna Anna in his opening productions

required frequent new productions. On the contrary, precisely because the Volksbühne's large membership only attended two or three performances a season Klemperer's Kroll was able to exist on the basis of a repertory far smaller than that required by a conventional subscribing public, which made more frequent visits to the opera.

28   Klemperer, 1929

255

of *Fidelio* and *Don Giovanni*.* These plans came to nothing. Singers of that calibre, Tietjen made plain, were reserved to the Linden Opera.[12] Thus productions at the Kroll were cast almost exclusively from the relatively small group of principal singers whom Klemperer and his colleagues had engaged in auditions over the past twelve months. Like Mahler, Klemperer was more concerned with intelligence and musicality than with purely vocal attainments.† His company contained some outstanding performers, such as Rose Pauly, Moje Forbach, Jarmila Novotna and Fritz Krenn, and a close-knit ensemble prevented first night standards from slumping in subsequent performances as they were liable to do both in Kleiber's Linden Oper and in the Städtische Oper under Walter. But in general the Kroll could not match the extremely high vocal standards frequently attained in Berlin's two other opera houses during the late twenties.

That was not the only limitation under which it suffered. As is revealed by Curjel's notes on a crucial meeting on 15 June, Klemperer at first proposed to include several large-scale works by Wagner and Strauss in his repertory. Here again, Tietjen, who held the purse-strings and was thus in a position to enforce his rulings, produced a list of works that were to remain the preserve of the Linden Opera. Other projects, such as a plan to give *Alcina* in modern dress, failed to materialise.‡ A production of Debussy's *Pelléas et Mélisande* was also abandoned.§ At one point consideration was given to setting up an experimental studio. As, however, one of the projects was a 'concentrated' version of *Tristan und Isolde* with 'musical sections linked by spoken narrative',[13] it is perhaps as well that it came to nothing. (But see p. 352.)

The Kroll repertory fell into three principal categories. Classical operas were performed and produced, as Klemperer put it, 'with an open mind',[14] by which he meant freed of traditional incrustation. Other works were included either because they were felt to be unduly neglected or as representatives of a given style. There was also a commitment to modern opera. It was hardly a recipe for success, least of all with a public largely provided by the Volksbühne. Yet the Kroll's reputation as a hotbed of radicalism has been exaggerated by its champions as well as by its foes. It differed from conventional opera houses on two grounds. In matters of

---

* Notes made in Curjel's hand at a *Regiesitzung* on 15 June 1927 (Curjel *Nachlass*). Leider (1888–1975) was the leading dramatic soprano of her generation.

† Many of Mahler's favourite singers, such as Gutheil-Schoder and Mildenburg, did not have conventionally beautiful voices.

‡ In view of the important role played by the Handel revival in Germany in the twenties, it remains surprising that none of his operas was staged at the Kroll.

§ In an interview with Heinrich Strobel (Südwestfunk, 11 February 1970), Curjel subsequently claimed that this was due to Klemperer's fear of the work. It was not, however, the first time he had planned to perform it (see p. 94).

staging and performance it was contemptuous of the naturalistic approach so dear to the average opera goer. It also set out to choose new and recent works on grounds of musical value rather than as a token gesture. These never comprised more than a modest proportion of the performances it offered. But a policy of performing new works and old works in new ways was to prove dynamite enough.

*　　　　　　*　　　　　　*

The presence of the Linden cuckoo in his nest gave Klemperer a welcome excuse to delay the all-important opening production of *Fidelio* until November. Tietjen, however, insisted that the new Kroll, which was already arousing intense expectation, should in the meantime present a couple of concerts. This was not inappropriate. In his contract Klemperer had stipulated that he should conduct no fewer than ten a year, the same number as Kleiber gave at the Linden Opera. Much of the musical impact of the new Kroll was in fact to stem from the concerts that Klemperer presented there with his section of the Staatskapelle. Whereas some of the operatic performances were to remain ill-attended, the concerts from the start evoked such enthusiasm that it was hard to get a seat without taking out a subscription. As Furtwängler and Walter also each conducted an annual series in Berlin, standards were extremely high and competition fierce.* But Klemperer's concerts rapidly developed a stamp of their own.

In its blend of old and new, the opening programme on 29 September 1927 hoisted the banner that Klemperer was to hold aloft during the coming four seasons; as Heinrich Strobel commented in the *Berliner Börsen-Courier* (30 September 1927), it left Berlin in no doubt of his musical convictions ('Gesinnung'). There was intense expectation when, with pale, drawn features, he appeared uncharacteristically late and bowed curtly to a packed house. The evening opened with a performance of Bach's Suite in D, which, as Strobel and others commented, seemed in its severity and avoidance of sentimentality to strip off the romantic veneer that the nineteenth century had imposed on the music. Alfred Einstein,† the newly appointed critic of the *Berliner Tageblatt*, found it unacademic, but right; the fugato firmly propelled, the gavotte fiery, the bourrée properly burlesque, the famous 'air' unemphatic to the point of coolness, with the melody hardly more prominent than the accompanying voices.[15] For a

---

* Perhaps no city has ever enjoyed such a rich orchestral life as Berlin during the later years of the Weimar Republic.

† Alfred Einstein (1880–1952), a musicologist of international repute (*The Italian Madrigal* (1949) was the first comprehensive study of the subject) and celebrated in wider circles for his studies of Mozart and Schubert, was also an outstanding critic, for whose well-balanced and well-expressed views Klemperer had much respect.

257

29   Janáček with Klemperer on the occasion of the first Berlin performance of his *Sinfonietta*, September 1927

soloist, Klemperer inevitably turned first to Schnabel. No pianist was closer
to him musically and many critics commented on the almost uncanny
unity that seemed to exist between them in a performance of Mozart's D
minor Concerto (K.466).

Klemperer took it as a matter of course that his opening concert should
contain a major work that was new to Berlin and he chose the Janáček
Sinfonietta which had so appealed to him, if not to his audiences, when he
had conducted it in Wiesbaden and New York during the previous season.
The composer himself arrived in Berlin on the evening before the concert.
The following morning Klemperer impressed him by singing and playing
the work at the piano by heart and, except for the prestissimo finale, which
was not fast enough for his taste, the tempi pleased him. The critics'
reactions were in the main tepid, but the audience was delighted and
Janáček was called out again and again to acknowledge applause. 'The
work has conquered', he noted that night in his diary.[16] So, too, had
Klemperer – at any rate for the moment. For the first time cries were heard

258

of 'Vive Kl'empereur' that were henceforth to greet his appearances in Berlin.

Klemperer, who had already made enquiries of Janáček's publishers about his most recent opera, *The Makropoulos Affair*, took the opportunity of the composer's presence in Berlin to press for the first German performance rights of *From the House of the Dead*, which was as yet incomplete. Janáček was hesitant. 'Ah well', he wrote in his diary on 29 September, 'They have persuaded me, although the stage seems small to me.'* What he would really like, he subsequently told Emil Hertzka, his publisher, in an undated letter, would be a production under Klemperer, 'in my opinion one of the most gifted of conductors', in the Linden Opera. Meanwhile, Klemperer, disturbed at what he took to be the evasiveness of Janáček's publishers, wrote on 11 October to tell the composer that he would not press the issue, 'Were not this work... artistically all-important to me, and did I not believe that our theatre, which wants to eliminate the star system in the bad sense, in particular offers the right conditions for a work of this sort'. In the course of the season he returned to the subject in at least two letters to Janáček. 'I hope with all my heart that I should be able to conduct the opera in Berlin', he wrote on 21 May 1928. But less than three months later, Janáček was dead, and when in its last gasp in June 1931 the Kroll eventually gave the opera its first German performance, it was not Klemperer who conducted it (see pp. 351, 372).

*   *   *

When apprehensive, as he had reason to be in the autumn of 1927, Klemperer was prone to rehearse with an intensity that even his wife regarded as excessive. 'Nicht tüfteln' ('don't be so finicky') was her recurrent warning. But he had never before set about preparing a production with such fanaticism as he brought to the *Fidelio* that was to launch the new Kroll. In his negotiations with Schillings four years earlier he had harshly condemned operatic conditions in Berlin and since then most influential critics in the capital had increasingly come to present him as the saviour who would bring regeneration. Now, as he must have been acutely aware, the time had come to back words with action. Simultaneously, he was confronted with the formidable task of welding a group of singers largely unknown to himself and to each other into an ensemble. He was also responsible for the stage production. As was his custom, he himself coached the entire cast from the earliest stages of the production, which had started in mid-August. Rehearsals thus stretched over three months and often lasted late into the evening. The tension was tremendous.[17]

---

* A surprising observation. It was certainly larger than that of the theatre in Brno, where most of Janáček's operas had their first performances.

The theatre was shut for three entire days before an event that was awaited by musical Berlin as a deed that would herald a new dawn.

Although there was much brave cheering, the première on 19 November 1927 came as an anti-climax. A handful of critics spoke up for the performance, notably Oscar Bie, for whom it had 'the indefinable strength of something entirely new'.[18] In the *Montagspost* Sling contrasted Walter's traditional approach to the work at the Städtische Oper with a performance that seemed to represent a new age.[19] That was, of course, precisely what upset more traditionally minded critics. But it was not merely the newness that offended. 'The performance', wrote Einstein in a review that well summed up a general reaction, 'has a fanatical exactitude that brings surprises for the most knowledgeable of listeners...[But] there is an exaggerated dependence on the conductor that borders on tyranny...In this opera about freedom there is no sense of freedom. Every detail has been thought out and worked on...In a certain sense everything is in order. Only necessity is lacking – and grace.'[20] This particularly applied to Klemperer's handling of the choral numbers. In the final scene, as each part of the chorus cried 'Heil' on its entries, arms shot into the air in salute as though at a pistol shot.[21] 'The Prussian parade-ground', wrote Paul Zschorlich, who was to become one of the leading right-wing scourges of the Kroll, '...is a model of personal improvisation in comparison to the gestures of the inmates of this state prison.'[22] Weissmann, who had done so much to raise Klemperer's reputation in Berlin to dizzy heights, concurred.

Now we know: what has been cooking for weeks, for months is this monomaniac exaggeration of new principles of performance, a realisation of the dogmatic...a one-sidedness that one may find splendid but that could have ominous consequences for opera.

The incontestable personality of Otto Klemperer has exercised a dangerous tyranny over all others responsible. It is necessary to restore a measure of artistic independence...

The ensemble wonderfully drilled. The singers reduced to infallible if cramped puppets. Did I say singers? I have never heard so much shouting on an operatic stage...

Fidelio under Klemperer [represents] the complete triumph of the conductor and producer over Beethoven.[23]

Much of the disappointment undoubtedly stemmed from a cast that Hanns Eisler, who at that period of his career was serving as music critic for the Communist daily paper, *Rote Fahne*, caustically described as 'provincial singers who had been excellently rehearsed'.* Rose Pauly's

* *Rote Fahne*, 22 November 1927. Hanns Eisler (1898–1962), who had by this time already broken with his teacher Schoenberg and started to dedicate himself to the Communist cause, was later to be an intimate collaborator with Brecht. He subsequently became the leading composer of the German Democratic Republic.

260

expressive Leonore was marred by a heavy vibrato, Hans Fidesser's Florestan was regarded as lacking in tragic stature.* There was also well-nigh unanimous disapproval of Dülberg's monumental cubist sets; only Heinrich Strobel found words of praise for their formal strength and the subtle range of greys, blues and whites which stood in such sharp contrast to the violent colours Dülberg had used in Wiesbaden.[24] Nor did the radical implications of a closing scene, in which Leonore's central position in the drama was usurped by the liberated crowds, win much approval. 'German shame everywhere one looks', thundered Zschorlich in a phrase calculated to associate the Kroll and its *Fidelio* with the humiliation that the Treaty of Versailles had inflicted on the young republic. The National Socialist organ, the *Völkische Beobachter*, enraged at Lunacharsky's description of Klemperer as 'the Piscator of the opera',† attacked Jewish influences at the Kroll. Klemperer, it claimed, was an *Obermusikjude*, who as a Jew was unable to enter Beethoven's world of feeling. He had needed so many rehearsals only in order to convert singers and musicians to the mangled caricature he had presented of the opera.[25] It was not, however, only reactionary critics who used such prophetic phraseology. In *Melos*, the distinctly progressive musical periodical, a collective review enthusiastically prescribed 'the submission of all concerned to the strong will of a leader' as a precondition of the sort of unified performance Klemperer had sought.‡

The critical mauling his opening *Fidelio* received was doubtless in part due to the exaggerated expectations that it had aroused, for it continued to be performed with success throughout the coming seasons without occasioning further attacks. Klemperer himself later maintained that the orchestral playing had been very fine. He also spoke up strongly for Pauly's Leonore (in spite of her admittedly poor intonation) and, above all, for Dülberg's sets. But the evening as a whole he regarded as one of his most

---

* When, four months later, Walter mounted a new rival production of *Fidelio* at the Städtische Oper, Lotte Lehmann, Lotte Schöne, Karl Oestwig and Alexander Kipnis were in the cast. In June 1928 Kleiber conducted a revival of the work at the Linden Opera with Frieda Leider, Richard Tauber and Friedrich Schorr. Such were the standards against which Klemperer's cast was measured.

† Erwin Piscator (1893–1966), Communist stage director, who in 1927 broke away from the Berlin Volksbühne in order to set up the politically activist Junge Volksbühne, on which account he became embroiled with the organisation's extremely unrevolutionary officials. Piscator had an important influence on the early development of Brecht's approach to the theatre. Lunacharsky probably saw the Kroll *Fidelio* when he was in Berlin in late November 1927 and also attended a performance of Toller's controversial *Hoppla, wir leben* at the Junge Volksbühne, which may have led him to suppose there was a parallel between Piscator and Klemperer. There was none.

‡ January 1928. The collective review was signed by Hermann Springer, Heinrich Strobel and Werner Wolffheim. Language with totalitarian implications was not infrequently used by some of Klemperer's more radical supporters.

261

resounding failures.[26] Indeed, at a party later that night, a mood of consternation spread among those who had been primarily responsible for bringing him to Berlin. Ever the diplomat, Tietjen felt a need to make a display of loyalty. Giving Klemperer his hand, he portentously declared himself 'in Treue fest' ('firm in loyalty'). Klemperer turned to Curjel, who was standing nearby, and said in a voice that Tietjen could not fail to hear, 'He has just betrayed me.'[27] Thereafter he regarded Tietjen with a suspicion and dislike that neither Curjel nor Zweig felt to be justified.

In the summer of 1926 Dülberg had designed sets for a production of *Die Zauberflöte* that had been abandoned on account of Klemperer's frequent absences from Wiesbaden during the ensuing season. At first Klemperer intended that these should provide the basis for their second collaboration at the Kroll. After much hesitation, however, he finally opted for *Don Giovanni*, influenced perhaps by the immense success that both he and Dülberg had enjoyed with their production of the work in Wiesbaden. Yet indecision continued to dog him and it was only after weeks of hesitation that he finally cast the opera.[28]

In the event, the production, which had its première on 11 January 1928, aroused little real enthusiasm: it was, as Marschalk wrote, at best 'a half-success'.[29] There was widespread praise for an immaculate ensemble and fine orchestral playing. There was also approval for the way in which, as in Wiesbaden, Dülberg's sets, again based on permanent lateral structures, made it possible to play each act without a pause. It would be hard, wrote Einstein, to conceive of a more urgent and rapidly moving production.[30] But, he observed, this pace had been achieved at a cost: the action seemed to take place in a series of empty spaces, which Dülberg's rich costumes did not succeed in enlivening. Nor was his attempt to match an essentially rectilineal style to a rococo curvaceousness regarded as successful.* As in his production of *Fidelio* two months earlier, Klemperer's staging of *Don Giovanni* seems to have revealed his lack of what Rabenalt subsequently described as 'theatrical fiction'.[31] In the field of music Klemperer's deep respect for facts provided a firm basis for his interpretative imagination. But because, like so many musicians, he was no *Augenmensch*, his scenic conceptions were liable to remain skeletons to which he could not add theatrical flesh and blood.†

There were as usual some who also found Klemperer's approach to

---

* In *Der Querschnitt* (February 1928) Hans von Wedderkop observed that the worlds of rococo and *neue Sachlichkeit* were irreconcilable. Though less rigid than those for Wiesbaden, Dülberg's designs for the Kroll *Giovanni* (in the Theatermuseum of Cologne University) remain inappropriately stiff. Kruttge, who saw both productions, was not alone in considering that at Wiesbaden superior.

† Hence his distinctly prosaic productions of *Fidelio* and *Die Zauberflöte* at Covent Garden in 1961 and 1962.

Mozart's music lacking in warmth and others who complained that he had done less than justice to the *giocoso* elements in the work. But much of the criticism again centred on the Kroll's vocal standards. Although he paradoxically announced it to be the best *Don Giovanni* Berlin had heard in years, Hanns Eisler dealt particularly harshly with both the cast and its subservience to Klemperer's will.

In the Staatsoper am Platz der Republic there is only one star... he is called Otto Klemperer and he tolerates no other gods in his proximity. He himself is an outstanding musician and certainly Berlin's most competent opera director. But that does not suffice for a good performance of a Mozart opera... which demands singers of stature... The star is in the wrong place. Instead of being on the stage, he is in the orchestral pit and he also produces. Everything is splendidly new and *sachlich*, only the singing is wretched and hardly any of the cast are able to breathe life into the roles they portray.[32]

Neither in *Fidelio* nor in *Don Giovanni* had Klemperer and Dülberg achieved a shadow of the triumphs they had enjoyed with these operas in Wiesbaden. So far, however, they had operated in familiar territory. Their third collaboration at the Kroll, a Stravinsky triple bill, consisting of *Oedipus Rex*, *Mavra* and *Petrushka*, took them on to more controversial territory and as the day of the première approached Klemperer was increasingly beset by doubt. While walking in the Tiergarten with a young musician on his staff, he anxiously asked his companion whether he thought *Oedipus* would last.[33] Scarcely more than two weeks before the opening night, Regi Elbogen wrote on 9 February to tell her sister, Marianne Joseph, that their brother's nerves were so badly overstretched that he even considered handing over the staging to an outside producer.

In the event he did not do so, which was as well, for at its première on 25 February 1928* both the work and its production were received with enthusiasm – at any rate in the press. With the exception of a weak protagonist, the musical performance was judged to be outstandingly fine and Dülberg's towering cubist construction to be well-matched to Stravinsky's monumental score. There were, inevitably, dissenters. Weissmann announced that Stravinsky had no sense of the theatre and could not write tunes.[34] Theodor Wiesengrund-Adorno,† who had already come to the conclusion that neo-classicism was intrinsically reactionary, a theme that he was to pursue through the thickets of his prose for the next forty years, compared the score to that of a Handelian oratorio stripped of its contents and filled with concrete.[35] Under a misapprehension

---

* Contrary to what is often asserted, this was not the work's first stage performance, which had taken place two days earlier at the Vienna State Opera.

† Adorno (1903–69), social philosopher, composer and critic, whose neo-Marxist writings on music have been more influential on the continent of Europe than in the Anglo-American world.

263

30   Stravinsky, Dülberg and Klemperer on the occasion of the Stravinsky
triple bill at the Kroll, February 1928

that the composer was a Jew, Zschorlich referred to 'Isidor – sorry,
Igor – Stravinsky'.[36]

Yet the evening as a whole was less than a complete triumph. *Mavra*
was widely dismissed as a feeble little joke, while critics such as Bie, who
had seen *Petrushka* when it had been danced by Diaghilev's company on
its first visit to Berlin in 1912, were not impressed by choreographic
standards at the Kroll.* But there was a further reason why the first night
failed to catch fire. The stalls had been sold to the Verein Berliner Kaufleute
und Industrieller, and a gathering of salesmen and manufacturers, hungry
for the supper-dance that was to follow, was not calculated to provide an
enthusiastic audience for a Stravinsky triple bill. That Tietjen permitted so
crucial an occasion to be turned into something akin to a closed performance
before a public that was bound to be unsympathetic does not speak well

---

* Ballet was never to be the Kroll's strong suit. In four seasons the only other work that was
danced was Debussy's *Jeux*, and that was on account of special factors. See p. 351.

264

for his commitment to the new Kroll. Inevitably, there was hissing in the stalls to which the gods responded with appropriate militancy.

Dinner-jacketed business men were not, however, the only occupants of the better seats. Both Hindemith and Schoenberg were in the audience. The former, according to Stravinsky, was 'hingerissen' (carried away).* The latter put an enraged pen to paper.

I do not know what I am supposed to like in *Oedipus*...It is all negative: unusual theatre, unusual setting, unusual resolution of the action, unusual vocal writing, unusual acting, unusual instrumentation – all this is 'un' without *being* anything in particular. I could say that all that Stravinsky has composed is the dislike his work is meant to inspire.

To his credit, Schoenberg soon had second thoughts:

* Igor Stravinsky and Robert Craft, *Dialogues and a Diary*, p. 25. But Hindemith's diary provides no evidence that he attended the première.

31   Ewald Dülberg: stage set for *Oedipus Rex*

My remarks about Stravinsky now strike me not only as less witty than they did a few hours ago, but as something almost equally bad: rather philistine...I know, after all, that the works which in every way arouse one's dislike are precisely those the next generation will in every way like. And the better the jokes one makes about them, the more seriously one will have to take them...And yet I can only say what I really think...I still believe that the work is nothing, even though I really liked *Petrushka*. Parts of it very much indeed.[37]

The composer himself was also not totally happy. On his arrival in Berlin he had been aghast to discover that, in place of the prescribed evening dress, the narrator in *Oedipus Rex* was to be clothed in a black pierrot costume. His protests were of no avail: 'Herr Professor Stravinsky', he was told, 'in our country only the Kapellmeister is allowed to wear *Frack*.'* But though he later declared that he 'winced' whenever he recalled the Berlin staging, he pronounced the musical performances of all three scores to be 'de premier ordre'.[38] The evening seems to have ended in high spirits: at a late party Stravinsky was observed dancing a minuet with Ernst Bloch.† Before he left Berlin he played his new and as yet unperformed *Apollo* to Klemperer. Klemperer was enthralled and promptly determined to give the work during the coming season. For the second performance of the triple bill six days later the house was packed and the audience enthusiastic, although Klemperer was so enraged at the inadequacy of the tenor that he forbad him to appear before the curtain to acknowledge applause and also refused to do so himself.[39]

*　　　　　　　　　　*　　　　　　　　　　*

Such behaviour indicated psychological stress, and indeed Klemperer's protracted hesitations about casting *Don Giovanni*, his uncertainty about the lasting value of *Oedipus Rex*, dark intimations that he had come to regard the entire Kroll project as utopian, his general unapproachability and the strained condition noted by his sister, Regi, who was living in Berlin, were all straws in a wind that had been blowing with increasing force since the beginning of the season. Curjel had observed that Klemperer had not been himself since his return from New York in March 1927. He had in fact for some time been moving towards a depression, and as the season advanced he grew ever more full of self-doubt. On 5 March 1928

---

* *Dialogues and a Diary*, p. 25. When the work was revived the following May, the narrator wore a dark suit. *BZ am Mittag*, 31 May 1928.
† Through his friendship with Klemperer, Bloch was close to the Kroll throughout its existence and contributed many notable essays to its programmes (several of which are collected in his *Zur Philosophie der Musik*). It was in one of these essays that he coined a phrase that aptly described Klemperer at this point of his career, 'Nirgends brennen wir genauer', an untranslatable expression perhaps best rendered as 'nowhere is passion so closely allied to precision'.

Georg Klemperer, who had experienced such periods in his cousin's youth, certified that he had been suffering for some months from sleeplessness and headaches 'as a result of overwork'. The following day Klemperer conducted *Fidelio* and then set out with his wife for the Côte d'Azur, where they stayed at Cap Martin. On 8 March the story leaked and the *Vossische Zeitung* announced that Klemperer had gone on leave on account of 'a nervous breakdown'.

The news could not have broken at a more awkward moment. With the exception of *Oedipus Rex* (which was not to prove a box office success when it was revived later in the season), the operas that Klemperer had himself produced and conducted had been less than wholly successful. Meanwhile the other works that had been added to the repertory had failed to make much impact on either the public or the press.* Smetana's *The Kiss*, Verdi's *Luisa Miller* (which had its first German performance at the Kroll on 10 December 1927) and Gounod's *Le Médecin malgré lui* were collectors' items that well merited revival but exercised limited appeal, and Puccini's *Il Trittico* and Auber's *Le Domino noir*, which were added in March and April, fell into much the same category.† The critics praised the refinement that Zemlinsky brought to the Puccini one-acters and the light touch that Zweig revealed in Gounod and Auber. But most of the singing was condemned as inadequate. Max Marschalk complained that, in *Luisa Miller*, 'the singers whom Otto Klemperer has assembled from the provinces – together with a few Berlin artists of second and third rank – are not able to meet the expectations that we have here...That becomes clearer with every performance. An ensemble of real quality can only be achieved with voices of real quality.'[40]

Georg Klemperer was of course well aware that his cousin's troubles did not have their roots merely in 'overwork'. Johanna had, however, not as yet taken the full measure of her husband's predicament. This was the first time in nine years of married life that she had experienced him in deep depression and, not unnaturally, she attributed his condition to the exceptional strains he had borne throughout the winter. He had, she believed, simply undertaken too heavy a burden. Hence she regarded a reduction of his responsibilities as essential and with characteristic energy set about persuading him to relinquish his position.‡

* It was not until the end of 1927 that the Kroll was in a position to provide the three weekly performances to which it was limited as long as the Linden company was squatting in the theatre.
† Characteristically, Curjel contrived in a programme essay to inscribe *Le Médecin malgré lui* under the banner of *die neue Sachlichkeit*. *Les Six* approved of it and Satie had written additional dialogue for the work. QED!
‡ So much is clear from the despairing letter that Curjel wrote to Georg Klemperer on 8 April. It is also significant that in an undated and strictly confidential letter written without

267

Curjel and Dülberg were aghast at what little they could gather of the course of events on the Côte d'Azur. Aware, as Johanna was not, that Klemperer's depression was basically endogenous, they realised that a failure to grasp this crucial point underlay her determination to bring about his resignation as director, and they feared that the new Kroll, which was so closely identified with his name, might founder if he now withdrew. On 25 March Dülberg wrote to Curjel, imploring him to invoke Georg Klemperer's aid as a means of counteracting Johanna's 'disastrous' influence. Consternation spread up as well as down the chain of command. After Johanna had belatedly written to ask for the extension of her husband's leave, which had expired in early April, and no word came from Cap Martin of plans to return, Tietjen told Curjel that it was essential that Klemperer should at least show himself in Berlin without delay: in view of the perfidious comments that had already appeared in the press, a prolongation of his absence might precipitate a crisis.

Though not fully restored, Klemperer was by the middle of April already sleeping better (an indication that the depression had passed its deepest point) and he returned to Berlin in time to attend the gala performance of *Die Zauberflöte*, with which the Linden Opera celebrated its return to its own quarters on 28 April.* On 2 May he himself conducted in the Kroll for the first time in eight weeks.

On 29 May Klemperer formally asked to be relieved of his position as director of the Staatsoper am Platz der Republik, although it was not until 3 July that his resignation and replacement by Ernst Legal were made public.† He himself remained *Generalmusikdirektor* with an assurance that, as he later claimed, he 'would preserve far-reaching influence on all artistic measures' and that a director who sympathised with his aims would succeed him.‡ Although his new contract provided for three months leave

Klemperer's knowledge from Cap Martin to Hans Schüler, who had produced the Wiesbaden *Cardillac*, Johanna held out the possibility of an unspecified position in Berlin, conceivably as assistant to Klemperer.

* The performance, which was far from well received, was described by malicious wags as the Kroll's greatest success to date (*Conversations*, p. 62).

† Two days later, on 5 July, Klemperer stated in the *Vossische Zeitung* that he had resigned of his own free will. Kestenberg later claimed that the resignation had only been brought about on the initiative of Becker and Tietjen (*Berliner Tageblatt*, 20 April 1931, 'Grosse Oper im Arbeitsgericht'. See also *Untersuchungsausschuss*, column 323). Thirty years later Tietjen in a WDR interview with Curjel claimed that he and Kestenberg had had the task of persuading Klemperer to resign as director.

Ernst Legal (1881–1955). Intendant in Darmstadt (1924–7) and in Kassel (1927–8), which, like Wiesbaden, was directly administered by the Prussian Kultusministerium. After two seasons at the Kroll he succeeded Leopold Jessner as Intendant of the Berlin Schauspielhaus. In 1945 he became *Generalintendant* of the Berlin State Opera (1945–52). Scornfully described by the producer, Arthur Maria Rabenalt as the 'embodiment of a mildly modern theatre administrator'.

‡ The phrase is drawn from Klemperer's submission to a labour tribunal (Arbeitsgericht), before which he subsequently brought an action against the Prussian exchequer

a year, his salary was only reduced from 55,000M to 45,000M. The Finance Ministry later angrily claimed that this was another item of expenditure* on which it had not been consulted.

*   *   *

As both Tietjen and Kestenberg later admitted, it had been a mistake to appoint as director a musician entirely lacking in administrative ability (and by temperament singularly ill-matched to the exigencies of Prussian bureaucracy).† But there was an additional reason why the Ministry was relieved to see Klemperer replaced as director. This lay in the difficult relationship that had already started to emerge between the Kroll and its principal client, the Berlin Volksbühne. The theatre itself had been developed as a full-scale opera house primarily to meet the post-war demands of the Volksbühne. Yet the Volksbühne had been consulted neither about Klemperer's appointment, nor about the controversial artistic policies that he proposed to put into effect.‡ Klemperer had behaved in a manner as nonchalant as the Kultusministerium. When asked in the 1927 Christmas number of *Vossische Zeitung* what the public might expect of the opera and the opera of the public, he ignored the first question and to the second answered that he looked for an unprejudiced attitude on the part of the public to old and new works in performances whose first duty was to realise the composer's will. As a description of his own policy the answer was characteristically succinct, but it indicated a blithe unawareness of the resistance such a policy might meet from an unsophisticated Volksbühne public. Nor had he or his staff made any attempt to win the confidence of its officials. That was to prove a serious omission, for, contrary to what was often assumed, the Volksbühne did not provide the Kroll with a captive audience. Its members, who in the 1928/9 season were taking more than 1400 seats on four days a week,§[41] paid separately for

---

(Fiskus), which turned largely on his conditions of employment at the Kroll (see pp. 356–7, 362–8).

* Expenditure in the sense only that Klemperer's salary was reduced by a smaller proportion than his commitments to the Kroll.

† Tietjen subsequently expressed the view (letter of 1 March 1930 to the Kultusminister) that a change had become necessary because 'Klemperer's individuality could not be reconciled with the demands of the position of opera director' (Klemperer's personal file, p. 106). See also *Untersuchungsausschuss*, columns 322 and 326.

‡ These facts were admitted by Kestenberg when on 29 October 1928 he gave evidence before a Court of Arbitration (Schiedsgericht) that had been set up to determine the price that the Volksbühne was to pay for its seats.

§ 800 at weekends and on holidays. The Kroll therefore looked to the Volksbühne to take rather more than half the seats in the house. On the basis of these (official) figures it would seem that the Volksbühne alone occupied an average of more than half the seats in the house. On 14 October 1929 Seelig (see p. 175) told the Landtag Hauptausschuss (Principal Committee) that the Volksbühne, together with its middle-class counterpart, the Bühne-volksbund (see p. 276) occupied no less than eight-ninths of the Kroll seats (Landtag Proceedings, Hauptausschuss).

each performance they elected to attend and were fully at liberty to withdraw at short notice from evenings that did not whet their appetite.[42]

Complaints from the Volksbühne about the repertory at the Kroll started to land on Tietjen's desk with increasing frequency. On 2 May its secretary-general, Siegfried Nestriepke,* informed him that in the month of April his membership had taken up their full quota of seats only for a single performance of *Fidelio*. Six days later Nestriepke followed this up with a memorandum pointing out that in the previous six weeks the Kroll's repertory had consisted of *Il Trittico*, *The Kiss*, *Le Médecin malgré lui*, *Fidelio* (once only), *Luisa Miller* and *Le Domino noir*. Presented with a list of what he termed 'abgespielte Spielopern' ('played-out light operas'), his members had taken up less than thirty per cent of their ticket allotment.[43] Such unpalatable facts must have concentrated the mind of the officials in the Kultusministerium on the future policy of the Kroll, and the cries of public outrage that greeted an expressionist forest scene in Dülberg's new setting of *Der Freischütz* on 21 May may have served to convince them that a change of course was necessary.†

In setting up Klemperer's Kroll to provide the Volksbühne with operatic performances, Kestenberg had allowed his idealism to seduce him into supposing that a natural bond existed between the representatives of a new society and new forms of artistic expression, and that any gap between them could be closed by education. The cause of operatic reform in the first half of the twentieth century was to pay a heavy price for that sentimental illusion. As Weissmann caustically observed, 'the so-called people want only the operas that are put before the wealthy bourgeoisie...They yearn for *Carmen* and *Aida* like anyone else ...'[44]

*　　　　　*　　　　　*

The first Berlin production of Hindemith's *Cardillac* on 30 June 1928 was the closing event of a season that had brought more than its fair share of the tribulations inseparable from any operatic undertaking. The work well merited a hearing in the German capital, but that no fewer than three of the four productions which Klemperer conducted during his opening season should have been of works that he had already given with notable success in Wiesbaden is indicative of his caution in periods of depression.

---

* Siegfried Nestriepke (1885–1963), Secretary-General of the Berlin Volksbühne since 1920, was the organisation's leading functionary. Nestriepke, who was described by the theatre critic, Herbert Ihering, as 'the Metternich of the Volksbühne', was a worthy but unimaginative organiser with limited cultural insight. He was to become one of the most dangerous opponents of Klemperer's Kroll.

† *Deutsche Allgemeine Zeitung*, 22 May 1928. A coloured illustration in Curjel's *Experiment Krolloper* (p. 261) suggests that this was nonetheless one of Dülberg's most profoundly imaginative achievements.

Contrary to his original intention that he and Dülberg should assume responsibility for the staging of operas he conducted, Klemperer did not himself produce.* The severity of Dülberg's sets again found little favour in the press, but there was much praise for the dramatic energy Klemperer infused into the music. The work itself was widely admired; the cast, headed by Fritz Krenn,† who had also sung in Wiesbaden, was regarded as strong.

Yet an opera by Hindemith was no more calculated to appeal to the members of the Volksbühne than a modernistic production of *Der Freischütz*. The evening drew fire from both ends of the political spectrum. Paul Schwers, the nationalist editor of the *Allgemeine Musikzeitung*, complained that, under cover of pursuing a social policy in the arts, Klemperer's henchmen were using the Kroll for Communist propaganda (13 July 1928). In the Party's official organ, however, Hanns Eisler assailed Hindemith's 'objectivisation' of music and his use of pre-classical forms as an attempt to evade the social issues of the time.‡

The tensions, social and political, musical and personal, that were to beset the Kroll Opera had already begun to gather. Commenting at the end of the season on Klemperer's resignation as director and the uncertain outlook for his theatre, Max Marschalk recalled that in the previous October, when the Kroll had not staged even a single production, Tietjen had told Berlin's assembled music critics that the city could not in the long run support three opera houses. 'One of them will have to be closed.' Then with Delphic ambiguity Tietjen had added, 'And you can imagine which one that will be.'§ The oracle had spoken.

---

* It is significant that after this traumatic opening season Klemperer did not again produce until the last months of the Kroll, when he was in a manic condition (see pp. 369–71). He did, however, continue to occupy himself with every detail of any production he conducted.
† Fritz Krenn (1887–1964) later celebrated for his performances of Baron Ochs in *Der Rosenkavalier*, which he sang under Klemperer at the Linden Opera (see pp. 339–40), Vienna and elsewhere.
‡ *Rote Fahne*, 3 July 1928. Eisler was attacking the phrase, 'objectivised expression', that Curjel had used in a jargon-laden introductory essay on *Cardillac* (*Blätter der Staatsoper*, June 1928).
§ *Vossische Zeitung*, 3 July 1928. There is no evidence that Marschalk was himself present on this occasion, and the report on it in the *Vossische Zeitung* (25 October 1927) makes no mention that Tietjen made such an observation, although it is clear that a discussion arose on the ability of Berlin to support three opera houses.

13 *The Kroll gets under way*

At the end of the 1927/8 season Johanna took the children to the North Sea while Klemperer remained in Berlin. As a result of the decision to establish an entirely separate orchestra and chorus at the Kroll there were musicians to be engaged and from the effort it cost him to reach decisions he realised that he had not entirely recovered from the depression that had incapacitated him earlier in the year. Even the impending move from the suburb of Grunewald to a spacious flat near Lützowplatz, from which he would be able to walk to work across the leafy expanses of the Tiergarten, filled him with apprehension. New scores were another burden. After a season in which his concert programmes had been predominantly conventional, he knew that he must strike out in new directions. But in his low spirits even Berlioz's *Symphonie fantastique*, a work he had not hitherto conducted, failed to make any appeal.* Of recent scores only Stravinsky's *Apollo* seemed of real consequence; and the more he studied the three one-act operas by Krenek that he was committed to conduct in the coming season, the less he liked them.[1]

He was, however, no longer averse from all human contacts, as when trapped in the eye of a depression. Since his first visits to the Soviet Union he had been increasingly open to the radical influences that were dominant in the cultural life of Berlin in the twenties, and it was to these circles that he sometimes gravitated when, exceptionally, he felt a need for company.† Thus at a reception at the Soviet embassy in July, he encountered Ernst Toller, through whom a few days later he met Erwin Piscator and Georg Grosz, all leading representatives of the radical intelligentsia.‡ On a more domestic level, there were excursions with his cousin Georg and his family to Potsdam and Wannsee to escape the heat of the Berlin summer. But he

---

* Klemperer was, however, to revise this negative view in America.
† Nonetheless Gerhard Meyer-Sichting's assertion that the Klemperer apartment had by 1929 developed into 'a mirror of the revolutionary intelligentsia of the twenties' (*Partitur eines Lebens*, pp. 47–9) should be taken with a grain of salt.
‡ Ernst Toller (1893–1939) had been a member of the short-lived revolutionary government, which had been set up in Munich in 1919, on whose collapse he had been jailed. Erwin Piscator, see p. 261n. A subsequent plan for Piscator to produce Auber's *La Muette de Portici* (see p. 329) at the Kroll came to nothing. The paintings, drawings and cartoons of George Grosz (1893–1959) have left a lasting image of social life in Germany during the early years of the Weimar Republic.

272

was still not sleeping well and he determined to travel to Switzerland, where he was to take his vacation, via Hamburg so as to consult Moses Goldschmidt, the *Internist* who had helped him in the grim year of 1916.

By 7 August he was in Flims. But the Swiss resort did not please him and within a few days he moved to the more familiar surroundings of the Waldhaus Hotel at Sils Maria, where among the many musicians on holiday there he encountered Strauss and Furtwängler. To his amazement, Strauss told him that he could not conduct a Beethoven symphony without having a programme in mind.* In spite of the bitter comments that Strauss had made about Klemperer less than four years earlier (see pp. 196–7n.), the meeting was as cordial as ever. The 64-year-old composer 'looked marvellous', Klemperer reported to his wife,[2] and, doubtless as a gesture of support for the Kroll, he agreed to conduct performances of the new production of *Salome* that was to open the coming season.†

The problems of his opera house continued to plague Klemperer in the Engadine. Dülberg, whose tuberculosis had attacked his intestines, was more seriously ill than either he himself or Klemperer yet realised. He was in any case temperamentally ill-suited to work within an organisation and already disenchanted with the Kroll. On 27 July he informed Curjel that, though he expected to be well enough to return to Berlin in October, the coming season would be his last; after that he would work for the Kroll only as a guest – with dictatorial powers. By the middle of August he had moved to a sanatorium in Arosa, from which he wrote to tell Klemperer that he would not be able to provide sets for a new production of *The Soldier's Tale*, which Klemperer was planning to couple with a revival of *Oedipus Rex*, or for Krenek's one-acters.

That was not the only shadow that clouded Klemperer's vacation. How would Ernst Legal, the new director and nominal head of the Kroll, fit in with the small and closely linked group of men who had hitherto run it? The intractable Dülberg, who saw only enemies around him, was pessimistic. 'I prophesy', he wrote to Curjel on 18 August, 'that "compromise" will stand in capital letters on our new flag.' On 3 September he returned to

* *Minor Recollections*, p. 36. Strauss's remark underlines how deeply his imagination remained rooted in the Lisztian world of the symphonic poem. Similarly, Klemperer's astonishment reveals the aesthetic gulf that separated Strauss from a younger generation influenced by Busoni's view of music as an absolute art.
† He conducted four performances in the course of the winter. Strauss never used his vast prestige to intervene in defence of the Kroll, but in an interview, 'Strauss persönlich', (*Vossische Zeitung*, 5 May 1932), given after it had been closed, H. H. Stuckenschmidt claimed that he had taken 'a very lively interest' in the Kroll and been sympathetic to the aims Klemperer had pursued there. Einstein (*Berliner Tageblatt*, 26 June 1930) also states that Strauss made a last-minute intervention on behalf of the Kroll. No further details have, however, come to light.

273

32   Klemperer and Furtwängler. Engadine, 1928

the attack. 'Inwardly', he told Curjel, 'I have separated myself from the Kroll and henceforth view this institution only as an employer.' In fact Dülberg's alienation from the theatre was not to come about, as he himself envisaged, through the intervention of the rather nebulous figure of Legal. It was Curjel who henceforth was increasingly to become the predominant influence on the visual side of the Kroll.

The first two months of the new season did, however, seem to confirm Dülberg's fears. It opened on 5 September with an unremarkable production of *Salome* by Legal himself. There was praise for Zemlinsky's conducting and a stirring performance by Rose Pauly in the title role, but the staging was dismissed by the critics as conventional. *Il Matrimonio segreto* on 6 October fared even worse. Both production and sets were regarded as disastrous and the singers were thought to lack the *bel canto* style that Cimarosa's music called for. Several critics commented on the air of boredom that pervaded the house, and Volksbühne members complained because the work had no choruses.

Carmen, which Tietjen had released from the list of works that were reserved to the Linden Opera in an attempt to strengthen the Kroll's repertory, aroused only a tepid reaction on its first night on 31 October. Zweig's neat and dextrous conducting was found deficient in dramatic attack, vocal flaws and a lack of physical seductiveness marred Rose Pauly's otherwise striking performance in the title role and Legal's production again failed to rise above a level of conventional competence. The critics were, however, divided on the merits of the sets and costumes by Caspar Neher, a young designer who only two months earlier had made his reputation with the staging of *Die Dreigroschenoper*, which was proving the hit of the season in the Theater am Schiffbauerdamm.*

Klemperer's first contribution to the season was a new production of *The Soldier's Tale* on 11 October. Both it and *Oedipus Rex* enjoyed a success so overwhelming that even the reticent Klemperer described it as 'kolossal' in a telegram he sent the following day to Stravinsky. Carl Ebert† was much praised as the Narrator. On the recommendation of Brecht and Weill (the latter was already closely associated with the Kroll), Jakob Geis produced. Traugott Müller provided an open set that was erected during the interval in front of the set for *Oedipus Rex* in a manner that Piscator

---

* Caspar Neher (1897–1962) was henceforth to be closely associated with both Brecht and Weill, as librettist as well as designer. He played a crucial role in the emergence of Brecht's distinctive style of theatre.
† Carl Ebert (1887–1980). Intendant in Darmstadt (1927–31) and at the Berlin Städtische Oper (1931–3). In 1934 he and Fritz Busch became artistic directors of the newly founded Glyndebourne Opera, of which, apart from a wartime interlude, he remained a mainspring until 1959. From 1956 until 1961 he was again Intendant of the West Berlin Deutsche Oper, as the former Städtische Oper was called after its post war reconstruction.

275

had already used and Brecht was to make familiar. Klemperer, dressed in a Russian peasant's blouse, conducted the band on stage.

The enthusiasm on the first night was intense. On such occasions the Kroll had already begun to gather a special public. Albert Einstein might be seen in the stalls near to the Papal nuncio, Cardinal Pacelli.* Stresemann, the German Foreign Minister, and his family were regular attenders, as was General von Seeckt, who as head of the army from 1920 to 1926 was one of the most powerful men in Germany. Brecht, Weill, Ernst Bloch and Walter Benjamin represented a rather different social perspective. On first nights such as that of 11 October 1928 the tension and air of expectation was immense. As H. H. Stuckenschmidt later recalled, 'The theatre was miraculously transformed into something more than a temple of the muses.' One felt that 'the heart of the world's spirit was beating within it'.[3]

It was, however, a very different audience that gathered for the third performance of the Stravinsky double bill nine days later. On that Saturday evening much of the theatre had been taken by the Bühnenvolksbund, a middle-class equivalent to the Volksbühne, which provided cheap seats on subscription.† After the difficulties of its opening season the Kroll had been glad to enter into such arrangements with any organisation that would occupy seats, but the *spiessig* Bühnenvolksbund public did not provide a sympathetic audience for such a programme. *Oedipus Rex* was received with what *Dresdner Neueste Nachrichten* (23 October 1928) described as 'speechless outrage'. The sight of stage hands erecting the sets for *The Soldier's Tale* on an open stage during the interval was greeted with loud laughter. It was, however, Stravinsky's impious use of a chorale that finally triggered an explosion and the demonstration that followed continued for ten minutes. There was whistling, hissing and shouting. Many of the audience jumped up from their seats. The solitary policeman on duty decided that discretion was the better part of valour. At one stage the uproar grew to a point where Klemperer seemed to falter, but Ebert raised his voice and the performance continued.

Such incidents remained comparatively rare. The Volksbühne public, which still preserved some residue of its original cultural ideals and a certain naive respect for the theatre, did not manifest the boorish philistinism of its middle-class counterpart. But it was no whit less disenchanted when confronted with an evening such as the Stravinsky

---

* Later Pope Pius XII.

† Nominally non-political, the Bühnenvolksbund described its *Anschauung* as 'Christian, German and popular', in contrast to the socialist affiliations of the Volksbühne. Like many German middle-class institutions, it became increasingly dominated after 1929 by the Nazis. (Gentsch, *Die politische Struktur der Theaterführung*)

276

double bill. As Nestriepke later observed, in *The Soldier's Tale* it saw only a reversion to the primitive travelling theatre that played in the working-class districts of industrial cities,* and from which it sought to escape into the world of *Bildung*.[4] No work presented at the Kroll occasioned so many written protests from members of the Volksbühne.† Thus the solitary artistic triumph that the Kroll enjoyed in the first months of its second season served only to deepen the gulf between it and its principal client.

Krenek's three one-acters caused no such disturbances when they were added to the repertory on 2 December, but they did little to bolster the Kroll's sagging reputation. The older critics praised their theatrical effectiveness; their more radical colleagues dismissed them as an attempt to pursue the eclecticism of *Jonny spielt auf* by allocating its components to individual works rather than by combining them in a single score. In *Der Diktator*, a lampoon on Mussolini, Krenek developed his neo-veristic vein; there were echoes of his teacher, Schreker, in the neo-romantic idiom of *Das geheime Königreich*; the jazz elements that had contributed so much to the triumph of *Jonny* were given their head in the comic *Schwergewicht*. For Klemperer's taste the last came too close to operetta for comfort and during the previous summer he had made an unsuccessful attempt to persuade Krenek to substitute another work.[5] The composer was also not content and later criticised the discrepancy between Oskar Strnad's imaginative sets and Legal's conventional productions. All told, it was not an event of much distinction.

Worse was to come. In an attempt to tap the Christmas trade, the Kroll mounted a modern dress production of *Die Fledermaus* that in other respects was unabashedly conventional. Johanna Klemperer, who earlier in the season had unsuccessfully attempted to establish herself in the spoken theatre,‡ sang the role of Adele under the pseudonym of Hanna Klee. The *Allgemeine Musikzeitung* unkindly described her as 'ein klein wenig zu massiv'. Zemlinsky conducted.§ From every point of view the venture was a failure. The critics were scathing about the production's artistic standard. The Kroll's intellectual supporters regarded it as an act

---

* In a sense that was just what Stravinsky and Ramuz had intended.
† In all, 102. It is symptomatic of the failure in communications between the Kroll and its principal client that these complaints were despatched by Nestriepke to Tietjen, who duly forwarded them to the Kroll – where the Volksbühne had its offices. (Rockwell, 'The Berlin State Opera', p. 237)
‡ In the previous October she had appeared as Amalia in Schiller's *Die Räuber* at the modest theatre of Coburg. In 1929 she also played a minor role in Wilhelm Dieterle's silent film, *Ludwig der Zweite, König von Bayern*. With the exception of *Die Fledermaus* she only sang on isolated occasions at the Kroll, generally as a stand-in.
§ When Klemperer himself subsequently took over three performances in May 1929, Adorno ('Berliner Opernmemorial', *Anbruch*, June 1929) observed that in the finale of the second act menace loomed behind the laughter.

277

of self-betrayal, and the Volksbühne audiences were disappointed with a production that was subsequently overshadowed by the far more imaginative staging that Reinhardt mounted at the Deutsches Theater the following June. A third of the second season had passed and, apart from the Stravinsky double bill which had occasioned hostile reactions from run-of-the-mill audiences, the Kroll had done little to fulfil the great expectations it had aroused. Were Dülberg's fears that the advent of Legal as director spelt the onset of compromise to prove justified?

*   *   *

At the beginning of 1929, fourteen months after it had opened under Klemperer's direction, the Kroll could be described as a leaky ship that had run into stormy seas with an unsteady captain at the helm. Its artistic successes had been few and far between, and, although they had sufficed to gain the fierce loyalty of Berlin's radical intelligentsia, they had so far failed to find a wider public or to win over the Volksbühne. Meanwhile opposition was gathering on grounds that were not purely artistic. In the chauvinistic and conservative columns of the *Signale für die musikalischen Welt*, Fritz Ohrmann complained after the ill-fated Krenek triple bill that under Klemperer the Kroll Opera

is not concerned with art alone. Here a 'line', which anyone with eyes can see aims at destruction and disintegration, is given every conceivable support. Through the distortion of old masterpieces. Through productions by backers of this line. Through huge state subsidies, without which this temple of the muses would be bankrupt...The question must be put to Klemperer, 'Are you not troubled that many circles are mistrustful of the enthusiastic support you give to works that assail a Christian view of the world?'...Even today, I am convinced that Otto Klemperer is inspired by the purest of artistic motives. But he has fallen victim to the ideology of literary coffee house chatterers.[6]

The legend of Klemperer as *Kulturbolschewist* was gaining ground.

It was just at this crucial moment in its destiny that the Kroll scored a bulls-eye with a production that was at once to gladden the hearts of its supporters and to drive its opponents to a new peak of fury, to fill the house and to resonate down the annals of twentieth-century operatic history. On a visit to Berlin to conduct *Salome* in November 1928, Strauss learnt that the Kroll was about to stage *Der fliegende Holländer*. It was he who suggested that the work should be given in its original version. In the Prussian State Library Klemperer and Curjel found the score from which Wagner himself had conducted the work at the Berlin Schauspielhaus in January 1844, only a year after its first performance in Dresden. The original orchestral material was borrowed from Zurich.

To the men of the Kroll Wagner's music dramas and the naturalistic manner in which they were still generally staged represented the epitome of a world they had rejected. Over the years Klemperer himself had grown increasingly resistant to orthodox Wagnerianism. He did not question the composer's greatness, but he regarded him as the culmination of a chapter of operatic history that had been initiated by Weber and Marschner, rather than the successor to Beethoven and the creator of music dramas that had rendered all other approaches to opera obsolete. For Klemperer, the world that had dawned in 1918 was basically 'in opposition to Wagner'.[7] His attitude had concrete musical implications. In the almost Mahlerian clarity of texture he had sought in performances in Cologne, he had already revealed his rejection of the sumptuous carpet of sound that was still widely regarded as authentic.

Between 1846 and 1860 Wagner had made a series of revisions to *Der fliegende Holländer*, partly to emphasise the work's 'philosophy', and partly to bring the scoring into line with that of his later practices. To strip away these accretions would be a means at once of demythologising the work and of recapturing the raw directness of the original scoring. The overture, like the opera itself, would again end, not with the reprise of the 'redemption' theme, but with a blast dominated by brass and timpani. Similarly, the Dutchman's appearance in Senta's parlour would be heralded by a trombone chord instead of a tasteful string pizzicato. The harp that Wagner added in 1860 would be eliminated. Klemperer could not, however, be persuaded to complete the restoration by performing the opera in a single act, as the radical young Wagner had originally conceived it.

The spirit of the enterprise is vividly evoked in an essay that Ernst Bloch wrote for the occasion and mischievously entitled 'Rettung Wagners durch surrealistische Kolportage'.* Like many intellectuals of his generation Bloch had been allergic to Wagner and the mystique surrounding him ever since he had been obliged to sit as a small boy through cycles of *The Ring*. To view *Der fliegende Holländer* as an adventure story, such as might have come from the pen of Captain Marryat yet with surrealist elements, appealed to him as offering a means of stripping the work of the 'Traumkitsch' in which, as he felt, Wagner had subsequently encased it.

The approach was equally acceptable to the other participants. Jürgen Fehling, whom Klemperer had enlisted as producer, was a less than avid Wagnerian.† Dülberg, who had returned to Berlin from Arosa to design the sets, was similarly disposed; indeed over the years he had done much

---

* Reprinted in *Zur Philosophie der Musik*, pp. 176–84.
† Jürgen Fehling (1885–1968). 1922–45 producer at the Berlin Schauspielhaus. Generally regarded as one of the outstanding theatrical directors of his day in Germany. Another manic-depressive.

279

to impregnate Klemperer with Busonian attitudes to Wagner. The undertaking was therefore in the hands of a team that was at one in its determination to escape from the pious traditionalism that had blocked all change at Bayreuth since Wagner's death almost fifty years earlier.

Fehling, who had not previously worked in an opera house, was handicapped by his lack of experience; as a result, much of the detailed preparation fell to Klemperer and Dülberg, who later complained bitterly that Fehling had received much credit for a production for which he, Dülberg, had been largely responsible. This marked a further stage in Dülberg's disenchantment with the Kroll. Klemperer was in a tense and excitable condition throughout. He took a particularly active part in the rehearsals, frequently leaping on to the stage to demonstrate a gesture or a movement, while singing a role. Moje Forbach, who had been cast as Senta,* found him an alarming figure, who simultaneously inspired fear and confidence. He had, she has recalled, an unhappy tendency to communicate his own anxieties. Yet, when the moment arrived to sing, he could impart such excitement that, at the start of Senta's ballad 'it was as though I were physically lifted up'.[8] As was his habit, he insisted that there should be no 'marking'; even in the earliest rehearsals, the cast was obliged to sing with full voice.

In spite of exacting rehearsals there was also much laughter. On one occasion Forbach held a note longer than Klemperer approved. 'How long do you intend to hold that G, Frau Forbach?' 'Excuse me, but it is marked *ad libitum*.' 'Which means?' 'According to taste.' 'And *whose* taste, Frau Forbach?' Forbach (with a curtsey as deep as her irony), 'Why *yours*, of course, Herr General.'[9] At the dress rehearsal Siegfried Wagner, the composer's son, made an unexpected appearance in Klemperer's dressing room. 'Nu, Ihr seht ja alle zum Piepen aus', was the only comment he could offer.† Klemperer proffered a chair. 'Bitte, Herr Wagner, entsetzen Sie sich.'‡ For all the tensions the Kroll was a pleasant theatre to work in. Forbach was struck by the undivided loyalty Klemperer commanded in spite of his unaccommodating character and abrasive tongue. More than one member of the company later described it as 'a family'.

There was, however, little merriment on 15 January 1929, when the head of the Berlin police telephoned to say that trouble was expected at the première that evening and that he would be stationing men around the auditorium.§ Bloch's sacrilegious comparison of the opera to an

---

* The role was originally to have been sung by Rosa Pauly. At an early rehearsal Forbach deputised to such effect that she was given the part.

† 'Well, you all look a little crazy.'

‡ *Sich setzen*: to sit down. *Sich entsetzen*: to be enraged. *Experiment Krolloper*, p. 58.

§ According to Curjel (*ibid.*), some arrests were made. The author has, however, found no reference to these in the Berlin newspapers of the following day.

adventure story had already given offence. More was taken when the curtain rose to reveal a Dutchman without a beard and sailors who might have been a gang of dock labourers; Senta's companions, dressed in plain blouses and skirts, did not spin but were occupied in the more prosaic task of making fishing nets.* Senta herself was no longer a submissive heroine, bent on immolation, but an ecstatic, red-headed visionary, who sang her ballad as though in a trance. (Einstein described Forbach as resembling a proletarian figure from the sketches of Käthe Kollwitz.) At his first appearance at the helm of his ship only the Dutchman's ghostly face was visible. In the last act Daland's seamen were hurled back from the Dutchman's ship as though they had been struck by a cyclone. Above all, wrote Adorno in 'Berliner Opernmemorial', out of Klemperer's account of the score, 'at once tumultuous...and utterly lucid', there emerged an engulfing sense of a 'turbulent, restless, menacing sea'. It was from this that the performance derived its 'basic impulse', so that Senta's parlour seemed to be 'the cabin of a ship toiling on the ocean'. 'Nothing like it had been seen on the operatic stage before', recalled Oskar Fritz Schuh almost half a century later.[10] For him and for many other young men of the theatre, the Kroll's *Flying Dutchman* represented an entirely fresh approach to Wagner, more than two decades before the New Bayreuth came into existence.

Much of the production's impact arose from an inner tension between Dülberg's severe, rectilinear sets and the expressionist intensity of the stage action, a synthesis that uncannily matched the disciplined fury that Klemperer unleashed in the music. But beneath this delivery of Wagner from 'metaphorical dust, hollow symbolism, theatrical piety and romantic costuming', Adorno sensed an even more blasphemous ingredient. In this production, he claimed that the Kroll had 'mobilised a reserve of actuality in Wagner...which will explode today or tomorrow'. It was to do so almost fifty years later on a scale that he can hardly have anticipated. To that extent, at any rate, the Kroll may be regarded not only as the father of Wieland Wagner's New Bayreuth but as a source of the new realism of Wagnerian producers such as Patrice Chéreau and Götz Friedrich, who took as their starting point the composer's youthful political radicalism and treated *The Ring*, in particular, as a parable of contemporary society.

Whether Klemperer and his collaborators regarded *Der fliegende Holländer* in this light is doubtful.† But many right-wing commentators, and

---

* It is not inconceivable that Tietjen's refusal to sanction funds for new costumes for the chorus may have precipitated rather than impeded this approach, in spite of the fact that Klemperer, Fehling and Dülberg protested against it (Stompor, 'Musiktheater').
† Certainly it did not match Dülberg's intentions, which were to provide settings that would not be so much 'modern' (a word both he and Klemperer despised) as 'relevant to the times' ('zeitgültig'). But, Dülberg cautioned, a designer should remember that his own contribution

particularly those in the musical periodicals, were convinced that they did, so that for the first time a production at the Kroll became a political issue. It was, wrote Fritz Stege, an act of 'unparalleled cultural shamelessness, which with a sneering grin has reduced a German cultural monument to ruins'.* In *Der Tag* (16 January 1929), Max Donisch concurred. 'What Herr Klemperer has done with this soiling of a German opera...can no longer be excused as mere wrong-headedness. It is an irresponsible attempt to destroy, and to that there can only be one answer, "Out with the pest".' In the *Signale für die musikalischen Welt* the editor, Max Chop, attacked those who 'looked on with sadistic pleasure at the martyrdom that was being inflicted on German art by a group of degenerates'.[11] It was, however, Paul Schwers, the editor of the *Allgemeine Musikzeitung*, who led the pack.

would be more ephemeral than the work itself (*Bühnentechnische Rundschau*, 1930, No. 1. 'Soll Wagner modern inszeniert werden?').

* *Berliner Westen*, 16 January 1929. Fritz Stege (1896–1967), who in 1929 joined Alfred Rosenberg's newly founded National Socialist Kampfbund für deutsche Kultur (see pp. 286–7), was to rise to prominence in the Third Reich as critic on the *Völkische Beobachter*, chairman of the Arbeitsgemeinschaft Deutscher Musikkritiker and press officer of the Reichsmusikkammer.

33   Ewald Dülberg: stage set for *Der fliegende Holländer*

The Dutchman, naturally beardless, looks like a Bolshevist agitator, Senta like a fanatical...Communist harridan, Erik...a pimp. Daland's crew resemble port vagabonds of recent times, the wretched spinning chamber a workshop in a woman's prison...What Klemperer and his helpmates offer...amounts to a total destruction of Wagner's work, a basic falsification of his creative intentions. That goes in almost equal degree for the musical performance, which coarsened the sound to an intolerable extent...Tempi were ridiculously overdriven, finer dynamic shadings eliminated and all expression reduced to a minimum...

...this proletarianised *Ur-Holländer*...[is] an *artistic betrayal of the people*...Yes, artistic betrayal of the people has been systematically practised on this 'experimental stage' in the Tiergarten ever since the fanatical, cranky Klemperer with his barren ideological preoccupations has been able to use the money and means that the state has entrusted to him...*The way the State Opera in the Tiergarten functions is damaging to Berlin's reputation as a cultural centre.* Either its methods must be changed...or it must be shut.[12]

When the Nazis staged their exhibition of degenerate music in Düsseldorf in 1938, the Kroll's *Fliegende Holländer* was singled out as one of the greatest cultural outrages of the Weimar Republic.[13]

Inevitably there were repercussions. The police returned for the second performance, which Klemperer did not conduct as he had left for Holland: a student organisation, the Hochschulring deutscher Art, had threatened stink bombs. Klemperer and others received threatening letters. The Richard Wagner Verband deutscher Frauen, the Bayreuther Bund deutscher Jugend, the Akademischer Richard Wagner Verband all demanded that the production be withdrawn. Klemperer himself, now highly manic, was not immune from this wave of rising temper. Enraged by a disparaging review in the *Vossische Zeitung* (16 January) by his former supporter, Max Marschalk, he marched into the paper's editorial offices, demanded that Marschalk be instantly dismissed, and, when this was refused, threatened to attack, or, according to some accounts, even to kill the offender. The episode provided further ammunition which the predominantly right-wing musical press was not slow to fire at the Kroll.[14]

Der fliegende Holländer was by no means the only event at the Kroll to cause public controversy that winter. On his return to Berlin earlier in the season Klemperer had attended a performance of *Die Dreigroschenoper*. It exercised such a fascination on him that he not only repeatedly returned to see it,* but commissioned from Weill an orchestral suite based on themes from the work. Thus emerged *Die kleine Dreigroschenmusik*, which Klemperer conducted at a Kroll concert on 7 February 1929.† Einstein

---

* Its producer, Ernst Josef Aufricht (*Erzähle damit du dein Recht erweist*, p. 82) claims that Klemperer attended no fewer than ten performances.
† Kruttge told the author that the work was earlier performed at the annual opera ball and David Drew, an authority on Weill, is also of this opinion. Yet the extensive press coverage of the evening makes no mention of such a performance.

perceptively pointed to the work's solid musical merits.[15] Others observed how neatly it fitted into a programme in which Bach joined hands with other neo-classical works by Hindemith and Stravinsky: here were various aspects of the new classicism alongside the old. But less open-minded critics (and, as *Der fliegende Holländer* had revealed, there were plenty of them in Berlin) failed to see beyond the use that Weill had made of rhythms and instruments associated with jazz. In particular they were shocked by the appearance of a saxophone, guitar and banjo within the portals of a German opera house. Such music, insisted the *Berliner Lokal-Anzeiger* (8 February 1929), always an accurate barometer of *spiessig* prejudice, belonged to the dance hall or the variety theatre.

Only five days later the Kroll delivered yet another affront to conventional taste. In the course of the season, a far-reaching shift had occurred in the influence of the individual members of the group who ran the theatre. Legal had proved less of a threat to radical policies than his colleagues had foreseen; he was content to handle administration and stage a series of unremarkable productions that were not always happily matched to their more innovatory settings.* Dülberg had returned to Arosa, his illness aggravated by the strains of *Der fliegende Holländer*. In his absence, Curjel emerged as the only member of the group with any real understanding of visual matters and the way was now open for him to put into effect his plans to bring about a renewal of scenic design in the opera house which was to go far beyond anything that Klemperer and Dülberg had envisaged. During the previous summer Klemperer had assured Curjel that 'in the field of stage design I also long for real structure and stand entirely on the side of progress'.† But, eager though he was to escape convention, Klemperer was not a man of much visual imagination and he was to be as much taken aback as were most of the critics by the production of *The Tales of Hoffmann* that the Kroll presented on 12 February with sets designed by László Moholy-Nagy.

Moholy-Nagy, who was still only in his early thirties, had never before designed for a fully equipped theatre, although during his years at the Bauhaus (1923–8) he had worked in its stage department with Oskar Schlemmer (see p. 330). In his approach to the theatre Moholy was influenced by Russian constructivism. Light and space, geometrical forms, photo-montage and films were combined to create what he subsequently defined as 'vision in motion'.[16] Curjel, who had been in contact with him during his period at the Bauhaus, had the wit to perceive that behind this

---

* In the 1928/9 season Legal was responsible for no less than five of the Kroll's ten new productions.

† 'In puncto Bühnenbild sehne auch ich mich nach wahrer Gestaltung und stehe ganz auf dem fortschreitenden Standpunkt.' Letter of 29 August 1928.

preoccupation with technological innovations lay a romanticism that could be used to illuminate the macabre visions of E. T. A. Hoffmann and Offenbach. A dream world would be evoked with modern materials. Machinery and human emotion would interact so as to reflect the ambivalence that gives the opera its special flavour.*

Moholy-Nagy delivered coloured geometrical drawings of astonishing beauty. His intention was, as he himself put it, 'to create space out of light and shadow...[so that] everything is transparent and all these transparencies contribute to an elaborate...pattern of shapes (Raumgleichung)'[17] Teo Otto, the youthful apprentice whom Dülberg had brought as an assistant from the Kassel Kunstakademie, was detailed to realise them as stage sets.† He later recalled Moholy as making 'a fascinating impression...of amiability and implacable tenacity' in the theatre.[18] Legal, who produced, was dismayed to discover that he did not have 'a dog on a lead', as he had been led (by Curjel?) to suppose, but 'a lion'.[19] How well the designs worked on the stage is hard to determine from the photographs that survive.‡ Predictably, Moholy's setting of the scene in Spalanzani's laboratory was widely considered the most effective: here the connection between the drama and his constructivist fantasy was readily apparent. Elsewhere even a critic as open-minded as Einstein found an unbridgeable gap between the two worlds. Bloch was one of the few to defend the production. What, he asked, could be 'more truly Hoffman-nesque than this power to bring ghosts into *our world*? Without nightgowns, but with machinery? In the cold, phosphorescent world of machines, in the empty chambers of our time, what is suppressed is here liberated in the form of what is to come...The ghosts that appear are new...[This] conspiracy in steel is worth seeing.'[20] Klemperer, who took over as a conductor from Zemlinsky for a single performance on 19 February, was less confident. To Dülberg he wrote, 'I believe that you would have found much that was artistic in *Hoffmann*', thereby implying that there were also elements of which his redoubtable friend might not have approved. Later, he expressed a less ambiguous view that the production had gone 'too far'.§

---

* It was on the basis of his experience at the Kroll that Moholy in 1930 developed his famous 'light-prop' ('Licht-maschine'). See Hans Curjel, 'Moholy-Nagy und das Theater', *Du*, November 1964.

† Teo Otto (1904–68) only came into his own in the final Kroll season of 1930/1, when he designed sets for Debussy's *Jeux*, Charpentier's *Louise* and a highly successful production of *Figaro* (see Chapter 15). Otto subsequently became one of the best known German stage designers of his generation, though in later years his productivity outran his imaginative powers.

‡ The art of stage photography was by no means as well developed in the late twenties as it was to become after the Second World War. This provides an obstacle to forming a reliable impression of the visual impact of productions at the Kroll.

§ *Conversations*, p. 66. '...two nearly naked girls on a swing, swinging in time with the music. Supposedly a new way for opera.'

The Soviet critic, Nikolay Malkov, who on a visit to Berlin early in 1929 found the theatres 'decades behind those in the Soviet Union', patronisingly dismissed the production as 'inoffensive (and pretty tasteless)'; from his point of view the Kroll offered nothing that was 'formally progressive'.[21] But the right-wing press in Berlin predictably denounced the whole enterprise as an abomination that made even Dülberg appear (as in some respects he was) a traditional figure. Stege demanded that the issue of the Kroll be debated in the Prussian Landtag,[22] while Paul Zschorlich, another exponent of the right-wing radicalism that was becoming increasingly strident, carried the debate on to an overtly racial level.

The Klemperer ensemble [he wrote], which consists mainly of aliens, is bit by bit devouring the entire repertory. It presents the best loved operas 'according to the spirit of the times', that is, according to the Jewish spirit. We observe this spirit in Klemperer's deeds, in the collaborators he chooses, in his artistic attitudes and in his affinity to the Soviet potentates, from whom he earns so well on guest appearances...The three-quarters Jewish public was once again delighted by the evening...Klemperer and Legal would do well...to declare their cultural bolshevist undertaking a 'Jewish Opera'. What goes on in it has nothing to do with German artistic spirit.[23]

The uproar coincided with the founding in Munich by Alfred Rosenberg* of the Kampfbund für deutsche Kultur under the auspices of the National

* Alfred Rosenberg (1893–1946) joined the National Socialist party on its foundation in 1919 and from 1925 edited its principal newspaper, the *Völkische Beobachter*. In 1933 appointed *Reichsleiter* of the Nazi party and from 1941 until the end of the war

34   László Moholy-Nagy: stage set for *The Tales of Hoffmann*

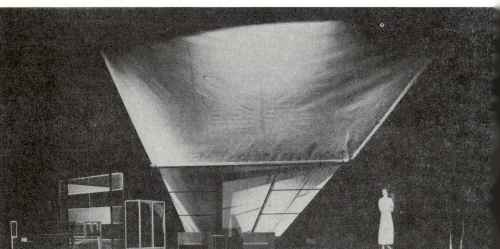

Socialist party with widespread academic support and the patronage of both Wagner's daughter and daughter-in-law, Eva Chamberlain and Winifred Wagner. Its programme was immediately endorsed by Alfred Heuss, the editor of Germany's oldest musical periodical *Zeitschrift für Musik*, who the following month lectured as a representative of the Kampfbund in Munich University on 'Die Krise in der Musik und im Musikleben'.[24] The assault on the Kroll was rapidly moving out of a purely cultural sphere. In an article ominously entitled 'Opernkulturkampf', Alfred Schattmann denounced the theatre's approach to opera as politically motivated. Invoking Pfitzner's *Die neue Aesthetik der musikalischen Impotenz* (see pp. 150–1) (almost a decade after its first appearance that bird was now coming home to roost), he called for a change in the country's political structure.[25]

The Kroll had indeed become a means of attacking the republican regime, and the right-wing parties in the Landtag were not slow to exploit the openings it offered. Two months earlier, the Deutschnationale Volkspartei, whose leadership had late in 1928 been taken over by the more extremist Hugenberg faction, had tabled a motion complaining of the high proportion of Jews employed in the Prussian state theatres.* On 20 February, three days after the publication of Schattmann's article, the DNVP tabled a further motion, condemning the Kroll as a centre of cultural Bolshevist experimentation (*Der fliegende Holländer* and *The Tales of Hoffmann* being singled out as notable outrages) and demanding that this state of affairs be brought to an end. Contrary to what Klaus Pringsheim claimed in the official socialist organ, *Vorwärts*,[26] the motion did not urge that the Kroll be shut. But the attack on its existence had begun, and on 19 February the *Berliner Börsen-Courier* published a symposium in which Hindemith and Weill, as well as Gropius† and Harry Graf Kessler,‡ rallied to its defence.

That the anticipated assault did not materialise was due to the fact that such attention as the Landtag could spare for opera was for the moment drawn elsewhere. As Weissmann had pointed out in the previous autumn in an article that was probably a trial balloon for a scheme that had been hatched by Bruno Walter to fuse the Linden Opera and the Städtische Oper

---

Reichsminister for the occupied eastern territories. Author of *Der Mythos der zwanzigsten Jahrhundert* (1930) and a fanatical racist, he was hanged after standing trial for war crimes at Nuremberg.

* Paradoxically, neither Klemperer nor any of his Jewish colleagues at the Kroll were mentioned. The targets on this occasion were Leopold Jessner, the Intendant of the Berlin Schauspielhaus, and Erich Kleiber, who denied he was a Jew.

† Walter Gropius (1883–1969), architect, founder of the Weimar (later Dessau) Bauhaus and its head until 1928. Alma Mahler's second husband.

‡ Harry Graf Kessler (1868–1937), diplomat, man of letters and collector, whose diaries are a valuable source of the intellectual life of the Weimar Republic. Co-author (with Hofmannsthal) of the scenario for Strauss's ballet, *Josefslegende* (see p. 94).

with himself as director, Berlin had in one form or another suffered from a perennial opera crisis ever since it had become an imperial capital in 1871. The roots of that crisis lay in the fact that the city could not support three full-scale opera houses. Hence a merger was essential.[27]

That argument was to be heard *ad nauseam* during the next two years, but for the moment it was not the Kroll but the Linden Opera that lay in the line of fire. In contrast to the Städtische Oper, which under Walter's direction had often attained an international level, the august State Opera had manifestly failed to find its feet since it had returned in April 1928 to its reconstructed quarters. On 6 February 1929 Einstein fiercely assailed two routine performances. Leading singers and conductors, he claimed, were too often abroad and their replacements were inadequate. Thus, when the Landtag debated the budget estimates for the state theatres on 13 March, the Kultusminister, C. H. Becker, called for a more intensive collaboration between the Linden and City houses, so that they would between them be able to match the fees that were attracting artists to New York.*

The debate occasioned much criticism of the large rise in the subsidies of the state theatres over the previous three years and a sub-committee was set up to consider the matter. This held four sittings during the spring and summer of 1929. But, in spite of the fact that much of the additional expenditure had been due to the establishment of an independent Kroll, Klemperer's opera house attracted little attention beyond desultory right-wing sniping. The representatives on the committee of the parties that supported Braun's coalition made it plain that they regarded the Kroll as an indispensable agent of *soziale Kunstpflege*. Berlin's opera problem was for the moment seen to lie primarily in the fact that the Städtische Oper had become an embarrassingly formidable competitor to the Linden Opera. For the moment the Kroll's existence was not in question. An official of the Kultusministerium felt confident enough in the early spring of 1929 to assure the Soviet critic, Nikolay Malkov, that 'although Klemperer's path is steep, if he can hold on for another year or two, he will win through'.[28]

*   *   *

In the course of the winter of 1928/9 Klemperer's mood had begun to undergo a sea change. When he conducted in Breslau in December (see p. 309), Anneliese Reich was among the audience. As the daughter of

---

* The Kultusministerium did not, however, press the point, probably because Böss and the Berlin *Magistrat* had no intention of permitting a fusion between the City Opera, which they had set up and of which they were justifiably proud, and the problem-ridden Linden Opera. Walter, unable to achieve his aims and discontented with a situation in which Tietjen had a foot in both houses, accordingly resigned on 4 April 1929.

Oskar Kohnstamm, in whose sanatorium in Königstein Klemperer had so frequently sought refuge from the psychological upheavals that had afflicted him with particular violence in his youth, she was familiar with his medical history. On this occasion she formed an opinion that he was in a distinctly manic condition.[29]

Her diagnosis was correct. On arriving in Breslau on 7 December, Klemperer wrote to inform his publisher, Willy Strecker, that he had added a new text to the coloratura aria he had earlier composed for *The Barber of Seville* in Cologne. He also told him that his wife would sing this, together with an excerpt from the opera he had composed in Königstein in 1915, at a concert he planned to conduct in Berlin on 6 January 1929. This renewed interest in compositions that he had left untouched for years was a clear indication that his psychic weathervane had swung from depression to euphoria. There were other symptoms. On Christmas Day 1928 the *Vossische Zeitung* published a brief symposium on 'Intellectuals and Sport'. In it Klemperer vouchsafed the information that he swam in the baths at the Luna Park,* climbed in the Alps, was prevented only by lack of time from riding – and was thinking of learning to drive a car. None of this was untrue; but that the usually reticent Klemperer was on this occasion willing to present himself in public as a sporting intellectual suggests a certain buoyancy of mood. This was not the only announcement of his activities to appear in the press. On 18 December the *Berliner Tageblatt* revealed that he had composed an opera, whose four parts all now bore purely musical titles, 'Allegro and Andante', 'Waltz', 'One Step' and 'Andante'. This was in fact the opera, *Eros*, which he had referred to in his letter to Strecker, had recently revised, and was shortly to rechristen *Das Ziel*.†

By this time, however, Klemperer had already left for Paris, where he was to conduct two concerts in the week before Christmas (see pp. 310–11). On the journey he stopped in Cologne to see his sister, Marianne, and toyed with the idea of giving her and her husband a small car (generosity on such a scale was further evidence of euphoria). He also played his opera to her and to Helmuth Plessner, who told him that he found it 'pretty, but somehow old-fashioned'.‡ Klemperer was unabashed. 'If that's so', he

* An amusement park in the Halensee district of Berlin.
† See p. 101. The four acts had titles that varied with the years. The strictly musical terms they bore in the twenties were intended to reflect the period of *neue Sachlichkeit*, as is confirmed by the fact that on 18 December 1928 Klemperer wrote from Paris to Helmuth Plessner (see footnote below) telling him that he had in mind a new sub-title for the entire work: 'Musikalische Einakter in neo-classizistischer Manier'.
‡ Helmuth Plessner (1892–   ). Professor of philosophy at Cologne and Göttingen universities. Long-standing friend of Marianne and Otto Klemperer.

wrote to Johanna from Paris (18 December), 'I don't find it such a terrible failing.'

After spending Christmas in Sils Maria, where the splendour of the Alps in winter enthralled him and he was able to skate daily for the first time in years, he returned to Berlin on New Year's Eve. On 6 January he conducted a Sunday morning concert of the low-grade Berlin Symphony Orchestra in aid of a charity. Johanna was ill (or so it was declared) and the performances of two arias from *Das Ziel* that had been announced were cancelled. Klemperer seems to have approached the concert with an uncharacteristic nonchalance that evoked sharp comment from the usually temperate Alfred Einstein. His account of Schumann's Symphony No. 1 had, Einstein wrote, 'been improvised, with all the heaviness and unevenness that improvisation always brings; admittedly also a few genuine musical surprises. But even Klemperer cannot afford such jests, and least of all before an unassuming public.'[30] Clearly, he was riding high, for only in such a condition would he have approached even the most modest task without adequate preparation. True to form, he had indeed already offered *Das Ziel* to Universal Edition. Hertzka, who was not a man to turn down a work by a powerful conductor much involved in new music, accepted it on 16 January and a contract was signed two weeks later.

*　　　　　　　　　*　　　　　　　　　*

Schoenberg had been living in Berlin since January 1926, when he had succeeded Busoni as the teacher of a master class in composition at the Prussian Academy of the Arts. He had thus been able to observe the Kroll at first hand and he was not enamoured of much that Klemperer chose to perform, nor of how he performed it. Perhaps under the impact of a Schubert concert that Klemperer had conducted a few days earlier (see p. 300), he wrote in his diary for 7 March 1928:

Klemperer is taken as a great expert in Berlin because he makes music in a way that is less laden with feeling (gefühlsbetont) than is usual here. In reality he is only continuing from where Mahler began, but he exaggerates. Whereas Mahler always brought out the form and had the art of accommodating each phrase within the narrowest space (which is one reason why he never needed to draw out the music for this purpose), Klemperer loses the form: he doesn't get away with it. He often sounds cramped.

Many of the Berlin critical adherents of *Sachlichkeit*, who are schooled against romanticism, find this in accordance with their principles. We are indeed living in an anti-romantic period... [But] it is of course a great exaggeration to make modern marionette music out of works characterised by a certain breadth that cannot be communicated without putting warm blood into their limbs. One must have a strong sense of form to get away with it. That is how it comes about that such spirits prefer music so impoverished in content and material that an emphatic performance is not only unnecessary but damaging, as it would reveal its inner emptiness...[31]

Although Schoenberg was often ready to take offence, his resentment was in this case understandable. In earlier years Klemperer had performed his music, if only intermittently, at least more frequently than most conductors of his generation. Mahler had provided an indirect link and there had also been a degree of personal contact. Not for nothing had Klemperer elected to make his début as a conductor in Berlin in 1921 with an all-Schoenberg programme. Yet during his first two seasons at the Kroll, he did not perform a single work either by Schoenberg or by the two principal members of his school, Berg and Webern. There was a reason for that neglect: Klemperer could not warm to the works written in the twelve-note technique which all three composers had been using since the middle twenties. Asked what his attitude had been to Schoenberg's music during the Kroll years, he later replied, 'I waited for a piece I could say "yes" to.'[32] That, however, does not explain his failure to perform any of their earlier, non-dodecaphonic works in a period when his programmes contained much music by Stravinsky, Hindemith and Krenek. Schoenberg was not mistaken in his belief that at this period of his life Klemperer had undergone a certain revulsion against his pre-war expressionist music, which younger men such as Curjel regarded as outdated. On 12 October 1928 (significantly, the day after Stravinsky and Klemperer had enjoyed triumph at the Kroll with *The Soldier's Tale*) Schoenberg complained bitterly in a letter to his publishers, Universal Edition, 'I do not count among my friends Kleiber, Klemperer, Walter and all the other apes of a *Sachlichkeit* that may be 'new' to them but isn't new to me.'* Hence it was not, as might have been expected, Klemperer, but Furtwängler, who gave the first performance of Schoenberg's *Variations for Orchestra*, Op. 31, his first dodecaphonic score for full orchestra.† Hence, too, there was virtually no personal contact between Schoenberg and Klemperer in Berlin.‡

Nonetheless, as soon as Klemperer learnt (probably from a newspaper report) that Schoenberg was at work on a comic opera, he telegraphed a request to Universal Edition on 13 October 1928 for the right to give its first performance. Schoenberg's publishers replied that they had no knowledge of any such work.§ In fact *Von Heute auf Morgen* was only completed in

---

* The assertion that Walter was in any way associated with *die neue Sachlichkeit* is, of course, absurd.
† Which Klemperer attended on 2 December 1928 and found 'very good' as a performance (CBC Interviews XV, p. 12).
‡ Information given to the author by Josef Rufer.
§ The most probable explanation for this puzzling ignorance is that Schoenberg, who firmly believed that the opera would be a success on the scale of *Jonny spielt auf*, already planned to publish it at his own expense.

draft on 1 January 1929, when Schoenberg was wintering in the south of France. But at some point there must have been contact between the two men, for on 10 March Klemperer wrote to Dülberg from Leningrad about his plans for the coming season.

Schoenberg has written a new opera: *Von Heute auf Morgen*. A one-acter, plays in the bedroom of a married couple (I don't know whether that will appeal to you). So far I have only seen the text. Very nice. Time: the present. But not without deeper meaning (herein the difference from Hindemith, who deliberately rejects any 'deeper meaning')...He [Schoenberg] has offered me the first performance, which I have accepted with joy (freudigst). We want to give it with *Erwartung*.

Klemperer was not the only conductor to show interest in *Von Heute auf Morgen*. Not being on good terms with Schoenberg, Kleiber made an approach through Berg, who reported on 20 March that the composer had already given Klemperer 'a half-promise' of the first performance. On 7 May, however, Berg wrote again to tell Kleiber that he believed that Klemperer no longer held an option on the work.* What caused Klemperer to withdraw remains unclear. It is significant that he had accepted unseen a score that he later described as 'complicated beyond all measure'.[33] There is, however, another possible explanation: his winter euphoria was beginning to wane, and the caution associated with depression was already beginning to reassert itself. At all events, *Von Heute auf Morgen* was not the only problematic new work from which to the exasperation of his colleagues Klemperer was to withdraw before the season had ended.

           *   *   *

On his return to Berlin on 20 April Klemperer's first task was to prepare the première of another operatic comedy of modern life, Hindemith's *Neues vom Tage*.† This was the only entirely new opera that the Kroll was to stage, and it was rehearsed with a thoroughness that drove the orchestra to the brink of revolt.‡ Klemperer was at first pleased with the score. 'Everything fits together charmingly', he wrote to his wife on 30 May after the first orchestral rehearsal, 'the instrumentation is a marvel.' Curjel was less enthusiastic, but, in a letter written to Weill only six days before the première on 8 June 1929, he nonetheless expressed confidence: 'The

---

* Berg, who had no reason to love the Kroll, added that Schoenberg would do better at Kleiber's Linden Opera than at Klemperer's '*Republik-Zirkus*'. 'That is something you could mention in a letter to Schoenberg', he slyly added, doubtless aware of his master's anger with Klemperer.

† *Zeitoper* was in the air, although in some respects its innovator could be said to have been Richard Strauss, whose *Intermezzo* dates from 1924. Klemperer thought little of it, however (Letter to his wife, 6 August 1924).

‡ According to Karl Ulrich Schnabel, who played one of the score's three piano parts. (Interview with the author)

orchestra sounds fascinating, a lot goes on on the stage, OK's *élan* compensates for much.' The first-night audience obliged with its customary enthusiasm, but the work was not at all well received by the press.* Alfred Einstein put his finger on its central defect: a disproportion between Marcellus Schiffer's almost cabaret-like libretto and an elaborate score that, in spite of its use of jazz and dance music, failed to achieve the requisite lightness.[34] Even Strobel, usually eager to applaud a new work by Hindemith, concurred.[35] In Bie's view the music achieved buffoonery rather than true comedy, while the instrumental style of the vocal writing hindered audibility of the text.[36] Donisch darkly hinted at a conspiracy between Le Corbusier, the Bauhaus, the Kroll and the Kremlin and went on to express his shock at a scene in which the heroine receives her admirers in the bath.† Conjuring with the clichés of the hour, Curjel in an essay disarmingly entitled 'The Triumph of the Commonplace' proclaimed an end to exalted conceptions of 'art' and the start of a reign of 'objective emotion' that would take the place of '*espressivo*'.[37] (Bie drily commented that it was easier to eliminate 'ecstasy' than to invent a new buffo style.)[38] Stuckenschmidt observed with satisfaction, 'Shares in operatic tragedy are falling' and added that even Mozart had composed silly texts – such as *Così fan tutte*.[39] In an attempt to defend *Neues vom Tage*, the Kroll's ideologues were clearly scraping the bottom of the barrel.

---

* The first performance of Hindemith's new comic opera was part of the annual Berlin Festival which had become the high point of the year's music making. In 1929 this attained a level scarcely equalled anywhere before or since. Between 19 and 29 May Toscanini conducted a season of six operas performed by La Scala, Milan, which Curjel described to Weill (letter of 2 June 1929) as 'musically [wonderful] beyond description, scenically ridiculous'. Klemperer, whose laudatory article on Toscanini was timed to coincide with the visit (see p. 169) attended performances of *Falstaff*, *Manon Lescaut* (which he did not like) and *Aida*. Between 1 and 11 June Strauss conducted six of his own operas, including the latest, *Die aegyptische Helene*. Furtwängler, whose appearances in Berlin's opera houses were rare, conducted *Tristan* and *Figaro*. Blech contributed *The Ring* and Busoni's *Dr. Faust*, Georg Szell was in charge of *André Chenier*, while Kleiber conducted *La Clemenza di Tito* and *Don Pasquale*. In addition to Hindemith's new opera, Klemperer gave performances of *Don Giovanni*, *Der fliegende Holländer* and the Krenek one-acters. His concerts during the festival included an all-Stravinsky programme with the composer as soloist (see p. 307). The Diaghilev ballet, conducted by Ernest Ansermet, also appeared in a number of Stravinsky scores. Walter's contribution was limited to a performance of *Das Lied von der Erde*. The city's musical life can never have seemed more cornucopian. The clouds that lay ahead were scarcely visible on the horizon of that brilliant sunset of the summer of 1929.
† *Der Tag*, 9 June 1929. He was not alone in this. In a public attack on Hindemith made at the Berlin Sportpalast on 6 December 1934, Goebbels singled out for special condemnation 'the vulgar and obscene scenes in which naked women appeared on the stage' (Wulf, *Musik im Dritten Reich*, pp. 376–8). He also erroneously described its musical idiom as 'atonal'. Hitler's dislike of Hindemith is sometimes similarly said to have stemmed from *Neues vom Tage*, but there is no evidence that he attended a performance of it, or indeed of any other opera at the Kroll.

293

Klemperer's own early enthusiasm did not survive. Forty years later he dismissed it as, 'Unfortunately, [not] a very good piece.'*

*   *   *

In an interview he had given in Paris in December 1928, Klemperer had confirmed that (as had already been announced at the beginning of the season) he would be conducting the first performance of *Der Aufstieg und Fall der Stadt Mahagonny*, on which Brecht and Weill had been intermittently at work since the summer of 1927 with a view to performance at the Kroll (see p. 246). The opera was eventually completed in April 1929 and within twenty-four hours of his return to Berlin from his Russian tour Klemperer asked Weill to play it to him.[40] Such precipitancy does not suggest that he as yet had any reservations about the work, and on 10 May the Kroll duly requested that a contract be drawn up for it to give the first performance. Klemperer had not, however, at this stage read the text, as Brecht's first two acts were only sent to him on 24 May. It is nonetheless apparent from the letter that Weill wrote to his publishers on the following day that hesitations had already arisen on both sides. Klemperer was bothered by the 'love' scene in which a group of men queue outside a brothel. Weill was troubled by the Kroll's notoriously timorous Volksbühne public; he was eager that his new opera should be seen by the audiences that had flocked to *Die Dreigroschenoper* throughout the season.† Both men were, however, agreed that Brecht should produce.‡ On 4 June Weill, who was in France, told Universal Edition that the Kroll was so bound ('angewiesen') to the project that all problems would prove surmountable.

Yet within a week Hertzka, who had been in Berlin for talks with Klemperer, Tietjen and Brecht, reported to Weill that he was trying to free *Mahagonny* from the Kroll.[41] The following day Weill admitted to his friend Curjel that he had from the start had doubts about launching his first full-length opera in Berlin and these had now been reinforced by the failure of *Neues vom Tage*, which had not sold out even at its première.

That such a silly affair could not succeed in Berlin was always clear to me. But that it would prove a disaster on such a scale I had not anticipated...For *Mahagonny* I have learnt one thing, that it was a correct instinct not to have planned it as a 'merry opera'...*Spielfreudigkeit* is now finally played out.[42]

---

* *Conversations*, p. 63. Nonetheless, in a letter of 28 February 1930 to Hindemith's publisher, Willy Strecker, he referred to the score as 'masterly and transparent'.
† The flaw in Weill's character is already apparent: he wanted to compose a full-scale opera and he also wanted to repeat the success of *Die Dreigroschenoper*. That desire to have his cake and eat it was to prove fatal during his later years on Broadway.
‡ The project collapsed because the Kroll could not afford the fee of 5,000M, which Brecht demanded (Curjel's letter to Weill, 2 June 1929).

If a new opera exercised so little attraction during a festival, could *Mahagonny* be risked in mid-season? That was not the only problem. On 22 June Weill wrote to tell Curjel that he had heard from Hertzka that Klemperer was still 'riding his hobby-horse' about Brecht's 'unchaste' text.* He for his part was more convinced than ever that the production should be moved to another theatre, but Klemperer was adamantly opposed.

On 4 July Weill informed his publishers that he was on his way to Berlin in response to an urgent telegram from the Kroll. Nine days later he reported to Hertzka on what had transpired.

The *Mahagonny* affair has now taken a very surprising turning. After playing Klemperer the third act, I left. Legal, who was particularly impressed, insisted on immediate acceptance of the work. Klemperer declared himself to be basically in agreement. Two hours later, however, he telephoned me at my flat to say that he wanted to come round at once. He arrived in a completely distraught condition and said with tears in his eyes that he had struggled with himself for two hours but that he could not do the work. He recognised its importance, he saw its musical beauties, but it was alien and incomprehensible to him.[43]

As a compromise Klemperer had proposed that the opera be first given in the provinces, after which, if it convinced him, he would conduct it at the Kroll.

Immediately after that encounter, there was a further meeting at the Kroll, where, Weill continued in his letter to Hertzka, Legal and Curjel had made it plain that they in no way shared Klemperer's attitude to the opera and would insist on performing it.

Legal said to Klemperer in my presence, 'From this day our theatre can no longer be called the Klemperer Opera'. Legal's position, to which...he will certainly stick, is this: 'I have no desire to direct an institution whose decisions are dictated by the entirely personal taste of a single man. The first performance of *Mahagonny* is a necessity of life for our theatre; therefore we must force it through, even if against K's will.'

From this Weill drew the conclusion that it would be feasible to perform the work at the Kroll, even if Klemperer did not conduct it. Hertzka was more realistic. In a caustic reference to Legal's grandiloquent *démarche*, he told Weill in his reply that 'inwardly and outwardly...the Kroll is the Klemperer Opera, not the Legal Opera'. The choice was therefore between a first performance there conducted by Klemperer himself, or a production in another theatre.[44]

That home truth only served to increase Weill's bitterness. Conveniently

---

* That Klemperer should have objected to *Mahagonny* on moral grounds may appear paradoxical in view of his own distinctly uninhibited behaviour when manic. But in depression his sexual attitudes verged on prudishness and there is reason to suppose that by the summer of 1929 the euphoria of the previous winter had spent itself.

forgetting his own earlier reservations about the Kroll, he declared that 'the complete blame for this situation is...Klemperer's'.[45] But he also perceived that more was at stake for Klemperer than for *Mahagonny*, which would find another berth more readily than the Kroll would find another new opera of equal calibre. 'The *Mahagonny* affair...' he wrote to Curjel on 2 August, 'is very damaging for Klemperer. The many voices that have always maintained that he is timid and that his boldness is so much bluff will be confirmed in their opinion and the news will spread quickly. A pity! He is a brilliant conductor. But to us he is worth no more than Furtwängler.'

Curjel was equally disillusioned. 'I must openly say', he wrote to Weill on 31 July, 'that I have lost almost all confidence [in Klemperer]. I constantly ponder whether the moment has not come to set up an uncompromising music theatre on a private basis...As you can see, I don't reckon any more on O.K....perhaps that's unfair of me...Perhaps illumination will still come to him!' On 6 August he accordingly wrote in a final attempt to persuade Klemperer to reconsider his decision.*

Please do not take it amiss if I once again feel obliged to tell you that the situation that has arisen represents the greatest danger that our institution has faced and that I believe that you personally have taken a step basically in conflict with the aims you have always stood for in the field of operatic theatre. It is not just a matter of the première...It is the question of artistic experiment, which we have espoused because experiment has proved to be the field in which the strongest and truest forces manifest themselves today. We have up to now supported experiment out of a will to create...Hence my anxieties about a stabilisation in our endeavours. During my last conversation with Kestenberg I felt clearly that he is basically quite happy with the stand you have taken over *Mahagonny*; he reeks of stabilisation...

That is why it seems to me that our work has reached a crucial point. After *Oedipus*...*Mahagonny* is the most decisive expression of a new musical theatre ...Naturally it contains much that is critical of the *status quo*...But precisely for that reason it is our duty to perform it. To be in favour of the work need not imply that one regards it as an absolute artistic fulfilment, but as a serious and genuine experiment.

It was bravely spoken. But when Klemperer, now on holiday in Sils Maria, replied two days later, he devoted almost his entire letter to the possibility of including Weill and Hindemith's new *Lindberghflug* as a cantata in a concert during the coming season.† Only in a brief final paragraph did he so much as allude to *Mahagonny*, 'The quite unforced (natürliche) pleasure

---

* It is indicative of Curjel's sympathies that he never similarly took up cudgels on behalf of *Von Heute auf Morgen*. Nor did he subsequently indicate in *Experiment Krolloper* or elsewhere that Klemperer had originally intended to give the first performance of Schoenberg's comic opera.

† This jointly composed cantata had had its first performance only two weeks earlier on 25 July at the Baden-Baden Festival.

I had in *Der Lindberghflug**...has made me aware of how little the conception of *Mahagonny* convinces.'[46]

The issue nonetheless rumbled on until the end of the year, as Klemperer had paradoxically still not abandoned his idea of performing the work at the Kroll, once it had proved itself elsewhere. After the vocal score arrived in Berlin in December, Zemlinsky, Dülberg and Zweig all again declared themselves in favour.[47] But Klemperer still refused to commit himself and on 6 January 1930 Weill informed his publishers that negotiations had finally been broken off. Three weeks later Weill met Klemperer at a concert, when, as he wrote to his wife, Lotte Lenya, 'He, too, was embarrassed, but genuinely so (out of a bad conscience) and also genuinely nice'. With time, good relations were restored.

On 9 March *Der Aufstieg und Fall der Stadt Mahagonny* was given its first performance by Gustav Brecher in Leipzig. The brothel scene that Klemperer had objected to was omitted on the insistence of the civic authorities, but the work occasioned one of the most resounding operatic scandals of the time, which has been memorably described by Alfred Polgar.[48] Klemperer was present. According to Stuckenschmidt, he left the theatre 'speechless'.†
Zemlinsky subsequently conducted the first Berlin performance on 21 December 1931. But by that time Klemperer's Kroll Opera had shut its doors for ever.

Thus, for one reason or another, in the course of his second season in Berlin Klemperer rejected *Von Heute auf Morgen* and *Der Aufstieg und Fall der Stadt Mahagonny*, both operas that would have shed lasting lustre on the Kroll.

*   *   *

Klemperer's attitude to his own compositions always provided the most reliable weather-vane to changes in his disposition. Throughout the winter of 1928/9 he had been much occupied with his opera, *Das Ziel*, and neither the disapproval of his elder sister, Regi, nor the embarrassed silence of his friends, had damped his ardour. In early March he had broken his journey from Rome to Leningrad in Vienna, in order to discuss publication details with Universal Edition.‡ On 10 March in Leningrad he had written to tell Dülberg that he had already discussed plans to perform the work at the Berlin Schauspielhaus with its Intendant, Leopold Jessner. Five days later

---

* See pp. 305–6.
† *Zum Hören geboren*, p. 117. Forty years later Klemperer still insisted that the work was a 'Schweinerei' (*Conversations*, p. 64).
‡ His manic condition is evident in an interview he gave to the *Neues Wiener Journal* in early March (date unknown). When the interviewer observed that he was composing and talking simultaneously, Klemperer replied, 'I always do two things at once.'

he told Johanna in a letter that he had composed an *Ave Maria* and a *Pater Noster*.

There are, however, no further references to *Das Ziel* in his correspondence with its publisher. His manic phase had spent its force. On 26 July, immediately on arrival at Sils Maria, where he was to spend his summer vacation, he wrote a terse, impersonal note. He would not, he informed Universal Edition, for the moment be returning the revised score, as he wanted to be free of musical tasks during his holiday. The wind had changed again. A fellow guest observed that he looked harassed and depressed.* On 5 August in a manifestly embarrassed letter he finally wrote to tell Hertzka that he had decided to withdraw *Das Ziel* for the time being.

The reasons for my request are purely artistic. For weeks now, doubts have been stirring in me that my work isn't yet completely finished, that it needs yet another thorough revision. It is very hard to be precise about such internal things. I have the feeling that something is lacking...At any rate I need more time. You will certainly object that in this way we shall lose the coming season. I *have* to reply: so be it. In the extraordinarily exposed position...that I occupy, which makes it my duty to reach decisions about works and their performances, I can only appear with a work of my own when I myself see no more flaws and weaknesses in it. Perhaps in the haste of my working last winter I brought in the harvest too quickly and I now see that not all the sheaves are ripe.

---

* In an interview with Philo Bregstein, Alex Pollak years later recalled his father, the conductor Egon Pollak, who was also on vacation in the Engadine, describing Klemperer as looking like Atlas, with all the cares of the world on his shoulders.

Much of Klemperer's fame stems from the operas he conducted, and in some cases produced, during his years at the Kroll. But his musical aims are more clearly apparent in the series of concerts which he gave each season with the Berlin Staatskapelle and which came to be regarded as an outstanding feature of the city's cultural life during the last years of the Weimar Republic. Here, at any rate, he was not enmeshed in the thousand-and-one non-artistic considerations that seem an inescapable adjunct of operatic endeavour.

It was, however, only in his second season at the Kroll that he was able to put an individual stamp on these concerts, so that they stood out from the annual series given by Furtwängler, Walter and Kleiber. In the opening season of 1927/8 he was a grossly overburdened man in the throes of depression. In addition to shouldering for the first time in his life a considerable administrative load, he was fully stretched by the tasks of moulding a new ensemble while preparing a series of new productions. Nor did he as yet have exclusive use of his own section of the Staatskapelle, but was obliged to share it on an *ad hoc* basis with the Linden Opera. He thus had neither the time to study nor the means of rehearsing new or unfamiliar works. Hence his programmes in 1927/8 were by his own standards in the main unadventurous.

There were other factors that at first prevented the Kroll concerts from making as profound an impact as those that had established Klemperer's reputation in Berlin earlier in the decade. Although the Staatskapelle was a first-rate orchestra, its strings were not the equal of those of its rival, the Berlin Philharmonic, and in addition the Kroll's concert acoustics were unsatisfactory.* There had also been something of a reaction to the cult-like reputation that the Berlin press had bestowed on Klemperer earlier in the decade. Absence makes a critical heart grow fonder; now that he was no longer an infrequent visitor to the capital, but could be heard regularly, his limitations became more apparent.

But there was a deeper reason for the absence of the almost ecstatic welcome that both the public and the critics had given to his earlier

---

* In the autumn of 1928, Dülberg made an unsuccessful attempt to remedy them with screens.

concerts. It was widely felt that in the intervening years Klemperer had allowed himself to be drawn too deeply into the chilly waters of the *neue Sachlichkeit*; by the late twenties he had come to be regarded, by supporters and detractors alike, as its very embodiment among conductors. And not without reason, for at this period of his career, his aim was 'to achieve the greatest possible objectivity...Objective faithfulness to the score is the main problem of interpretation.'[1] One commentator on his years at the Kroll has, however, suggested that in this Klemperer was to some extent a victim of the tendency of the Berlin press to present him as an opposite in all matters of style to Furtwängler and Walter, and that this in turn may have pushed him towards a degree of interpretative 'objectivity' in keeping with only a part of his musical character.[2]

Even his Bruckner, which four years earlier had been enthusiastically received in Berlin and elsewhere, met a relatively cool reception when he conducted the Symphony No. 7 in E flat on 3 November 1927. There was also a distinctly reserved reaction to a Beethoven concert that followed on 1 December, when Klemperer's approach to the 'Pastoral' Symphony, was widely felt, even by his admirers, to lack the warmth and expressiveness that Furtwängler brought to the score.[3] The dramatic fire and architectural strength he revealed in the Symphony No. 7 in the same concert were much praised, but his account of the Symphony No. 5 later in the season was widely regarded as over-emphatic and over-driven. Even Strobel, champion of the *neue Sachlichkeit*, criticised its heavy accents and unrelenting rhythms, as well as an undue lack of *espressivo* in the andante.[4]

It was, however, an all-Schubert concert on 1 March that brought a perceptible disenchantment with Klemperer's interpretations to a head.* Much though he loved the 'Great' C major Symphony, it was a score that filled him with special apprehension, as it indeed continued to do for the remainder of his life. The level-headed Schrenk observed that he had approached it

as though he were conducting Beethoven's Symphony (No. 5) in C minor; hard, very taut in rhythm, almost heroic in its expressive austerity. But where was the sweet breath of this music, the tender melancholy of the andante, the lilting Viennese rhythms of the scherzo? Klemperer deprived the work of its carefree, happy, singing quality. He killed Schubert with a rigid beat that suffocated all warmth and sensuality...[5]

Heads had earlier also been shaken over a Brahms concert that Klemperer had conducted on 13 January. Einstein, who described the outer movements as unduly fast, found his account of the Symphony No. 1 in C minor lacking in emotional commitment.[6] Strobel and Schrenk both

---

* For Schoenberg's unfavourable comments, probably on this concert, see pp. 291–2.

commented on a lack of pathos, the former with approval, the latter with reservations.[7] Similarly, while Walther Hirschberg criticised a lack of romantic lyricism, Klaus Pringsheim singled out that very quality for praise as heralding a new world of feeling, far removed from the interpretations of conductors such as Furtwängler and Walter.[8]

Yet in comparison to these reactions a performance of Brahms's C minor Symphony, recorded only three weeks after he had conducted the work at the Kroll, today makes a less controversial impression, particularly when compared with two post-war performances that are also available on disc.* If the tempi of the outer movements are faster in the 1928 recording, they are more rigorously sustained in both the later versions. Fifty years ago many Berlin critics accused Klemperer of unyielding tempi. But to judge from the 1928 performance he was at that time more inclined to linger over modulations and bridge passages than he was to be a generation later. Thus a comparison of these recordings in no way supports the widespread view that Klemperer had 'mellowed' by the fifties.† If any conclusion is to be drawn, it is that performances that startled Berlin audiences and critics in the late twenties had a generation later come to be regarded as orthodox. In the far-ranging change of approach to the classics that was to occur within the next twenty-five years Klemperer played a greater part than any other conductor with the possible exception of Toscanini.

*   *   *

It was only in his second season at the Kroll that Klemperer's Berlin programmes began to develop a special physiognomy. By the autumn of 1928 he had secured exclusive control of the one hundred and six members of the Staatskapelle who were on attachment to the Kroll and he had been able to appoint his own leaders.‡ His new contract also gave him more time to study and prepare new scores and the fruits were immediately apparent in programmes which, particularly in their combination of Bach with composers such as Stravinsky, Weill and Hindemith, came to be regarded as characteristic of his years at the Kroll.

Klemperer was, however, never doctrinaire in his musical sympathies. In spite of an absence of music by Schoenberg and his school, his programmes included new works by composers, such as Eduard Erdmann

---

* The recording was made on 3 February 1928 (information provided by Michael Gray) and has been reissued on EMI Electrola (see discography, no. 17). The post-war recordings were made with the WDR Symphony Orchestra, Cologne (1955) and the Philharmonia Orchestra, London (1956/7).
† Held by, among others, Eigel Kruttge, a perceptive observer, who had many opportunities to hear Klemperer conduct both before 1933 and after 1954.
‡ Josef Wolfsthal (1899–1931), a violinist of great distinction whose early death came as a blow to Klemperer, and Max Strub (1900–66), who later formed a well-known trio with Elly Ney and Ludwig Hoelscher.

301

and Josef Matthias Hauer,* who may not have survived the test of time but cannot be regarded as representatives of the new classicism. He also continued to conduct Mahler, whose reputation went into decline during the years of the *neue Sachlichkeit*. But even here his interpretations, which stood in sharp contrast to those of Walter, seemed to break new ground, as is evident in an account by Strobel, who had little sympathy for the music, of a performance that Klemperer gave of the Symphony No. 2 during the Berlin Festival of 1930.

He conducts the work with the greatest energy and tautness. No savouring of emotional passages, no decorative orgies of sound... [He] grasps Mahler as we have today once again learnt to understand music: from its inner organism and its energy-laden formal tensions. Klemperer also seeks to free the symphony as far as possible from the programmatic ideas on which it is based. In spite of this attempt, the finale makes a monstrous and theatrical impact. But the fault is certainly not Klemperer's... The trouble lies in... the contradiction... between the [work's] symphonic-ethical idea and its musical realisation.[9]

The gulf between Klemperer and other leading conductors in Berlin was nowhere more apparent than in his approach to Bach. As a boy in Hamburg, he had been taken by his mother to Good Friday performances of the St Matthew Passion in the Michaeliskirche and he had been drawn into the world of Bach during his years in Strasbourg (see p. 103). But he did not himself conduct any of his music until after the war, when at the opening concert of the first Rhenish Chamber Music Festival at Schloss Brühl on 23 May 1921 he had directed a performance of the Brandenburg Concerto No. 1 in F major from a harpsichord. His decision to give the work with solo instruments (a decision that excited much comment) suggests that, unlike most conductors of his generation, he no longer conceived the music in terms of nineteenth-century orchestral sonorities.† When three years later he included the work in one of his early Berlin concerts (21 November 1924), he again performed it with solo instruments. That he on this occasion played the continuo on a grand piano can be attributed to the size of the Philharmonie. Later in that season, on 22 June

---

* Eduard Erdmann (1896–1958), German pianist of some standing who composed in an idiom generally described as 'expressionist'. Klemperer conducted his Piano Concerto with the composer as soloist on 4 October 1929. Josef Hauer (1883–1959), Austrian composer who in 1919 devised 'a law of the twelve notes' which thus predated the publication of Schoenberg's twelve-note system in 1923. Klemperer conducted his *Sinfonietta* (13 December 1928), *Wandlungen* (chamber oratorio – 14 June 1930) and excerpts from his opera, *Salambo* (see p. 368).

† In a sleeve note to the German edition of Klemperer's 1960 recordings of the Brandenburg Concertos (Electrola IC 187-00532-3), Kruttge recalled that Furtwängler performed and in 1930 recorded the third concerto with the full strings of the Berlin Philharmonic Orchestra (Decca CA 8013-4, Polydor 95417-8). In No. 5, he was in the habit of imposing improvisatory flourishes on crucial cadences in a continuo in the manner of Reger.

302

1925 in Wiesbaden, he also gave an all-Bach concert – a rarity at the time.

Nonetheless it was only with time that the full measure of Bach's genius revealed itself to him. From Moscow on 15 March 1929, he wrote to Johanna, 'Bach slowly becomes for me an even greater miracle...In *essentials* music has not advanced since 1750 [Bach's death].' It was thus not until his second season at the Kroll that Bach started to figure regularly in his programmes. The impact of his interpretations was immense. In 1929, musicological investigations into eighteenth-century *Aufführungspraxis* were still in their infancy. Two great musicians had, however, already brought about far-reaching changes. From 1913 to 1919 Wanda Landowska had directed a newly established harpsichord course at the Berlin Musikhochschule.* A more immediate influence on Klemperer was Busoni, who shortly before the outbreak of war had started to prepare a complete edition of Bach's keyboard music that marked a distinct reaction against the heavily romanticised editions of the Inventions and Preludes and Fugues which he had himself published in the 1890s. Following the example of Busoni in his last years, Klemperer used the *Urtexte* in his performance of Bach's instrumental music, and in the case of the Brandenburg concertos was able to study the original manuscripts in the Prussian State Library.

Although he occasionally consulted expert opinion, Klemperer, like most conductors, was neither versed in, nor in the final resort much concerned with, musicological minutiae. But he had an instinctive understanding that Bach had been falsified by the heavy romantic veneer that had been imposed on the music in the nineteenth century. He recognised that 'expressive' dynamics still preferred by most conductors were inappropriate and in their place substituted terraced dynamics. He dispensed with string vibrato, even in slow movements. He also grasped the need for far slimmer instrumental sonorities and more lithe rhythms. Above all, he strove for clarity. But decorations and appoggiaturas remained to the end an unexplored field: Klemperer's Bach was plain and unadorned.

Today, it is apparent that a misconception underlay his purism. As the musicologist Hermann Roth pointed out in a letter to Curjel, after Klemperer's performance of the D major suite at the opening Kroll concert (see p. 257), to play its famous air solely with Bach's own bowings was equivalent to dispensing with appoggiaturas on the ground that they did not appear in the manuscript. An authentic Bach style,

* Klemperer may well have heard Landowska (1879–1959), the musician largely responsible for the revival of the harpsichord, at a Gürzenich concert in Cologne, at which she appeared as soloist and continuo player, in December 1917. (Kruttge, sleeve note)

Roth insisted, could not be based exclusively on literal fidelity to the notes.* Such insights had, however, only gained limited currency in the late twenties, as can be gauged from the approval that Klemperer's Bach performances earned from scholars as reputable as Alfred Einstein and Hugo Leichentritt. And, indeed, in the life brought to inner voices, the lightness of textures and the absence of *espressivo*, even in slow movements, his interpretations represented a distinct advance on contemporary practice. In his approach to Bach, Klemperer was undoubtedly much influenced by the tenets of the *neue Sachlichkeit*. But it would be a mistake to suppose that his performances were therefore cold or mechanical. Max Strub later recalled how in a slow movement of the Suite in D major, which Klemperer conducted virtually without gestures, he brought such inner concentration to the music that he burst into a profuse sweat.[10]

Klemperer opened his concert of 7 February 1929 with a performance of the Brandenburg Concerto No. 6, which he himself directed from a harpsichord and in which all seven parts were played by soloists who included Wolfsthal, Hindemith and Eva Heinitz on instruments borrowed from the Musikhochschule.† In Einstein's view, it was a performance that revealed stylistic insight as well as the utmost musicality.[11] By no means all critics shared his enthusiasm. When, on 25 April 1929, Klemperer opened another Kroll concert with the Brandenburg Concerto No. 4 in G major, performed with the three soloists accompanied by only a small group of ripieno strings, Marschalk criticised the relentless severity of the interpretation. 'When one sees him standing guard over the tempo, one cannot help feeling that a metronome would do as well.'[12] He also objected to the reductions of all dynamics to forte and piano, while Fritz Ohrmann asserted that Klemperer's motorised rhythms drained the music of emotion.[13] But Einstein, on this occasion supported by a majority of his colleagues, asserted that the performance was 'as lively as it was "historically" right...perfect in balance and in its union of severity, delicacy and fire – at last Bach without a ritardando at every cadence'.[14]

When in the following season Klemperer ventured an all-Bach concert, empty seats on 14 November 1929 served to underline the unusualness of such an event, even in a city as musically alert as Berlin. Once again, the old guard put up stiff resistance. Otto Steinhagen denounced terraced dynamics as an error of the times;[15] others renewed their complaints at what they took to be a suppression of emotional response to the music. But Einstein again came to Klemperer's defence.

* Hermann Roth (1882–1938), editor of Bach and Handel. Letter of 10 October 1927.
† Among them a viola da gamba, an instrument at that time so rare that Eva Heinitz claims to have been the only player of it in Berlin.

The many listeners who...avoided Otto Klemperer's second concert deprived themselves of one of the real 'events' of the Berlin musical winter: the performance of Bach's Brandenburg Concerto No. 1. One hardly ever hears it; conductors are frightened of the harsh sounds of the exposed horns, which they seek to wrap up in a welter of strings...Klemperer has the courage and the sense of style: the baroque humour of the first movement, the boldness and subtlety of the adagio, the bucolic high spirits of the minuet, with the uncouth and tender episodes that are part of a *fête champêtre*, all come into happy prominence. They even managed to lay hands on a violino piccolo...It is not just a matter of a faithfulness to the text, the avoidance of the usual vices of today, such as an exaggeration of cadences, that distinguishes Klemperer's Bach interpretations. It is his fiery feeling for the inner...life of every voice, his lack of academicism, the naive strength which seems in Bach not an 'old classic', but music for today and always.[16]

In later years Klemperer's Bach came to be widely regarded as heavy-handed and old-fashioned, and nowhere more so than in London in the 1960s, by which time he had taken to performing the Suites with a larger orchestra than he had used in Berlin.[17] When, only eight days after his all-Bach concert at the Kroll, he made his first appearance in London on 20 November 1929, Francis Toye was not alone in finding his account of the Suite No. 3 in D major 'very heavy, almost lumpy',[18] though Ernest Newman was inclined to attribute these defects to shortcomings in the orchestral playing.[19] But in Berlin Klemperer's Bach found widespread recognition, even among musicians who did not go along with everything that occurred in his opera house.

      *   *   *

It was not mere coincidence that Hindemith was the solo violist in the performance of the Brandenburg Concerto No. 6 on 7 February 1929 and that the same concert included recent works by Stravinsky, Weill and Hindemith himself. Programmes of this sort, which thereafter became a feature of the Kroll, in themselves embodied a programme. By linking such composers with works by Bach, Klemperer was nailing neo-classical colours to his mast-head.

In spite – or, as Weill himself suspected[20] because – of his rejection of *Mahagonny*, Klemperer was eager to give the first performance of his new cantata, *Lindberghflug*, a revised version of the *Lehrstück* by Brecht that Hindemith and Weill had originally composed as a joint undertaking for the Baden-Baden festival of 1929. A quarrel had subsequently occurred between Hindemith, for whom the work's pedagogic purpose was exclusively musical, in the sense that it provided a score that could be sung by amateurs, and Brecht, for whom it was primarily a means of political indoctrination. With Hindemith's agreement, Weill accordingly recomposed the text as a concert piece, completing it less than a fortnight before Klemperer gave its first performance on 5 December 1929. Almost exactly a year later, on 7 December 1930, *Der Jasager*, a subsequent *Lehrstück* for children that had had a first and controversial performance at the Berlin Festival of 1930, was also given at the Kroll by schoolchildren in the teeth of the composer's opposition.* That more works by Weill were not performed at the Kroll was due only to the fact that during the years of the theatre's independent existence he composed little (apart from *Mahagonny*) that was suitable either to its concerts or to its operatic repertory.

In contrast, Hindemith provided a steady flow of orchestral pieces of all shapes and sizes that found ready acceptance at the Kroll. The concert that saw the first performance of Weill's *Lindberghflug* also included the first Berlin hearing of Hindemith's early Cello Concerto (*Kammermusik No. 3*) with Emmanuel Feuermann as soloist.† That was, however, by no means the first orchestral score by Hindemith to be heard at the Kroll. As early as 3 November 1927, and with the composer as soloist, Klemperer had conducted the first performance of his new Viola Concerto (*Kammermusik No. 5*), which had been commissioned for the occasion. This had been followed on 11 May 1928 by the first Berlin performance of the Concert Music for Wind Orchestra, Op. 41. On 7 February 1929 Josef Wolfsthal had played the Violin Concerto (*Kammermusik No. 4*). On 27 November 1930 Hindemith was again the soloist in his recent Concert Music for Solo Viola and Chamber Orchestra, Op. 48; in his last concert at the Kroll on 25 April 1931, Klemperer accompanied Walter Gieseking in the first Berlin performance of the recently composed Concert Music for Piano, Brass and Harps, Op. 49. During his four years at the Kroll, he conducted no fewer than three operas and six orchestral works by Hindemith.‡

But if Hindemith, who was living in Berlin at the time, led the field in

---

* Weill regarded the work as quite out of place in a professional theatre (letter to Universal Edition, 11 November 1930).

† Klemperer had got to know Feuermann (1902–1942) when the prodigiously gifted sixteen year old had arrived after the war in Cologne, where he had become leader of the cello section of the Gürzenich Orchestra and a teacher at the Conservatory. On 30 June 1923 Feuermann was the soloist in a performance of Dvořák's Concerto at one of Klemperer's opera house concerts. In 1929 he moved to Berlin and it is indicative of the high regard in which Klemperer held him that he at once seized the chance to work with him again. The two men appeared together on several occasions in America before Feuermann's sudden and premature death.

‡ A further collaboration was planned, though not in connection with the Kroll. In November 1928, Diaghilev commissioned a score from Hindemith to be based on a scenario about a six-day bicycle race. It was to have been entitled *No. 27* and a few days before his death in August 1929 Diaghilev showed his travelling companion, the young Igor Markevitch, a letter in which Klemperer had agreed to conduct the work, together with a new ballet score by Markevitch. Neither project came to fruition. Thus Diaghilev's death prevented the only occasion on which the disparate worlds of the Ballets Russes and the Kroll might have momentarily impinged on each other. (See Buckle, *Diaghilev*, pp. 516–17, and Markevitch, *Être et avoir été*, p. 187.)

306

quantity, Klemperer owed a far deeper allegiance to Stravinsky. During the Kroll's four years of existence Klemperer regularly gave the first Berlin performance of each new work, often immediately after it had become available, and the composer appeared on no less than three occasions as soloist in his own music. *Apollo*, which had so enchanted Klemperer when Stravinsky had played it to him on the piano on the occasion of his visit to Berlin for the staging of *Oedipus Rex*, led the way on 1 November 1928. It was not, however, well received, Strobel finding its simplicity 'affected' and its harmony 'sweet'.[21] A reason for this failure only became apparent when Klemperer repeated the work at an all-Stravinsky concert given as part of the Berlin Festival of 1929. On this occasion the composer, who was to play his own Piano Concerto, was present at a rehearsal. Klemperer had hardly begun *Apollo* when Stravinsky stood up. 'I hear nothing. It is all soup', he called, and there and then halved the numbers of the first strings, making corresponding reductions in the other parts.* There was an immediate improvement. That was not, however, Stravinsky's only interruption. At one point he called out, 'Herr Klemperer! Metronome 108. You have 112.' Klemperer unhesitatingly complied.[22]

On 17 June the theatre was packed to its rafters; the stalls teemed with representatives of the city's intellectual and cultural life, the balconies were full of young people.[23] *Apollo* was received with an enthusiasm conspicuously lacking earlier in the season. There was much applause for Stravinsky's playing of his concerto. But the triumph of the evening was the concluding performance of *Les Noces*. Georg Szell and Fritz Zweig were among the four pianists and the chorus had been prepared by Karl Rankl.† Its success with both critics and public was so great that Klemperer repeated the work on 5 December 1929.

On 23 January 1930 Stravinsky appeared again at the Kroll, on this occasion as soloist in his most recent work, *Capriccio*, which had had its première in Paris only six weeks earlier.‡ The concert opened with another recent work, the suite from *Le Baiser de la fée*, which had also not previously been heard in Berlin. This cool confrontation with the romantic genius of Tchaikovsky confounded the entrenched attitudes of many Berlin critics. The conservatives found themselves praising what they chose to regard as

---

* This story, which was related to the author by Gerhard Meyer-Sichting, one of the violinists concerned, is confirmed in Stravinsky's *Chroniques de ma vie*, Vol. 2, pp. 117–19, where details of the reduction (but no date) are given.

† Karl Rankl (1898–1968). Chorusmaster at the Kroll (1928–31), musical director at the German Opera House in Prague (1937–9) and the Royal Opera House, Covent Garden (1946–51). Rankl also conducted a number of performances at the Kroll during its last two seasons and served as chorusmaster of the Berlin Philharmonic Chorus (see p. 383).

‡ On 6 August 1929, three months before he completed the work, he had written to his Berlin agents, Wolff und Sachs, 'I do not want to deprive myself of the pleasure of playing my new concerto with Klemperer in the first year of its existence.'

Stravinsky's new-found warmth; the advance guard had difficulty in squaring its admiration for Stravinsky with this unexpected evolution in his style. The doctrinaire Strobel in particular cautioned that it would lead to 'a dangerous reaction', were weaker personalities to dally with an 'Empfindsamkeit' ('sensibility') rejected by new music in general, and by Stravinsky in his strongest periods of creativity.[24]

Klemperer harboured no such doubts about *Capriccio*. On receiving the score he at once wrote to the 'Hochverehrter Meister' to express admiration for 'the new and original way in which your spirit again expressed itself'.* At his request Stravinsky arrived in Berlin early enough to permit three orchestral rehearsals to be devoted exclusively to the work. Yet, though Klemperer had described the music as 'difficult', it was the composer who seems to have suffered stage fright after the dress rehearsal, when he announced that he had damaged a finger and for a while insisted that he would not be able to perform.[25] In Berlin both the work and the performance were warmly received. But when Stravinsky and Klemperer repeated it seven days later with the Gewandhaus Orchestra in Leipzig, Adolf Aber dismissed it as no more than the product of 'a witty conversationalist',[26] a not uncommon view of the 'Parisian' Stravinsky in the German provinces during the Weimar Republic. Outside Berlin, indeed, Stravinsky's neo-classical works had made so little headway in Germany that the composer's agents had been unable to arrange for him and Klemperer to perform *Capriccio* in any other cities.[27]

*   *   *

Klemperer regarded the Berlin Staatskapelle as a first-rate orchestra, well able to meet his requirements, even if on occasions he resented the bureaucratic attitudes its members were prone to adopt as state employees. They in their turn resented his tendency to over-rehearse. As a result, only a minority seem to have regarded him with much affection. With time, however, his hard-driven instrumentalists came to realise that his exigence stemmed, not from a mere desire to impose his will, but from a passionate concern with the matter in hand. As its leader, Max Strub, later recalled, the members of the Staatskapelle 'felt themselves from the start seized by the undertaking [of the Kroll]. What was at first a sort of curiosity was transformed into engagement (Arbeitsinteresse)...The demands made of the players were enormous and there were fusses and upsets in abundance, but these were outweighed by the results.'[28]

In other cities relations between Klemperer and orchestras that knew him less well were often tense and on occasions turbulent. His revised contract of July 1928 enabled him to make more guest appearances in

---

* Letter of 1 January 1930. In his reply of three days later Stravinsky addressed Klemperer as 'Mein lieber Freund'.

the German provinces and abroad than had been possible since leaving Wiesbaden. But these visits were usually of short duration and thus provided insufficient time for orchestras to come to terms with their exacting taskmaster. Nor were they always in a position to meet his technical demands. Klemperer hated subservience in personal dealings. But on the platform he was a ruthless authoritarian, who sometimes seemed bent on breaking an orchestra's will as a preliminary to securing its co-operation.* On more than one occasion these tactics drove an orchestra to open revolt. Yet trials of strength, such as occurred in early 1930 in Erfurt and Dresden, generally ended in triumph. In the final resort Klemperer had an uncanny ability to overcome resistance he had himself awakened.†

On 24 October 1928 Klemperer conducted an orchestral concert in Hamburg for the first time since the scandal sixteen years earlier. On arrival, he was delighted to find himself once again in the city in which he had grown up, though distinctly apprehensive lest his return should lead to references to the incident in the press.[29] But the welcome his concert received from the critics made his home-coming doubly gratifying. When, three months later, he returned for a further concert whose success was even greater, old Ferdinand Pfohl, the critic of the *Hamburger Nachrichten*, who had witnessed his triumphant début with *Lohengrin* in 1910, wrote glowingly of the maturity he had since achieved. Like a fine wine, he had become *durchgegoren* (matured) with the years.[30] Henceforth Klemperer returned with fair regularity to the city that he still regarded as his home town.

Early in December 1928 he made another pilgrimage into his past: for the first and last time in his career, he conducted in Breslau, where he had been born. Paradoxically, the return of the native did not evoke special enthusiasm: the critics in the remote Silesian capital found his Bach dry, his Mozart lacking in poetry and Stravinsky's *Pulcinella* suite a matter of 'musical grimaces'.

---

* Similar treatment was sometimes meted out to soloists, as when at short notice the 22-year-old Claudio Arrau was called to Wiesbaden in February 1925 to deputise for Schnabel in Schumann's Piano Concerto. During rehearsal he was unnerved by a ceaseless battery of criticism from Klemperer, who afterwards retained the young pianist to demonstrate himself precisely how he wanted the work to be played. 'Klemperer was so nasty', Arrau later recalled. 'After many, many years when we played together again and I had become much more assured, I said, "Do you remember what you did to me in Wiesbaden?"...He couldn't believe it when I told him about it – how much damage it had done to me, at a moment when I was still developing' (Joseph Horowitz, *Conversations with Arrau*, pp. 17–18). Later collaborations were more harmonious.

† Karl E. Hesse, a member of the Dresdener Staatskapelle, has recalled how after some particularly tense and unfriendly rehearsals the orchestra determined on passive resistance at the concert (4 April 1930). To Hesse's amazement, as soon as Klemperer raised his baton, the orchestra played with unparalleled warmth and intensity, such as it did not provide even for its permanent conductor, Fritz Busch.

As his reputation spread, invitations to appear abroad arrived with increasing frequency. On 21 and 23 December he conducted for the first time in Paris. Once again, the city delighted him. As he noted in a letter (18 December 1928) to his friend Helmuth Plessner, 'It's curious. In fact nothing at all is happening either at the opera or in the theatre...In spite of that the [place as a] whole is so stimulating and refreshing that finally one can only suppose that it lies in the air.' Although he described the players as 'excellent' his initial encounters with them did not go smoothly. The youthful Orchestre Symphonique de Paris, which had only been established earlier in the year by Pierre Monteux,* found him a harsh taskmaster, prone to terrifying rages.† At a wrong entry in Beethoven's Symphony No. 7, Klemperer turned to observe the leader of the orchestra pulling what he took to be a disrespectful face. Unaware that the man had suffered facial injury in the First World War, his fury rose to new heights. Equally enraged, the leader replied, 'That is the face *you* gave me.' For a moment it seemed as though there would be physical violence.³¹ Once he was made aware of the facts, Klemperer hastened to apologise. But the leader, nursing his hatred of *les boches*, declined to accept his hand and refused to play at the concert.

Nonetheless, Klemperer's force of character and musicianship again triumphed. The young orchestra finally succumbed to his uncanny ability to convey 'the idea as well as the sound',³² while he found its woodwind much to his taste, notably in Stravinsky's music. His plain, unadorned approach to Bach met with a mixed response from an audience whose taste had been largely conditioned by Casals's more romantic interpretations, and neither Hindemith's *Concert Music for Wind Orchestra* nor Krenek's *Kleine Symphonie*,‡ both of which were new to Paris, aroused more than respectful interest. But after the second concert a correspondent of the *Berliner Tageblatt* (27 December 1928) reported that Stravinsky's *Pulcinella* suite and Beethoven's Symphony No. 7 had given rise to such 'indescribable enthusiasm' that an early return to Paris seemed certain.

In a letter written after the first concert on 21 December Arthur Lourié (see p. 213) reported to Stravinsky that Klemperer had given *Pulcinella* with unusual accuracy and precision. 'What an excellent conductor he is, despite his strange movements and mannerisms.'³³ After the second concert Lourié was even more enthusiastic. He also gained a different view

* As conductor of Diaghilev's Ballets Russes, Monteux (1875–1964) gave the first performances of Stravinsky's *Petrushka* and *The Rite of Spring*, Ravel's *Daphnis et Chloe* and Debussy's *Jeux*. He was subsequently conductor in Boston (1920–4), San Francisco (1936–52) and London (LSO, 1961–4).

† These manifestations of his manic condition were recalled forty-five years later by Marc Pincherle in his obituary of Klemperer. *Les Nouvelles Littéraires* (16 July 1973).

‡ Klemperer had conducted its first performance at a Kroll concert on 1 November 1928.

from the orchestra of Klemperer as a man. 'Beside being a magnificent conductor, I think he's a kind and straightforward fellow, warm and sincere.'[34] Before Klemperer had left Paris, plans (which came to nothing) had been made for him to return during the summer to conduct a series of concerts in which Stravinsky himself would play the solo part in his Piano Concerto and Ida Rubinstein would dance in *Le Baiser de la fée.** On 5 January 1929 the *BZ am Mittag* announced that Rubinstein would also appear at the Kroll with Klemperer conducting, but this uncharacteristic flirtation with the world of ballet also proved abortive.

Less than a month later, Klemperer for the first time appeared at the head of the Amsterdam Concertgebouw, which he conducted in three concerts at The Hague and Amsterdam on 19, 20 and 24 January 1929. Here too, not all the players cared for his harsh ways in rehearsal, but, perhaps because Klemperer found the orchestra to be 'the best...I have conducted'† no serious difficulties arose.[35] As a result, he was invited to stand in for Willem Mengelberg three months later, when in concerts on 13, 17 and 18 April he conducted Mahler's Symphony No. 2 and *Das Lied von der Erde* with notable success, though a majority of the critics compared his interpretations unfavourably with Mengelberg's more familiar and leisurely approach.‡

In the last week of February Klemperer and his wife set out for Italy, which she had never visited. Their destination was Rome, where for the first time he conducted the Santa Cecilia Orchestra in two programmes that contained Casella's *Scarlattiana* with the composer as soloist (27 February) and Hindemith's *Concert Music for Wind Orchestra* (3 March), which was accorded a distinctly cool reception. A light schedule for once enabled him to combine work with relaxation and he took special pleasure in showing Johanna a city he was coming to love almost as much as Paris. From Rome they travelled to Vienna, making a brief stop in Venice, which enthralled Johanna and appealed to him far more than it had done in the lonely summer of 1914 (see p. 94). In Vienna, Johanna made no difficulty about a visit to Elisabeth Schumann and they enjoyed 'a particularly nice lunch

* Ida Rubinstein (1885–1960) scored initial success as a mime in Diaghilev's first Paris season of 1909. She subsequently left his company and in 1911 commissioned music from Debussy for d'Annunzio's *Le Martyre de Saint-Sébastien*, in which she danced the title role. In 1934 she similarly commissioned and danced in Stravinsky's *Perséphone*.
† Letter to Dülberg, Leningrad, 10 March 1929. On a card written to Anneliese Reich from Amsterdam on 24 January 1929, he described it as 'grandios'.
‡ Willem Mengelberg (1871–1951), who was conductor of the Amsterdam orchestra from 1895 until 1945, was responsible for raising it to the front rank of European orchestras. He was also one of Mahler's earliest champions. But after the performance of the Symphony No. 2 on 13 April 1929 *De Courant Nieuws van de Dag* commented that Klemperer's faster tempi (he apparently took 87 minutes as against Mengelberg's 110 minutes) were closer to Mahler's own.

with R. Strauss in his grandiose house'.* Later that day in an interview with the *Neues Wiener Journal* Klemperer declared that he 'counted himself with pride among those who honour this musician above all others ...nothing is more precious to me than an hour in the presence of this master'. His respect for creative genius was always deep, but both the sentiment and the rather extravagant language in which it was expressed were uncharacteristic. He was, of course, manic (see pp. 289ff.).

From Vienna Klemperer travelled alone to Russia, where he was to make his longest visit since December 1925. All plans to return in the intervening years had been curtailed. The project that he should conduct *Fidelio* and a complete Beethoven cycle in Leningrad in the centenary year of 1927 had foundered on the refusal of the Prussian Kultusministerium to grant him the requisite leave so soon after his return from a long absence in New York. All that survived in the fourteen days conceded were two performances (19/20 April 1927) with the former Imperial Chapel Choir of the *Missa Solemnis*, a work he had not previously conducted. A visit arranged for the spring of 1928 had similarly been reduced in length owing to the sick-leave he had been obliged to take in the two preceding months (see pp. 267–8). Thus it was not until March 1929 that he was again able to embark on an extensive series of concerts in the Soviet Union.

By this time, however, conditions there were changing; the cultural buds that, especially in Leningrad, had blossomed in the mid-twenties were already beginning to feel a frost that was to harden as Stalin established his grip on power. In 1928 he had felt secure enough to launch his first Five Year Plan and to embark on a ruthless policy of collectivisation of agriculture. In January 1929, Trotsky, who had already been dismissed from his positions within the Party, was exiled. Lunacharsky was on the point of resignation.†

Musical life did not remain untouched by these developments; indeed its evolution during the twenties mirrors the differences that had begun to arise within the Party after Lenin's death in 1924. During the years of the NEP (1921–7), the liberally minded Association for Contemporary Music (ACM) felt free to pursue its open-door policies with a freedom that

---

* Letter from Klemperer to Dülberg, Leningrad, 10 March 1929. On his resignation as director of the State Opera in 1924, the municipality of Vienna had presented Strauss with a site overlooking the gardens of the Belvedere Palace. On it he had built a substantial villa, which the municipality had helped to furnish in princely style. In return, Strauss undertook a number of conducting commitments in Vienna and presented the manuscript score of *Der Rosenkavalier* to the Austrian National Library.

† Although his resignation was not announced until the following September, he offered it in the spring of 1929, after his Commissariat had been stripped of its responsibility for higher education (Fitzpatrick, *Education and Social Mobility in the Soviet Union, 1921–34*, p. 290).

Trotsky had advocated (see p. 213). But as Stalin started to press forward with 'socialism in one country', the opposition group, the Russian Association of Proletarian Musicians (RAPM), whose aims have been described by a moderately minded commentator as 'violently anti-modern, anti-Western, anti-jazz and often anti-classical',* began to gain in importance. In the mid-twenties, it had been no more than 'a small, noisy but unimportant group of second-rate composers'.[36] Early in 1929, however, it felt strong enough to launch a new periodical, *Proletarskiy muzïkant*, whose aim was to combat the influence of 'decadent' bourgeois music.[37] In June 1929 an All-Russian Music Conference was convened in Leningrad, nominally to resolve differences in musical policies, in fact to enforce the Party's support of the RAPM.† Members of the ACM, which died a natural death, henceforth hastened to join their opponents. Contemporary music from the West largely ceased to figure in orchestral programmes after the 1929/30 season. Stravinsky's new works were not heard after 1929.[38] The Stalinist ice-age had dawned.

Blithely unaware of these gathering tensions, Klemperer had on this visit elected to perform a number of works that, for one reason or another, were liable to arouse controversy. His opening programme on 12 March 1929, which included the first performance in Russia of *Das Lied von der Erde* was comparatively innocuous. Until the mid-twenties Russia had evinced little enthusiasm for either Bruckner or Mahler.‡ But thereafter interest in Mahler began to grow, at any rate in Leningrad, after two decades of neglect.§ After 1926 Central European conductors started to perform the

---

* Schwarz, *Music and Musical Life in Soviet Russia, 1917–1970*, p. 58. It would, of course, be an error to regard such attitudes as intrinsically Marxist. Realism and national folk-song, together with suspicion of *l'art pour l'art* and Western aestheticism, figure prominently in Russian nineteenth-century music. Under Stalin, however, nationalism, which had previously been musically 'progressive', allied itself to anti-modernism and to the Party's search for proletarian roots. It is not mere coincidence that both the style of music favoured and the terminology in which it was advocated bore a distinct resemblance to subsequent developments in Germany under the Nazis, even to the point of a common pejorative use of the word 'Left' (see Gojowy, *Neue sowjetische Musik der 20er Jahren*, pp. 5–14). In both countries (as so often in the subsequent history of the twentieth century), socialism and nationalism discovered themselves to be natural allies.
† This has been denied, presumably on the ground that in 1932 the RAPM was itself swallowed up in the Union of Composers, henceforth the instrument the Party used to enforce its will on musical life. But the policies pursued by the Party in the years of Stalin's rule evolved directly out of those advocated by the RAPM.
‡ When on 13 April 1927 Klemperer conducted what appears to have been the first Russian performance of Bruckner's Symphony No. 8, Nikolay Malkov had found the music's 'static monumentality and...length...oppressive' (*Zhizn' iskusstva*, 19 April 1927).
§ Fried had conducted the Symphony No. 2 in 1906 and Mahler himself the Symphony No. 5 in 1907. Only lack of rehearsal time and a shortage of instrumental resources had prevented Klemperer from performing Nos 2 and 9 in 1924 and 1925 (*Zhizn' iskusstva*, 24 March 1925, interview with Klemperer).

313

symphonies there with some regularity and their impact on members of the younger generation was immense. In particular, Ivan Sollertinsky and his close friend, Dmitry Shostakovich, became fervent Mahlerians.* According to the conductor, Nikolay Mal'ko, Sollertinsky even approached Klemperer, with whom he later became well acquainted, in the street with a request that he include works by Mahler in his programmes.†

Sollertinsky subsequently maintained that he had never heard so deeply satisfying an account of the last movement of *Das Lied von der Erde* as that given by Klemperer.‡ In *Zhisn' iskusstva* he hailed the performance as a blow struck against the widespread Russian prejudice that Mahler was yet another German composer of his time who attempted to 'disguise the poverty of his musical thought...through the convulsive clamour of a gigantic orchestra'. On the contrary, Sollertinsky maintained, his use of trivial and popular melodies, which were then subjected to elaborate contrapuntal and instrumental development, presaged a new form of symphonic music that was 'urban, "democratised"...and (despite its exceptional complexity) meant to be grasped by the broad masses', while harmonically it led straight into the world of Schoenberg.[39] When, however, Klemperer repeated the work in Moscow on 31 March, reactions varied in a way that reflected the growing tensions within Russian musical life. While *Muzïka i revolyutsiya* (1929, No. 2), the organ of the ACM, described it as 'a work of great feeling...whose gloom is akin to the tragic pathos of antiquity', *Proletarskiy muzïkant* (1929, No. 2), the new mouthpiece of the RAPM, dismissed as 'utterly trivial', 'eclectically tasteless' and 'absolutely formless' music that, it claimed, expressed nothing but 'the depression and boredom of the German philistine'.§

Weill's *Kleine Dreigroschenmusik*, which Klemperer included in his first Moscow programme on 16 and 17 March, pedictably aroused even fiercer controversy. A packed hall (Meyerhold and Tairov, both of whom afterwards joined a supper party given for Klemperer, were among the audience) greeted the work with enthusiasm, while the 'Kanonenlied' aroused so much laughter that it had to be repeated. Other reactions were markedly less favourable. Even before the concert had taken place, Nikolay Golovanov,

* Ivan Sollertinsky (1902–44), critic and musicologist. Lector (1929–41) and artistic director (1941–4) of the Leningrad Philharmonic Orchestra. Author of studies of, among others, Mahler and Schoenberg. Shostakovich dedicated his Piano Trio (1944) to the memory of his lifelong friend.
† Mikheyeva (ed.), *Pamyalï I. I. Sollertinskogo*, p. 144. The present writer has a similar recollection of the performance that Klemperer conducted in London on his eighty-fifth birthday.
‡ Mikheyeva, p. 108.
§ Mahler's music later fell into disfavour as 'reactionary' and only began to be performed again in the Soviet Union after 1956 (Blaukopf, 'Zur Mahler Rezeption in Russland', *HiFi Stereophonie*, December 1980).

who was preparing it for Klemperer prior to his arrival from Leningrad, described it in a letter (13 March) as 'pretty rubbishy'.* The critics shared that view. *Muzïka i revolyutsiya* (1929, No. 2) frowned on what it described as an example of 'the jazz-band music that has swamped the West and has...even penetrated to us', and in its next issue denounced the inclusion of the work in a concert as 'entirely unjustified'. *Proletarskiy muzïkant* (1929, No. 2) similarly dismissed it as 'characteristic of post-war bourgeois Germany', and added, 'It is hard to suppose that a musician such as Klemperer takes this "art" seriously.'

There is, however, every reason to suppose that he did. Anticipating that the work was likely to be misunderstood, as it had been at its first performance in Berlin only a month earlier, he went to the trouble of writing a brief introduction for the programme.† When, at the party afterwards, a guest suggested that the music was meretricious, Klemperer sat down at a piano and played it through, after which he turned to his audience and said, 'It's really a classical piece, even if not in the Viennese style'.[40]

Paradoxically, Janáček's *Sinfonietta*, whose folk-song material might have been expected to appeal to the RAPM's organ, was rejected by *Proletarskiy muzïkant* on the grounds that the composer's use of it was 'coarse' and 'mechanical'. *Muzïka i revolyutsiya* concurred: 'the music is fresh and sincere...But what poverty of development, what slightness of form, what an absence of symphonic thinking in the true sense of the word.' Klemperer had no more success as an advocate of Janáček's music in Slav Moscow than he had had in Cologne or New York.

Stravinsky fared little better. The enthusiasm that *Pulcinella* had aroused in 1925 had not been extended to the first Russian performance of the Suite No. 2, which Klemperer conducted in Leningrad on 10 April 1927, when Nikolay Malkov had sourly described the little pieces as 'the extremely unattractive grimaces' of a talented composer, 'who is reduced to making coarse jokes...as if he had nothing else to say'.[41] Nor was there a warm response to the first Russian performance of *Apollo*, which Klemperer gave in Moscow on 31 March 1929. *Proletarskiy muzïkant* passed the event over in silence. *Muzïka i revolyutsiya* (1929, No. 2) found the work 'monotonous and feeble' and branded its composer as a 'child of musical fortune'.

* Golovanov, *Literaturnoye naslediye. Perepiska. Vospominaniya sovremennikov*, p. 96. Golovanov (1891–1958), chief conductor at the Bol'shoy Theatre (1919–28 and 1948–53) and of the USSR All-Union Radio Orchestra (1937–58). Married to the celebrated soprano Antonina Nezhdanova (1873–1950). It was Golovanov who gave the post-concert party, after which he noted in a letter to his wife (18 March 1929) that Klemperer had begun to understand and even to speak a little Russian.

† Letter to Johanna Klemperer, Moscow, 15 March 1929. The note does not, however, seem to have been published.

Braudo also considered that it had left no deep impression.[42] Only Sollertinsky, who described it as 'serious, beautiful if rather cool music with a tendency towards classicism in the best sense of the word',[43] seems to have taken the measure of Stravinsky's most recent score after Klemperer repeated it in Leningrad on 2 and 3 April. But it was Moscow, the stronghold of the RAPM, that was increasingly to set the tone of Soviet reactions to new music.

Modernism was, however, not the only category of music to draw frowns. In an atheistic state, religious and liturgical works were inevitably regarded with disfavour. When two years earlier Klemperer had conducted the *Missa Solemnis*, a work that had not been heard in Leningrad since the revolution, the critics had found it necessary to minimise the work's religious significance. *Zhizn' iskusstva* (3 May) tactfully described it as 'a majestic hymn to nature...thoroughly imbued with an optimistic spirit' and went on to praise Klemperer's brisk tempi as suitably 'secular'. Thus, concurred Valerian Bogdanov-Berezovsky in *Rabochiy i teatr*, 'the religious emotions that perhaps gave impulse to the work's creation disappeared'.*

There was a similar reaction when on 27 and 28 March 1929 Klemperer conducted a concert of excerpts from *Parsifal*, including the entire last act. That he should have chosen to do so comes as a twofold surprise. The cloudy Christian mysticism of Wagner's 'sacred' opera was hardly calculated to appeal to the authorities. Nor was it a work to which Klemperer himself was attached. Indeed, as a Catholic, he regarded it as not far short of blasphemous, which may account for the fact that he had conducted it only rarely and did not do so again after 1929. But the fact that there was no prospect of hearing the opera in the theatre may have led to demands that excerpts be given in the Philharmonic, demands which may have awoken Klemperer's ever-lively spirit of opposition. That such an event was still possible early in 1929 in Leningrad (it is perhaps significant that the performances were not repeated in Moscow) indicates that a liberal spirit still survived in the old capital. Nonetheless in the semi-official *Zhizn' iskusstva* (7 April) Nikolay Malkov chose his words carefully. The work's religious and mystical emotions, he wrote, were not relevant to the present times or to present-day composers. It should accordingly be regarded in its historical perspective, so that its ideological content would be rendered harmless and attention concentrated on the beauties of the music. Such an event, continued Malkov, might have been redeemed by a performance of high calibre. Unfortunately, that had not been the case.

This was by no means the only complaint about the level of the

---

* When Klemperer conducted the work three years later in Berlin it was widely felt that, on the contrary, he had restored spiritual significance to a score that was too often approached as concert music (see p. 325).

performances that Klemperer conducted in Leningrad during his 1929 visit. As Malkov admitted, the authorities were partly to blame for foisting on him a back-breaking schedule which obliged him to give within a period of a month no fewer than seven taxing programmes (those in Leningrad were repeated) with two orchestras, neither of which was familiar with much of the music it was called on to perform. Klemperer was indeed a grossly over-burdened man. 'Today', he wrote to his wife from Moscow on 22 March, 'I have had a stroke of luck; an orchestral rehearsal has been cancelled...that has been a great joy (when each week one conducts three concerts and eight rehearsals it's understandable, isn't it?)...Tomorrow... the rehearsal grind begins again.' Such complaints were uncharacteristic of a conductor who more usually complained about a lack of rehearsals.

His manic condition added to tensions, and the shortcomings of the Leningrad orchestra led to scenes. In a rehearsal for *Das Lied von der Erde* he obliged the harpist to repeat a phrase until she burst into tears. Klemperer sarcastically called for valerian drops and added, 'The dear lady seems too nervous to work in an orchestra'.* Such behaviour, which was regarded by Russian musicians as all too characteristic of visiting German conductors, may have contributed to a collaboration that was less than whole-hearted. At all events, Klemperer, who felt the orchestra to be handicapped by poor instruments, was dissatisfied with the results he achieved in his second Leningrad concert.[44] So, too, were the reviewers, whose dissatisfaction grew increasingly open with each successive concert. *Zhizn' iskusstva* (1 April) criticised unwieldy sonorities in a Bach suite and slow tempi and a lack of Russianness in *Petrushka*. Sollertinsky was not alone in noticing what he described as 'a degree of indifference' in performances (the first Klemperer had ever given) of Brahms's *Ein deutsches Requiem* in Leningrad on 2 and 3 April. Such a deficiency, he added, was particularly perceptible to those who recalled the memorable account of Brahms's Symphony No. 4, with which he had made his début in the same hall four seasons earlier.[45]

Wind of the tension that had been gathering in Leningrad since Klemperer's first concert there in mid-March may have reached Moscow, where Golovanov, who was preparing the recently formed Sofil Orchestra†

---

* Ginzburg, *Izbrannoye*, p. 76, who tells of another occasion when an orchestral player neatly turned the tables on his tormentor. When the first flute made an error, Klemperer caustically observed, 'It seems as though you've never played in Beethoven's Seventh Symphony.' The flautist gravely nodded assent, whereupon Klemperer yelled, 'You should be in a waxworks, not an orchestra.' The flautist quietly replied, 'Ask the maestro if he knows Glinka's *A Life for the Tsar*.' Klemperer (who may not have been familiar with the Russian title): 'What's that?' Flautist: 'Tell the maestro that there is a spare place beside me in the waxworks.'

† Sofil (Sovetskaya Filarmoniya), an all-Union organisation had been founded in 1928 to remedy, among other deficiencies, the endemic disorganisation of Moscow's concert life

for Klemperer's concerts, was apprehensive lest it fail to satisfy a notoriously exacting visitor.[46] Contrary to Golovanov's fears, Klemperer was delighted. The Sofil Orchestra, he wrote on 15 March to his wife, was 'very good (much better than Leningrad). It plays *Petrushka* as I've never heard it played, so earthily (urwüchsig).' That favourable impression survived throughout the visit, and his Moscow concerts attracted none of the unfavourable comment those in Leningrad had aroused. 'Of all the musicians from abroad', wrote *Komsomol'skaya pravda* (26 March) 'Klemperer is closest to us in his artistic cast of mind.' *Vechernyaya Moskva* (22 March) described him as 'a striking example of a new type of per- former...who transforms the vast culture of the past...into a weapon of the present-day'. Both journals, however, felt obliged to salute him as an 'optimist' and 'a life-affirming artist'.

Perhaps in part because the orchestra was more to his taste, Klemperer on this visit soon reversed his earlier preference for Leningrad (see pp. 223–4). 'I have been here for two days', he wrote to his wife on 15 March, 'and I must say that this city is much more agreeable than Leningrad...the people of today fit much better into *this* architecture than into the "aristocratic" ("fein") architecture of Leningrad.' In Moscow, Klemperer and the young orchestra manifestly warmed to each other. Before he left he wrote a glowing testimonial to its 'quality of tone, musical virtuosity and, not least, [its] thoughtful attitude',[47] and on the day before his departure the orchestra in its turn gave him a farewell party.*

Before Klemperer left Moscow there were discussions with the Bol'shoy Theatre about a new production of *Fidelio*.[48] But he was not to return to the Soviet Union for six years. Events were moving fast and the party leaders, such as Trotsky, Lunacharsky and Chicherin, with whom he had come into contact, had either fallen from power or were about to do so.† The cultural climate which had drawn him to the Soviet Union and in

(*Iskusstvo*, 1929, pp. 123–4). Sofil founded a concert orchestra, which the capital had hitherto lacked. This first played in public on 16 November 1928. It soon collapsed, however, and in 1931 the Moscow State Philharmonic Orchestra arose out of its ashes.

* The speech that Klemperer made on this occasion was published in *Sovetskaya Filarmoniya* (19 April). In it he referred to the conductorless Persimfans Orchestra, which he had heard perform Beethoven and Tchaikovsky symphonies so impressively that, as he put it, 'I was obliged to ask myself a serious question: is a conductor really necessary? In the last analysis I remain the opinion that [he is]. First, there are new works of such complexity that an assured performance without a conductor is scarcely possible. Secondly, however precisely detail is prepared in rehearsal, at the actual concert there is always an improvised "something"...in respect of rhythm or dynamics and this can only derive from a conductor. This improvisation inspires a performance and...makes...a conductor essen- tial. Otherwise a performance is machine-like...whereas music is a part of life itself.'

† On 25 April 1927 Lunacharsky had himself introduced Klemperer's Beethoven centenary concert in Moscow (see also p. 261 and n.). Chicherin, who ceased to be Foreign Minister in 1930, had made at least two visits to hear him conduct in Wiesbaden (see p. 247).

318

which he had on earlier visits enjoyed triumphs unprecedented in his career, was giving way to a cruel and obscurantist tyranny whose musical policies were correspondingly primitive.

*   *   *

It was not until November 1929 that Klemperer first appeared in London, the city that was to be so intimately connected with the final phase of his career. The delay was not, however, due to insular unawareness of his stature. In 1927 he had turned down one invitation from London in favour of another from the Royal Philharmonic Society to give the first British performance of *Oedipus Rex* with the actor, Herbert Marshall, as narrator, a project which foundered when he insisted on more than the three rehearsals earlier agreed and subsequently refused to accept a Beethoven programme as an alternative.[49] Lack of rehearsal (one single run through on the morning of the concert was all that was often considered necessary) and a pernicious deputy system, whereby players who had appeared for rehearsal were not bound to play at the concert, between them ensured that the concert life in Europe's largest and richest city remained on a comparatively low level. But in the spring of 1929, Elizabeth Courtauld, whose husband, Samuel, was head of a great textile concern, determined to remedy the situation. Mrs Courtauld had met Schnabel at the house of his friend, Robert Mayer,* where he had fired her enthusiasm for a plan to set up in London a series of concerts after the pattern of those that Kestenberg had established at the Berlin Volksbühne. There was to be a minimum of three rehearsals for each concert (more in the case of new works), and subscription tickets were to be available at modest prices. Malcolm Sargent was appointed conductor.† Partly on account of the lavish receptions given after the concerts by their *patronne*, the Courtauld–Sargent Concerts, which remained a feature of London's musical life until their demise in 1940, developed on a social pattern very different from that of their model in Berlin. But for the first time in many years London benefited from the existence of a concert-giving organisation with a coherent artistic policy.‡

It was Schnabel who urged Klemperer's merits on Elizabeth Courtauld and he was duly engaged to conduct the second concert of her opening

---

* Sir Robert Mayer (1879–   ), with his wife, Dorothy Moulton, founder of the first series of children's concerts to be established in London. A far-sighted musical benefactor and patron.

† Sir Malcolm Sargent (1895–1967). From 1928 conductor of the Royal Choral Society. Chief conductor of the BBC Symphony Orchestra, 1950–7.

‡ The BBC Symphony Orchestra, which more than any other institution breathed new life into the city's orchestral scene, was not established until 1930. Beecham launched his London Philharmonic Orchestra two years later.

season.* As in so many other cities, he chose to make his London début with Bruckner's Eighth Symphony.† If he was aware that Bruckner was little performed and even less admired in England, those were not considerations calculated to deter him.‡ He was, however, dismayed by orchestral playing that remained as indifferent at the last rehearsal as it had been at the first. That was not altogether surprising: several members of the brass section that performed at the concert were different from those he had rehearsed. The orchestra, he wrote on a later visit to London, was simply 'unsuitable for Bruckner'.§

Nor did the players warm to this alarming German giant. The first flute subsequently described Klemperer as 'a recrudescence of Prussianism', who was 'more concerned to terrorise us than anything else, and with war memories not far away, it did not make for full mutual understanding'.[50] Other survivors from Klemperer's pre-war London appearances confirm that what they regarded as his bullying methods excited an almost mutinous atmosphere. At one point in rehearsal Klemperer marched over to a brass player and seized from his stand the newspaper he was reading.‖ Tension rose further when he extended a rehearsal beyond its allotted span. 'Are you musicians or workmen?' he angrily shouted in a heavy accent. 'Well', replied a violinist, 'we are engaged as musicians but we are sometimes treated like workmen.'¶ A chasm of misunderstanding opened up between Klemperer's fanatical devotion to the task in hand and an English tendency to be satisfied with performances that were 'good enough'.

A lack of sympathy between himself and the orchestra may have contributed to the failure of his Bruckner to win the lavish plaudits it had earned him elsewhere. With the solitary exception of Ernest Newman,[51] not a single critic suggested that Bruckner's music might warrant serious consideration. *The Times* dismissed it as 'childlike';[52] to Francis Toye it represented 'a typical example of German bad taste'.[53] 'We have never', wrote A. H. Fox-Strangways, 'heard such a number of platitudes and mannerisms within an hour...But the melodies are worst: they really have

---

* Schnabel was the soloist at the inaugural concert on 22 October 1929, when, with Sargent conducting, he performed concertos by Beethoven (in C major) and Brahms (in D minor).

† Prefaced by Bach's Suite No. 3 in D major (see p. 315).

‡ Neglect of Bruckner's music in England persisted until the late fifties, when such few performances as occurred still attracted meagre audiences.

§ Letter to Johanna Klemperer, London, 6 February 1932. In *Conversations*, p. 82, he described the playing as 'very bad'.

‖ A practice that still exists in London!

¶ Information provided by Messrs Lionel Bentley, Andrew Brown and Jack Robinson. Unfortunately it has not proved possible to establish precisely at which of Klemperer's pre-war appearances in London these incidents occurred.

no meaning.'[54] Small wonder that Klemperer concluded that Bruckner symphonies were 'not good for the (London) audience's artistic digestion'.[55] But that was not to prevent him from returning to the assault two seasons later (see p. 388).

(see p. 388).

         *   *   *

Guest engagements alone do not account for the fact that during 1929/30 Klemperer conducted markedly fewer operatic performances at the Kroll than he had during the preceding season (49 as against 69). In the summer of 1929 he had acquired a new commitment that was to make greater demands on his time and energy than he can have foreseen. As a student in Berlin he had attended concerts of the Philharmonic Chorus under its conductor, Siegfried Ochs, which were a feature of the city's musical life; in this way he had first heard Bach's B minor Mass, Beethoven's *Missa Solemnis* and Brahms's *Ein deutsches Requiem*, performances that remained among the most vivid memories of his youth.[56] Ochs had established his predominantly Jewish chorus, over which he ruled as a despot, in 1882, at a time when choral singing in Germany was largely overshadowed by the country's thriving instrumental and operatic life, and his impact in this field can be compared to that which Hans von Bülow, the founder of the Berlin Philharmonic Orchestra and the prototype of the modern professional conductor, had had on orchestral music. It was after a successful collaboration with von Bülow in Beethoven's Choral Symphony in 1888 that Ochs's choir had won the right to call itself the Berlin Philharmonic Chorus.

Ochs did more than achieve new standards of choral singing in Germany. He also brought about a far-reaching extension of the choral repertory. He reintroduced music by Schütz and Bach (notably the cantatas and the B minor Mass) that had suffered neglect for so long that much of it was virtually unknown.* He performed works rarely heard in Germany, such as Berlioz's *Grande messe des morts* and Liszt's *Missa Choralis*, and, in contrast to the more conservatively minded Singakademie, he laid special emphasis on new works. In 1885 the 26-year-old Strauss attended a performance of his *Wandrers Sturmlied* – one of the first occasions on which his music was heard in Berlin. The following year the Chorus sang Bruckner's *Te Deum* in the presence of the composer, and in 1899 it gave a performance of Verdi's recently composed *Quattro pezzi sacri*. Advancing years did not abate Ochs's enterprise: after 1918 he introduced new works by composers as diverse as Zemlinsky and Honegger.

---

* Ochs's approach to Bach nonetheless remained essentially Wilhelmine in its pathos and in the massive forces he employed. A page of his annotated score of *Christ lag im Todesbanden*, reproduced in Kurt Singer's *Siegfried Ochs: der Begründer des Philharmonischen Chors*, shows a forest of dynamic hairpins.

321

At some point the young Klemperer must have attracted Ochs's attention, for as a student he found occasional work accompanying rehearsals. A warm mutual regard sprang up between the two men, and the crusty old chorusmaster seems to have developed a liking for his talented accompanist. Klemperer subsequently recalled that Ochs had treated him 'as a colleague, which awoke an agreeable feeling that he took me seriously. That is the best thing that can happen to a young man.'[57] Over twenty years later, shortly after his unsuccessful *Fidelio* at the Kroll, he had been gratified to receive a letter of support from his old colleague 'at a time when most people said "no" to me and only a very few "yes"'.[58]

Thus when Ochs died at the age of seventy in February 1929 Klemperer was a natural choice to conduct the Chorus at a memorial concert. So impressive were the results that he was invited to become its musical director, and the Kultusministerium gave its consent provided that he confined himself to two concerts a season. But Klemperer characteristically threw himself into his new task with such energy that it proved a larger commitment than he had foreseen.

For his inaugural performance of Bach's *St John Passion* on 18 December 1929 he insisted on no fewer than thirty rehearsals and opened proceedings by going through the text in detail, drawing special attention to its anti-Semitic implications.[59] It did not at first prove easy for the many elderly members of the choir to adjust themselves to his requirements. But he set about instilling them with every means at his disposal, 'with gestures, grimaces and by singing...in a voice that any soloist might have envied',[60] which often proved the only method of indicating what he wanted. 'The *Johannes Passion*', he wrote to Dülberg three days prior to the event, 'makes such demands that I cannot think of anything else.' Before the concert Eva Heinitz observed him in silent prayer in a corner of the conductor's room at the Philharmonie.

The performance divided the press. There was no dispute about its exceptionally high technical level, but the more conservative critics frowned on Klemperer's fast tempi, the deliberate suppression of dramatic expression in the chorales, the absence of ritardandos on final cadences and the severely objective style imposed on the Evangelist. To Fritz Ohrmann, he seemed a prisoner of an anti-expressive aesthetic that was at odds with the inner spirit of the work;[61] yet paradoxically other critics shared Eva Heinitz's view that the performance had unparalleled dramatic intensity. Einstein was able to resolve these differences. He noted that Klemperer had indeed set out with some unduly rigid notions.

But again and again these are thrown overboard by his musicianship: The rigid dynamics that hardly seem to admit to any stages between forte and piano (and yet do so permit); the rigid adherence to a tempo that even on cadences permits of no tarrying (and yet here and there does so tarry); the rigid adherence to the letter of Bach's score, out of which the sense and the music has to bloom (and does so bloom). Only occasionally is he a victim to this rigidity...for example in the *fermate* in the chorales, which he observes with religious scrupulousness and literalness. Yes, they are there, but quite rightly no musician heeds them...

For the rest this *Johannes Passion* is unusual, but it is right and it makes a profound impact. It is a drama that reaches its highpoint in the first half of the second part..., where a wild tumult embraces not only the *turbae*...but also the chorales and arias; it is an impassioned interaction that takes away one's breath...Dramatically, stylistically...and above all musically it is the only true approach.[62]

Einstein (and others) were, however, critical of a lack of balance between chorus and orchestra. Though Klemperer had reduced the strings of the Berlin Philharmonic Orchestra (and introduced several old instruments), he retained the traditional full-scale chorus used by Ochs. In this respect his hands were tied: the Philharmonic Chorus had some two hundred singing members, all of whom expected to take part. Eyebrows were also raised at a total absence of appoggiaturas. Elisabeth Schumann, who was making her first appearance on a platform with Klemperer since the Hamburg scandal of 1912, was not considered a convincing Bach singer, but there was much enthusiasm for the young evangelist, Julius Patzak, who had not previously appeared in Berlin.* Heinrich Rehkemper sang the bass arias and Günther Ramin, to whom Klemperer often turned at this period for advice on questions of *Aufführungspraxis*, presided at the harpsichord.† Klemperer's first concert with the Philharmonic Chorus was hailed by Einstein as a significant date in the history of Berlin's musical life. In its singular blend of musical sobriety and dramatic passion, which stood in stark contrast to the aura of solemn religiosity and textural opulence that still enveloped most interpretations, this (uncut) performance of a neglected masterpiece did much to put a seal on his reputation as a Bach interpreter and as a conductor who seemed to embody a new world of feeling.

By this time Klemperer had emerged as an antipole to the romantically inclined Furtwängler. The contrast between the two conductors turned less on what they performed than on how they performed it. During the twenties Furtwängler had indeed rivalled Klemperer in his advocacy of new works.‡ But in his musical sensibilities he, like Pfitzner, remained rooted

---

* Julius Patzak (1897–1974), whose exceptional musicality and reedy tenor voice (it resembled an oboe d'amore!) made him an ideal Bach singer.

† Günther Ramin (1898–1956). From 1918 organist of the Thomaskirche, Leipzig, from 1939 until his death Thomaskantor. In 1933 he succeeded Klemperer as conductor of the Berlin Philharmonic Chorus.

‡ In some respects he had outshone him. He had twice performed *The Rite of Spring*, a work that Klemperer never ventured to conduct (see p. 162). He gave the first performance of Schoenberg's *Variations for Orchestra*, Op. 31 (see p. 291), and on one occasion conducted the *Five Orchestral Pieces*, Op. 16, which Klemperer studied but never programmed (see p. 74). Furtwängler was also an early advocate of Hindemith's music.

in an earlier age. Thus when the question arose in 1930 of whether he
or Klemperer should give the first performance of Hindemith's new Concert
Music for Piano, Brass and Harps, Op. 49, the composer's publisher, Willy
Strecker, advised him that the work would receive a better performance
from Klemperer.[63]

In spite of his assured position as conductor for life of the Berlin
Philharmonic Orchestra, Furtwängler was surprisingly prone to envy.*
When, in the summer of 1928, the two men had met by chance in Sils
Maria, Furtwängler had been disconcerted to discover that they both
planned to conduct Bruckner's Symphony No. 4 during the coming season.
He had promptly asked the date of Klemperer's concert, so that, as he
naively admitted, he could perform it first.† Given this sense of rivalry, it
was probably not mere chance that Furtwängler chose to give Beethoven's
Missa Solemnis no more than twelve days before Klemperer was to conduct
it for the first time in Germany on 15 March 1930. From the moment that
Klemperer had become a force in Berlin's musical life the critics had lost
no opportunity to contrast his interpetations with Furtwängler's. The close
proximity in time of two performances of a work so taxing and rarely heard
as Beethoven's Mass inevitably added grist to their mill.

The bludgeoning that the Philharmonic Chorus had received during the
preparations for the *St John Passion* was as nothing compared to the
treatment that Klemperer meted out during the two and a half months in
which he rehearsed the *Missa Solemnis*. Unlike most orchestral conductors,
he did not regard a chorus as a ready-made instrument, to be polished in
a few final rehearsals, but material to be hammered into shape over a
lengthy period. That process could be painful. Oblivious that he had before
him, not professional musicians, but amateurs pursuing a pastime, he
insisted on repeating passages again and again until he had what he
needed. The smallest deficiency was liable to evoke frightening rages. At
one point, when the sopranos could not manage their exposed high notes
in 'Et vitam venturi saeculi', Klemperer obliged each of them to sing the
line in turn. As one lady faltered, her neighbour, knowing that she was
the next to mount the scaffold, went into a dead faint.[64]

Yet an account of an early rehearsal goes far to explain the devotion
he nonetheless commanded.

Twenty times, one after another, he stops at a certain point to repeat a few bars
until he has achieved the sound he must have. Time and place disappear for him.
He is no longer aware that before him he has people with legs who grow weary
of standing; he sees, hears and feels only the vocal instruments which he must
make sound – at all costs. He reaches into the chorus almost literally with his
wonderfully expressive hands, kneading the sound, hurling it on high, hammering

---

* His subsequent rivalry with von Karajan was notorious.
† Bregstein Interviews, III, p. 10. Furtwängler did indeed include the work in his opening
  concert of the following season on 7 October 1929.

it with artistic fury or blessing it with a tenderness lost to the world. He himself sings...encourages, beseeches, commands – and then, with a gesture of despair puts down his baton...He suddenly notices that the ladies and gentlemen of the chorus, exhausted as flies...have sat down. For a moment he seems absolutely unable to grasp this fact, but himself sits with a gesture of resignation that makes everyone smile. And then he smiles himself, a smile that somehow goes to the heart, because it is the smile of a pure, childlike man, who only a moment earlier was raging like a demon.[65]

The rehearsals bore fruit: by general consent the choral singing far outstripped that in the performance conducted by Furtwängler, and the sopranos who had suffered in rehearsal doubtless found compensation in the special praise won by their full, homogeneous tone in high-lying passages. In Einstein's view Furtwängler's approach to the work had been primarily instrumental; whereas he had striven to obtain twenty different degrees of forte, Klemperer had been content with one. Similarly, whereas Furtwängler had sought subtle transitions between one section and another, Klemperer simply stood them alongside each other. Yet the stature of the work had not been diminished. Furtwängler, Einstein suggested, treated a score that was still used for liturgical purposes in Vienna as a concert piece.[66] In contrast, wrote Schrenk, Klemperer had performed it 'with a religious devotion that had turned the concert hall into a church'.[67]

*   *   *

The first new production of the 1929/30 season at the Kroll was a triple bill of one-act operas by contemporary French composers, consisting of Ravel's *L'Heure espagnole*, Milhaud's *Le Pauvre Matelot* and Ibert's *Angélique*, the last of which had two years earlier enjoyed a huge success in Paris. Klemperer and Curjel again looked to the spoken theatre for a producer. During the previous winter they had together attended a late-night performance of Cocteau's *Orphée* and, impressed by the production, afterwards went backstage to meet the rising young actor who was responsible for it. It was thus that Gustav Gründgens came to make his bow as an opera producer at the Kroll.* Rehearsals were about to begin when Gründgens's eye fell on a young singer of exceptional beauty who had just joined the company. He begged Klemperer to allow her to sing the role of Concepción in *L'Heure espagnole* and it was in this part that Jarmila Novotna made her first appearance at the Kroll.†

* Gustav Gründgens (1899–1963), perhaps the outstanding German actor of his generation, who was later particularly celebrated for his performances as Mephisto in both parts of Goethe's *Faust*. In 1934 Gründgens was appointed Intendant of the Staatliches Schauspielhaus in Berlin, in which position he enjoyed the favour of Goering and his actress wife, Emmy Sonnemann. In 1947 he became head of the Düsseldorf Schauspielhaus and in 1955 moved to a similar position in Hamburg. In 1930/1, 1931/2, and 1932/3 he collaborated on three productions with Klemperer.

† Jarmila Novotna (1907–   ). Czech soprano, who sang a number of leading roles at the Kroll. Novotna was subsequently a member of the Vienna State Opera (1933–8), and the Metropolitan Opera House, New York (1939–53).

In spite of these auspicious débuts, Zemlinsky's deft conducting and sets by Caspar Neher, the evening aroused little enthusiasm. Of the three works, all of which were new to Berlin, Milhaud's was the best received.* But the composer's presence on the opening night occasioned a startling personal attack. Milhaud, wrote Paul Zschorlich in the nationalist *Deutsche Zeitung* (28 September 1929) 'had the typical features of a boxer...a square head and a deceitful look, puffy cheeks and thin, arrogant lips. A head whose coarse, materialistic features betray strength of will and egotism, but not a trace of intelligence.' It was an unrecognisable portrait of a notably affable character, but Milhaud was a Jew and the racial animosities that had long been simmering beneath the surface in Germany were now coming into the open.

Klemperer and Dülberg had planned a production of *Die Zauberflöte* as early as 1924 and the project was revived three years later when Klemperer had intended to include the opera in his opening season at the Kroll. By 1929, however, when he again returned to the idea, relations with Dülberg had deteriorated badly. Angered by what he considered to be Fehling's ineffectiveness as a producer of *Der fliegende Holländer* and further annoyed by Curjel's choice of Moholy-Nagy as designer of *The Tales of Hoffmann*, Dülberg had brusquely informed Klemperer that he would in future only provide sets if he were also responsible for the production.[68] Klemperer would hardly have accepted such a condition from any other man. But Dülberg was one of his very few close friends as well as a touchstone in all matters relating to the stage, and the entire staging of *Die Zauberflöte* was accordingly placed in his hands.

Although Klemperer subsequently rated the production as one of Dülberg's most successful achievements,[69] that was not the view of the Berlin critics, several of whom after the première on 10 November compared his semi-abstract assembly of arches, pillars and steps to a cinema organ.† As in his *Don Giovanni*, curtains were again used to ensure rapid changes of scene. But on this occasion Dülberg's attempt to enliven the stage with brilliantly coloured and elaborate costumes did not find favour, and critics as open-minded as Bie condemned his approach as over-theoretical.[70] To an increasing extent he was seen as falling between two stools: his stiff, semi-abstract style offended conservative eyes without convincing those attuned to the advanced art of the period. 'To nail those silly blocks together, to stick romanesque arches on top of them and then

---

* Milhaud enjoyed a considerable reputation in Germany in the late twenties. In 1930 Kleiber conducted the first performance of his *Christophe Colomb* at the Linden Opera, one of the few occasions when the achievements of the Kroll were emulated by its senior sister.
† Such few and indifferent photographs as survive (Theatermuseum, Cologne University) have an art deco flavour, although that can hardly have been Dülberg's intention.

to paint the whole thing like a gigantic bonbon – if Herr Dülberg wants to sell us that as modern decor, then', wrote Hans von Wedderkop in the intellectual monthly, *Der Querschnitt* (December 1929), 'one also must say that – like his *Don Giovanni* – it reveals a timeless lack of talent. But our great Otto Klemperer seemingly cannot have enough of it.' Leichentritt among others praised the clarity, detail and sense of proportion that distinguished Klemperer's account of the score.[71] Friedrich Schorr, who had been seconded from the Linden Opera, was an impressive Speaker and the cast, which included singers of the calibre of Novotna, Käthe Heidersbach, Hans Fidesser and Fritz Krenn, was on a higher level than the Kroll had fielded in earlier productions. Yet the evening as a whole evoked little enthusiasm.

It is, however, not certain that Dülberg completed his production. He was taken ill during rehearsals and on his return discovered that many alterations had been made during his absence. 'Shaking with rage', he told his son to return his production book to Legal. 'That was the end.'* Yet, to judge from the warm letter that Klemperer wrote to his friend in Arosa on 15 December, more than a month after the première, their personal relations were good enough for Klemperer to raise the question of a further collaboration. That never came to pass, although later in the season Dülberg did produce and design a *Rigoletto*, whose first performance on 17 May 1930 was conducted by Zemlinsky with what was felt to be more finesse than *brio*. But the staging attracted widespread criticism; even Strobel, who had been one of the few to defend Dülberg's *Fidelio*, regarded his cool, constructivist style as being at odds with Verdi's passionate score.[72] Dülberg, cussed as ever, subsequently described it as 'the only pure pleasure' he had had in the theatre.[73] The production was, however, to be his last completed work for the Kroll, or indeed for any opera house. At some point, probably in the autumn of 1930, he prepared designs for an abortive production of *Tristan und Isolde*.† But before the end of the year another quarrel occurred between Klemperer and Dülberg.‡

Sick, cantankerous, inflexible and frequently absent from Berlin, Dülberg had proved physically and psychologically ill-equipped to realise Klemperer's dream that he should determine the visual image of the Kroll, as Roller had determined that of the Vienna Opera during the latter years of

* Verbal communication to the author by Peter Dülberg, who was acting as assistant to his father.
† See p. 352. Dülberg dismissed these designs, which are in the Theatermuseum of Cologne University, as a 'misuse' of his talent. Paradoxically, they stand among his most fascinating achievements in the subtlety of colour and romantic aura that here pervades his severe, linear style. The design for Act 1 is reproduced in colour in *Experiment Krolloper*, p. 437.
‡ As Dülberg freely acknowledged, it did not prevent Klemperer from making it possible for him to return to Arosa.

Mahler's rule. Once he had ceased to be the dominant influence, Klemperer's own conceptions of staging and design proved too ill-defined to prevent Curjel from seizing the initiative in this field. Klemperer disapproved of much that was done ('Sometimes I think we went too far').[74] But he never carried that disapproval to the point of open opposition, as he did not hesitate to do where musical issues were involved.

Dülberg, however, was enraged by Curjel's approach to the stage. In an angry letter to his former colleague, written after the closure of the Kroll, he laid bare the roots of their differences.

Your basic error is to believe that *living* theatre means *zeitnahes* theatre (close to the time). But in every art, as you should know as an art historian, the really *living* element is almost always directed *against* its time...How can you speak of a *kernel* [of artists who had worked at the Kroll] and then conjure up such dummies (Schiessbudenfiguren) as Moholy, Gründgens, Schlemmer, Reinking, Neher and Fehling? And why this emphasis on productions such as those of *Figaro*...which, together with *Falstaff*, revealed the total bankruptcy of the Kroll idea.

The catastrophe of my Berlin theatrical activity...and quite certainly the source of the unbridgeable differences between you and me, has probably been that I exist on another level and thus can never see theatrical matters from the same point of view as you, Klemperer *e tutti quanti*.[75]

As he made plain in a radio talk in the summer of 1931, Dülberg left the Kroll a profoundly disillusioned man. In particular, he disapproved of the degree to which the recreative arts of the producer and designer had (as he saw it) come to take precedence over the creative art of the composer. He also objected to the excessive importance that had come to be attached to 'stage decorations', an element without which, as he pointed out, the theatre had successfully survived from ancient Greece to the Renaissance.[76] In Dülberg's mind Klemperer had enticed him back to the theatre after he (Dülberg) had turned his back on it, only to betray him by compromising their joint ideals.[77]

Curjel had already come to be regarded as the Kroll's grey eminence and his influence further increased when in January 1930 he was appointed Legal's deputy.* Arthur Maria Rabenalt, who came into frequent contact with him in the course of staging a number of productions, later described him as 'a man who bridged music and the visual arts, the theatre and the lecture hall, himself uncreative, but clever..., crafty and not over-loyal'.†[78] In Rabenalt's view, Curjel was 'an ideal *Galerist*, a born mounter of exhibitions, a lively instigator of *vernissages*...[who] was responsible for

---

* Legal had been appointed to succeed Jessner as Intendant of the Berlin Schauspielhaus, although he continued to serve as director of the Kroll until the end of the season. As the house was by then under sentence of death, no successor was appointed, so that Curjel acted as *de facto* director during the final season of 1930/1.

† 'Keinesfalls der Erfinder der Nibelungentreue'.

the *embarras de richesse* of visual art on the stage of Kroll. His mistake was to suppose that every important painter was also a gifted stage designer.' Yet the latter-day reputation of the Kroll as a source of visual regeneration in the staging of opera stemmed in large part from the producers and designers that Curjel engaged. Unfortunately it proved easier to bring about innovation on this level than to conjure into existence a rebirth of *dramma per musica*, such as had long haunted Klemperer's imagination.

*   *   *

Having rejected both *Von Heute auf Morgen* and *Der Aufstieg und Fall der Stadt Mahagonny*, Klemperer found himself without a new opera for the 1929/30 season. As a result he had no alternative but to opt for Krenek's latest work, *Das Leben des Orest*. The prospect did not fill him with enthusiasm.* Nor, as Klemperer realised, was it calculated to appeal to Dülberg. Casting around for a designer for Krenek's 'classical-surrealist' work, Curjel alighted on the ingenious idea of inviting Giorgio de Chirico, whose dreamlike urban landscapes made use of classical architectural features placed in a contemporary context. De Chirico travelled to Berlin, where the score was played to him, but all that arrived a few weeks later were tiny *gouaches*, which Teo Otto had the difficult task of realising on a larger scale.[79] Klemperer was no happier about Legal's production than he was about the score,[80] and after its first night on 4 March 1930 the Berlin critics found the staging inferior to that which the work had received in Leipzig at its première there six weeks earlier.† Krenek's attempt to resuscitate Meyerbeerian formulae in what he described as a 'grand opera in five acts' did not arouse much enthusiasm. He had, wrote Bie, an instinct for the pulse of the times. But recourse to a miscellany of stylistic features that happened to be in favour at the moment, such as classical subject-matter, jazz, hard-edged instrumentation, bold melodic writing and large-scale operatic conceptions, could not disguise the superficiality of the score.[81] *Das Leben des Orest* provided neither a popular nor a critical success at a time when the Kroll was badly in need of one (see pp. 338–9).

The last major event of the 1929/30 season was even less calculated to arouse popular enthusiasm.‡ After Klemperer's withdrawal from *Von*

---

* When the author snidely enquired whether the opera was an improvement (*Verbesserung*) on *Mahagonny*, Klemperer replied with an intellectual agility remarkable in a man of eighty-four, 'No, [but] it was a *Verwässerung* (dilution)' (*Conversations*, p. 65).

† Krenek was of the same opinion. Letter to Heinsheimer (Universal Edition), 5 March 1930.

‡ Other new productions (neither conducted by Klemperer) staged in the course of the season were of *The Bartered Bride* and Auber's *La Muette de Portici*, in which, to Klemperer's irritation, disproportionate emphasis was given to the work's revolutionary background. 'The tragedy is more the tragedy of a dumb woman than of the Italian people' (*Conversations*, p. 66). Neither made much artistic impact, but the production of *La Muette* excited much criticism on account of its political implications.

Heute auf Morgen, the Kroll was clearly under an obligation to do something about Schoenberg. He was indisputably the greatest composer living in Berlin, yet a Berlin opera house that had been established, at any rate in part, to perform new works had totally neglected his music. Furthermore, at the time that he had engaged Zemlinsky, Klemperer had given him an assurance that he would conduct a production of *Erwartung.** A decision was eventually taken to perform it with *Die glückliche Hand,* another short one-act opera that had suffered even greater neglect since Schoenberg had completed it in 1913. Klemperer elected to conduct the latter, but, to judge from his subsequent comments on the work, there is no reason to suppose that he embarked on the task with enthusiasm.

Schoenberg had a precise conception of how he wanted *Die glückliche Hand* to be staged and on 14 April 1930 he delivered his instructions in a letter to Legal.†'Objects and localities', he wrote, '...should be as clearly recognisable as pitches. When there is something puzzling on the stage...and the spectator has to ask himself what it means, he misses a part of the music.' He also expressed his intense dislike of stylised settings. For all his musical radicalism and involvement in the visual arts, in his approach to the stage Schoenberg remained rooted in nineteenth-century naturalism.

At Curjel's instigation Oskar Schlemmer was engaged to design both operas. It was a brilliant choice. In January 1913 Schlemmer, then a young man of only twenty-four, had been so deeply impressed by a performance of *Pierrot Lunaire* on its first tour of Germany that he had asked Schoenberg to compose a ballet score.‡ Nothing came of his approach, but at this period he had noted in his diary a description of a sequence of colours and music that bears a remarkable resemblance to the combination of the two elements that Schoenberg called for in the (as yet unpublished) score of *Die glückliche Hand.*[82] Although he had joined the Bauhaus, where from 1923 to 1929 he had been director of its stage workshop and had evolved an individual brand of cubism, Schlemmer had never entirely cut his links with his early expressionism.§ To Curjel Schlemmer seemed predestined to design Schoenberg's one-acters. But his largely abstract style was remote from the naturalism on which the composer had insisted in his letter to Legal. The stage was set for one of those confrontations in which Schoenberg was a past master.‖

* Zemlinsky had conducted the first stage performance in Prague in 1924.
† That Schoenberg chose to address himself to Legal is a further indication of the cool relationship at that time obtaining between himself and Klemperer.
‡ Oskar Schlemmer (1888–1943) was also a dancer.
§ In 1921 he had designed sets for Hindemith's early, one-act expressionist operas.
‖ Curjel subsequently claimed that Schoenberg had agreed to Schlemmer's engagement, if 'with some doubts' (letter to Gertrud Marbach, 18 January 1962). His claim that Rabenalt,

That was not the only source of tension. On 3 May Schoenberg noted in his diary that his brother-in-law, Zemlinsky, had admitted to him that Klemperer regarded *Die glückliche Hand* as a product of a vanished epoch.* Schoenberg was beside himself with fury. 'How many people', he wrote in his diary, 'has this man of power trodden under foot (über den Haufen gerannt) and before how many new doors has he stood? How should he find access to my music?' Thereafter Schoenberg communicated his wishes to Klemperer through his assistant, Josef Rufer.[83]

It was not until 11 May that Schlemmer first visited the composer and only thereafter that he started work on his designs.†On 5 June, only two days before the first night, Schoenberg appeared with his wife at the first rehearsal at which the sets were in position. According to Curjel the lighting instructions in the score of *Die glückliche Hand* were unfortunately not yet functioning.‡Tension rose and Schoenberg left the theatre in what Schlemmer in his diary described as 'Kampfstimmung' ('warlike mood'), threatening to disown the entire undertaking. Another rehearsal was hastily arranged for that very evening at the unusual hour of eleven and Curjel had the difficult task of persuading the outraged composer to attend, if possible without his wife, who, it was felt, had failed to pour oil on troubled waters earlier in the day.§ Schoenberg finally consented to appear and, if not content with what he saw, was to some extent appeased by the attempts that had been made to meet his wishes by the time the rehearsal ended at four o'clock the following morning.[84]

Stuckenschmidt, who had attended the only two previous stagings of *Die glückliche Hand*, described the Kroll's production as the best of the three.[85] Whereas in Prague in 1924 a harmonium had been used to keep the soloist in tune in *Erwartung*, Moje Forbach required no such assistance. But neither opera evoked much enthusiasm. The conservative critics attacked both works as products of a diseased imagination, while their more

who produced, similarly agreed to Schlemmer as a partner must, however, be regarded with scepticism. Rabenalt's appointment only occurred after other producers, notably Gründgens, had declined. According to Schlemmer's diaries, he first met Rabenalt on 27 May 1930 – only ten days before the première on 6 June and two weeks after Schlemmer had started work on his designs.

* In 'Das Heute in der Musik' (a series of brief observations published in the *Berliner Börsen-Zeitung* of 1 January 1931) Klemperer was careful to pay tribute to Schoenberg's stature but did not disguise his approval of the return of tonality evident in the works of young composers, such as Hindemith, Weill and Krenek.

† He thus had little more than three weeks in which to complete them. In spite of Klemperer's meticulous habits of rehearsal, the Kroll was not, it seems, always a model of long-term planning.

‡ According to Klemperer they were never used (*Conversations*, p. 65).

§ Which the author, having had the benefit of Gertrud Schoenberg's views on Peter Hall's production of *Moses und Aron* at Covent Garden in 1965, can well believe. Nothing short of a staging by Cecil B. de Mille would have satisfied her demand for naturalistic spectacle.

progressive colleagues shrugged them off as relics of a bygone age. Schoenberg's 'romantic pessimism', wrote Karl Westermeyer, 'is diametrically opposed to the...affirmative spirit of the younger generation.'[86] There were also complaints about an evening that consisted of less than an hour's music and *L'Heure espagnole* was accordingly added to the two further performances that the double bill received before the end of the season.* Even so, the attendances remained poor. Nor was there much enthusiasm for the works within the Kroll itself. Schlemmer subsequently confessed that, though he had found the music beautiful, he had felt ill at ease in its *Jugendstil* atmosphere. Klemperer regarded *Die glückliche Hand* as a theatrical disaster, which probably accounts for his failure to revive it in the following season.† The composer, satisfied though he declared himself to be with the musical performances, remained as angry as ever about the staging.

It was not long before he found an opportunity to give vent to his spleen.

* Owing to Zemlinsky's illness, at the second performance on 11 June *Le Pauvre Matelot* was substituted for *Erwartung*, so that Schoenberg's one-acters were only heard together on two occasions. *Erwartung* had two further performances in 1930/1.
† Schoenberg had 'no idea of theatre, really none at all' (*Conversations*, p. 65).

35   Oskar Schlemmer: stage set for *Die glückliche Hand*

In July, Klemperer, on holiday in a lighthouse near Kampen, wrote to Schoenberg. Though he could see no possibility of performing his recently completed Choruses for male choir, Op. 35, with the Philharmonic Chorus, he would, he told the composer, like to give the first performance of another new work, *Begleitmusik zu einer Lichtspielszene*, at a Kroll concert during the coming season. Would Schoenberg, Klemperer enquired, consider a proposal (which doubtless stemmed from Curjel) that the score be played against the background of an abstract film, to be designed by an artist such as Moholy-Nagy. The idea was not without its appeal to Schoenberg, but, characteristically, he raised difficulties:

After much reflection on its pros and cons I find your suggestion of an abstract film very attractive, because it solves the problem of this 'Music for no film'.

Only one thing: the shock of the Berlin productions of my stage works, the atrocities that were committed by scepticism, lack of talent, ignorance and frivolity and which, in spite of the musical achievements, proved deeply damaging – this shock is still too much with me for me not to be very cautious. How can I protect myself against this sort of thing?

I do not know Herr Moholy. But what if I am particularly unfortunate and he weds the rascally, ignorant scepticism of Herr Rabenalt to the unimaginative decency of Herr Schlemmer?

There is only one way: that Herr Moholy should work on the film with me. (That will ensure that there will be at least one person with ideas.)[87]

Predictably, nothing came of Klemperer's proposal.*

Nonetheless the Film Music enjoyed a substantial success when, prefaced by Schoenberg's orchestration of Bach's Prelude and Fugue in E flat, it was given its first performance at the Kroll on 6 November 1930. Klemperer did not care for the massive instrumentation, which was at odds with his own approach to Bach's music. But this was the first dodecaphonic score that he warmed to. Yet it remained the only Schoenberg première he conducted at the Kroll. Later in Los Angeles, when the composer was again a close neighbour, Klemperer claimed that in Berlin 'the permanent fight against all reactionary elements made it difficult to work for Schoenberg at that time'.[88] That was a very partial statement of the truth. The opposition to Schoenberg's music had stemmed from 'progressive' as well as reactionary elements and these had been present within the Kroll as well as outside it. In this instance, at any rate, Schoenberg's proneness to paranoid resentment was not wholly without justification.

*   *   *

* The work has, however, since been performed on a number of occasions in the manner that Klemperer foresaw.

During the last days of the season Tietjen appeared unannounced in Klemperer's office and declared 'quite casually' that the Kroll would be shut during the following year. 'We thought he had gone mad.'[89] The machiavellian *Generalintendant* was not mad. While Klemperer had been immersed in his musical tasks, Tietjen, dispassionate as ever, had observed the clouds that had been gathering over the Kroll. The storm was about to break.

15   The end of the Kroll

On 26 September 1929 the Prussian Oberrechnungskammer published a report on its examination of the accounts of the state theatres for the years 1924, 1925 and 1926. Between 1924 and 1929, it pointed out, the deficit met from public funds had risen more than fourfold.* The Oberrechnungskammer, which sat in Potsdam and enjoyed quasi-judicial status, had been established in 1717 to examine public spending. It was entirely independent of ministerial control. Its president was *ex officio* head of the Rechnungshof, which accounted for all expenditure by the state, and its members, who were mostly very senior officials, were appointed for life and empowered to make proposals as well as to exercise critical supervision. When the Oberrechnungskammer spoke, ministries clicked their heels.

In its view the increase that had occurred in public expenditure on the state theatres was unacceptable and by implication reflected on the control exercised by the Kultusministerium. Berlin, declared the Oberrechnungskammer, could not support three major opera houses 'with more or less the same repertory' and it called in the first place for economies at the Kroll. In this connection, it criticised the contract that the Prussian state had made with the Berlin Volksbühne in 1923, whereby it in effect met three-fifths of the cost of every seat it provided for the Volksbühne. A warning shot had been fired. The Kroll was under attack.

On this occasion, however, the press rallied to its defence, and in any case the years covered by the report dealt with a period before the Kroll had been established as an independent artistic entity under Klemperer's direction. For the moment the Landtag showed little disposition to follow the Oberrechnungskammer's lead. When the issue of the Berlin opera houses arose in October and November criticism still centred on the overlapping functions of the Linden Opera and the Städtische Oper. Speaking before the Landtag's Principal Committee (Hauptausschuss) on 14 October 1929, Seelig (see p. 175) was able to claim that the Kroll was developing favourably. Its income was stable and its repertory was in the main now designed to meet the tastes of lower income groups. For the first time in history, he proudly added, a government and a parliament had

---

* The *Denkschrift*, which forms part of the Proceedings of the Prussian Landtag (Drucksachen), is dated 7 July 1929. The deficit on the State theatres had risen from 1,601,179M (1924) to 6,919,561M (1929).

335

collaborated to bring into existence an opera house devoted exclusively to social aims.[1] With his political flank thus secure, the Kultusminister, C. H. Becker, turned to deal with the Finance Minister, the formidable Hermann Höpker-Aschoff, who had already identified himself with the views of the Oberrechnungskammer.* In a sharply worded letter of 6 December 1929 Becker reminded his colleague that the issue of the Kroll had been the subject of continuous consultation between their respective ministries, that in view of the contract with the Volksbühne no changes in existing arrangements were possible, nor would he countenance them in view of the social functions (*soziale Kunstpflege*) that the theatre fulfilled.† The letter served its purpose.‡ When Höpker-Aschoff spoke in a debate on the budget estimates in the Landtag seven days later, he conceded that in 1928/9 expenditure in the state theatres had exceeded estimates by almost 50 per cent but went on to claim that steps had been taken to ensure that this did not recur. Short of shutting a theatre, however, he could not see how subsidies could be materially reduced. To close the historic opera house on Unter den Linden was out of the question and the state had legal and social commitments to the Kroll. There matters might well have rested, had not events combined to change the entire course of German politics.

*   *   *

On 3 October 1929 Gustav Stresemann died at the age of only fifty-one. Klemperer was not slow to grasp the significance of that event.§ First as Chancellor and subsequently as Foreign Minister, Stresemann had since 1923 been primarily responsible for the stabilisation of the currency and the reintegration of Germany into Western Europe. The prosperity enjoyed by Germany during those years can be deduced from the fact that the purchasing power of the wages of metal and building workers had

---

* Hermann Höpker-Aschoff (1883–1954), Prussian Finance Minister (1925–31). In the Federal German Republic a prominent member of the Free Democratic Party (FDP) and from 1951 President of the Bundesverfassungsgericht. In spite of (or, perhaps, because of) strong but conventional musical interests, a determined adversary of the Kroll. Klemperer later claimed that Höpker-Aschoff was opposed to him 'because my tempi are different from those he takes when he plays piano duets with his wife at home'.

† Pp. 17–18 in *Betrieb und Leitung der Staatstheater*, the state theatre file of the Staatsministerium (i.e. the office of the Prussian Prime Minister). This file, indispensable to understanding of the ministerial struggle surrounding the Kroll, survives in the Geheimes Staatsarchiv, Preussischer Kulturbesitz, Berlin (Dahlem) GStA. Pk, I HA, Rep 90/2406, and is subsequently referred to as Staatsministerium theatre file.

‡ Becker's defiant letter to Höpker-Aschoff was nonetheless the first document to be entered in a new file opened by the Kultusministerium with the ominous title 'Closure of the Kroll Opera' (*Untersuchungsausschuss*, columns 13–14).

§ At the time it occurred he described Stresemann's death as 'a day of destiny also for us', i.e. for the Kroll (Stuckenschmidt, *BZ am Mittag*, 4 July 1931). So it was indeed to prove.

doubled.[2] But the economic well-being, which had enabled the Kultus-ministerium to pursue an expansionary opera policy, had been achieved on the unstable basis of foreign loans. As early as November 1928 Stresemann had warned the Reichstag that 'if a crisis arose and the Americans called in their short-term credits, we should be faced by bankruptcy'.[3] That prophecy was fulfilled within twelve months.

On Black Friday, 24 October 1929, only three weeks after Stresemann's death had already shaken confidence in Germany's political stability, the New York stock market collapsed. The world had begun to lurch into the deepest depression it was to experience in the first half of the twentieth century and its impact was felt with particular sharpness in an economy dependent on foreign money. In an attempt to prevent its withdrawal, German interest rates were raised so sharply that between October and December unemployment increased from 1,760,000 to 3 million. Political tension rose correspondingly. On 23 January 1930 a National Socialist regime was elected to power in Thuringia, where Wilhelm Frick became Minister of the Interior.* The agony of the Weimar Republic was already at hand and the fate of the Kroll was to foreshadow that of the regime which had called it into existence.

The deterioration of the political and economic situation soon made itself felt in the operatic field. On 7 January 1930 the small right-wing Deutsche Fraktion tabled a motion in the Landtag calling for the closure of the Kroll. On the same day a Deutschnational deputy, Pastor Julius Koch, who was to emerge as one of the theatre's most vitriolic critics, wrote to make a similar proposal to Höpker-Aschoff. That seed fell on receptive ground. Two days later the Finance Ministry informed the Kultusministerium of what had already become evident in informal exchanges: it was no longer merely seeking economies at the Kroll but its closure. The Kroll was, however, by no means the only opera house to find its very existence imperilled. Frankfurt, Darmstadt and Mainz were all in difficulties and there were plans for amalgamations in the Ruhr.[4] There were also threats to the existence of the theatres in Breslau and Königsberg. These carried more immediate political implications, for both were regarded as bastions of *Deutschtum* in a slavonic hinterland.

The situation in Königsberg was particularly delicate. The city was the capital of the province of East Prussia, which at the Treaty of Versailles had been physically separated from the remainder of Germany by the Polish corridor. It was also the homeland of Otto Braun, the Prussian Prime

---

* Wilhelm Frick (1877–1946), who was hanged at Nuremberg as a major Nazi war criminal, was the Minister of the Interior during the Third Reich from 1933 to 1943. His Thuringian government only lasted fifteen months, but its cultural policies during that period provided a foretaste of what was to come when the Nazis finally gained power in 1933.

Minister.* As a social democrat, Braun was in principle well disposed to an opera house that had been called into existence to serve the needs of the Volksbühne. But he was particularly sensitive to distress signals from his native province. As the head of a fragile coalition, he was also alert to an issue that could easily become a hot potato.

At this moment an event occurred that was gravely to weaken the Kroll's position. For purely political reasons Braun felt obliged to refashion his cabinet, which rested on a coalition between his own SPD and the Catholic Zentrum, together with the small Democratic Party, to which Becker nominally belonged.† The SPD, which had hitherto been under-represented in the cabinet, demanded another portfolio, and Braun found himself obliged to give the post of Kultusminister to a member of his party. Becker was accordingly succeeded on 30 January by Adolf Grimme, a decent but ineffectual schoolmaster with no special understanding of music or the arts.‡ The whiggish Becker had prided himself on his 'non-political' policies. But, as in 'der Fall Schillings', his lack of political backing on this occasion proved his undoing. With his resignation the Kroll lost a stalwart and enlightened patron. Thereafter the Kultusministerium was rudderless and the implications of its weakness were soon to become apparent.

On 8 February Braun addressed himself personally to Grimme. Neither the Breslau nor the Königsberg opera houses could be allowed to founder. As no additional funds could be made available, savings would have to be made in the state's theatre budget. A rationalisation of Berlin's operatic life was thus an urgent necessity; the capital could not support three opera houses at a time when the very existence of provincial theatres of such crucial importance was threatened.[5] It took the new Kultusminister no more than five days to propose that the necessary savings be made by closing the Kroll at the end of the 1930/1 season.[6] On 26 February Höpker-Aschoff threw his weight into the scales by urging the Haupt-

---

* Otto Braun (1872–1955), headed the coalition of Social Democrats, Zentrum and Democrats that ruled Prussia with brief intervals from 1920 to 1932. Its dissolution in 1932 (see p. 396) in effect sealed the fate of the Weimar Republic.

† The Deutsche Demokratische Partei, founded by Friedrich Naumann, was supported by the liberally minded middle class, a diminishing segment of society in the later years of the Weimar Republic. Up to 1930 it won a majority of Jewish votes, though it sought to evade the reputation of being a Jewish party by largely avoiding Jewish candidates. Hannah Arendt (*The Origins of Totalitarianism*, p. 25) unkindly described it as a party of 'respectable and bewildered gentlemen' who were gullible enough to look to the state as a guarantor of democratic values. In 1930, having allied itself to moderate right-wing elements, it re-emerged as the Deutsche Staatspartei. But this bizarre coalition collapsed and henceforth the party rapidly declined, thus mirroring the polarisation of political life that did so much to undermine the Weimar Republic in its last years. (See Niewyk, *The Jews in Weimar Germany*, pp. 72–3)

‡ Adolf Grimme (1889–1963). 1946–8, Kultusminister, Lower Saxony. 1948–56, Intendant of the North-West German Radio.

ausschuss of the Landtag, which since 17 February had been debating the Kultusministerium's budget for the coming financial year, to make no provision for the Kroll after summer 1931.[7]

In the course of that debate a new factor emerged that was further to undermine the position of the Kroll. Up to this point the Catholic Zentrum had been well enough disposed to the Kroll as an agent of *soziale Kunstpflege*. Now, however, it declared itself to be as concerned with the precarious condition of the theatres in the areas in the west that bordered on France and Belgium* as was Braun with their counterparts in the east. On 28 February an influential member of the party, Albert Lauscher,† tabled a motion, urging the Kultusministerium to enter into negotiations with the Berlin city council with a view to transferring the social functions exercised by the Kroll to the Städtische Oper. The Kroll would thus serve no special purpose and could, it was implied, accordingly be closed at the end of the 1930/1 season, so that the savings achieved might be applied to the frontier theatres.

That, however, was not sufficiently drastic for the right-wing Deutschnationale Volkspartei, which regarded the Kroll as a hotbed of *Kulturbolschewismus*. With the intention of bringing about the theatre's immediate demise, it proposed that 600,000M should be deducted forthwith from its budget and made available to the Prussian Landesbühne.‡ Even before this occurred, Aloys Lammers, the Secretary of State of the Kultusministerium and thus its senior official, had twice intervened in the deliberations of the Hauptausschuss to emphasise that the minister would 'naturally' look for a solution along the lines it indicated. Thus by the end of February 1930 the government and two of the three largest parties in the Landtag were at one in a willingness to sacrifice the Kroll to operatic life in the provinces.

A furious debate at once broke out in the press with the heavy guns rallying to the cause of the beleaguered theatre. Among its most effective defenders was Alfred Einstein. He pointed out that the most stimulating

---

* These areas were the principal stronghold of the Catholic Zentrum, which, it is relevant to note, had in December 1928 moved decisively to the Right under a new chairman, Prälat Kaǎs (see p. 339), but remained of crucial importance to Braun as an indispensable component of his coalition. In spite of earlier French attempts to foster separatism in the Rhineland, the Zentrum's claims that the German nature of the area was threatened bordered on fantasy. But they well illustrate the extent to which a rising tide of German nationalism had begun to infect even political circles that had not hitherto been prone to chauvinism.

† Albert Lauscher (1872–1944), professor of theology at Bonn University and papal domestic prelate, henceforth led the opposition to the Kroll within the Zentrum.

‡ Set up as an unofficial body in 1922 with the original purpose of advising the Kultusministerium on theatrical life in the provinces, the Landesbühne had become particularly concerned with the theatres in the frontier areas both in the east and the west (Brodbeck, *Handbuch der deutschen Volksbühnenbewegung*, pp. 386–92).

opera house in Berlin was by far the cheapest to maintain.* Furthermore, it was the only house to maintain a proper ensemble, so that subsequent performances of a new production did not decline, as they were prone to do at the Linden Opera and the Städtische Oper.[8] The city's most influential intellectual periodicals, *Das Tagebuch* and *Die Weltbühne*, also took up cudgels on behalf of the Kroll. In contrast, outright attacks were largely confined to mass circulation right-wing dailies. In the *Berliner Illustrierte Nachtausgabe* (1 March 1930), Josef Buchhorn claimed that the end of the 'Kestenberg opera house' would signal a rebirth of the German theatre.† In windy rhetoric he proclaimed that

The theatre will then play a crucial role in the renewal of the German people's sense of national awareness, in the revival of those powers of will and faith...will open a new period for the Germans...The theatres in Saarbrücken, Trier, Breslau, Königsberg and Tilsit...are not theatres in the usual sense of the word. No, they are essential bulwarks in the struggle for a new German land of the soul...They are bases for the renewal of German spirit and faith. Our mission to the peoples of Europe cannot and must not be halted merely because...military and political misfortune have temporarily blocked our way to inner fulfilment...The struggle for the Kroll is thus not merely of financial and political importance, but of national and ethical significance.

When the Zentrum and Deutschnational motions were debated (and passed) in a plenum session of the Landtag on 4 April, the right wing pressed its attack on the Kroll.‡ Pastor Koch in particular launched into a furious denunciation of its artistic policies which, he maintained were

working for an anti-German and anti-Christian culture...and its replacement with Jewish pessimism...To this is added a curious feature of our times that I would describe as its negroid character...this nigger-culture reaches us in the form of jazz...We have seen a disgusting performer, Josephine Baker, celebrate triumphs in the west end of Berlin...[This is] the Jewish-Negroid period of Prussian art.[9]

Economic pressures and political prejudice were joining hands around the throat of the Kroll.

       *   *   *

* Its budget for singers was on a par with that of a middle-sized provincial theatre, such as Magdeburg, and less than half of that of the Linden Opera (Stephan Stompor, 'Oper im zwanzigsten Jahrhundert: Die Entwicklung des Musiktheaters von Gustav Mahler bis Walter Felsenstein' (henceforth 'Musiktheater').
† Josef Buchhorn (1875–1954). Deutsche Volkspartei member of the Landtag, prolific writer, dramatist and journalist who was later associated with *Deutsche Kulturwacht*, a National Socialist periodical.
‡ Only the SPD and the KPD (the Communists) voted against these motions. The latter had, however, hitherto chosen to regard the Kroll as an organ of a reactionary regime and a purveyor of bourgeois culture. That did not prevent it from supporting the theatre when its existence was threatened as a means of embarrassing Braun's government.

340

No sooner had the Zentrum and its right-wing allies mounted their attack in February, than the Berlin Volksbühne submitted a memorandum in defence of its position to members of the Landtag.[10] The Volksbühne pointed out that the closure of the Kroll would infringe legal rights that it enjoyed under the agreement made with the state in 1923, when, in return for handing over the theatre, it had been guaranteed seats in it for twenty-five years (see pp. 184–7). Thus, claimed the Volksbühne, the Kroll could not be shut without its consent. (Indeed, it went further and argued that, as the theatre had been reconstructed to meet its requirements, it was morally its own.) This legal argument, rather than any sympathy for Klemperer's achievements, was to prove the main obstacle to an early closure of the Kroll.

The Volksbühne's close links with the SPD ensured it of the backing of the largest party in the Landtag,* and it was not long before that party began to make its views known at the highest level. On 24 February, Herbert Weichmann, a young official on Braun's personal staff, sent a memorandum to his immediate superior, questioning Grimme's plan to make the savings that the Prime Minister had demanded by shutting the Kroll.† Having attended the debate on 28 February in the Hauptausschuss, he followed this up on 4 March with a further memorandum to Braun himself, in which he argued that the necessary economies could be achieved by collaboration between the Linden and Städtische opera houses.[11] Braun was impressed and on 12 March wrote to Grimme. A state that acknowledged social responsibilities could not, he now maintained, countenance the closure of the one Berlin opera house that fufilled a social function. A republic had a duty to maintain a theatre that made art available to a large number of people at modest prices, and the Kultus-ministerium should reconsider the whole issue from that aspect.[12] The impact of this snub to the inexperienced Grimme was increased by the support it won from the other socialist member of the cabinet, Heinrich Waentig.‡ The wind was now blowing from another direction and on 3 April Tietjen, who a month earlier had been appointed *Theaterreferent* in the Kultusministerium as well as *Generalintendant* of all the Prussian theatres,§ felt confident enough to assure union officials at the State Opera that in all probability the Kroll would not be shut.[13] But Höpker-Aschoff, who had already indicated his support of the Zentrum's motion in the Landtag, insisted on a *Chefbesprechung* between Braun, Grimme and

* Cultural considerations played a very subordinate part in the SPD's opposition to closure.
† Herbert Weichmann (1896–   ), *Oberbürgermeister* of Hamburg, 1965–71.
‡ Heinrich Waentig (1870–1943), Prussian Minister of the Interior, February–October 1930.
§ The *Berliner Tageblatt* (2 March 1930) commented that the prime purpose of these appointments had been to remove the theatres from the control of Kestenberg and Seelig.

himself. This took place on 10 April.* It seems that at it he was rebuffed, for two days later the Staatsministerium produced a document, indicating how the savings he required could be met without closing any of Berlin's opera houses.[14] On 3 May the cautious Tietjen, now well placed to observe the state of play and alert as always to the mood of his political masters, informed the Oberrechnungskammer that, though savings would be made, complete closure of the Kroll was not feasible.[15]

For the moment the tide seemed to have turned in the Kroll's favour, at any rate within the cabinet. But a time bomb had meanwhile been ticking away in the Landtag: Lauscher's motion that the government enter into negotiations with the Berlin *Magistrat* to investigate the possibility of accommodating the Volksbühne at the Städtische Oper so as to facilitate the closure of the Kroll had been making its way through parliamentary procedures and debates. On 6 May it was finally passed by a majority consisting of members of the right-wing parties and of the Zentrum. The solution it advocated proved not to be feasible, but its passage transformed the situation. The Zentrum, which was an indispensable component of Braun's precarious coalition, had given notice that it was not prepared to support his attempts to prevent the closure of the Kroll. Braun henceforth seems to have forsaken a policy that risked incurring the anger of his political allies; at any rate there is no evidence that he intervened further on the theatre's behalf.

Repercussions soon became evident elsewhere. Now that the Landtag had added its weight to that of the Finance Ministry and the Oberrechnungs-kammer, the Kultusministerium abandoned further resistance and informed the Volksbühne that it could no longer prevent closure. The Volksbühne, which earlier in the year had so vigorously championed 'its' theatre, also resigned itself to the inevitable. Less than two weeks after Lauscher's bill had been passed by the Landtag it meekly agreed in principle to accept rights at the Städtische Oper similar to those it enjoyed at the Kroll. To all appearances, that settled the issue, as in the opinion of the government's advisers the theatre could only legally be shut with the Volksbühne's consent. Even the press, which earlier in the year had so effectively championed the Kroll, now seemed resigned to its early demise. It was probably at about this time that Tietjen appeared unannounced in Klemperer's office to tell him that closure was inevitable (see p. 334).

What had brought about the Volksbühne's abrupt change of front? Over the years the organisation had lost the missionary spirit of its founding

* Tietjen was the only other person present. For reasons best known to himself, he subsequently insisted (in a letter to the author, dated 1 August 1965) that he had not attended the meeting. A document in the Staatsministerium theatre file (p. 104) indicates beyond doubt that he did.

fathers. The schoolmasterly bureaucrats who had increasingly come to exercise control continued to mouth fine sentiments and lofty slogans at annual general meetings, but their artistic policies had grown steadily more timid and conventional. That process had come to a head in 1927, when many young and radically minded members, alienated by the organisation's lack of sympathy for new developments in the theatre, had rallied to Piscator's schismatic Junge Volksbühne.* This inner malaise was not the only cause of the Volksbühne's weakness. As the slump had deepened, its finances had inevitably felt the impact of rising unemployment. The 1929/30 season had opened tolerably well, but by February not only was membership falling but a steadily increasing proportion of it was failing to take up its ticket allocation. By June, the Volksbühne admitted that the proportion of unoccupied seats was 'frightening'.† Nestriepke subsequently claimed that he had changed his attitude to the Kroll under pressure from the Kultusministerium.[16] But if the proposal that the Volksbühne should move to the Städtische Oper had originated from that source, it had undoubtedly fallen on fruitful ground.

The Volksbühne had never warmed to the 'experiments' that Klemperer had provided at the Kroll. In a memorandum that probably dates from the spring of 1930, and was thus drafted at a time when it was still eager to preserve the theatre in some form or another, its secretary-general, Siegfried Nestriepke, had made it plain that what his organisation really wanted was 'a popular opera house in the best sense of the word' and one that would specifically exclude the experimental.‡ Or, as Klemperer many years later more trenchantly observed, 'the Volksbühne wanted big singers, big arias, big applause'.[17] Dissatisfaction with Klemperer's Kroll began to be an important factor as soon as the prospect arose of alternative arrangements at the Städtische Oper, whose conventional repertory and style were more to its taste. The Charlottenburg opera was by no means eager to share its theatre with the Volksbühne, but as the Volksbühne's membership diminished from month to month, it became more feasible for it to meet Nestriepke's reduced requirements.

By the middle of June 1930 the Volksbühne was ready to be bought out. Thus when the government held out an offer of a five-year subsidy as an added inducement to forgo its rights at the Kroll, it swallowed the bait. In doing so, it finally undermined the efforts of those elements in the SPD and

---

* The split was, however, as much political as artistic (see p. 261).
† According to its own figures, it amounted in the second week of that month to no less than 45 per cent (*Denkschrift über die Sicherung der Volksbühne vor Mitgliederabfall*, no date).
‡ 'Neuaufbau der Berliner Opernwirtschaft'. From the fact that Nestriepke's estimates provided a sum for conductors that would have made it impossible to meet Klemperer's salary, it may be deduced that the Volksbühne attached little importance to securing his services as musical director of a 'popular' Kroll opera.

in Braun's cabinet which had striven to prevent closure, for the grounds on which they had defended the Kroll stemmed from loyalty to the principle of *soziale Kunstpflege*, as embodied in the state's contract with the Volksbühne, rather than from any enthusiasm for Klemperer's policies. But the board of the Städtische Oper, which had financial difficulties of its own, now proved a stumbling block. By the end of the month no agreement had been reached on the terms on which it would meet the Volksbühne's ticket requirements and at this point the summer holidays intervened.

As *Das Tagebuch* (28 June 1930) observed, the parties concerned had manoeuvred themselves into a bizarre situation. Economic conditions, it argued, had made it inescapable that one of Berlin's three opera houses would be shut. But instead of examining which of them represented the greatest cultural asset at the least cost (and, once the question had been posed in that form, the answer could only be the Kroll) the Prussian Kultusministerium, the Berlin municipality and the Volksbühne, all nominally pledged to *soziale Kunstpflege*, were engaged in horsedealing to ensure that the Kroll would be closed, so that the two costly representational opera houses, whose functions largely overlapped, might continue to exist. The *Tagebuch*'s argument was unassailable in logic. But it overlooked the fact that the ministry had no control over the Städtische Oper and was thus in no position to close it.

*　　　　　　　*　　　　　　　*

During this entire period Klemperer remained surprisingly inactive in defence of his theatre. On New Year's Eve of 1929, when the threat was little more than a cloud on the horizon, he was already aware that its existence was menaced and had indeed told his elder sister that in his view the issue was basically political – a position from which he never deviated.* But he himself made no attempt to enter the fray, even after Tietjen had declared that closure was inevitable. On the contrary, having conducted a revival of *Neues vom Tage*, he left Berlin early in July for a two and a half month holiday on Kampen, the first vacation he and Johanna had taken on the North Sea since 1923. Looking back on that summer of 1930, he later described it to Johanna as the happiest time they had spent together. It was to be a last period of calm and contentment before the storms that lay ahead.[18]

He interrupted the holiday only to make a brief visit to Bayreuth, his first since 1909. What caused him to desert the tranquillity of Kampen for the hubbub of a festival city was the prospect of hearing Toscanini conduct

* Regi Elbogen, letter to Marianne Joseph, 1 January 1930. *Conversations*, p. 67. 'Naturally, it was political. People saw in us a danger and that's why we were closed...'

344

*Tristan und Isolde.** About Wagner himself Klemperer's reservations were as great as ever. 'So much genius', he wrote within a few days of his return, 'and yet also dross (Erdenreste), such as one hardly finds... in any other genius.'† But about Toscanini he had no doubts. At one point Klemperer sat in the orchestral pit. The way in which his great colleague conducted Act 3, he wrote, 'silences all comment'. 'His performances are more than beautiful, they are right.'[19]

*   *   *

By the time the holidays were over, the outer world had grown even darker. In March 1930 Heinrich Brüning had been appointed Chancellor. Having failed to get his drastic financial measures (Notverordnungen) through the Reichstag, he had dissolved it and at elections on 14 September both the extreme Left and, to an even greater degree, the extreme Right had made dramatic gains.‡ The non-Catholic middle-class voters had in large part gone over to the Nazis, and henceforth Prussia stood as a democratic bastion in a rising tide of totalitarianism.§ The results led to further withdrawals of foreign credits and by December 1930 the number of unemployed had risen to more than four million.

When the new Reichstag met on 13 October, Nazi mobs demonstrated in the Leipzigerstrasse, smashing the windows of Jewish department stores in Berlin's main shopping street. That evening rowdies gathered in the Potsdamerplatz, shouting slogans, such as 'Deutschland erwache' and 'Juda verrecke', which were henceforth to be heard on the squares of German cities with ever-increasing frequency. Late in the night, before the Fürstenhof Hotel, where Klemperer sometimes ate, one eye-witness observed gangs of adolescent *Lumpenproletariat* in larger numbers than he had ever seen in the centre of the city. From the fact that some of them appeared to provide a patrol service, he deduced that they were paid.[20] Having established a foothold in parliament, the National Socialists were moving towards control of the streets.

Brüning's *Notverordnungen* had a devastating impact on German operatic

---

* This was the first year that Toscanini conducted at Bayreuth. He returned in 1931 and was due to do so in 1933, when he cancelled as a protest against Nazi treatment of Jewish musicians.
† Letter to Gerhard Meyer-Sichting, 11 August 1930.
'Uns bleibt ein Erdenrest zu tragen peinlich,
Und wär er von Asbest, er ist nicht reinlich.'
Goethe, *Faust*, Part 2, Act 5

‡ The Communists increased their seats from 53 to 77. The National Socialists won no fewer than 107 as opposed to 12, polling 6,400,000 votes as against 810,000.
§ Between 1928 and 1932 there were only eight National Socialist deputies in the Prussian Landtag. Hence the minor role they played in the affairs of the Kroll.

345

life. Between 1928 and 1931 theatre subsidies were reduced from 60,000,000M to 35,000,000M and the number of theatres whose season extended around the year with only a brief summer break declined from 106 to 82. Premières of new operas fell from 60 to 28 and the Dresden state theatres went so far as to remove from their repertory all works on which royalties were payable, a step which virtually eliminated recent music.* A pall of operetta spread over the land, engulfing even major theatres, such as the Linden Opera, which had hitherto staged such works only exceptionally.[21] But behind this need for retrenchment there lay a more sinister change in the cultural atmosphere. A period of exuberant experimentation had come to an end. Intendants who were considered unresponsive to the new wave of 'deutscher Kulturwille' were threatened with dismissal. Universal Edition began to receive requests from German theatres to confirm that Alban Berg was an 'Aryan'.[22] Kurt Weill observed that there had been a 'noticeable retreat from all works that dealt in a new or exposed manner with the problems of form or content in opera'.[23] Indeed Weill himself was only one of several leading composers who seemed ready to accommodate the new mood of conservativism.† The Kroll was by no means alone in feeling the pressure of the time.

As the economic situation grew more menacing Höpker-Aschoff became increasingly insistent on the need to reduce subsidies in the coming budget. Yet having failed to reach an agreement with the Berlin municipality, the Kultusministerium was by the autumn considering whether it might not prove cheaper to maintain the Kroll on a reduced scale than to compensate the Volksbühne and provide it with seats at the stiff price demanded by the Städtische Oper.[24] Braun finally resolved to cut the Gordian knot. On 10 October he called Höpker-Aschoff and Grimme to another *Chefbesprechung*, at which it was agreed that, irrespective of the outcome of the negotiations with the Städtische Oper, the Kroll would be closed at the end of the current season in 1931.

The axe had fallen. But the decision could not be made public until alternative arrangements had been reached to accommodate the Volksbühne elsewhere.‡ It was not until 6 November that the government was officially able to announce that the Kroll would be shut. It also declared

---

* The *Sozialistische Monatshefte*, December 1931, commented that, as the savings amounted to no more than 1,890M, they seemed to be inspired less by a desire to economise than by a dislike of new works.

† Panofsky (*Protest in der Oper*, p. 203) points out that whereas in 1928 Schoenberg, Hindemith, Krenek and Weill were all involved in *Zeitoper*, by 1931 they had all embarked on less controversial and more traditional projects, i.e. *Moses und Aron, Das Unaufhörliche, Karl V* and *Die Bürgschaft*.

‡ Nonetheless on 31 October Tietjen informed the *Betriebsrat* (employees council) of the Staatsoper that the closure of the Kroll was now inevitable (Merseberg, 2.10.6, Nr. 889).

that a further fall in the Volksbühne's membership had made it possible to meet its reduced demand for seats at the Linden Opera, where Monday evenings would be set aside for it. Negotiations would be opened with the Volksbühne to determine the financial compensation it would receive in return for forgoing its rights at the Kroll.[25]

With every month that passed the Volksbühne's ability to offer resistance had grown weaker. It was in debt to the city of Berlin, its theatre on the Bülowplatz was mortgaged, its operations were running at a deficit.[26] To these troubles was added a further severe fall in membership. The gale-like proportions of the crisis that had struck the German economy are apparent from the fact that by the opening of the 1930/1 season the Volksbühne's membership numbered 26,000 less than the 86,000 it had anticipated when it had entered into its commitments for that season only a few months earlier.* In such conditions it was eager to lay its hands on any compensation that could be squeezed out of the Kultusministerium.

It is a measure of the remoteness of Klemperer and his staff that they only became aware of the precarious condition of the Volksbühne when, early in October, its chairman, Curt Baarke, visited the Kroll to convey the complaints of its members at the revival of *Neues vom Tage*. Two or three weeks later, Curjel, who was acting director, belatedly invited Siegfried Nestriepke to discuss their mutual difficulties. Conversation had hardly begun when Klemperer appeared. It was his first meeting with the Volksbühne's leading functionary and it did not run smoothly. Klemperer abruptly asked why the Volksbühne was ready to abandon its rights at the Kroll. Nestriepke launched into a catalogue of complaints about the repertory, but then conceded that his organisation's membership had fallen to a point where it could no longer take up its quota of tickets. Klemperer leapt on that admission: the Volksbühne, he told Nestriepke, was demanding compensation from the state for the abrogation of a contract it could no longer fulfil.[27]

---

* 'Berliner Volksbühne und Krolloper', *Die Volksbühne*, 5 December 1930. The propensity of the Volksbühne to look for protection to the state was to contribute to its ignominious end. As early as the summer of 1933, its organ, *Die Volksbühne* (No. 5/6, pp. 3–4, quoted in Schwerd, *Zwischen Sozialdemokratie und Kommunismus*, p. 135,) after dismissing the Nazi policy of *Gleichschaltung* as 'a superficial matter', went on to claim that 'The social aims of the Volksbühne...have today become the general policy of the rulers of the state. On this point the organisational ideas of the Volksbühne clearly correspond with the intentions of the government.' This is not the only instance in twentieth-century history of left-wing *étatisme* finding common ground with right-wing authoritarianism. The Nazis made great play with their 'social policies' and the Volksbühne fell for it.

The Bühnenvolksbund, which had been occupying almost as many seats as the Volksbühne, was also feeling the pinch. On 26 August 1930 it informed Tietjen that in the coming season it would be reducing its ticket requirements by a third (Stompor, 'Musiktheater', pp. 2511–13).

The encounter stung Klemperer into action. The following day he and Curjel went to see Tietjen, who referred them to Grimme. The Kultusminister offered expressions of regret and blamed Höpker-Aschoff. Klemperer then moved on to the Landtag, where he saw Lauscher, whose motion had played a crucial role in undermining the government's will to fight for the Kroll, and a couple of deputies on the far right who had attacked his artistic policies with particular virulence. He then called on Höpker-Aschoff himself. The Finance Minister vouchsafed the information that he disliked Wagner. In that case, replied Klemperer, he should have sympathy for a theatre that had only one opera by Wagner in its repertory. There was an argument about figures, which Höpker-Aschoff cut short by dryly remarking that this at any rate was a field he understood. 'That's just as well', retorted Klemperer, 'It's what you're paid for.'[28]

At all these meetings Klemperer made great play with his sense of outrage that money which might have helped to maintain the Kroll should be used to indemnify the Volksbühne for the annulment of a contract it was unable to fulfil. In doing so, he found himself in a bizarre alliance with those right-wing members of the Landtag who regarded the proposed compensation announced on 13 November as further evidence of the favoured treatment that the organisation had over the years received from its friends in the Kultusministerium. That was not the only paradox: precisely those political circles which were most eager to close the Kroll were most unwilling to approve a deal that was an essential precondition to doing so.

On 11 December an agreement between the Volksbühne and the Prussian state was finally tabled in the Landtag and six days later passed by a small majority of Zentrum and SPD deputies in the Hauptausschuss against the opposition of the right-wing parties. On 19 December the issue was again debated at a plenum session of the Landtag. But the discussions, which were delayed by a sudden vote of confidence on another matter, took longer than foreseen, and before a vote could be taken, the Landtag adjourned for its six-week Christmas break. Weimar democracy was giving abundant evidence of its ineffectiveness and the comedy was far from over.

*　　　　　　　*　　　　　　　*

The government's announcement on 6 November that it had decided to close the Kroll occasioned a storm of protest. Now that Klemperer's theatre was near the point of extinction, there was a sudden awareness of what, with all its shortcomings, it had come to represent. Article after article pointed to its unified style, its strong ensemble and its adventurous repertory, in all of which it was held to be markedly superior to the Linden and city operas. On 9 November Klemperer conducted a matinée

348

performance of *The Soldier's Tale* attended by Stravinsky. When the two men appeared together on stage they were greeted by demonstrative storms of applause.[29] Three days later in an interview Stravinsky expressed his amazement that such a unique institution as the Kroll was about to be closed. 'In no other city have I and my works met with such interest and understanding as in Berlin. For that I have to thank above all Otto Klemperer and the Kroll Opera, in which not just individual works but almost my entire output has been performed, so that it has been possible to gain an overall picture of it.'[30] Stravinsky also joined Thomas Mann, Weill, Hindemith and others in an appeal for the preservation of the Kroll that appeared in *Das Tagebuch* on 15 November. Mann, who led the protest, asked why the opera house that cost the least and offered the most intellectual stimulus should be singled out as a victim of the difficult times the German economy was going through.

> Why? Because the Kroll Opera occupies a strong position on the intellectual left, because it stands at the crossroads of social and cultural interests and is a thorn in the eye of...obscurantism (Verstocktheit). If opera today is still or has once again become an intellectual issue and a subject of intellectual discussion, that is in the first place the merit of *this* institution...I do not know how the Berlin opera crisis is to be solved, but it should certainly not be solved at the cost of the Kroll...

Leading figures in German theatrical life joined in the campaign, the *Betriebsrat* of the State Opera petitioned the Landtag and agitation in the press gained momentum. Desperate and implausible plans, in some of which Klemperer himself was involved, were drawn up to incorporate the Kroll in the Landesbühne, to turn it into a touring company or a privately subsidised experimental studio, while Tietjen obligingly produced a scheme for maintaining it with a more popular repertory and a reduced subsidy. For an institution that had been condemned to death, it was belatedly showing remarkable powers of resistance.

*   *   *

These battles occurred during the early months of a season that had got off to an inauspicious start. For the opening production of *The Barber of Seville* Curjel engaged Arthur Maria Rabenalt and Wilhelm Reinking, a young team of producer and designer that had already made a name for itself in Darmstadt, notably with its radical approach to light opera. In an article provocatively entitled 'Die Entbürgerlichung der Spieloper' and published in the same month as the duo made its Berlin début at the Kroll, Rabenalt outlined his plan of campaign. *Spieloper* had become a bastion of 'cosy and complacent philistinism'. 'A surgical-dramaturgical knife' must be taken to its 'oozing sentimentality'. Entire scenes should, where necessary, be excised and old characters replaced with new ones, so as to tighten the action. 'A musical dramaturgy must be established, which is not founded on...old musical forms, but on the dynamic law of our dramatic sensibility today.'[31]

In accordance with this programme, Rabenalt and Reinking brought the action forward to 'around the middle of the nineteenth century' and used modern dress.[32] That was common practice in the German theatre of the time and Reinking's sketches seem to have occasioned no adverse comment when he presented them earlier in the summer. By September, however, the political situation had been transformed by the huge gains made by the National Socialists in the general election. Four days after those elections, on 19 September, Tietjen appeared at the dress rehearsal. As soon as Count Almaviva made his entry in a blazer and Oxford bags Reinking observed the usually impassive Intendant nervously drumming his fingers on the balustrade of his box. When Figaro raised the shutters of his barber's shop to reveal two massively bosomed and elaborately coifed wax customers Tietjen leapt to his feet, shouted 'curtain' and stormed out of the auditorium.[33]

As a result of this intervention, the première was postponed. But Tietjen was not alone in his disapproval of the production. Reinking subsequently accused Klemperer and Zweig, who was conducting and had distinctly conservative tastes in the matter of staging, of having 'demonstratively opposed my approach before and after the première'.* Curjel alone fought for the production. But having made his point with uncharacteristic flamboyancy, Tietjen wavered. Through photographers who had witnessed the incident the press got wind of what had occurred; comments were far from favourable. After almost a fortnight's indecision, he suddenly gave permission for the production to be staged with minimal alterations.† Nothing essential was altered. But the wily *Generalintendant* had made his point; through his intervention he had dissociated himself publicly from an event that was liable to attract criticism in the right-wing circles, whose power was clearly in the ascendancy.

It was not Tietjen's only means of distancing himself from the liberal and socialist men in the Kultusministerium on whose backs he had risen

* Letter to Tietjen, 5 November 1930. Klemperer subsequently made no bones about his disapproval. In an interview with *La Plata Post* (Buenos Aires, 29 May 1931) he stated his view that a work imposed certain limitations of style. Rabenalt had overshot these in search of 'mere theatrical effectiveness...One cannot arbitrarily alter the form and expression of a work of art.' Zweig, who had the ear of his Intendant, has stated that he complained to Tietjen about the production. (Undated typescript memoirs in Curjel's *Nachlass*, confirmed in conversation with the author)
† In a letter (1 December 1981) to the author, Reinking claimed that he agreed to these alterations only as a means of saving Tietjen's face and that they were not finally put into effect.

to power. The second production of the season was to be the first German staging at the end of October of Janáček's posthumous opera, *From the House of the Dead*, which Klemperer had himself intended to conduct since the time of the composer's visit to Berlin in September 1927. In late September, however, anti-German demonstrations in Prague led to a ban on German films on the ground that their showing might occasion further disorder. As a protest Tietjen on 28 October announced the postponement of the production, which was on the point of opening.*

As a result, the only new production in which Klemperer was directly involved during the first half of the season was of Hindemith's miniature opera, *Hin und zurück*, whose first performance he had attended at Baden-Baden in 1927 (see p. 245n). This came to pass in a bizarre manner. Eckart von Naso, who had succeeded Curjel as *Dramaturg*, was a member of the Rot-Weiss tennis club, whose annual dinner-dance was an event in the Berlin social calendar. It was customarily preceded by a theatrical entertainment, in the choice of which von Naso had a say. It thus came about that the Kroll agreed to provide a show to precede the more convivial part of the evening. Von Naso later recorded his amazement at the care and total lack of cynicism with which the Kroll set about preparing for the event.[34] But the fare it chose to set before an audience of socialites and sportsmen in *grande toilette* also suggests a degree of unworldliness.

The programme opened on 29 November with a revival of *L'Heure espagnole* under Zemlinsky and continued with a spanking account from Klemperer of the *Kleine Dreigroschenmusik*, which, predictably, proved the hit of the evening. Then followed items that had been specially prepared for the occasion. The Kroll had hitherto turned a cold, even contemptuous shoulder on ballet. To entertain an audience of tennis enthusiasts it now chose to stage Debussy's *Jeux*, whose amorous frolics take place around a tennis court. It was a nice pleasantry, but the music was sufficiently recondite to lead to a premature exit of those members of the audience whose mind was already turning to their supper. Hindemith's *Hin und zurück*, whose action goes into reverse motion half way through the piece, completed what was intended as a light-hearted evening *à la* Kroll. But in spite of the fact that Klemperer conducted, Moholy-Nagy contributed a witty set, Curjel for the first time set his hand to production and Johanna scored a notable success in one of the two principal roles, it failed to raise

---

* *Berliner Tageblatt*. Klaus Pringsheim later asserted that Tietjen had acted on instructions from the German Foreign Office (*Vorwärts*, 29 May 1931). Similar pressure may also account for his carpeting in March 1930 of Zemlinsky and Novotna on the grounds that they had taken part in a performance in Prague of Beethoven's Ninth Symphony, sung partly in Czech! Curjel's *Nachlass* contains a note in which he lists this incident among 'Tietjens *Eingriffe*'.

much laughter. Within fifteen minutes the auditorium was transformed into a ballroom, Marek Weber and his orchestra dispensed tangos, slow foxtrots and English waltzes, and Jarmila Novotna, the belle of the Kroll, took the floor with one of the many tennis stars who were present.[35]

Two weeks before this heterogeneous evening, the *Vossische Zeitung* announced that Klemperer would be conducting a new production at the Kroll of *Tristan und Isolde* with Moje Forbach as the heroine and, following Toscanini's example at Bayreuth, another soprano (instead of the more usual mezzo) as Brangäne. The relationship of this production to the projected studio version is unclear (see pp. 256 and 327n). That Dülberg designed sets for one or other is certain, and Moje Forbach has stated that it was intended that Fehling should produce.[36] Solo rehearsals had been in progress since October and stage rehearsals were planned to start before Christmas.[37] But the project was abandoned at an early stage,* and Klemperer was never again to conduct an opera with which he had been so closely associated earlier in his career.

Its place was taken by a production of *Figaros Hochzeit* that was mounted on 25 January 1931 as part of the celebrations of the one hundred and seventy-fifth anniversary of Mozart's birth. It was to provide the Kroll with what it desperately needed: an artistic triumph that also filled the theatre. As Dülberg declined to collaborate and Curjel's attempt to involve Moholy-Nagy came to nothing,† the sets were handed over to the young Teo Otto, who had hitherto played only a subordinate role at the Kroll. His designs were closer to Goya than to Boucher: instead of the customary pink, gold and blue, the colours were predominantly grey and realistic.[38] Such an approach was well matched to the view of the opera taken by both Klemperer and his producer Gustav Gründgens, who, in spite of differences in temperament, worked in surprising harmony on what was to be the first of three collaborations. Otto subsequently recorded his amazement at the detailed consideration they gave to the opera's political background.‡ Their determination to stress the social tensions that underlie the action inevitably attracted criticism, and Erich Bachmann, among others, complained that the result was closer to Beaumarchais than to da Ponte.[39] But Oscar Bie, who had attended a performance under Mahler in Vienna, maintained that the work's pre-revolutionary aspects had on that

---

* A note in Curjel's *Nachlass* suggests that there were casting difficulties.
† According to Stompor ('Musiktheater', p. 2396), Moholy worked on designs for *Figaro*, but abandoned the project after three weeks.
‡ WDR interview with Curjel. As Szabo's film, *Mephisto*, based on the novel of the same title by Gründgens's brother-in-law, Klaus Mann, indicates, the future *Staatsrat* and Intendant of the Berlin Schauspielhaus during the Third Reich, was at this time in an early 'progressive' phase of his development.

occasion been even more drastically underlined than they were at the Kroll.[40]

In the opinion of Walther Schrenk Klemperer occasionally over-emphasised the score's shadows and asperity, while Einstein considered the accents in the overture (taken at a rattling pace) too vehement. But both agreed that the music had been made to articulate the drama to an unusual degree. Einstein claimed that he could not recall a more profoundly unified account of the extended finale to the second act.[41] Many critics detected a new tenderness in Klemperer's interpretation, and Victor Zuckerkandl also found him more attentive to the needs of the singers.[42] That corresponded with their own impressions. Novotna (Cherubino) subsequently recalled him as more approachable and relaxed than he had been during the rehearsals for *Die Zauberflöte* a year earlier, while the breathless hush that had seemed to surround the chords that introduce 'Deh vieni' was years later still a vivid memory to Irene Eisinger, who scored a notable success as Susanna.* A rising young baritone, Willi Domgraf-Fassbänder, made a particularly strong impression in the title role.† But what by general consent gave the performance its outstanding distinction was an immaculate ensemble that extended to the last detail. Klemperer was the hero of the evening. To the irritation of the handful of hostile critics who had been baying for his theatre's closure, he was greeted at every appearance with tumultuous applause, as young people in the balcony repeatedly chanted his name as a demonstration of support for the condemned Kroll. Had Klemperer and his company achieved such a triumph earlier in their chequered history, the outcome of the struggle surrounding the theatre might have been different.

*   *   *

Two days later Klemperer left for London, where on 2 and 3 February he conducted a programme consisting of Schoenberg's orchestral transcription of Bach's Prelude and Fugue in E flat and Beethoven's Ninth Symphony. The former did not go down well. 'We disliked Schoenberg's orchestration', pronounced *The Times* (3 February 1931), 'which seemed to emulate the worst qualities of the modern German organ – to English ears intolerably crude and coarse.' Klemperer's account of the Choral Symphony, with which twenty-six years later he was to put a seal on his reputation in London, divided the critics. Eric Blom in particular found nothing to praise

---

* Both comments were made in interviews with the author. It is worth noting that whereas in Strasbourg Klemperer had made an issue of casting the role of Susanna with a sizeable, 'womanly' voice, at the Kroll he used a soubrette, a practice he had so trenchantly condemned fifteen years earlier.
† As he did three years later in the *Figaro* with which Glyndebourne opened its doors.

in the first three movements.[43] But although Ernest Newman agreed that the performance had begun 'in a rather sober, Kapellmeisterlike style', it has grown in power and finished magnificently. 'For once, criticism of the purely musical quality of parts of the finale was silenced; one was swept away by the mighty impulse that underlies the sometimes commonplace realisation of the pious sentiments of Schiller's poem...'[44] W. J. Turner, Klemperer's sole advocate among the pre-war London critics, went much further.

Mr Klemperer much impressed all perceptive English musicians who heard him for the first time...last year. But he put a seal on his reputation in England this week, for he revealed a virtuosity of the highest degree subserving a wholly artistic conception. Delicacy and refinement went together with vitality and power, and added to them was that personal force which can magnetise an orchestra and chorus...and weld them together into one instrument working with the conductor in the service of art...

A performance of such outstanding quality – so pure, so straight, so sensitive and so overwhelming...serves to destroy for ever the absurd idea that Beethoven did not know what he was doing when he wrote a choral finale to the Ninth Symphony...I was overjoyed and exhilarated by a performance of such magnificence that if Beethoven had been living one can only imagine him embracing Klemperer as he embraced Weber and saying: 'You are a splendid fellow.'[45]

The players disliked him every bit as much as they had done on his first appearance in London fifteen months earlier (see p. 320), but several of those most bitterly resentful of his behaviour in rehearsal later conceded that the performance of the Choral Symphony had been outstanding. And for once Klemperer seemed well content with what he had achieved. From Rome, where he arrived on 6 February, he wrote to his wife,

These two evenings in London were really very good (schön). The success splendid beyond all measure. Very important for me that I was once again able to experience the Ninth quite strongly, after I had to some extent over-conducted it in the many performances I gave in Russia. The Courtaulds were enchanting to me. For the first time I really got to know them properly and to esteem them as human beings.[46]

Again Rome delighted him. The sun shone, the sky was blue, the women attractive, 'only they have the effect of antique statues, which one does not touch', as he cautiously added in his letter to Johanna. In the first of his two concerts the principal work was again Bruckner's Seventh Symphony, at that time virtually unknown in Italy. To the evident surprise of the critics, who showed little enthusiasm for the music, the audience listened attentively and applauded warmly.

Between rehearsals Klemperer spent his spare time sitting out of doors in the gardens of the Villa Borghese or taking walks along the Tiber with a new acquaintance, Roger Sessions.* Sessions asked him to describe Stravinsky's new *Symphony of Psalms*, whose first German performance he was to conduct in Berlin on 19 February. Klemperer reflected, and then with a single word replied, 'Ravenna'. They also discussed Beethoven's Choral Symphony, and when Sessions revealed that he had never heard the work without Wagner's instrumental retouchings, Klemperer invited his young American friend to Berlin to hear him conduct it in this form.†

But Klemperer's mind was never far from the Kroll. On 26 January, the day after the première of *Figaro*, the *Berliner Tageblatt* had published an article by him entitled, 'In eigener Sache'. Never a man who readily took up a pen, he now for the first time addressed himself, over the heads of the politicians and administrators he had hitherto lobbied, to the general public. In terse, trenchant language, he recounted how his hatred of repertory opera and the mediocre standards it involved had led him to the conception of a theatre in which a limited number of productions could be maintained at a high level, and how the Volksbühne's commitment to the Kroll had seemed to promise conditions in which that ambition could be realised. And to a considerable extent, he insisted, it *had* been fulfilled.

Every work was completely newly studied and designed. We never gave more than ten to twelve operas at any one time. The terrible *Leitmotiv* of German operatic life, 'We don't have the time', was at last abolished in our theatre. Thus we could give each production a strength that enabled it to stand up to frequent performances.

Klemperer went on to point out that modern works had formed no larger a proportion of the repertory than they did in most provincial theatres.‡ The Kroll had also proved a singularly economical opera house.

And now we are to be struck down in mid-course. Of course we have made mistakes. Periods of enthusiastic progress have given way to spells of hesitancy, as is inevitable in any long campaign. We are in mid-course and the work is to be taken out of our hands. So be it. Then whoever comes next will have to continue what we have begun. Whenever this concept of opera is taken up again, a beginning will have to be made where we have been obliged to leave off. Our theatre may be closed, but the idea behind it cannot be destroyed.

In Rome Klemperer seized the opportunity to call on Pacelli, who, on leaving his post as Nuncio in Berlin, had been appointed Secretary of State at the Vatican. The future Pope Pius XII had been a frequent visitor to the

---

* Roger Sessions (1896–   ), subsequently one of America's most esteemed and influential composers. A late developer, Sessions, who had studied with Ernest Bloch, had in 1931 not yet found his creative feet and was living in Europe.
† Klemperer arranged for Sessions to stay with Max Strub for several weeks in March and April. It was to be only the first of several visits that he made to Berlin.
‡ For instance, while *Fidelio* had been given fifty-eight performances, *Oedipus Rex* – one of the most successful and most performed productions of modern works at the Kroll – had been seen no more than eleven times.

Kroll and Klemperer found him understanding. Pacelli suggested that he approach Prälat Kaas, the leader of the Catholic Zentrum, and the Chancellor, Heinrich Brüning, who was a member of the same party. The advice was shrewd, for, while the Socialists and Democrats were well disposed to the opera house they had called into existence, and the right-wing parties were for that very reason opposed to it, the Zentrum's withdrawal of its earlier support had, more than any other single factor, undermined the Kroll's position. Back in Berlin Klemperer saw Kaas, to whom he unrealistically suggested that the Reich might perhaps be persuaded to assume responsibility for the theatre.[47] But an interview with the beleaguered Chancellor put an end to any such illusions. Brüning told Klemperer that the Kroll had been called into existence at the wrong time: instead of building theatres Germany should have paid its debts. So far as he was concerned, the decision to close it was a belated step in the direction of financial responsibility.*

That decision was now to all intents and purposes irreversible. As though to emphasise the point, Nestriepke told a meeting of the Betriebsrat at the State Opera on 9 February that the Volksbühne had no intention of remaining at the Kroll, even if it were to be spared: the arrangements that the Kultusministerium had made for performances at the Linden Opera were manifestly more to its liking. On 26 February Höpker-Aschoff informed the Landtag sub-committee, which was considering the state theatres' budget for the coming financial year, that all personnel at the Kroll not on long-term contracts would be given notices of dismissal the following day and this duly occurred.[48]

As his contract did not expire until 1937, Klemperer himself was not directly affected. But pouncing on a clause in it, he wrote on the following day, 28 February, to Tietjen, to point out that, in the event of the closure of the Kroll, he was bound to perform similar duties at the Linden Opera. These duties, he maintained, were described in his contract as those of 'a functioning musical director in the fullest sense' ('amtierender General-musikdirektor in vollem Umfang'). In view of the fact that Kleiber already occupied that position at the Linden Opera, he asked what steps the Prussian government would take to fulfil its commitment. Tietjen was absent in Kassel when this letter landed on his desk on the morning of Monday, 2 March, and that evening he had to attend a meeting of the Landtag sub-committee on the budget for his theatres. At two o'clock in the afternoon of the following day Klemperer abruptly announced to the

---

* Autobiographical sketch, p. 21. On 1 March 1931, after he had conducted Stravinsky's *Symphony of Psalms* in the Berlin Philharmonie at a concert in memory of St Augustine, sponsored by the Katholischer Akademiker-Verband, Klemperer met the German Chancellor more informally and found him 'an uncommonly sensitive and understanding man'.

press that, as he had received no reply from Tietjen, he would take legal action to ensure that the terms of his contract, as he interpreted them, would be fulfilled. 'Klemperer brings an action against the state' ran the headlines in the evening edition of the *Berliner Tageblatt*.

That very evening Tietjen wrote to tell Klemperer that he was 'absolutely amazed' to learn of the step he had taken, but that in the circumstances there was nothing he could do but let the law take its course. The Kultusministerium was also astonished because it had that morning been informed by Tietjen that he planned to invite Klemperer to a meeting the following day. Whether Klemperer's precipitancy or a degree of dilatoriness on Tietjen's part was more to blame for the situation that had arisen was of little moment. Klemperer was again entering a manic phase that was to prove the most intense he had suffered since his years in Strasbourg. The rough time he had given orchestral players in London, his eye for women in Rome, the growing zest with which after a period of inactivity he had belatedly thrown himself into the battle for the Kroll were all evidence of his condition.

As an invariable concomitant of such a period, Klemperer had once again started to compose. On 9 February he had sent Willy Strecker of Schotts a new song from Rome, and shortly after his return to Berlin had followed it up with settings of 'Ave Maria' and 'Pater Noster', which he had composed in Leningrad in March 1929 (see p. 297) but since allowed to gather dust. Meanwhile he had reverted to the project he had abandoned two years earlier of performing his opera, *Das Ziel*. To that end Universal Edition had already agreed to print the score. To his credit, Willy Strecker proved less amenable.

You have [he wrote on 24 February] such a great position in musical life today and the entire younger generation looks up to you as to a born leader, whose judgement and decisions serve as guiding principles. [Thus] anything that comes from you...is examined under a magnifying glass...One thinks of Virgil's dictum, 'Parturiunt montes nascietur ridiculus mus'.* As a friend, I would advise you simply to have this 'Pater Noster' performed and only to make a decision about publication at a later date...

It was bravely spoken, particularly by a publisher to some extent dependent on Klemperer's sympathetic consideration of new works. But Klemperer, riding high, brushed aside this sound advice and insisted on publication 'even at the risk that young Germany rebukes me for being reactionary'.†

He was now in a frame of mind in which he would brook no constraint.

---

* The quotation, 'The mountains labour, a ridiculous mouse is born', comes not, as Strecker imagined, from Virgil but from Horace's *Ars Poetica*, 139.

† Letter to Willy Strecker, 27 February 1931. The works in question were duly published in the course of the year.

Just as he rejected Strecker's warning words, so he dismissed the advice of his friend and lawyer, Fritz Fischer, that the prospects of succeeding in his claim against the Prussian state were remote,* and a first hearing before a labour tribunal was accordingly fixed for 21 March. Klemperer later insisted that his purpose in bringing the action was to preserve his right to determine the operas he could be asked to conduct at the Linden Opera. It was, however, widely interpreted as an attempt to ensure that he would exercise there the powers that he had enjoyed at the Kroll, in spite of the fact that Kleiber's contract, which was not due to expire until August 1932, contained a clause stipulating that no other conductor was to be engaged as his superior. Tietjen subsequently claimed that he had already made Klemperer aware of this situation, when at the close of the previous season he had first warned him that the days of the Kroll were numbered.[49] Klemperer nonetheless chose to persist in his action.

If his recourse to legal proceedings seemed from the start doomed to defeat, Klemperer's lobbying of the Landtag belatedly began to yield surprising fruit. Confronted for the first time in the flesh by the *Kulturbolschewist* bogeyman they had supposed him to be, right-wing members were surprised to discover how far removed he was from the image they had had of him. To general amazement, when in the first week of March the Hauptausschuss debated the budgetary estimates of the state theatres, which naturally made no provision for the Kroll's continuance, a minority of the Deutschnational deputies, who had only a few weeks earlier been most eager to end its existence, began to have second thoughts. In particular, Pastor Koch, while maintaining his assaults on 'republican art', asserted that Klemperer had shown signs of reform and on that account raised the question of whether the Kroll could not be maintained as a *Filialbetrieb*. Tietjen, who appeared as a witness on 6 March, rightly dismissed the scheme, which had in effect been tried between 1924 and 1927 and found wanting, as impractical. But a split had opened in the ranks of the Kroll's fiercest adversaries. Thus when a vote was taken on closure it was passed by a majority of only one, with two Deutschnational members of the committee joining with the Socialists and Communists in opposing it.

After a ten-week interval the debate on the Volksbühne's contract was simultaneously resumed at a plenum session of the Landtag on 5 and 6 March. The public gallery was filled to the last seat – a rare spectacle – mainly by members of the Kroll with their musical director at their head. According to Domgraf-Fassbänder, who was present, Klemperer became

---

* Author's interview with Fritz Fischer, October 1964. Fischer (1888–1972) was a close friend of Schnabel, through whom he had come to know Klemperer well.

very excited and noisily interrupted the debate.[50] 'It is natural', commented the Nazi organ, *Der Angriff* (6 March 1931), 'that these disciples of Moscow should seize the opportunity to make a little theatre.' To the irritation of his colleagues, Pastor Koch reverted to his new role as a defender of the Kroll. He pointed out that a plenum session of the Landtag had never voted for the theatre to be closed,* and in the course of the protracted struggle over its continued existence it had come closer than any other state theatre in meeting the estimates for the last financial year. Klemperer's public quarrel with the Volksbühne had earned him some strange allies.

The network of issues and aims had indeed become farcically entangled. A Socialist member opposed the closure of the Kroll, but urged acceptance of a new Volksbühne contract, whose prime purpose was to make that closure possible in law. Conversely, most (but not all) the right-wing deputies were torn between opposition to compensating the Volksbühne and determination to close the theatre, while a minority opposed the contract yet sought to preserve the Kroll in some other form. The Communists, who had hitherto opposed subsidies to all state theatres as organs of a bourgeois regime, now instanced the government's desire to shut the Kroll as evidence of its intention to abolish *soziale Kunstpflege*. The KPD spokesman therefore opposed compensation for the Volksbühne. Thus when a vote was taken, the Communists and right-wing parties joined in abstaining. But as twenty-three members of the Zentrum also abstained, the government coalition nonetheless failed to achieve a quorum. The ineffectiveness of German democracy could not have been more cruelly exposed than in this bizarre failure of the Prussian government to bring about the closure of an opera house.

Meanwhile a ground-swell of support for the Kroll continued to gather momentum, as the moderation that Klemperer's former enemies now claimed to detect in his policies was reflected in new productions at the Kroll. As Einstein pointed out, the theatre seemed in *Louise*† and *Figaro* to have made a breakthrough that had eluded it in earlier seasons.[51] In the twilight of its existence the Kroll now went from success to success. On 23 February, Zemlinsky conducted a new production of *Madam Butterfly*, the first full-length opera to be presented at the Kroll by a composer it had

---

* Technically correct. At Höpker-Aschoff's insistence the right-wing motion to cut the Kroll's budget so as to oblige it to shut its doors had been withdrawn on 16 May 1930 on the grounds that the theatre could not be deprived of the means of meeting its legally incurred commitments. The Zentrum's motion, passed on 7 May 1930, had merely called for negotiations with the Berlin municipality so as to *enable* the government to shut the Kroll. When these negotiations had broken down the government had without consulting the Landtag simply removed the theatre from the budget for the coming season and subsequently dismissed its staff.

† On 12 December 1930 Zemlinsky had conducted a new production with considerable success.

hitherto regarded with disdain. Jarmila Novotna was an alluring heroine and Charles Kullman, a young American tenor still studying at the Hochschule, made an auspicious début as Pinkerton.* Curjel's production and even Moholy-Nagy's sets were cordially received. As though to emphasise that a period of experimentation was over, Moholy abandoned the radical innovations he had made in *The Tales of Hoffmann*. In sets which consisted of a delicate bamboo framework that could be transformed into a variety of shapes, all seen against a backcloth depicting a bird's eye view of Nagasaki harbour, a place was found even for naturalistic details such as glow-worms and a real fountain.† That Klemperer himself took over the second performance on 26 February of an opera that he had only previously conducted on one isolated occasion in Cologne is further evidence of how far he was now prepared to go to appease his critics.‡

The Kroll's next bid for public favour was, however, more in accordance with his taste. Since his début with Reinhardt in 1906, Klemperer had been a fervent admirer of Offenbach's operettas, a devotion he shared with Karl Kraus, the Viennese satirist and critic who was celebrated for 'readings', or *Theater der Dichtung*, as he preferred to call them, in which he sang and recited his own drastically revised versions of the texts. Klemperer had earlier met Kraus in Berlin at a performance of *Die Dreigroschenoper*, after which negotiations were set on foot for the Kroll to perform his new version of *La Périchole*.[52] Most German opera houses included one or two operettas in their repertory and Kraus seemed to provide an opportunity to present a specimen with more intellectual edge than the genre usually offered. Zweig, who earlier in his career had accompanied Kraus's recitations on the piano, conducted, a producer and a number of singers who specialised in operetta were engaged and, in accordance with the Kroll's usual practice of commissioning introductions to new productions for the *Blätter der Staatsoper*, Walter Benjamin contributed an essay entitled 'Offenbach – gesehen von Karl Kraus'.

In spite of these elaborate preparations, rehearsals did not go smoothly. Like most of Offenbach's operettas, Kraus's versions were designed to be played in a small auditorium. In a large theatre such as the Kroll much

---

* Charles Kullman (1903–1983) has recalled to the author how Klemperer suddenly appeared at an audition and demanded a high note. Kullman responded with a ringing A flat on 'America for ever' and was promptly engaged. Thereafter he made numerous appearances under Klemperer and recorded *Das Lied von der Erde* under Walter. From 1935 to 1960 he sang at the Metropolitan Opera House in New York.

† Sibyl Moholy-Nagy claims that by 1930 Moholy-Nagy had ceased to believe that opera could be modernised. By the time of *Madam Butterfly* he had also abandoned the mechanical features that had figured prominently in his settings for *The Tales of Hoffmann* two years earlier (*László Moholy-Nagy, ein Totalexperiment*, p. 52).

‡ These are the only two occasions on which Klemperer conducted any opera by Puccini.

360

of the text went for little and pace was lost. Kraus became dissatisfied and tension rose further when he refused to countenance any cuts.* On the first night (27 March) he is said to have sat in the balcony and instigated booing. If the story is true, it did not prevent him from appearing on stage to acknowledge applause at the end of the evening. The Kroll had scored another success and Klemperer, who was usually loath to conduct an isolated performance of a production he had not himself prepared musically, again did so on 6 April.

*   *   *

On 18 March the Prussian government made yet another attempt to push its new agreement with the Volksbühne through the Landtag and yet again failed to secure a quorum. Meanwhile, Klemperer had made progress in a last ditch effort to secure private support for the Kroll,† and within twenty-four hours of the inconclusive vote in the Landtag three of the most influential daily newspapers in the capital – the *Vossische Zeitung, Berliner Tageblatt* and the *Berliner Börsen-Courier* – combined to urge that the relatively small amount of money that he would require to reconstitute the theatre as a modest *Volksoper* be made available from public funds. In his manic condition, he himself seemed oblivious of the artistic implications of such a step. Having for so long stood aside from the struggle to preserve the Kroll, he now seemed ready to do so at almost any price.

On 25 March the government once more failed to secure a quorum for the Volksbühne bill. On the same day, however, the Zentrum, confronted with a further rise in the deficit of the state theatres, determined to grasp the nettle by presenting a bill to close the Kroll that had already passed the Hauptausschuss by a narrow majority on 6 March. The right-wing parties supported the motion, the Socialists abstained and only the Communists, who were henceforth to pose as the sole defenders of a theatre that they had so often attacked, opposed it. Klemperer and many members of his company were in the Landtag to witness its death sentence. Walking through the Tiergarten with Curjel on his way home, as was his habit, Klemperer was attacked in broad daylight by a group of young Nazis. Only a passing taxi enabled him to escape.[53]

As the *Berliner Tageblatt* pointed out the following day, a grotesque situation had now arisen: the Kroll's existence had formally been ended,

---

* He subsequently repeated these complaints in his periodical, *Die Fackel* (No. 852, pp. 25–6), quoted in Stompor ('Musiktheater', p. 2446), but was obliged to admit that on the second night the performance had run 47 minutes less than at the première.
† Some of the organisations that responded to his appeal – such as the Verband deutscher Motorradfahrer and the Verein chinesischer Studenten – can hardly have been motivated by anything beyond the possibility of cheap seats.

thus confirming *de jure* a situation that had been established *de facto* since the previous November, when Höpker-Aschoff had refused to make provision for the theatre after the end of the current season. Yet the original Volksbühne agreement of 1923, which presupposed the theatre's existence, was still operative, owing to the Landtag's inability to reach agreement on a replacement.

At this point, however, the right-wing opponents of the new Volksbühne bill agreed to abandon their obstructive tactics on condition that the Landtag set up a formal committee to investigate the relationship of the Volksbühne and the Kroll to the Kultusministerium since the war, in the confident expectation that light would be cast on some shady aspects of the government's *Kulturpolitik*. Even this course of action was at first blocked by a failure of the coalition parties and their opponents to agree on the number of members who should sit on the committee. On 21 March, however, the government gave way and a committee of twenty-nine deputies, which was to conduct its investigations in public, was duly set up. In the coming weeks Berlin was to be entertained by two public spectacles and in both of them Klemperer was to play a central role.

*   *   *

On 24 March Klemperer appeared before the Labour Tribunal that was to hear his suit against the Prussian state. As the contesting parties were not permitted to be represented by lawyers, he was obliged to conduct his own case, which he proceeded to do with a vigour that kept his name in the headlines.

At the plaintiff's desk, the huge figure of Klemperer, the sharply cut, passionate, almost fanatical features, with glasses and a mop of black hair, bowed over his papers. Sometimes looking around him when the door of the courtroom opens or there is whispering at the press table. Even here demanding silence, as though he were conducting a concert. Entirely absorbed in the issue he is fighting for. An artist through and through, even in this situation. In general, not noisy or vehement in his speech. Rather, quiet and intensely concentrated. Very often parrying his opponent with delicate irony and only on occasion jumping up to give vent in a ringing voice to his indignation.[54]

Klemperer opened his case by insisting that, in referring to him as an 'amtierender Generalmusikdirektor', his contract of 1928 was describing the function he was to exercise at the Kroll after he had ceased to be its director, in contrast to the purely honorary significance of the title he had been awarded in Cologne. 'I am not', he declared, 'demanding to become a functioning music director. I already am one.' He then went on to claim that his contract, in stating that in the event of a closure of the Kroll he would be obliged to fulfil identical functions at the Linden Opera, entitled him to serve there as functioning *Generalmusikdirektor*. The defence contested his claims, arguing, somewhat disingenuously, that the title was purely honorary. Thus far Klemperer seemed to be standing on firm ground and the mood at the court's opening session was light-hearted. Referring to rumours (which were to prove well-founded) that Tietjen had opened negotiations with Furtwängler and Walter to conduct at the Linden Opera alongside himself and Kleiber, Klemperer declared amid laughter, 'My nose is large. But to have four gentlemen dancing on it is too much.'

Two weeks before the second session on 10 April Fritz Fischer met an official from the Linden Opera in an attempt to settle out of court a claim that he openly regarded as ill-founded, and an agreement was reached whereby at the Linden Opera his client would conduct only productions in whose preparation he had himself been involved and revivals only at the specific behest of Tietjen. But Klemperer rejected the compromise and when the court sat again the atmosphere was more tense. The defence then put its finger on the weak point in his case. The vexatious phrase 'amtierender Generalmusikdirektor', it claimed, had only been added to Klemperer's revised contract of 1928 at his own request, as a means of establishing that he should receive parity with Kleiber. How, the defence argued, could he now in good faith interpret his contract to mean that he would enjoy in the Linden Opera the same powers which that same contract by implication described Kleiber as already exercising there. Klemperer was enraged at the implication that he was acting in bad faith. Tempers began to rise as he constantly interrupted the proceedings, attacking the right-wing press for giving the case a political flavour and stressing that it was not his fault that he had been appointed to the Kroll by the Social Democrats.* But his case had been fatally undermined.

Public interest had become so great that the third session on 20 April had to be transferred to a larger courtroom. Tietjen, cool, considered and weighing every word, insisted that there was no such position as musical director; the phrase had only crept into Klemperer's contract in an attempt to define the scope of his duties at the Kroll after he had resigned as director. With the bit between his teeth, Klemperer compared his situation to that of Dreyfus. 'They don't want to send me to Devil's Island', he yelled at the top of his voice, 'but to deport me to the Linden Opera.'[55] He assailed Höpker-Aschoff, who had become a *bête noire*. Himself he described (not inaccurately) as 'a radical conservative' and went on to declare that he could not square it with his conscience to become part of a theatre in which *Die Walküre* might be performed without cuts on one evening and with cuts two days later, according to who happened to be conducting it.

* In fact the only socialist directly involved in Klemperer's appointment was Kestenberg.

36 Klemperer before the Labour Tribunal. Berlin, 21 April 1931

The court made a last-minute attempt to bring about a reconciliation. As ever the diplomat, Tietjen also tried to effect a meeting. But in his manic condition Klemperer was not disposed to compromise. He did, however, put out a feeler that further damaged his case. He would, he said, be willing to put his suit in abeyance for a year, if he were given an assurance that he would succeed Kleiber, whose contract was due to expire in August 1932. At a stroke he seemed to confirm what his enemies had alleged from the start: that the real purpose of his case was to secure the eviction of Kleiber from the Linden Opera.* The court accordingly threw out his claim. It found that, at the time he signed his 1928 contract, he was aware that, should the Kroll be shut and he be transferred to the State Opera's other theatre on Unter den Linden, he would find there a conductor who exercised powers similar to his own at the Kroll. He was therefore not justified in interpreting the contract to mean that he should now be set above Kleiber. That adverse judgement did not, however, prevent Klemperer from lodging an appeal, while subsequently modifying his claim to one that he be given a special position at the Linden Opera.†

Only a day after Klemperer's case had been rejected the curtain rose on the second spectacle in which he was a leading player. On 21 April the Landtag's investigatory committee sat for the first time. Its enquiries centred on the Volksbühne's legal claim to compensation on the closure of the Kroll. Most of its members were, however, more concerned to score political points than to conduct an investigation. Those on the right, in particular, seized the opportunity to assail Kestenberg as the man who, more than any other, had been responsible both for establishing the Kroll and for forging its links with the Volksbühne. But by that time Kestenberg's star, which had stood in the ascendant as long as Becker was Kultusminister, had already waned. Tietjen's appointment as *Theaterreferent* in the Kultusministerium in March 1930 had clipped his wings,‡ and from the moment, two months later, when the Landtag had in effect voted for the closure of the Kroll, Klemperer had noted a distinct change in his old patron's

---

* Had Klemperer played his cards differently, been less openly contemptuous and mistrustful of Tietjen, and not made his own manic instability so public, this might well have come to pass, for in spite of the fame Kleiber enjoyed in later years, in Berlin before 1933 he was regarded as a comparatively light-weight conductor, whose drawing power was not to be compared to Klemperer's (see p. 402). Thirty years later Tietjen maintained that he had indeed proposed to the Kultusministerium that Klemperer be appointed musical director at the Linden Opera after the closure of the Kroll. (Curjel interview with Tietjen, WDR 1962)

† This appeal was heard and rejected in Klemperer's absence in South America on 20 July. Even that rebuff did not restrain him from lodging a further appeal to the Reichsgericht in Leipzig. Before this could be heard, however, his manic phase had begun to ebb and on 21 December Fischer was able to inform Tietjen that his client had finally withdrawn it.

‡ See p. 341. In his autobiography, *Bewegte Zeiten* (p. 77), Kestenberg later observed that by 1930 he was already regarded as 'a dead man'.

attitude towards the opera house that he had done so much to bring into existence.* In his evidence before the committee Kestenberg made an ignominious attempt to shuffle out of the crucial role he had played in establishing it as an independent opera house under Klemperer's direction.† In Klemperer's view he thereby betrayed his cause and a breach occurred between the two men that was only to be healed after the war. It is hard to see what, in the absence of a Kultusminister more resolute than Grimme, Kestenberg could have done to save the Kroll. But his behaviour before the Landtag committee cast a melancholy twilight over a career that in its earlier stages had been distinguished by a rare blend of imagination, energy and courage. No man did more to shape the musical life of Berlin that was one of the few glories of the short-lived Weimar Republic.‡

Klemperer himself appeared before the investigatory committee on 21 and 23 April. In the course of the hearings of the Labour Tribunal his manic condition had clearly grown more acute, and at his appearances before the Landtag committee he cast aside any remaining restraint. In doing so he brought a refreshing gust of theatre into its interminable wrangles. He delighted in paradoxical assertions. He cracked jokes about his new-found friends in right-wing circles. He gave smart answers. Told that members of the Volksbühne, who only attended the opera on two or three occasions each season, had complained of hearing the same work twice, he replied that if a work was good, it was worth hearing twice. Asked whether performances at the Kroll were well attended, he replied that it was not customary for a conductor to face the public. He teased the members of the committee by pretending, as 'an irresponsible musician', to be unable to grasp the point of their questions. Maddened at his inability to extract a clear answer, Josef Buchhorn (see p. 340n), the Deutsche Volkspartei member who had throughout been one of the most virulent and demagogic critics of Klemperer's artistic policy, cried, 'Herr Generalmusikdirektor, let

---

* Curjel had observed a similar change. See p. 296.
† *Untersuchungsausschuss*, column 73. Rockwell ('The Prussian Ministry of Culture and the Berlin State Opera', pp. 287–8) goes so far as to claim that he lied. Certainly it is hard to square his assertion that he had never discussed the project with Klemperer before Becker authorised him to offer the post of director in August 1926 (see p. 241) with Klemperer's repeated claim that Kestenberg had held out the position on a visit to Wiesbaden in the spring of that year (e.g. *Conversations*, p. 57).
‡ Kestenberg's German career came to an abrupt end after Franz von Papen, who had succeeded Brüning as Chancellor on 1 June 1932, arbitrarily dissolved Braun's legally elected Prussian government. On 1 December 1932, four days after his fiftieth birthday, Kestenberg was summarily dismissed from the Kultusministerium. In 1934 he fled to Prague, where he founded and directed the International Society for Musical Education. In 1938 he emigrated to Palestine, where he became manager of the Palestine (now Israel Philharmonic) Orchestra and set up a college for training music teachers. It was in Israel that a reconciliation with Klemperer took place, probably in 1951.

us drop the matter.' 'No', shouted Klemperer in his high-pitched ringing voice. The *rapporteur* repeatedly but in vain called him to order for the irrelevance of his replies.

For all the laughter he caused, Klemperer was determined to ventilate his intense disillusionment and anger with his former allies, who had in his view failed the Kroll. He assailed the Kultusministerium and in particular Kestenberg for the bland assurances it had given him that the Volksbühne was inspired by genuine cultural ambitions, whereas in his view it had revealed itself to be no more than an organisation for distributing cheap tickets. Now that the Volksbühne was no longer in a position to take up its allocation of tickets, the state was proposing to compensate it to the tune of two million marks for its failure to fulfil its part of the 1923 contract, while the Kroll was to be shut for want of 400,000M.*

Both figures were bogus. The compensation that the Volksbühne was to receive stretched over the unexpired eighteen years of its old contract. The sum that Klemperer gave for preserving the Kroll was based on a number of uncertain assumptions and on running it as a *Volksoper* with a popular repertory. But the argument was of course balm to the ears of the right-wing members of the committee. Hitherto Klemperer had appeared to them as the musician most closely identified with the regime that had set up the Kroll. Now he seemed intent on dissociating himself from his former patrons and in the fatal year of 1933 he was to the dismay of his friends to carry that process a step further. Many of his shafts found their target, but an awareness that he had not presented himself in an altogether happy light is apparent in his final words to the committee on 23 April.

I have a personal request. As the proceedings have been very lively – and I have certainly contributed something to that – I would like to ask the deputy chairman to request the press not to present my evidence in such a sensational manner. I am ashamed every day that I pick up a paper. It is quite dreadful. I haven't meant all these things so maliciously (bös)...After all, I'm just a conductor.[56]

After a series of sittings that had extended over two months the committee's *rapporteur* finally admitted on 22 June that it had not been possible to reach any agreement on the obligations of the state to the Volksbühne. A motion, proposed by the Zentrum and the Democrats, that

---

* Klemperer's plan to continue the Kroll with a subsidy of a mere 400,000M was laid before the Untersuchungsausschuss and printed as appendix 22 of its proceedings. The unreality of this plan can be gauged from the fact that on 11 April 1930 Tietjen's estimate of the subsidy that the Kroll would require in the season of 1930/1 was 6,120,200M (Merseburg 2.10.6, Nr. 128, p. 50). The untenable assumptions underlying this and similar plans were subjected to devastating analysis in an article entitled 'Dilettantismus um neue Kroll-Projekte' (*Die Welt am Abend*, 4 May 1931).

the report be approved, was nonetheless passed by a narrow majority of two votes. A second motion, approved by fifteen votes to ten, accepted that no individual had been guilty of any dereliction of duty.* When both motions were referred to the Landtag on 9 July, they were finally passed by a majority of 227 to 2 (the coalition parties having voted in its favour, while the opposition abstained).

*   *   *

At few other periods of his career did Klemperer throw himself into conducting activities with such indiscriminate energy as in the early spring of 1931. At a benefit concert in the vast Sportpalast he contributed uncharacteristically impromptu readings of Weill's *Kleine Dreigroschenmusik* and Johann Strauss's waltz, *Wiener Blut*. He conducted several isolated performances at the Kroll of operas he had not himself prepared, and on 10 April he undertook a concert for the Berlin branch of the International Society of Contemporary Music. This also was not in keeping with his usual practice. Klemperer greatly resented the label of modernist frequently pinned on him; such new works as he conducted, he normally undertook only after long consideration. But of the four scores in a programme arranged at short notice only one, two scenes from Hauer's opera, *Salambo*, is likely to have been his own choice. For the first time in his life he tackled a work by Webern.† The Symphony, Op. 21, was received with such 'loud laughter' that Klemperer was obliged to quell it with 'furious Mussolini-like glances'.[57] Heinrich Strobel, in later years a champion of post-Webernian serialism, dismissed it as 'a bloodless abstraction' of 'a fanatical ideologist', who 'lacked all personality' and had 'abandoned all meaningful musical construction'.[58] Einstein was almost alone in pointing to Webern's ability to match 'complete thematic consistency' to expressivity.[59] The sole success of the evening was a brilliant performance by Feuermann as the soloist in Ernst Toch's early concerto for cello and chamber orchestra.

Klemperer was equally active in propagating his own compositions. On 23 March he sent the embarrassed Strecker a new version of his Psalm 42 and followed this up a month later with a suggestion that Schott's publish the *Faust-Musik*, which had lain forgotten since 1917, to celebrate

---

* By the time the committee had examined almost a score of witnesses, including Klemperer, Tietjen, Nestriepke and Curjel as well as all the officials concerned, its report extended to over 565 columns. In spite of a forbidding title the *Bericht des 26. Ausschusse (Untersuchungsausschuss Krolloper)*, Drucksache No. 7431, 23 June 1931, is a vital source of information about the Kroll and the cross-currents beneath the surface of Berlin's operatic life during the Weimar Republic.

† The score of the Symphony was despatched to Klemperer only a little more than two weeks before the performance took place.

the coming bicentenary of Goethe's birth. On 29 March, three days after she had sung under his direction in another performance by the Philharmonic Chorus of the *St John Passion*,* he sent Elisabeth Schumann his song, 'Der König von Thule'. But his attention was by this time concentrated on *Das Ziel* and on 8 April he wrote to tell Universal Edition that he had arranged a private rehearsal of the work in the concert hall of the new radio building in the Masurenallee. Before doing so, he also played the work to Elisabeth Schumann.†

The guests at the run-through of *Das Ziel* on the Sunday morning of 19 April included many distinguished musicians, figures in the city's intellectual life and members of the Kroll. No critics were invited.[60] The atmosphere was uncomfortable; Schnabel, in particular, was seen to be shaking his head sorrowfully.[61] Klemperer, however, was jubilant. In the interval he wandered round with his eleven-year-old son, greeting his guests. That evening he despatched a cable to Universal Edition, 'Private rehearsal satisfactory nothing stands in the way of publication from my side'. When in Hamburg a week later, he informed Universal Edition on 29 April that the First Conductor at the opera, his old friend, Egon Pollak, would perform the work during the following season at the Stadttheater. At one point indeed the production was announced.[62] But no other evidence of the project has survived and on 4 November Hans Heinsheimer informed Klemperer on his return from South America that it had been dropped. That was the last to be heard of *Das Ziel* for many years.

*   *

Amid all the excitement occasioned by his appearances in his own court case and before the Landtag committee, Klemperer had been busy preparing Verdi's *Falstaff*, the last opera he was himself to mount at the Kroll.‡

---

* Einstein (*Berliner Tageblatt*, 27 March 1931) described the performance as being of rare greatness, the only remaining defect being the size of the chorus (80–90 voices), which Klemperer himself had seemed to find excessive. His abandonment of long fermatas in the chorales, the reintroduction of appoggiaturas and a proper balance between woodwind and strings were among the details singled out for praise by Heinz Pringsheim (*Allgemeine Musikzeitung*, 3 April 1931).

† Recollections of Roger Sessions, who had arrived in Berlin at Klemperer's invitation (see p. 355). It is symptomatic of Klemperer's manic state that for the first time since the scandal of 1912 he went out of his way to see Schumann. He attended the recital she gave in Berlin on 28 March and afterwards wrote an affectionate letter, praising the natural and unaffected ('vernünftig') quality of her singing. On the morning of the recital she even visited him at his home, a call that he described in his letter as having been 'happy and harmonious', which says much for Johanna's forbearance.

‡ Whether by chance or design it was not the only work he conducted in the season of 1930/1 by a composer with whom he was otherwise little associated. On 18 December he directed the Philharmonic Chorus in the only performance he gave in the course of his entire career of the *Requiem Mass*. The critics admired its fire and intensity but found it stiff and

Although he had never previously conducted the work, it was an opera for which he had developed a special attachment since he had first heard it in Barcelona in 1924, when he had written, 'Strauss's *Rosenkavalier* has quality, until one hears the genuine (legitim) sounds of Verdi's *Falstaff* (it is just being given here with the splendid Amato). *"Das ist ein Anderes."* Indescribable.'* Nonetheless he seems to have prepared it with less than his customary care and caution. On 11 March, no more than six weeks before the première, Dülberg had written an angry letter of protest to the administration of the Kroll. 'Herr Generalmusikdirektor Klemperer', as he now stiffly referred to his old friend, had, he complained, repeatedly pestered both him and his doctor on the telephone with requests for him to design *Falstaff*. For five months, Dülberg bitterly observed, the Kroll had made no use of his services. Now he was expected to throw together designs for an opera he particularly loved. 'I must repeat', he wrote, 'that on principle I am not prepared to work in this manner on the masterpieces of operatic literature.' This stinging condemnation of Klemperer's failure to maintain the standards both men had fought so stubbornly to uphold was to be their last professional contact.†

The haste with which Klemperer in this instance set to work was not the only evidence of his manic condition. Although he planned to produce *Falstaff* himself, he engaged as assistant Natalia Satz, the young director of the Central Children's Theatre in Moscow, where he had met her in 1925. It was a bizarre appointment. For all her talents, Satz had had no previous experience of opera and spoke little German or Italian. In Berlin, she attended Berlitz language courses, while Klemperer prepared her musically by playing the music repeatedly on the piano. He talked much of Toscanini's approach to Verdi.‡ Yet his young collaborator subsequently claimed that he described the music as being 'as true to life and coarse as a brothel'.[63]

unyielding in lyrical passages. Two weeks later, on 1 January, he conducted a studio performance of *Otello* at the Berlin Radio with Lauritz Melchior in the title role and Herbert Janssen as Iago. It was a score he had not touched since his galley years in Cologne, but it met with a very favourable critical reaction. Josef Rufer (*BZ am Mittag*, 2 January 1931) observed that the music had so vividly illuminated the drama that the absence of a stage representation had scarcely been noticeable.

* Letter of 25 January 1924 to Eigel Kruttge. Pasquale Amato (1878–1924) was one of the most celebrated interpreters of the title role. The quote is from *Parsifal*, Act One.
† In the summer of 1933 the friendship was patched up in letters that have not survived. A few weeks later Dülberg, ravaged by tuberculosis, died at the age of only forty-five. In an obituary (*Neue Freie Presse*, 30 July 1933) Klemperer, customarily so reserved in print, laid bare his grief and sense of loss. When, twenty-three years later, the present writer first met him for the purpose of preparing a biographical article, Klemperer devoted much of the interview to stressing Dülberg's significance. No man outside his immediate family circle came closer to him.
‡ Less than two years earlier he had heard Toscanini conduct the work on the occasion of the visit of the Scala, Milan, to Berlin (see p. 293n).

If Klemperer uttered such a strange opinion, it does something to explain why the production was assailed by many Berlin critics for its tastelessness and vulgarity. To Oscar Bie's amazement Sir John sported a monocle, Fenton appeared in plus-fours, while Bardolph and Pistol appeared as Pat and Patachon.* It was, he wrote despairingly, 'half a fancy dress ball, half an English weekend',[64] with little sense of period or place and much clowning that was out of keeping with the music. In the last scene a fountain played in the depths of Windsor Forest.†

The musical side of the evening was as heavy-handed as the production. Klemperer, who earlier that day had spent seven hours in court and was greeted with prolonged cheering, set about the score as though he were conducting *Elektra*. Stamping noisily in the pit, as he had not done in years, he hammered out accents, exaggerated dynamic contrasts and gave the brass its head. Verdi's light *parlando* vocal writing was undermined, ensembles were ragged and several critics noted a lack of the disciplined precision that had marked the performances that Toscanini had conducted in Berlin less than two years earlier. Even his young American admirer, Roger Sessions, recalled the musical style as 'boisterous and violent' rather than sparkling.[65] Klemperer's manic condition was particularly apparent in the finale, where, rising to his full height, he loudly sang with the chorus 'Lauter gefoppte', in a clear reference to the unsuccessful outcome of his court case earlier that day.‡

Klemperer was, however, only able to conduct two further performances of the opera before he left Berlin to undertake a season of conducting at the Teatro Colón in Buenos Aires. His farewell appearance took place on 25 April at a concert at which he accompanied Gieseking in the first Berlin performance of Hindemith's new Concert Music for Piano, Brass and Harps, Op. 49, which received a mixed reception from the critics, and then conducted a performance of Beethoven's Choral Symphony. For the first time in his career he on this occasion deleted the retouchings, which Wagner had made in 1846 and were still in general use, so as to give the work in its original orchestration. Four years earlier, in an interview in New York,[66] Klemperer had still maintained that such amendments were necessary if, for instance, the main theme of the scherzo were to be fully audible. In the meantime, however, he had (at any rate for the time being) moved closer to accepting the overriding importance of *Werktreue*. But another factor was involved. If he now abandoned many of the retouchings

* German equivalent of Laurel and Hardy.
† Klemperer, however, remained delighted with the production. When it was revived at the Linden Opera a year later (see p. 393), he struggled to re-engage Natalia Satz. When he failed to do so, he wrote on 27 March 1932 to tell her that 'Your work on *Falstaff* is the brightest memory I have in the theatre so far as production is concerned.'
‡ 'All made fools of'. 'Tutti gabbati' in the original (*BZ am Mittag*, 21 April 1931).

he had felt to be necessary earlier in his career, it was, as he subsequently admitted, because he had since learnt how to make the score sound effectively without them.[67]

Klemperer's overwrought condition was apparent in rehearsals. Scenes, such as were liable to mark his guest appearances with strange orchestras in and out of Germany, were rare at the Kroll, where the Staatskapelle was used to his methods. On this occasion, however, Klemperer stormed out after a string player had made a wrong bowing and was only with difficulty persuaded to return. In spite of the performance's overwhelming dramatic fury, several critics felt that it had fallen short of his highest standards. Fritz Brust found his handling of both the trio and adagio unyielding;[68] Stuckenschmidt described the presto in the finale as so fast as to be scarcely audible.[69] But the audience was determined to pay tribute to the conductor whose concerts had become such a feature of the city's musical life, and at the end of the evening, as ovation followed ovation, it rose to its feet, shouting 'Wiederkommen, Wiederkommen'.

Yet it was not a happy farewell. As Klemperer had become more involved in attempts to save the Kroll, he had grown uncharacteristically eager to compromise. To Curjel's dismay, he had in the course of the winter shown himself increasingly ready to drop his plans to conduct the first German production of Janáček's *From the House of the Dead* in favour of a repertory work, such as *Der Rosenkavalier* or *Die Meistersinger*, and only the united opposition of his colleagues had prevented him from doing so. Worse was to come. In January 1931 he had been approached by his old friend, Max Hofmüller,* who had been appointed director for the coming season of the Teatro Colón in Buenos Aires. To Curjel's amazement, Klemperer accepted a five-month engagement, which necessitated his departure from Berlin more than two months before the end of the Kroll's final season. But Tietjen, doubtless glad to be rid for a while of a figure who was causing so much disturbance, readily granted permission for Klemperer to go on leave on 27 April. Thus when Janáček's posthumous opera, which was the last production to be mounted at the Kroll, was finally performed to a half-empty house on 29 May, he had already arrived in Buenos Aires. In his absence the work was conducted by Fritz Zweig and produced by Curjel with sets by Caspar Neher. A prison-camp setting was, as Klemperer had foreseen, hardly calculated to exercise public appeal and such profoundly idiosyncratic music inevitably divided the critics. But the opera provided a final offering worthy of the ideals that the Kroll had set out to serve.

On 3 July the Kroll Opera finally shut its doors with a performance of *Figaro*, in which the music's underlying anguish overshadowed its merriment. As the curtain fell, the audience rose as a man. The entire

* See biographical glossary and pp. 92 and 103.

company appeared on the stage, stage hands as well as singers, musical staff as well as the orchestra, prompters as well as secretaries. Suddenly, a voice was raised above the tumult. From a proscenium box, Edgar Schmidt-Pauli, a friend of Klemperer from his Hamburg days, launched into a denunciation of the Landtag, the government and, above all, the Finance Minister, Höpker-Aschoff. Curjel replied from the stage and, whenever Klemperer's name was mentioned, it was drowned in cheers.[70] But no word came from Buenos Aires, Tietjen was in Bayreuth and even the Kultusministerium did not trouble to send a representative. In its last hour the Kroll was abandoned by the men who had done most to launch it on its course.

Curjel wrote what must have been a bitter letter of reproach to Klemperer,* who replied from Buenos Aires on 13 August at unwonted length, clearly in a more sober frame of mind than that in which he had left in the spring.

I wanted to send a telegram at the time of the final performance, but what was I to say? Every word seemed banal, even ridiculous. After all that I had *fruitlessly done* and *sacrificed* for our theatre, it seemed impossible to spin words. There are deaths at which one cannot even offer condolences. You reproach me on my tactics in my efforts to save our theatre. How unjust! If a tactic has no success that does not mean that it is wrong...In clear awareness that I was right, I brought my suit for *our opera* and my rightness is not lessened by the fact that so far I have failed *legally* and lost a lot of money...For the rest I can only say five words that even my enemies cannot deny: I did what I could.

That Klemperer felt obliged to defend himself at such length by attempting to relate two quite separate issues suggests that, as his manic phase had started to wane, he had begun to feel a need to justify the legal action he had so rashly embarked on and unease at the charge that he had abandoned the Kroll in its final agony. Thirty years later, in an interview with Eigel Kruttge, he admitted that, though his visit to Buenos Aires had been financially rewarding, 'today I much regret that I went'.[71]

* It has not survived.

16 *The Kroll: an epilogue*

Klemperer's Kroll, as it was often called, so unmistakable was the personal stamp he put on it, arose out of a widely held belief that traditional opera was dying, together with the society that had given it birth.* A new society demanded new forms of artistic expression, and it was in part as a means of bringing these into existence that the Kroll was set up as an artistically independent organisation in 1927. At the same time it was to serve as the Volksbühne's opera house and no one seems to have paused to consider whether these two aims were compatible. On both counts the Kroll became an object of controversy. Because it was regarded, by its foes as well as its friends, as an expression of a new regime and a new epoch, and because of its close links with the socialist Volksbühne, the Republikoper (as it was also called) aroused suspicion and even hatred among adherents of the old order, which had been destroyed by military defeat yet retained the loyalty of a large part of the population, especially among the middle classes.

Klemperer had been a supporter of the young republic since 1918 and vaguely radical in his political sympathies. But he was not in the least concerned with theories about art and society. His aims were at once more limited and more concrete. He wanted to abolish what he regarded as the abuses of repertory opera. He wanted to reform the staging of opera by bringing it into line with the innovations that had occurred in the spoken theatre. He wanted to introduce new works into a stagnant repertory. Above all, he sought a new unity of music and drama. Such aims were, however, sufficient to attract the wrath of traditionalists. That he himself was a Jew by birth and that of the group around him only Dülberg and Legal were 'Aryans', made it easier for the radical Right to depict the Kroll as an alien organism in German cultural life.

Klemperer's policies proved far harder to achieve than either he or Kestenberg had foreseen. During its opening season the Kroll was bedevilled by the problems of sharing its premises with the Linden company and of building a new ensemble. He himself proved ill-suited to the administrative burden he had assumed for the first time in his life, and throughout the

---

* As is exemplified in the writings of Kurt Weill, who, at any rate in the late twenties, argued that new musico-dramatic forms could only arise out of a new view of the world (e.g. 'Zeitoper', *Melos*, March 1928). The influence of Weill's thinking on the Kroll is particularly apparent in Curjel's essay, 'Neben der Oper' (*Blätter der Staatsoper*, October 1928).

374

winter of 1927/8 he was in the throes of a deep depression. It was only in the course of its second season that the Kroll began to fulfil its potential, notably in the production of *Der fliegende Holländer* and in Klemperer's concerts. Yet hardly had it done so than conservative and Catholic forces in the Landtag moved to close it. For the last year of its existence the Kroll was under sentence of death. That so much was achieved in such conditions says much for Klemperer's powers of leadership.

A large part of the Kroll's failure to stay the course can be attributed to the delay that occurred in establishing it as an artistically independent entity. Had the Kultusministerium been quicker to grasp the fact that a mere *Filiale*, such as was opened (already belatedly) in 1924 would not prove viable, had Schillings not blocked the path to artistic independence (and it is no coincidence that steps to that end were only initiated after his dismissal in December 1925), its history might have taken a more favourable course. Had it been set up in the early years of the Weimar Republic, it might well have been able to establish itself as an operatic equivalent of the Bauhaus, before it was assailed by economic blizzards and right-wing radicalism.

The nub of the Kroll's problem lay in its relations with the Volksbühne. The closer it came to fulfilling its role as midwife to a new operatic age, the less it pleased its principal client. Had the Volksbühne been consulted on Klemperer's appointment and policies, had he and his staff treated it with more understanding and consideration, had, above all, Kestenberg, who alone had a foot in both camps, succeeded in reconciling their divergent views, it might have felt a deeper sense of loyalty. In the minds of the socialist democratic politicians, who formed its defence in the Prussian Landtag, the Kroll had been set up primarily for the benefit of the Volksbühne; almost to a man, they were unconcerned with, even unaware of, its cultural significance. Hence, when in the hour of decision the Volksbühne revealed its disenchantment with the Kroll, the carpet was pulled from under the feet of those very politicians who sought to preserve the theatre. More than any single factor, it was the failure of the Volksbühne to stand shoulder to shoulder with the Kroll that destroyed Klemperer's ambitions.

Too late in the day, its founders perceived that the twin aims it had been set up to realise were irreconcilable. After the theatre had closed, C. H. Becker admitted that as Kultusminister he had made a mistake in supposing that an uninformed public could be attracted to advanced art.[1] For that error of judgement, Kestenberg's blithe belief that an enlightened musical patron lay hidden within the breast of every worker, that 'education' could bridge the ever-widening gulf between contemporary music and the general public, bore a heavy responsibility. Without Kestenberg's idealism the Kroll

375

might never have come into existence. Yet the naive and unrealistic assumptions that underlay his conception of a *Republikoper* sowed the seeds of its undoing.

The Kroll itself contributed to its own demise. In the course of four years it did not hold a single press conference. Until the die was cast, it showed an astonishing obliviousness to the power of publicity. Internally, it remained unified in the face of the pressures that beset it, and there were no defections among its principal participants.* Yet that inner sense of solidarity led it to turn its face away from an increasingly hostile world. And when Klemperer himself belatedly entered the fray, it was to complete the alienation of the Volksbühne and thus finally to sever the branch he was sitting on.

There were inevitably artistic errors. Klemperer himself made misjudgements in the works he chose and rejected. Scenic renewal proved an elusive target and Dülberg, on whom Klemperer's hopes had rested, temperamentally and physically ill-suited to the strains of theatrical life. As Einstein admitted in a judicious and largely laudatory survey of the Kroll's achievements, 'Many experiments were made on unsuitable subjects, the style of performance did not always match the style of the work.'[2]

Yet the ultimate source of the difficulties that confronted Klemperer's Kroll throughout its brief existence lay deeper. The times themselves were ill-disposed. The operatic repertory was already ceasing to renew itself and such fresh shoots as emerged no longer appealed to the broad mass of its audience. 'Basically', Einstein continued, 'the Kroll foundered on the lack of operatic creativity today, on the inner difficulties of the operatic situation in the present time, which one may or may not call a "crisis", but which conditions the outer crisis.' In the final resort the Kroll was a victim of a situation it had, at any rate in part, been called into existence to remedy.

*   *   *

If political prejudice, economic distress, human shortcomings and the sickly condition of opera in the early twentieth century combined to destroy the Kroll before it had been able to reveal more than a small part of its potential, it cannot on that account be dismissed as a failure. As Einstein observed, 'For the first time on such a scale a German opera house had basically turned its back on museum-like attitudes and set out in quest of living art.'[3] In the process the Kroll established a far wider repertory and more close-knit ensemble than existed at either of the other Berlin opera houses. It introduced new works of real importance and made bold innovations in

---

* Dülberg quarrelled with Klemperer, not because he defected from the aims of the Kroll, but because he considered that Klemperer and Curjel had betrayed them.

the field of production and design. And on those occasions when it achieved a unity between work and performance, between music and theatre, it achieved what Einstein described as 'das Grösste'. Above all, it established a model for the future. As Klemperer himself wrote as his theatre was in its death throes, 'Whenever this approach to opera is revived, it will have to start where we have been obliged to leave off. They may shut our theatre, but the idea underlying it cannot be killed.'[4]

That prophecy has been amply fulfilled. When, after the physical and spiritual devastation wrought by the Third Reich, German operatic life sought a new point of departure, Klemperer's Kroll provided an example to which it could look. Both the New Bayreuth under Wieland Wagner and Walther Felsenstein's Komische Oper set out in very different ways to pursue paths it had opened. In his awareness of the ultimate incompatibility of repertory opera, as then practised in Central Europe, and decent standards of performance, Klemperer was also ahead of his time, even if for a solution he looked to what he termed *Serientheater*, rather than to the *stagione* system that has since replaced permanent companies in most of the world's leading opera houses.*

In part due to Curjel's rosy-hued recollections, the Kroll has indeed come to enjoy a mythological status that has only a limited relationship to fact. Just as, during its existence, hostile critics in the press and in political life sought to create the legend of a hotbed of *Kulturbolshewismus*, so it has subsequently come to be regarded as the very prototype of an avant-garde opera house. That was never Klemperer's intention; paradoxically, many of the deeds for which the Kroll is most celebrated today were done without his approval. In so far as it was the first major opera house to pursue a systematic policy of experimentation in the fields of production and stage design, it can claim credit for the great impulse of renewal it eventually brought to opera. By the same token it cannot escape a degree of responsibility for the excesses committed by many producers and designers in recent years.†

What lifted the Kroll above ideology and experimentation was the presence of Klemperer, who dominated the theatre from start to finish and ensured that musical considerations generally remained paramount. It was he who gave many of its performances an impact that still lives in the accounts of those who were fortunate enough to experience them. He was also the only leading conductor of his generation who systematically set

* Klemperer was not opposed to ensemble opera (quite the reverse, indeed), only to the nightly changes rung on a vast repertory, as was habitual in Central Europe until jet aircraft and the recording industry finally rendered the system unworkable, at any rate at an acceptable level of performance.

† A number of German provincial opera houses, notably Darmstadt, where Carl Ebert was Intendant from 1927 to 1931, pursued similar policies, though on a more modest scale.

out to bring new intellectual impulses into an opera house. And just as Klemperer was the keystone around which the Kroll was built, so it formed the keystone of his career. For all the anguish and disappointment they brought, the four years in which he guided its destiny enabled him to fulfil himself as he was never to do again. In a real sense his earlier years were a long apprenticeship for the role he was to play in Berlin. In his own mind, the later decades, in which he came to be regarded with veneration, ironically as a source of traditional musical values, remained an anti-climax to his achievements at the Kroll.

Today the scene of Klemperer's labours no longer exists. Reduced to ruins in the war, what remained of the Kroll was subsequently levelled to make way for roads and parks and no stone or plaque marks its site. Yet the memory endures. As Oscar Bie wrote after the Kroll's curtain had fallen for the last time, 'The four years... will remain a gleaming chapter in the history of opera, full of art and humanity, with human weaknesses and human error, but with all the grandeur of true endeavour and conscientious labour. May the devil take a time that cannot support that.'[5]

17 *On Devil's Island*

Before embarking from Cuxhaven for Buenos Aires on 29 April, Klemperer spent twenty-four hours in Hamburg, where he took the opportunity to consult Moses Goldschmidt, the *Internist* to whom he had more than once turned at moments of stress. That he sought medical advice in periods of euphoria is evidence that even during manic periods he was aware of the pathological nature of his high spirits.

On board, the weather was fine, even in the Bay of Biscay, so that Klemperer was able to spend most of his time on deck reading and composing. Before the first week was out, he had completed the text of a new opera, *Bathseba*, which he dedicated to Johanna.* Somewhat to his own surprise, he also passed hours playing *Skat*, although he ruefully noted that skill at card games was not a talent he had inherited from his father.[1] Among his fellow-passengers was a group of Jewish emigrants, who were travelling steerage. Moved by their poverty, he and Johanna gave a concert for their benefit. The proceeds were not, however, received without suspicion when the recipients learnt that their beneficiary was a convert to Catholicism. 'Never mind', one of them observed. 'He has not lost his Jewish heart.'[2]

When Klemperer and his wife disembarked at Buenos Aires on 16 May the commission that ran the Teatro Colón was assembled on the quayside to greet them. The dignitaries, attired with appropriate Latin formality, were disconcerted when a towering figure descended the gangway, dressed in Bavarian *Tracht*, complete with Tyrolean hat, *Lederhosen* and stockings.[3] The commission itself had recently been reconstituted. In the previous autumn the city council had taken over its opera house, which had until then been administered by a series of private impresarios, and a new theatre commission had been charged to bring a degree of artistic coherence into its disordered affairs. One of its first acts had been to appoint Max Hofmüller director.†

Hofmüller's task was to 'Europeanise' the Colón by modernising its technical equipment and introducing a more up-to-date approach to production and design, which had hitherto been largely left to look after

---

* That she subsequently used the exercise book in which he had written it to inscribe details of a slimming regime suggests that she did not take her husband's creative labours over-reverently. The book was nonetheless among her possessions on her death.
† See biographical glossary and p. 372.

itself. As what was in part doubtless an exercise in *Kulturpolitik*, a revolving stage and lighting bridge had been despatched from Berlin, sets based on Hofmüller's designs had been made in the workshops of the Cologne opera, and German technicians had been sent out to initiate the Argentinian staff into recent developments in stagecraft.[4] Klemperer was engaged as chief conductor of the German repertory, which, in spite of visits from guest ensembles under Weingartner (1922) and Strauss (1923), had suffered neglect in a city where such operatic tradition as existed was predominantly Latin.

The season got off to a good start with a new production by Hofmüller of *Die Meistersinger*, which Georg Sebastian had prepared musically prior to the arrival of Klemperer and the soloists.* Klemperer was agreeably surprised by the quality of both the orchestra and the chorus[5] and the performances were enthusiastically received by press and public alike. But Johannes Franze sounded a warning in the *Argentinisches Tageblatt* (23 May 1931). After dwelling on the miseries of past Wagner performances at the Colón and welcoming the introduction of German methods, he asked whether these would be able to establish themselves in the Latin soil of Buenos Aires.

Franze's foreboding proved well-founded. The German advisers soon began to attract the resentment of their Latin colleagues, who were used to running the Colón in their own way and felt that they were being elbowed to one side. Opposition extended to within the commission itself, which started to interfere in matters that Hofmüller regarded as his prerogative. Virulent polemics broke out in the press, part of which asserted that Hofmüller had arrived with the idea of bringing *Kultur* to savages, but was himself ignorant of any art that was not German.[6] To make matters worse, the manic Klemperer quarrelled with the orchestra and then tried to force Hofmüller to engage Johanna to sing the role of Adèle in *Die Fledermaus*, although there had been no prior agreement that she should do so. Hofmüller had been close to Klemperer during euphoric phases in Strasbourg, but he had never before experienced his old friend in such ungovernable rages.[7] On 22 June, his health undermined by the strains of his position and a severe bout of influenza, he left Buenos Aires on sick leave. On his return on 15 July he resigned, attributing his decision to interference from the commission, which, he claimed, was dominated by a Francophile majority.[8] The conception of a 'Kulturtheater' was, he maintained, incompatible with Argentinian mentality and the conditions prevailing at the Colón.[9]

* Georg (originally György, subsequently Georges) Sebastian (Sebastyen) (1903–) settled in 1946 in Paris, where for a number of years he conducted much of the German repertory at the Opéra.

380

Thereafter the entire season began to disintegrate. Klemperer, who had arrived in Buenos Aires with ambitious plans for a series of concerts, which were to include Bach's B minor Mass as well as symphonies by Bruckner and Mahler, was obliged to confine himself to a programme consisting of Bach's Brandenburg Concerto No. 1 and the Choral Symphony, which, as in Berlin earlier in the year, he again conducted in Beethoven's original orchestration.* A projected production of *Der Rosenkavalier* also came to nothing, so that more than three months passed between the opening performance of *Die Meistersinger* and a new staging of *Le nozze di Figaro*, which Klemperer conducted on 23 August.† At his insistence Natalia Satz was engaged to produce and a strong cast included Delia Reinhardt (the Countess), Alexander Kipnis (Figaro) and Salvatore Baccaloni (Bartolo).‡ But the evening was above all a triumph for Klemperer, who conducted a much reduced orchestra from the harpsichord. Such ensemble, the German critics agreed, had never before been heard on the boards of the Colón, and John Montés claimed that Klemperer's 'commanding intelligence was the axis of the evening'.[10]

Natalia Satz nonetheless found that contact was less close than it had been during the free and easy weeks during which she and Klemperer had together prepared *Falstaff* in Berlin. Indeed as his return to Germany grew nearer, his mood perceptibly darkened. 'Denk ich an Deutschland in der Nacht, so [correctly, dann] bin ich um den Schlaf gebracht', he wrote to an unknown correspondent on 5 August.§ Eight days later, in a letter to Curjel, he wrote that 'theatrical work is appallingly difficult here, as everything is in a primitive condition. But I must admit that I think more about the coming winter than I do about my work here and my thoughts are heavy.' The exuberance that had hitherto sustained him through a difficult year was ebbing.

His final operatic task was to conduct a new staging of *The Ring*, which had not been heard in its entirety in Buenos Aires since 1922, when the cycle had been given for the first time in the Argentine by a company from the Vienna State Opera under Weingartner. A cast that included Frieda Leider, Lauritz Melchior and Kipnis assured high vocal standards, but the

---

* In spite of the fact that the chorus sang in Italian, the two performances he gave on 10 and 18 June made an overwhelming impression. Franze maintained (*Argentinisches Tageblatt*, 19 June 1931) that Buenos Aires had never before experienced such disciplined playing from its orchestra.
† For the first and last time in his career he conducted an Italian opera by Mozart in its original language in the theatre.
‡ Delia Reinhardt (1891–1974), a soprano much admired in Mozart and Strauss. Alexander Kipnis (1891–1978), one of the outstanding basses of his generation. Salvatore Baccaloni (1900–1969), a great *buffo* bass.
§ Heine, 'Nachtgedanken' (*Neue Gedichte*, 1844). 'When in the night I think of Germany, I am robbed of sleep.'

occasion was dogged by misfortune. Some of the sets ordered from Cologne failed to arrive and no substitute was found for Hofmüller, who was credited with the *mise en scène* in spite of his absence. John Montés blamed Klemperer's relentless rehearsing for the weariness evident in the orchestral playing in *Das Rheingold* on 1 September. Five days later *Die Walküre* was given a gala performance in the presence of the new president. The audience was inattentive and to ensure that its patience should not be overtaxed severe cuts were made, even in the scene between Fricka and Wotan. Klemperer's tempi were found fast and his interpretation lacking in inner commitment. *Siegfried* on 17 September fared little better and cuts were again so extensive that Wotan put only a single question to Mime and even his crucial encounter with Siegfried was curtailed. Not surprisingly, Klemperer seemed to Montés not to be 'entirely gripped by his task'.[11] *Götterdämmerung* on 29 September was, however, considered by one critic to have far outstripped in dramatic intensity the performance given by Weingartner nine years earlier.[12] But Klemperer had by this time quarrelled with Melchior, whom he found artistically 'inadequate'[13] as Siegfried. Indeed, according to one recollection, relations with leading members of the cast were so tense that they refused to acknowledge applause in his company.[14] By this time the season was in any case running so far behind schedule that *Götterdämmerung* received no more than a single performance: no sooner had the curtain fallen than the principal singers, their bags already packed, made for the docks to embark that very night for Europe. Klemperer was never again to conduct *The Ring*.

He himself was in no such hurry to return to Berlin. As though to postpone his departure until the last possible moment, he took a further week's leave, so as to be able to conduct twice (5 and 7 October) a programme consisting of Beethoven's 'Eroica' Symphony and the first performances in Latin America of Stravinsky's *Symphony of Psalms*. Again, the impact was immense. Johannes Franze wrote that not since the visits of Nikisch and Strauss had such an outstanding personality taken part in the musical life of Buenos Aires. 'His successes were extraordinary, his influence on the inner working of the Teatro Colón will long endure.'[15] But now the evil day could no longer be postponed. Like an unhappy boy returning to school, Klemperer embarked on 7 October for what was to be one of the most miserable periods of his life.

*   *   *

In 1930 Hindemith, on the rebound from his unhappy collaborations with Brecht,* approached the expressionist poet, Gottfried Benn,† with a request for a text for an oratorio. The result was *Das Unaufhörliche*, which in scale and in manner marked a distinct break with the predominantly light-hearted manner he had cultivated since 1924 and the onset of what he later regarded as his mature style. Hindemith was well aware that the time had come when the dancing had to stop, that a new traditionalism was making itself felt. Shortly after he had heard Klemperer give the first German performance of Stravinsky's *Symphony of Psalms* in Berlin in February 1931, he observed in a letter to Willy Strecker that 'a new wave of serious and great music is on the way'.‡ Both Benn's mystical text and the monumental dimensions of much of the score were well calculated to match that new mood.

In the same letter Hindemith expressed his preference for a first performance by the Berlin Philharmonic Chorus under Klemperer. Strecker concurred and Rankl (see p. 307) started rehearsals in the course of the summer. But it was only on disembarking in Genoa on 23 October that Klemperer received the score. Three days later in Berlin he held his first rehearsal. Gertrud Hindemith, the composer's wife, was present.

It is a pity [she wrote to Willy Strecker] that you were not still here on Sunday. In the evening Klemperer arrived straight from the ship in fine form. Monday and today choral rehearsals, which made an incredible impression. What this man achieves, how people suddenly get moving (loslegen), how he drives them, mercilessly, to the uttermost, is something to be seen. And to be heard. Today everything went with an immense swing. He knows the score inside out, sings all the solo parts, permeates everything with his own particular intensity. You will be amazed.[16]

Das Unaufhörliche, which was by far the largest non-operatic score Hindemith had as yet composed, aroused intense expectation, and perhaps for that very reason the first performance on 21 November came as an anti-climax. The composer's new-found solemnity met with varying reactions. But even those who saluted it as the belated onset of maturity detected an underlying lack of stylistic unity. While some sections still echoed the *enfant terrible* who had emerged in the twenties, others seemed to look back to Pfitzner and Reger; it was, commented Heinz Pringsheim, as though new music were extending a hand to late romanticism.[17] Robert

* See p. 305. A quarrel between the two men took place in the summer of 1930 when Hindemith, as a member of the committee of the 1930 New Music Festival in Berlin, rejected Eisler's cantata, *Die Massnahme*, composed to a text by Brecht. That marked the end of Hindemith's brief flirtation with 'progressive' circles.
† Gottfried Benn (1886–1956). A practising doctor of medicine, Benn was the only German writer of stature actively to support the Nazis. He subsequently broke with them and in 1938 was expelled from the Reichsschrifttumskammer.
‡ Letter of 2 March 1931. See p. 346 for other examples of this change of wind.

Oboussier observed influences as diverse as Gregorian chant, Bach's passion music, Beethoven and even Mahler.[18] Schrenk spoke for many of his colleagues when he described the result as 'Stückwerk', impressive in part, but lacking organic unity.[19] There was, however, unanimity that the performance represented a triumph for Klemperer and his choir. Hindemith was so delighted that he inscribed at the head of a number in Klemperer's copy of the score, 'With heartfelt thanks for so much – and on this occasion quite especially.' Klemperer's reaction was less enthusiastic. He later tersely described the music as 'good', the text as 'incomprehensible'.[20]

*   *   *

Klemperer had sailed for Buenos Aires still under the illusion that the Kroll could somehow or other be saved. On 25 April he had submitted a plan for preserving the theatre on a more modest scale to the Landtag investigatory committee and two days later he and Curjel had called on Tietjen to discuss the project. Tietjen was characteristically non-committal, though his scepticism is apparent in a brief handwritten comment that he subsequently added to his memorandum on the meeting.* Before they parted, he put a direct question. On the assumption that the Kroll would not survive, would Klemperer be willing to fulfil his contractual obligations at the Linden Opera? Klemperer replied that, subject to the outcome of his appeal against the dismissal of his court case, he would put himself at Tietjen's disposal.†

As both men must have been well aware, that seemingly conciliatory answer begged the crucial question: what role was Klemperer to play on his transfer to the Linden Opera? If his appeal against the rejection of his plea by the Labour Tribunal were upheld by a higher court, he would exercise there powers similar to those he had held at the Kroll. That prospect was not calculated to appeal to Tietjen. Not only would his own prerogatives inevitably be circumscribed, but the presence of the overbearing Klemperer in a position of authority threatened personal friction. Klemperer had made no bones of his mistrust of the *Generalintendant* and on occasion had treated his official superior with open contempt.‡ Tietjen suffered such insults with apparent insouciance, but even before the Labour Tribunal had reached its verdict, he took steps to secure his position. On 13 April he announced

---

* Subsequently yet another plan was launched for the Kroll to be run by the Reichsrundfunk-gesellschaft (the German equivalent of the BBC), and, when that collapsed, Klemperer, through an intermediary (probably Prälat Münch) made a further appeal to Brüning. Documents in the Bundesarchiv (Koblenz) indicate that it predictably fell on stony ground.

† Or so Tietjen's memorandum of the meeting phrases it.

‡ Hofmüller (Bregstein interview, I, p. 28) later recalled that Klemperer had spoken to Tietjen 'like a bootblack', when he had 'requested' five months leave to enable him to fulfil his Buenos Aires engagement.

that in the coming season he would himself assume artistic direction of the Linden Opera; Kleiber would cease to function as musical director;* and in spite of the fact that he would have on his staff no fewer than three senior conductors who ranked as *Generalmusikdirektoren* (Blech and Kleiber as well as Klemperer), Walter and Furtwängler, neither of whom had previously been associated with the State Opera, would each conduct a new production. Klemperer's contribution would be a new staging of Gluck's *Iphigénie en Tauride*.[21] It was a policy of divide and rule, and as a result few opera houses can have entered a new season with a roster of conductors equal to that which Tietjen had at his disposal at the Linden Opera in 1931/2 at the very trough of the slump. In this way, he ensured that, in the improbable event of Klemperer winning his court case, he would find plenty of competition under the lime trees.

If that was the old fox's game, his adversary played into his hands. On 25 September Klemperer wrote to Tietjen from Buenos Aires to ask that *Iphigénie en Tauride* be postponed on account of the heavy commitment of *Das Unaufhörliche* and because no adequate orchestral material was available for the original version, which he wanted to perform. Thus when Klemperer finally returned to Berlin on 25 October, almost two months after the start of the new season, no plans had been made for his future activities at the Linden Opera, an omission that had already attracted unfavourable comment in the press and concern in the Kultusministerium. Such a situation could clearly not be allowed to continue, and when the two men met again for the first time in five months on 29 October, Tietjen launched his thunderbolt. To Klemperer's amazement, 'He proposed that we should simply forget my old contract and make a new one, whereby I would only be available during special periods.'[22]

On the face of it there was much to be said for the proposal. Any possibility that Klemperer would be able to exercise at the Linden Opera powers remotely comparable to those he had wielded at the Kroll had long since faded. Yet he abhorred conventional repertory work, to which he was in any case temperamently ill-suited. Under Tietjen's scheme he would be able to fulfil special tasks according to his taste in Germany's leading opera house, while retaining freedom for guest appearances elsewhere. But Klemperer sensed a deeper purpose in Tietjen's proposal. 'He wanted to get rid of me. So I refused.' Both men were henceforth locked in a strained relationship, a situation that might have endured until the expiry of Klemperer's contract in 1937, had not the Nazi seizure of power intervened to sever the knot.

---

* When, in the course of the following season, Kleiber's contract came up for renewal it was not extended (see p. 393).

It was not until a month later that the State Opera was able to announce that, in addition to undertaking three concerts with the Staatskapelle, Klemperer would conduct a new production of *Così fan tutte*. It was thus with this work that, after an eight-month absence from Berlin's operatic life, he made his bow on 15 December in the theatre he had described as 'Devil's Island'. Tietjen did what he could to meet Klemperer's requirements; Gustav Gründgens and Teo Otto, with whom he had worked so successfully on *Figaro* at the Kroll earlier in the year, were engaged as producer and designer at his behest. On this occasion, however, the collaboration went less smoothly. Gründgens staged the work with a degree of elaboration that did not meet Klemperer's wishes for the utmost simplicity.* While he was well pleased with Helge Roswaenge and Willi Domgraf-Fassbänder as the officers,† the sisters did not arouse his enthusiasm. Above all, he was miserable in the working conditions of the Linden Opera, where he missed the family spirit that had prevailed at the Kroll. In particular, he was irked to be greeted on arrival at the stage door with 'Gut'n Morgen, Herr General'. 'Ich *bin* kein General', he shouted back to no avail.[23]

There was much praise for the transparent textures and chamber music intimacy of the playing that Klemperer drew from an orchestra of only forty players. Einstein considered his handling of the harpsichord accompaniment to the recitative less *buffo* in spirit than Strauss's, but Walter Berten found his approach at once livelier and more harmonious than it had been when he had last conducted the work in Cologne.[24] But even in sophisticated Berlin the opera itself had still not come to be regarded as part of the canon of Mozart's mature stage works. Schrenk dismissed the plot as embarrassingly silly, while even Bie, among others, found the score long and monotonous and criticised Klemperer's decision to restore arias, such as 'Tradito, schernito', which was still so frequently cut that Einstein admitted that he had not heard it in fifty productions.[25]

On 21 December 1931 Fritz Fischer informed the *Intendanz* of the State Opera that Klemperer had finally withdrawn his appeal to the Reichsgerichtshof against the dismissal of his court case, but confirmed that he would not agree to any alteration of his contract. The problem of how he was to be employed at the Linden Opera could therefore no longer be evaded. On 8 January 1932, shortly after Klemperer had returned from conducting in Paris, where his account of Brahms's Symphony No. 1 had won an enthusiastic reception from a small audience,[26] Tietjen invited him to discuss the matter. The negotiations did not go smoothly.[27] Tietjen first not unreasonably requested Klemperer not to take the leave to which he

* Klemperer subsequently expressed a preference for *Così fan tutte* to be produced with a minimum of stage action. (Information provided by Lotte Klemperer)
† Helge Roswaenge (1897–1972), outstanding Danish tenor, who sang at the Berlin State Opera from 1929 to 1945 and thereafter in Vienna.

was entitled in the form of short absences that made planning difficult. Klemperer declined to meet his wishes. Tietjen then suggested that he revive a production that he had himself prepared at the Kroll. To this Klemperer consented and in the course of the season he conducted performances of *Figaro* and *Falstaff*. Tietjen also reverted to Klemperer's earlier suggestion that he should prepare a new production of *Der Freischütz* with a producer and designer of his own choice. To this Klemperer also agreed, but the project subsequently collapsed because (as Tietjen had feared) he turned out to be too frequently absent on leave during periods when the stage was free for the large number of rehearsals he required.

Tietjen then turned to the issue that lay at the root of their difficulties. He explained that as the current economic difficulties had led to a cut in the State Opera's budget, it was imperative that all the three *Generalmusik-direktoren* on its staff should be fully employed.* Blech and Kleiber were both available to conduct routine repertory performances; indeed, Tietjen observed with apparent satisfaction, Kleiber had even taken over a revival of *Die Meistersinger* without rehearsal. Therefore he must require Klemperer to conduct such performances, though 'naturally with rehearsal...and only of works that corresponded to his artistic inclinations'.

Klemperer was appalled at the prospect of returning to the conditions of repertory opera from which he had over so many years struggled to extract himself. Indignantly he told Tietjen, 'In other words you want me to work inartistically, because that is what would be involved if I were to take over operas that I had not myself prepared.' Tietjen again assured Klemperer that there was no question of his being asked to appear without rehearsal, although that in his view could be required of any experienced conductor. But Klemperer remained obdurate: Tietjen was challenging the very principles on which he had based his professional life. At Klemperer's request an official who was present was sent from the room. When they were alone Klemperer asked Tietjen whether he really intended to insist on his demands. Tietjen assured him that he did, whereupon Klemperer formally declared that he could not accept them. The issue was referred to the Kultusministerium, where Kestenberg and Seelig gave Tietjen unreserved support. There the matter rested while Klemperer fulfilled a guest engagement in London.

*   *   *

On 23 January Klemperer wrote anxiously to Schnabel, who had continued to act as intermediary between him and the Courtauld–Sargent concerts. He was, he explained, concerned about inadequate rehearsals for a coming

---

* This economic stringency had not, however, prevented Tietjen from engaging Walter and Furtwängler as guests (see p. 385).

concert in London. 'I have Bruckner Seven (always difficult and time-consuming to rehearse in London because of the tubas), Hindemith's concerto (very taxing for the wind) and only four rehearsals. Bear in mind that Bruckner and Hindemith are quite new to the orchestra.'* The visit turned out no better than he had foreseen. Elizabeth Courtauld had died since he had last been in London and he was oppressed by the uncanny quiet that now pervaded the great house in Portman Square, previously a scene of such liveliness. The weather was foggy, the hotel (he had thriftily taken a room without bath) unduly expensive. 'The orchestra', he wrote to Johanna (6 February 1932), 'is unsuited to Bruckner. You certainly recall how difficult it was when we were first here.' He walked in Hyde Park, with which he was in later years to become so familiar, but, as for so many continental visitors of the period, the seemingly closed world of London had for him none of the appeal of Paris or Rome.

Bruckner's Symphony No. 7 went down not a whit better than the Eighth had done two seasons earlier. *The Musical Times* declared that 'London endures a great deal from these continental reputations. That of Bruckner, one suspects, is kept alive chiefly by conductors who, having explored all the ordinary avenues towards notoriety, seek a fresh one by showing their intimacy with sixty-minute works that no one cares about...[The symphony] is not merely naïve, it is uneducated, badly conceived, badly worked out, badly orchestrated. In fact, it is not worth discussing.'[28] Fox-Strangways pronounced it 'a mass of platitudes and clichés. Burn it!',[29] while Neville Cardus described Bruckner as the Austrian equivalent of 'our own Elgar (in his local appeal), excepting that he has not a penn'orth of Elgar's technical skill'.[30] Provincialism was still riding high in *das Land ohne Musik*. Only *The Chesterian* praised the score's 'surpassing beauty'. But its critic, whose taste for Bruckner seems to have been nurtured on the heavily romanticised interpretations still current, condemned the performance for a want of suppleness and 'inner fervour'.[31]

Hindemith's work, which was receiving its first performance in London made little appeal and only W. J. Turner spoke up for Klemperer's account of the 'Prague' Symphony which he described as 'direct and pure' in welcome contrast to the perfumed Mozartian style preferred in England.† London clearly cared no more for Klemperer than he cared for it and more than fifteen years were to pass before he returned.

*   *   *

* In addition to the Bruckner symphony, the programme consisted of Mozart's 'Prague' Symphony and Hindemith's Concert Music for Piano, Harps and Brass, in which Beveridge Webster, Schnabel's young American pupil, appeared as soloist.

† Doubtless a reference to the interpretations of Beecham and Walter. *The New Statesman and Nation*, 13 February 1932.

On 20 February Tietjen wrote to tell Klemperer formally that his contract required him to take his share in conducting the general repertory. He therefore instructed him to prepare himself to take over *Die Meistersinger*, *Fidelio*, *Der fliegende Holländer* and *Die Zauberflöte* when these works came up for revival. There would, he added, be rehearsals of a number he would himself determine, but he warned Klemperer that he might nonetheless be required to conduct without any, should circumstances make that necessary. The letter was an ultimatum; Tietjen required an answer within seven days. After almost a year of stubborn refusal to make himself available on any terms other than his own, Klemperer suddenly capitulated. On 23 February he assured Tietjen with surprising meekness, 'As I attach importance to closer contact with the institution, I am very ready to take part also in the general repertory.'

It was an astonishing volte-face. But the manic condition in which he had so heedlessly sailed into battle with the authorities had long since given way to depression, in which caution determined his actions. In the course of the winter the depression had steadily deepened until it had become more severe even than that which, four seasons earlier, had led to his resignation as director of the Kroll. Essentially a recessive character, Klemperer was usually so successful in disguising his ups and downs, even from quite close associates, that few of the singers at the Kroll had been aware that he was a manic-depressive. But in the winter of 1931/2 even acquaintances perceived that all was not well. Arthur Lourié, who met Klemperer when he conducted in Paris in late December, wrote to tell Stravinsky that 'he made a wild and distressing impression. He's not at all the same person I knew two years ago...He exhibits an hysterical instability bordering on madness. If this is a consequence of what is happening in Germany, it is terrifying.'[32] Roger Sessions recalled long, silent walks in the Tiergarten, during which Klemperer could hardly be induced to utter a phrase beyond a lugubrious '*Finden* Sie?'.[33]

At such periods anxiety would attach itself like a creeper to anything that momentarily caused him concern. In the depression of 1931/2 he was worried not only about his position at the Linden Opera and his conducting technique, but also about Johanna, about her health, her tendency to overeat and overdrink and hence to put on weight, about her inability to economise, about her career, which seemed to be coming to a premature close, in part due to the unsparing use she had made of her voice in earlier years. At such a period letters were liable to be full of pleas, remonstrations and injunctions, as though he had assumed the *persona* of a severe and puritanical mother – his own, maybe.

Your letter...[he wrote to Johanna from Vienna on 25 February 1932] worries me in two ways. Above all the cramps. I hope with all my heart that the condition doesn't recur before your return. As soon as you are here, I shall straightaway send you for a medical examination. It can't go on like that...You really have an enormous amount to do, if in addition to your daily work you are to learn this role.* You must come back to Berlin with the part *ready*. Take this really seriously, so that you do credit to yourself and are perhaps re-engaged.

When recently I wrote that you should not borrow (anpumpen) from your colleagues, but rather write to me...I begged you...to live *really economically*. Why don't you do so? You get 180M from the Musikbühne, you get 100M from me in addition, and you can't manage on 280M? It must be possible. To prevent worse (as I regard borrowing) I am sending the 30M you asked for, but it is *impossible* to send more.

I am sure that the cramps are at any rate in part connected with the fact that you eat and drink too much. When the liver and spleen are overburdened, especially by alcohol, they become rebellious and tax the whole system. It's so frightfully silly to have to say the same thing again and again. I personally, for instance, would now (it's about half past ten) like to have a nice snack. In the afternoon I also wouldn't mind having a cup of chocolate and cakes, because I enjoy them. I don't do so, because I would become too fat and would suffer more from a tummy than from the mild abstinence I impose on myself. It is simply *foolish* to indulge in pleasures that one must pay for with greater unpleasantness. Only children live like that...I don't like preaching...

Nonetheless, the following day he returned to the same themes. They were strange letters for a wife to receive from a husband who, apart from substantial fees for guest engagements, earned a yearly salary of 45,000M, and who in a different frame of mind was all too prone to throw to the winds the abstinence and self-discipline he enjoined on her.

Such was the form that Klemperer's love for his wife was liable to take when he was beset by the black dog of depression. Contrary to the impression given to outsiders by his inability in manic periods to resist a pretty face, that love had deepened with the years. On 15 June 1925, the day before the sixth anniversary of their marriage, he had written to Johanna,

My beloved *Alterchen*. Today...is Rembrandt's birthday and tomorrow our wedding day. Even though Rembrandt's day is far more important for the world...we know what this day means *to us*. Because [on it] we have built for ourselves and with our little ones a world that, God willing, will endure *in goodness*. My mother always said that it is difficult for married people to congratulate each other on their wedding day...That I am happy and grateful to be and live with you, you know, at least you ought to know, even without my telling you. And you know that elevated words don't come easily to me. Take – in thought – a tender kiss and believe in the true bonds that bind us...Goodbye, my dearest, and remain mine as I am for ever yours...Your six-year-old Otto.

Such expressions of emotion did not come easily to a man for whom any sort of effusion (in music or in life) was alien. Yet in spite of their unflowery

---

* Johanna Klemperer had been engaged by the Deutsche Musikbühne (see note, p. 395) to sing the role of the Countess in *Figaro*.

style, his letters to his wife bear constant witness to his devotion. 'Just before your letter came', he wrote in the summer of 1928, when he was emerging from a depression, 'I felt how strong the bond between us is...One doesn't feel it all the time. But when I do, I want for once to tell you, *mein guter Esel.*'[34]

The marriage brought tensions in plenty. Johanna had a fiery temper and even Klemperer's most childish flirtations would drive her into paroxysms of jealousy. Their sexual characters had indeed developed in contrasting directions. Fame and fortune had made it easier for Klemperer to indulge his whims in manic phases; there were always plenty of women who felt flattered by the attentions of a famous conductor. Johanna, whose pre-marital life had not been chaste, after marriage never even considered infidelity. That did not make it easier to listen to the detailed 'confessions' her husband inflicted on her once a manic phase had started to ebb, particularly as these often involved women whom she knew well. Yet she had become the rock on which his life was founded, as he himself recognised when he wrote, 'Do you sometimes think of me, as you solemnly promised? *Alter*, my conducting depends on it. And then there is also peace and quiet at home. My Hans, love me as I love you.'[35] A love had come into existence that was to survive the many storms that lay ahead.

Klemperer's depressions (like his periods of euphoria) were considered by his doctors to be basically endogenous in origin. Yet outer circumstances undoubtedly exacerbated them and early in 1932 he had good reasons to be in low spirits. In a presidential election on 13 March Hitler polled no less than 30 per cent of the votes cast, an increase of 86 per cent over the figures at the general election of only eighteen months earlier. The significance of these results did not escape him. When, on his arrival to conduct in Königsberg later in the month, his hosts apologised for the smallness of the car they had sent to collect such a large man, he wryly responded, 'Ein bisschen gedrückt sitzt ja heute jeder' ('Today everyone is sitting a little uncomfortably').[36]

Conditions at the Linden Opera served as a further depressant. 'In Berlin', Klemperer wrote to Stravinsky (16 February 1932), 'it is very sad. The business of a typical repertory opera is not for me.' Even in periods of great success, Klemperer always remained self-critical. Now, however, he began even to doubt his abilities. Depression engulfed him to such an extent that on occasions Johanna was obliged to call the family doctor to persuade him to conduct.* At one point, indeed, he came to believe himself

* Professor Ernst Wollheim has recalled that Klemperer would offer no explanation, but simply announce as a matter of fact that he was unable to conduct. (Interview with the author)

391

to be so technically inadequate that he engaged a younger colleague, Leo Borchard, to attend rehearsals in order to point out his faults.* It was probably with reference to this that at about this period he wrote to Johanna, 'I am pleased rather than otherwise when I can learn something. That it should be *necessary* understandably worries me.'[37]

Most of this was in the mind. On his reappearance with the Staatskapelle at the Kroll on 30 January after an absence of nine months he was greeted with prolonged ovations and the concert itself was enthusiastically received.† Einstein commented that his interpretation of Bach's Suite in D major, which had so sharply divided opinion when he had similarly opened his first Kroll concert four seasons earlier, had in the meantime come to be generally regarded as 'right and natural', as an approach that bridged Bach's own time and the present day. He described an uncut performance of Bruckner's Symphony No. 8 as unsurpassed in its 'concentration and unity'.[38] Most critics concurred, although there was much shaking of heads over the total absence of new or rarely heard works in Klemperer's programmes for the season.‡

It would be a mistake to imply that there was any direct relationship between Klemperer's psychological condition and the quality of his concerts. Euphoria could cause him to be satisfied with less than his best, while, conversely, depression frequently had the effect of spurring him to greater efforts. Yet nothing he conducted in the remainder of the season met with a fraction of the success he had hitherto usually enjoyed in Berlin. His second concert on 17 February, in which he gave a classical programme, curiously reminiscent of that with which he had established himself in the capital in April 1924, was tepidly received.§ He had conducted, wrote Otto Steinhagen, as though he was hacking the music out of stone with a hammer.[39] Sessions subsequently recalled the Brahms as 'lifeless'. Schnabel left the concert deeply cast down.[40] Four days later, a revival of *Figaro* at the Linden Opera was widely dismissed as no more than a pale shadow of the previous year's triumphant performances at the Kroll.

An uncut performance of the *St Matthew Passion* on 13 March failed to make the impact of his earlier Bach interpretations. There was as usual

* Leo Borchard (1899–1945) conducted the first concert to be given by the Berlin Philharmonic Orchestra after the end of the war on 26 May 1945. Three months later, he (like Webern) was shot by a trigger-happy American soldier. Had he not died, he, and not Sergiu Celibidache, would probably have become the orchestra's conductor, at any rate during the period when Furtwängler was forbidden to appear in public, pending denazification proceedings.

† The Kroll was of course otherwise no longer functioning as a part of the State Opera.

‡ Tietjen had, however, earlier refused the use of the State Opera Chorus for a performance of Schoenberg's *Gurrelieder* that Klemperer had planned to give in conjunction with the Philharmonic Chorus. He never conducted the work in its entirety.

§ See pp. 192–3. The first halves of both programmes were identical: Haydn's Symphony No. 95 in C minor and Mozart's 'Jupiter' Symphony. In 1932 he substituted Brahms's Fourth Symphony for Beethoven's Seventh.

praise for its clarity and precision, but widespread reservations about what was regarded as a lack of expressive life. A performance of Beethoven's Choral Symphony on 7 April impressed in its intensity and in the elemental force of the finale. Yet many critics expressed reservations about its harsh angularity and almost brutal violence. Paradoxically, in a revival of *Falstaff* on 19 April, he was praised for showing more restraint and achieving a greater degree of precision than he had done a year earlier at the Kroll. But in spite of the fact that a new director had been engaged to eliminate some of the more grotesque features of the production, Klemperer's musical approach was still widely felt to be heavy-handed.

It says much for Tietjen's discretion and artistic understanding that in these circumstances he did not press his advantage. Although Klemperer had in principle agreed to conduct repertory performances, in practice Tietjen never compelled him to do so.* During the eighteen months that he spent at the Linden Opera he never conducted a performance of a production that he had not been involved in from the start. In the entire season of 1931/2 he gave no more than twenty-one performances of only three operas: *Così fan tutte*, *Figaro* and *Falstaff*.

His under-employment did not go unremarked by the ever-vigilant Oberrechnungskammer, which on 20 June demanded an explanation from the *Generalintendanz*. Tietjen's confidential reply throws light on the difficulties he had in accommodating Klemperer at the Linden Opera. He first explained that, owing to Klemperer's presence, he had not renewed Kleiber's contract, which expired at the end of the season. Yet Klemperer's insistence on taking the three months' leave to which he was entitled in a number of short periods made it hard to use him systematically. But the problem, Tietjen went on, had deeper roots. For a new production Klemperer required half as much time again as any of his colleagues and, during that period, the opera house was hamstrung. Singers were so exhausted by his rehearsals that they were frequently incapable of appearing in the evening. Similarly, he was unable to undertake revivals with less than eight days' rehearsal, which involved some use of both the stage and the orchestra, whereas other conductors were able to make do with one or two rehearsals.†

Tietjen went on to explain that he had not forced the issue because he

---

* An alarm did, however, occur in the following season. In early January 1933, when his total contribution to the Linden Opera's season had amounted to little more than a handful of performances of a new production of *Der Rosenkavalier* (see pp. 399–400), Tietjen attempted to persuade him to take over a revival of *Die Walküre* with no more than a single *Verständigungsprobe* and Fritz Fischer advised that he had no legal grounds for refusing. 'For several weeks this apparition hung over me like a nightmare. But it came to nothing. Chance? There is no chance, says Schiller' (*Conversations*, p. 68).

† Fritz Zweig, for instance, told the author that at the Linden Opera, where he was engaged after the closure of the Kroll, he never received more than a single rehearsal for a revival.

was convinced that these difficulties were not due to ill-will on Klemperer's part.

On the contrary he makes every effort to fit in with the demands of the daily repertory which have become alien to him. *But he cannot*; and, as that inability stems from factors that are psychological as well as artistic, he never will be able to do so. Herr Klemperer is one of those strange but unique artistic phenomena, around whom an entire organisation has to be geared to the last degree, if it is to function without friction. That was the secret of his strength at the Kroll, which...had, and could only have had, a single artistic hub and that was *Klemperer*. There the relatively limited number of works that were performed in the course of a season could be rehearsed for months. There were instances in which – with quite outstanding results, be it noted – we had to concede three months of rehearsal time to Herr Klemperer.

The Linden Opera is quite different. This organisation, as the first opera house in the *Reich*, is entirely *unklempererisch*, that is,...it can only be run on the basis of a permanently changing repertory. That is alien to Herr Klemperer. Conversely, Herr Klemperer is an alien body in its machinery, and he always will be.[41]

In that balanced assessment there is no trace of the malice or hostility that Klemperer believed his Intendant to bear him, and which might indeed have been excusable in view of the manner in which he had himself treated Tietjen. Tietjen was a man who assessed situations with coolness and clarity and adjusted himself accordingly. Thus he had supported the Kroll as long as its existence was assured, but had not been prepared to fight for it once it was seriously threatened. His attitude to Klemperer himself, whom he had earlier described as 'as easy to lead as a child',[42] was similar. He was a problem that had to be lived with, and he proceeded to do so with his customary adroitness.

*   *   *

In spite of Tietjen's malleability Klemperer continued to feel so thwarted at the Linden Opera that towards the end of the season he seems even to have toyed with the idea of abandoning his career in the theatre.[43] In vain he sought new operas from Stravinsky and Hindemith that might provide a task worthy of his energies.[44] To escape from the misery of his existence in Berlin and a political situation that from week to week looked more ominous, he again rented for the summer the lighthouse on Kampen, where he and his wife had been so happy two years earlier that he had come to look back on it as a last idyllic period before the clouds had begun to gather around the Kroll and Germany itself.[45] But Johanna, who was rehearsing with the Deutsche Musikbühne, a small touring company she had joined that spring, could not join him.* The prospect of solitude

---

* The Deutsche Musikbühne was established early in 1932 by Prince Heinrich XLV of Reuss, who was also its artistic director, to tour modest but carefully rehearsed operatic

lowered his spirits further and to be with her he moved to Schloss Elmau in Upper Bavaria, where rehearsals were in progress. Klemperer spent his time working and reading. But inner peace eluded him. 'This year', he wrote to Curjel, 'it is difficult even to be on holiday, because there are always rumblings at the centre.'[46]

Storm signals were indeed not wanting. The advance of the National Socialists seemed irresistible. In the elections of 24 April 1932 for the

productions in the German provinces. Its conductor was Hans Oppenheim (later of Glyndebourne). The first productions of *Figaro* (in which Johanna Klemperer sang the role of the Countess) and Handel's *Rodelinda* were well received, though there was some criticism of the company's vocal standards. In the summer the troupe reassembled to rehearse Humperdinck's *Hänsel und Gretel* and Strauss's *Intermezzo*, in which Johanna Klemperer was to sing the principal role of Christine.

37   Strauss and Klemperer at rehearsals for *Intermezzo*. Schloss Elmau, July 1932

395

Prussian Landtag they had increased their seats from 9 to 162. Democratic government in Prussia, which up to this point had provided a bulwark of stability in the increasingly turbulent political life of the *Reich*, was fatally undermined, and though Braun continued for the moment to lead a caretaker government, henceforth he was a broken man. Five weeks later Franz von Papen succeeded Brüning as Chancellor.* Throughout the summer there was increasing violence on the streets† and on 20 July this gave von Papen the excuse he needed to dismiss the legally elected Prussian government and to establish authoritarian rule in a *Land* that comprised two-thirds of the area of Germany. The end of the Weimar Republic, with which Klemperer's career had been so closely identified, was at hand.

Three days after this *Putsch* Strauss invited Klemperer to tea at his home in Garmisch, only a few miles from Elmau. The purpose of his visit was to question the composer about *Der Rosenkavalier* and *Ein Heldenleben*, both of which he was to conduct at the Linden Opera during the coming season. Over 'Kaffee und Kuchen' the great man airily waved aside the problems that Klemperer raised. 'Oh, you know, I'm always glad when I'm over those passages.' The conversation then inevitably turned to the menacing political situation and in particular to its implications for the many Jews – a number of them friends of Strauss – who occupied prominent positions in German musical life. The composer's formidably forthright wife, Pauline, turned to Klemperer and in her broad Bavarian accent declared, 'If the Nazis give you any trouble, Herr Klemperer, just you come to me. I'll tell those gentlemen who's who.' Strauss raised his eyebrows in amazement. 'That will be just the moment to stand up for a Jew.'[47] Klemperer was flabbergasted by the shamelessness of the observation. But the composer whose attitudes so strikingly epitomised the political stance of the German middle classes of the period had unwittingly revealed what was to be expected of him in the moment of need.

In the Reichstag elections that took place a week later, the Nazis were returned as by far the largest party,‡ and in the following September Goering was duly elected President of Germany's parliament. The hour of reckoning was at hand. Within twelve months the man who was regarded as Germany's greatest living composer would have deputised for Walter, when the Nazis made it impossible for him to conduct in Berlin, stood in for Toscanini after he had in protest withdrawn from Bayreuth,

---

* Franz von Papen (1879–1969), more than any single parliamentarian, was to open the door to Hitler through his influence with the ageing President Hindenburg and the circle around him. When Hitler finally came to power on 30 January 1933, von Papen became Vice-Chancellor.
† During the night of 17 July seventeen people were killed in a pitched battle in Altona.
‡ In fact they won more seats than had ever been held by a single party in the history of the German parliament (Taylor, *Literature and Society in Germany, 1918–1945*, p. 31).

396

and accepted the position of President of the Reichsmusikkammer, an organisation set up by Goebbels as a means of exercising control over German musical life. In that capacity he would offer Hitler and Goebbels 'the warmest thanks of all German musicians' for the prospect they held out of the restoration of a new link between 'the German people and its music'.[48]

18 *Crossing the Red Sea*

During much of the autumn of 1932 Klemperer was immersed in preparations for a performance of Bach's B minor Mass that was to celebrate the fiftieth anniversary of the founding of the Berlin Philharmonic Chorus. He had never before conducted the work and few undertakings in his entire career caused him so much anxiety. To Johanna, who had left Berlin on another tour with the Musikbühne, he wrote on 17 November, 'The Bach Mass is the hardest thing I have as yet had to conduct. It is giving me a great deal of worry.' A week later he was still troubled: 'You cannot imagine how difficult the Mass is chorally.'[1] Rehearsals extended over several weeks and, once again, there were lengthy consultations with Günther Ramin on musicological issues (see p. 323).

His fears proved ill-founded, for the performance on 5 December made as deep an impression as anything he ever conducted in Berlin. Many critics contrasted his essentially architectural approach to music in which Ochs had sought dramatic intensity and subjective piety. Klemperer's interpretation was seen to represent a distinct break with this tradition. To achieve greater contrapuntal clarity, he reduced the strings in proportion to the number of woodwind employed. Dynamics were terraced, there was a complete absence of expressive nuances and Einstein commented (with approval) that in the course of the entire evening there was no more than a solitary ritardando – at 'Et sepultus est'.[2] Only in his continuing use of a chorus of no fewer than 250 voices did Klemperer adhere to traditional practice and here his hands were tied by the number of active members in his choir. Yet the performance aroused little of the outraged opposition that had greeted the *St John Passion* three years earlier. Though a few conservatively minded critics continued to complain of a lack of 'expression' and the correspondent of the *New York Times* (21 January 1933) attacked the interpretation as 'a shocking demonstration of that arch-fallacy of "letting the music speak for itself"', Berlin as a whole had made its peace with Klemperer's 'objective' Bach interpretations.

After the performance the choir and its guests repaired to the Esplanade Hotel for a celebratory banquet, at which many of the city's leading musicians, including Furtwängler and Walter, were present. Schoenberg was, however, conspicuous by his absence. Although he attended the concert, he refused an invitation to the party, because, as he put it in a letter of 4 December to Klemperer, 'I feel happy in the company of friends of my achievements and prefer not to consort with alien solar systems. Therefore I can send you my best wishes for the celebration, but cannot personally take part in it.' Clearly the double bill of *Erwartung* and *Die glückliche Hand* and the first performance of the Film Music had not sufficed to appease his rancour at the neglect he considered his music to have suffered at the Kroll.

Of all the great artists based on Berlin during the Weimar Republic, Artur Schnabel was closest to Klemperer. He attended his friend's performances whenever possible and Klemperer attached great importance to his comments. It was therefore natural that he should be invited to propose Klemperer's health and he did so in words that, convoluted though they were, revealed his deep understanding of Klemperer's complex artistic character.

As a colleague, I would like to thank Klemperer for his exemplary behaviour as an artist...[An artist is confronted] by questions, not of personal advantage and security, but of truthfulness at any price, even at the price of lifelong insecurity, which is finally the hallmark of continuing creative development and the real source of sustenance and satisfaction. Klemperer knows that the struggle between opposites is particularly strong in an artist, and he knows...that pressure to conformism...is also strong. But an artist of his calibre is able to resist it.

[Artists like] Klemperer are at once conservative, liberal *and* revolutionary; they are aristocrats and anarchists; they are for freedom and for discipline. Again like Klemperer, they have an inner independence that obliges them simultaneously to do justice both to what is timeless and to what is of their own time.[3]

*   *   *

In planning the 1932/3 season at the Linden Opera Tietjen had gone some way to meet Klemperer's wishes by agreeing that he should conduct new productions of *Der Rosenkavalier* (a work he had earlier been eager to perform at the Kroll) and *Tannhäuser*, in each case with a producer and designer of his own choice. *Der Rosenkavalier* was rather coolly received on 22 September. On the following day in a letter to his wife, Klemperer described the public as polite rather than enthusiastic and the critical reception as mixed. There was as usual praise for the clarity and precision of the orchestral detail, but Stuckenschmidt expressed a widespread reservation when he wrote that Klemperer

lacks the right touch for this score, the elegant lightness and carefreeness it calls for. While he overdrives the prelude, he draws out the dialogue and the interludes. Pitiless dynamics often endanger the voices and the atmosphere. The waltzes also emerge as curiously abstract...[only] towards the end, from the trio on, does he (almost against his will, so it seems) allow himself to be immersed in the broad and generous stream of Strauss's vocal and orchestral sound.[4]

399

In this letter to Johanna, written after he had read the press notices, Klemperer expressed his resentment at 'this dog collar of "severe and objective" that is hung around my neck in Berlin and makes it hard for me to have success in such a work'. Usually impervious to newspaper criticism, favourable or unfavourable, he strongly resisted any suggestion that he was an exponent of the *neue Sachlichkeit* or any attempts by its embattled supporters to foist on him their narrow doctrinal sympathies.* Although by no means content with what he had achieved in *Der Rosenkavalier*, his dissatisfaction did not stem, as Stuckenschmidt had implied, from any lack of sympathy with the work itself. In an account of the first night that he sent to Strauss on 27 September (their encounters during the previous summer had triggered off their first correspondence for years) Klemperer assured the composer that 'in its burgeoning strength your work is every bit as captivating as it was twenty years ago'.†

His sense of dissatisfaction stemmed basically from conditions in the Linden Opera, where star singers came and went and he missed the devoted teamwork that had been the hallmark of the Kroll. Of the cast of *Der Rosenkavalier* only 'the very sympathetic Fräulein Fuchs from Dresden' entirely satisfied him in the role of Oktavian.‡ In such conditions he found it hard to give his best. To Johanna, who was on tour with the Musikbühne, he wrote (23 September), 'the joylessness that arose out of a lack of contact with my colleagues also certainly had an effect on my own perform-ance...*Mein Alter*, you have no idea how happy you should be that you are able to work with people you like.'

Nor had the staging satisfied him. Nothing had troubled Klemperer more insistently after Dülberg's withdrawal from the Kroll than the difficulty he had experienced in finding producers and designers who could breathe life into his somewhat negative desire for sets that would avoid a weak-kneed naturalism without lapsing into waywardness and licence. In the alien Linden Opera the problem seemed insoluble. To Strauss, he described the merits of Gustav Gründgens's production as its 'unpretentiousness and lack of gimmickry', but he was critical of what he regarded as a characteristically modern lack of colour and contrast.§ In his reply of 16 October Strauss

---

* He continued to do so until the end of his life.
† In this connection it is worth noting that shortly after he had conducted *Ein Heldenleben* on 15 December in Berlin, Klemperer again went out of his way to assure Strauss that 'To me, who for the first time have had an opportunity to conduct this great work, it has given immense pleasure' (letter of 26 December 1932).
‡ Letter to Strauss, 27 September 1932. Martha Fuchs (1898–1974) subsequently developed into an outstanding dramatic soprano, who sang the roles of Brünnhilde and Isolde at Bayreuth during the late thirties and early forties. To his wife (23 September 1932) Klemperer wrote of her: 'she is musically secure and has temperament'.
§ Subsequently he was less circumspect: 'I don't like it at all!' (Heyworth (ed.), *Conversations*, p. 69). That comment casts light on an episode subsequently related by Gründgens. After

came down firmly against designers' licence. 'Hardly anyone could do better than what Roller achieved here.* After two hundred years a baroque house remains a baroque house.' To which Klemperer replied, 'I agree entirely with what you write about Roller...The question of production remains so completely unsolved that it can deprive one of all pleasure in conducting opera.'[5]

Indeed opera, as conventionally practised, had come to revolt him. Later that month in Frankfurt, Hans Wilhelm Steinberg, his former assistant in Cologne, invited him to attend a performance of *Die Entführung aus dem Serail*, a work for which he had long had particular affection. To Johanna he afterwards wrote, 'I don't want to see any more opera. I find the whole thing so disgusting.'[6] From a congenital man of the theatre, that was a cry of despair.

In the first four months of the new season, from its opening in early September to the Christmas holidays, Klemperer in fact conducted no more than eleven performances at the Linden Opera. Owing to the absence from Berlin of Jürgen Fehling, who at Klemperer's insistence had been engaged to produce, preliminary work on *Tannhäuser* did not begin until mid-November. For a man of his immense energies, who had always been used to working at full stretch, such inactivity was hard to bear, even if it had been largely brought about by his own unwillingness to conduct repertory performances. Now he in vain sought new tasks that would provide an escape from operatic routine. He wrote to ask Strauss to support his wish to conduct the Berlin production of the recently completed *Arabella*, parts of which the composer had shown him on his visit to Garmisch earlier in the year. He tried fruitlessly to win Tietjen for a new production of *Oedipus Rex*.[7] He had earlier expressed interest in Hindemith's new opera, which Strecker had in the spring described to him as 'a completely unlaid egg',[8] but which was now in the process of revealing itself as *Mathis der Maler*. The problem of what he described as 'my unnatural situation in the theatre' continued to prey on his mind.[9]

           *   *   *

Yet at a period when his operatic activities seemed to have reached a nadir, his career as a concert conductor started to flourish as never before. In the previous season the programmes and standards of performance at the Berlin Staatskapelle concerts had come in for criticism. This had been aimed

Der Rosenkavalier had been staged, the two men were walking across the Tiergarten; Klemperer, sunk in gloom, was inveighing against the miseries of operatic life. 'And the worst of it is, Gründgens, that one never finds a decent producer.' Not surprisingly, that seems to have been their last meeting (WDR interview with Gründgens, p. 6).

* Roller, see pp. 27–8. Designer of the first production of *Der Rosenkavalier* at Dresden in 1911.

primarily at Kleiber, whose evenings had been markedly less well attended than Klemperer's.* When a need for economy obliged Tietjen to reduce the number of concerts in 1932/3 to no more than four, Kleiber withdrew, leaving Klemperer in possession of the field.

For his opening concert, he chose a programme identical to that with which he had five years earlier bidden farewell to Wiesbaden: Beethoven's *Grosse Fuge* and Bruckner's Symphony No. 5 in B flat. The latter work produced another clash over programmes with Furtwängler, who, when he got wind of Klemperer's intention, asked him through the *General-intendanz* to abandon the Bruckner, which he himself intended to conduct in Berlin during the coming season. Tietjen's office passed on the request, but on this occasion, no doubt mindful of the fact that this was not the first time that Furtwängler had asked him to give way, Klemperer on this occasion declined to do it.†

In contrast to the tepid reception his Staatskapelle concerts had met earlier in the year, the programme that Klemperer conducted on 13 October in the Linden Opera provided him with one of the most over-whelming triumphs he ever enjoyed in Berlin. Critical opinion was divided on the merits of what was described as a 'black and white' account of the *Grosse Fuge*: his abstract conception was entirely without the symphonic drama that Furtwängler sought to give the work. But there was virtually unanimous praise for his Bruckner, where the inevitable comparison with his great rival was decisively to Klemperer's advantage. Ernst Schliepe, the critic of the *Deutsche Allgemeine Zeitung*, observed that, whereas Furt-wängler's approach to the score was essentially romantic in sound and feeling, the sharper outlines and clear, cooler light of Klemperer's perform-ance combined to illuminate its architectural and contrapuntal structure.[10] How, after such a performance, Strobel asked, could anyone ever have complained of the work's formal defects or lack of measure?

There was not the slightest break, not a single illogical passage, not a trace of those 'holes'...which are usually so disturbing. Klemperer gave the enormous symphony all the splendour of colour, the pathos, the hymn-like fervour it calls for. But he performed it so simply, so naturally, that one seemed to be listening to a new work...The lines were not fashioned so much as allowed to intertwine, as though of their own accord as in a Schubert symphony. The structure was entirely clear, never before has one experienced the intellectual unity of the finale so strongly..., the adagio melodies have never had such solemnity – precisely because Klemperer never exaggerated...The performance had tension and power..., real religious

---

* Box office receipts for two concerts that Kleiber had conducted in January and February had been less than a third of those for the two concerts Klemperer had conducted in the same period (Merseburg, 2.10.6, No. 540, p. 56).

† See p. 324. Klemperer's letter to Müller (*Generalintendanz*), Schloss Elmau, 18 July 1932 (Merseburg, 2.10.6, No. 540, p. 143). Furtwängler did not conduct the work that season.

feeling and naivety, but everything was contained by a calm that comes with complete maturity.[11]

The critics divided along predictable lines after a Staatskapelle concert on 15 December in which Klemperer paired *Ein Heldenleben* with Hindemith's Concert Music for Brass and Strings, Op. 50. Otto Steinhagen, who dismissed Strauss's score as 'atavistic', regarded the programme as an attempt to embody an irreconcilable contrast between what was dying in the music of the time and what was coming to life.[12] Max Marschalk, who after early championship of Klemperer in Berlin had been so critical of his subsequent development, in contrast rejoiced that on this occasion 'he had luxuriated in the massive sounds [of Strauss's score] as though neither the Old nor New Objectivity had ever existed'.[13] But there was unanimous praise for the chamber music-like intensity and delicacy of a performance of Mozart's Piano Concerto in C (K. 467), in which Klemperer had

38   Hindemith, Gieseking and Klemperer. Berlin, December 1932

persuaded Walter Gieseking to abandon his cadenza in favour of one by Busoni.

Busoni, whose music had not figured in Klemperer's programmes since Wiesbaden, also featured in his next Staatskapelle concert on 12 January 1933. But neither the Violin Concerto, in which Max Strub was soloist, nor the *Berceuse élégiaque* made much impact. 'Busoni's beautiful Berceuse was received with icy silence', Klemperer reported to his wife. 'Friends say, "From emotion". *Na, na,* I'm not so sure.'[14] But the evening ended in triumph with Janáček's *Sinfonietta*, which was received by both press and public with an enthusiasm that had been conspicuously lacking when he had first conducted it in Berlin five years earlier (see pp. 258–9). At last Klemperer's long championship of Janáček's music in Germany seemed to be bearing fruit.

*   *   *

In the coming months a series of performances of Bruckner's Symphony No. 5 brought widespread recognition of his growing stature as an interpreter, rather as nine winters earlier his accounts of the Eighth had done much to carry his name round Central Europe (see pp. 182 and 204). Within a week of the performance he had conducted in Berlin on 13 October, he was gratified to receive an invitation to repeat the work at the next year's Salzburg Festival, and, when on 28 and 30 October he again gave it twice in Frankfurt, Karl Holl, the principal critic of the *Frankfurter Zeitung*, described him as

the same and yet changed...Once a fanatic, who not only made the work blaze but in the process allowed the sparks of his temperament to fly around, now he is purified and completely at the service of what he performs. He allows the fires of a work to radiate through him, without imposing his own temperament on the music, so he appears an instrument of the music in the spirit as well as in the flesh.[15]

The directors of the Frankfurt Museum Concerts were so impressed that they at once asked him to return the following year.

It was also with Bruckner's Symphony No. 5 that he chose to mark his return to Leipzig for the first of three concerts with the Gewandhaus Orchestra, which he had earlier described as the foremost in Germany,[16] and again his interpretation made a profound impression. Adolf Aber commented that 'in the history of the Gewandhaus the chronicler must look far back before he finds a New Year's Concert of such inner and outer grandeur'.[17] Even Alfred Heuss, who had transformed the *Zeitschrift für Musik* into a National Socialist organ, admitted that Klemperer had conducted 'with fanatical faithfulness and complete clarity, even if the warmth that is an essential part of Bruckner's music was often lacking'.[18]

There was similar enthusiasm when he conducted a Beethoven programme in Hamburg on 30 January 1933. In his home town his career had naturally been followed with keen interest, especially by those who recalled his turbulent years at the opera before the First World War. Among them was Heinrich Chevalley, the critic of the *Hamburger Fremdenblatt*, who in an extensive review of the concert wrote:

Otto Klemperer seems to be in an important new phase of his development, the third since we have known him in Hamburg. When, many years ago, he was a conductor at the Opera, he went through his *Sturm und Drang* period: fanatical, as though possessed by music, each time he conducted he whipped up his own temperament to white-hot intensity and his conducting was remarkable for the violence of his gestures and the physical energy he expended. Later, as a pioneer of the most modern music, especially during his time as head of the Kroll Opera in Berlin, he subscribed entirely to the cause of musical objectivity; it was a period in which he was known for his concentration on iron rhythms and definition of line to the exclusion of colour and expression. One called him *l'homme machine*. But that was for him no more than a time of transition in which he was moving towards...a new clarity and self control in his conducting. This is clear from the present stage in his development, which forms a synthesis of the earlier periods. Klemperer remains austere and strict. But he now dispenses with the despotic treatment of an orchestra that formerly seemed more calculated to constrain and intimidate rather than to release its energies. Today his manner of music-making is at once severe and yet tender.

His Beethoven of today is distinguished from his earlier Beethoven performances in that he now does full justice to the sense of personal struggle in the music...His Fifth Symphony, which grips attention literally from the first bar, is transformed into a soul-shaking experience. Without lapsing into sentimentality and emotional indulgence, it illuminates a sense of personal declaration in the music, even projects an ideal figure of Beethoven himself. But the transformation in Klemperer was also evident in his interpretation of the Symphony No. 2...Never before has he attained such manly grace, such subtlety of sound...as yesterday.

The evening was thus a great and indisputable artistic success for Klemperer, in whom we have one of the most important and valuable conductors in the world today...[19]

True to the demands of the hour, the Nazi *Hamburger Tageblatt* (31 January 1933) sourly commented that 'a large number of followers, mostly members of his own race' had given the conductor a wildly enthusiastic reception. The evening was indeed a triumph and, back in Berlin, Klemperer wrote (1 February 1933) to tell his wife that he had been engaged to give four concerts in his home town during the following season. In the same letter he informed her that he had been offered the permanent conductorship of the Frankfurt Museum Concerts. Two days later the Berlin papers carried the news that Hindenburg had awarded him the Goethe medal for services to German music. If his situation in the Linden Opera remained as frustrating as ever, he was plainly achieving new recognition in other fields.

That did nothing to diminish his interest in the activities of his colleagues. Unlike most conductors, he remained almost to the end of his life an assiduous attender of other men's concerts, even if he rarely stayed the course, frequently leaving without making much effort to disguise his departure and afterwards entertaining his companions with caustic comments. No conductor of his generation intrigued him as much as Furtwängler. The friendly relations of their youth had not survived the competitive positions they had come to occupy in Berlin and when in high spirits Klemperer was liable to give cruelly telling imitations of his rival's high priestly manner on the platform. But he was never in doubt about his stature as a musician.

There were, however, aspects of Furtwängler's musicianship which did not appeal to his more austere taste. Their approaches to Bach were too different for either man to find much to admire in the other's interpretations. Furtwängler considered that Klemperer's insistence on performing the *St Matthew Passion* in its entirety imposed an excessive burden on twentieth-century ears;[20] Klemperer was shocked by Furtwängler's omission of the coda to the first movement of the Suite in B minor.* Nor was he greatly taken by a performance of *Die Meistersinger* that he heard at the Linden Opera in the season 1932/3; though the orchestral playing was on a notably high level, he detected a lack of responsiveness to the stage.†

But on 17 October 1932, the day after he had attended a rehearsal of Reger's *Variations and Fugue on a Theme of Mozart* he wrote to tell his wife that not only had he been 'absolutely carried away by the music' but had found Furtwängler's performance 'fine'. Nothing, however, made as deep an impact as the performance of Tchaikovsky's Symphony No. 5 he attended on 5 February 1933. At a time when he himself regarded the work with reserve, he was much impressed by the passionate commitment that Furtwängler brought to it. Yet there was irony in his comment, 'Is that *German?*'‡, on this achievement of a conductor who, in contrast to Klemperer himself, was regarded as the very embodiment of Germanic *Gesinnung*.[21] That was to be the last occasion on which Klemperer heard Furtwängler conduct, and they never met again.

*　　　　　　　　*　　　　　　　　*

On 15 November 1932 Klemperer, always an assiduous theatre-goer, attended a performance of Gerhard Hauptmann's *Gabriel Schillings Flucht*,

---

* It is probable that Klemperer heard him conduct the work in April 1932 and that it was on this occasion that Hindemith, who was otherwise well-disposed towards Furtwängler, exclaimed, 'Oh. Furtwängler simply doesn't understand Bach' (*Conversations*, p. 91).

† *Conversations*, p. 92. Klemperer was not alone in regarding Furtwängler as primarily a concert conductor, as is illustrated by Carl Hagemann's comment, 'Furtwängler ist kein Theatermensch' (*Bühne und Welt*, p. 99).

‡ A wry reference to Wagner's essay, 'Was ist deutsch?' (*Sämtliche Schriften und Dichtungen*, Volume 10).

in which he found Elisabeth Bergner 'enorm'. Afterwards, Carl Ebert persuaded him to join Hauptmann and Bergner for supper at the Hotel Adlon. At the end of the evening, as Klemperer rose to go, the old writer, who cultivated a prophet-like appearance and had doubtless noticed his companion's gloom, took his hand and said, 'You still have a lot before you. I feel it from your handshake.'[22] Klemperer was touched and grateful. Indeed, he would have liked to talk further with the great man, had he not already bidden him goodnight. The prediction was to be fulfilled. But before it came to fruition Klemperer was to live through long years of tribulation. Even as the conversation flowed around that urbane dinner table, events were in motion that were to bring about a rupture in the lives of most of those present.

On 4 January 1933 a secret meeting in Cologne between Hitler and von Papen prepared the way for the National Socialist leader to become Chancellor and on 30 January Hindenburg invited him to form a government. Klemperer learnt of the fatal news from an evening paper on the following day as he was on his way to conduct in Hamburg (see p. 405). Behind closed doors Jews and people associated with left-wing causes trembled for their future. But on the streets there was an atmosphere of jubilation. 'Tonight', wrote Graf Kessler in his diary, 'Berlin is in carnival spirits. SA and SS troops and uniformed Stahlhelm* fill the streets and on pavements stand the spectators ... As we came out, an endless SA procession goose-stepped past some prominent personage.'[23]

Klemperer made no reference to these events in the letter he wrote to Johanna on returning from Hamburg to Berlin on 1 February. Yet he was usually alert to the significance of what was going on in the world around him and he cannot have been unaware of their sinister implications for a musician who was not only a Jew by birth but was regarded by Germany's new rulers as a leading *Kulturbolschewist*. Some years earlier, at a time when Hitler was no more than a cloud on the horizon, he had ruefully observed that, while the sound of the Horst Wessel song in the streets could be supported as no more than a minor irritant, the sight of the Nazi leader's face on Germany's postage stamps would be more disagreeable.[24] That day was now fast approaching, and he had in the meantime experienced in his own person the violence that was an inevitable concomitant of the growth in political radicalism.

Many, if not most, of Klemperer's closest friends and associates were also Jews, and in the autumn of 1932 he may have felt a need to strengthen his 'Aryan' connections. Though in later years he did not hide his resentment of Pauline Strauss's crass, if well-meant, assurance of support

---

* Quasi-military supporters of the Nazis' Deutschnational allies.

should the Nazis come to power, it may have made him aware that an association with Germany's leading composer might offer a degree of protection in such an eventuality. That, in its turn, may not be unconnected with the number and the cordiality of the letters he wrote to Strauss in the months after their meetings during the summer. Further evidence of Klemperer's apprehensions in the early winter of 1932/3 is provided by a letter from Hindemith to his publisher and close friend, Willy Strecker. Klemperer, wrote Hindemith, whose bonhomous exterior masked a waspish tongue, 'is deeply unhappy about the course of events and looks in every direction for support, comfort and backing. That's why he's performing the Boston piece for strings and brass here and I have to be present – apparently as *Renomiergoi*.'*

Yet as the events he had feared came to pass, Klemperer seemed to observe developments with almost nonchalant unconcern. On the evening of his return to Berlin from Hamburg on 1 February, he listened to Hitler's radio address to the nation. Kruttge noted in his diary that he seemed 'almost fascinated'. In fact the depression that had set in on his return from Buenos Aires almost a year and a half earlier had already started to give way to a manic phase, which was to prove the most intense he had suffered since his Strasbourg years and was at times to rob him of all sense of reality.† As a result, he was to move like a somnambulist through some of the most critical months of his career, as though providentially sheltered from full awareness of the implications of the events he was living through.

Within a week of the Nazis' coming to power, Klemperer was involved in a potentially dangerous incident in Leipzig, though whether what occurred was a result of misadventure or of design is impossible to determine. On 7 February, while rehearsing *Ein Heldenleben* for the second of his three concerts with the Gewandhaus Orchestra,

the balustrade at the back of the podium suddenly gave way, so that Klemperer fell approximately five feet into the auditorium...[he] was restored to consciousness by a doctor who was called and brought to the house of the publisher, Dr Jollowicz, with whom he is staying. He has suffered bruising on the left side which makes it impossible for him to conduct the concert.[25]

* 'Gentile who by association lends renown'. The 'Boston piece' is the Concert Music for Brass and Strings, which Klemperer conducted at a Berlin Staatskapelle concert on 15 December 1932. (Letter of 16 November 1932.)
† It is hard to determine when this manic phase first made itself felt. An indication is perhaps provided by Klemperer's curious belief that Goering's attendance at his performance of Bach's B minor Mass on 5 December 1932 was a favourable omen. There is no evidence that Goering was in fact present.

In fact he had been concussed and was obliged to remain in bed for two days.*

*   *   *

The fiftieth anniversary of Wagner's death fell on 13 February 1933 and the event could not have been better timed to suit the convenience of Germany's new rulers. The Nazis had not yet secured a firm hold on the levers of power and were accordingly eager to seize any means of underlining the national and traditional aspects of their 'revolution'. In Wagner they saw a figure who could be presented as a forerunner of Nazism. 'The decisive struggle has begun', announced *Der Angriff* on the anniversary of his death, 'and Richard Wagner takes part in this fight.' On the morning of 12 February Hitler, Goering and Frick, accompanied by Winifred Wagner and her sixteen-year-old son, Wieland, attended a commemorative celebration at the Gewandhaus in Leipzig, which was the composer's birthplace.† That evening Hitler attended a performance of *Tristan und Isolde* in Weimar.

The Linden Opera was naturally involved in these celebrations. Months before the Nazis had come to power, Tietjen had planned a cycle of Wagner's operas from *Das Liebesverbot* to *Parsifal*. On the anniversary itself Strauss conducted a performance of *Tristan und Isolde*, and on 12 February, the very day on which Hitler and his entourage were paying homage to the composer in Leipzig, Klemperer was to conduct a new production of *Tannhäuser*. In view of what occurred, Tietjen had reason to congratulate himself that the new *Machthaber* had not opted to attend the Linden Opera.

Klemperer's approach to Wagner was at the best of times liable to affront traditionalists. Nothing he had done at the Kroll had caused so much

---

* According to Frau Eva Morel (interview, 20 October 1980), Klemperer himself maintained that the balustrade had deliberately been weakened and, in view of the animus against conductors of Jewish birth that was already evident barely more than a week after the Nazis had come to power, the explanation cannot be excluded. Medical opinion does, however, firmly discount a suggestion, made even in Klemperer's family circle, that the fall was the cause of the brain tumour that was removed in autumn 1939 and left him seriously disabled on his right side. The incident did, on the other hand, probably give rise to the severe back pains from which he started to suffer a year later. Owing to the final rehearsals for *Tannhäuser* at the Linden Opera and a foreign tour that followed shortly afterwards, Klemperer did not trouble to have himself X-rayed.

† Winifred Wagner (1897–1980), the composer's English-born daughter-in-law, was one of the earliest and most fervent supporters of the Nazi cause (see also p. 287). After the death of her husband, Siegfried, in 1930, she ran the Bayreuth Festival until the collapse of the Third Reich in 1945. From 1931 Tietjen served her both as artistic director and subsequently as guardian of her young family.

Wieland Wagner (1917–1966), elder son of Siegfried and grandson of the composer, who successfully revived the discredited festival on new political and artistic lines. He regarded the Kroll's *Fliegende Holländer* as a crucial forerunner of the New Bayreuth.

outrage as the production of *Der fliegende Holländer* on which he had collaborated with Jürgen Fehling (see pp. 278–83). Now, at the very moment when the Nazis were in the process of annexing Wagner as the patron saint of their movement, he presented *Tannhäuser* on similar lines. He again opted to give the work in its original version. Fehling was once more the producer and the sets were by Oskar Strnad, who had also had associations with the Kroll.* But it was Klemperer who, quite rightly, was regarded as the mainspring of the entire undertaking, and at his reappearance in the orchestral pit before the beginning of the last act he was met, as he later recalled, by 'a gale of whistling such as I have never heard. My supporters clapped against it. It was deafening. I sat and waited patiently for ten minutes.'[26]

Much of the press presented the production as an act of cultural vandalism. Particular exception was taken to Strnad's stylised sets (Act Two was dominated by a vast symbolic harp on a pedestal) and Fehling's treatment of the chorus as an undifferentiated mass. But the attack was concentrated on Klemperer, who had insisted on their engagement. Several critics commented ironically on the fact that he should have instigated such a staging only a few weeks after an article had appeared in which he had protested against producers' licence in Wagner. They failed to notice that in it he had gone on to call for 'a free, imaginative and courageous treatment' of the composer's stage instructions.[27] There was praise for the lucidity of the orchestral textures and the unusual prominence he gave to inner voices, but little enthusiasm for his decision to perform the work in its original version. Ernst Schliepe complained that the music was too sharply defined, at once fevered and cold.[28] But implicit in Klemperer's choice of the Dresden version was a determination to avoid the satin carpet of sound that so many of his colleagues sought in their performances of Wagner.

Right-wing critics expressed anger at the choice on such an occasion of a production that recalled the worst excesses of the Kroll. Paul Zschorlich urged the new Kultusminister, Bernhard Rust, to ban 'this presumptuous attack on Wagner and German culture'.[29] Fritz Stege protested against the staging of 'an artistic falsification at a time of German spiritual renewal'.† There were widespread calls for Tietjen to restore order in his house. A minority of critics bravely defended the production with praise that was almost equally one-sided. Oscar Bie was one of the few to keep his head. He defended the cause of innovation and reform, without claiming this

* Oskar Strnad (1879–1935), Viennese architect, subsequently stage designer, who worked much with Reinhardt. He had previously provided sets for Krenek's three one-acters at the Kroll (see p. 277).
† *Der Berliner Westen*, 13 February 1933. Stege, see p. 282.

Tannhäuser to be a notably successful instance of it. Klemperer's contribution, he wrote, had grandeur and power, but vocally the evening had been undistinguished and the production had lacked the unified impact of *Der fliegende Holländer* at the Kroll.[30] In the Third Reich, however, Klemperer's *Tannhäuser* came to be regarded as one of his gravest offences against German culture.

It is particularly significant that as late as 13 [sic] February 1933, and after the National Socialist seizure of power, the Jewish *Generalmusikdirektor* Klemperer had the impudence on the occasion of the fiftieth anniversary of Wagner's death to mount a production of *Tannhäuser* at the Berlin State Opera that ranked as a deliberate insult to the great German master and an affront to all people with decent feelings.[31]

On 16 February the *Vossische Zeitung* announced that, owing to the after-effects of the fall he had suffered in Leipzig, Klemperer was again confined to bed and would be unable to conduct the second performance of *Tannhäuser* on the following evening. On 20 February Stege, who had close contacts with the new regime, revealed in *Der Berliner Westen* that the production would be withdrawn and the old staging used for further performances. But the Nazis had yet to establish full control of cultural life and when Klemperer conducted on 26 February and 1 March Strnad's sets were still in use. Thereafter *Tannhäuser* disappeared for several weeks from the repertory. When it was revived on 26 April, Klemperer was no longer in Germany. Leo Blech, who conducted, reverted to the Paris version of the opera and an earlier naturalistic production replaced that of Fehling and Strnad.* Convention had triumphed, as it was so often to do in the cultural life of the Third Reich.†

*　　　　　*　　　　　*

In the course of February Goering, now Prussian Minister of the Interior, had established his hold on the police, as a first step in the process of installing a totalitarian regime. But the Nazis were still anxious to reassure middle-of-the-road opinion, which in its turn was eager to believe that the new government was yet another in the series of short-lived, right-wing coalitions that had ruled Germany since March 1932. Many Germans took comfort from the fact that, unlike Mussolini, Hitler had staged no 'march on Rome', but had come to power through constitutional means, and that the Nazis were in possession of only three ministries as against the nine

---

* Blech enjoyed protection at the Lindenoper because, though a Jew, he had been appointed *Generalmusikdirektor* in 1913 by Wilhelm II and was therefore not regarded by the Nazis as a product of the hated Weimar 'system'.
† Among those who welcomed the restoration of 'the good old production', in which 'one felt again the fresh air of German mountains and woodlands', was Walter Abendroth, the newly appointed critic of the *Lokal Anzeiger* (27 April 1933). See p. 109 and n.

held by their *Deutschnational* allies. Among those who suffered from the illusion that no decisive rupture had occurred in German political life was none other than Vice-Chancellor, Franz von Papen. Countering a charge that he had unleashed a tiger, he answered with glib assurance, 'You are wrong. We have hired one.'[32]

Another was Klemperer. The burning of the Reichstag on 27 February, which the Nazis successfully presented as the signal for an abortive Communist *Putsch*, provided the new government with an excuse to introduce emergency legislation that drastically curtailed the guarantee of personal liberty contained in the Weimar constitution, and a wave of arrests followed. But, like many of his compatriots, Klemperer could not bring himself to believe that a German government had engineered the burning of its own parliament,[33] and the continuing readiness of musical organisations to engage him for future events doubtless served to confirm his belief that the political developments of the past month presented no threat to his livelihood. Plans were agreed with the Berlin Philharmonic Chorus for concerts in the coming season* and on 3 March the board of Frankfurt Museum Concerts announced his appointment as their permanent conductor.†

The presence of von Papen at a performance Klemperer conducted of the *Missa Solemnis* on 5 March must have further bolstered his confidence. In Hugenberg's *Berliner Illustrierte Nachtausgabe* (6 March 1933) Alfred Schattmann denounced the reproduction in the programme of the words, 'a plea for inner and outer peace', which Beethoven had himself written in the score at the head of the 'Dona nobis pacem', as 'tasteless as it was suspect'. In the *Völkische Beobachter* (11 March 1933) Hugo Rasch, who took to appearing at concerts in SA uniform,[34] attacked the use of foreign singers, such as Kipnis and Kullman. But Klemperer was demonstratively applauded on his appearance in the Philharmonie and many critics, including Einstein, who wrote he had never heard the work performed with such inner power and naturalness, were not afraid to express their enthusiasm.[35] It was the last concert he was to conduct in Berlin for fifteen years.

The following morning Klemperer left the city in high spirits for a tour that was to take him to Hungary and Italy. On the train he met Fritz Busch, who was travelling to Dresden, and the two conductors enjoyed such an animated lunch that they attracted the disapproving attention of a senior SA officer, seated at a nearby table.‡ On 11 March he conducted for the

---

* Among the works announced for the coming season on 5 March was Handel's *Israel in Egypt*!
† On 25 February Klemperer informed Arthur Judson, later to be his American agent, of his German commitments without giving the least indication that these might be threatened.
‡ Busch, *Aus dem leben eines Musikers*, pp. 196–7. The SA officer, Manfred von Killenger, was

412

first time in Budapest, and then left for Florence, where he had a concert on the 19th and Sessions had given him an introduction to Bernard Berenson. The celebrated art historian and his companion, Nicky Mariano, were amazed at their guest's euphoric view of Germany under the Nazis.[36]

Meanwhile the situation in the Reich continued to deteriorate daily. Terrorism, already intensified after the Reichstag fire, grew more widespread. Commissions were set up in place of constitutionally elected provisional governments. On 13 March SA troops invaded the Berlin Städtische Oper and 'deposed' its Intendant, Carl Ebert.* Three days later the Leipzig police cancelled a concert that Bruno Walter was to give in the Gewandhaus. On the morning of 21 March, 'the day of Potsdam', the Nazi government staged a series of events carefully calculated to convey the grip they had established on the state and its principal institutions. In the morning, a ceremonial service before the tomb of Frederick the Great in the Garrison Church at Potsdam underlined the support of the army for the new regime. The aged President Hindenburg attended, as did the *Generalität*. Hitler wore morning dress. In the afternoon, the centre of attention moved back to Berlin, where the Führer, now attired in the uniform of a leader of the SA, attended a brief inaugural session of the Reichstag, which had taken up its new quarters in the nearby Kroll. That evening there were torchlight processions, while Hitler and the government attended a performance in the Linden Opera of *Die Meistersinger* conducted by Furtwängler.

Klemperer learnt of these events from newspapers in Italy, yet he still failed to take the measure of their significance. With one part of his mind he realised that his position in Germany was threatened. With another part he clung to the hope that by showing loyalty to the new regime he could keep out of trouble. Both attitudes are apparent in a birthday letter he wrote to his thirteen-year-old son on 20 March. He first told Werner that, in accordance with his wish, he had bought him 'a beautiful silver pen with a gold nib', and that he would also give him the Shakespeare that he himself had received from his parents at his bar mitzvah on his own thirteenth birthday. He reminded his son that two years earlier he (Werner) had for the first time received Holy Communion and urged him 'at all times to hold fast...to the Roman Church...Then you will always live in happiness and tranquillity, even in times when life brings difficulties. Particularly in such times only faith and trust in God can bring salvation.' Only after playing the heavy father did he turn to events in Germany.

prominent among those who the following evening prevented Busch from holding a rehearsal of *Rigoletto*. Five days later Busch requested indefinite leave from the Dresden State Opera. In 1934 he became Glyndebourne's first musical director.

* When the ever-resourceful O. W. Lange briefly got a foot in the door (see p. 194n).

You know that it is possible that I may lose my position. If that happens, let us not complain. 'What is, is good.'* You must not allow the joy that Germany will rightly take in its solemn, national holiday on Tuesday to worry you.† *We all* celebrate this day of the *rinascimento*...of Germany, the Germany of Goethe, Bach, Mozart and Beethoven. We celebrate the victory over the devilish powers of Communism, which preaches atheism and the denial of God. You may certainly carry the old black, white and red colours in your buttonhole.‡ Your father voted deutschnational. (You don't need to advertise the fact, on the other hand there is no need to hide it.) We are Catholics who think in a German-National way, even if we do not officially belong to the German-National party.§ I read that Tuesday is to be a school holiday. And the beginning of spring. What a happy coincidence! It will be terribly full on the streets, so you would all probably do best to remain at home. The times are still so turbulent that one must behave as discreetly as possible. *Now listen to me*. Never talk about politics, get on quietly with your work and live *privately*.

Klemperer's attempt to shield his son from perils he was himself still trying to evade had resulted in a bizarre mixture of realism and an ostrich-like refusal to recognise the true state of affairs. But before he left Florence that evening for Turin he learnt of an event that, as he later recalled, momentarily caused the scales to fall from his eyes: Bruno Walter had been obliged to abandon his concerts in Berlin and had left for Austria.

I thought my last hour had also come. From Turin, I telephoned my cousin, Georg Klemperer, in Berlin and [told him that] I did not want to return. Now, he told me, particularly now, you must return. Now we Jews must show...I still didn't know what we were supposed to show.[37]

*   *   *

Tietjen had also drawn his conclusions from Walter's experiences. On 22 March he wrote to Klemperer in Turin.

---

* A favourite saying of Klemperer's mother and as such much quoted in the family.
† A reference to 'the day of Potsdam'.
‡ The colours of imperial Germany, as opposed to the black, yellow and red of the Weimar Republic.
§ Hugenberg's Deutschnationale Volkspartei was the largest component in Hitler's coalition government. Bizarre though Klemperer's decision to vote for a party that had allied itself to the Nazis may now seem, he was by no means the only Jew to do so. The 'Verband Deutschnationaler Juden', which dismissed Hitler's anti-Semitism as 'background noise', endorsed Hugenberg's party in the election of 5 March, in the expectation that it would exercise a moderating influence. The Socialist party similarly tended to regard the Nazis' anti-Semitism as a demagogic trick to gain power and hence believed that they would become more moderate on attaining it. The Nazis played skilfully on that belief.
    It also has to be remembered that anti-Semitic violence had been virtually unknown in modern Germany (in contrast to eastern European countries). For that reason it was at first widely supposed that under the Nazis life for the Jews would be unpleasant rather than intolerable, that they would suffer disadvantages rather than outright persecution, let alone extermination; in other words, that they would live in conditions to which the diaspora had long accustomed them. (See Niewyk, *The Jews in Weimar Germany*.)

Although you have been absent from Berlin for some time, you are probably aware of the extent to which conditions in German theatrical and concert life have altered and will alter further.

At the moment I cannot foresee how far this will affect your position at the State Opera. But the following measures have in any case shown themselves to be necessary and I would ask you to consider them as primarily preventative. Among them is the postponement of the première of *Kreidekreis** for an indefinite period. Only today it has also become evident that the fourth symphony concert cannot take place next week under your direction. As I would like to avoid transferring this concert to another conductor, I have cancelled it.†

That letter only caught up with Klemperer on his return to Berlin on the morning of 27 March and the following day he went to see Tietjen. Tietjen emphasised that the cancellation of his concert was intended purely as a precautionary measure to spare him the disagreeableness that Walter had experienced in Leipzig and Berlin. Klemperer then asked about further prospects and urged Tietjen to speak frankly. Tietjen replied that no one could give any assurances about his future at the State Opera. Klemperer replied that he had heard that a limited number of non-Aryans would be permitted to perform and that he hoped to be included among them. He went on to assure Tietjen that he was in complete agreement with the course of events in Germany: even if he were to be one of those adversely affected, the country could not continue to be run as it had been – that he could say in the light of his experiences with personalities such as Kestenberg.‡

He then enquired whether he himself was regarded as a 'cultural bolshevist'. Tietjen tactfully replied that his artistic abilities were acknowledged in the highest quarters, even by Goering himself, but that the tendencies of his collaborators at the Kroll had possibly damaged his reputation. Klemperer protested that he had never been politically engaged. In the upheavals of 1918/19 he had embraced Catholicism out of

---

* *Der Kreidekreis*, opera by Zemlinsky, who, after the closure of the Kroll, had declined a position as musical director in Wiesbaden in order to devote himself entirely to composition. Klemperer was to have conducted its first performance later in the season. In spite of the fact that Zemlinsky was also a Jew, the work was subsequently staged under another conductor at the Berlin State Opera on 23 January 1934, after it had had its first performance three months earlier in Zurich.

† Klemperer's personal file at the Berlin State Opera. Klemperer was to have conducted his fourth and last Staatskapelle concert on 30 March. Hans Hinkel, the newly appointed State Commissar in the Prussian Kultusministerium, offered another explanation for its cancellation. In the Kampfbund organ, *Deutsche Kulturwacht* (II/8, 1933), quoted in Prieberg, *Musik im Dritten Reich*), he wrote 'we need our SA and SS for more important things than to protect the hall for Herr Klemperer...The German public has for so long been provoked by not a few Jewish frauds in artistic life that – regrettable though it may be – Klemperer and Bruno Walter have to suffer from public feeling (Volksstimmung).'

‡ Klemperer regarded the Weimar Republic and its agents as having betrayed the Kroll Opera. That was undoubtedly a factor in his disillusionment with the republican regime and, it may be, in his otherwise surprising political attitudes early in 1933.

415

deliberate opposition to 'the red flood'.* At the Kroll he had performed works only out of artistic conviction, and for that reason had refused to mount *Der Aufstieg und Fall der Stadt Mahagonny* in spite of Kestenberg's insistence that he should do so.† If his contract were to be dissolved, he requested that, like Furtwängler, he be engaged for guest performances, as an association with the State Opera was for him a matter of artistic necessity.‡ Finally, he asked Tietjen to arrange an audience with Goering.§

Almost forty years later, in the last months of his life, Klemperer read the official memorandum, in which Tietjen had recorded the course of their discussion and which had survived in his personal file in the archives of the Berlin State Opera.‖ Characteristically, he made no attempt to deny or excuse what he had himself earlier described as his 'foolishness' ('Leichtsinn')[38] at this time. And indeed there was no explanation other than his psychological condition. During the very days when his entire future and that of his family was hanging in the balance he had been able to sketch an entire new opera, *Der verlorene Sohn*, designed as a prelude to *Bathseba* (see p. 379). He also composed a *Chanson russe*, which he dedicated to Micha May, a pretty young medical student of Russian origin, in whom he had late in 1932 become infatuated, in spite of the fact that she was shortly to marry the young son of his old friend and doctor, Oskar Kohnstamm. The manic fires were raging wildly.

Yet a sense of reality intermittently asserted itself: on 28 March, directly after his meeting with Tietjen, he sent Johanna, who was again on tour with the Musikbühne, a composed and rational account of what had transpired and its implications for their future. Tietjen, he wrote,

was *very nice*, but whether I can remain or not is questionable. Therefore we must – as you with your feminine instinct rightly prophesied – be prepared for everything...The main thing they have against me is not my race, but that I am regarded as a man of the Left...One could also call that tragic irony or tragic misunderstanding...Ah well, calm and patience. I should very soon have discussions with the ministry. *Perhaps* there is a chance of a short guest contract.

But he was, as he himself later recalled, 'in a dreamlike state',[39] and as the situation worsened, his attempts to rationalise his optimism grew more extravagant. On 27 March, at supper at the Strubs, where Carl Flesch and Edwin Fischer were among the guests, he argued passionately that it was

---

* He was doing himself less than justice. See pp. 135–8.
† Not true. See p. 296.
‡ A striking change of tone from his attitude over the past eighteen months.
§ In his autobiographical sketch (p. 23) Klemperer claimed that Tietjen had told him that Goering regarded him as 'the most interesting conductor at the Berlin State Opera'. He may also have been influenced to request a meeting by the fact that Goering is reputed to have received Fritz Busch after his dismissal from the Dresden State Opera (H. H. Stuckenschmidt, *Frankfurter Allgemeine Zeitung*, 6 December 1980).
‖ Merseburg, HA Rep. 119 Neu, pp. 355–6. Klemperer's rather different version appears in *Conversations*, p. 69.

the duty of the Jews to remain in Germany. Flesch told him to his face that his political views were 'nazionalist'.* When asked by Wolfgang Stresemann, the half-Jewish son of the German statesman, what his plans were, he angrily replied, 'I am a Catholic and a pupil of Pfitzner' and turned on his heels.[40] On 1 April, which had been declared Jewish Boycott Day 'to forestall [as the Nazis put it] events that otherwise might be hard to control', he invited Roger Sessions to tea and read him a prose-poem he had written in praise of the New Order in Germany.[41] On the following day he urged the baptism of all Jews on his orthodox brother-in-law, Ismar Elbogen, on the ground that the Jewish question was basically a religious issue, and even recommended that a Jewish palatine guard be formed to protect Hitler.[42]

But at this point an event occurred that suddenly shattered the cocoon of euphoria in which he had been living. On the very next day, 3 April, he learnt from his cousin, Georg, who had until the previous year been the director of the Moabit Hospital, that the head of its neurological department had been arrested in broad daylight. Apart from the fact that the man was a Jew, no one knew why this had occurred or where he had been taken. At a stroke, Klemperer became aware of the danger in which he stood. 'I thought, my goodness, it is time to leave.'[43]

Having reached that conclusion, he acted without delay. After agreeing with Johanna that she should follow with the children and Fräulein Schwab, he went the following morning to the police to have his passport stamped with a permit to leave Germany. To his wife's amazement and anger, he tried to persuade Micha May to accompany him to Switzerland. But at Johanna's request Georg Klemperer intervened decisively. Mindful of what had occurred twenty years earlier, when his cousin had eloped with Elisabeth Schumann, Georg explained that depression and remorse would inevitably follow euphoria, so that the invitation was not to be taken seriously. In the midst of packing, Klemperer telephoned Fritz Zweig to tell him that he was handing over the Philharmonic Chorus to him, and angrily brushed aside Zweig's protests that as a Jew he would hardly be a suitable successor.[44] Finally he went to bid farewell to Tietjen. Tietjen politely enquired about his destination and, on learning that it was the celebrated Bircher-Benner Clinic in Zurich, sought refuge from his embarrassment in a discussion of the relative merits of the diets it offered.

In the early afternoon of 4 April, Johanna, weeping bitterly, brought her husband to the Anhalter Station. The carriages to Basle were full of Jews leaving Germany. That night, as he entered Switzerland, Klemperer felt as relieved 'as the Jews when they had crossed the Red Sea'.[45] But the world he had entered was to prove no Promised Land.

* Information provided by Eigel Kruttge, who was also present. Carl Flesch (1877–1944), Hungarian-born violinist and a great teacher of the instrument.

Notes

1 Childhood

1 Letter to Alma Mahler, 26 November 1911.
2 Heyworth (ed.), *Conversations with Klemperer*, pp. 22–3 (henceforth *Conversations*).
3 Simon Bischheim, letter to his parents, 24 May 1910.
4 Autobiographical sketch, pp. 3–4.
5 *Conversations*, p. 25.

2 A student in Berlin

1 Heyworth (ed.), *Conversations*, p. 26.
2 Ilse Fromm-Michaels, a fellow student, to the author.
3 *Le Ménestral*, 13 August 1905.
4 *Wege eines Komponisten*, p. 34.
5 *Allgemeine Musikzeitung*, 22 June 1906.
6 *Conversations*, p. 89.
7 *Ibid.*, p. 30; *Minor Recollections*, pp. 12–13.
8 Felix Holländer, 'Zum Engagement Otto Klemperer', *8 Uhr Blatt*, 28 September 1926.
9 Verbatim account as related by Klemperer to his daughter, Lotte, in November 1972.
10 *Conversations*, p. 29.
11 Otto Klemperer, 'In eigener Sache', *Berliner Tageblatt*, 26 January 1931.
12 *Minor Recollections*, pp. 13–14.
13 Letter to Alma Mahler, 26 November 1911.
14 *Allgemeine Musikzeitung*, 12 February 1907.
15 Alfred Roller, 'Mahler und die Inszenierung', *Anbruch*, April 1920.
16 *Illustriertes Extrablatt*, 9 September 1903. Quoted in Blaukopf, *Mahler*, p. 174.
17 Roller, 'Mahler'.
18 *Conversations*, p. 37.
19 *Ibid.*, p. 38.
20 *Ibid.*

3 Apprenticeship in Prague

1 *Prager Tagblatt*, 21 December 1910, 'Angelo Neumann und das deutsche Prag'.
2 Richard Batka, 'Angelo Neumann', *Der Merker*, 1911, No. 7.
3 Richard Rosenheim, *Die Geschichte der deutschen Bühnen in Prag*, p. 50.
4 Heyworth (ed.), *Conversations*, p. 39.
5 *Ibid.*, p. 97.

418

6   *Ibid.*
7   *Minor Recollections*, p. 17; *Conversations*, p. 31.
8   *Arbeiter-Zeitung*, 20 December 1920.
9   Alma Mahler, *Gustav Mahler: Memories and Letters*, p. 305 (where it is incorrectly dated 22 September). The performance took place on 19 September.
10   Grete Fischer, *Dienstbote Brechts und anderen*, pp. 77–8.
11   Klemperer's account of the incident on 25 July 1966.
12   *Conversations*, p. 39.
13   The letter is undated.

4   Hamburg

1   Mahler's undated letter to Alma Mahler. Alma Mahler, *Gustav Mahler: Memories and Letters*, p. 331.
2   *Minor Recollections*, p. 26.
3   Heyworth (ed.), *Conversations*, p. 34.
4   CBC transcripts, tape 14, p. 18; tape 2, p. 11.
5   *Minor Recollections*, p. 20.
6   *Ibid.*, pp. 32–3.
7   Ferdinand Pfohl, *Hamburger Nachrichten*, 6 September 1910.
8   Lotte Lehmann, *Wings of Song*, p. 92.
9   *Hamburger Nachrichten*, 1 December 1910.
10   *Hamburger Correspondent*, 1 December 1910.
11   *Hamburger Nachrichten*, 9 November 1910.
12   *Hamburger Fremdenblatt*, 5 September 1910.
13   *Conversations*, p. 40.
14   *Ibid.*
15   Saint-Saëns, *Ecole buissonière*, pp. 228–31.
16   'Über eine Opernaufführung im Théâtre du Jorat, mitgeteilt von einem reisenden Enthusiasten' (July 1911), in *Über Musik und Theater*, pp. 121–8.
17   Richard Wagner, 'Ein Einblick in das heutige deutsche Opernwesen', *Musikalisches Wochenblatt*, 3, 10 and 17 January 1873.
18   Letter to Helene Hirschler, 4 February 1945.
19   *Minor Recollections*, pp. 43–4.
20   *Conversations*, p. 75.
21   *Ibid.*, p. 43.
22   *Minor Recollections*, pp. 36–7, where the remark appears in quotation marks.
23   *Ibid.*, p. 64.
24   The letter is undated.
25   Letter of 26 November.
26   Letter of 7 February 1912.
27   Letter to Regi Elbogen, 9 January 1912.
28   *Die Musik*, March 1912.
29   *Allgemeine Musikzeitung*, 16 February 1912.
30   *Hamburger Nachrichten*, 9 February 1912.
31   Letter of 5 May 1912.

5   Shipwreck

1   Carl Hagemann, *Die Kunst der Bühne*, p. 414.
2   *Hamburger Theater-Rundschau*, 15 September 1912.
3   *Hamburger Fremdenblatt*, 3 September 1912.
4   *Ibid.*
5   *Hamburger Neueste Nachrichten* 3 September 1912.
6   *Hamburger Fremdenblatt*, 5 September 1912.
7   *Hamburger Nachrichten*, 4 September 1912.
8   *Hamburger Nachrichten*, 21 September 1912.
9   *Hamburger Fremdenblatt*, 28 September 1912.
10   *Hamburger Fremdenblatt*, 1 October 1912.
11   *Neue Freie Presse*, 30 July 1933.
12   Dülberg, 'Versuch einer Selbstdarstellung', *Der Merkur*, 1951, No. 3, pp. 253–67.
13   *Hamburger Nachrichten*, 21 October 1912.
14   *Minor Recollections*, p. 43. Essay in *Schoenberg*, ed. Armitage.
15   *Minor Recollections*, p. 43.
16   Lotte Lehmann, *Wings of Song*, pp. 117–18.
17   Interviews with the author (20 July 1972) and Bregstein (typescript).
18   *Hamburger Fremdenblatt*, 2 December 1912.
19   Mathis, 'Elisabeth Schumann', p. 131.
20   Interview with Mrs Robert Müller-Hartmann.
21   *Hamburger Nachrichten*, 1 December 1912.
22   *Hamburger Fremdenblatt*, 30 November 1912.
23   Letter to Desmond Shawe-Taylor, London, 12 January 1965.
24   Letter to his parents, Schiltigheim, 10 December 1911.
25   *Conversations*, p. 91.
26   Minutes of the Barmer Theaterverein, 23 January 1914.
27   Dent, *Mozart's Operas*, p. 190.
28   *Barmer Zeitung*, 12 March 1914.
29   *Conversations*, p. 44.

6   With Pfitzner in Strasbourg

1   Letter to Hans Rectanus, 23 October 1968.
2   26 January 1913. See Walter Abendroth, *Hans Pfitzner*, p. 190.
3   Hans Pfitzner, *Eindrücke und Bilder meines Lebens*, pp. 46–7.
4   Abendroth (ed.), *Hans Pfitzner, Reden, Schriften, Briefe*, p. 85.
5   January 1915, No. 11.
6   January 1915, No. 9.
7   January 1915, No. 11.
8   January 1915, No. 8.
9   25 March 1915.
10   *Conversations*, p. 45.
11   Information provided by Max Hofmüller.
12   *Bürgerzeitung*, 12 January 1915.
13   Marguerite Hugel's recollection in her 'Memoiren einer danebengeratenen Pfitzner-schülerin' (unpublished typescript) of a performance she heard Klemperer conduct in 1917.

14   *Strassburger Post*, 1915, No. 254.
15   1915, No. 222.
16   *Strassburger Post*, 1915, No. 714.
17   Dülberg, 'Vita', typescript excerpts, p. 3.
18   Siegbert Elkuss's letter of 25 May 1915 to his fiancée, S. von der Schulenberg.
19   *Neue Zeitung*, 17 May 1915, No. 136.
20   Letters from Elkuss to von der Schulenberg.
21   Both extracts are from a letter of 15 July 1915 to Else Nürnberg.
22   Information given to the author by Ludwig Strecker, 27 November 1975.
23   Ludwig Strecker to Klemperer, 2 September 1915.
24   Based on an account by Hofmüller.
25   *Hamburger Nachrichten*, 27 October 1915.
26   *Neue Musikzeitung*, 3 February 1916.
27   *Hamburger Fremdenblatt*, 27 October 1915.
28   Letter to Ludwig Strecker, 2 November 1915.
29   *Neue Badische Landeszeitung*, 2 December 1915.
30   Letter from Else Nürnberg to the author, 6 October 1975.
31   *Allgemeine Musikzeitung*, 14 January 1916; *Neue Musikzeitung*, 19 October 1916.
32   Ida Klemperer to Elli Sternberg, 16 January 1916.
33   Letter to Hans Rectanus, 23 October 1968; *Conversations*, p. 45.
34   Letter to Helmut Grohe, 10 January 1967.
35   Minutes of the Theatre Commission meeting, 12 February 1916 (Archives municipales, Strasbourg, file C 12–19).
36   Abendroth, *Hans Pfitzner*, p. 206.
37   Letter from Helmut Grohe to Lotte Klemperer, 27 January 1975.
38   *Conversations*, p. 45.
39   By Mlle Marguerite Hugel, who provided this information.
40   Sitting of 10 March 1916 (Archives municipales, file C 13/78).
41   *Neue Zeitung*, 3 April 1916.
42   Charlotte Bloch, a fellow patient. Interview with the author.
43   Letter to Helene Hirschler, undated, *c.* July 1939.
44   Theaterbetriebsausschuss, 30 December 1916.
45   *Kölner Tageblatt*, 9 January 1924.
46   *Kölnische Zeitung*, 7 January 1917.
47   *Kölnische Volkszeitung*, 8 January 1917.
48   April 1917, No. 86.
49   This phrase is also drawn from Marguerite Hugel's diary.
50   May 1917, No. 116.

7   Cologne: conversion and marriage

1   Letter to Helene Hirschler, 18 August 1917.
2   Carl Niessen, 'Das Kölner Theaterwesen', *Handbuch von Köln 1925*.
3   Ludwig Strecker to Klemperer, 5 July 1917. Confirmed by comment of Max Hofmüller to the author.
4   Heyworth (ed.), *Conversations*, p. 46.
5   *Kölnische Zeitung*, 28 January 1918.
6   '*Don Juan* und die neue Stilbühne', *Kölnische Zeitung*. No date ascertainable.
7   *Kölnische Volkszeitung*, 28 January 1918.

8 *Kölner Tageblatt*, 13 May 1918.
9 Letter of 11 May 1918.
10 Dahn, *Allerhand, Durcheinand*, p. 38.
11 Julius Gless, typescript reminiscences.
12 von Hofmannsthal and von Andrian, *Briefwechsel*, p. 286.
13 *Minor Recollections*, p. 61.
14 Dülberg, 'Vita', typescript excerpts, p. 4.
15 Wilhelm Kemp in the *Blätter der Bücherstube*, n.d. (Wiesbaden).
16 *Conversations*, p. 50.
17 *Kölnische Zeitung*, 4 March 1919.
18 *Conversations*, p. 47.
19 Letter of 21 November 1918.
20 Markham, *A Woman's Watch on the Rhine*.
21 Details of the occupation are drawn mainly from de Jonge's *Weimar Chronicle*.
22 *Westdeutsche Wochenschrift*, 2 May 1919.
23 Historisches Archiv der Stadt Köln, Bestand 46/12/11, No. 176.
24 *Kölner Tageblatt*, *c*. 28 April 1919, 'Die Kölner Theater am 1 Mai'.
25 Letter to Helene Asch-Rosenbaum, 2 January 1919.
26 Letter to Helene Asch-Rosenbaum, 18 February 1919.
27 See *Conversations*, p. 54.
28 Letter to Helene Asch-Rosenbaum, 20 June 1919.
29 *Ibid*.
30 *Westdeutsche Wochenschrift*, 4 July 1919.
31 *Kölnische Volkszeitung*, 17 June 1919.

8 Cologne: galley years

1 Letter of 16 July 1921.
2 Letter to Helene Asch-Rosenbaum, 27 October 1919.
3 *Kölnische Zeitung*, 6 October 1919.
4 Interview with the author, 3 February 1972.
5 *Ibid*.
6 *Conversations*, p. 33.
7 *Kölnische Zeitung*, 19 January 1920.
8 Letter to Klemperer, 16 January 1916.
9 Letter to Helene Asch-Rosenbaum, 14 June 1920.
10 *Rheinische Zeitung*, 13 October 1919.
11 *Kölner Stadt Anzeiger*, 13 October 1919.
12 Autobiographical sketch, p. 15.
13 Letter to Mimi Pfitzner, 13 April 1920.
14 Letter to Hans Rectanus, 23 October 1968.
15 Details provided by Schmitz in an interview with and letters to the author.
16 *Rheinische Volkswacht*, 7 December 1920.
17 *Westdeutsche Wochenschrift*, 7 January 1921.
18 Letter to Helene Asch-Rosenbaum, 15 December 1920.
19 *Neues Wiener Tagblatt*, 20 December 1920.
20 *Der Merker*, January–March 1921.
21 Letter to Busoni, Nordeney, undated, *c*. August 1920.
22 Letter to Johanna Klemperer, Paris, 22 December 1920.
23 Typescript reminiscences of Julius Gless, who sang Marke and Rocco.
24 Letter to Johanna Klemperer (back in Cologne), 23 January 1921.

25 Letter to Johanna Klemperer, Barcelona, 29 January 1921.
26 *BZ am Mittag*, 23 April 1921.
27 *Deutsche Allgemeine Zeitung*, 25 April 1921.
28 *Berliner Börsen-Courier*, 20 May 1921.
29 *BZ am Mittag*, 26 January 1922.
30 *Deutsche Allgemeine Zeitung*, 31 January 1922.
31 Letter of 3 January 1923.
32 Paul Bekker, 'Neue Musik' (1919) and 'Deutsche Musik der Gegenwart' (1921), both in *Neue Musik*, pp. 112 and 185.
33 Letters of 5 and 12 October 1921.
34 Schreker to Universal Edition, 16 July 1922.
35 *Conversations*, p. 61.
36 Information provided by Adrian Boult.
37 Letter to Johanna Klemperer, 22 November 1921.
38 Lord Rothschild, *The Times*, 20 June 1975.
39 The direct speech is taken from *Conversations*, p. 46.
40 *Kölnische Zeitung*, 9 December 1922.
41 *Kölnische Volkszeitung*, 10 December 1922.
42 *Rheinische Volkswacht*, 11 December 1922.
43 Letter of 15 September 1922.
44 Letter of 18 September 1922.
45 Letter to Johanna Klemperer, 28 December 1922.
46 Letter to Johanna Klemperer, 4 January 1923.
47 Letter to Johanna Klemperer, 28 December 1922 (the order of the excerpts quoted has been reversed for purposes of clarity).
48 Letter to Johanna Klemperer, 3 January 1923.
49 *Giornale d'Italia*, 28 December 1922.
50 *Das Tagebuch*, 25 May 1929.
51 Adolf Weissmann, 'Otto Klemperer', *Die Musik*, May 1928.

9 Berlin beckons

 1 Heyworth (ed.), *Conversations*, pp. 58–9.
 2 Werner Bollert, *50 Jahre Deutsche Oper, Berlin*, pp. 13–19.
 3 Letters to his wife, 8, 10, 13 and 16 January 1923.
 4 Information provided by Fritz Zweig.
 5 Memorandum from Max von Schillings on subsequent and quite distinct negotiations with Klemperer. See p. 179.
 6 Letter to Ludwig Strecker, 12 August 1919.
 7 Kurt Singer, 'Staatsoper Kalamitäten', *Anbruch*, December 1921.
 8 Kestenberg, *Bewegte Zeiten*, p. 9.
 9 Kestenberg to Gerhard Braun, 23 February 1952. Braun, *Die Schulmusikerziehung in Preussen*, p. 72.
10 Braun, *Schulmusikerziehung*, p. 72.
11 Raupp, *Max von Schillings*, pp. 216–18.
12 Autobiographical sketch, p. 16.
13 *Conversations*, p. 56.
14 Hans Curjel, ed. Eigel Kruttge, *Experiment Krolloper*, pp. 193–5.
15 Historisches Archiv der Stadt Köln, Bestand 46/13/14, Nos. 106–8.
16 Loewenberg, *Annals of Opera*.

17 *Saturday Review*, 27 May 1965, 'Early Days with Klemperer'.
18 Walther Jacobs, *Kölnische Zeitung*, 30 November 1923.
19 *Bohemia*, 11 December 1923.
20 *Vorwärts*, 17 August 1919.
21 See especially Paul Bekker, *Kritische Zeitbilder*, pp. 212–17, 231–3.
22 *Vossische Zeitung*, 24 June 1923.
23 Zuckmayer, *Als wär's ein Stück von mir*, quoted in Taylor, *Literature and Society in Germany, 1918–1945*, p. 16.
24 *BZ am Mittag*, 23 February 1924.
25 *Musikblätter des Anbruch*, May 1924.
26 *Dresdner Neueste Nachrichten*, 30 March 1924.
27 *BZ am Mittag*, 28 March 1924.
28 *Neue Zürcher Zeitung*, 3 April 1924.
29 *Frankfurter Zeitung*, 29 March 1924.
30 *Vossische Zeitung*, 29 March 1924.
31 *Conversations*, p. 48.
32 Wolfgang Stresemann, *…und Abends in der Philharmonie*, pp. 92–5.
33 *Berliner Tageblatt*, 12 April 1924.
34 *Berliner National-Zeitung*, 11 April 1924.
35 *Vossische Zeitung*, 27 August 1924.
36 *Vossische Zeitung*, 9 December 1924.
37 Historisches Archiv der Stadt Köln, Bestand 902/103/1, Nos. 489–91.
38 Historisches Archiv der Stadt Köln, Bestand 46/13/14, No. 144.
39 Information provided by Eigel Kruttge.
40 Historisches Archiv der Stadt Köln, Bestand 902/155/1, Nos. 929–30.
41 Details and dates concerning Klemperer's Wiesbaden engagement are taken from his personnel files in the theatre's archives, which were among the few to escape destruction in the Second World War.

10 Wiesbaden: the world opens up

1 Carl Hagemann, 'Gustav Mahler als Opernleiter', *Wiesbadener Theateralmanach*, 1926.
2 Bengsch, 'Carl Hagemann und die Szenenreform der Schauspielbühne', pp. 33–7.
3 Hagemann, *Die Kunst der Bühne*, pp. 257–8, 261.
4 Quoted in Panofsky, *Protest in der Oper*, p. 178. (A very free translation.)
5 Ewald Dülberg, 'Musik und Szene', *Von neuer Musik*, ed. Eigel Kruttge.
6 Dülberg, 'Vita' excerpts p. 5.
7 *Neue Freie Presse* (Vienna), 30 July 1933.
8 *Pult und Taktstock*, October 1924.
9 *Wiesbadener Tagblatt*, 2 July 1925.
10 *Vossische Zeitung*, 4 October 1924.
11 Siegfried Pisling, *Berliner National-Zeitung*, 28 October 1924.
12 *Vossische Zeitung*, 24 October 1924.
13 *Deutsche Allgemeine Zeitung*, 24 October 1924.
14 *Deutsche Allgemeine Zeitung*, 7 October 1925.
15 *Berliner Tageblatt*, 26 November 1925.
16 *Der Morgenpost*, 27 November 1925.
17 *Deutsche Allgemeine Zeitung*, 27 November 1925.

18 For a general assessment of Klemperer at this stage of his development, see Adolf Weissmann's essay in *Der Dirigent im zwanzigsten Jahrhundert* (1925).
19 'Le Coq et l'arlequin', in *Le Rappel à l'ordre*, p. 31.
20 Letter of 27 October 1922.
21 *Zhizn' iskusstva*, 23 April 1925.
22 *New York Herald Tribune*, 16 January 1926.
23 *Krasnaya gazeta*, 7 April 1925.
24 Heyworth (ed.), *Conversations*, p. 61.
25 *Wiesbadener Tagblatt*, 19 November 1925.
26 Interview with Frau Eva Morel, who attended rehearsals.
27 Confirmed by Eigel Kruttge. Interview with the author, 26 July 1975.
28 Leonid Sabanejew, 'Die Musik und die musikalischen Kreisen Russlands in der Nachkriegszeit' (*Musikblätter des Anbruch*, March 1925) and Victor Belaiev (*Christian Science Monitor*, 7 February 1925). See also Schwarz, *Music and Musical Life in Soviet Russia, 1917–1970*.
29 Gojowy, *Neue sowjetische Musik der 20er Jahren*, p. 16.
30 Trotsky, *Literature and Revolution* (1923), quoted in Krebs, *Soviet Composers and the Development of Soviet Music*, pp. 34–5.
31 Trotsky, *Literature and Revolution*, quoted in Schwarz, *Music and Musical Life in Soviet Russia, 1917–1970*, p. 48.
32 Gauk, *Memuarï. Izbrannïye stat'i. Vospominaniya sovremennikov*, p. 77.
33 Letter to Lotte Klemperer, 7 January 1982.
34 Bregstein interview, I, pp. 10–11.
35 Gauk, *Memuarï*, p. 76.
36 Ginzburg, *Izbrannoye. Dirizhorï i orkestrï*, p. 75.
37 *Conversations*, p. 57.
38 Autobiographical sketch, p. 17.
39 Yudin, *Musïkal'naya zhizn'*, 21 November 1973.
40 *Krasnaya gazeta*, 26 March 1925; *Pravda*, 7 April 1925.
41 Yudin, Memoirs, p. 117.
42 *Ibid.*, p. 115.
43 *Krasnaya gazeta*, 26 March and 15 April 1925.
44 Information provided by the Leningrad State Theatre Museum.
45 Yudin, Memoirs, pp. 117–19; Gauk, *Memuarï*, p. 77.
46 Asaf'yev, *Kriticheskiye stat'i, ocherki i retsenzii*, p. 273.
47 *Musical Courier* (New York), 11 February 1926.
48 *Krasnaya gazeta*, 2 December 1925.
49 *Conversations*, p. 57.
50 Letters to Johanna Klemperer, 3 and 12 December 1925.
51 Letter to Johanna Klemperer, 3 December.
52 *Pravda*, 11 December 1925.
53 *Neue Musikzeitung*, 1926, No. 5, p. 329.
54 Letter to Dülberg, Wiesbaden, 3 January 1926. Interview with *The Musical Digest*, 9 February 1926.
55 Robert A. Simon, *The New Yorker*, 6 February 1926.
56 *New York Times*, 25 January 1926.
57 *New York Herald-Tribune*, 25 January 1926.
58 *New York Herald-Tribune*, 29 January 1926.
59 *Musical Courier*, 11 February 1926.
60 *New York Telegram*, 5 February 1926.

61 *New York Times*, 27 February 1926.
62 *New York Herald-Tribune*, 22 March 1926.
63 W. J. Henderson, *New York Sun*, 26 March 1926.
64 *Prager Presse*, 8 December 1926.
65 Letter of 15 July 1926.
66 Letter to Hans Heinsheimer (Universal Edition), 14 December 1926.
67 Pitts Sanborn, *New York Telegram*, 19 February 1927.

11 The call comes

1 Dülberg, letter to Klemperer, 3 February 1929.
2 *BZ am Mittag*, 3 January 1924.
3 *Musikblätter des Anbruch*, March 1924.
4 *BZ am Mittag*, 11 April 1925.
5 Friedrich A. Lange, *Gross-Berliner Tagebuch*, p. 96.
6 Bruno Walter, *Theme and Variations*, p. 298.
7 *Berliner Tageblatt*, 29 November 1925.
8 *Der Jungdeutsche*, 28 November and 2 December 1925.
9 *Vossische Zeitung*, 14 December 1925.
10 Personal file, State Opera archives in Zentrales Staatsarchiv, Merseburg.
11 Curjel, ed. Kruttge, *Experiment Krolloper*, p. 19.
12 Zentrales Staatsarchiv, Merseburg, 2.10.6, No. 126, pp. 332–7.
13 Autobiographical sketch, pp. 18–19.
14 Verbal communication to the author, July 1973.
15 Stravinsky, *Themes and Conclusions*, p. 225.
16 Heinsheimer, 'Meine Erinnerungen an Alexander Zemlinsky', Hamburg State Opera programme book, 20 September 1981.
17 *Musical America*, 19 February 1927.
18 Exchange of letters between Gertrud Hindemith and Willy Strecker, 21 and 23 April 1926.
19 *Minor Recollections*, p. 55. Confirmed by Paul Gergely, repetiteur in Wiesbaden at the time.
20 Busoni, 'Entwurf eines Vorwortes zur Partitur des *Doktor Faust*...' (1921), in *Von der Einheit der Musik*.
21 Krenek, letters to his parents of 12 October and 28 December 1926.
22 Stravinsky, ed. Craft, *Selected Correspondence*, Vol. 1, pp. 106–8.
23 *Neue Wiesbadener Zeitung*, 4 July 1927.
24 Hagemann, *Bühne und Welt*, pp. 101–3. (Free translation)

12 Klemperer's Kroll opens

1 Letter from Klemperer to his wife, Berlin, 1 September 1927.
2 Curjel, ed. Kruttge, *Experiment Krolloper*, p. 21.
3 Ginzburg, *Izbrannoye. Dirizhorï i orkestrï*, pp. 79–80.
4 *Über Musik und Theater*, p. 88.
5 Such is the view expressed by his widow, Louise Zemlinsky, to the author.
6 Letter of 6 March 1930 (?), quoted in Weber, *Alexander Zemlinsky*, p. 38.
7 'Angewandte Musikpolitik', *Berliner Tageblatt*, 21 September 1922.
8 *Experiment Krolloper*, p. 71.
9 Heyworth (ed.), *Conversations*, p. 58.

10 Arthur-Maria Rabenalt, 'Die Legende der Krolloper', Appendix to Reinking *Form und Spiel*, pp. 257–63.
11 Hans Curjel, 'Erinnerungen an Kurt Weill', *Melos*, March 1970, pp. 81–5.
12 *Conversations*, p. 60.
13 Curjel, in *Experiment Krolloper*, p. 41.
14 *Conversations*, p. 67.
15 *Berliner Tageblatt*, 30 September 1927.
16 This and other details in the above paragraph are largely drawn from diaries made available by the Janáček Archives, Brno.
17 Recollections of Irene Eisinger (Marzelline), related to the author.
18 *Berliner Börsen-Courier*, 21 November 1927.
19 22 November 1927.
20 *Berliner Tageblatt*, 20 November 1927.
21 Heinz Pringsheim, *Berliner Volkszeitung*, 21 November 1927.
22 *Deutsche Zeitung*, 21 November 1927.
23 *BZ am Mittag*, 21 November 1927.
24 *Thüringer Allgemeine Zeitung*, 25 November 1927.
25 *Völkischer Beobachter*, 24 March 1928.
26 *Conversations*, p. 60.
27 Curjel gave various accounts of this incident, the fullest in an interview with Strobel (Südwestfunk, 11 February 1970).
28 Information provided by Fritz Zweig.
29 *Vossische Zeitung*, 12 January 1928.
30 *Berliner Tageblatt*, 12 January 1928.
31 Interview with the author, 18 June 1978.
32 *Rote Fahne*, 14 January 1928.
33 Information provided by Helmut Grohe, the musician in question.
34 *BZ am Mittag*, 27 February 1928.
35 *Neue Musikzeitung*, 1928, pp. 416–20.
36 *Deutsche Zeitung*, 27 February 1928.
37 *Style and Idea*, pp. 482–3.
38 *Chroniques de ma vie*, Vol. 2, p. 109.
39 Letter from F. Von Weber to Stravinsky. See Stravinsky, *Selected Correspondence*, Vol. 1, endnote 192.
40 *Vossische Zeitung*, 12 December 1927.
41 *Untersuchungsausschuss*, column 523.
42 Nestriepke, 'Kritik und Volksbühne', *Berliner Tageblatt*, 29 December 1928.
43 Zentrales Staatsarchiv, Merseburg, 2.10.6, No. 747, pp. 167, 169.
44 *Vossische Zeitung*, 1 September 1928, 'Musik und Volk'.

13 The Kroll gets under way

1 Letter to Johanna Klemperer, Berlin, 19 July 1928.
2 Letter of 28 August 1928.
3 Curjel, ed. Kruttge, *Experiment Krolloper*, p. 73.
4 S. Nestriepke, 'Volksbühne und neue Musik', *Melos*, January 1930.
5 Universal Edition (Heinsheimer) to Krenek, 30 May 1928.
6 Issue of 12 December 1928.
7 Heyworth (ed.), *Conversations*, p. 51.
8 Interviews with the author.

9   Ernst Bloch's recollections in *Experiment Krolloper*, p. 72.
10   Oskar Fritz Schuh in the catalogue of an exhibition devoted to Fehling's productions (Akademie der Künste, West Berlin, 1978). Many of the details of the production are drawn from his description of it.
11   23 January 1929, 'Ein neues Attentat auf ein deutsches Meisterwerk'.
12   25 January 1929, 'Der entwagnerte *Holländer*'.
13   Ziegler, *Entartete Musik: eine Abrechnung*, p. 25.
14   *Allgemeine Musikzeitung*, 8 February; *Signale*, 20 February 1929.
15   *Berliner Tageblatt*, 8 February 1929.
16   Terence A. Senter, 'Moholy-Nagy's Vision of Unity' (catalogue of the Arts Council exhibition, London, 1980, p. 12). See also Moholy-Nagy's own, rather cloudy, essay, 'Theater der Totalität' in *Von Material zu Architektur*.
17   Moholy-Nagy, 'Theater, Zirkus, Variété', reprinted in *Von Material zu Architektur*, p. 219.
18   *Experiment Krolloper*, pp. 50–1.
19   Sibyl Moholy-Nagy, *László Moholy-Nagy, ein Totalexperiment*, p. 52.
20   *Der Querschnitt*, March 1929.
21   *Zhizn' iskusstva*, 21 April 1929.
22   *Berliner Westen*, 13 February 1929.
23   *Deutsche Zeitung*, 13 February 1929.
24   Brenner, *Die Kunstpolitik des National-Sozialismus*, pp. 9–11.
25   *Der Tag*, 17 February 1929.
26   22 February 1929, 'Klemperer und die Republikoper'.
27   *BZ am Mittag*, 4 November 1928, 'Wie ist unsere Opernkrise zu lösen?' See also Walter's letter of 20 September 1928 to Oberbürgermeister Böss, *Briefe*, pp. 217–22.
28   *Zhizn' iskusstva*, 21 April 1929.
29   Interview with the author.
30   *Berliner Tageblatt*, 9 January 1929.
31   In the library of the Schoenberg Institute, Los Angeles.
32   *Conversations*, p. 75.
33   *Ibid.*
34   *Berliner Tageblatt*, 10 June 1929.
35   *Melos*, August 1929.
36   *Berliner Börsen-Courier*, 9 June 1929.
37   *Blätter der Staatsoper*, June 1929, 'Triumph der Alltäglichkeit'.
38   *Berliner Börsen-Courier*, 10 June 1929.
39   *Blätter der Staatsoper*, June 1929, 'Einbruch des Kabaretts in der Oper'.
40   Weill to Universal Edition, 21 April 1929.
41   Universal Edition (Hertzka) to Weill, 12 June 1929.
42   Weill to Curjel, St. Cyr s. Mer, 13 June 1929.
43   Weill to Hertzka, Ammersee, 13 July 1929.
44   Hertzka to Weill, 18 July 1929.
45   Weill to Universal Edition, Ammersee, 22 July 1929.
46   Letter to Curjel, Sils Maria, 5 August 1929.
47   Weill to Universal Edition, 16 December 1929.
48   Drew (ed.), *Über Kurt Weill*, pp. 69–72.

14   The Kroll in midstream

1   *La Plata Post*, 29 May 1931.
2   *Nuova Rivista Musicale Italiana*, 1974, No. 1, Jan Meyerowitz, 'Otto Klemperer e la Krolloper'.
3   *Die Weltbühne*, 1928, No. 1, Joachim Beck.
4   *Berliner Börsen-Courier*, 16 June 1928.
5   *Deutsche Allgemeine Zeitung*, 9 March 1928.
6   *Berliner Tageblatt*, 16 January 1928.
7   *Berliner Börsen-Courier*, 15 January 1928. *Deutsche Allgemeine Zeitung*, 20 January 1928.
8   *Signale für die musikalischen Welt*, 18 January 1928. *Vorwärts*, 19 January 1928.
9   *Berliner Börsen-Courier*, 19 June 1930.
10   Curjel, ed. Kruttge, *Experiment Krolloper*, p. 44.
11   *Berliner Tageblatt*, 8 February 1929.
12   *Vossische Zeitung*, 27 April 1929.
13   *Signale für die musikalischen Welt*, 1 May 1929.
14   *Berliner Tageblatt*, 27 April 1929.
15   *Berliner Börsen-Zeitung*, 15 November 1929.
16   *Berliner Tageblatt*, 16 November 1929.
17   Interview with Eigel Kruttge, 24 June 1978.
18   *Morning Post*, 21 November 1929.
19   *Sunday Times*, 24 November 1929.
20   Weill, letter to Universal Edition, 1 October 1929.
21   *Melos*, November 1928.
22   Strub, WDR interview with Curjel.
23   *Berliner Morgenpost*, 19 June 1929, Kastner.
24   *Berliner Börsen-Courier*, 24 January 1930.
25   Curjel, 'Stravinsky in Berlin', *Melos*, 1972, pp. 154–6.
26   *Leipziger Neueste Nachrichten*, 31 January 1930.
27   Letter of 8 August 1929.
28   *Experiment Krolloper*, p. 44.
29   Information provided by Mr John Woolf, who met Klemperer on his arrival at the station.
30   *Hamburger Nachrichten*, 29 January 1929.
31   Mr Leon Temerson, member of the orchestra.
32   *Ibid.*
33   Lourié to Stravinsky, 22 December 1928.
34   Lourié to Stravinsky, Paris, 28 December 1928.
35   Interviews with players undertaken by Mr N. P. H. Steffen.
36   Krebs, *Soviet Composers and the Development of Soviet Music*, p. 49.
37   Willett, *The New Sobriety*, p. 183.
38   Gojowy, *Neue sowjetische Musik de 20er Jahren*, pp. 38–40.
39   17 March 1929.
40   Ginzburg, *Izbrannoye. Dirizhorï i orkestrï*, p. 77.
41   *Zhizn' iskusstva*, 19 April 1927.
42   *Die Musik*, September 1929.
43   *Zhizn' iskusstva*, 14 April 1929.
44   Letter to Johanna Klemperer, Moscow, 15 March 1929.

45 *Zhizn' iskusstva*, 14 April 1929.
46 Golovanov, letter to Nezhdanova, Moscow, 13 March 1929.
47 Published in *Sovetskaya Filarmoniya*, 31 March 1929.
48 *Muzĭka i revolyutsiya*, 1929, No. 3.
49 Minutes of the Royal Philharmonic Society, 3 August–27 October 1927.
50 Jackson, *First Flute*, p. 77.
51 *The Sunday Times*, 24 November 1929.
52 23 November 1929.
53 *The Morning Post*, 21 November 1929.
54 *The Observer*, 24 November 1929.
55 Heyworth (ed.), *Conversations*, p. 82.
56 Speech given by Klemperer on 5 December 1932 at a banquet to celebrate the Chorus's fiftieth anniversary.
57 *Ibid.*
58 *Ibid.*
59 Recollections of Mr Axel Hubert, a member of the Chorus.
60 Stappenbeck, *Chronik des Philharmonischen Chors in Berlin*, p. 57.
61 *Signale für die musikalischen Welt*, 1 January 1930.
62 *Die Musik*, February 1930.
63 Letter from W. Strecker to Hindemith, 1 September 1930.
64 Recollections of Mr Axel Hubert.
65 Edgar Schmidt-Pauli, 'Klemperer als Chordirigent', *Politik und Gesellschaft*, 16 December 1929.
66 *Die Musik*, April 1930.
67 *Deutsche Allgemeine Zeitung*, 17 March 1930.
68 Letter of 3 February 1929.
69 *Neue Freie Presse*, 30 July 1933.
70 *Berliner Börsen-Courier*, 11 November 1929.
71 *Die Musik*, December 1929.
72 *Berliner Börsen-Courier*, 19 May 1930.
73 'Versuch einer Selbstdarstellung', *Der Merker*, 1951, No. 3, p. 260.
74 *Conversations*, p. 66.
75 Dülberg, letter to Curjel, 17 November 1931.
76 'Die Bühnendekoration der Gegenwart', *Berliner Funkstunde*, 5 August 1931.
77 Dülberg, letter to Curjel, 28 February 1932.
78 'Die Legende der Krolloper', Appendix to Reinking, *Spiel und Form*, p. 261.
79 Curjel, 'Zu de Chiricos Berliner Bühnenbildern', *Du*, November 1964. Teo Otto's recollections in *Experiment Krolloper*, p. 51.
80 *Conversations*, p. 62.
81 *Berliner Börsen-Courier*, 5 March 1930.
82 Curjel, 'Oscar Schlemmer und die abstrakte Bühne', *Melos*, 1963, pp. 331–8.
83 Information provided by Professor Rufer.
84 Curjel, letter to Gertrud Marbach, 18 January 1962.
85 *BZ am Mittag*, 10 June 1930.
86 *Berliner Tageblatt*, 11 June 1930.
87 Letter to Klemperer, 18 July 1930.
88 Armitage (ed.), *Schoenberg*, p. 184.
89 *Conversations*, p. 68.

15 The end of the Kroll

1 Proceedings of the Prussian Landtag, 89th session, 14 October 1929, columns 9 and 14.
2 Laqueur, *Weimar: A Cultural History*, p. 23.
3 Quoted in Taylor, *Literature and Society in Germany 1918–45*, p. 25.
4 *Vossische Zeitung*, 12 January 1930; *Berliner Tageblatt*, 14 January 1930.
5 Staatsministerium theatre file, pp. 49–53.
6 Staatsministerium theatre file, pp. 58–61.
7 Stompor, 'Musiktheater', p. 2329.
8 'Um die Krolloper', *Berliner Tageblatt*, 20 February 1930.
9 Proceedings of the Prussian Landtag, 157th session, 4 April 1930, columns 13456–69.
10 Dated 21 February 1930.
11 Staatsministerium theatre file, pp. 62, 79–90.
12 Staatsministerium theatre file, pp. 81–4.
13 Merseburg, 2.10.6, No. 1446.
14 Statsministerium theatre file, pp. 105–7.
15 *Untersuchungsausschuss*, column 346.
16 *Untersuchungsausschuss*, columns 215–16.
17 *Conversations*, p. 65.
18 Letter from London, 6 February 1932.
19 'Der Dirigent Toscanini', *Das Tagebuch*, 25 May 1929.
20 Kessler, *Tagebücher*, p. 646.
21 'Das deutsche Theater und seine Mitglieder in der Krise', *Der neue Weg*, May 1932; Panofsky, *Protest in der Oper*, p. 180; Hans Heinsheimer, 'German Music on the Breadline', *Modern Music*, March/April 1932.
22 Hans Heinsheimer, 'Neues vom Tage', *Anbruch*, January 1931.
23 'Situation der Oper', *Melos*, February 1931.
24 *Untersuchungsausschuss*, columns 288–9.
25 *Vossische Zeitung*, 8 November 1930.
26 *Die Weltbühne*, 14 October 1930 (Hans von Zwehl, 'Volksbühnen-Defizit') gives a picture of the Volksbühne at this stage of its disintegration.
27 *Untersuchungsausschuss*, columns 64, 70, 78, 197–201.
28 *Untersuchungsausschuss*, column 66.
29 *Berliner Börsen-Courier*, 11 November 1930.
30 *Tempo*, 12 November 1930.
31 *Deutscher Theaterdienst*, October 1930. Reprinted in *Experiment Krolloper*, pp. 378–80.
32 Reinking, *Spiel und Form*, pp. 114–21.
33 *Ibid.*
34 *Ich liebe das Leben*, pp. 506–8.
35 *BZ am Mittag*, 1 December 1930.
36 Interview with Moje Forbach.
37 Stompor, 'Musiktheater', p. 2360.
38 *Frankfurter Zeitung*, 29 January 1931.
39 *Berliner Börsen-Zeitung*, 26 January 1931.
40 *Berliner Börsen-Courier*, 26 January 1931.
41 *Deutsche Allgemeine Zeitung*, 26 January 1931; *Berliner Tageblatt*, 27 January 1931.

42 *Tempo*, 26 January 1931.
43 *Manchester Guardian*, 4 February 1931.
44 *The Sunday Times*, 8 February 1931.
45 *The New Statesman*, 7 February 1931.
46 Letter to Johanna Klemperer, 7 February 1931.
47 *Experiment Krolloper*, p. 81.
48 *Vossische Zeitung*, 27 February 1931.
49 Klemperer's submission to the Labour Tribunal, 24 March 1931, pp. 6–7. Evidence of Tietjen and Curjel, as reported in the *Berliner Tageblatt* of 20 and 21 April 1931.
50 Stompor, 'Musiktheater', p. 2552 (interview with Domgraf-Fassbänder).
51 *Berliner Tageblatt*, 19 February 1931.
52 Aufricht, *Erzähle, damit du dein Recht erweist*, p. 82.
53 *Experiment Krolloper*, p. 82.
54 Edgar von Schmidt-Pauli, *Politik und Gesellschaft*, 30 April 1931.
55 *Berliner Börsen-Courier*, 21 April 1931.
56 *Untersuchungsausschuss*, column 257.
57 Fritz Stege, *Zeitschrift für Musik*, June 1931.
58 *Berliner Börsen-Courier*, 16 April 1931.
59 *Berliner Tageblatt*, 16 April 1931.
60 *Vossische Zeitung*, 21 April 1931.
61 Recollections by Roger Sessions, who was present.
62 *Melos*, July 1931.
63 Satz, *Novellen meines Lebens*, p. 254.
64 *Berliner Börsen-Courier*, 21 April 1931.
65 Roger Sessions's description in a CBC interview with Robert Chesterman, 15 January 1970.
66 *Musical America*, 19 February 1927.
67 *Experiment Krolloper*, p. 42.
68 *Allgemeine Musikzeitung*, 8 May 1931.
69 *BZ am Mittag*, 27 April 1931.
70 Von Naso, *Ich liebe das Leben*, pp. 518–19, and newspaper reports.
71 WDR interview, London, 26 February 1961.

16 The Kroll: an epilogue

1 Related to the author by C. H. Becker's son, Professor Hellmut Becker.
2 'Nachruf auf die Krolloper', *Berliner Tageblatt*, 5 June 1931.
3 *Ibid.*
4 'In eigener Sache', *Berliner Tageblatt*, 27 January 1931.
5 *Berliner Börsen-Courier*, 4 July 1931.

17 On Devil's Island

1 Letter to Marianne Joseph, Lisbon, 3 May 1931.
2 Mariano, *Forty years with Berenson*, p. 214.
3 John Montés, letter to the author, 7 March 1981.
4 *La Plata Zeitung*, 17 and 21 May 1931.
5 Letter to his children, 22 May 1931. Also interview in *La Plata Zeitung*, 19 May 1931.

6   Unidentified newspaper of 21 June 1931.
7   Interviews with the author, November 1973 and February 1975.
8   *Argentinisches Tageblatt*, 16 July 1931.
9   *La Plata Zeitung*, 17 and 19 July 1931.
10 *Argentinisches Tageblatt*, 25 August 1931.
11 *Argentinisches Tageblatt*, 2, 7 and 18 September 1931.
12 *La Plata Zeitung*, 30 September 1931, Johannes Franze.
13 Autobiographical sketch, p. 22.
14 Information provided by John Montés.
15 *La Plata Zeitung*, 7 October 1931.
16 Letter of 29 October 1931.
17 *Allgemeine Musikzeitung*, 27 November 1931.
18 *Frankfurter Zeitung*, 25 November 1931.
19 *Deutsche Allgemeine Zeitung*, 23 November 1931.
20 Autobiographical sketch, p. 22.
21 *Berliner Tageblatt*, 13 April 1931, 'Die neue Spielzeit der Staatstheater'.
22 *Conversations*, p. 68.
23 Author's interview with Professor Ernst Wollheim.
24 *Berliner Tageblatt*, 16 December 1931; *Germania*, 17 December 1931.
25 *Deutsche Allgemeine Zeitung*, 17 December 1931; *Berliner Börsen-Courier*, 16 December 1931.
26 *Le Courrier musical*, 15 January 1932.
27 Klemperer's personnel file (pp. 319–20) contains Tietjen's memorandum on their discussion.
28 1 March 1932, William McNaught.
29 *The Observer*, 14 February 1932.
30 *The Manchester Guardian*, 11 February 1932.
31 L. Dunton Green, *The Chesterian*, March 1932.
32 Letter to Stravinsky, 4 January 1932.
33 Roger Sessions, letter to the author, 12 August 1979.
34 Letter to Johanna Klemperer, Sils-Maria, 28 August 1928.
35 Letter to Johanna Klemperer, Ludwigshafen, undated.
36 Information provided by Bruno Vonderhoff.
37 Undated letter, probably of April 1932.
38 *Berliner Tageblatt*, 1 February 1932.
39 *Die Musik*, April 1932.
40 Letter from Roger Sessions to the author, 12 August 1979.
41 Heinz Tietjen, letter to the Oberrechnungskammer, 4 July 1932.
42 Prussian Landtag (Hauptausschuss) proceedings, 6 March 1931, column 21.
43 Undated letter from Regi Elbogen to Marianne Joseph.
44 Letters to Stravinsky (16 February 1932) and Willy Strecker (31 March 1932).
45 Letter to Johanna Klemperer, London, 6 February 1932.
46 Letter of 2 July 1932.
47 *Conversations*, p. 42.
48 Speech at the opening session of the Reichsmusikkammer, quoted in Wulf, *Musik im Dritten Reich*, p. 194.

18 Crossing the Red Sea

1 Letter to Johanna Klemperer, 24 November 1932.
2 *Berliner Tageblatt*, 6 December 1932.
3 Artur Schnabel, 'Spruch für Klemperer'. *Vossische Zeitung*, 6 December 1932. (Free translation.)
4 *BZ am Mittag*, 23 September 1932.
5 Letter of 29 October 1932, Frankfurt am Main.
6 Brussels, 2 November 1932.
7 Letter to Stravinsky, Frankfurt, 27 October 1932.
8 Letter of 4 April 1932.
9 Letter to Johanna Klemperer, 22 October 1932.
10 Issue of 14 October 1932.
11 *Berliner Börsen-Courier*, 14 October 1932.
12 *Die Musik*, February 1933.
13 *Vossische Zeitung*, 16 December 1932.
14 Letter to Johanna Klemperer, 14 January 1933.
15 Issue of 1 November 1932. (Free translation.)
16 *Musical America*, 23 January 1926.
17 *Leipziger Neueste Nachrichten*, 2 January 1933.
18 *Zeitschrift für Musik*, March 1933.
19 *Hamburger Fremdenblatt*, 31 January 1933.
20 Information provided by Frau Hilde Firtel.
21 *Conversations*, pp. 91–2.
22 Letter to Johanna Klemperer, 17 November 1932.
23 Kessler, *Tagebücher*, p. 704.
24 Observation made to Eduard Rosenbaum, who related it to the author.
25 *Vossische Zeitung*, 8 February 1933.
26 Autobiographical sketch, p. 23.
27 *Anbruch*, January 1933.
28 *Deutsche Allgemeine Zeitung*, 14 February 1933.
29 *Deutsche Zeitung*, 13 February 1933.
30 *Dresdener Neueste Nachrichten*, 17 February 1933.
31 Berndt, *Gibt mir vier Jahre Zeit*, p. 232.
32 Bracher, *Die Auflösung der Weimarer Republik*, p. 729.
33 Autobiographical sketch, p. 24.
34 H. H. Stuckenschmidt, 'Die Musen und die Macht', *Frankfurter Allgemeine Zeitung*, 6 December 1980.
35 *Berliner Tageblatt*, 6 March 1933.
36 Mariano, *Forty Years with Berenson*, p. 214.
37 Autobiographical sketch, p. 23.
38 Letter to Micha Konstam (May), Los Angeles, 22 May 1935.
39 Autobiographical sketch, p. 24.
40 Stresemann, *...und Abends in der Philharmonie*, pp. 97–8.
41 Information provided by Roger Sessions.
42 Information provided by Micha May.
43 *Conversations*, p. 69.
44 Stresemann, *...und Abends*, pp. 97–8.
45 *Conversations*, pp. 70–1.

Appendix: The Berlin opera houses during the Weimar Republic

No fewer than four opera companies were at one moment performing in Berlin during the Weimar Republic. Three of them underwent changes of title and function and are accordingly referred to in the text under different names, occasionally English as well as German. The following list attempts to guide the reader through the maze.

Berlin State Opera (Staatsoper). The former court opera house on Unter den Linden, where, after rebuildings, it still stands. On account of its position it was often referred to as the Linden Opera (Lindenoper), particularly in order to distinguish it from the State Opera's second theatre (the Kroll). To-day the Deutsche Staatsoper (East Berlin).

Kroll Opera (Krolloper). Until 1923 properly called the Theater am Königsplatz, thereafter Theater am Platz der Republik, where it occupied a site adjacent to the Reichstag. From 1919 to 1923 the Kroll was leased to the Volksbühne. In 1924 it reopened after reconstruction as a branch (*Filial*) of the State Opera. In 1927 it was reconstituted as an artistically independent opera house (though administratively it remained an integral part of the State Opera) with Klemperer as director. Destroyed in the war.

Berlin City Opera (Städtische Oper). Originally the Deutsches Opernhaus, it was also often referred to as the Charlottenburg Opera on account of its location in that suburb. Initially the property of a private company which went bankrupt in 1924, it was then acquired by the city council (*Magistrat*) of Berlin, which reopened it as the Städtische Oper in 1925 whereafter it became a rival to the Linden Opera. In 1933 the theatre reverted to its original title. It was destroyed in the war, but the West Berlin Deutsche Oper today stands on its site in the Bismarckstrasse.

Die Grosse Volksoper. A purely private undertaking founded in 1919, it played from 1922 until its bankruptcy in 1924 in the Theater des Westens, an operetta theatre still standing close to the Zoo.

435

Biographical glossary

Bekker, Paul (1882–1937). One of the leading German critics of his generation, who subsequently made a career as a theatrical administrator. Bekker was an early and highly effective champion of the music of both Mahler and Schreker. After a lengthy period (1911–25) as chief critic of the influential *Frankfurter Zeitung*, he was appointed Intendant of the Prussian theatres of Kassel (1925–7) and Wiesbaden (1927–33). In spite of his close links with the Prussian Kultusministerium he emerged during this latter period as a vocal opponent of the artistic tendencies pursued by Klemperer at the Kroll. In 1934, he emigrated to New York, where he resumed his career as a critic on the local German-speaking daily newspaper, *Die Staatszeitung*.

Blech, Leo (1871–1958). German conductor associated for over half a century with operatic life in Berlin, where he was conductor at the Court (later State) Opera from 1906–23 and from 1926–37. From 1923–4 he was musical director of the Deutsches Opernhaus. In 1937 he sought refuge as a Jew in Riga and subsequently in Stockholm, but returned in 1949 to West Berlin, where he conducted for a number of years at the Städtische (later Deutsche) Oper.

Bloch, Ernst (1885–1977), not to be confused with the composer, *Ernest* Bloch, was one of the most idiosyncratic Marxist thinkers of his time, who, in *Vom Geist der Utopie* (1918) and his *magnum opus, Das Prinzip Hoffnung*, made an attempt to reconstruct 'a philosophy of hope' on the basis of Marxism and Jewish utopianism. After emigrating to America after 1933 Bloch returned in 1948 to what was still the Soviet Zone of occupied Germany, where he was appointed professor of philosophy in Leipzig. In 1961 he moved to West Germany, where he held a guest professorship at Tübingen for the remainder of his life. Bloch was one of Klemperer's few close friends and on Klemperer's death delivered at the age of eighty-eight a lengthy extempore eulogy on German television. A versatile essayist and a knowledgeable music lover, he also made notable contributions to the Kroll's programme books.

Bodanzky, Artur (1877–1939). Austrian conductor. After a period as violinist in the orchestra of the Vienna Court Opera, Bodanzky became a repetiteur on Mahler's staff there in 1903. In 1907 he was appointed First Conductor at the German Opera in Prague at the same time as Klemperer joined the company as chorusmaster. Two years later he moved to Mannheim, where he remained until 1915, when he became principal conductor in the New York Metropolitan Opera. Thereafter his career was centred on America, where he established a reputation primarily as a Wagnerian, but also gave a number of transatlantic first performances, including that of *Das Lied von der Erde*. Bodanzky was one of a number of exceptionally talented musicians who were drawn into Mahler's orbit.

Brecher, Gustav (1879–1940). After a brief period under Mahler in Vienna, Brecher was appointed First Conductor in Hamburg in 1903. In 1911 he moved to a similar position in Cologne, where he was succeeded in 1917 by

436

Klemperer. From 1916 he conducted in Frankfurt and in 1924 was appointed music director in Leipzig, where he conducted the first performances of Krenek's *Jonny spielt auf* and Weill's *Der Aufstieg und Fall der Stadt Mahagonny*. Brecher, who was also well known for his translations of opera libretti, lived for many years with the celebrated American dramatic soprano, Edyth Walker (1870–1950), who sang the role of Brünnhilde in Klemperer's first *Ring* cycle in Hamburg in 1912. In 1940 Brecher and his wife disappeared in mysterious circumstances in Ostend, while attempting to flee to Britain.

Busch, Fritz (1890–1951). German conductor, brother of the violinist Adolf Busch. Music director of the Dresden State Opera (1922–33), where he conducted the first performance of Strauss's *Intermezzo* (1924), Busoni's *Dr. Faust* (1925) and Hindemith's *Cardillac* (1926). His collaboration with Carl Ebert on a production of *Un Ballo in maschera* (1932) at the Berlin Städtische Oper was a milestone in the revival of interest in the operas of Verdi's middle period outside Italy. In 1933 Busch left Germany, having refused to deputise at Bayreuth for Toscanini (who had withdrawn in protest against the Nazis' anti-Jewish policies). In 1934 Busch and Ebert became joint artistic directors of the newly established Glyndebourne Opera, for whose success they were largely responsible.

Curjel, Hans (1896–1974). German art historian, conductor and producer. After publishing a thesis on Hans Baldung Grien in 1923, Curjel joined the staff of the Karlsruhe Kunsthalle but was drawn to the world of theatre. In 1924 he briefly served as conductor at Louise Dumont's Düsseldorf Schauspielhaus. From 1927 to 1930 he was Klemperer's *Dramaturg* at the Kroll Opera and deputy director during its final season of 1930/1, when he also produced. In 1933 he emigrated to Zurich, where he became director of the Corso Theatre. From 1945 to 1948 he was director of the Stadttheater in Chur, where on his initiative the first post-war Brecht production of *Antigone* was staged. In later years he was more preoccupied with the visual arts. Curjel's massive documentary study, *Experiment Krolloper*, was published posthumously.

Dessau, Paul (1894–1979). German composer and conductor and lifelong friend of Klemperer. In 1919 he was engaged by Klemperer as repetiteur and conductor at the Cologne Opera. In 1925 he joined the Berlin Städtische Oper under Bruno Walter. He first began to make a mark as a composer in the late twenties. After emigrating to France in 1933, Dessau moved to the United States, where his long collaboration with Brecht began. In 1948 Dessau settled in East Berlin, where after Eisler's death in 1962 he came to be regarded as the nestor of composers in the German Democratic Republic.

Dülberg, Ewald (1888–1933). Artist and stage designer whose career was torn between these two aspects of his creativity, but who was a decisive influence on Klemperer's approach to all matters of staging and whose neo-classical sympathies had an impact on the evolution of Klemperer's musical taste in the twenties. Dülberg started his theatrical career at the Hamburg Stadttheater. For a brief period after the war he worked at the Berlin Volksbühne, but in 1920 turned his back on the stage to develop his interests in wood-cutting, stained glass, weaving and mosaics and to teach, first at the Odenwaldschule and from 1922 at the Kassel Kunstakademie. It was only in 1924 that Klemperer and Dülberg were finally able to put their ideas into practice in the *Fidelio* with which Klemperer opened his three years in Wiesbaden. In 1927 Dülberg became designer and producer at the Kroll Opera, where through his close friendship with Klemperer his influence was at first paramount in all visual matters. After 1930 he ceased to work at the Kroll and three years later the tuberculosis from which he had long suffered killed him.

Fried, Oscar (1871–1941) was born of poor Jewish parents and for a while worked as an itinerant musician, a clown and a circus kennel-master. Later, he earned a living as a dog-breeder. Although he received some musical instruction from Humperdinck, it was not until his late twenties that he started to study counterpoint with Philipp Scharwenka. He also composed, and the success of a choral work, *Das trunkene Lied* (1904) helped to win him the conductorship of the Stern'sche Gesangsverein, whose rehearsals Klemperer accompanied while still a student. Mahler and (with reservations) Klemperer thought well of him as a conductor and he was one of the few regularly to introduce new music in pre-1914 Berlin. In 1921 he became the first German conductor to visit the Soviet Union, whither he emigrated in 1933, becoming conductor in Tiflis. He later took Soviet citizenship.

Furtwängler, Wilhelm (1886–1954). After working as repetiteur at Zurich and Munich, Furtwängler was appointed chorusmaster at Strasbourg in 1910. A year later he became music director at the Lübeck opera, and from 1915 held a similar position in Mannheim. In 1920 he emerged in the front rank of German conductors as director of the concerts of Berlin Staatskapelle. Two years later, on the death of Nikisch, he was appointed conductor of both the Gewandhaus Orchestra and the Berlin Philharmonic Orchestra and his career was henceforth centred on the concert platform rather than the opera house. In 1925 he made his transatlantic début with the New York Philharmonic Orchestra and in 1936 was invited to succeed Toscanini as its permanent conductor. By this time, however, he had become involved in political issues, and, in spite of the fact that he had defended Hindemith's music and colleagues such as Walter and Klemperer, he withdrew after a storm of protest. The Allies forbade him to conduct in Germany after the war and he did not resume his activities until May 1947. His last years continued to be clouded by controversy over the equivocal role he had played in the Third Reich.

Gutheil-Schoder, Marie (1874–1935). Leading soprano celebrated for her musical accomplishment and the dramatic intensity of her performances. In 1900 she was engaged by Mahler as a member of the Vienna Court Opera, where she continued to appear until 1926. A distinguished recitalist and soprano soloist in the first performances of Schoenberg's String Quartet No. 2 (1908) and *Erwartung* (1924).

Hofmüller, Max (1881–1981). Originally trained as a conductor, Hofmüller joined Pfitzner's opera school in Strasbourg as a tenor in 1910, subsequently becoming a member of the Stadttheater, where he remained until 1918. After five years (1923–8) as *Oberspielleiter* at the Bavarian State Opera in Munich, he was appointed *Generalintendant* of the Cologne municipal theatres, a position from which he resigned in January 1933. In the season of 1931 he served as artistic director of the Teatro Colón in Buenos Aires.

Kleiber, Erich (1890–1956). Austrian conductor and father of Carlos Kleiber (1930–). After several provincial appointments, Kleiber leapt into prominence when, following the collapse of negotiations with Klemperer and others, in 1923 he was appointed First Conductor and music director of the Berlin State Opera, where he continued to work until he emigrated from Germany in 1935. From 1936 until 1949 Kleiber was mainly active at the Teatro Colón in Buenos Aires. In 1925 he conducted the first performance of Berg's *Wozzeck*, which was among a number of works that he gave with notable success at Covent Garden in the years before his death.

Klemperer, Georg (1865–1946). Distinguished physician and author of *Neue deutsche Klinik* (*1928–1932*). From 1906 until 1932 medical director of the Moabit Hospital in Berlin, as well as of a university clinic. In 1922 he attended Lenin in what was to prove his last illness. In 1936 he emigrated to America and settled near Boston, where in 1939 Otto Klemperer (his first cousin) underwent an operation for a brain tumour.

Korngold, Erich Wolfgang (1897–1957). Austrian-born composer, son of Julius Korngold, Hanslick's successor as principal music critic of the *Neue Freie Presse* (Vienna). At the age of ten was pronounced a talent by Mahler, who recommended that he study composition with Zemlinsky (q.v.). This he did to such good effect that three years later his ballet, *Der Schneemann*, was performed at the Vienna Court Opera. Schnabel (q.v.) similarly championed an early piano sonata. *Violanta* and *Der Ring des Polykrates* were his first operatic successes. In 1920 his opera, *Die tote Stadt*, was given simultaneous premières in Hamburg and in Cologne, where Klemperer conducted it. In 1934 Reinhardt (for whom he had in 1929 prepared a successful version of *Die Fledermaus*) invited him to Hollywood, in whose film studios he could be said to have found his true *métier*, and where he and Klemperer were on cordial terms. After the war Korngold returned without notable success to the field of concert music and Klemperer conducted the first European performance of his Violin Concerto in Vienna in 1947.

Krenek, Ernst (1900–). Together with Hindemith and Weill, a leading member of the generation of composers which emerged in Central Europe after the First World War. Prolific in a succession of styles, he scored worldwide success in *Jonny spielt auf* (1927). After 1933, Krenek, who had been a pupil of Schreker (q.v.) converted to Catholicism and returned to his native Austria, where in 1934 he completed his largest scale opera, *Karl V*. In 1938 he emigrated to the United States.

Kruttge, Eigel (1899–1979). 1922–4 musicological assistant to Klemperer at the Cologne Opera, 1925–7 continued his piano studies with Schnabel. Thereafter active as a harpsichordist, as which he played in some of Klemperer's concerts at the Kroll. From 1931 on the music staff of the Berlin and Hamburg radio stations. From 1952 in the music department (its deputy director 1957–66) of the West German Radio in Cologne, where he was responsible for the many concerts Klemperer conducted there between 1954 and 1966. Editor of Curjel's documentary study, *Experiment Krolloper*.

Lehmann, Lotte (1888–1976). After a shaky start in Hamburg, due to an uncertain technique, Lehmann had by 1916 made sufficient mark to be engaged by the Vienna Court Opera, where she soon gained recognition as the Composer in the first performance of the revised version of Strauss's *Ariadne auf Naxos*. Thereafter she remained until 1938 the leading lyric-dramatic soprano in Central Europe, particularly celebrated for her performances in Wagner and Strauss, and above all as the Marschallin in *Der Rosenkavalier*. Strauss chose her as his first Färberin (*Die Frau ohne Schatten*) and Christine (*Intermezzo*). Lehmann's style was marked by a remarkable intensity and range of dramatic utterance.

Mahler, Alma (1879–1964) née Schindler. When Mahler in 1901 met and fell in love with this talented daughter of the Austrian landscape painter, E. J. Schindler, she was studying composition with Alexander von Zemlinsky (q.v.).

They married in the following year. After Mahler's death Alma remarried, first the architect Walter Gropius and subsequently the Czech expressionist writer Franz Werfel.

Nikisch, Arthur (1855–1922). Austro-Hungarian conductor. After occupying positions at Leipzig, Boston and Budapest, where he was musical director at the opera from 1893–5, Nikisch became within the space of a few years permanent conductor of the Berlin Philharmonic and the Leipzig Gewandhaus orchestras and of the Hamburg Philharmonic concerts. For the last twenty-five years of his life he was thus the dominant figure in German concert life. An early advocate of both Bruckner and Tchaikovsky, who heard and much admired his interpretation of his Symphony No. 5, Nikisch was regarded as a supreme exponent of romantic music.

Pfitzner, Hans (1869–1949). German composer, who established his reputation with two early operas, *Der arme Heinrich* (1895) and *Die Rose vom Liebesgarten* (1901). His masterpiece, *Palestrina*, on which his enduring fame largely rests, dates from 1917. Thereafter his star waned as a deep-rooted revulsion from romanticism swept Germany after the end of the First World War. From 1897 to 1907 he taught composition and conducting at the Berlin Stern Conservatory. From 1908 until 1918 he was director of the Strasbourg conservatory and the city concerts. From 1909 to 1916 he also served as director of the city's opera house. An embittered polemicist in defence of romantic musical values. In spite of his intense nationalism Pfitzner occupied no official position during the Third Reich.

Pollak, Egon (1879–1933). Czech conductor, who began his career as chorusmaster at the German Theatre in Prague in 1901. After engagements in Bremen and Leipzig, he was appointed First Conductor at Frankfurt in 1912. From 1917 to 1931 he was engaged in a similar position at the Hamburg Stadttheater.

Schillings, Max von (1868–1933). German composer and conductor. Between 1892 and 1915 Schillings wrote a number of operas in a late romantic idiom, of which the last, *Mona Lisa* (1915), was the most successful. From 1911–18 he was musical director at the Stuttgart Opera, from 1919 to 1925 Intendant of the Berlin State Opera. In 1932 he became president of the Prussian Academy of the Arts (see pp. 239–40). In March 1933 Schillings was appointed director of the Berlin Städtische Oper, but died only four months later.

Schnabel, Artur (1882–1951). Perhaps the most celebrated classical pianist of his generation, Schnabel excelled in Viennese music from Mozart to Brahms. He also composed in a radical style that was influenced by Schoenberg's twelve-tone system.

Schreker, Franz (1878–1934). Austrian composer whose reputation was established by *Der ferne Klang* (1912) and further extended by *Die Gezeichneten* (1918) and *Der Schatzgräber* (1920), all of which enjoyed such widespread esteem and popularity that in the years immediately after the First World War Schreker seemed poised to challenge Strauss as the leading opera composer in Central Europe. But with *Irrelohe*, whose first performance Klemperer conducted in 1924, the boom burst and Schreker's reputation fell so rapidly that the arrival in power of the Nazis in 1933 did no more than finish a career that was already in shreds. The style of his music, which was unkindly described by Adorno as 'pubescent', bridged late romanticism and 'modernism', rather as the Vienna Secession did in the field of the visual arts. In 1921

Schreker was appointed by the Prussian Kultusministerium to the influential position of director of the Berlin Hochschule für Musik, where Krenek (q.v.) was among his composition pupils.

Schumann, Elisabeth (1888–1952) joined the Hamburg company in 1909 and remained there until 1919, when at Strauss's request she joined the Vienna State Opera. She continued to sing there until the *Anschluss*, after which she went to New York, where she died. 'A beautifully controlled high soprano of delicate ringing timbre and crystalline purity, and a charming stage presence, especially in demure, mischievous parts' (Desmond Shawe-Taylor) made her one of the outstanding Mozart singers of her time. The role of Sophie in *Der Rosenkavalier*, which first brought her fame when she sang it in Hamburg in 1911, was also ideally suited to her gifts. In spite of the light weight of her voice, her taste, technique and spontaneity made her an entrancing Lieder singer, even at the age of sixty. The author recalls her with delight as an artist who made singing sound as though it were the most natural thing in the world.

Steinberg, William (originally Hans Wilhelm) (1899–1978). American conductor of German birth. After studying conducting at Cologne Conservatory with Hermann Abendroth, he was engaged as assistant to Klemperer at the Cologne Opera. In 1927 he succeeded Zemlinsky (q.v.) as music director of the German Opera in Prague. In 1929 he moved to Frankfurt, where in 1930 he conducted the first performance of Schoenberg's *Von Heute auf Morgen*. He emigrated in 1936 to Palestine, where with Huberman he founded an orchestra that subsequently became the Israel Philharmonic Orchestra. He was later musical director of orchestras in Buffalo (1945–52), Pittsburgh (1952–76), Boston (1969–72). From 1958–60 he was also music director of the London Philharmonic Orchestra.

Stiedry, Fritz (1883–1968). Another conductor who was launched on his career by a recommendation from Mahler. From 1914 to 1923 Stiedry conducted at the Berlin State Opera. After five years as director of the Vienna Volksoper, where he gave the first performance of Schoenberg's *Die glückliche Hand*, he returned to Berlin as principal conductor of the Städtische Oper, where he collaborated with Carl Ebert on productions of *Macbeth* and *Simone Boccanegra* that did much to foster a taste for Verdi in Germany during the latter years of the Weimar Republic. After a period in the Soviet Union, Stiedry went to the United States, where, after Klemperer had declined the position, he was appointed musical director of the newly formed New Friends of Music. Stiedry, who of all conductors of his generation was closest to Schoenberg, a fellow-Viennese, conducted regularly at the New York Metropolitan Opera House. He also appeared at Glyndebourne (*Orfeo*, 1947) and Covent Garden (*The Ring*, 1953/4).

Strecker, Willy (1884–1958). With his brother Ludwig, co-proprietor of Schotts and one of the outstanding music publishers of his generation. A collection of mainly French pictures of the late nineteenth and early twentieth centuries that now hangs in the Wallraf–Richartz Museum in Cologne bears witness to an artistic discernment that also extended to the visual arts. A close friend of Hindemith, whose entire works he published.

Szell, Georg, subsequently George (1897–1970). Hungarian-born conductor. Engaged by Strauss as a member of the music staff of the Berlin Court Opera in 1915, Szell held a number of appointments as conductor in German provincial theatres, including Strasbourg, where he succeeded Klemperer in

1917, before returning to the Berlin State Opera in 1924. From 1929 to 1937 he was musical director of the German Theatre in Prague. After a brief spell in Glasgow with the Scottish National Orchestra (1937–9) he emigrated to the USA, where from 1946 until his death he conducted the Cleveland Orchestra, which he made into one of the world's leading orchestras.

Toscanini, Arturo (1867–1957). Italian conductor. Music director of the Teatro alla Scala, Milan (1898–1903) and of the New York Metropolitan Opera House (1908–15). Artistic director of the Scala (1920–9), conductor of the New York Philharmonic Symphony Orchestra (1928–36) and of the NBC Orchestra (1937–54).

Walter, Bruno (1876–1962). Like Klemperer, Walter was closely linked both to Mahler and to Pfitzner. He first came under Mahler's spell on joining the Hamburg Stadttheater at the age of only eighteen, and in 1901 he followed his mentor to the Vienna Court Opera, where he remained until 1913. After Mahler's death, it was Walter who gave the first performances of *Das Lied von der Erde* and the Ninth Symphony and, partly through recordings, came to be viewed as the authoritative interpreter of his music, until his mellow, nostalgic readings were implicitly challenged by Klemperer's more astringent approach. In 1913 he was appointed music director in Munich, where he became a friend of the music-loving Thomas Mann and Pfitzner, whose *Palestrina* he conducted in 1917. Walter's international career flowered in the early twenties when he became a popular and highly esteemed visitor to New York, London and Paris. In 1925 he became a notably successful music director of the Berlin Städtische Oper and began a close association with the Salzburg Festival that lasted until the *Anschluss* of 1938. In 1929 he succeeded Furtwängler as conductor of the Gewandhaus concerts in Leipzig, while in Berlin he also established an annual series of concerts that bore his own name and formed a counterpart to those conducted by Furtwängler and Klemperer. On leaving Germany in 1933 he held positions with the Amsterdam Concertgebouw Orchestra and the Vienna State Opera. In 1939 he settled in America where he conducted regularly at the New York Metropolitan Opera between 1941 and 1957, as well as acting as musical adviser to the New York Philharmonic Orchestra from 1947 to 1949. After Toscanini and Furtwängler, Walter was perhaps the most widely admired conductor of his generation.

Weingartner, Felix von (1863–1942). Austrian conductor and composer. From 1891–8 conductor at the Berlin Court Opera, whose concerts he continued to head until 1907, when he succeeded Mahler as director of the Vienna Court Opera. He remained there for four seasons, although he continued as conductor of the Vienna Philharmonic Orchestra's own concert series until 1927. From 1912–14 Weingartner was principal conductor at the Hamburg Opera. He also returned (1935/6) to Vienna as director of the opera. But his international fame rests on his achievements as a concert musician. Prolific composer of a number of operas, including *Cain und Abel* (1914) and other instrumental scores.

Zemlinsky, Alexander von (1871–1942). Austrian composer and conductor. After appointments in Vienna, Zemlinsky in 1911 became chief conductor at the German Opera in Prague, where he remained until 1927. In 1924 he conducted the first stage performance of *Erwartung* by his brother-in-law, Schoenberg. From 1927 to 1931 he was an assistant conductor under Klemperer at the Berlin Kroll Opera. Thereafter he held no permanent position but devoted most of his energies to composition. In his early years Zemlinsky was fostered as a composer by Brahms. In 1900 Mahler gave the first performance of *Es war einmal* at the Vienna Court Opera and only his unexpected resignation in 1907 prevented him from likewise conducting the première of *Der Traumgörge*. Klemperer gave the first performance of *Der Zwerg* in Cologne in 1922. Zemlinsky instructed Schoenberg in counterpoint for some months shortly after the two men met in 1893 and also advised him on several early compositions. He died, a forgotten figure, in New York State, but in recent years his compositions have attracted renewed attention.

Zweig, Fritz (1893–   ). Czech-born, later American conductor. Zweig was an early pupil of Schoenberg, whose influence he, however, rejected. In 1913 Bodanzky engaged him as assistant conductor in Mannheim. In 1921 he moved to Barmen, where Klemperer heard him conduct *Die Meistersinger*. Thereafter a friendship developed. In 1923 Zweig became First Conductor of Lange's Grosse Volksoper in Berlin and was instrumental in Klemperer's abortive acceptance of a position as its director. From 1925 to 1927 he worked under Walter at the Berlin Städtische Oper. In spite of his conservative inclinations in 1927 he joined Klemperer at the Kroll, where he remained until 1931, when he moved for two years to the Linden Opera. In 1933 he was dismissed from this position as a Jew. In 1934 he joined the staff of the German Opera in Prague. After a period in Paris from 1938 to 1940, he emigrated to the United States, where his career was cruelly cut short by illness.

Discography: commercial recordings by Otto Klemperer

by Michael H. Gray

Introduction

This discography of Otto Klemperer's commercial gramophone recordings is divided into two parts. Recordings for Polydor/Deutsche Grammophon, Parlophone and His Master's Voice appear in this volume of the biography; records made for Vox, Hungaroton and EMI appear in the second volume of the biography. Unauthorised recordings derived from broadcasts or concert performances appear in sequence with the normal commercial issues.

Klemperer was one of many notable conductors to make records in Weimar Germany. His first contract was with Polydor/Deutsche Grammophon for whom he made four acoustic and ten electrical recordings between 1924 and 1931. Three of the acoustic sets were complete symphonies; the fourth was the Adagio from the Bruckner Symphony No. 8. All were made in 1924 as part of a Polydor plan to build a broad catalogue of major masterworks on records, an aim keenly in competition with other German companies, notably Parlophone, pursuing the same goal at the same time with other artists. Klemperer's electrical records, made in 1926 and possibly early 1927, included only one symphony, the Beethoven Eighth, a repeat of his acoustic version. The absence of substantial repertoire may have been one reason for his move to HMV and then to Parlophone for whom he made eight works between 1927 and 1929, though the repertoire there was in fact no more substantive than that left on Polydor. Whatever his reasons for shifting companies Klemperer returned to Polydor for what became his final recording of his German career, Weill's *Kleine Dreigroschenmusik*, made on four ten-inch sides in 1931.

Because Deutsche Grammophon's recording books and other materials were destroyed during World War II the recording dates for Klemperer's records for that company have been lost. To provide a rough chronology these recordings have been arranged in matrix number order. Because no information is available on unpublished Polydor recordings the existence of test pressings of Bach's Brandenburg Concerto No. 1, reportedly heard in February 1925, cannot be confirmed. This report appears in reminiscences by Eigel Kruttge, a long-time Klemperer associate, who is quoted in the liner notes for Electrola's issue of the Philharmonia recordings of Bach's Brandenburg Concertos on set 1C 187-00532/3. If Kruttge's report is correct this recording would have been made during the acoustic sessions of 1924.

Klemperer's work for Parlophone and HMV is easier to document since recording books and cards still exist for these records. With the exception of the Auber and Offenbach overtures the repertoire chosen could easily have been that of the conductor's Indian summer for EMI. The Parlophones enjoyed wide circulation through that company's international branches and clearly formed a small but key part of its catalogue. The HMVs circulated less widely on its release schedules, though all three recordings were published in Germany and England, two of HMV's principal territories at the time.

444

Discography

Klemperer's recording career came to an effective end in October 1929 when the final two sides of Strauss's *Don Juan* were made in Berlin. With the exception of the 1931 *Dreigroschenmusik* Klemperer did not make records again until July 1946 when Vox Productions arranged sessions in Paris during Klemperer's first tour to Europe since leaving Germany in 1933. The story of these records and the flowering of his recording career under Walter Legge is the subject of Part Two of this discography.

Acknowledgements

Many people helped me to compile this discography. Alan Sanders and David Hamilton checked and corrected the manuscript of Parts One and Two and furnished much additional release information. Eric Hughes of the British Institute of Recorded Sound added many additional numbers from the WERM files and Derek Lewis provided help from information in the catalogues of the BBC Gramophone Library.

I am indebted to many others for help with Part One. Richard Warren, Jr, at the Yale Historical Sound Recordings Collection checked the entire draft and provided corrections and clarifications. Mr Geoffrey Bibby surpassed my expectations and furnished a complete matrix list for all of Klemperer's 78 rpm discs plus additional material on Polydor issues in Nazi Germany. Don Hodgeman and Steve Smolian checked the draft and provided valuable matrix information. Johann Landgraf of Electrola, Cologne, and Keith Hardwick of EMI, London, furnished recording dates for the Parlophones and HMVs. Hajime Suga of Tokyo, Japan, found additional information on Japanese 78 rpm issues on Polydor and Parlophone not possible for me to find otherwise. Christopher Dyment reviewed the draft and found one key correction.

For Part Two I am grateful for assistance on the Vox records to Ms Pat Willard of the Moss Music Group and Mr George Mendelssohn of Pantheon Productions. Mr Georges Zeisel of Radio France and Mr Peter Heyworth provided information on the Vox recording dates and matrix numbers not otherwise available to me. Mr Paul Robinson of Toronto and Mr John Endrenyi called my attention to some obscure but important releases on the Hungaroton label. For the EMI portion of the discography I owe much to the staff of the International Classical Division, EMI Music, London, and particularly to Mr John Watson and Mr Peter Higgins who took time from otherwise busy schedules to help me compile information and to answer my later queries. Mr Werner Unger offered invaluable help in documenting unauthorised LP issues of Klemperer broadcasts.

I also owe much to Frau Lotte Klemperer, who encouraged me in this work and who continued to provide me with valuable information on unofficial issues of Klemperer performances on records. Mr Peter Heyworth has graciously permitted this discography to form part of his biography. I also received much assistance from the staff of the Rodgers and Hammerstein Archives at New York Public Library and staff members of the Library of Congress Motion Picture, Broadcasting and Recorded Sound Division.

I am also indebted to Mr Malcolm Walker's discography of Klemperer's commercial recordings which appeared in Peter Heyworth's *Conversations with Klemperer* and to the compilers of the Klemperer discography which appeared in the German translation of *Conversations*.

For those whose help I have forgotten to acknowledge I offer my apologies.

445

Discography

Abbreviations used in Part One

Record labels	Bruns.	Brunswick
	Elec.	Electrola
	HMV	His Master's Voice (applies to all countries using this trademark)
	Parl.	Parlophone
	Poly.	Polydor
	Vic.	Victor

Countries	Czech.	Czechoslovakia
	Eng.	England
	Fr.	France
	Ger.	Germany
	Holl.	Holland
	It.	Italy
	Jap.	Japan
	Swed.	Sweden
	Switz.	Switzerland
	US	United States

Other		Mechan. copyr. Mechanical copyright
		Roman numerals in entries for symphonies signify movement numbers

Part One: Polydor, Parlophone and HMV recordings

1. Beethoven: Symphony No. 1 in C, Op. 21 (Acoustic recording)
   Orchester der Staatskapelle Berlin; recorded 1924

Matrix	Side Number	
1768 as	B 20458	I
1769 as	20459	I
1767 as	20460	II
1766 as	20461	II
1763 as	20462	III
1764 as	20463	IV
1765 as	20464	IV

Release: Ger. = Poly. 69760/3, 66231/4; LP = Ger. DG 2535 811

Note: Side 8 on both sets is Beethoven Quartet Op. 18, No. 5: Minuet with the Wendling Quartet (Side Number B 20465)

Note: 69760/3 reviewed in the *Gramophone* Feb. 1926; a reference to it appears in *Gramophone* Sept. 1925. The recording is announced for issue in the Polydor advertisement in the 1 December 1924 number of the *Phonographische Zeitschrift*.

2. Bruckner: Symphony No. 8 in c. Adagio (Acoustic recording)
   Orchester der Staatskapelle Berlin; recorded 1924

Matrix	Side Number
1770 1/2 as	B 20466
1771 as	20467
1772 as	20468
1773 as	20469
1774 as	20470
1775 as	20471
1789 as	20472

Release: Ger. = Poly. 69764/7, 66325/8

Note: Side 8 on both sets is Dittersdorf Quartet in E Flat: Andante with the Wendling Quartet (Side Number B 20473)

Note: This recording announced for issue in the Polydor adverstisement in the 1 December 1924 number of the *Phonographische Zeitschrift*.

3. Schubert: Symphony No. 8 in b, D. 759, 'Unfinished' (Acoustic recording)
   Orchester der Staatskapelle Berlin; recorded 1924

Matrix	Side Number	
1912 as	B 20507	I
1915 as	20508	I
1916 as	20509	I
1910 as	20510	II
1911 as	20511	II
1913 as	20512	II

Release: Ger. = Poly. 69778/80, 66338/40

Note: Appears in the Polydor June 1925 catalogue.

4. Beethoven: Symphony No. 8 in F, Op. 93 (Acoustic recording)
   Orchester der Staatskapelle Berlin; recorded 1924

Matrix	Side Number	
1977 as	B 20553	I
1978 as	20554	I
2004 as	20555	II
1965 as	20556	III
2005 as	20557	IV
2006 as	20558	IV

Release: Ger. = Poly. 66264/6, 69786/8

Note: Appears in the Polydor May 1925 catalogue.

5. Ravel: *Alborada del gracioso*
   Orchester der Staatskapelle Berlin; recorded 1926

Matrix	Side Number
296 bm	B 20782
297 bm	20783

Release: Ger., Spain = Poly. 66463; Eng. = Bruns. 80012;
         LP = DG 2563 251 in set 2721 070

447

Discography

6. Beethoven: Symphony No. 8 in F, Op. 93 (Electrical recording)
Orchester der Staatskapelle Berlin; recorded 1926

Matrix	Side Number	
321 1/2 bm	B 20776	I
322 bm	20777	I
323 bm	20778	II
324 bm	20779	III
325 bm	20780	IV
326 bm	20781	IV

Release: Ger., Spain = Poly. 66460/2

7. Debussy: Two Nocturnes
Orchester der Staatskapelle Berlin; recorded 1926

Matrix	Side Number	
331 bm	B 20784	Nuages, pt 1
332 bm	20785	,, pt 2
319 bm	20786	Fêtes, pt 1
320 bm	20787	,, pt 2

Release: Ger., Spain = Poly. 66464/5; Eng. = Bruns. 80016/7

8. Beethoven: *Coriolan Overture*, Op. 62
Orchester der Staatskapelle Berlin

Matrix	Side Number
387 1/2 bi	B 20910
388 bi	20911

Release: Ger., Spain, Fr. = Poly. 66599; Ger. = Poly. 57022;
Fr. = Poly. 516636 (post 1936); Eng. = Decca CA 8091;
Jap. = Poly. 40155; LP = DG 2535 811
Mechan. copyr. 1927.

9. Beethoven: *Egmont*, Op. 84. Overture
Orchester der Staatskapelle Berlin

Matrix	Side Number
389 1/2 bi	B 20912
390 bi	20913

Release: Ger. = Poly. 66600; Jap. = Poly. 40156; LP = DG 2535 811
Mechan. copyr. 1927.

10. Beethoven: *Leonore Overture No. 3*, Op. 72a
Orchester der Staatskapelle Berlin

Matrix	Side Number
391 bi	B 20914
392 bi	20915
393 bi	20916

Release: Ger., Fr., Spain = Poly. 66601/2 (3 sides); Ger. = Poly. 57070/1;
Jap. = Poly. 40191/2 (3 sides); LP = DG 2535 811
Note: 78 coupled with Mendelssohn: *A Midsummer Night's Dream*. Overture,
Op. 21
Mechan. copyr. 1927.

11. Wagner: *Siegfried Idyll*
    Orchester der Staatskapelle Berlin

Matrix	Side Number
394 bi	B 20920
395 bi	20921
396 bi	20922
397 bi	20923

    Release: Ger., Fr., Spain = Poly. 66604/5; Ger. = Poly. 57043/4; US
    = Bruns. 90135/6; Jap. = Poly. 40194/5
    Mechan. copyr. 1927.

12. Mendelssohn: *A Midsummer Night's Dream*. Overture, Op. 21
    Orchester der Staatskapelle Berlin

Matrix	Side Number
398 bi	B 20917
449 bm	20918
400 bi	20919

    Release: Ger., Fr., Spain = Poly. 66602/3 (3 sides); Jap. = Poly. 40206/7
    (3 sides)
    Note: Coupled with Beethoven: *Leonore Overture No. 3*, Op. 72a
    Mechan. copyr. 1927.

13. Weber: *Euryanthe*. Overture
    Orchester der Staatskapelle Berlin

Matrix	Side Number
450 bm	B 20935
456 bm	20936

    Release: Ger., Fr., Spain = Poly. 66629
    Mechan. copyr. 1927.

14. Weill: *Kleine Dreigroschenmusik*
    Mitglieder der Staatskapelle Berlin

Matrix	Side Number	
2743 1/2 BH II	(C 41042)	No. 2, Die Morität von Mackie Messer
2744 BH II	(C 41043)	No. 4, Die Ballade vom angenehmen Leben
2746 BH II	C 41044	No. 5a, Tango-Ballade
2745 BH II	41045	No. 6, Kanonen-Song

    Release: Ger., Fr., Austria = Poly. 24172/3; US = Vox set 451; Jap. = Poly.
    30082/3, D 158/9; LP = US Past Masters PM-31
    Note: Side numbers of first disc inferred from the sequence of the second disc.
    Mechan. copyr. 1931.

449

15. Brahms: *Academic Festival Overture*, Op. 80
    Orchester der Staatsoper Berlin; recorded 23 June 1927, Berlin Singakademie;
    recordist Robert Beckett.

Matrix	Side Number
CDR 4713-2	4-040578
4714-1	4-040579
4715-2	4-040580

    Release: Ger. = Elec. EJ 152/3; 1C 053-28939; Eng. = HMV D 1853/4;
    Austria, Czech. = HMV ES 699/700; Jap. = Vic. JD 319/20
    Note: Coupled with Mozart: Divertimento in D, K. 334: Minuet (Blech/BS00;
    Matrix CDR 4464-2, Side number 4-040581)

16. Wagner: *Tristan und Isolde*. Act I: Prelude (1859 version)
    Orchester der Staatsoper Berlin; recorded 23 June 1927, Berlin Singakademie;
    recordist Robert Beckett.

Matrix	Side Number
BDR 4716-1	8-40571
4717-1	8-40572
4718-1	8-40573
4719-1	8-40574

    Release: Ger. = Elec. EW 27/8; Eng. = HMV E 476/7; It. = HMV AV 4223,
    4225; Austria, Czech. = HMV ER 245/6

17. Brahms: Symphony No. 1 in c, Op. 68
    Mitglieder der Staatskapelle Berlin; recorded 3 February 1928

Matrix	
2-20511-1	I
2-20512-2	I
2-20528-1	I
2-20529-1	I
2-20530-1	II
2-20531-2	II
2-20590-2	III
2-20591-4	III
2-20858-1	IV
2-20859-2	IV
2-20860-1	IV
2-20861-2	IV

    Release: Ger., Norway, Belgium = Parl. P 9615/20; Finland, It., Switz.,
    Fr. = Parl. P 9812/3, 9818, 9839/40; Eng. = Parl. E 10807/12;
    Ger. = Odeon O-6890/5; US = Decca 25487/92; Jap. = Parl.
    17013/8; LP = Ger. Elec. 1C 053-28939

18. Strauss: *Salome*, Op. 54. Salome's Tanz
    Orchester der Staatsoper Berlin; recorded 25 May 1928, Berlin Philharmonie; recordist Douglas Larter.

Matrix	Side Number
CLR 4212-1	4-040659
4213-2	4-040660

    Release: Ger. = Elec. EJ 276; Eng. = HMV D 1633; Fr. = HMV W 1007; Spain = HMV AB 538; LP = BASF set 9822177-6; Acanta MA 22177

19. Auber: *Fra Diavolo*. Overture
    Mitglieder der Staatskapelle Berlin; recorded 22 May 1929

    Matrix
    2-20862-2
    2-21431-2

    Release: Holl., Finland, Norway, Swed., Belgium, Switz., Ger. = Parl. P 9406; Eng. = Parl. E 11201; Spain = Parl. P 55.030; Fr. = Parl. 57.055; US = Col. G-50250-D, G-7286-M; Jap. = Parl. 15069

20. Offenbach: *La Belle Hélène*. Overture
    Mitglieder der Staatskapelle Berlin; recorded 22 May 1929

    Matrix
    2-21432-1
    2-21433-1

    Release: Ger., Switz, Swed., Norway, Holl. = Parl. P 9469; Fr., Belgium = Parl. 57.051; It. = Parl. P 56015; Spain = Parl. P 55.032; Eng. = Parl. E 10935; Ger. = Odeon O 6889; US = Decca 25145

21. Strauss: *Till Eulenspiegels lustige Streiche*, Op. 28
    Mitglieder der Staatskapelle Berlin

Matrix	
2-21452-1	3 June 1929
2-21453-1	,,
2-21513-1	24 June 1929
2-21514-1	,,

    Release: Ger., Switz, Holl. = Parl. P 9859/60; Ger., Holl. = Parl. P 9650/1; Belgium = Parl. P 61900/1; Fr. = Parl. 58.503/4; Eng. = Parl. E 10925/6; Jap. = Parl. 17029/30; US = Decca 25421/2; Odeon 5191/2; Ger. = Odeon O-7628/9

22. Strauss: *Don Juan*, Op. 20
    Mitglieder der Staatskapelle Berlin

    Matrix
    2-21523-1   28 June 1929
    2-21524-1   ,,
    2-21615-1   25 October 1929
    2-21616-1   ,,

    Release: Ger., Switz., Holl., Norway = Parl. P 9495/6; Fr. = Parl. 59.524/5;
               Spain = Parl. P 55.047/8; Eng. = Parl. E 11051/2; Jap. = Parl.
               E 15104/5; US = Decca 25444/5; LP = US Past Masters PM-31

Bibliography

I Books

Abendroth, Walter, *Hans Pfitzner*. Munich 1935
  Ich warne Neugierige. Munich 1966
Abendroth, Walter (ed.), *Hans Pfitzner, Reden, Schriften, Briefe*. Berlin 1955
Aksyuk, S. V. (ed.), *Mariya Veniaminovna Yudina*. Moscow 1978
Arendt, Hannah, *The Origins of Totalitarianism*. London 1958
Armitage, Merle (ed.), *Schoenberg*. New York 1937
Asaf'yev, Boris. V., *Kriticheskiye stat'i, ocherki i retsenzii*. Moscow–Leningrad 1967
Aufricht, Ernst Josef, *Erzähle, damit du dein Recht erweist*. Berlin 1966
Bekker, Paul, *Kritische Zeitbilder*. Berlin 1921
  Neue Musik. Stuttgart & Berlin 1923
Berndt, Alfred-Ingemar, *Gebt mir vier Jahre Zeit*. Munich 1937
Blaukopf, Kurt, *Mahler*. London 1973
Bleuler, Eugen, *Lehrbuch der Psychiatrie*. Berlin 1960
Bloch, Ernst, *Zur Philosophie der Musik*. Frankfurt a.M. 1974
Bollert, Werner, *50 Jahre Deutsche Oper, Berlin*. Berlin 1963
  'Musical Life', in H. Herzfeld (ed.), *Berlin und die Provinz Brandenburg in 19 &*
    20 Jahrhunderte. Berlin 1968
Bracher, Karl Dietrich, *Die Auflösung der Weimarer Republik*. Stuttgart 1955
Braun, Gerhard, *Die Schulmusikerziehung in Preussen*. Kassel & Basle 1957
Braun, Otto, *Von Weimar zu Hitler*. New York 1940
Brenner, Hildegard, *Die Kunstpolitik des National-Sozialismus*. Hamburg 1963
Brodbeck, Albert, *Handbuch der deutschen Volksbühnenbewegung*. Berlin 1930
Buckle, Richard, *Diaghilev*. London 1979
Busch, Fritz, *Aus dem Leben eines Musikers*. Zurich 1949
Busoni, Ferruccio, *Von der Einheit der Musik*. Berlin 1922
Cahn, Peter, *Das Hoch'sche Konservatorium 1878–1978*. Frankfurt 1979
Cocteau, Jean, *Le Rappel à l'ordre*. Paris 1926
Cunz, Rolf (ed.), *Deutsches Musikjahrbuch*. Essen 1923
Curjel, Hans, ed. Eigel Kruttge, *Experiment Krolloper 1927–1931*. Munich 1975
Dahn, Felix, *Allerhand, Durcheinand*. Cologne 1929
Dent, Edward J., *Busoni*. London 1933
  Mozart's Operas. London 1947 (2nd rev. edn)
Dominicus, A. *Strassburgs deutsche Bürgermeister. Bach und Schwander*. Frankfurt
  1939
Drew, David (ed.), *Über Kurt Weill*. Frankfurt 1975
Eyck, Erich, *Geschichte der Weimarer Republik*. Zurich 1956
Fischer, Grete, *Dienstbote Brechts und anderen*. Freiburg i.B. 1966
Fitzpatrick, Sheila, *The Commissariat of Enlightenment*. Cambridge 1971
  Education and Social Mobility in the Soviet Union, 1921–1934. Cambridge 1979
Frajese, Vittorio, *Dal Costanzi al Teatro dell'Opera*. Rome 1977
Freitag, Eberhard, *Schönberg*. Hamburg 1973

Fuerst, Walter René & Hume, Samuel J., *Twentieth Century Stage Decoration*. London 1928

Gauk, A. V., *Memuarï. Izbrannïye stat'i. Vospominaniya sovremennikov*. Moscow 1975

Gay, Peter, *Freud, Jews and other Germans*. New York 1978

Gentsch, Adolf, *Die politische Struktur der Theaterführung*. Dresden 1942

Ginzburg, Leo M., *Izbrannoye. Dirizhorï i orkestrï*. Moscow 1981

Gojowy, Detlef, *Neue sowjetische Musik der 20er Jahren*. Regensburg 1980

Golovanov, Nikolay, *Literaturnoye naslediye. Perepiska. Vospominaniya sovremennikov*. Moscow 1982

Haegy, Xavier (ed.), *Das Elsass von 1870–1932*. Colmar 1938

Hagemann, Carl, *Bühne und Welt*. Wiesbaden 1948
  Die Kunst der Bühne. Berlin 1921

Hayman, Ronald (ed.), *The German Theatre*. London 1975

Heinsheimer, Hans & Stefan, Paul (eds.), *25 Jahre neue Musik. Jahrbuch 1926 der Universal-Edition*. Vienna 1926

Heller, Friedrich C. (ed.), *Briefwechsel Arnold Schönberg–Franz Schreker*. Tulzing 1974
Handbuch von Köln, 1925

Hevesi, Ludwig, *Altkunst, Neukunst, Wien 1894–1908*. Vienna 1909

Heyworth, Peter (ed.), *Conversations with Klemperer*. London 1973

Hofmannsthal, Hugo von & Andrian, Leopold von, *Briefwechsel*. Frankfurt 1968

Horowitz, Joseph, *Conversations with Arrau*, London 1982

Jackson, Gerald, *First Flute*. London 1968

Jaspar, Gottfried (ed.), *Von Weimar zu Hitler*. Cologne/Berlin 1968

Jonge, Alex de, *Weimar Chronicle*. New York 1978

Kessler, Harry Graf, *Tagebücher*. Frankfurt 1961

Kestenberg, Leo, *Musikerziehung und Musikpflege*. Leipzig 1921
  Bewegte Zeiten, Wolfenbüttel and Zurich 1961

Klemperer, Otto, *Minor Recollections*. London 1964
  Über Musik und Theater. Berlin (GDR) 1982

Krebs, Stanley D., *Soviet Composers and the Development of Soviet Music*. London 1970

Kruckl Karl, 'Das Strassburger Stadttheater 1871–1918', in *Wissenschaft, Kunst und Literatur in Elsass-Lothringen 1871–1918*, ed. G. Wolfram. Frankfurt 1934

Kruttge, Eigel (ed.), *Von neuer Musik*. Cologne 1924

Lange, Friedrich A., *Gross-Berliner Tagebuch*. Berlin 1951

La Nier Kuhnt, Irmhild, *Philosophie und Bühnenbild: Leben und Werk des Szenikers Hans Wildermann*. Emsdetten 1970

Laqueur, Walter, *Weimar: A Cultural History 1918–1933*. London 1974

Lehmann, Lotte, *Wings of Song*. London 1938

Loewenberg, Alfred, *Annals of Opera*. 3rd edn, London 1978

Lunacharsky, A. V., *O teatr i dramaturgii*. Moscow 1958

Mahler-Werfel, Alma, *Mein Leben*. Frankfurt 1960
  Gustav Mahler: Memories and Letters. 3rd edn, London 1973

Maisenbacher, Fritz, *Bühne und Leben in Strassburg*. Strassburg 1932

Mann, Thomas, *Betrachtungen eines Unpolitischen*. Frankfurt 1956
  Tagebücher, 1918–1921. Frankfurt 1979
  Briefe, 1889–1936. Frankfurt 1962

Mariano, Nicky, *Forty years with Berenson*. London 1966

Markevitch, Igor, *Etre et avoir été*. Paris 1980

Markham, Violet R., *A Woman's Watch on the Rhine*. London 1920

Bibliography

Meyer-Sichting, *Partitur eines Lebens*. Lahnstein n.d.
Mikheyeva, L. (ed.), *Pamyalï. I. I. Sollertinskogo*. Leningrad 1978
Moholy-Nagy, László, *Von Material zu Architektur*. Mainz 1968 (reprint)
Moholy-Nagy, László & Schlemmer, Oskar, *Die Bühne im Bauhaus*. Munich 1925
Moholy-Nagy, Sibyl, *László Moholy-Nagy, ein Totalexperiment*. Mainz & Berlin 1972
Moldenhauer, Hans, *Anton von Webern*. London 1978
Müller-Blattau, J., *Hans Pfitzner*. Potsdam 1940
Naso, Eckart von, *Ich liebe das Leben*. Stuttgart & Hamburg 1953
Neumann, Angelo, *Erinnerungen an Richard Wagner*. Leipzig 1907
Niessen, Carl, *Deutsche Oper der Gegenwart*. Regensburg 1944
Niewyk, Donald L., *The Jews in Weimar Germany*. Manchester 1980
Olkhovsky, Andrey, *Music under the Soviets*. London 1955
Ouelette, Fernand, *Edgard Varèse*. London 1973
Panofsky, Walter, *Protest in der Oper*. Munich 1966
Pfitzner, Hans, *Vom musikalischen Drama*. 2nd edn, Munich 1920
   Eindrücke und Bilder meines Lebens. Hamburg 1947
Prieberg, Fred. K., *Musik im Dritten Reich*. Frankfurt 1982
Raupp, Wilhelm, *Max von Schillings: der Kampf eines deutschen Künstlers*. Hamburg 1935
Reinking, Wilhelm, *Spiel und Form*. Hamburg 1979
Rosenheim, Richard, *Die Geschichte der deutschen Bühnen in Prag*. Prague 1938
Sachs, Harvey, *Toscanini*. London 1978
Saint-Saëns, C. C., *Ecole buissonière*. Paris 1913
Satz, Natalia, *Novellen meines Lebens*. Berlin (GDR) 1973
Schlemmer, Oskar, *Briefe und Tagebücher*. Munich 1958
Schoenberg, Arnold, *Style and Idea*. London 1975
Schreiber, Wolfgang, *Mahler*. Hamburg 1971
Schrott, Ludwig, *Die Persönlichkeit Hans Pfitzners*. Zurich 1959
Schwarz, Albert, *Die Weimarer Republik*. Konstanz 1958
Schwarz, Boris, *Music and Musical Life in Soviet Russia, 1917–1970*. London 1972
Schwerd, Almut, *Zwischen Sozialdemokratie und Kommunismus*. Wiesbaden 1975
Silverman, Dan T., *The Reluctant Union*. London 1972
Singer, Kurt, *Siegfried Ochs: der Begründer des Philharmonischen Chors*. Berlin 1933
Stahl, Ernst Leopold, *Das Mannheimer Nationaltheater*. Berlin & Leipzig 1929
Stappenbeck, Martin, *Chronik des Philharmonischen Chors in Berlin 1882–1932*. Berlin 1932
Stargardt-Wolff, Edith, *Wegweiser grosser Musiker*. Berlin 1954
Staude, John Raphael, *Max Scheler*. New York 1967
Stravinsky, Igor, *Chroniques de ma vie*. Paris 1935
   Themes and Conclusions. London 1972
Stravinsky, Igor, ed. Robert Craft, *Selected Correspondence*. London 1982
Stravinsky, Igor & Craft, Robert, *Dialogues and a Diary*. London 1968
Stravinsky, Vera & Craft, Robert, *Stravinsky in Documents and Pictures*. London 1979
Stresemann, Wolfgang, *...und Abends in der Philharmonie*. Munich 1981
Stuckenschmidt, H. H., *Busoni*. London 1970
   Schoenberg, Leben, Umwelt, Werk. Zurich 1974
   Zum Hören geboren. Munich 1979
Taylor, Ronald, *Literature and Society in Germany, 1918–45*. Sussex 1980
Tiessen, Heinz, *Wege eines Komponisten*. Berlin 1962
Tuohy, F., *Occupied 1918–1930*. London n.d.

455

Bibliography

Vincent, Vincent, *Le Théâtre du Jorat*. Lausanne 1933
Vom Dadamax bis zum Grüngürtel: Köln in der zwanziger Jahre. Exhibition catalogue. Cologne 1975
Walter, Bruno, *Theme and Variations*. London 1947
  Briefe, 1894–1962. Frankfurt 1969
Weber, Horst, *Alexander Zemlinsky*. Vienna 1977
Weissmann, Adolf, *Der Dirigent im zwanzigsten Jahrhundert*. Berlin 1925
Wende, Erich, *C. H. Becker, Mensch und Politiker*. Stuttgart 1959
Willett, John, *Expressionism*. London 1970
  The New Sobriety. London 1978
Wiskemann, Elizabeth, *Czechs and Germans*, London 1938
Woikowsky, Biedan, *Der Kampf um das Deutsches Opernhaus*. Berlin 1925
Wollenberg, Robert, *Erinnerungen eines alten Psychiaters*. Stuttgart 1931
Wulf, Joseph, *Musik im Dritten Reich*. Gutersloh 1963
Yudin, G. Ya., *Za gran'yu proshlïkh dney*. Moscow 1978
Zentner, Wilhelm, 'Der Komponist Hans Pfitzner und Strassburg', in Ekkhart, *Jahrbuch für den Oberrhein 1942*.
Ziegler, Hans Severus, *Entartete Musik: eine Abrechnung*. Dusseldorf 1938
Zuckmayer, Carl, *Als wär's ein Stück von mir*. Vienna 1966

II Unpublished typescripts, dissertations, memoires etc.

Bengsch, Hans-Jürgen, 'Carl Hagemann und die Szenenreform der Schauspiel-bühne'. Dissertation. Munich 1951
Drew, David, 'Kurt Weill: life, times, and works'
Dülberg, Ewald, 'Vita', typescript excerpts from autobiography
Gless, Julius, Reminiscences
Hugel, Marguerite, 'Memoiren einer danebengeratenen Pfitzner-Schülerin'
Klemperer, Otto, Autobiographical sketch (1962)
Mathis, Alfred, 'Elisabeth Schumann: the chronicle of a singer's life'
Rockwell, John, 'The Prussian Ministry of Culture and the Berlin State Opera, 1918–1931'. Dissertation. University of California (Berkeley) n.d.
Scheper, Dirk, 'Das triadische Ballett und die Bauhausbühne'. Dissertation. Vienna 1970
Stompor, Stephan, 'Oper im zwanzigsten Jahrhundert: Die Entwicklung des Musiktheaters von Gustav Mahler bis Walter Felsenstein'. (Unfinished)

III Transcriptions of interviews

Bregstein Interviews. Interviews with Klemperer, and many of those associated with him, for a film (1972) made by Philo Bregstein.
WDR Interviews. Interviews with Klemperer and others associated with the Kroll for a four-hour radio programme on the Kroll Opera, first transmitted by Westdeutsche Rundfunk in 1962. The text of this programme is reprinted as an introduction to Curjel's *Experiment Krolloper*.
CBC Interviews. Original text of interviews of the present author with Klemperer, August 1969, which subsequently formed part of *Conversations with Klemperer*.

IV Libraries and archives containing the principal documents consulted

Berlin (W)

Geheimes Staatsarchiv, Preussicher Kulturbesitz
 Proceedings of the Prussian Landtag
  Plenum sessions; Hauptausschuss; Untersuchungsausschuss Krolloper
  (Drucksachen Nr 7431); reports of the Oberrechnungskammer
 Betrieb und Leitung der Staatstheater, file of the Staatsministerium (Rep. 90/2406)
  C. H. Becker–Archiv
 Akademie der Künste
  Heinz–Tietjen–Archiv

Brno

Janáček Archives

Cologne

Historisches Archiv der Stadt Köln
Theatermuseum und Theaterwissenschaftliches Institut der Universität zu Köln

Frankfurt

Paul-Hindemith–Institut

Los Angeles

Schoenberg Institute, University of Southern California

Mainz

B. Schott Söhne. Archives

Marbach a. N.

Deutsches Literatur–Archiv
 Hans Curjel *Nachlass*, which contains an extensive collection of letters, documents,
  cuttings and interviews relating to the Kroll Opera

Merseberg

Zentrales Staatsarchiv
 Files of the Berlin State Opera, including Klemperers personnel file

New York

Library of the Performing Arts
 Papers of the New York Symphony Orchestra

Strasbourg

Archives municipales
 Pfitzner's personnel files; Klemperer's personal file; Proceedings of the Theatre
  Commission

Bibliography

Vienna
Musiksammlung der Nationalbibliothek
Musiksammlung der Stadtbibliothek
  Correspondence between Universal Edition and its composers (including Klemperer) to 1933
Staatsarchiv
  Vienna State Opera archives

Wiesbaden
Hessisches Staatstheater
  Klemperer's personnel file.

Index

by Frederick Smyth

The name of Otto Klemperer appears on almost every page of the text. To avoid an unnecessary overloading of the sections under his name many references to him have been placed under other relevant headings.

Throughout the index his name has been abbreviated to 'OK'. The word 'critic' may be taken to imply, unless otherwise qualified, 'music critic'. Unless stated otherwise, all recordings referred to were conducted by Klemperer.

Stage works, listed under the names of their composers, are – unless identified as something else – operas. These are further distinguished by the dates of first performance.

An asterisk (*) following a single page reference indicates that the performance, operatic or orchestral, was under Klemperer. Where the asterisk precedes a series of page references, all those references relate to Klemperer performances.

Bold figures (**234**) indicate the more important references; *italic* figures (*234*) denote illustrations or their captions. 'q.' stands for 'quoted'; 'q.v.' for '*quod vide*' (which see). '*bis*' conveys that there are two references to the same subject on the page concerned; '*passim*' (e.g. 234–50 *passim*) means that references to the same subject are scattered throughout the group of pages, not necessarily on every page. '*n*' ('*nn*') directs attention to one or more footnotes.

Index

Ansermet, Ernest (1883–1969), conductor, 127n

Appia, Adolphe (1862–1928), stage designer, 27–8, 83 & nn, 84, 201; La musique et la mise en scène (1899), 83

Arbeitsgemeinschaft Deutscher Musikkritiker, 282n, 410n

Arbeitsrat für Kunst, 130

Arendt, Hannah, The Origins of Totalitarianism (1958), 338n

Argentinisches Tageblatt, Das, 380, 381n

Arimondi, Vittorio (1861–1928), singer, 39

Arrau, Claudio (b. 1903), pianist, & OK, 309n

Artobolevska, Anna D., on Mariya Yudina, 221n

Asaf'yev, Boris ('Igor Glebov', 1884–1949), critic & musicologist, 215, 215n, 218 bis, 221 bis, q. 223, 224

Asch, Joseph, 119n

Asch-Rosenbaum, Helene ('Leni', 1894–1979), Marianne Klemperer's friend, 136, 145n, 190

Association for Contemporary Music (Russia), 213, 312–14

Auber, Daniel (1782–1871), 91
Domino noir, le (1837), 267
Fra Diavolo (1830), 110,* overture recorded, 451
La Muette de Portici (1828), 113, 272n, 329n

Auden, Wystan Hugh (1907–73), poet, 162n

Aufricht, Ernst Josef (1898–1971), producer, 283n

Ausdruckstanz, development from eurhythmics, 59

Baarke, Curt, chairman of the Volksbühne, 347

Baccaloni, Salvatore (1900–69), bass, 381 & n

Bach, Carl Philipp Emanuel (1714–88), his sonatas played by OK, 12

Bach, Johann Sebastian (1685–1750), 103, 130
Brandenburg Concertos, 303; recordings (Klemperer, Furtwängler), 302n, 444
  No. 1 in F, * 216, 302, 305, 381
  No. 3 in G, 302n*
  No. 4 in G, 304*
  No. 6 in B flat, 304–5*

Concerto in D minor for Piano & Orchestra, 63–4*
Suite No. 2 in B minor, 406 & n
Suite No. 3 in D, * 257, 303–5, 319n, 392
Chromatic Fantasy and Fugue in D minor, played by OK, 15
Chorale Preludes (arr. Schoenberg), 211*
Prelude and Fugue in E flat (arr. Schoenberg), * 333, 353
arias, 136
Mass in B minor, 321 bis; * 398, 408n
St John Passion, * 322–3, 369 & n, 398
St Matthew Passion, 11, 56, 302; * 392, 406

Bachmann, Erich, critic, 352

Bachur, Max, theatre director, 49–50

Backhaus, Wilhelm (1884–1969), pianist, 16 & n

Baden-Baden: Festival (1929), 296n; the former Donaueschingen Festival (1927), 245

Badische General-Anzeiger, Der (1915), 106

Bahr-Mildenburg, Anna (1872–1947), soprano, 26 & n, 27, 256n

Baker, Josephine (1906–75), entertainer, 340

Barcelona, Gran Teatro del Liceo, 82n, 154–5, 155n, 162n, 162–3

Barmen, theatre, 80–6 passim, 443

Barmer Zeitung, Die, q. 82, q. 84, 86

Bartók, Béla (1881–1945), 16
Rhapsody for Piano and Orchestra, op. 1, 16
Bluebeard's Castle (1917), 193
The Miraculous Mandarin, ballet (1928), 190
The Wooden Prince, ballet (1918), 190.

Bassi, Amedeo (1874–1949), tenor, 167 & n

Batka, Richard (1868–1922), critic, 29, 34n, 35n, 42n

Battistini, Mattia (1856–1928), baritone, 188

Bauhaus, school of architecture, Weimar & Dessau (1919–33), 284, 287n, 330

Bayreuth, Festival, 31, 60n, 103n, 237n, 377

Beaumarchais, Pierre Augustin Caron de (1732–99), dramatist, 97

Beck, Joachim, critic, 104n

Becker, Carl Heinrich (1876–1933), Prussian Kultusminister, 177 & n, 234 & n, 242, 338, 375; & OK, 179, 180n, 240, 268n; & the State Opera & Kroll, 235–8, 237n, 239–40, 288

Index

Brodbeck, Albert, *Handbuch der deutschen Volksbühnenbewegung* (1930), 339*n*
Bruch, Max (1838–1920), 91; *Odysseus*, for chorus & orchestra, 81
Bruckner, Anton (1824–96), 158, 320*n*, 440
  Symphonies
    No. 4 in E flat, 324 & *n*
    No. 5 in B flat, * 247, **402**, 404 *bis*
    No. 7 in E, 155; * 182*n*, 233, 300, 354, **388**
    No. 8 in C minor, * **182** & *n*, 204, 205, 228, 313*n*, 320, 392, 404; recording, 444, 447
  Te Deum, 321
Brüning, Heinrich (1885–1970), German Chancellor (1930–2), 136*n*, 345 *bis*, 356 & *n*, 366*n*, 384*n*, 396, 412*n*
Brust, Fritz, critic, q. **98**, q. 110, 372
Buchhorn, Josef (1875–1954), Landtag member, q. **340**, 340*n*, 366–7
Buckle, Richard (b. 1916), critic & writer, *Diaghilev* (1979), 306*n*
Budapest, opera, 440
Buenos Aires, Teatro Colón, 168, 372, 379–82, 438
Buffalo Philharmonic Orchestra, 441
Bühnentechnische Rundschau, q. 281–2*n*
Bühnenvolksbund, Berlin, 269*n*, 276 & *n*, 347*n*
Bülow, Hans von (1830–94), conductor, & the Berlin Philharmonic Orchestra, 321
Bürgerzeitung, Die (Strasbourg), 92*n*
Busch, Adolf (1891–1952), violinist, 437
Busch, Fritz (1890–1951), conductor, 159, 245, 275*n*, 309*n*, 412–13, 416*n*; biography, **437**; *Aus dem Leben eines Musikers* (1949), 413*n*
Busoni, Ferruccio (1866–1924), **21** & *n*, 178, 208, 244; as a pianist, 61, 63*n*; meets Stravinsky, 127*n*; and Dülberg, 201; and Kestenberg, 175, 177
  influences on OK, 23, 127, 303; letters, from OK, 128, 131, 152, 165*n*, 167; to OK, q. **167**; opinion of OK, 21, 37; OK's opinion of him, 127, 208, 208–9*n*; is visited by OK (1918), **126–7**, 128
  Entwurf einer neuen Aesthetik der Tonkunst (1907), 126 *bis*; 'Junge Klassizität' (1920), 126 & *n*; his edition of Bach's keyboard music, 303
  Berceuse élégiaque, op. 42, 404*

Piano Concerto, 147 & *n*
Violin Concerto, 404*
Cadenza for Mozart's Concerto K.467, 404
violin sonatas, 130*n*
Arlecchino (1917), 126 & *n*, 130, * 132, 229
Die Brautwahl (1912), 190
Doktor Faust (1925), 209*n*, 293*n*, 437
Turandot (1917), 126 & *n*, 130, 132*
BZ (*Berliner Zeitung*) *am Mittag* (Berlin), 196*n*, 266*n*, 311, 336*n*, 370–1*nn*

Calderón de la Barca, Pedro (1600–81), playwright, 85
Cardus, Neville (1889–1975), critic, q. 388
Carelli, Emma (1877–1928), opera director, 167–9
Caruso, Enrico (1873–1921), tenor, 50, 53, 74*n*
Casals, Pau (1876–1973), cellist & conductor, 310
Casella, Alfredo (1883–1947), composer & conductor, 49*n*, 168 & *n*; as pianist, 311; *Scarlattiana*, 311
Celibidache, Sergiu (b. 1912), conductor, 392*n*
Chaliapin, Feodor (1873–1938), bass, 181
Chamberlain, Eva (1867–1942), Wagner's daughter, 287
Charpentier, Gustave (1860–1956), *Louise* (1900), 158*n*, 285*n*, 359 & *n*
Chelius, Oscar von (1859–1923), soldier & composer, *Die vernarrte Prinzessin* (1905), 122–3*
Chéreau, Patrice, producer, 281
Cherubini, Luigi (1760–1842), *Les Deux Journées* (*Der Wasserträger*) (1800), 149 & *n**
Chesterian, The (journal), 388
Chevalley, Heinrich (1870–?), critic: on OK the conductor, q. 50, 54, q. **64**, q. **72–3**, q. 76, q. 191, q. **405**; on OK's songs, 65, 104; on other people & subjects, 50–1, 51*n*, 69, 74*n*, q. 75
Chicago Opera, 158 & *n*, 159
Chicherin, Georgy (1872–1936), Russian Foreign Minister, 247 & *n*, 318 & *n*
Chirico, Giorgio de (1888–1978), painter, 329
Chop, Max (1862–1929), composer & editor, q. 282
Chopin, Frédéric (1810–49), Piano Concerto in F minor, 115*n*
Chur, Stadttheater, 437

464

Index

Cimarosa, Domenico (1749–1801), *Il Matrimonio segreto* (1792), 275
Claudel, Paul (1868–1955), poet & dramatist, 150 & *n*; *L'Annonce faite à Marie* (1912), 150*n*
Cleveland Orchestra, 442
Coburg, theatre, 277*n*
Cocteau, Jean (1889–1963), writer, 207 & *n*, 246*n*; *Orphée* (1926), 325; essay, 'Le Coq et l'arlequin' (1918), 207 & *n*
Cologne
  Conservatory, 306*n*
  Gesellschaft der Künste (1918), **129–30**, 134–5, 148
  Gürzenich Hall, 133, 143
  Gürzenich Orchestra & Concerts, 114 & *n*, **133–4**, 146, 164–5, 303*n*, 306*n*; and OK, 114, 134, 164, 174
  Hotel Disch, Rococo Saal, 130
  Konzert-Gesellschaft, 133
  municipal theatres, 438
  Opera, 120–1, 153*n*; its chorus, 131–2, 148; its Künstlerrat, **129**; its orchestra, 133, 148; OK at, 88*n*, 114–15, **121–69**
  Opera House Concerts, **145–8**
  opera houses, 120 & *n*
  St Maria im Kapitol, church, 120*n*
  University, 136; its Theatermuseum, 84*n*, 212*n*, 262*n*, 326–7*nn*
  Vereinigung geistiger Arbeiter Kölns, 134
  Westdeutsche Rundfunk (WDR), 439
  WDR Symphony Orchestra, 301*n*
Contemporary Music, Association for (Russia), 213, 312–14
Cooke, Deryck (1919–76), musicologist, his reconstruction of Mahler's Tenth Symphony, 205*n*
Cornelius, Peter (1824–74), 91; *Der Barbier von Bagdad* (1858), 85
Corriere della Sera, Il (Italian journal), 169
Courant Nieuws van de Dag, De (Dutch newspaper), 311*n*
Courtauld, Elizabeth d. 1931, concert patron, 319, 388
Craft, Robert, ed. Stravinsky, *Selected Correspondence* (1982), 213*n*
Craig, Edward Gordon (1872–1966), stage designer & director, 27–8, 83 & *n*; *The Art of the Theatre* (1905), 83
Culp, Julia (1880–1970) mezzo-soprano, 39
Curjel, Hans (1896–1974), art historian, writer & *Dramaturg*, 197 & *n*, 251,

278, 366*n*; biography, **437**; as conductor, 197*n*; as *Dramaturg* at the Kroll, 197, 241, 249, 284, 325, 437; as deputy director at the Kroll, 328–33 & *nn passim*, 347–52 *passim*, 368*n*, 372–3, 437; his ideas and influence, 251–2, 253; interviewed on WDR, 352*n*, 365*n*; and the *neue Sachlichkeit*, 252, 267*n*; his notes & recollections, 256 & *nn*, 262
  and OK, 236*n*, 266–8 & *nn*, **296**, 361, 372–3; on OK, q. 254; and Dülberg 273–5, 328; and Moholy-Nagy, 284, 285*n*, 326; and Weill's operas, 245*n*, 246 & *n*
  his letters: to G. Klemperer (1928), 267*n*; to OK (1929), q. **296**, (1931), q. **373**; to Gertrude Marbach (1962), 330–1*n*; to Weill (1929), q. 292–3, 293–4*nn*, q. **296**
  essay on *Cardillac* (*Blätter der Staatsoper*, 1928), 271*n*; *Experiment Krolloper* (1975), 270*n*, 280*nn*, 296*n*, 327*n*, 437; 'Moholy-Nagy und das Theater' (*Du*, 1964), 285*n*; 'Neben der Oper' (*Blätter...*, 1928), 374*n*; 'Neue Kriterien – neue Masstäbe' (*Melos*, 1932), 251*n*; 'The Triumph of the Commonplace' (*Blätter...*, 1929), 293; his *Nachlass*, 256*n*, 350–2*nn*
Curtius, Ernst Robert (1886–1956), writer, 102*n*, 138*n*
Czech Philharmonic Orchestra, 38, 230

Dahn, Felix, producer, 124, 166
D'Albert, Eugene (1864–1932), 14; *Tiefland* (1903), 82
Dalcroze, Jacques (1865–1950), music teacher and propounder of eurhythmics, 59, 83*n*
Dame Kobold, Die, opera (1909) from Calderón, using Mozart's music from *Così fan tutte*, 85
Damrosch, Walter (1862–1950), conductor, 222, 225 & *n*, 227–8, 230 & *n*, 233
Daniel, Oskar, singing teacher, 189*n*
d'Annunzio, Gabriele (1863–1938), *Le Martyre de Saint-Sébastien*, 311*n*
Daubler, Georg, stage designer, 90
Debussy, Claude (1862–1918), 21, 131
  Après-midi d'un faune, L', 58*n*
  Ibéria, * 229, 232
  Nocturnes, recording, 448

465

Index

Index

Index

478

Index

Milan, La Scala Opera House & Company, 167–8*nn*, 169, 200*n*, 293*n*, 370*n*, 442

Milhaud, Darius (1892–1974), 207, **326** & *n*
  Christoph Colomb (1930), 326*n*
  L'Enlèvement d'Europe (1927), 245*n*
  Le Pauvre Matelot (1927) * 325–6, 332*n*

Mochi, Walter (1870–1955), opera director, 168

Moholy-Nagy, László (1895–1946), stage designer, **284–5**, 285*n*, 328, 333, 351–2, 352*n*, 360 & *n*; his *Hoffmann* set (1929), **286**, 326, 360 & *n*

Moholy-Nagy, Sibyl, *László Moholy-Nagy, ein Totalexperiment* (1972), 360*n*

Moissi, Alexander (1880–1935), actor, 24, 60

Montagspost (Berlin journal), 260

Montés, John, critic, 381–2

Monteux, Pierre (1875–1964), conductor, 310 & *n*

Morel, Eva, 212*n*, 409*n*

Moscow
  Bol'shoy Opera, 216–17 and *nn*
  Bol'shoy Theatre Orchestra, 214, 222, 224, 314*n*, 318
  Central Children's Theatre, 217 & *n*, 370
  Conservatory, 214
  Hebrew Theatre, 217
  Moscow State Philharmonic Orchestra (1931), 317*n*
  Persimfans Orchestra, 318*n*
  Sofil Orchestra (1928), 317*n*, 317–18
  Sovetskaya Filarmoniya (1928), 317*n*

Motta, José Vianna da (1868–1948), pianist & composer, 175 & *n*

Mottl, Felix (1856–1911), conductor, 60*n*

Mozart, Wolfgang Amadeus (1756–91), 57, 91, 97*n*, 98–9, 293
  piano concertos, 10
    No. 20 in D minor (K.466), 258*
    No. 21 in C (K.467), 403–4*
    No. 23 in A (K.488), 192*n**
  symphonies
    No. 38 in D ('Prague', K.504), 388*
    No. 40 in G minor (K. 550), * 147, 215
    No. 41 in C ('Jupiter', K.551), * 192; 392*n*
  Clemenza di Tito, La (1791), 293*n*
  Così fan tutte (1790), 60, 81, 91, 113, 126*n*, 293; * **85–6**, 121*n*, **148–9**, **386**
  Don Giovanni (1787), 11, 17, 27–8, 30, 194, 202; OK's intentions, 58, 99,

106; * (1917–22), 117, 122, 148, 152–3, (1924–8), **211–12**, 212*n*, **247**, **262–3**; OK's paraphrase on its themes, 103

  Entführung aus dem Serail, Die (1782), 401; * 116, **132–3**

  Nozze di Figaro, Le (1786), **71**, 106, 285*n*, 353*n*, 359; * (1912–23), 75–6, **97–9**, 104, **121–2**, 164, 353*n*; (1925–32), 203, **352–3**, **372–3**, 381 & *n*, 392; (1970), 99*n*; other conductors, 60, 293*n*; Johanna Klemperer's roles, 117, 395*n*

  Zauberflöte, Die (1791), 44, 69, 106, 262, 268; * 200*n*, 262*n*, **326–7**

Muck, Karl (1859–1940), conductor, 21 & *n*, 33, 37, 41, 43

Müller, Traugott (1895–1944), stage designer, 275

Müller-Blattau, Josef (1895–1976), *Hans Pfitzner* (1940), 109 & *n*

Müller-Hartmann, Robert (1884–1950), critic, q. **51**, q. 65, 104

Münch, Ernst (1859–1928), organist & choirmaster, 103

Münch, Prälat Franz-Xaver (1883–1940), 136–8 & *nn*, 195, 384*n*

Munich
  Bavarian State Opera, 438
  Court Opera, 60*n*
  Mozart Festival, 117
  Residenztheater, 60, 83, 199*n*
  Tonkünstler Orchestra, 60

Musica (Italian journal), 168*n*

Musical Times, The (London), 246*n*, 388

Musik, Die (German journal) 151*n*, q. 215, 218–20

Musikblätter des Anbruch (Viennese journal) see *Anbruch*

Mussolini, Benito (1883–1945), 168, 412

Mussorgsky, Modest (1839–81): *A Night on a Bare Mountain*, tone-poem, 218;* *Boris Godunov* (1870), **181–2**,* 182*n*, 189–90

Muzïka i revolyutsiya (organ of the ACM, Russia), 314–15

Muzïkal'naya zhizn (Russian periodical), 214*n*

Nardi, Luigi (d. 1956), tenor, 167

Naso, Eckart von (1895–1976), *Dramaturg* at the Kroll, 351

Nathan, Ida, *see* Klemperer, Ida

Nathan, Marianne (*née* Rée, 1810–87), OK's grandmother, **2–3**, 4–5, 5*n*

Index

Paderewski, Ignacy Jan (1860–1941), pianist, 14

Palestine (Israel Philharmonic) Orchestra, 366n

Panofsky, Walter, *Protest in der Oper* (1966), 346n

Papen, Franz von (1879–1969), German Chancellor, 178, 366n, 396 & n, 407, 412 *bis*

Paris
Opéra, 380n
Opéra-Comique, 58n
Orchestre Symphonique de Paris, 310

Patzak, Julius (1897–1974), tenor, 323 & n

Pauly, Rose (1894–1975), soprano, 166 *bis*, 196, 256, 260–1, 275 *bis*, 280n

Pfitzner, Hans (1869–1949), composer, conductor and director, *89*, 108nn, 113, **151**n; his marriage, 13n; at the Stern Conservatory, 20n, **20–1**; at Strasbourg (1907–16), 40, 43, 57, 87–99 *passim*, **107**, 440; biography, **440**

a nationalist, 108 & n, 126, 151, 440; his satirical poem (1907), q. 120 & n; his musical conservatism, 21, 126; and later sociological interpretation, 151; a reactionary in later years, 90

antipathy to Busoni, 21, 26; relations with Thomas Mann, 20n, 108, **151**n; and Bruno Walter, 108n, 183n, 442

teaches and advises OK, **20–1**, 23, 29, 34, 40; OK performs his music, 118, 147 (*see also* his operas, *below*); and discards it, 210; OK's opinions of him, 87, 90; conflict with OK, 43, 95–6, 98, **107–11**, 151; they meet again, 109, 149, 151; letters from OK, *see under* Klemperer, Otto

Futuristengefahr, pamphlet, 126; *neue Aesthetik der musikalischen Impotenz, Die* (1920), **150–1**, 287; *Vom musikalischen Drama* (2nd edn, 1920), 90n

his compositions, 21, 147, 178
violin sonatas, 130n
arme Heinrich, Der (1895), 20, 97,* 440
Christelflein (1906), 122, 151; overture conducted by OK, 118
Palestrina (1917), 87, 92–3, 108, 118, 150n, 440, 442; * **149–50**, 150n

Rose vom Liebesgarten, Die (1901), 20, 42–3, 108 & n, 118,* 440;
Vom deutscher Seele, cantata, 151
songs, 65, 120n

Pfitzner, Mimi (*née* Kwast, d.1926), wife of Hans, 13n, 59, 109

Pfohl, Ferdinand (1862–1949), composer, writer & critic: on concerts conducted by OK (1912, 1928), q. **64**, 309; on operas conducted by OK (1910–12), q. **50–1**, q. 53–4, q. 72; on OK's songs, q. **65**, q. 103–4; other reviews, q. 74, q. 76

Piccaver, Alfred (1884–1958), tenor, 36 & n, 114n

Pincherle, Marc (1888–1974), musicologist, recalling OK's manic condition, 310n

Piscator, Erwin (1893–1966), stage director, **261**n, 272 & n, 275, 343

Pittsburgh Symphony Orchestra, 441

Plato (*c*.427–348 BC), *The Republic*, q.251n

Plessner, Helmuth (b.1892), philosopher, 289 & nn, 310

Polgar, Alfred (1873–1955), writer & critic, on the première of *Mahagonny*, 297

Polignac, Winnaretta, Princesse de (1865–1943), patroness of the arts, 246 & n

Pollak, Alex (b.1911), son of Egon, interviewed, 298n

Pollak, Egon (1879–1933), conductor at Frankfurt & Hamburg, 77, 80, 298n, 369; biography, **440**

Poulenc, Francis (1899–1963), 207

Prager Abendblatt, Das, q. 34–5, 42

Prager Presse, Die, q. **166**

Prager Tagblatt, Das, 34, 36, 42, 44 & n

Prague
German Ständetheater, 30 & n, 31
(Czech) National Theatre (1881), 31–2, 46, 82n
New German Theatre (1888), referred to in the text as the German Theatre (*now* the Smetana Theatre), 31 & n, **32–7**, 35nn, 82n; OK as conductor, 29, **34–46**, 182; other conductors, 60, 243, 307n, 436, 440–3

Pravda (Moscow newspaper), 214, 216–17, 217n, 220

Prieberg, Fred K., *Musik im Dritten Reich* (1982), 415n

Pringsheim, Klaus (1883–1972), conductor, composer & critic, 287, 301, 351n, 369n, 383

Index

485

Index

Stravinsky, Igor (*cont.*)
    classicistic style, 207; as a
    conductor, 246 & *n*; as a pianist,
    211, 246, 307–8
  is admired by Auden, 162*n*, and
    Dülberg, 201; admires Zemlinsky,
    243; meets Busoni, 127*n*;
    Stravinsky on Schoenberg, 211;
    Schoenberg on Stravinsky, q.
    265–6; on 'words', q. 127*n*; on the
    Kroll, q. **349**
  OK first meets Stravinsky (1914), 94*n*;
    OK's commitment to his music, 162,
    210–11, 232, 266, **307–8**, 394;
    OK with Stravinsky at
    performances, 211, 266, 307–8,
    349; he writes to Stravinsky, q. 308
    & *n*, q. 391; OK on Schoenberg &
    Stravinsky, q. **210–11**
  Chroniques de ma vie (1935), 307*n*;
    Dialogues and a Diary (with R. Craft,
    1968), 265–6*nn*; *Selected*
    Correspondence (ed. Craft, 1982),
    213*n*; Asaf'yev's monograph
    (1929) on Stravinsky, 215*n*
  Capriccio for Piano & Orchestra,
    Stravinsky as soloist, **307–8***
  Piano Concerto, 311; with Stravinsky as
    soloist, * **211** & *n*, **307**
  Suite No.2. * 232, 315
  Symphony of Psalms, * 355, 356*n*,
    382–3
  Apollo, ballet music, 266, 272; * **307**,
    315
  Baiser de la fée, Le, ballet suite, 307,*
    311
  Histoire du soldat, L' (1918), 127*n*, 203*n*,
    277*n*; * 202–3, 273, 275–7, 349
  Mavra (1921–2), 263–4*
  Noces, Les, ballet music, 307*
  Oedipus Rex (1928), 263*n*, 355*n*, 401;
    conducted by Stravinsky, **246**;
    * 249, **263–6**, *265*, 273, 275–6
  Persephone, melodrama (1934), 311*n*
  Petrushka, ballet music, 94 & *n*, 266,
    310*n*; * **162**, 190, 229, 263–4,
    317–18
  Pulcinella, ballet suite, * 203, 205, 211,
    218 *bis*, 309–10, 315
  Rite of Spring, The, ballet music, 162,
    310*n*, 323*n*
Strecker, Ludwig (1883–1978), director of
    Schotts, 101 & *n*, 119
Strecker, Willy (1884–1958), director of
    Schotts: and Hindemith's works,
    142*n*, 324, 383, 401, 408; and

OK's works, 289, 357 & *nn*, 368;
    and OK's visit to New York, 225;
    his letter (1931) to OK, q. **357**;
    biography, **441**
Strelitzer, Hugo (1896–1981),
    chorusmaster, 124*n*, 128*n*
Strel'nikov, Nikolay (1888–1939),
    composer & critic, 215
Stresemann, Gustav (*c*. 1878–1929),
    German Chancellor & Foreign
    Minister, 181, 192*n*, 207, 276,
    336–7, 417
Stresemann, Wolfgang (b.1904),
    conductor, composer & Intendant,
    192*n*, 417; on OK's Berlin concert
    (1924), q. **192–3**
Strnad, Oskar (1879–1935), architect &
    stage designer, 277, 410*n*; Berlin
    Tannhäuser (1933), 410–11
Strobel, Heinrich (1898–1970),
    musicologist & critic: on OK, 257,
    261*n*, 300–1, q. **302**, q. **402–3**;
    other reviews, 261, 293, 307–8,
    327, q. 368; interviewed (1970),
    256*n*
Strohbach, Hans, producer at the Grosse
    Volksoper, Berlin, 188
Strub, Max (1900–66), violinist, 301*n*,
    304, 308, 355*n*, 404, 416
Stuckenschmidt, Hans Heinz (b.1901),
    critic & writer, 273*n*; on OK, q. 276,
    q. 293, 331, 372, q. **399**, 416*n*;
    Zum Hören geboren (1979), 297 & *n*
Stuttgart Opera, 440
Sudermann, Hermann (1857–1928),
    dramatist, 13
Sun, The (New York), q. 243
Szabo, Isztvan (b.1938), film director,
    Mephisto, film, 352*n*
Szell, Georg(e) (1897–1970), conductor,
    115, 293*n*; as a pianist, 115*n*, 307;
    biography, **441–2**
Szenkar, Eugen (1891–1977), conductor,
    188 & *n*, 195 & *n*
Szigeti, Joseph (1892–1973), violinist,
    247*n*

Tag, Der (German newspaper), q. 25, q.
    282, 293*n*
Tagebuch, Das (Berlin periodical), 225*n*,
    340, 344, 349
Tairov, Alexander (1885–1950), Moscow
    theatre director, 217, 314
Tauber, Richard (1892–1948), tenor, 261*n*
Tchaikovsky, Piotr Ilyich (1840–93), 440
  Symphony No. 5 in E minor, 406, 440

Index

Index